APPLICATIONS

Advertising, 536, 592

Agriculture, 401, 584, 592

Airline scheduling, 584

Amortization schedules, 311

Annuities, 299

Assignment problems, 78

Ballot counting, 25–30

Carbon dating, 343

Channel assignment, 247, 265

Chemical bond graphs, 105

Codes, 19, 147, 148

Communication networks, 140

Compound interest, 291

Consumer price index, 350

Decision problems, 224

Determination of cost of operation, 247

Diagnosis, 217

Diet determination, 380, 392, 418, 553

DNA, 17, 109

Dominance relations, 445

Elections, 2, 619

Energy efficiency, 247

Food web, 44

Games, 180, 582

Genetics, 17, 109, 263

Gross national product and the deficit, 240, 260, 263

Homogeneity of bimetallic objects, 132

Income taxes, 258, 280

Individual retirement accounts, 309

Inflation, 340

Installment loans, 310

Investments, 391, 394, 588

Land development, 596, 603, 615

Leontief input-output models, 500

Lotteries, 180, 182, 625

Markov chains, 446

Newton's law of cooling, 344

One-way street assignments, 121

Paired comparison experiments, 27, 241, 278

Personal decision making, 31, 602

Political campaigns, 3, 588

Population growth, 490

Probability, 20, 172, 189, 212

Production problems, 490

Profit maximization, 397, 402, 418

Psychological scaling, 281

Psychology experiments, 380, 401

Quality control, 24, 167, 175

Radioactive decay, 341

Representative sampling, 268

RNA chains, 19, 56

Road construction, 130

Sampling with defectives, 167, 175

Scheduling problems, 38, 148, 401

Searching, 116

Sensitivity analysis, 561

Shortest route problems, 38, 148, 401

Sinking funds, 305

Sorting, 107, 276

Spread of information and disease, 345

Survey sampling, 9, 222

Tournaments, 277

Toxic waste disposal, 616

Transportation problems, 136, 393, 402, 417, 479

Traveling salesman, 65, 147

Voting power, 156, 170

Mathematics and Its Applications

Mathematics and Its Applications

To Management, Life, and Social Sciences
With Finite and Discrete Mathematics

MARGARET B. COZZENS & RICHARD D. PORTER, NORTHEASTERN UNIVERSITY

D. C. Heath and Company • *Lexington, Massachusetts* • *Toronto*

Cover photo: David F. Hughes/Stock, Boston

Acquisitions Editor Mary Lu Walsh
Production Editor Kim Rieck Fisher
Designer Mark T. Fowler
Production Coordinator Mike O'Dea

International Standard Book Number: 0-669-09368-8

Library of Congress Catalog Card Number: 86-81263

Preface

Students majoring in business and the social and biological sciences are often required to take a one-semester course in finite mathematics. Traditionally, this course consists of such topics as logic, sets, algebra, probability, and statistics. With the increased use of computers in business and other areas, the applications in this course have become computer oriented. To provide the necessary background for these new applications, we have added topics in discrete mathematics to the traditional core topics.

As in any freshman or sophomore level finite mathematics text, the only prerequisite is high school algebra. Material that students have seen before, such as graphing linear equations and solving linear equations in two unknowns, is reviewed as it occurs in the context of problem solving.

Features

Applications These are numerous and varied. Throughout the text we have introduced 800 applied examples and exercises to give students concrete evidence of the role mathematics plays in such disciplines as business, social science, and biological science. Some applications recur as new techniques are developed. For example:

RNA and DNA chains appear first in Chapter 1 on sets. Eulerian paths are used in Chapter 2 to assemble an RNA chain from its fragments. Finding the number of different possible chains appears in Chapter 4 as an application of counting.

Gauss-Jordan elimination is used in Chapter 10 to solve systems of equations. This forms a bridge from geometric solutions to linear programs (Chapter 9) to the simplex algorithm solutions (Chapter 11).

The probability theory in Chapter 5 is combined with matrices in Chapter 10 to describe Markov chains. For 2-by-2 systems, the existence of a steady state is reduced to a problem about difference equations solved in Chapter 8.

Graph coloring is introduced in Chapter 2 in relation to scheduling problems. In Chapter 6, polynomials are applied to count the number of different ways to color graphs.

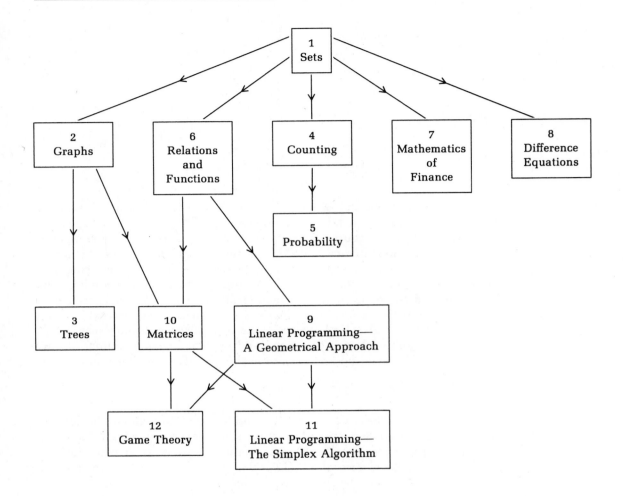

Exercises   Each section has an extensive set of exercises ranging from routine to more challenging problems. Answers to odd-numbered exercises are in the back of the book.

Practice Examples   Each section contains practice examples for students to check their understanding of a just described idea or technique. Solutions are given at the end of each section.

Chapter Summaries   The chapter summaries give an overview of the material presented in the chapter and help students prepare for tests.

Review Exercises   Each chapter ends with a set of review exercises.

Flexibility   We have included more topics in this text than can be covered in one semester. Teachers may choose those chapters and topics most appropriate for the level and interest of their students. The above chart shows the dependencies among chapters.

Supplements

The *Instructor's Guide* contains solutions to all the exercises.

Acknowledgments

Our families have contributed to this book with their comments, typing, drawings, and unfailing encouragement. Without their support this book would not have been written. We thank Edward Comstock and Conrad Caligaris for sharing their ideas and giving us source material for some applications in the text.

We wish to thank the following reviewers whose comments improved this book: Sally Fischbeck, Rochester Institute of Technology; Rochelle Leibowitz, Wheaton College; Joseph Malkevitch, York College; Robert Moreland, Texas Tech University; Carl Simon, University of Michigan; Donald Small, Colby College; and James Vick, University of Texas, Austin.

We thank Melanie Drozdowski, Fang Guang Xiong, Laura Kelleher, Dah-Wing Lee, Xiaoyun Ma, and Wijiang Zhang who helped us with the solutions to the exercises, and our typist, Patricia Nally.

It has been a pleasure to work with Mary Lu Walsh and Kim Rieck Fisher, editors at D. C. Heath. To these people and the others who have helped us, we express our appreciation.

Margaret B. Cozzens
Richard D. Porter

Contents

1 Sets 1

1.1 Mathematical Language: Sets and Politics   2
1.2 Survey Sampling   8
1.3 More on Sets   17
1.4 Ballot Counting   25

Chapter Summary   33
Review Exercises   33

2 Graphs 37

2.1 Scheduling Problems—Coloring   38
2.2 RNA Chains—Eulerian Paths   49
2.3 Traveling Salesman Problem—Hamiltonian Paths and Circuits   65
2.4 Assignment Problems—Matching   78
2.5 Shortest Route Problems   86

Chapter Summary   98
Review Exercises   99

3 Trees 105

3.1 Trees to List and Count the Possibilities   106
3.2 Games and Search I   114
3.3 Search II—One-way Streets   121
3.4 Minimum Spanning Trees   130

Chapter Summary   137
Review Exercises   137

4 Counting 141

4.1 Sum and Product Rules—DNA Revisited   142

4.2 Permutations   *149*
4.3 Voting Power   *156*
4.4 Combinations   *162*
4.5 Probability   *171*

Chapter Summary   *182*

Review Exercises   *183*

5 *Probability* 185

5.1 Probability Spaces   *185*
5.2 Conditional Probability and Independent Events   *200*
5.3 Probability Trees—Bayes' Theorem   *212*
5.4 Expected Value   *224*

Chapter Summary   *234*

Review Exercises   *234*

6 *Relations and Functions* 239

6.1 Relations   *240*
6.2 Functions—Input-Output   *247*
6.3 Polynomial Functions—Coloring Revisited   *258*
6.4 Equivalence Relations—How to Cut up the Pie   *268*
6.5 Order Relations   *275*

Chapter Summary   *287*

Review Exercises   *288*

7 *Mathematics of Finance* 291

7.1 Savings Accounts—Compound Interest   *291*
7.2 Annuities and Sinking Funds—Accumulating Capital   *299*
7.3 Amortization Tables—Installment Loans   *310*

Chapter Summary   *321*

Review Exercises   *322*

8 *Difference Equations* 325

8.1 Introduction to Difference Equations—The Tower of Hanoi   *326*
8.2 Applications—Radioactive Decay, Newton's Law of
     Cooling   *340*

8.3 Solving Difference Equations by Iteration *352*

Chapter Summary *358*

Review Exercises *358*

9 Linear Programming—A Geometrical Approach *361*

9.1 Graphing Linear Equations *362*
9.2 Algebraic Solutions to Systems of Linear Equations *370*
9.3 Graphing Linear Inequalities *380*
9.4 Linear Programming—Problem Formulation *392*
9.5 Linear Programming—Geometrical Solutions *403*

Chapter Summary *416*

Review Exercises *416*

10 Matrices *419*

10.1 Matrices, Relations, and Graphs *419*
10.2 Matrix Arithmetic *428*
10.3 Markov Chains—Transition Matrices *446*
10.4 Gauss-Jordan Elimination: Systems with a Unique Solution *462*
10.5 Gauss-Jordan Elimination: Systems with More than One Solution *476*
10.6 Inverses—Leontief Input-Output Models *491*

Chapter Summary *513*

Review Exercises *515*

11 Linear Programming—The Simplex Algorithm *521*

11.1 Simplex Algorithm—Getting Started—Pivoting *522*
11.2 Simplex Algorithm—Finding the Optimum *532*
11.3 Minimization and Duality *545*
11.4 Using a Computer for the Simplex Method *557*

Chapter Summary *577*

Review Exercises *578*

12 Game Theory   581

12.1   Introduction to Game Theory—Strictly Determined Games   582
12.2   Mixed Strategies   589
12.3   Mixed Strategies Through Linear Programming   603
12.4   General Games   614

Chapter Summary   622

Review Exercises   623

Answers to Odd-Numbered Exercises A1
References A71
Index A75

Mathematics and Its Applications

Sets

1

In this chapter we develop some of the machinery involved in problem solving. Identifying what is important and what is not, and selecting (or creating) a suitable mathematical structure are crucial to solving any type of problem. The mathematical structure varies from problem to problem, but most problems have a common base structure, called sets. A *set* is simply a collection of objects. Sets are used to examine mathematical systems, to understand the concept of counting, and to characterize aspects of applied problems.

Even though the study of sets had its formal origin in 1850, sets have been known intuitively for centuries. The theory of sets was developed by Cantor in the middle 1800s as an important new branch of mathematics. Even arithmetic, it was discovered, could be defined using sets. It was not until the 1960s, the post-Sputnik era, that the language of sets was introduced to school children. Even then, there was controversy about what was "new" and what was "old" math. The belief today is that the language and concepts of sets both clarify mathematical ideas and provide a structure or framework into which many problems can be placed.

People often encounter problems that require the solver to understand the nature of the problem and to put the problem into a mathematical setting, using the language of mathematics. In the first section of this chapter we introduce the language of sets in the context of attempting to solve certain political problems. It is hoped that the student will learn the language of sets and at the same time begin to gain insight into the problem-solving process.

In the second section we introduce an application of sets to data collection and analysis. In this section Venn Diagrams of sets and set operations are used to solve specific counting problems.

The third section presents a preview of "things to come" in the remainder of the book. At the same time this section indicates the tremendously wide range of problems whose structure includes sets. Writing codes (as in Morse codes and DNA codes) is introduced and studied later in Chapter 2. An introduction to probability is given here as a preview to Chapter 5.

Section 1.4 discusses a number of possible solutions to the problem of how to count ballots in an election, pointing out that there is no "perfect" solution to the problem. Here, as in the previous sections, sets form the framework of the problem, but the whole analytical process of problem solving is discussed.

1.1   *Mathematical Language: Sets and Politics*

One of the basic concepts in mathematics is that of a set. For our purposes we shall consider a **set** to be a collection of objects, called **elements**. We generally use capital letters for sets and small letters or numbers for elements of sets. For example, consider $A = \{1, 2, 3\}$. We use the notation $a \in A$ to mean "a is an element of set A," and $a \notin A$ to mean "a is not an element of set A." In the example above, $1 \in A$ and $4 \notin A$. Two sets are equal if they have exactly the same elements. A set A is a **subset** of another set B, denoted $A \subseteq B$, if every element of set A is an element of set B. $\{1, 3\} \subseteq A$. A set A is a **proper subset** of a set B, denoted $A \subsetneq B$, if $A \subseteq B$ and $A \neq B$. To get a feel for working with sets, look at an application to political structures.

Let A be the set of people who have to vote to reach a decision about a piece of legislation, a candidate, etc., and assume that each member of A must vote either for or against the legislation or the candidate. A **winning coalition** is a subset of A whose members as a whole have enough votes to win. The number of votes necessary to win not only depends on the size of A, but also on a preestablished formula or rule. In some cases a simple majority (more than one-half) is sufficient to win, while in others two-thirds of the total number of votes cast is necessary to win. In other situations, as in the United Nations, certain members have veto power, and therefore their votes are necessary, regardless of numbers, to pass a resolution.

When sets are small we often use the brace notation to describe the elements in the set. For example, the set consisting of a, b, and c can be written as $\{a, b, c\}$. Only those listed within the braces are elements of the set.

EXAMPLE 1 $A = \{a, b, c, d\}$. Each member has one vote, and a simple majority decides the issue. Hence a winning coalition must have at least three votes. The winning coalitions are the subsets $\{a, b, c\}$, $\{a, b, d\}$, $\{a, c, d\}$, $\{b, c, d\}$, and $\{a, b, c, d\}$. The first four are called **minimal winning coalitions**: they are winning coalitions and no proper subset of them is a winning coalition. ■

Suppose we change the rule slightly but do not change the set.

EXAMPLE 2

Let $A = \{a, b, c, d\}$. Each member has one vote, and in case of a tie vote, a, as chairperson, has the deciding vote. Otherwise the simple majority rule is in effect. The winning coalitions of the previous example are still winning coalitions, but now $\{a, b\}$, $\{a, c\}$, and $\{a, d\}$ are too. Certain police courts that consist of three jurors and a judge operate with this system. ■

In many situations, a person may not have just one vote. For example, a representative of an election district has a number of votes proportional to the population of his or her district. The number of votes a stockholder in a company has corresponds to the percentage of shares the stockholder owns in the company.

EXAMPLE 3

Let $A = \{a, b, c, d\}$, and members a, b, c, and d have 6, 5, 5, and 1 votes, respectively. A three-fourths majority, or 13 votes, is needed to win. The winning coalitions are $\{a, b, c\}$, with 16 votes, and $\{a, b, c, d\}$, with 17 votes. Only $\{a, b, c\}$ is a minimal winning coalition. In other words, d is powerless. ■

The number of votes a person has does not always correspond to his or her real power.

EXAMPLE 4

Let $A = \{a, b, c\}$, and let members a and b have 4 votes and member c have only 1 vote. A simple majority, or 5 votes, is needed to win. The minimal winning coalitions are $\{a, b\}$, with 8 votes, $\{a, c\}$, with 5 votes, and $\{b, c\}$, with 5 votes. Thus, each member has the same power, yet not nearly the same number of votes. ■

In the previous examples, in order to determine the winning coalitions, we determined the number of votes necessary to win and looked for those subsets whose total vote count equaled or exceeded this amount. An alternative to this method is to write out *all* of the subsets of the set of voters, and assign to each subset the total number of votes it possesses. Thus, in Example 4, we would have the subsets

$\{a\}$ with 4 votes
$\{b\}$ with 4 votes
$\{c\}$ with 1 vote
$\{a, b\}$ with 8 votes
$\{a, c\}$ with 5 votes
$\{b, c\}$ with 5 votes
$\{a, b, c\}$ with 9 votes

The **empty set**, the set with no elements, denoted $\varnothing$, is a subset of every set. Therefore, we also have the $\varnothing$ with 0 votes. Now, the winning coalitions are those subsets listed with greater than or equal to 5 votes.

The set of all subsets of a set A is called the **power set** of A, and is denoted $P(A)$. Thus if $A = \{a, b, c\}$, then

$$P(A) = \{\varnothing, \{a\}, \{b\}, \{c\}, \{a, b\}, \{a, c\}, \{b, c\}, \{a, b, c\}\}$$

In Chapter 4 we will actually prove that there are 2^n subsets of an n-element set. Thus, we did not have to write out $P(A)$ to see that there are 8 subsets of A. Similarly, if A has 4 elements, then $P(A)$ has 16 elements, so there are 16 subsets of A. As the size of A increases, this method takes considerably longer than just looking for winning coalitions directly.

The **complement** of a subset B of A, denoted $A - B$, or just B', when A is the largest set in the discussion, is the set of elements that are in A and not in B. For example, if $A = \{1, 2, 3, 4, 5\}$ and $B = \{1, 2, 5\}$, then $B' = \{3, 4\}$. A subset B is a **blocking coalition** if B is not a winning coalition, and, when the members of B vote against an issue, the remaining members of A cannot combine to pass the issue. Therefore, if B is a blocking coalition, then B' is not a winning coalition, and B is not a winning coalition.

EXAMPLE 5   Let $A = \{a, b, c, d\}$, and members a, b, c, and d have 4, 4, 3, and 3 votes, respectively. If a simple majority is required for a win then 8 votes are needed, and the winning coalitions are $\{a, b\}$, $\{a, c, d\}$, $\{b, c, d\}$, $\{a, b, c\}$, $\{a, b, d\}$, and $\{a, b, c, d\}$. However, $B = \{b, c\}$, $C = \{b, d\}$, $D = \{a, c\}$, and $E = \{a, d\}$ are all blocking coalitions, since they are not winning coalitions and $B' = \{a, d\}$, $C' = \{a, c\}$, $D' = \{b, d\}$, and $E' = \{b, c\}$ are not winning coalitions. ∎

If a person with *veto power* is one whose vote is necessary to pass any piece of legislation, then in Example 3, each of a, b, and c has veto power. On the other hand, a *dictator* is defined to be one who single-handedly carries a decision, that is, the legislation passes if and only if the dictator votes in favor of the legislation. None of a, b, or c is a dictator.

EXAMPLE 6 $A = \{a, b, c, d\}$ and members a, b, c, and d have 5, 1, 1, and 1 votes, respectively. For even the simple majority rule, $\{a\}$ is a winning coalition, and it is the only minimal winning coalition. There are no blocking coalitions. ∎

PRACTICE EXAMPLE 1   A committee that passes judgment on the amount of violence in a TV show consists of the president, vice president, treasurer, and station manager, or simply $\{P, V, T, S\}$. If these members have 5, 4, 3, and 2 votes, respectively, and a simple majority is required to allow a TV show to be broadcast, list all winning coalitions and blocking coalitions as sets. Which of those listed are minimal winning coalitions? Suppose the requirement is changed to a two-thirds majority needed for approval. What changes are made in these three types of coalitions? Answer the same questions if the vote distribution changes to 15, 12, 9, and 6 votes, respectively. ■

In politics, coalitions are not born; they are created to either block a resolution, or pass a resolution, block a person from winning an election, or elect a particular individual. Often persons are convinced to join a coalition in return for favors once the election is over. When two sets B and C are combined, we call it the **union** of sets B and C, denoted $B \cup C$. $B \cup C$ is the set consisting of the elements that belong to B or C or both.

EXAMPLE 7   Let $A = \{$Hart, Mondale, Glenn, Jackson, Askew, McGovern$\}$, or simply $\{$H, M, G, J, A, Mc$\}$. H and M have 30 votes each, G and J have 15 votes each, and A and Mc have 5 votes each. If a simple majority is necessary to win, then 51 votes are needed. No single element subset is a winning coalition, but if H can combine with the coalition $\{$G, J$\}$ by offering certain favors if elected, then $\{$H$\} \cup \{$G, J$\} = \{$H, G, J$\}$ is a winning coalition with 60 votes. $\{$M, A, Mc$\}$ is not even a blocking coalition, since it has only 40 votes. ■

PRACTICE EXAMPLE 2   Let $A = \{a, b, c, d, e\}$, and members a, b, c, d, and e have 3, 3, 5, 6, and 1 votes, respectively. There are 12 votes required to pass a resolution. Let $B = \{a, b\}$, $C = \{b, c\}$, $D = \{c, d\}$, and $E = \{e\}$. Find $B \cup C$, $B \cup D$, $C \cup D$, $D \cup E$, $B \cup E$, $C \cup E$, $B \cup E'$, $C' \cup D$. Which of these sets are winning coalitions and which are blocking coalitions? ■

Sometimes coalitions will overlap. In the previous example coalitions B and C have the element b in common. Formally, if B and C are two sets, then the **intersection** of B and C, denoted $B \cap C$, is the set consisting of the elements that belong to both B and C. For example, $\{$H, M, J, G$\} \cap \{$M, J, Mc, A$\} = \{$M, J$\}$. In the context of politics, one might say that Mondale = M and Jackson = J are both wanted in the same two coalitions.

A useful way of picturing the operations union, intersection, and complement on sets is by depicting the sets as circles contained in a box, which represents subsets of a whole set. This type of diagram is called a **Venn diagram**. The three operations are shown pictured with Venn diagrams in Figure 1.1.

Figure 1.1

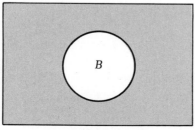

$B' = $ Shaded area

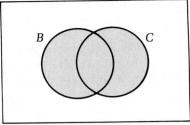

$B \cup C$ = Shaded area

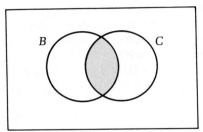

$B \cap C$ = Shaded area

In the next section we use Venn diagrams to help us count and organize data when surveys are taken.

CONCEPTS

set
element
subset
proper subset
winning coalition
minimal winning coalition
complement of a set

blocking coalition
empty set
power set
union
intersection
Venn diagram

SOLUTIONS TO PRACTICE EXAMPLES

1. Total votes = 5 + 4 + 3 + 2 = 14, simple majority requires 8 votes.
   Winning coalitions:
   {P, V}, {P, T}, {V, T, S} minimal
   {P, V, T, S}, {P, V, T}, {P, T, S}, {P, V, S} nonminimal

   Blocking coalitions: {V, T}, {P, S}
   Two-thirds vote required = 10 votes

Winning coalitions:

{P, V, T}, {P, T, S}, {P, V, S} minimal

{P, V, T, S} nonminimal

Blocking coalitions: {P}, {T, S}, {P, S}, {V, S}, {P, T}, {P, V}, {V, T}, {V, T, S}.

Vote changes: $15 + 12 + 9 + 6 = 42$ total, simple majority requires 22 votes.

Winning coalitions:

{P, V}, {P, T}, {V, T, S} minimal

{P, V, T}, {P, V, S}, {P, T, S}, {P, V, T, S} nonminimal

Blocking coalitions: {P, S}, {V, T}.

Two-thirds vote required $= 28$ votes

Winning coalitions:

{P, V, T}, {P, V, S}, {P, T, S} minimal

{P, V, T, S} nonminimal

Blocking coalitions: {P}, {P, T}, {P, V}, {P, S}, {V, T}, {V, T}, {T, S}, {V, T, S}.

2. $B \cup C = \{a, b, c\}$ 11 votes—blocking coalition

$B \cup D = \{a, b, c, d\}$ 17 votes—winning coalition

$C \cup D = \{b, c, d\}$ 14 votes—winning coalition

$D \cup E = \{c, d, e\}$ 12 votes—winning coalition

$B \cup E = \{a, b, e\}$ 7 votes—blocking coalition

$C \cup E = \{b, c, e\}$ 9 votes—blocking coalition

$B \cup E' = \{a, b, c, d\}$ 17 votes—winning coalition

$C' \cup D = \{a, c, d, e\}$ 14 votes—winning coalition

EXERCISES 1.1

1. At the 1980 Republican convention there were two contenders for the presidential nomination: Ford and Reagan. At the Democratic convention there were three contenders for the presidential nomination: Carter, Humphrey, and Mondale. A public opinion poll was used to determine in advance the voters' preference for each possible pair in the November election. How many different pairs must the voters be questioned about? Write them as sets.

2. A committee has 12 members, each member has one vote, and a simple majority is sufficient to pass any legislation. How many members are necessary for a winning coalition? How many members are necessary for a winning coalition if the committee has $2m$ members?

3. Let $A = \{a, b, c, d, e\}$, and let each member have one vote.
   (a) If a simple majority is required for a measure to pass, list all winning coalitions, minimal winning coalitions, and blocking coalitions.
   (b) If two-thirds of the membership must vote in favor of the measure for the measure to pass, list all winning coalitions, minimal winning coalitions, and blocking coalitions.

4. Answer the same questions as in Exercise 3 if the members of A have 10, 8, 5, 5, and 3 votes, respectively.

5. The Security Council of the United Nations has 15 members. These include the 5 permanent large nation members and 10 others elected for a two-year term. For a measure to pass, 9 votes are required, but these 9 votes must include all 5 of the permanent members. Find the minimal winning coalitions and the blocking coalitions.

6. In Nassau County, New York, in 1964, the Board of Supervisors consisted of 6 members, with a vote distribution of 31, 31, 28, 21, 2, and 2 votes. There were 59 votes needed to win. List all minimal winning coalitions and blocking coalitions. Discuss what your answers say about the political strength of each member.

7. In the Australian government, each of the 6 states gets 1 vote and the federal government gets 2 votes. There are 5 votes needed to win, but in the case of a 4−4 tie the federal government makes the decision. List all minimal winning coalitions. To eliminate any problem with ties we could give the federal government 3 votes instead of 2. List the minimal winning coalitions under this plan. Are they the same?

8. Let $A = \{a, b, x, y\}$. A coalition wins if at least a or b is in it, and at least x or y is in it. List all winning coalitions, all minimal winning coalitions, and all blocking coalitions.

9. Consider a committee of three senators and three representatives. A measure passes this committee if it receives the support of at least two senators and at least two representatives. Set up a set A, and give all minimal winning coalitions and blocking coalitions.

10. A committee consists of three Democrats: a, b, c; three Republicans: x, y, z; and one Liberal: p. A simple majority is needed to pass any measure. Look at the coalitions: $B = \{a, b, c\}$, $C = \{x, y, z\}$, $D = \{p\}$, $E = \{a, b, p\}$, $F = \{x, y, p\}$, $G = \{c, z, p\}$. Using set operations and only these sets, describe three winning coalitions and three blocking coalitions.

11. What is the power set of $A = \{a, b, c, d\}$?

12. How many elements are in $P(S)$ when $S = \{1, 3, 5, 7, 9\}$?

13. Give an example in everyday life where both a set and its complement can win.

14. Find the vote distribution and the number necessary to win in Exercise 5.

15. Is it possible to determine the number necessary to win in Exercise 8? Why?

1.2 Survey Sampling

An interesting application of sets, set operations, and the use of Venn diagrams comes in **survey sampling**. After a survey is taken and data collected, you need an efficient way to analyze the data.

Since each Venn diagram consists of a set of regions in a box, we can think of these regions as describing specific subsets of the large set or universal set. For example, the Venn diagram shown in Fig. 1.2 for two sets A and B divides the universal set into four regions: region I represents those elements in A and not in B, equivalently $A - B$; region II represents those elements in both A and B, equivalently $A \cap B$; region III represents those elements in B and not in A, equivalently $B - A$; and region IV represents those elements not in A and not in B, equivalently $(A \cup B)'$, or $A' \cap B'$.

Figure 1.2

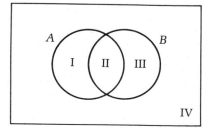

If we can determine from the data collected the number of elements in each of the basic regions, we can answer other questions about the data.

EXAMPLE 1   Suppose an advertising agency asked 100 people if they liked three brands of coffee, brand A, brand B, and brand C, and recorded the information in a Venn diagram as shown in Figure 1.3. (Being in A means "liked" brand A.)

Figure 1.3

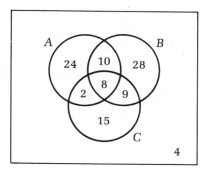

The following questions can be easily answered from Figure 1.3.

1. How many people liked all three brands? 8—the overlap of all three circles.
2. How many people did not like any of the brands? 4—the region outside all of the circles.
3. How many people liked only coffee B? 28—the region in B and not in A or C.
4. How many people liked brands A and C only? 2—the region where A and C overlap that is not part of B.

5. How many people liked at least one brand of coffee? 96—the number in any one of the regions within the circles = the number in $A \cup B \cup C$; or can be computed as $100 - 4$, all but the outside region.

6. How many people liked coffee A or coffee B, but not coffee C? $24 + 10 + 28 = 62$ or $100 - 4 - 15 - 2 - 8 - 9 = 62$—the number in $(A \cup B) - C$, or the total number — the number not in $A \cup B \cup C$ — the number in C.

This time suppose we are not given the Venn diagram with numbers filled in, but only the results of the survey.

EXAMPLE 2

A high school guidance counselor surveys 100 freshman to see their interest in taking the three languages offered at the high school: French, Spanish, and Russian.

5 expressed interest in all three
8 expressed interest in French and Russian
19 in Spanish and Russian
15 in Spanish and French
41 in Spanish
29 in French
26 in Russian

Because of the way the survey was taken and recorded, he does not know how many did not want to take any language and would now like to determine this number. By constructing a Venn diagram with three intersecting circles, one representing Spanish = S, one representing French = F, and one representing Russian = R, this number, as well as other numbers of interest, can be determined.

STEP 1 Put 5 in the space corresponding to S ∩ F ∩ R, representing those that expressed interest in all three languages (Figure 1.4).

Figure 1.4

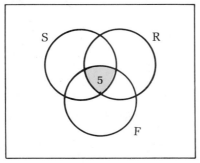

5 in all three

STEP 2 Put 8 in the intersection of R and F, but since 5 is already in the three-way intersection, $8 - 5 = 3$ is placed in the section denoting *only* R ∩ F and not R ∩ F ∩ S. Similarly, $19 - 5 = 14$ is placed in the section denoting S ∩ R and not R ∩ F ∩ S, and 15 − 5 = 10 is placed in the section denoting only S ∩ F and not S ∩ F ∩ R (Figure 1.5).

Figure 1.5

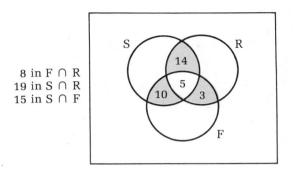

8 in F ∩ R
19 in S ∩ R
15 in S ∩ F

STEP 3   Forty-one are interested in Spanish, yet the Spanish circle already includes 14 + 5 + 10 = 29, so 41 − 29 = 12 is placed in the remaining area of the circle denoting Spanish. Similarly, 29 are interested in French, but 10 + 3 + 5 = 18 are already included in the French circle, hence 29 − 18 = 11 is placed in the remaining section. Finally, 26 are interested in Russian, yet 14 + 5 + 3 = 22 are already included, so 26 − 22 = 4 are placed in the remaining area (Figure 1.6).

Figure 1.6

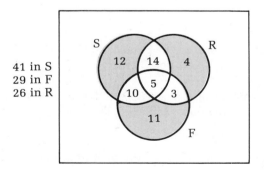

41 in S
29 in F
26 in R

STEP 4   To find out how many are interested in no language at all, we simply add all of the numbers in the circles and subtract this sum from 100, the total number in the survey.

$$12 + 14 + 4 + 10 + 5 + 3 + 11 = 59 \text{ and } 100 - 59 = 41.$$

Thus 41 are in (S ∪ R ∪ F)′ as shown in Figure 1.7.

Figure 1.7

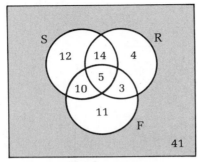

Total = 100

To see how many people are interested in only one language, we can use the diagram and add the numbers 11 + 4 + 12 = 27. Even more questions can be answered using the final diagram. ◾

A survey of 1000 people showed that prior to the first Democratic primary in 1984:

    250 people liked Mondale
    230 people liked Glenn
    220 people liked Hart
      80 liked Mondale and Glenn
      70 liked Mondale and Hart
      60 liked Glenn and Hart
      20 liked all three

How many people surveyed liked none of these three? How many people surveyed liked only one of the three? How many of those surveyed liked Mondale, but not Hart and not Glenn? ◾

Often, it is not as easy to set up the Venn diagram to solve the problem as it was in the previous problems. This will be illustrated in the next example.

EXAMPLE **3**

A random sample of 50 undergraduate students and 35 graduate students was surveyed to determine preference for the semester system versus the quarter system. It is known that 33 students favored the quarter system, and 23 undergraduates favored the semester system, but all of the remaining data were lost. Can you determine how many favored the semester system? To answer this question, we will go back to the very beginning of this section where we talked about sets in a Venn diagram dividing the universal set into regions. There are basically two kinds of people and their complements. We have graduate students and their complement, undergraduates, and we have those who favor the quarter system and their complement, those who favor the semester system. We make one of the basic sets in the Venn diagram G for graduate students, and the other Q for those favoring the quarter system. This results in the Venn diagram shown in Figure 1.8, with region I, the set of graduate students favoring the semester system; region II, the set of graduate students favoring the quarter system; region III, the set of undergraduates favoring the quarter system; and region IV the set of undergraduates favoring the semester system.

Figure 1.8

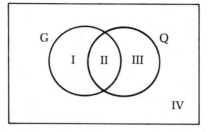

From the data we have, we know that G has 35 elements in it and G′ has 50 elements in it. We also know that Q has 33 elements in it, therefore Q′ has $(35 + 50) - 33 = 52$ elements in it. Since 23 undergraduates favored the semester system, region IV has 23 elements in it. This region corresponds to $(G \cup Q)'$. Since Q′ has 52 elements, the shaded area G–Q must have $52 - 23 = 29$ elements (Figure 1.9).

Figure 1.9

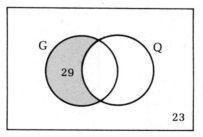

Now, since G has 35 elements, $G \cap Q$ must have $35 - 29 = 6$ elements (Figure 1.10).

Figure 1.10

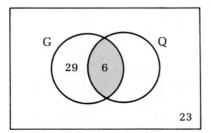

Finally, since Q has 33 elements, we can complete the diagram by computing the number of elements in Q–G, namely, $33 - 6 = 27$ (Figure 1.11). ◼

Figure 1.11

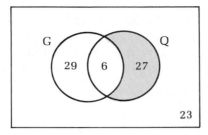

By now the observant student probably realizes that using Venn diagrams for more than three distinct sets or classes would be very difficult. Even for four sets, we would need to draw the circles not as circles, but as blobs in order to get a distinct region to represent the intersection of all four sets, regions to represent the three-way intersections (there are four of these), the six two-way intersections, as well as single regions for the part of each set that does not intersect the other three. In other words, we need 16 distinct regions as shown in Figure 1.12. With three sets we needed eight regions, making it possible to use the three-ring symbol to picture the sets.

Figure 1.12

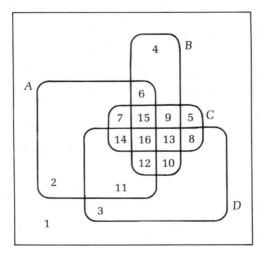

PRACTICE EXAMPLE 2   A survey was conducted of 100 college students who voted in the 1984 election for president. Of the students, 50 were freshmen, 55 voted Republican, and 35 were nonfreshmen who voted Democratic. Use a Venn diagram to determine how many freshmen voted Republican. ◼

In the next section we use sets and set operations to describe a variety of situations. At the same time we introduce some of the topics that will be discussed in detail in future chapters.

CONCEPTS

survey sampling
numerical Venn diagrams

SOLUTIONS TO PRACTICE EXAMPLES

1.

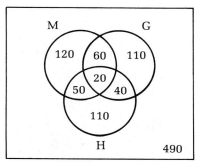

Total = 1000

490 = number of people who liked none of the three.
120 + 110 + 110 = 340 = the number of people who liked only one of the three.
120 = the number of people who liked Mondale, but not Hart and not Glenn.

2.

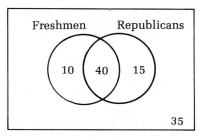

Since 35 were nonfreshmen who voted Democratic, 100 − 35 = 65 belong to F ∪ R. But 50 + 55 = 105 − 65 = 40 must belong to F ∩ R. Therefore F–R has 10 elements and R–F has 15 elements. The number of freshmen who voted Republican is 40.

EXERCISES 1.2

1. A mathematics class has 25 students. Of these, 15 are freshmen, 14 are business majors, and 6 are neither. Use a Venn diagram to determine how many are freshmen business majors.

2. If set A has 17 elements, set B has 13 elements, and $A \cap B$ has 9 elements, how many elements does $A \cup B$ have?

3. If set A has 16 elements, set B has 10 elements, and $A \cup B$ has 20 elements, how many elements does $A \cap B$ have?

4. In the Venn diagram below, identify the region corresponding to each of the following.
   (a) $E–F$ (b) $F–G$ (c) $G–E$
   (d) $E \cap F \cap G$ (e) $(E \cap F)–(E \cap F \cap G)$
   (f) $E' \cap (F \cap G)$

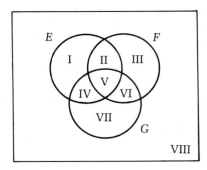

5. A survey of 100 people in Hanover showed that:

   33 read *Newsweek*

   29 read *Yankee*

   22 read *People*

   13 read *Newsweek* and *Yankee*

   6 read *Yankee* and *People*

   14 read *Newsweek* and *People*

   6 read all three

   (a) How many read none of the three?
   (b) How many read only one of the magazines?
   (c) How many read *Newsweek* and *Yankee* but not *People*?

6. If set A has 29 elements, set B has 11 elements, set C has 12 elements, set $A \cap B$ has 1 element, set $A \cap C$ has 5 elements, set $B \cap C$ has 2 elements, and set $A \cap B \cap C$ has 1 element, $A \cup B \cup C$ has how many elements? How many elements are not in any of the sets A, B, C?

7.   A survey of 1000 businesspeople showed that:

   10 drove a car, took the subway, and walked to work

   60 drove a car and took the subway

   10 took the subway and walked

   50 drove a car and walked

   450 drove a car

   300 took the subway

   200 walked

   (a) How many businesspeople surveyed did not get to work in any of these three ways?
   (b) How many businesspeople surveyed only drove a car?
   (c) How many businesspeople surveyed used only one of the three modes of transportation?

8.   Among a group of 30 applicants for a job with a computer firm, 2 are over 40 years old with a degree in computer science and previous experience. There are 5 who have previous experience and a degree in computer science, 3 are over 40 and have a degree in computer science, and 6 are over 40 with previous experience. Of the total applicants 10 are over 40, 15 have previous experience, and 12 have a degree in computer science.
   (a) How many of the applicants have no previous experience, are not over 40, and do not have a degree in computer science?
   (b) How many of the applicants do not have a degree in computer science or do not have previous experience?
   (c) How many of the applicants are over 40 and do not have a degree in computer science.

9.   A survey was made of 36 children in grades 6 and 7 to see if they wanted to take a language in junior high school. There were 20 sixth graders, 18 of whom said that they wanted to take a language, and 8 seventh graders who did not want to take a language. How many seventh graders wanted to take a language? How many sixth graders did not want to take a language?

1.3   More on Sets

In the previous two sections we introduced sets and set operations to look at two types of real-world situations. In this section, we will see that sets and set operations can be used to look closely at a wide variety of problems. We will also generalize the notion of coalition to situations where voting is not directly involved.

A **code** is a set of sequences of symbols, letters, or numbers used to represent (and transmit) information.

EXAMPLE 1   Deoxyribonucleic acid, **DNA**, is a basic material in chromosomes and carries the inherited characteristics during reproduction. DNA is a chain in which each link of the chain, called a *base*, is a member of the set of chemicals:

Figure 1.13
(By Lloyd K. Townsend, © 1984 National Geographic Society)

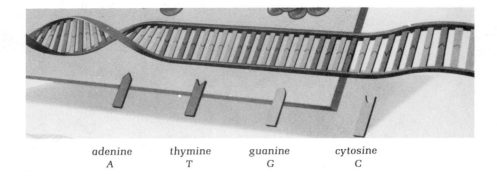

adenine   thymine   guanine   cytosine
A   T   G   C

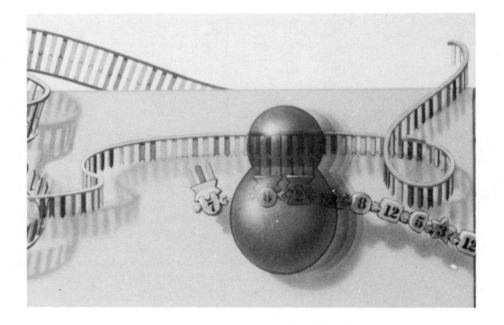

B = {thymine = T, cytosine = C, adenine = A, guanine = G}. They appear in pairs in a ladderlike structure as shown in Figure 1.13. Adenine and thymine are paired, and guanine and cytosine are paired as rungs of the ladder. Sugars and phosphates make up the boundary of the ladder. Sequences of bases read along one side of the ladder encode (represent) certain genetic information. Cells produce thousands of proteins by making a small opening at some point in a DNA molecule and separating it to expose the bases whose sequence is the blueprint for the protein. Subunits of these proteins are called *amino acids*. A single part of a DNA chain will encode one such amino acid.

If we look at two-element DNA chains, we have 16 possible chains, given by: $\mathscr{C} = \{$TC, TA, TG, TT, CT, CA, CG, CC, AT, AC, AG, AA, GT, GC, GA, GG$\}$. Since there are 20 basic amino acids, we need longer than two-element DNA chains to encode all of them. Here sets are used to represent the possibilities, with members as the various possible chains.

RNA, ribonucleic acid, a messenger molecule found in chromosomes, copies the DNA blueprint. The bases of an RNA chain come from the set $F = \{$A, C, G, U = uracil$\} = (B - \{$T$\}) \cup \{$U$\}$. The ordering of bases in an RNA chain determines the combination of amino acids that forms a protein. Enzymes act on RNA chains to break them into pieces, called *fragments*. In Chapter 2 we will show how to reconstruct RNA chains from sets of fragments.

PRACTICE EXAMPLE 1

Write out the set of all three-base RNA chains starting with U.

EXAMPLE 2

In Morse code, letters of the alphabet are transmitted using sequences of dots and dashes. For example, a is the sequence $* -$, and k is the sequence $- * -$. Only six of the letters of the alphabet can be encoded using one or two element sequences of dots and dashes. The set of one and two element sequences is $S = \{*, -, * *, - -, * -, - *\}$. We would need to use one, two, three, and four element sequences to encode all 26 letters of the alphabet. Why?

Codes such as the Morse code that use just two symbols are called *binary codes*. These codes form the basis for computer technology today. If we use sequences of elements from the set $\{0, 1\}$, we can encode numbers, letters, instructions, etc. Complicated statements can be encoded and then translated into the design of switches (on–off) in a circuit.

The elements of a sequence in a binary code using members of the set $S = \{0, 1\}$ are called **bits**. For example, the number 5 can be encoded using three bits, 101, since $5 = 1(2^2) + 0(2^1) + 1(2^0)$ and the number 8 can be encoded using four bits, 1000 $= 1(2^3) + 0(2^2) + 0(2^1) + 0(2^0)$. If we want to indicate signed numbers, one possible method is to reserve one bit, the leftmost, for the sign. If the number is positive the first bit is 1, otherwise the first bit is 0. Therefore, $+5$ is encoded with 1101, and -5 is encoded with 0101.

Everyone is familiar with *experiments*, situations which can be repeated many times, the results of which cannot be predicted in advance. Researchers in biology, chemistry, physics, and psychology, perform experiments as part of their research. When we repeatedly play various games, we are conducting an experiment. Each time a set of Megabucks lottery numbers is rolled out, we witness the experiment: "given 36 numbers, choose 6 at random." What does this have to do with sets? The collection (set) of all possible outcomes of an experiment is called the **sample space** for the experiment. The outcomes, or elements, of the sample space are called **simple events**. A familiar example can be used to illustrate these ideas. Toss a coin and observe whether a head or tail appears. The sample space $S = \{H, T\}$, H for head and T for tail. If two coins are tossed the sample space becomes $S = \{HH, TT, HT, TH\}$, indicating the outcomes of two heads, two tails, a head on the first coin and a tail on the second coin, and a tail on the first coin and a head on the second coin.

EXAMPLE 3

A subject in a behavioral psychology experiment is asked which color—red, blue, green, or yellow—he finds most pleasing to the eye. Using r for red, b for blue, g for green, and y for yellow, the sample space can be given as $S = \{r, b, g, y\}$. ∎

PRACTICE EXAMPLE 2

When penicillin was first discovered, experiments were conducted on pneumonia patients to see if the patient improved, died, or showed no change after treatment with penicillin. Write the sample space for these experiments. ∎

EXAMPLE 4

A die (one dice) is rolled and the number on the top is recorded. The sample space for this experiment is $S = \{1, 2, 3, 4, 5, 6\}$. Each of the elements of S, considered as a singleton set, is a simple event. An **event** is any subset of the sample space S. Therefore, an event can be considered as the union of simple events. Usually events are described in words related to the experiment. For example, the event that a number less than 3 appears is the subset $E = \{1, 2\}$. The event that an even number appears is the subset $F = \{2, 4, 6\}$. We can use set operations to describe other events from these events. The event that an even number less than 3 appears is given by $E \cap F = \{1, 2\} \cap \{2, 4, 6\} = \{2\}$. The event that an even number or a number less than 3 appears is given by $E \cup F = \{1, 2\} \cup \{2, 4, 6\} = \{1, 2, 4, 6\}$. The event that an odd number appears is given by $F' = \{2, 4, 6\}' = \{1, 3, 5\}$.

If we involve union, intersection, and complement all at the same time, we can get events like the following. The event that a number greater than or equal to 3 and odd appears is given by $E' \cap F' = \{1, 2\}' \cap \{2, 4, 6\}' = \{3, 4, 5, 6\} \cap \{1, 3, 5\} = \{3, 5\}$. Notice that this is precisely the same set as $(E \cup F)' = \{1, 2, 4, 6\}' = \{3, 5\}$. Similarly, the event that a number greater than or equal to 3 or an odd number appears is given by $E' \cup F' = \{1, 2\}' \cup \{2, 4, 6\}' = \{3, 4, 5, 6\} \cup \{1, 3, 5\} = \{1, 3, 4, 5, 6\}$, but this is exactly the same as the set $(E \cap F)' = \{2\}' = \{1, 3, 4, 5, 6\}$. ∎

The two equivalences given in the last example $(E \cup F)' = E' \cap F'$ and $(E \cap F)' = E' \cup F'$, are not coincidences. These are statements of **De**

Morgan's laws for pairs of sets E and F, named after Augustus de Morgan, a British mathematician and logician of the nineteenth century. They say that to form the complement of a union (intersection) form the complements of the sets and change unions to intersections (intersections to unions).

We will use Venn diagrams to describe $(E \cup F)'$. In Figure 1.14a we have shaded $(E \cup F)'$, and in Figure 1.14b we have shaded E' lightly and F' darker, so that $E' \cap F'$ is the darkest shaded area. The lightly shaded area of 1.14b is the same as the shaded area of 1.14a, thus verifying the first of De Morgan's laws.

Figure 1.14

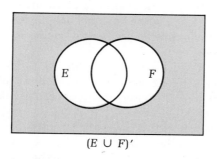

$(E \cup F)'$

(a) Shaded area

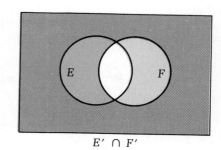

$E' \cap F'$

(b) Darkest shaded area

We can do the same for $(E \cap F)'$. In Figure 1.15a, we have shaded $(E \cap F)'$, and in Figure 1.15b, we have shaded E' lightly and F' darker. The total of all shaded parts of Figure 1.15b corresponds to $E' \cup F'$, and is the same as the shaded area of Figure 1.15a, namely $(E \cap F)'$, thus verifying the second of De Morgan's laws.

Figure 1.15

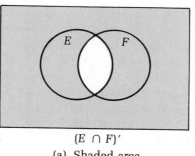

$(E \cap F)'$

(a) Shaded area

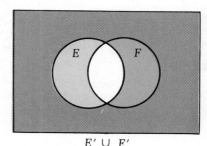

$E' \cup F'$

(b) All shaded area

In Chapter 4 we will use sample spaces, events, set operations, and these laws to compute probabilities of events.

PRACTICE EXAMPLE 3

A child's game has a spinner that determines how many spaces the child is to move. The spinner can land on spaces numbered from 1 to 8 and cannot land on a line. If the experiment is to spin the spinner and record the number it hits, what is the sample space? Let E be the event that an odd number is hit, and F be the event that a number greater than 4 is hit. Write out these two events as sets. Write out in words the event corresponding to E', and the event given by F'. Write out the set corresponding to the event that an even number less than or equal to 4 is hit. Write out the set corresponding to the event that an odd number or a number less than or equal to 4 is hit. What other set is this last set equivalent to (using the sets and set operations)?

We will end this section with examples of various kinds of nonvoting coalitions. We want to determine the basic set of "players" (voters in Section 1.1), and identify what constitutes a **winning coalition**.

EXAMPLE 5

An agency of the federal government has offered 10 states $6 million for development of waste treatment facilities, provided the states can agree on a distribution of the money. If no agreement is reached the federal government will hold the money.

$A = \{1, 2, 3, 4, 5, 6, 7, 8, 9, 10\}$, the set of 10 states each given a number, is the set of players. A winning coalition in this example is a subset of A such that the subset can guarantee itself money to be distributed. Therefore, the only winning coalition is the whole set A, since any other subset (coalition) would forfeit all the money, as no agreement would be reached. The **value of a coalition** is the amount of payoff the coalition can guarantee itself. In this example, the value of the coalition A is $6 million. The value of any other coalition is 0.

EXAMPLE 6

Each of eight people has a bag of garbage that he or she must drop in the yard of one of the eight people.

Let $A = \{1, 2, 3, 4, 5, 6, 7, 8\}$, corresponding to the eight people with garbage to dump, be the set of players. It is assumed that the players will cooperate and form coalitions. If, as a coalition, the players receive *less* garbage than they start out with as a group, the coalition is said to be a winning coalition. The coalition $\{1, 2, 3, 4, 5, 6, 7\}$ can agree to dump its garbage in the yard of player 8. The worst that can happen is that player 8 drops his or her garbage in the yard of one of the players in the coalition. Thus the coalition would receive at most one bag, substantially less than the 7 they started out with. However, the coalition $\{1, 2, 3, 4\}$ can agree to dump its garbage in yards of the other four, but each of the other four could drop their garbage in the yards of the players in the coalition. Thus, $\{1, 2, 3, 4\}$ would not constitute a winning coalition, whereas $\{1, 2, 3, 4, 5, 6, 7\}$ would constitute a winning coalition. The winning coalitions that would receive the least amount of garbage are the subsets: $A - \{1\}$, $A - \{2\}$, $A - \{3\}$, $A - \{4\}$, $A - \{5\}$, $A - \{6\}$, $A - \{7\}$, and $A - \{8\}$.

Situations such as those discussed in Examples 5 and 6 are examples of games. A *game* is defined as any competition or conflict between opponents, called *players*. These, and other types of games, will be discussed in Chapter 12.

PRACTICE EXAMPLE 4

Each of six countries has the means to destroy each one of the others. Write a set A to represent the players. Discuss what would constitute a winning coalition.

In the next section we will use sets to represent sets of candidates for an election, to represent legislation to be voted on, and to represent voter's preferences in an election. We will attempt to solve the problem of determining a winner in an election.

CONCEPTS

code	event
DNA	De Morgan's laws
RNA	winning coalition
sample space	value of coalition

SOLUTIONS TO PRACTICE EXAMPLES

1. {UAC, UAG, UCG, UAA, UCC, UGG, UUA, UUC, UUG, UUU, UCA, UGA, UGC, UAU, UCU, UGU}.

2. $S = \{I, D, N\}$, where I stands for improved, D stands for died, and N stands for no change.

3. $E = \{1, 3, 5, 7\}$ and $F = \{5, 6, 7, 8\}$.
   E' is the event that an even number is hit.
   F' is the event that a number less than or equal to 4 is hit.
   $E' \cap F' = \{2, 4\}$.
   $E \cup F' = \{1, 2, 3, 4, 5, 7\} = (E' \cap F)'$.

4. $A = \{1, 2, 3, 4, 5, 6\}$, where a number represents each country, is the set of players. A is the only winning coalition, since any country not in the coalition could destroy the ones in the coalition.

EXERCISES 1.3

1. Write out the set of all three-base DNA chains that begin with A and end with G.

2. $F = \{AC, C, U, AGC\}$ is a set of fragments that make up an RNA chain. For example, the RNA chain might be ACAGCUC. Write out all of the other possibilities.

3. The files of 10 people must be stored in a vault. Before these files are stored, each file is given a code number that uses only 0's and 1's. Only the person whose file is stored knows the number of his file and has access to it. Using sequences of at most 3 elements set up a coding scheme for these files.

4. A political poll surveys a group of people as to their preferences for a political party: Republican, Democratic, or Liberal, in the upcoming election. What is the sample space when this polling is viewed as an experiment?

5. A manufacturer of a particular computer chip insists on quality control. He samples 5 chips each hour and records the number defective. What is the sample space for this experiment? Describe the event "there are at least two defective chips" as a subset of your sample space.

6. Jane has a bag of 5 red balls numbered from 1 to 5, and 3 blue balls numbered from 6 to 8. The experiment consists of choosing a ball at random and recording its number and color.
    (a) What is the sample space for the experiment?
    (b) What is the event that a red ball appears?
    (c) What is the event that a ball numbered from 1 to 4 appears?
    (d) What is the event that a blue ball numbered 2 appears?
    (e) What is the event that a blue ball numbered less than 8 appears?
    (f) What is the event that a nonred ball numbered 4 or 7 appears?

7. A letter is chosen at random from the letters in the words "computer concepts."
    (a) What is the sample space for this experiment?
    (b) What is the event that a vowel is chosen?
    (c) What is the event that a letter preceding m in the alphabet is chosen?

8. In a version of a roulette game, the even numbers from 2 to 16 are colored red and the odd numbers from 1 to 15 are colored black. A ball is rolled and lands on one of the colored-numbered spots.
    (a) What is the sample space for this experiment?
    (b) Let E be the event that a number less than 10 is hit, and F be the event that a red number is hit. Describe in words the following events:
        (i) E'
        (ii) F'
        (iii) $E \cup F$
        (iv) $E \cap F$
        (v) $E' \cup F'$
        (vi) $(E \cup F)'$
        (vii) $(E \cap F')'$
    (c) Write each of the sets in part (b) as subsets of the sample space.

9. A card is drawn at random from the set of face cards (ace, jack, queen, king) in a deck of cards. The color and suit and name of the card are observed.
    (a) What is the sample space?
    (b) What is the event that a red queen is drawn?
    (c) What is the event that a spade or diamond is drawn?
    (d) What is the event that any king or the jack of clubs is drawn?

10. Using De Morgan's laws, what are each of the following equivalent to?
    (a) $(E \cup F')'$
    (b) $E' \cap F'$
    (c) $(E' \cap F)'$

11. A given tract of land is currently worth $100,000 to its owner while he uses it for farming. A shopping center developer can sell the land for $200,000, and a housing developer can sell the land for building lots for $300,000. Both the shopping center developer and the housing developer would like to buy the land. There are no other prospective buyers for the land. Let f represent the owner-farmer, s represent the shopping center developer, and h represent the housing developer. Therefore, the set $A = \{f, s, h\}$ is the set of players. Write out the set of subsets (coalitions) of A and discuss whether each can be considered as a winning coalition. Assign some kind of monetary gain to each coalition. For example, the coalition $\{f, s\}$ could be assigned $200,000, and the coalition $\{s\}$ could be assigned $0.

1.4   *Ballot Counting*

In this section we look at the problem of determining the winner (or winners) in an election. Not a mathematical problem, you say—but just wait and see! Here sets are used to describe the collection of candidates and the voters' preference for these candidates. The candidates may be people, brands of a product, or alternative pieces of legislation. The voters may be people voting in an election, consumers taking a taste test, or legislators voting on issues.

Little thought is given to how ballots are counted in an election, yet the procedure used can vastly affect the outcome of an election. The most interesting cases occur when the voters are asked to vote by **preferential ballot** (list the candidates in order of preference). We will assume for the moment that each voter must list *all* candidates in order of preference, and that an individual voter cannot be indifferent between two candidates.

The most common method of counting ballots does not initially take into account these preferences, but simply counts the total number of first place votes. The one receiving the greatest number of first place votes wins and is called the **plurality winner**. A slight variation of this procedure is to insist on a **majority winner**, namely, one who receives more than half of the first place votes. If no one does, all but the top two are crossed off the lists, and the votes are counted again. This is called the **run-off procedure** and may sometimes be used if there is a tie in the plurality method. In both cases, if the voters have voted preferentially, there is usually no need to have a second election when there is no majority winner.

We will describe the results of a preferential vote by displaying **preference orders** for the voters. For example,

B_3
B_2
B_1

means that the particular voter put B_3 in first place, B_2 in second place, and B_1 in third place on the ballot. To avoid listing the same preference order repeatedly, we will simply write the particular preference order once and list below it the total number of ballots with this preference order.

EXAMPLE 1   Three people are running for office: B_1, B_2, B_3. Under preferential balloting the following orders are possible.

	B_1	B_1	B_2	B_2	B_3	B_3
	B_2	B_3	B_1	B_3	B_1	B_2
	B_3	B_2	B_3	B_1	B_2	B_1
Votes cast	52	100	25	126	0	148

B_1 has $52 + 100 = 152$ first place votes, B_2 has $25 + 126 = 151$ first place votes, B_3 has $0 + 148 = 148$ first place votes. Thus, B_1 is the plurality winner, but B_1 does not have a majority. In a run-off, B_3 is eliminated, and we have the following:

	B_1	B_1	B_2	B_2	B_1	B_2
	B_2	B_2	B_1	B_1	B_2	B_1
Votes cast	52	100	25	126	0	148

B_1 now has $52 + 100 + 0 = 152$ first place votes, and B_2 has $25 + 126 + 148 = 299$ first place votes. Consequently, B_2 is the winner with more than half of the first place votes.

Maybe we should give candidates credit not only for the number of first place votes received, but also for the number of second place votes, third place votes, etc. The total number of points a candidate receives under this scheme is called the **borda count** of the candidate, after Jean-Charles de Borda, the developer of this method in the 1700s. The candidate with the highest number of points is declared the winner. For example, if each place in the preference order counts as follows:

first place = 2 points
second place = 1 point
third place = 0 points

then for the preference schedules given in the previous example, we get

	B_1	B_1	B_2	B_2	B_3	B_3
	B_2	B_3	B_1	B_3	B_1	B_2
	B_3	B_2	B_3	B_1	B_2	B_1
Votes cast	52	100	25	126	0	148

$$\text{count}(B_1) = 2(52) + 2(100) + 25 + 0 = 329$$
$$\text{count}(B_2) = 52 + 2(25) + 2(126) + 148 = 502$$
$$\text{count}(B_3) = 100 + 126 + 0 + 2(148) = 552$$

Thus, B_3 is declared the winner under the borda count method. ▪

It should be clear from this example that in many close races, the method of counting ballots and declaring a winner can completely alter the results. "A little knowledge is a dangerous thing"—to the opposition.

A fourth method was proposed by Marie Jean Antoine Nicolas Critat, the Marquis de Condorcet, in the 1700s, and is called the **condorcet criterion**. Suppose we can find one candidate who beats each of the other candidates in two-man races. "He should be the winner," said Condorcet. In the preference orders given above, we would have B_1 over B_2 in the first, second, and fifth, for a total of 152, and B_2 over B_1 in the third, fourth, and sixth, for a total of 199. Therefore, in a two-man race between B_1 and B_2, B_2 would win. We would also have B_1 over B_3 in the first three, giving B_1 a 177 total, and B_3 over B_1 in the last three, giving B_3 a 274 total. Thus, B_3 beats B_1 in a two-man race. Finally, we have B_2 over B_3 in the first, third, and fourth preference orders, for a total of 203, and B_3 over B_2 in the second, fifth, and sixth, for a total of 248. Thus, B_3 beats B_2 in a two-man race. B_3 is declared the winner by the condorcet criterion since he beats both B_1 and B_2 in two-man races.

Unfortunately, the condorcet criterion will not always produce a winner.

EXAMPLE 2   The following are the preference orders with nonzero votes in a three-product taste test.

	B_1	B_2	B_3
	B_3	B_1	B_2
	B_2	B_3	B_1
Votes cast	5	11	7

B_1	B_2	B_2		B_1	B_1	B_3		B_3	B_2	B_3
B_2	B_1	B_1		B_3	B_3	B_1		B_2	B_3	B_2
5	11	7		5	11	7		5	11	7

B_1 over B_2 with 5 B_1 over B_3 with 16 B_2 over B_3 with 11

B_2 over B_1 with 18 B_3 over B_1 with 7 B_3 over B_2 with 12

Thus, B_2 beats B_1 in a two-brand race between B_1 and B_2; B_1 beats B_3 in a two-brand race between B_1 and B_3; and B_3 beats B_2 in a two-brand race between B_2 and B_3. Therefore, neither B_1, B_2, nor B_3, beats the other two in a two-brand race, and no winner can be declared. ■

The following preference orders were the only orders appearing on ballots cast by high school students for the best pizza parlor. Determine the best pizza parlor under each of the following methods of counting ballots: plurality, majority and run-off (if necessary), borda count (first place = 3 points, second place = 2 points, third place = 1 point, and fourth place = 0 points), and the condorcet criterion.

A_1	A_2	A_3	A_2
A_4	A_3	A_2	A_4
A_2	A_1	A_1	A_1
A_3	A_4	A_4	A_3

| Votes cast | 15 | 9 | 4 | 3 |

In the last five years, another election procedure called **approval voting** has appeared. The idea behind approval voting is quite simple. In an election of three or more candidates for a single office, voters are not restricted to voting for just one candidate, nor to giving a complete preferential order to the candidates. Instead, each voter can vote for or "approve of" as many candidates as he or she wishes. Each candidate is given a point for each voter who votes for him or her. Thus, the winner is simply the candidate getting the largest number of points.

Two of the strongest proponents of approval voting, who have done extensive research on the procedure, are Steven Brams of New York University and Peter Fishburn of ATT. Their belief is that approval voting would improve the conduct of elections, leading to the selection of the candidate with the most widespread support. Approval voting would also counteract some of the negative aspects of exit polling. (*Exit polling* is a survey of how people voted that is made as they leave the polls.)

As an example of where approval voting could have made a difference, consider the U.S. Senate election in New York in 1980. Alphonse D'Amato defeated Elizabeth Holtzman and Jacob Javits with a 45% plurality. Holtzman had 44%, and Javits had 11%. An ABC exit poll of voters revealed that if Javits had not been in the race, twice as many of his supporters would have opted for Holtzman as for D'Amato, easily making Holtzman the winner in a two-candidate contest. Ironically, the Liberal party nominee (Javits) helped defeat the most liberal of the three Senate candidates (Holtzman).

Look at Example 1 again. Suppose each of the voters with preference order B_1, B_2, B_3 under approval voting approved of his first and second choice. Then B_1 and B_2 would each receive 52 votes. If those with preference order B_1, B_3, B_2 approved of B_1 and B_3, then B_1 and B_3 would each receive 100 votes. Similarly, if those with preference order B_3, B_2, B_1 approved of B_2

and B_3, both B_2 and B_3 would receive 148 votes. However, suppose those that thought B_2 should win (those who had B_2 in first place on their preferential ballot) did not like any of the other candidates, so that in approval voting they only approved of B_2. B_2 would now receive 151 votes from these two preference orders. With this system, B_1 would have $52 + 100 = 152$ votes, B_2 would have $52 + 148 + 151 = 351$ votes, and B_3 would have $100 + 148 = 248$ votes. Thus, B_2 would be declared the winner.

A case can be made for approval voting in national party conventions. If there had been approval voting in the 1972 Democratic convention, George McGovern might not have been his party's nominee. Not only did he not have strong support from his party's rank and file, but he was given little chance of winning in the general election. Based on ratings of the candidates taken from the University of Michigan's Center for Political Studies *1972 American National Election Study Survey*, it is estimated that Hubert Humphrey would have been approved of by 64.1% of Democratic voters to McGovern's 58.0%, lending support to the contention that McGovern was not the strongest choice of the Democratic party in 1972. Humphrey was also the strongest candidate under the borda count method. He lost to McGovern only under plurality voting in a field of four candidates that also included Edmund Muskie and George Wallace. McGovern received 33% of the vote compared to Humphrey's 29.4%. In opposition to approval voting, it is said that the procedure encourages more candidates to run in an election, thus weakening the two-party (three-party) system.

After reading and studying this section, you probably realize that there is not one, but many, solutions to the problem of determining a winner in an election. The way votes are cast and the method of counting the ballots can have a profound effect on the outcome of the election. In fact, Kenneth Arrow, Nobel Prize winner in economics in 1951, showed that it is impossible to find a fair election procedure. Arrow listed a set of fairness conditions for an election which include no dictator, no outside intervention, and consistency.

> **ARROW'S IMPOSSIBILITY THEOREM**   There does not exist an election procedure that ranks three or more candidates based on the individual preferences of at least two voters that obeys all of the fairness conditions.

(For more detailed information on the fairness conditions and further discussion of Arrow's theorem, see Luce and Raiffa 1957.)

PRACTICE EXAMPLE 2   The following preference orders are considered valid for the 1970 U.S. Senate election in New York. B stands for James Buckley, O stands for Richard Ottinger, and G stands for Charles Goodell. The total votes listed are actually percentages for each of the preference orders.

B	O	G	G
G	G	B	O
O	B	O	B

Votes cast	39	37	12	12

(a) Who was declared the winner using the plurality method?

(b) Who would be declared the winner if the simple majority method and run-off procedure had been used?

(c) Who would have been the winner if the borda count method had been used, where first place = 2 points, second place = 1 point, and third place = 0 points?

(d) Would there have been a winner if the condorcet criterion was used? If so, who?

(e) Under approval voting, it seems plausible that half the Buckley and Ottinger supporters would have also voted for Goodell, and half the Goodell supporters would have voted for their second choices. What would be the total vote count for each candidate under these assumptions and approval voting? Who would have been declared the winner? ■

CONCEPTS

plurality winner	run-off procedure
majority winner	borda count
preferential ballot	condorcet criterion
preference order	approval voting

SOLUTIONS TO PRACTICE EXAMPLES

1. Total votes = 31, therefore 16 votes are required for a simple majority. Plurality winner is A_1.

No one is the winner under the simple majority rule. Using the run-off procedure with A_1 and A_2, A_2 is declared the winner with 16 votes.

count (A_1) = 3(15) + 1(9) + 1(4) + 1(3) = 61

count (A_2) = 1(15) + 3(9) + 2(4) + 3(3) = 59

count (A_3) = 2(9) + 3(4) = 30

count (A_4) = 2(15) + 2(3) = 36

Thus, A_1 is declared the winner using the borda count method. Using the condorcet criterion, we have A_2 beating A_1 in a two-man race with 16 votes, A_1 beating A_3 in a two-man race with 18 votes, A_1 beating A_4 in a two-man race with 28 votes, A_2 beating A_3 in a two-man race with 27 votes, A_2 beating A_4 in a two-man race with 16 votes, and A_4 beating A_3 in a two-man race with 18 votes. Therefore, A_2 beats A_1, A_3, and A_4 in two-man races. Thus, A_2 is declared the winner.

2. (a) Plurality winner is Buckley.
   (b) In a run-off between B and O, B (Buckley) would be declared the winner with a total of 51 votes.
   (c) count (B) = 2(39) + 1(12) = 90
       count (O) = 2(37) + 1(12) = 86
       count (G) = 1(39) + 1(37) + 2(12) + 2(12) = 124
       Goodell is declared the winner using the borda count method.
   (d) Goodell would be declared the winner using the condorcet criterion, since in two-man races Goodell beats Buckley with 61 votes, Goodell beats Ottinger with 63 votes, and Buckley beats Ottinger with 51 votes.
   (e) Under the approval voting method, Goodell would have 19 + 18 + 24 = 61 votes, Buckley would have 39 + 6 = 45 votes, and Ottinger would have 37 + 6 = 43 votes. Thus, Goodell would be declared the winner under this system.

EXERCISES 1.4

1. A student is trying to decide which college to attend. He or she has narrowed his choices to B_1, B_2, and B_3. The student polls 36 teachers to get their preferences. Determine the plurality winner and the winner by simple majority coupled with the run-off procedure for the set of preference orders.

B_1	B_3	B_2
B_2	B_1	B_3
B_3	B_2	B_1

Votes cast	12	11	13

2. Suppose points are assigned in a four-brand taste test according to the following systems: 3 points for first place, 2 points for second place, 1 point for third place, and 0 points for fourth place. Compute the borda count for each of the brands for the set of preference orders.

A_1	A_1	A_3	A_2
A_4	A_2	A_1	A_3
A_2	A_3	A_2	A_1
A_3	A_4	A_2	A_4

Votes cast	12	3	10	8

   Which brand is the winner under the borda count method?

3. In Exercise 2, which brand would be declared the winner using the plurality method? Which brand would be declared the winner using the simple majority method?

4. Using the same set of preference orders as in Exercise 2, assign 6 points for first place, 3 points for second place, 2 points for third place, and 1 point for fourth place. Compute the borda count for each of the four brands using this point count. Does the winner change?

5. Suppose there are four candidates in an election. Could the following two procedures result in different candidates being elected?
   (a) Use the run-off procedure with the two candidates with the most first place votes.
   (b) Eliminate the candidate with the fewest first place votes. Now determine the two highest first place vote getters and use the run-off procedure with these two.

6. For the set of preference orders:

C_1	C_2	C_3	C_2
C_4	C_3	C_2	C_4
C_2	C_1	C_1	C_1
C_3	C_4	C_4	C_3

| Votes cast | 15 | 9 | 4 | 3 |

   (a) Who would be declared the winner using the plurality method?
   (b) Who would be declared the winner using the simple majority method with the run-off procedure?
   (c) If first place is assigned 4 points, second place is assigned 3 points, third place is assigned 2 points, and fourth place is assigned 1 point, who would be declared the winner using the borda count method?
   (d) Who would be declared the winner using the condorcet criterion?

7. Can a winner be declared using the condorcet criterion for the set of preference orders listed below?

A_1	A_2	A_3
A_3	A_1	A_2
A_2	A_3	A_1

| Votes cast | 5 | 11 | 7 |

8. Construct an example to show that a person who prefers A_1 and A_2 first and second in a three-candidate election can improve the chances of A_1 winning by ranking A_2 last, assuming the election will be decided by using the borda count method.

9. In a four-candidate race, if no candidate receives a majority, could one decide the election by the following procedure: Rank the candidates first, second, third, and fourth by their total number of first place votes. Pair the candidates that were first and third in a two-man election, and find a winner. Pair the candidates that were second and fourth in a two-man election, and find a winner. Finally, have an election between these two winners. Can you name instances where this procedure is used?

10. In the 1980 presidential election, Ronald Reagan won with 51% of the popular vote, to Jimmy Carter's 41% and John Anderson's 7%. An ABC exit poll indicated that if each voter had been allowed to vote for as many candidates as he or she wished, 25% would have voted for Carter and Anderson, 38% would have voted for Reagan and Anderson, 18% would have voted for Carter alone, 11% would have voted for Reagan alone, and 8% would have voted for Anderson alone. Under approval voting, if percentages are converted to votes, how many votes would each candidate get? Would the results of the election have changed?

CHAPTER SUMMARY

A *set* is a collection of objects, called *elements*. We looked at *subsets* of sets of voters that constitute winning and blocking coalitions. The set operations of *complement*, *union*, and *intersection* were defined and applied to the formation of coalitions. *Venn diagrams* were used to represent sets and set operations, and were used to analyze information gained in *survey sampling*. Sets can be used to represent *codes* such as the Morse code and *DNA* codes.

A *sample space* is the set of possible outcomes from an experiment, and an *event* is a subset of the sample space. Set operations were used to describe various events, as a prelude to a discussion of probability in Chapter 5.

Nonvoting coalitions were discussed in relation to games. Methods and procedures for voting and ballot counting in elections were presented, including *plurality*, *majority*, *borda count*, *condorcet criterion*, and *approval voting*. Arrow's Theorem says that there is no "perfect" voting procedure.

REVIEW EXERCISES FOR CHAPTER 1

1. A committee has members *a*, *b*, *c*, *d*, and *e*. Member *a* has 5 votes, member *b* has 3 votes, members *c*, *d*, and *e* each have one vote. If a simple majority is required for a measure to pass, list all minimal winning coalitions and all minimal blocking coalitions.

2. In the committee of Exercise 1, if a two-thirds vote in favor of a measure is required for passage, list all minimal winning coalitions and all minimal blocking coalitions.

3. If a committee has 5 members, four of whom have one vote each, how many votes should be assigned to the fifth member to make him or her a dictator? How many votes should be assigned to the fifth member to give him or her veto power?

4. A group has 5 members. How many distinct committees can be formed if each committee must have between 2 and 4 members? How is this related to the power set of a set?

5. An organization has members $\{1, 2, 3, 4, 5, 6, 7, 8\} = Q$. The finance committee is the set $F = \{2, 4, 6, 8\}$; the social committee is the set $S = \{1, 3, 6, 7\}$; the education committee is the set $E = \{1, 3, 5, 8\}$, and the nominating committee is the set $N = \{2, 3, 4, 5\}$. Find each of the following sets: $E \cap F$, $E \cup F$, $(E \cup F) \cap N$, $N \cup (S \cap E)$, $E{-}F$, and $S \cap E \cap N$.

6. An accounting class has 32 members. Of these, 15 are freshmen, 25 are business majors, and 5 are neither. Use a Venn diagram to determine how many freshmen in the class are business majors.

7. A sample of 100 new cars contains cars with the following defects:

    23 have faulty windshield wipers

    26 have a faulty horn

    30 have a headlight out

    7 have faulty windshield wipers and horn

    8 have faulty windshield wipers and a headlight out

    10 have a faulty horn and a headlight out

    3 have all three defects

    (a) How many cars have no defects?
    (b) How many cars have at least one defect?

8. In the Venn diagram below, the numbers were recorded as indicated. How many elements are in each of the following?

    $A{-}B$

    $A \cap B$

    $A \cap B \cap C$

    $B{-}C$

    $A \cup B \cup C$

    $A' \cup (B \cap C)$

    $A \cap (B \cup C)'$

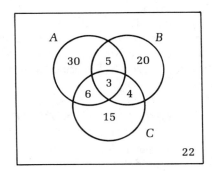

9. If a set E has 10 elements and a set B has 20 elements, and $A \cup B$ has 15 elements, how many elements are in $A \cap B$?

10. A survey was made of 25 Democratic congresspeople and 28 Republican congresspeople as to their preference about strict quotas on Japanese imports. Strict quotas were favored by 30; 10 Republicans did not favor strict quotas. Use a Venn diagram with $A = \{\text{Democrats}\}$ and $B = \{\text{favors quotas}\}$, to determine how many Republicans favored strict quotas.

11. A die (single dice) is rolled.
    (a) What is the sample space?
    (b) What is the event that an even number is rolled?
    (c) What is the event that a number greater than or equal to 4 is rolled?
    (d) What is the event that the number 2 is rolled?

12. In Exercise 11 if E is the event in (a) and F is the event in (b), describe in words and as sets $E \cap F$, $E' \cap F'$, and $(E \cup F)'$.

13. A code consists of sequences of $*$ and $\$$. Write out all possible sequences (code words) with less than or equal to three elements.

14. In Exercise 13, if one chooses a code word at random, what is the event that a two-element code word will be chosen? What is the event that the only symbol in the code word will be $*$?

15. Using De Morgan's laws, write an equivalent expression for:
    (a) $(A \cup B)'$
    (b) $(A' \cap B)'$
    (c) $A' \cup B$

16. The following preference orders for brands of cola were obtained.

a	b	c
b	a	b
c	c	a
Votes cast 32	28	25

    Determine the plurality winner and the simple majority winner, using the run-off procedure if necessary.

17. For the preference orders given in 16, assign 3 points for first place, 2 points for second place, and 1 point for third place. Compute the borda count for each brand. Which brand wins using the borda count?

18. For the preference orders in 16, is there a winner using the condorcet criterion? Explain.

19. In a poll 40 residents approved of zoning a piece of property residential or limited commercial, 30 approved of zoning it limited commercial or commercial, 32 approved of zoning it only residential, and 18 approved of commercial zoning only. Which type of zoning—residential, limited commercial, or commercial—was established under approval voting rules?

20.

x	y	z	w
z	z	x	x
y	x	y	y
Votes cast 8	10	4	5

    (a) Who is the majority winner with run-off? Is it the same as the plurality winner?
    (b) Assign points: 3 for first, 2 for second, and 1 for third. Who is the borda count winner?

2 Graphs

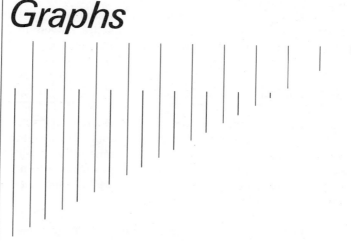

In this chapter we consider such problems as:

1. How can the meeting times for several committees be scheduled so that people on more than one committee can attend all their meetings?
2. How many colors will you need to color in a map so regions that touch are colored with different colors?
3. A salesperson wants to visit clients in several different cities. How should the trip be planned so the total cost is as small as possible?
4. Several people have applied for openings in a company. Is it possible to fill each of the available jobs with an applicant qualified to do that job?
5. A person wants to drive from Chicago to New York City. What is the shortest route? What is the quickest route?
6. The owner of a small company is going to buy a truck. Next year and each year after that the truck can be traded in for a new one or run for another year. If the total cost of having a truck over the next five years is to be as small as possible, then in which years should the owner buy a new truck?

We introduce graphs and show how the problems above can be viewed as questions about graphs. Here, graphs provide the mathematical structure for these problems. We give a sampling of general techniques in graph theory and use the techniques to solve problems such as the ones above.

In Section 2.1, we introduce graphs to solve scheduling problems and discuss the four-color problem, which was solved in 1976, more than one hundred years after it was first posed. In Section 2.2, we introduce paths in a graph and give Euler's solution to a problem called the Königsberg bridge problem. Euler's solution in 1736 is among the earliest applications of graph theory. As a contemporary application of Eulerian paths, we show how to reconstruct an RNA chain from its fragments. In Section 2.3, we discuss problems called traveling salesman problems. Problems such as that of matching applicants to available jobs are solved in Section 2.4, while shortest route problems are solved in Section 2.5.

2.1   *Scheduling Problems—Coloring*

Assigning broadcast frequencies to radio stations, scheduling final exams, coordinating tours of a factory or school, and assigning work spaces to workers in a factory are examples of **scheduling problems**. In this section we show how to translate scheduling problems into problems about coloring the **vertices** of a **graph**. We give the definition of a graph and discuss the four-color problem.

EXAMPLE 1   An aide to the Senate majority leader in a state legislature is asked to schedule weekly meeting times for several Senate committees. The available times are 9–11 A.M., on Monday, Wednesday, and Friday. The schedule must be arranged so that committees with a member in common do not meet at the same time.

In Figure 2.1 each dot (called a **vertex**) stands for one of the committees: Agenda, Education, Finance, Appropriations, and Ways and Means. Two vertices are joined by a line (**edge**) if the two committees on either end of the edge have one or more members in common, and so must be scheduled to meet at different times.

Figure 2.1

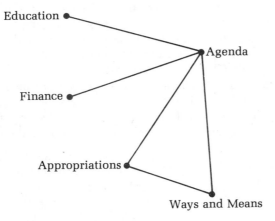

To schedule the committees, we will put a letter, M, W, or F, next to the vertices in Figure 2.1 to show which day of the week the committee is scheduled to meet. We start by assigning a meeting time to the Agenda

Committee and continue to pick meeting times for the remaining committees one at a time. Choose Monday as the meeting time for the Agenda Committee. Place an M next to the vertex labeled Agenda in Figure 2.1. Next schedule the Education Committee. Since there is an edge joining the Education and Agenda committees, these committees have one or more members in common, and so must meet at different times. The Education Committee can be scheduled for Wednesday or Friday, but not Monday. Choose Wednesday as the time for the Education Committee to meet, and place a W next to the vertex labeled Education in Figure 2.1. We can schedule the Finance Committee for Friday and the Appropriations Committee for Wednesday. Figure 2.2 pictures the scheduling done so far.

Figure 2.2

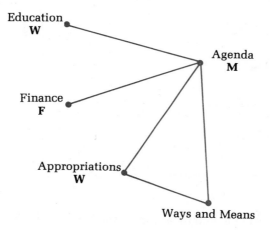

There is an edge between the Appropriations Committee and the Ways and Means Committee. The Ways and Means Committee has members in common with both the Agenda Committee and the Appropriations Committee. Since the Agenda Committee is scheduled for Monday and the Appro-

Figure 2.3

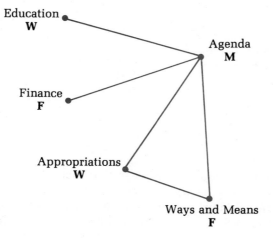

priations Committee for Wednesday, the only time available for the Ways and Means Committee is Friday. The completed schedule is pictured in Figure 2.3 on page 39. We made choices in constructing this schedule. It can be shown, using the counting techniques in Chapter 4, that there are 24 different schedules that would be just as acceptable as the one shown in Figure 2.3. (See Section 4.3.)   ■

PRACTICE EXAMPLE 1   Put one of the letters: R, B, or G, next to the vertices 3, 4, and 5 in the graph shown in Figure 2.4, so that vertices joined by an edge are given different letters. (Solutions to the practice examples are given at the end of the section.)   ■

Figure 2.4

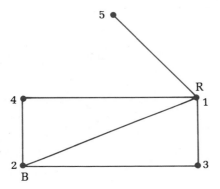

EXAMPLE 2   Freshmen have signed up to take advanced placement tests during the week before classes start. In Figure 2.5 we have shown a graph with one vertex for each test, and two vertices joined by an edge if one or more people signed up for both tests.

Figure 2.5

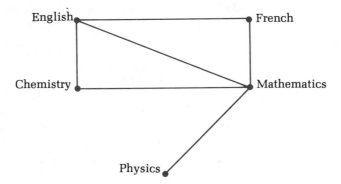

We want to schedule the tests so that each person will be able to take the tests for which he has signed up. The test times are Wednesday, Thursday, and Friday, from 8 to 11 in the morning. If we schedule the English test for Wednesday and the Mathematics test for Thursday, then from Figure 2.6 we see that the French and Chemistry tests must be scheduled for Friday. The Physics test can be scheduled for either Wednesday or Friday. ■

Figure 2.6

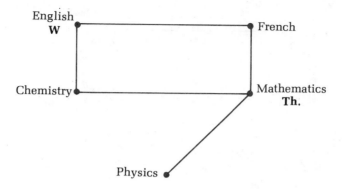

The problems solved in Examples 1 and 2 are called **graph coloring** problems. The "colors" in these examples are the meeting days. The problem is to color the vertices of the graph so that any two vertices joined by an edge are colored differently. In the practice example the colors are the letters R, B, and G.

Coloring the vertices of a graph is similar to coloring the regions of a map (such as a map of the United States divided into states) so that regions with a common boundary line are given different colors. To color the regions A, B, C, D, E, F, in the map in Figure 2.7 it is enough to color one point, say the capital, of each region.

Figure 2.7

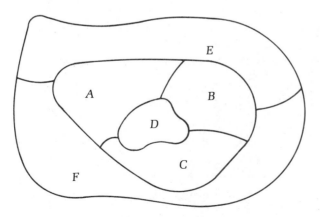

Join two capitals by an edge if the two regions share a common boundary line. If we erase the map, leaving only the capitals and edges, we get the graph shown in Figure 2.8.

Figure 2.8

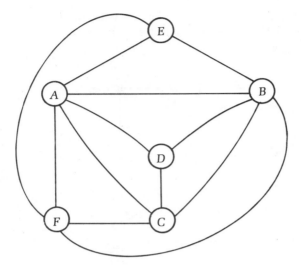

Coloring the vertices of the graph in Figure 2.8 is the same as coloring the regions of the map in Figure 2.7. Figure 2.9 gives a coloring of the vertices of this graph. See if you can color the map of Figure 2.7 to correspond to this coloring.

Figure 2.9

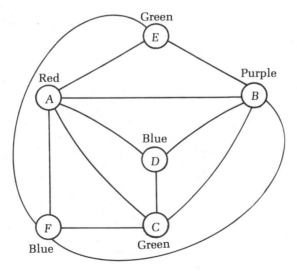

Every coloring of the map in Figure 2.7 uses at least four colors. Whether or not there exists a "map" that requires five colors is the classical four-color problem.

FOUR-COLOR PROBLEM   Show that every map in the plane can be colored with four or fewer colors, or find a map that requires more than four colors.

The first known statement of the four-color problem dates back to 1852. "Proofs" that every map can be colored with four colors were published in 1878 and 1880. Errors were found in these proofs, which left the problem still unsolved. For most of this century, the four-color problem was one of the famous unsolved problems of mathematics. In 1976 Wolfgang Haken and Kenneth Appel, of the University of Illinois, announced they had solved the problem. Every map in the plane can be colored with four or fewer colors. To solve the problem, they constructed a list of 1482 maps and showed that if every map on their list could be colored with four colors, then all maps could be colored with four or fewer colors. It required 1200 hours of computer time to check that each map on their list can be colored with four colors (see Appel and Haken 1978).

From the solution to the four-color problem and the relationship between maps and graphs, we can say that if a graph comes from a map in the plane, then the vertices of the graph can be colored with four or fewer colors. The graphs that come from maps in the plane are the graphs that can be drawn on a piece of paper so edges meet only at vertices. The graph in Figure 2.10 is an example of a graph that does not come from a map in the plane.

Figure 2.10

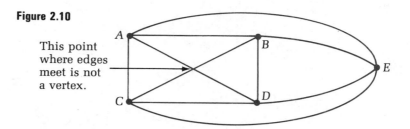

This point where edges meet is not a vertex.

Next we give a definition of graph. From the examples, you can see that a graph contains a set of vertices and a set of edges. In Figure 2.1, the vertex set is {Education, Agenda, Finance, Appropriations, Ways and Means}. In Figure 2.4 the vertex set is {1, 2, 3, 4, 5}. To draw a picture of a graph we need to know the vertex set, the edge set, and the vertices of each of the edges.

PRACTICE EXAMPLE 2

Draw the graph with vertex set $\{a, b, c, d\}$ and edge set $\{e_1, e_2, e_3, e_4, e_5\}$ if the vertices of the edges are:

Edge	Vertices of the Edge
e_1	$\{a, b\}$
e_2	$\{c, d\}$
e_3	$\{a, c\}$
e_4	$\{b, d\}$
e_5	$\{b, c\}$

Figure 2.11

(Adapted from a drawing by Susan LeVan/WGBH)

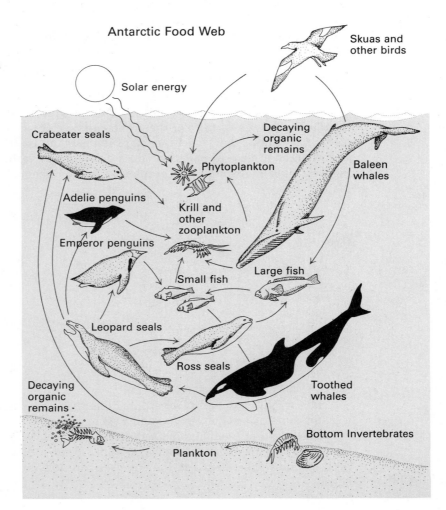

> DEFINITION   A **graph** consists of a set V of vertices and a set E of edges where the vertices of each edge are specified.

Graphs can be used to picture other relationships. For example, if we are given a food web in some ecological setting, we can construct the **competition graph** for that food web. The vertices of the graph are the species, and there is an edge between species *a* and species *b* whenever they have a common prey. Consider the food web shown in Figure 2.11 on page 44. In this figure the arrows point from a predator to its prey. A graph with arrows (direction) on the edges is called a **directed graph**. Figure 2.12 shows the directed graph representing this food web.

Figure 2.12

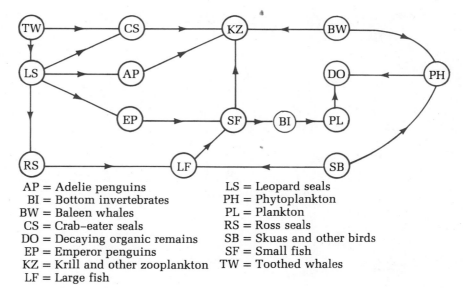

AP = Adelie penguins
BI = Bottom invertebrates
BW = Baleen whales
CS = Crab–eater seals
DO = Decaying organic remains
EP = Emperor penguins
KZ = Krill and other zooplankton
LF = Large fish

LS = Leopard seals
PH = Phytoplankton
PL = Plankton
RS = Ross seals
SB = Skuas and other birds
SF = Small fish
TW = Toothed whales

Figure 2.13 gives the competition graph.

Figure 2.13

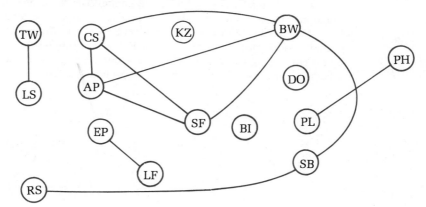

In the next sections of this chapter we will see graphs used to represent such things as a town's street network, RNA chains, airplane routes, and job-employee relationships. In Chapter 3 we look carefully at a very specific type of graph and see even more applications.

CONCEPTS

graph   scheduling problems
vertices   graph coloring
edges   directed graph

SOLUTIONS TO PRACTICE EXAMPLES

1.

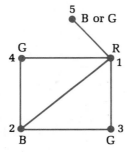

2.

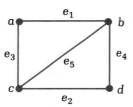

EXERCISES 2.1

In Exercises 1 through 11 the vertices in the graphs represent committees, and two vertices are joined by an edge if the committees have one or more members in common. Suppose the available meeting times are M = Monday, T = Tuesday, W = Wednesday, and F = Friday from 9 to 11 A.M. In each exercise schedule the committees by putting an M, T, W, or F next to each vertex so that vertices joined by an edge are given different letters. After finding a schedule, check to see if a schedule with fewer meeting times can be constructed.

1.

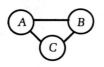

2.

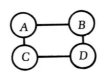

3.

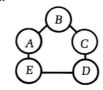

4.

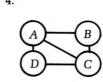

5.

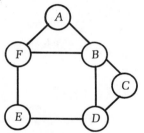

6.

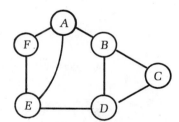

7.

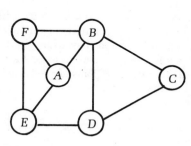

8.

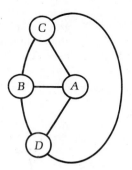

9.

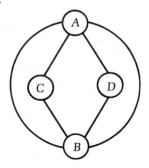

10.

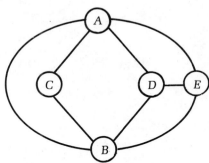

11.

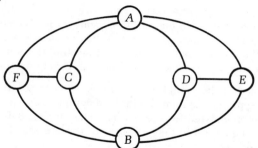

In Exercises 12, 13, and 14, draw the graph with the given vertices and edges.

12. vertices = $\{1, 2, 3\}$
     edges = $\{\{1, 2\}, \{2, 3\}, \{1, 3\}\}$

13. vertices = $\{A, B, C, D\}$
     edges = $\{\{A, B\}, \{C, D\}, \{A, C\}\}$

14. vertices = $\{A, B, C, D, E\}$
     edges = $\{\{A, E\}, \{B, D\}, \{C, E\}, \{A, C\}\}$

15. The annual convention of owners and managers of Volvo dealerships includes special seminars on consumer complaints, the Volvo warranty, sales, safety features, parts, service, and a seminar for owners of dealerships. Based on preconvention information the convention organizers have made the following graph. The vertices represent the seminars, with two seminars joined by an edge if one or more people indicated they want to attend both of those seminars. The times set aside for the seminars are MI = Monday 9–9:45 A.M., MII = Monday 10–10:45 A.M., TI = Tuesday 9–9:45 A.M., and TII = Tuesday 10–10:45 A.M. Schedule the seminars.

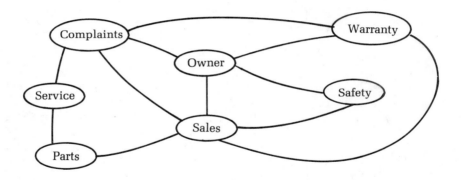

16. Suppose the membership of the subcommittees of the student council consists of:

> F = Fund Raising = {Foster, Hall, O'Neill, Ramsey, Snider}
> C = Concert Committee = {O'Neill, Ramsey, Snider}
> L = Lectures = {Barker, Foster}
> S = Special Events = {Hall, O'Neill, Ramsey, Snider}

(a) Draw the graph whose vertices are the committees and whose edges join committees with one or more members in common.

(b) The student council wants to schedule weekly meetings of each committee. What is the smallest number of meeting times needed if committees with members in common are to meet at different times?

17. The head of the graduate program is going to schedule the graduate courses for the spring. The numbers in the diagram below indicate how many students have preregistered for the courses. The number 8, for example, means that 8 people signed up to take all three of the courses Combinatorics, Algorithms, and Analysis.

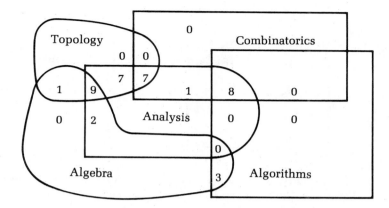

(a) Draw the graph whose vertices are the courses. Join two courses by an edge if one or more people have preregistered for both courses.

(b) Find a schedule for the courses if the available times are I, 3–4 on Monday, Wednesday, and Friday; II, 3–4:30 Tuesday and Thursday; and III, 4:10–5:10 Monday, Wednesday, and Friday.

2.2   *RNA Chains—Eulerian Paths*

In this section we introduce the idea of **paths in a graph**, and give Euler's solution (1736) to the Königsberg bridge problem. As a contemporary application we show how to reconstruct an RNA chain from its fragments. If you think of a graph as a road map, then a path is a truck route over the roads (edges) which starts at an intersection (vertex) and ends at an intersection (vertex). You are not allowed to stop, or turn around, part way along a road (edge). Usually a path is given by listing the vertices in the order they are visited.

Figure 2.14

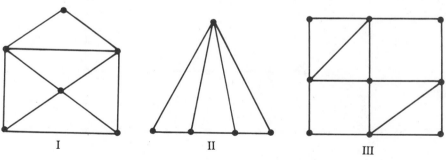

I   II   III

From Figure 2.14, which of the following shapes can be drawn without removing your pencil from the paper and without retracing any lines? For example, look at graph I and trace it using the numbers next to the vertices in Figure 2.15. The path starts at the vertex with 1 next to it, and then goes to 2, then 3, then to the vertices consecutively numbered to 9.

Figure 2.15

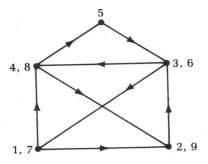

Actually, if you start any place but one of the two bottom corners you cannot do it. Note we do not end up back where we started. Likewise in graph II, if we start at either of the middle points shown in Figure 2.16 it is possible. Otherwise it is not.

Figure 2.16

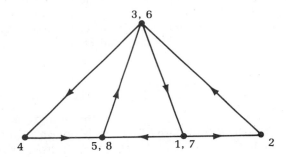

Graph III in Figure 2.17 is easier. We can start at any point, and we end up where we started.

Figure 2.17

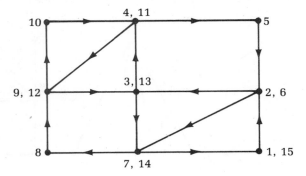

If the graphs I, II, and III are roads in a rural postal route with all mailboxes on one side of the road, then tracing the graph without removing your pencil from the paper, and without retracing any lines, gives a route for the postman so that the mail is delivered (each edge is traced) with the least amount of driving (no edge is retraced). Similar problems are faced by people who map out routes for such vehicles as garbage trucks and snow-plows.

The solution to this type of problem dates back to 1736. The problem was originally posed in a different context. The city of Königsberg in Prussia (now Kaliningrad in the Soviet Union) consisted of two islands linked to each other and to banks of the Pregel River by seven bridges. In the warm summer evenings the citizens of Königsberg would stroll through the city and cross over some of the bridges. On a long stroll one could cross all seven bridges. This posed an interesting problem called the *Königsberg bridge problem*. Could someone begin at one of the land areas, walk across each bridge exactly once, and return to the starting point? (See Figure 2.18.)

Figure 2.18

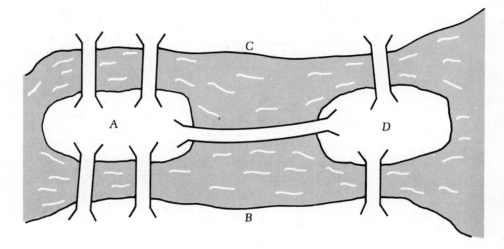

Redrawn as in Figure 2.19 and restated, the problem is: can the following graph be drawn without removing your pencil from the paper, and without retracing any line, so that you always get back to where you started?

Figure 2.19

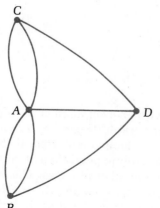

The vertices represent the land masses, and the edges represent the bridges. Euler showed that for a stroll across each bridge exactly once and back to the starting point to be possible, each vertex must be the meeting point of an even number of edges. Count how many edges meet at each vertex in Figure 2.19.

Since an odd number meet at each vertex, it cannot be done. Go back and count the edges meeting at each vertex for the graphs in Figure 2.14.

Figure 2.20

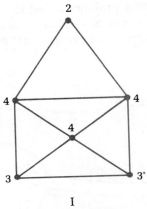

I

There are two vertices with an odd number of edges.

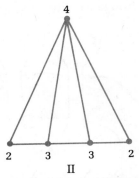

II

There are two vertices with an odd number of edges.

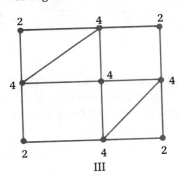

III

All vertices have an even number of edges.

Graph III is the only one with an even number of edges meeting at each vertex. Therefore we know that graph III can be drawn without retracing edges, and you can get back to where you started. If the starting point is allowed to be different from the ending point then all but two vertices must be the meeting point of an even number of edges. These two vertices must be the beginning and ending points, as in I and II. A path which traces each edge in a graph once and only once is called an **Eulerian path**. We summarize Euler's results by stating the two situations in which a graph has an Eulerian path.

A GRAPH HAS AN EULERIAN PATH IF

   1. Each vertex has an even number of edges. In this case the path can start at any vertex and must end where it started.
or 2. All but two of the vertices have an even number of edges. In this case the path can start at either of the odd vertices and must end at the other odd vertex.

An Eulerian path that ends where it started is called an **Eulerian circuit**. The following procedure constructs an Eulerian circuit and explains how Euler found his result. The basic idea is that since each vertex has an even number of edges, a path can always leave any vertex the path enters (with the possible exception of the starting/ending vertex).

PROCEDURE

To find an Eulerian circuit in a graph in which each vertex has an even number of edges:

STEP 1:   Pick any one of the vertices to be the starting and hence ending vertex. Put the letter s (for start) by this vertex.

STEP 2:   Starting at vertex s trace a path that ends at s. To see that this can always be done, notice that as you trace the path, each time you enter a vertex (other than s) there are an odd (and hence nonzero) number of edges at the vertex that are not yet used in the path. This is because each vertex has an even number of edges. It follows that the path can always leave any vertex different from s, and so it is always possible to trace a path that begins and ends at s.

If the path constructed in Step 2 is not an Eulerian circuit, you must proceed to Step 3 in order to add edges to the circuit.

STEP 3:   Given a circuit C that starts and ends at s but does not contain all the edges in the graph:
(a) Find the first vertex in the circuit C that has edges that are not in C.
(b) Use the procedure in Step 2 to construct a circuit that starts and ends at the vertex found in (a). Only use edges not in C.
(c) The new circuit is obtained by tracing C until you reach the vertex found in (a), tracing the circuit constructed in (b), then tracing the rest of the circuit C.
The result is a circuit that begins and ends at s and has more edges than the circuit C. Keep repeating Step 3 until an Eulerian circuit is obtained.

Can you see how to modify this procedure so it constructs an Eulerian path in a graph where all but two of the vertices have an even number of edges?

EXAMPLE 1   Use the procedure above to construct an Eulerian circuit for the graph in Figure 2.21.

Figure 2.21

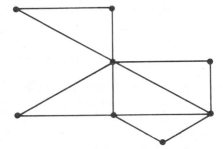

STEP 1:   We choose the vertex labeled s in Figure 2.22 to be the starting vertex.

Figure 2.22

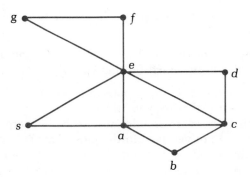

STEP 2:   Set C equal to the circuit passing (in order) through the vertices *sabcdefges*.

STEP 3:
(a) *a* is the first vertex in C with edges that are not in the circuit.
(b) The circuit *acea* starts and ends at the vertex *a* and uses only edges that are not in C.
(c) The new circuit is *saceabcdefges*.
This new circuit uses all the edges, so the procedure is completed.

EXAMPLE 2   Figure 2.23 is a map of a rural postal route where all mailboxes are on one side of the street. Can the postman deliver the mail and return to the starting point without driving along any road twice?

Figure 2.23

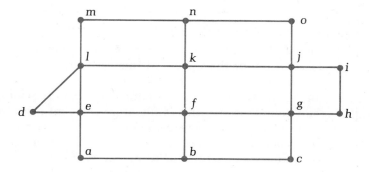

Count the number of edges at each vertex. The vertices b and n have an odd number of edges and the other vertices have an even number of edges. Since some of the vertices have an odd number of edges, the postman cannot deliver the mail and return to the starting point without driving along some of the roads at least twice. Since there are exactly two vertices, b and n, with an odd number of edges, the graph has an Eulerian path. The postman can start at b, deliver all the mail, and end the delivery at n. Find an Eulerian path from b to n. ■

Which of the graphs in Figure 2.24 has an Eulerian path that traces each edge in the direction given by the arrow on that edge?

Figure 2.24

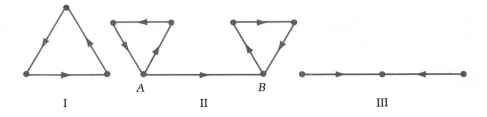

I   II   III

In graph I you can start at any vertex, follow the arrows, and end at the vertex where you started. Note that each vertex in graph I has the same number of arrows pointing into the vertex as point out of the vertex. In graph II the path starts at A, follows the arrows around the triangle with A as a vertex, goes to B, then around the triangle with B as a vertex, and ends at B. In graph II the starting vertex, A, has one more arrow pointing out of the vertex than pointing into it; and the ending vertex, B, has one more arrow pointing into the vertex than out of it. For each of the other vertices in graph II the same number of arrows point into the vertex as point out of it. There is no Eulerian path in graph III that follows the arrows. There are two situations in which a **directed graph** has an Eulerian path that traces the edges in the direction given by the arrows.

A DIRECTED GRAPH HAS AN EULERIAN PATH IF

1. Each vertex has the same number of arrows pointing into the vertex as point out of the vertex. In this case the path can start at any vertex and must end where it started.
2. One of the vertices has one more arrow pointing out of the vertex than points into it—this is the first vertex in the path. One of the vertices has one more arrow pointing into the vertex than out of it —this is the last vertex in the path. All the other vertices have the same number of arrows pointing out of the vertex as point into it.

Next we will use Eulerian paths to reconstruct an **RNA chain** from its fragments. Recall from Chapter 1 that an RNA chain is made up of bases from the set {A, C, G, U}. As enzymes act on a chain, the chain is broken into fragments. Some enzymes break the chain after every G base; others break the chain after every U and C base. The fragments arising from an enzyme acting on the chain to break it after each G base are called **G fragments.** **U-C fragments** occur when an enzyme breaks the chain after each U and each C base. For example, the RNA chain GACGAUACG has G fragments: G, ACG, AUACG, and U-C fragments: GAC, GAU, AC, G. In practice, the sequence of bases in a fragment can be determined by experiment, but the longer sequence of bases in an unfragmented RNA chain cannot be found directly. We can view the G and U-C fragments as a partial code of the RNA chain. Our task is to decode the fragments and find the chain. We begin by making a graph out of the G and U-C fragments.

EXAMPLE 3

G Fragments	U-C Fragments
G	C
ACG	AC
AUCG	GC
	GAU

STEP 1: Hyphenate the fragments. Put a hyphen after the first U or C and after the last U or C in each G fragment (reading the fragment from left to right). Put a hyphen after the first G and after the last G in each U-C fragment. Do not put in a hyphen unless it separates letters. The fragments that are not hyphenated will be omitted when we make the graph. For our example the hyphenated fragments are:

Hyphenated G-fragments	Hyphenated U-C fragments
G̶	C̶
AC-G	A̶C̶
AU-C-G	G-C
	G-AU

We have marked with an X the fragments that do not get hyphenated. The hyphenated fragments will be the edges in the graph. The vertices of an edge will be the first piece and the last piece of the fragment.

STEP 2:   Circle the first piece and the last piece of each hyphenated fragment. These are the vertices of the graph. Now make a list of the vertices.

Circling the first and last piece of each fragment in our example we get:

$$\widehat{AC}—\widehat{G} \qquad \widehat{G}—\widehat{C}$$
$$\widehat{AU}—C—\widehat{G} \qquad \widehat{G}—\widehat{AU}$$

The vertices are: AC, G, AU, C. Circled pieces that occur more than once, such as G, C, and AU in our example, are recorded only once in the list of vertices.

STEP 3:   Draw an edge for each hyphenated fragment. The vertices of the edge are the circled pieces. Draw a line segment, labeling the left-hand end point with the first circled piece and labeling the right-hand end point with the circled piece on the right. Put an arrow on the line pointing to the right. If there is a piece between the circled ends, then write this piece above the line. Now make a list of the edges. For our example, the edges are:

$$AC \longrightarrow G \qquad G \longrightarrow C$$
$$AU \overset{c}{\longrightarrow} G \qquad G \longrightarrow AU$$

STEP 4:   Draw the graph by attaching the edges to the vertices. For our example the graph is shown in Figure 2.25.

Figure 2.25

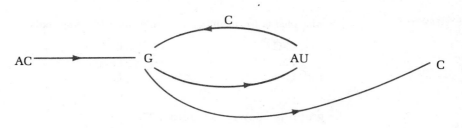

PRACTICE
EXAMPLE **1**

Draw the graph for the RNA chain with the following fragments.

G Fragments	U-C Fragments
AG	GAC
G	C
AC	AGGU
UCG	

To recover the RNA chain from the graph, find an Eulerian path in the graph that follows each edge in the direction of the arrow. As you trace the path, write down (from left to right) the symbols on the vertices and edges.

In our example there is only one such path. It starts at AC, goes to G, then to AU, then back to G, and ends at C. The corresponding RNA chain is ACGAUCGC. Check to see that the G and U-C fragments of ACGAUCGC are those with which we started. ■

PRACTICE EXAMPLE 2

Find the RNA chain with the graph shown in Figure 2.26.

Figure 2.26

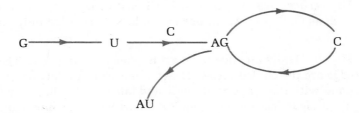

■

If there is only one Eulerian path that follows the arrows, then there is only one RNA chain with the same G and U-C fragments used to construct the graph. In our example, the path begins at the vertex that has more arrows pointing out of the vertex than pointing into it, and the path ends at the vertex that has more arrows pointing into it than out of it. An Eulerian path can also exist if each vertex has the same number of arrows pointing out as in. Then the path would start and end at the same vertex. To recover the RNA chain in this case, we need to know the starting vertex.

EXAMPLE 4

Hyphenated G fragments	Hyphenated U-C fragments
C-G	C
AC-U-G	G-AC
C	U
	G-C

The graph is shown in Figure 2.27.

Figure 2.27

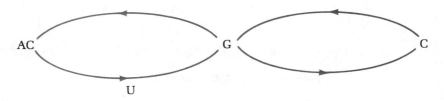

Each vertex in the graph has the same number of arrows pointing into the vertex as pointing out. Therefore, the path begins and ends at the same vertex. To find the starting (and ending) vertex, look for an unhyphenated G fragment that does not end with G, indicating the chain was not broken at that point. In the example it is C. Therefore the chain must end at C. If all unhyphenated G fragments have the last letter G, then there must be an unhyphenated U-C fragment that does not end with either a U or C. The path begins and ends there.

In our example the path begins and ends at C. There is only one such path, and the corresponding RNA chain is CGACUGC.   ■

Here is a summary of the steps used to reconstruct an RNA chain from its fragments.

TO RECONSTRUCT AN RNA CHAIN FROM ITS FRAGMENTS
1. Hyphenate the fragments.
2. Draw the graph whose edges are the hyphenated fragments.
3. Find an Eulerian path in the graph; if it is a circuit locate the beginning/end vertex.
4. Write down the RNA chain by reading the symbols on the graph as you trace out the Eulerian path.

If there is more than one Eulerian path with the correct starting and ending vertices, then these Eulerian paths give all the RNA chains with the given G and U-C fragments. (This method for finding the sequence of bases in an RNA chain using Eulerian paths is described in Hutchinson 1969. Applications of Eulerian paths to computer graph plotting, street sweeping, and coding theory are given in Chapter 11 of Roberts 1984.)

CONCEPTS

path in a graph	directed graph
Eulerian path	RNA chain
Eulerian circuit	G, U-C fragments of an RNA chain

SOLUTIONS TO PRACTICE EXAMPLES

1.
$$AG \xrightarrow{\text{G}} U \xrightarrow{\text{C}} G \longrightarrow AC$$

2. GUCAGCAGAU

EXERCISES 2.2

In Exercises 1 through 6 circle each vertex that is the meeting point of an odd number of edges and decide if the figure can be drawn without removing your pencil from the paper and without retracing any lines.

1.

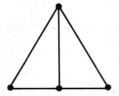

2.

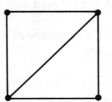

3.

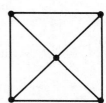

4.

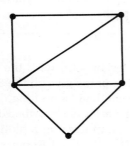

5.

6.

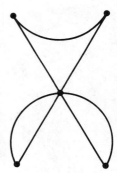

In Exercises 7 through 12 find an Eulerian path that starts at *S* and ends at *E*. Indicate your path by putting numbers next to the vertices as in Figures 2.15, 2.16, and 2.17.

7.

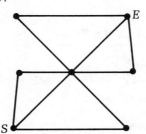

8.

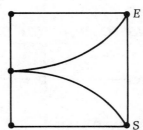

9.

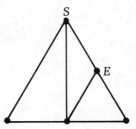

10.

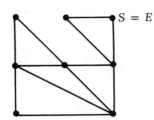

11.

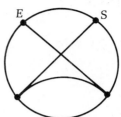

12.

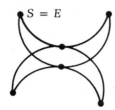

The figures in Exercises 13 through 16 picture rivers with bridges and islands. In each exercise draw a graph corresponding to the picture and decide if it is possible to take a walk that crosses each bridge once and only once and returns to the start.

13.

14.

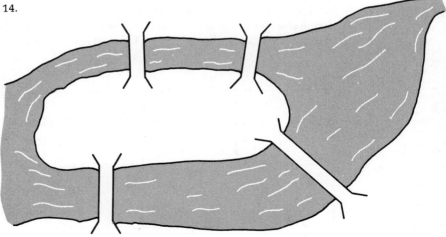

15.

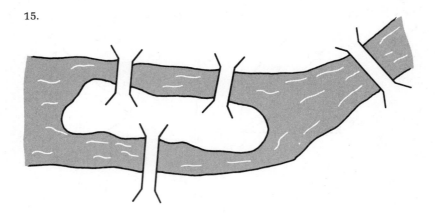

16.

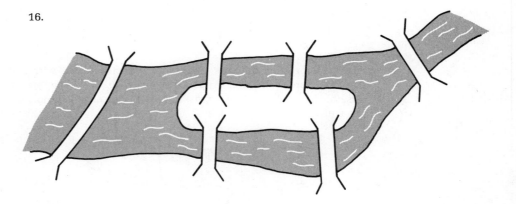

The figures in Exercises 17 through 20 are floor plans of houses. In each exercise decide whether it is possible to start either in a room or outdoors and walk through every doorway once and only once. If it is possible, then find such a route.

17.

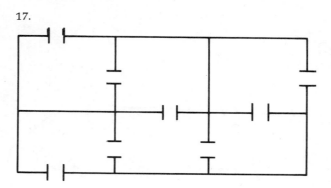

18.

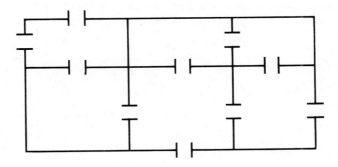

19.

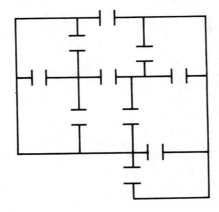

20.

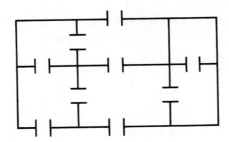

In Exercises 21 through 25 find the RNA chain whose graph is given. If there is more than one chain, then list all the RNA chains with the given graph.

21.

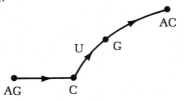

22.

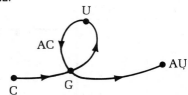

23.

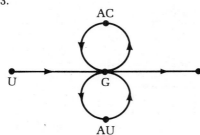

24.

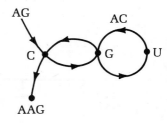

25.

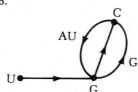

In Exercises 26 through 30:

(a) Hyphenate the fragments

(b) Draw the graph from the hyphenated fragments

(c) Find all the RNA chains with the given fragments

26.   *G fragments*   *U-C fragments*

      CG   C

      UCAG   C

                 AG

                 GU

27. | G fragments | U-C fragments |
|---|---|
| AC | C |
| AG | AGU |
| UCG | GAC |

28. | G fragments | U-C fragments |
|---|---|
| G | U |
| CAG | AG |
| CAAG | GC |
| UUAAG | AAGC |
| | AAGU |

29. | G fragments | U-C fragments |
|---|---|
| C | C |
| G | AGC |
| CG | GGC |
| CAG | |

30. | G fragments | U-C fragments |
|---|---|
| C | C |
| UCG | C |
| CAUG | AU |
| | GC |
| | GU |

2.3 Traveling Salesman Problem—Hamiltonian Paths and Circuits

In this section we introduce Hamiltonian paths and circuits and discuss the traveling salesman problem. Recall from the last section that an Eulerian circuit in a graph is a path that uses each edge just once and ends at the starting vertex. A path in a graph that passes through each vertex once and only once is called a **Hamiltonian path**. A path that passes through each vertex once and then ends at the starting vertex is called a **Hamiltonian circuit**. A salesman who visits each of several customers and then returns to his starting point is tracing out a Hamiltonian circuit in a graph whose vertices are the customers and whose edges are the routes between customers. If a number is put by each edge to indicate the cost of traveling between customers along that edge, then the sum of the numbers on the edges in a Hamiltonian circuit is the cost of using that circuit to visit the customers. Different circuits will generally have different costs. The **traveling salesman problem** is the problem of finding the cheapest route for the salesman.

EXAMPLE 1

Suppose a businessman in Washington, D.C., wants to plan a trip that includes visits to Richmond, Providence, and Philadelphia. Figure 2.28 gives the cost of flying from one city to another. The cost of the trip will depend on which city he visits first, which city he chooses to visit second, and so on. For example, if he goes to Philadelphia first, then to Richmond, and then to Providence before returning to Washington, the air fare is $75 + 100 + 130 + 90 = \$395$. If he goes to Richmond, then to Providence, then to Philadelphia, and then back to Washington, the air fare is $50 + 130 + 80 + 75 = \$335$ ($\$60$ less than the first route). If the businessman plans his trip by always choosing as his next stop the city he has not yet visited that costs the least to visit, then he visits Richmond first, then Philadelphia, then Providence, and then returns to Washington for an air fare of $50 + 100 + 80 + 90 = \$320$. ■

Figure 2.28

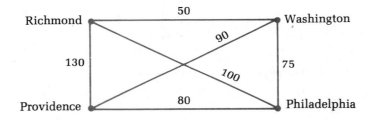

The procedure of always choosing as the next city the one not yet visited that costs the least to visit is called the **nearest neighbor rule**.

PRACTICE
EXAMPLE 1

Use the nearest neighbor rule to plan a trip from Washington that visits each of the other cities and returns to Washington (Figure 2.29).

Figure 2.29

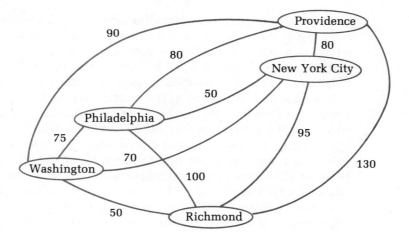

EXAMPLE 2   In Figure 2.30 the vertices represent cities, and the numbers on the edges give the cost of traveling between cities. List all the routes that start at 1, visit each city, and then return to 1. Find the cost of each route.

Figure 2.30

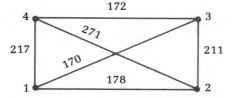

To make a list of the routes and the cost of each, we break the process of planning a route into steps. The first step is to pick the first city to be visited. The second step is to pick the second city to be visited and so on. Figure 2.31 indicates the different choices that can be made at each step together with the travel cost between cities.

Figure 2.31

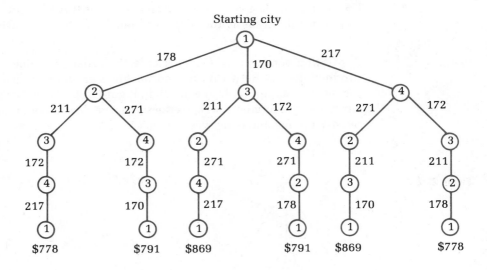

The graph in Figure 2.31 is an example of a special type of graph called a *tree*. Trees are discussed in the next chapter and used throughout the text. Each path from the top to the bottom of the tree in Figure 2.31 gives a route that starts at 1, visits each city, and returns to 1. Adding the numbers along a path gives the cost of the trip (listed in the bottom row). From Figure 2.31, we can construct a table of routes and costs.

Route	Cost
1, 2, 3, 4, 1	$778
1, 2, 4, 3, 1	$791
1, 3, 2, 4, 1	$869
1, 3, 4, 2, 1	$791
1, 4, 2, 3, 1	$869
1, 4, 3, 2, 1	$778

In this table, the cities are listed in the order they are visited. The sequence 1, 3, 2, 4, 1, for example, corresponds to the route: from 1 go to 3 to 2 to 4 to 1. The route given by the nearest neighbor rule is 1 to 3 to 4 to 2 to 1 for a cost of $791. This is $13 more than $778, the cost of the least expensive of the routes. So, in this example (and in general), the nearest neighbor rule does not give the least expensive route. Later in this section we give a table that indicates how long it takes to solve a traveling salesman problem by hand and by computer using the method of listing all the routes. ■

The next example gives a problem similar to the traveling salesman problem except in this example the path does not return to the starting point.

EXAMPLE 3   A printing company wants to decide the order in which to schedule its production runs. Between runs the machines are shut down and made ready for the upcoming run. In the graph in Figure 2.32, the vertices represent the runs, and the numbers on the edges give the downtime in hours needed to modify the machines between runs.

Figure 2.32

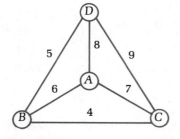

The company starts with a type *A* production run. In what order should the *B*, *C*, and *D* runs be scheduled so that the total downtime is as short as possible?

Figure 2.33

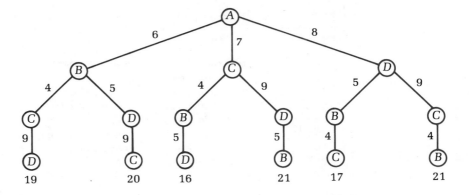

The tree in Figure 2.33 lists the options available to the company together with the total downtime for each option (bottom row). A path that starts at the top of the figure and goes to the bottom gives a scheduling of production runs. Adding the numbers on the edges of a path gives the total downtime for the production schedule. Looking at the bottom row of numbers in Figure 2.33, we see that the smallest possible downtime is 16 hours for the schedule: after A, run C, then B, then D. The nearest neighbor rule in this setting says always choose the next run to be the one that requires the least time to set up. This strategy gives the production schedule: after A, run B, then C, then D, with a total downtime of 19 hours.   ■

We have two methods for trying to solve a traveling salesman or production run problem: the nearest neighbor rule and check all the routes. If we check all the routes, we will get the best (optimal) solution. The nearest neighbor rule is easier and quicker, but it does not always give the optimal solution. If we assume a person can do one edge computation per minute and a computer can do one billion edge computations per second, then we can make tables that indicate how long it would take someone to do a typical traveling salesman problem by each of these methods. No matter which method you use, the more cities there are, the longer it will take.

From the tables it seems reasonable to conclude that to check all the routes is impractical by hand computation when there are more than 6 cities and by computer computation when there are more than 17 cities. On the other hand, the nearest neighbor rule gives an answer quickly, but it may not be the best answer. The problem of finding a fast method that will give the best answer to any traveling salesman problem is one of the outstanding

TABLE 1   Time to solve the traveling salesman problem by hand

Number of cities	Nearest neighbor	Check all routes
4	4 min.	6 min.
6	6 min.	2 hours
8	8 min.	4 days 16 hours
10	10 min.	more than 8 months

TABLE 2 Time to solve the traveling salesman problem by computer

Number of cities	Nearest neighbor	Check all routes
10	less than 1 sec.	less than 1 sec.
15	less than 1 sec.	1 min. 27 sec.
16	less than 1 sec.	21 min. 47 sec.
17	less than 1 sec.	5 hours 48 min.
18	less than 1 sec.	4 days
19	less than 1 sec.	2 months 16 days
20	less than 1 sec.	3 years and 10 months
25	less than 1 sec.	more than 19 million years

unsolved problems in mathematics. The current belief is that there is no quick solution.

A path which passes through each vertex once and only once is called a *Hamiltonian path*. A path that starts at a vertex, passes through each other vertex once and only once and then returns to the start is called a *Hamiltonian circuit*.

In Section 2.2, we saw that a graph has an Eulerian path if the number of odd vertices is zero or two. However, there is no known procedure for quickly determining whether a graph has either a Hamiltonian path or a Hamiltonian circuit. The graph in Figure 2.34 is an example of a graph that has no Hamiltonian paths or circuits.

Figure 2.34

The questions we have considered in the first three sections of this chapter illustrate three fundamental types of mathematical problems: **existence problems**, **optimization problems**, and **counting problems**. Determining whether a graph has Eulerian paths or circuits, Hamiltonian paths or circuits, scheduling problems, and the four-color problem are examples of existence problems. In an optimization problem the objective is to find the "best" way to carry out some task such as visiting all cities or scheduling production runs. Finding the cheapest Hamiltonian circuit (as in a traveling salesman problem) and finding the cheapest Hamiltonian path (as in Example 3) are examples of optimization problems. Determining how long it would take to solve a traveling salesman problem by listing all the routes reduces to counting the number of computations involved and is an example of a counting problem. Counting techniques are the main topic of Chapter 4. Tables 1 and 2 are constructed using techniques presented in Chapter 4.

The problems considered in this chapter illustrate a variety of possible answers to mathematical problems. The question of whether a graph has Eulerian paths or circuits, is quickly settled by counting the number of vertices with an odd number of *edges*. A proof that there is no map in the plane requiring five colors was found only after a great deal of effort by many mathematicians over a 100-year period. The question of whether a graph has Hamiltonian paths or circuits has no practical solution at this time.

In the next section, we present another general type of existence problem, matching problems, and give a procedure for solving them. In Section 2.5, we present an additional example of an optimization problem and give its solution.

CONCEPTS

traveling salesman problem
nearest neighbor rule
Hamiltonian circuit
Hamiltonian path

SOLUTION TO PRACTICE EXAMPLE

1. The route given by the nearest neighbor rule is: Washington to Richmond to New York City to Philadelphia to Providence and back to Washington for a cost of 50 + 95 + 50 + 80 + 90 = $365.

EXERCISES 2.3

In the graphs for Exercises 1 through 14, the vertices represent cities and the numbers on the edges give the cost of traveling between cities. For Exercises 1 through 6, use the nearest neighbor rule to find a path that starts at A, visits each other city once, and returns to A.

1.

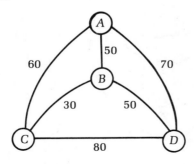

2.

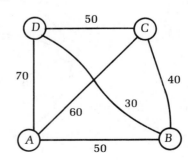

3.

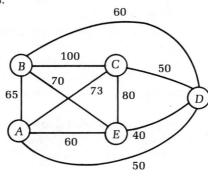

4.

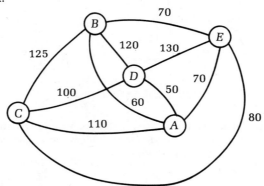

5.

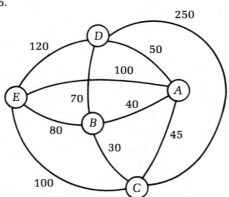

6.

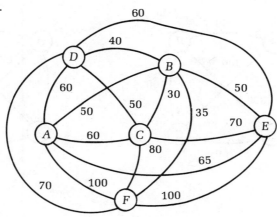

In Exercises 7 through 14:

(a) List (as in Figure 2.33) the paths that start at A, visit each other city once, and then return to A.

(b) Find the cost of each path in your answer to (a).

(c) Find the path (or paths) that cost the least.

(d) Does the nearest neighbor rule give a path of least cost?

7.

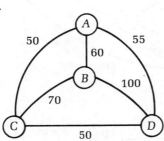

8.

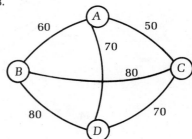

9.

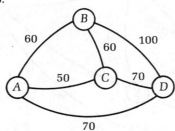

10.

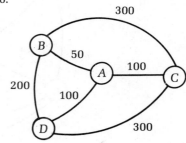

11.

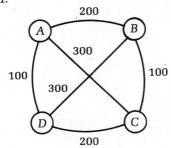

12.

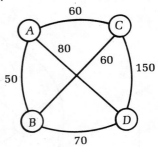

13.

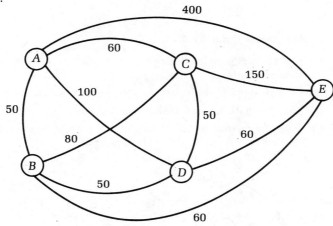

14.

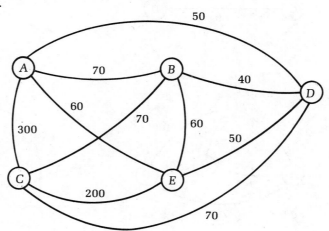

In the graphs for Exercises 15 through 19, the vertices represent the different products to be manufactured in a factory during the next month, and the numbers on the edges give the cost of converting the machinery between production runs. Suppose the first item to be manufactured is A. Decide the order in which the remaining products should be produced so that the cost of converting the machinery is as small as possible.

15.

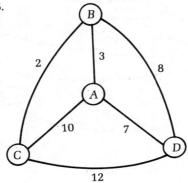

16.

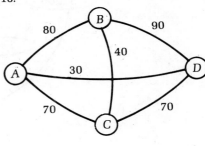

17.

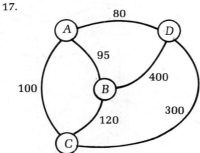

18.

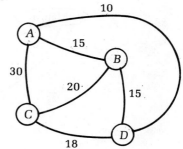

19.

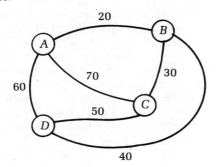

20. Find a Hamiltonian circuit in the graph:

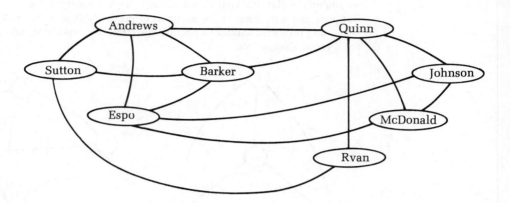

21. Find a Hamiltonian path in the graph:

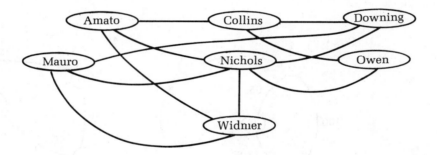

22. In the graph for Exercise 20, two people are joined by an edge if they know each other. Draw the graph with the same vertices as in Exercise 20 but with two people joined by an edge if they do not know each other. Find a Hamiltonian circuit in your graph.

23. For the graph in Exercise 21, two people are joined by an edge if they know each other. Draw the graph with the same vertices as in Exercise 21 but with two people joined by an edge if they do not know each other. Find a Hamiltonian path in your graph.

24. Use your answer to Exercise 20 to seat the people Andrews, Barker, Espo, Johnson, McDonald, Quinn, Ryan, and Sutton at the table illustrated by putting the first vertex in your path in seat 1, the second vertex in your path in seat 2, the third vertex in your path in seat 3, and so on. Since edges in the graph for Exercise 20 join people who know each other, people will know the people sitting on either side of them.

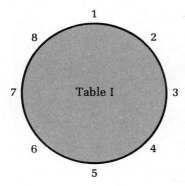

25. Use your answer to Exercise 21 to seat the people Amato, Collins, Downing, Mauro, Nichols, Owen, and Widmer at the table illustrated so that they all know the people they are sitting next to.

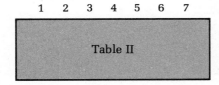

26. Use your answer to Exercise 22 to seat the people Andrews, Barker, Espo, Johnson, McDonald, Quinn, Ryan, and Sutton at Table 1 so that no one knows either of the people he or she is sitting next to.

27. Use your answer to Exercise 23 to seat the people Amato, Collins, Downing, Mauro, Nichols, Owen, and Widmer at Table II so that none of them know anyone they are sitting next to.

28. In the game of chess a knight is allowed to move by going two squares vertically or horizontally and then one square in a perpendicular direction. The *L*'s in the figure on page 78 mark the squares a knight at *S* can reach in one move. Given a playing board divided into squares, can a knight moving according to the rules of chess visit each square exactly once and return to the start? In order to translate this question (called the knight's tour puzzle) into graph theory, construct the tour graph whose vertices are the squares on the playing board and join two vertices by an edge if a knight can move from one vertex to the other in one move. A knight's tour of the board is then the same as a Hamiltonian circuit in the tour graph. The game board for chess is an 8-by-8 block of squares. The corresponding tour graph has 64 vertices, 168 edges, and several Hamiltonian circuits.

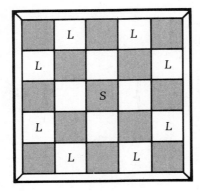

(a) Construct the tour graph for the 3-by-3 game board.

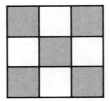

(b) Is there a Hamiltonian circuit in this tour graph?

(c) Is there a knight's tour which visits all but one of the squares and returns to the start?

2.4   Assignment Problems—Matching

In this section, we present a general type of existence problem called **matching** problems. Filling each of several job openings from a pool of candidates is an example of a matching problem.

EXAMPLE 1   A drugstore chain has a pool of employees who move from store to store as needed. Figure 2.35 gives a graph whose vertices are the workers in the pool and the locations of the stores that currently need an additional worker. A worker is joined by an edge to a store location if the store is within commuting distance of the worker. Match up the workers and stores so that each store is supplied with a worker within commuting distance.

Figure 2.36 pictures a matching of workers to stores by putting hash marks on an edge to show that the worker at one vertex of the edge is assigned to the store at the other vertex.

Figure 2.35

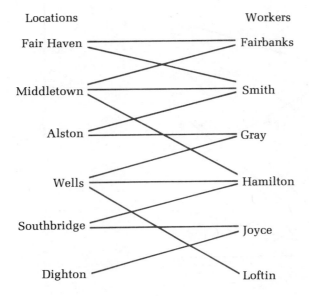

Figure 2.36

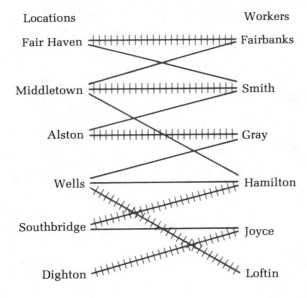

EXAMPLE 2   For the graph in Figure 2.37, the vertices J_1, J_2, and J_3, represent job openings with a company, and the vertices A_1, A_2, A_3, A_4, A_5, and A_6 represent applications for the jobs. An edge joins a job to an applicant qualified for the job. Match the applicants with the jobs so that each job is filled by a qualified applicant.

Figure 2.37

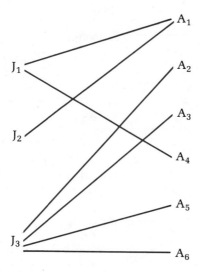

A matching is pictured in Figure 2.38 where hash marks on an edge indicate the applicant at one vertex is given the job at the other vertex.

Figure 2.38

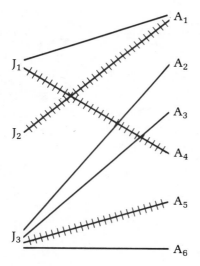

DEFINITION   A **matching** in a graph is a collection of edges with no two edges in the matching meeting at a vertex.

Note that two hashed edges meeting at a vertex in Figure 2.39 would correspond to assigning two people to the same job (if the shared vertex is a job) or assigning different jobs to the same person (if the shared vertex represents a job applicant).

A graph is called a **bipartite graph** if the vertices can be divided into two sets, X and Y, with no elements in common, so that each edge in the graph has one vertex in X and the other vertex in Y. In Example 1, we can take the towns for the vertices in X and the workers for the vertices in Y. In Example 2 we can let the jobs be the vertices in X and the applicants be the vertices in Y.

Next we give a method for solving matching problems for bipartite graphs.

STEP 1:   Put hash marks on as many edges as you can as long as no vertex is the vertex of more than one edge with hash marks. (The result will depend on the choices you make.)

Applying Step 1 to the graph in Figure 2.39 we obtain the graph in Figure 2.40.

Figure 2.39

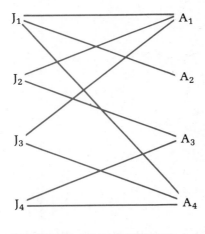

Figure 2.40

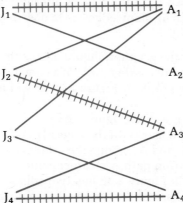

STEP 2: Circle all the vertices that are not on any of the edges with hash marks.

In our example, we circle the vertices J_3 and A_2.

STEP 3: Look for an **alternating path** in the graph that starts and ends at a circled vertex so that the edges in the path alternate: the first edge in the path has no hash marks, the second edge in the path has hash marks, the third edge has no hash marks, . . . , the last edge has no hash marks.

In our example, the path from J_3 to A_1, to J_1, to A_2 is an alternating path.

STEP 4: Use the path found in Step 3 to change the matching by putting hash marks on those edges in the path that do not have them and removing the hash marks from the edges in the path that do have them.

Applying Step 4 to the path from J_3 to A_1, to J_1, to A_2 we get the matching pictured in the graph in Figure 2.41.

Figure 2.41

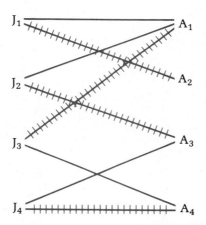

STEP 5: Repeat Steps 2–4 until there is no alternating path (Step 3). Now you have a matching with as many edges as is possible for any matching in the graph.

Since each vertex in the graph in Figure 2.41 is the vertex of an edge in the matching, there is no alternating path. We conclude from Step 5 that all of the matchings for the graph in Figure 2.39 have four edges or less.

EXAMPLE 3   Apply Steps 1–5 to the graph in Figure 2.42.

In Step 1, we put hash marks on the edges $\{J_1, A_1\}$ and $\{J_2, A_3\}$. In Step 2, we circle the vertices J_3 and A_2, giving the graph marked as in Figure 2.43. Since there is no alternating path, we can conclude from Step 5 that every matching for the graph in Figure 2.42 has two edges or less. If we think of the J's as representing jobs, and the A's as representing applicants, with the

Figure 2.42

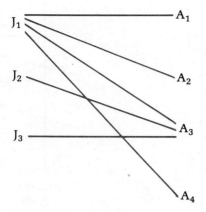

Figure 2.43

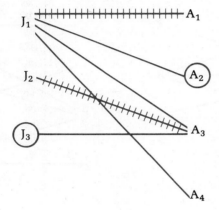

edges joining jobs to qualified applicants, then Figure 2.40 pictures an unsuccessful attempt to find a matching that fills all the jobs. The job J_3 goes unfilled. For the graph in Figure 2.43 there is no way to fill each job with a qualified candidate.

CONCEPTS

matching
bipartite graph
alternating path

EXERCISES 2.4

In Exercises 1 through 6, the J vertices represent jobs, the A vertices represent applicants, and edges join jobs to qualified applicants. Fill each job with a qualified applicant.

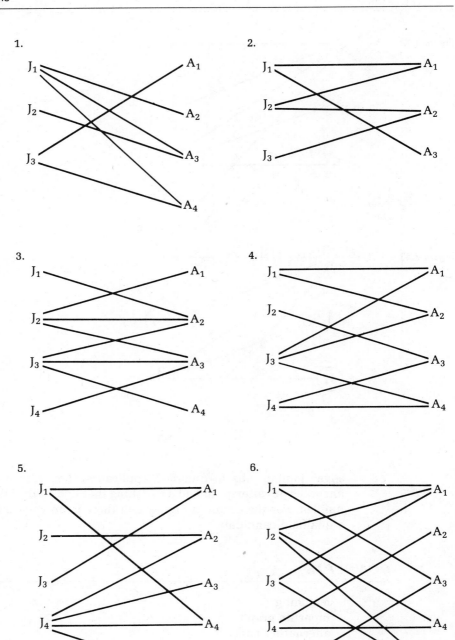

In Exercises 7 through 12 find the largest number of edges in any matching in the graph.

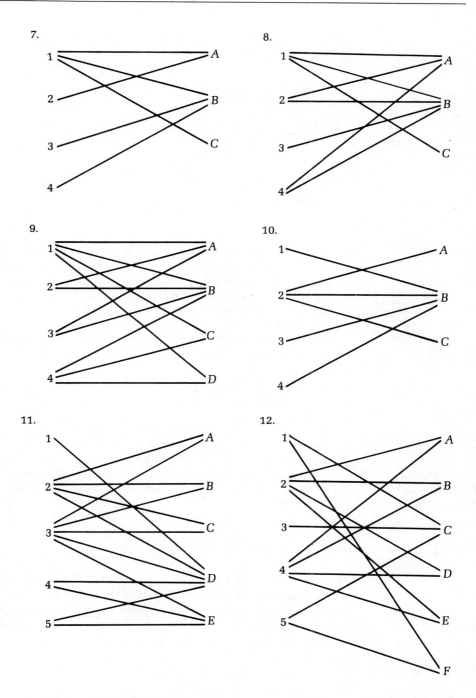

7.

8.

9.

10.

11.

12.

13. The computer center has four files, F_1, F_2, F_3, and F_4, to be stored. Each of the possible storage locations, L_1, L_2, L_3, and L_4, can hold at most one of the files. In the graph below an edge joins a file to a location if there is enough room in

the location at one vertex of the edge for the file at the other vertex. Decide where to store the files.

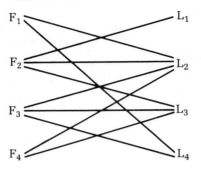

14. A high school has openings for five teachers, one opening in each of the subjects: mathematics, physics, chemistry, French, and history. The applicants are: Mrs. Adams (major—French, minor—history), Mr. Conti (major—mathematics, minor—physics), Mrs. Douglas (major—mathematics, minor—chemistry), Mrs. Dupre (major—chemistry, minor—physics), Mrs. Scott (major—chemistry, minor—history), and Mr. Wilson (major—French, minor—chemistry). Fill the openings with qualified teachers so that as many people as possible are assigned to teach the subject of their major and everyone is assigned to teach the subject of either their major or minor.

15. The committee membership of the Faculty Senate is: Agenda Committee (Clark, Taylor, Hastings, Walsh), Curriculum Revision Committee (Taylor, Hastings, Walsh), New Programs Committee (Taylor, Hastings, Beard), Program Review Committee (Smith, Beard, Walsh), Executive Council (Beard, Clark, Smith). The work of each committee is to be reviewed by a Senate member who is not on the committee. Draw the graph whose vertices are the committees and the members of the Senate and whose edges join committees to Senate members not on the committee. Assign a different reviewer to each committee.

2.5   Shortest Route Problems

In this section, we give an example of a general type of optimization problem called **shortest route** problems. Finding the shortest route from one town to another and finding the least expensive airline route from one city to another are examples of shortest route problems. In general, shortest route problems arise in situations where paths in a graph correspond to strategies for completing some task, and the shortest route corresponds to the "best" way to complete the task. We give a procedure, **Dijkstra's algorithm**, for solving shortest route problems.

EXAMPLE 1   In the graph in Figure 2.44, the vertices represent towns and the edges represent roads, with the mileage between towns given by the number next to the edge. What is the shortest route from Lewes to Bodiam? The shortest route from Lewes to Bodiam is 8 miles. Can you find it?

Figure 2.44

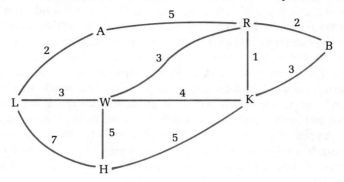

A = Alston   H = Hove   L = Lewes   R = Rodmell
B = Bodiam   K = Kingston   W = Wells

In a shortest route problem, the numbers on the edges do not have to be distances. For example, if the numbers in the graph in Figure 2.44 are travel times instead of mileages, then the "shortest route" is the path from Lewes to Bodiam which takes the least time. If the graph in Figure 2.44 represents airline routes, with the numbers on the edges giving the cost of a flight from one airport to another, then the "shortest route" is the one that costs the least. Shortest route problems arise in settings where paths correspond to strategies for completing some task, and the shortest route corresponds to the "best" strategy.

EXAMPLE 2

The owner of a small company is going to buy a truck. Next year and each year after that the truck can be traded in for a new one or kept for another year. The problem is to decide in which years the owner should buy a new truck, so that the total cost of having a truck over the next three years is as small as possible.

Figure 2.45

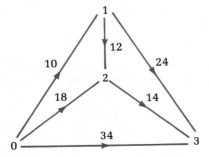

In the graph in Figure 2.45, the vertices correspond to years, with 0 representing the present. The numbers on the edges give the cost to the company, in thousands of dollars, of buying a new truck at the year indicated on one vertex of the edge and trading it in at the year on the other vertex. The number 24 on the edge {1, 3} means that if the owner buys a new truck 1 year from now, keeps it for 2 years, and then sells the truck 3 years from now, the cost of the truck over those 2 years is $24,000. The cost to the company includes purchase price, maintenance, insurance, and taxes minus the value of the truck when it is traded in.

A path from 0 to 3 is a buy-sell strategy for the owner. For example, the path from 0 to 1 to 3 corresponds to: buy a new truck now, after 1 year trade the truck in for a new one, then trade in that truck 3 years from now. The cost to the company over the 3 years is the sum of the numbers on the edges in the path from 0 to 1 to 3, 10 + 24 = 34 (thousand dollars). The shortest route from 0 to 3 gives the best buy-sell strategy. In this example the best buy-sell strategy is given by the path from 0 to 2 to 3 with a total cost of $32,000. ▪

Next we give a method, **Dijkstra's algorithm**, for solving shortest route problems. In general, a sequence of instructions that solves all instances of a well-defined problem is called an **algorithm**. If the problem is to find the shortest route from a vertex A to a vertex D, then the algorithm first finds the vertex closest to A and the shortest route from A to that vertex. Then the algorithm finds the next closest vertex to A and so on until the vertex D occurs.

The best way to learn the method is to work through examples. We will find the shortest route from A to D in the graph in Figure 2.46.

Figure 2.46

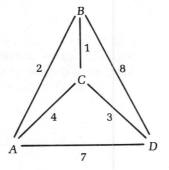

Copy Figure 2.46 onto a piece of paper and carry out the steps as we describe them. We are going to add symbols to the graph so make your graph big.

DIJKSTRA'S ALGORITHM:

STEP 1: Circle the beginning vertex. Put the number 0 next to the vertex and circle it. Underline the numbers on each edge joined to the beginning vertex.

In our example, A is the beginning vertex. After Step 1 you should have the graph marked as in Figure 2.47.

Figure 2.47

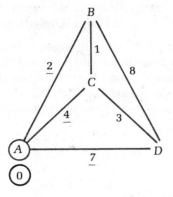

STEP 2:   Look at the edges that have one vertex circled and one vertex not circled. From these edges pick the edge with the smallest underlined number (in case of a tie pick from among the edges with the smallest of the underlined numbers). Then

(a) Put hash marks on the edge.
(b) Circle the not yet circled vertex of the edge.
(c) Write the underlined number (on the hash-marked edge) next to the newly circled vertex, and circle the number.

In our example, the edges with one vertex circled and one vertex uncircled are $\{A, B\}$, $\{A, C\}$, and $\{A, D\}$. The corresponding underlined numbers are 2, 4, and 7. In Step 2 we must pick the edge $\{A, B\}$ and put hash marks on it. Circle the vertex B, write the number 2 next to vertex B, and circle the 2. At this point you should have the graph in Figure 2.48. (B is the vertex closest to A. The shortest route from A to B is the edge $\{A, B\}$.)

Figure 2.48

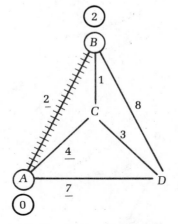

The next step adds more underlined numbers to the graph.

STEP 3:   Look at the edges that have one vertex circled, one vertex uncircled, and no underlined number on the edge. For each of these edges put on the edge the sum of the number originally on the edge and the circled number that is next to the circled vertex of the edge. Underline this number.

At this stage, $\{B, D\}$ and $\{B, C\}$ are the edges with one vertex circled, one vertex uncircled, and no underlined number. Now the edge $\{B, D\}$ gets the underlined number 10 since 8 (number originally on the edge $\{B, D\}$) + 2 (circled number next to the circled vertex of $\{B, D\}$) = 10. The edge $\{B, C\}$ gets the underlined number 3 (1 + 2). Now the picture is as in Figure 2.49.

Figure 2.49

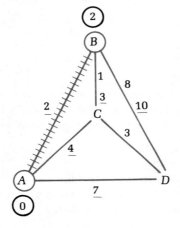

STEP 4:   Continue to carry out Steps 2 and 3 until the end vertex is circled. Then go to Step 5.

To do this for our example, follow the instructions in Step 2. The result is Figure 2.50.

Figure 2.50

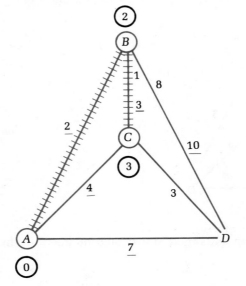

Now follow the instructions in Step 3 and you will get Figure 2.51.

Figure 2.51

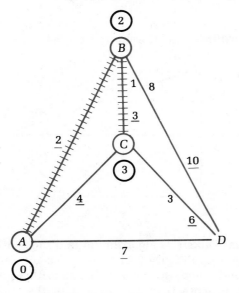

(After *B*, the vertex closest to *A* is *C*. The shortest route from *A* to *C* is *A* to *B* to *C*.)

After carrying Step 2 again, vertex *D* is circled (Figure 2.52).

Figure 2.52

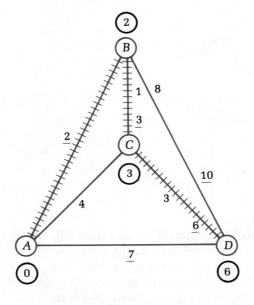

STEP 5: The shortest route from the beginning vertex to the end vertex is the path from beginning to end that uses only hashed edges. (There is only one such path.) The length of the path is the circled number at the ending vertex.

Step 5 tells us the shortest route from A to D is A to B to C to D. The length is 6.

PRACTICE EXAMPLE 1

Figure 2.53

Use Dijkstra's algorithm to find the shortest route from A to F in Figure 2.53.

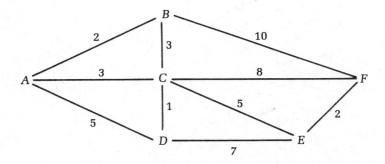

Now we will use Dijkstra's algorithm to find the shortest route from L to B in Figure 2.44. Copy Figure 2.44 onto a piece of paper. Use L as the beginning vertex and follow the steps of the algorithm until you reach the point where there is more than one edge with the smallest underlined number on the edges having one vertex circled and one vertex uncircled. Your graph should be as in Figure 2.54.

Figure 2.54

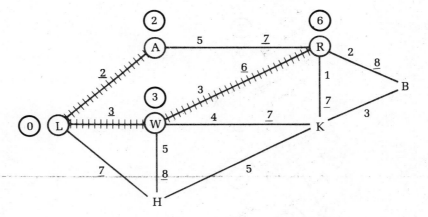

The smallest underlined number on an edge with only one vertex circled is the number 7, which occurs on the edges {L, H}, {W, K}, and {R, K}. Step 2 directs us to choose one of these edges. We choose the edge {R, K}. If you continue to carry out the steps in the algorithm until the end vertex B is circled, you should get the graph shown in Figure 2.55. The shortest route from L = Lewes to B = Bodiam is: L = Lewes to W = Wells, to R = Rodmell, to B = Bodiam. This route is 8 miles long.

Figure 2.55

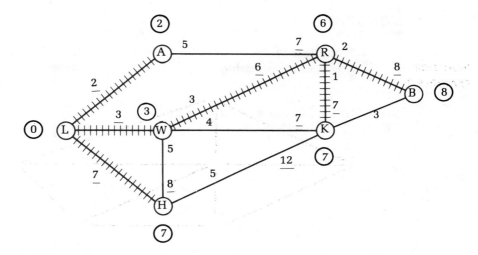

The procedure also works if the edges have arrows on them to indicate the direction the edge must be traveled (as in Example 2). The only change in the instructions occurs in Steps 1 and 3 where you place underlined numbers on the edges. Now, an underlined number is placed on the edge only if the arrow on the edge points from the circled vertex to the uncircled vertex.

If you apply Dijkstra's algorithm to the graph in Figure 2.45, then you will get the graph in Figure 2.56. The shortest route from 0 to 3 is: 0 to 2 to 3 with a length of 32. As we indicated in Example 2, the buy-sell strategy of least cost over 3 years is to buy a new truck now, after 2 years trade it in for a new one, and finally sell the truck 3 years from now. The cost to the company is $32,000.

Figure 2.56

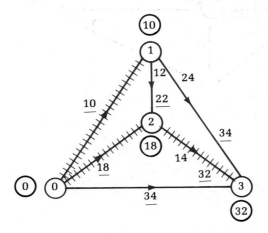

CONCEPTS

shortest route
Dijkstra's algorithm

SOLUTION TO PRACTICE EXAMPLE

1.

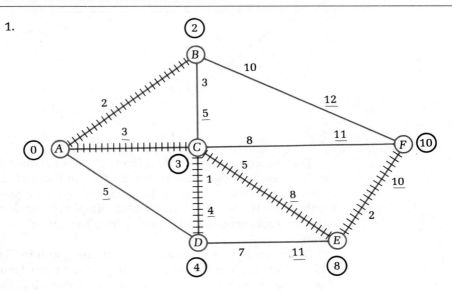

EXERCISES 2.5

In Exercises 1 through 5, find the shortest route from S to E.

1.

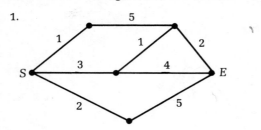

2.

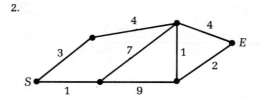

3.

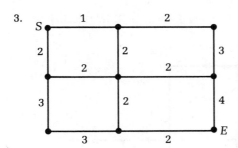

4.

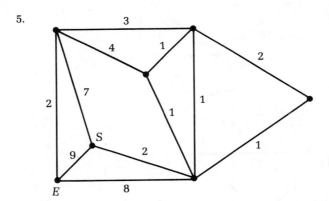

5.

6. A person in Bentonville wants to drive first to Newton and then to Newport.
    Find the shortest route.

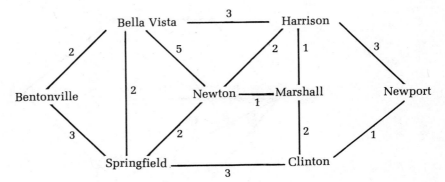

Find the shortest route from S to E in the directed graphs for Exercises 7 through 11.

7.

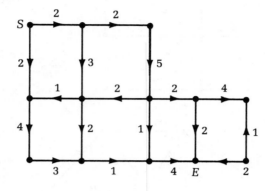

8.

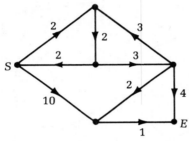

9.

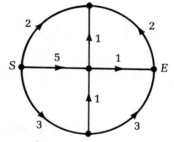

10.

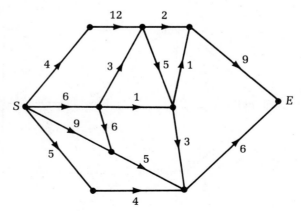

11.

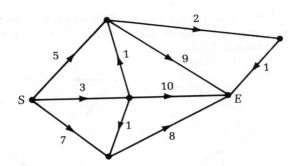

12. After buying a tractor this year, a farmer will have the option next year and each year thereafter of trading in the tractor for a new one or keeping the tractor for another year. The numbers on the edges in the graph below give the cost to the farmer, in thousands of dollars, of buying a new tractor at the year indicated on one vertex of the edge, and trading it in at the year on the other vertex. Apply Dijkstra's algorithm to the directed graph and use the result to decide the best buy-sell strategy for a farmer who plans to sell the farm and not have a tractor at the end of:

(a) 2 years

(b) 3 years

(c) 4 years

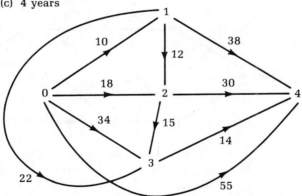

13. An assembly line will be set up to produce sofa frames from roughly shaped pieces of wood. The steps in the process are: sand, spray on protective coating, assemble the parts, put on the company nameplate. The company wants to know the order in which these steps should be done so that the frames are produced as quickly as possible.

In the graph below, the label on a vertex is a list of the steps that have been done so far. The edges with arrows pointing out of a vertex give the possible next steps in the process and how long in minutes that step will take. A path from start to finish corresponds to a possible ordering of the steps in the manufacture of a sofa frame with the sum of the numbers on the edges giving the time it takes to carry out the steps. For example, the path that traces out the edges SPNA in order corresponds to: first sand, then spray on the protective coating, then put on the nameplate, then assemble the pieces. This takes

$5 + 8 + 1 + 4 = 18$ minutes. The problem of finding the ordering of the steps that minimizes production time is the same as finding the shortest route from start to finish.

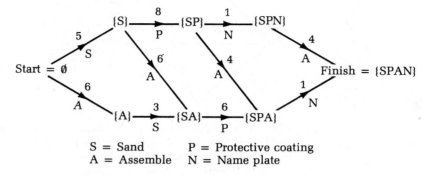

S = Sand   P = Protective coating
A = Assemble   N = Name plate

14. The last steps in the manufacture of a table are to assemble, sand, varnish, and polish the precut pieces.
   (a) In what order should these steps be carried out if the production time is to be as small as possible? The numbers in the diagram below give the time to carry out the steps.
   (b) In what order should the steps be done if the last step must be polishing and the production time is to be as small as possible?

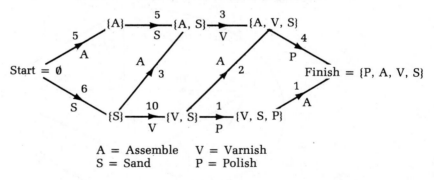

A = Assemble   V = Varnish
S = Sand   P = Polish

CHAPTER SUMMARY

In this chapter we introduced graphs and interpreted a variety of problems in terms of graphs: *scheduling problems* and *graph coloring* (section 1), reconstructing an RNA chain from its fragments and Eulerian paths (section 2), the *Traveling Salesman Problem* (section 3), assignment problems (section 3), and shortest route problems (section 4). For most of these problems we were able to find solutions. On the other hand the Traveling Salesman Problem is one of the important unsolved problems in mathematics. In Chapter 6 we return to graph coloring and find a procedure that counts the number of different ways to color a graph with any given number of colors. In the next chapter we consider a special type of graph called a *tree* and solve a variety of problems with algorithms.

REVIEW EXERCISES FOR CHAPTER 2

In Exercises 1 through 3, the vertices in the graphs represent committees, and two vertices are joined by an edge if the committees have one or more members in common. Suppose the available meeting times are M = Monday, T = Tuesday, W = Wednesday, and F = Friday from 9 to 10 A.M. In each exercise, schedule the committees by putting a M, T, W, or F next to each vertex so that vertices joined by an edge are given different letters. Do not use any more meeting times than necessary.

1.
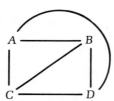

2.
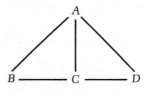

3.
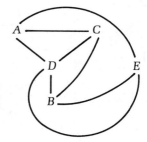

4. Draw the graph with vertices {1, 2, 3, 4, 5} and edges {{1, 3}, {1, 4}, {2, 3}, {2, 5}, {3, 4}, {3, 5}}.

5. Suppose the membership of the subcommittees of the student council are:

   F = Fund Raising = {Adams, Cohen, Kelly}
   C = Concerts = {Cohen, Kelly, Howland}
   L = Lectures = {Adams, Lambert, Phelan}
   S = Special Events = {Lambert, Kelley, Howland, Sullivan}

   (a) Draw the graph whose vertices are the committees and whose edges join committees with one or more members in common.
   (b) The student council wants to schedule weekly meetings of each committee. What is the smallest number of meeting times needed if committees with members in common are to meet at different times?

6. For the graphs below circle each vertex that has an odd number of edges and decide if the graph has an Eulerian path.

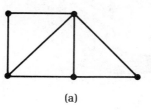

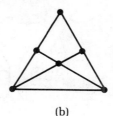

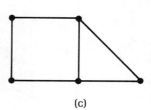

(a)   (b)   (c)

7.   Find an Eulerian circuit that starts and ends at the vertex s.

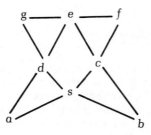

8.   Find an Eulerian path that starts at S and ends at E.

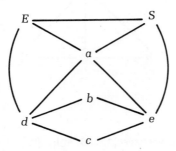

9.   The figure below pictures rivers with bridges and islands. Draw the corresponding graph. Is it possible to take a walk that crosses each bridge once and only once and returns to the start?

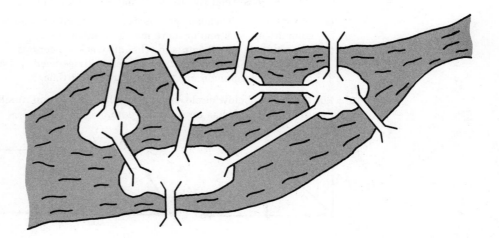

10. Find the RNA chain whose graph is:

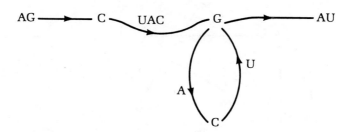

11. (a) Hyphenate the fragments given below.
     (b) Draw the graph from the hyphenated fragments.
     (c) Find all RNA chains with the given fragments.

G fragments	U-C fragments
AU	C
CG	AC
UACG	GAU
	GU

In the graphs for Exercises 12 and 13, the vertices represent cities and the numbers on the edges give the cost of traveling between cities. Find the Hamiltonian circuit of least cost that starts and ends at A. Is this the circuit given by the nearest neighbor rule?

12.

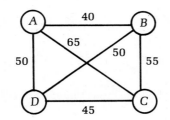

13.

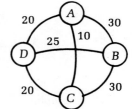

In the graphs for Exercises 14 and 15, the vertices represent different products to be manufactured during the next week. The numbers on the edges give the cost of converting the machinery between production runs. The first item to be manufactured is A. Decide the order in which the remaining products should be produced so that the total cost of converting the machinery is as small as possible.

14.

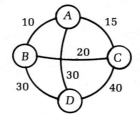

15.

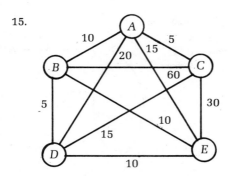

16. In the graph below the vertices represent people. Vertices are joined by an edge if the two people know each other. Find a Hamiltonian path in the graph and use the path to give a seating arrangement at the table so that they all know the people they are sitting next to.

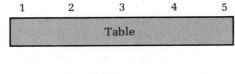

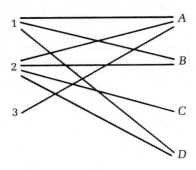

In Exercises 17 and 18 find the largest number of edges in any matching in the graph.

17.

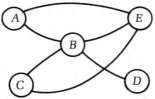

18.

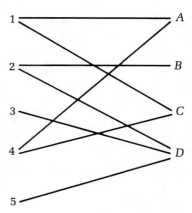

19. In the graph below the vertices on the left correspond to teachers. The vertices on the right correspond to courses. Vertices are joined by an edge if the teacher at one vertex of the edge is qualified to teach the course at the other vertex. Match teachers with courses so that each teacher is qualified to teach the course assigned.

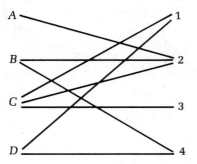

20. Find the shortest route from A to F in the graph below.

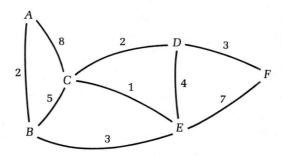

21. Find the shortest route from S to F in the directed graph below.

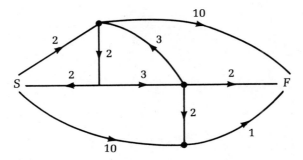

22. An assembly line will be set up to carry out four steps indicated by A, B, C, D. In the graph below, the label on a vertex is a list of the steps that have been done so far. The edges with arrows pointing out of a vertex give the possible

next steps and how long in minutes that step will take. In what order should the steps be carried out in order to minimize production time?

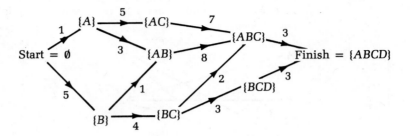

Trees

3

This chapter is devoted to a special kind of graph called a **tree**. Kirchoff developed the theory of trees in 1847 in order to solve systems of linear equations arising from electrical networks. He translated an electrical network with its resistances, condensers, and inductances into a graph and proceeded to find subgraphs that included all the vertices and, at the same time, were trees (spanning trees).

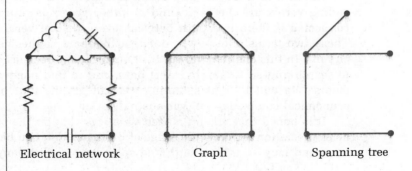

Electrical network   Graph   Spanning tree

In 1857 Cayley independently discovered trees while trying to count the isomers of saturated hydrocarbons, chemical compounds of the form C_nH_{2n+2}. The graphs (trees) corresponding to these saturated hydrocarbons are called **bond graphs.** A vertex is labeled C if it is bonded to four other vertices (carbon has chemical valence 4) and H if it is bonded to one other vertex (hydrogen has chemical valence 1).

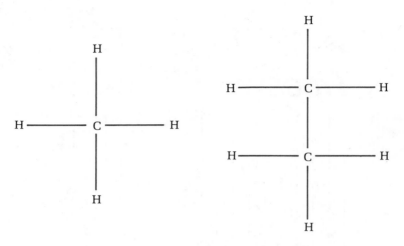

Methane   Ethane

In the early 1900s, in order to find the most economical layout in a power line network, Boruvka assigned weights to the edges of a graph corresponding to the cost. To solve his problem, he developed the first algorithm for finding a **minimum spanning tree** in a graph (a tree subgraph that includes each vertex and has the least total weight).

Today, trees are an indispensable tool to the computer scientist. Computers are asked to sort data, search for a piece of data, and insert data. The techniques used to perform these tasks rely heavily on the structure of trees. Trees have been applied to such varied subjects as computer and communication networks, power networks, transportation networks, picture processing, speech recognition, classification problems, and homogeneity of bimetallic objects. (For references and further applications, see Graham and Hell 1982.)

Recall that a **circuit** in a graph is a path whose starting vertex and ending vertex are the same, and no other vertex is repeated. A graph is **connected** if there is a path between every pair of vertices in the graph. These two terms allow us to define a **tree** as a connected graph with no circuits. In this chapter we will look at various properties of trees to count, to search and sort data, to insert data, and to find one-way street assignments. We will look at spanning trees of graphs that provide the most economical connections in various networks.

It is hoped that when finished with this chapter the student will have an appreciation for the wide range of problems that can be solved by using trees and may even be able to find some new applications of trees.

3.1   Trees to List and Count the Possibilities

In this section, we use trees to list and count various possibilities, and we give some of the properties of trees important in applications.

In the traveling salesman problem discussed in the last chapter we used a tree to indicate the possible routes a salesman could take to visit all assigned cities, starting at city 1.

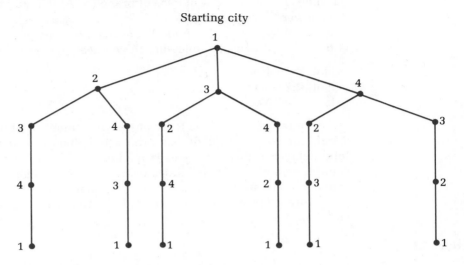

Starting city

A basic problem one encounters when working with data is sorting. If data are numerical, then one usually wants to sort in numerical order. In other instances, the sorting may be by letter of the alphabet, age, or sex. If we sort by comparisons, we can use a tree that represents the results of the decision made at each step, called a **decision tree**. For example, Figure 3.1 shows a decision tree for sorting three distinct numbers a, b, and c, by size.

Figure 3.1

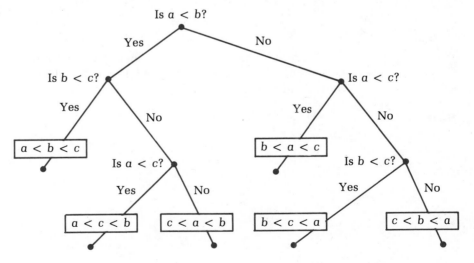

This decision tree not only shows the various possibilities, but it also shows that, at most, three questions need to be asked to find the correct order. Depending on the answer to the first question, one follows one of the two main branches of the tree. Depending on the answer to the second question, one follows one of two subbranches. At that point, either we know the answer (in our example $a < b < c$ or $b < a < c$), or we need to ask only one more question to find the answer. For example, if the actual order is $b < c < a$, then the following three questions are asked, in order:

Is $a < b$? No.
Is $a < c$? No.
Is $b < c$? Yes.

A vertex of degree one (only one edge incident to it) in a tree is called a **leaf**. The leaves of the decision tree are the possible final outcomes. The total number of final outcomes is the total number of leaves. Thus we can count the number of possibilities by counting the number of leaves. In our example there are six leaves, or six orderings of three distinct numbers.

Figure 3.2 gives additional examples of trees (connected graphs with no circuits).

Figure 3.2

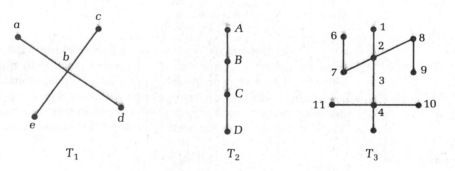

T_1 T_2 T_3

If a graph has only one piece, then there are paths between any pair of vertices and the graph is connected. Figure 3.3 gives an example of a graph that is not a tree, since it is not connected.

Figure 3.3

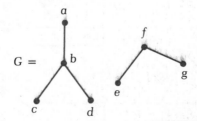

There are no circuits in any of the graphs in Figure 3.2 or 3.3. If we start at any vertex, we cannot get back to that vertex without repeating intermediary vertices. Figure 3.4 gives a graph that is not a tree because it has a circuit, b-c-d-e-b.

Figure 3.4

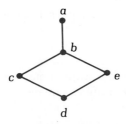

Recall from Chapter 1 that DNA chains are sequences of bases, thyamine (T), cytosine (C), adenine (A), and guanine (G). Three-element parts of these DNA chains encode various amino acids. How many three-element sequences of T, C, A, and G are there? We can use a tree to count the possibilities for three-element sequences from {T, C, A, G}. As shown in Figure 3.5, we use one extra vertex, called the *root* of the tree, to start the tree growing. The number of leaves of the tree is 64, therefore there are 64 three-element sequences.

Figure 3.5

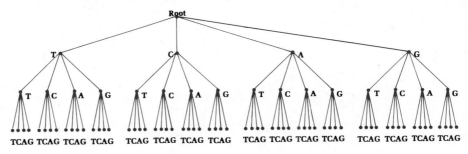

By starting at the root and reading vertices along each path to the leaves, we can list all of the three-element sequences, TTT, TTC, TTA, TTG, TCT, . . . , GGG.

Since computer scientists started using them, trees are grown downward, with the root at the top and the leaves at the bottom (probably because printer paper rolls that way), and most of our trees will be drawn that way. Those working in probability theory often grow their trees from left to right. A tree can be drawn with any vertex designated as the root. Figure 3.6 shows the tree T_1 of Figure 3.2 drawn as a rooted tree, first with *b* as the root, then with *a* as the root. Note in III that *a* is drawn as a root, but could be considered to be a leaf instead.

Figure 3.6

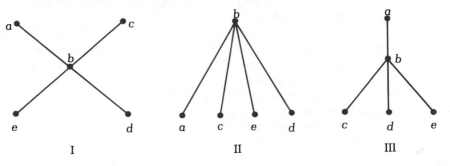

PRACTICE
EXAMPLE 1   Draw a tree that illustrates all the four-element sequences of 0's and 1's.

■

A campus mail room wants to sort the student mail so that it eventually gets into the correct boxes. Each box number consists of four digits from 1 to 9. One way to sort the mail is to initially sort by first digit, and then by second digit, then by third digit, and finally by fourth digit. We can represent this sorting by a tree as shown in Figure 3.7. There are $9 \times 9 \times 9 \times 9 = 6561$ possible mailbox numbers, and each mailbox number corresponds to a path through the tree. In the next section, we will see how this sorting can be done more efficiently.

Figure 3.7

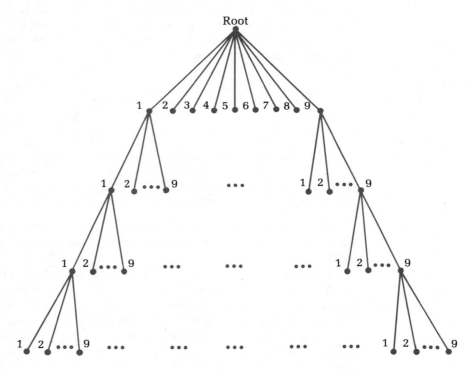

Often we want to distribute information to people in the fastest way possible. We can construct a communications tree to accomplish this distri- bution. As an example, suppose a president of a small university wants to let the faculty know that they are to receive a 10% raise in salary. The president can pass this information on to his vice president, who in turn passes it onto the various deans. The deans pass the information to the department chairpersons, who finally pass it on to the faculty members in their respective departments. Figure 3.8 shows an example of the communi- cations tree for the small university.

Figure 3.8

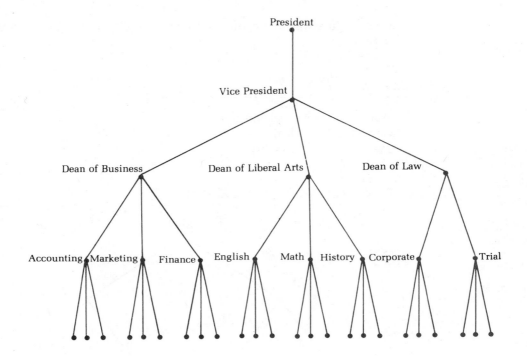

Trees are a simple kind of graph with many structural properties. We will list some of these properties here and use some of them later in the chapter. (For proofs of these properties, see any book on graph theory including Harary 1969, and Bondy and Murty 1976.)

PROPERTY 1   The number of edges of a tree e, equals the number of vertices, n, minus 1. $e = n - 1$.

PROPERTY 2   Every tree has a vertex of degree 1. If a tree has more than one vertex, then it has at least two vertices of degree 1.

PROPERTY 3   There exists a unique path with no repeated vertices between any two vertices.

PRACTICE EXAMPLE 2

Verify the formula, $e = n - 1$, for the trees in Figure 3.2.

In this section, we have introduced trees and have given some basic definitions concerning trees. Trees were used to display information in an orderly fashion so that the various possibilities could be listed and counted. The communications tree indicated the passage of information, and the decision tree provided a way of ordering data. In the next section, we will use trees in a way analogous to decision trees to search for an item in a set of data.

CONCEPTS

circuit	decision tree
connected	leaf
tree	$e = n - 1$

SOLUTIONS TO PRACTICE EXAMPLES

1.

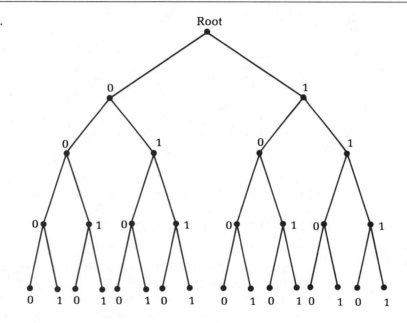

2. (a) T_1: $n = 5$ and $e = 4$. $4 = 5 - 1$
    (b) T_2: $n = 4$ and $e = 3$. $3 = 4 - 1$
    (c) T_3: $n = 11$ and $e = 10$. $10 = 11 - 1$

EXERCISES 3.1

1. Draw a tree with:

    (a) one vertex.

    (b) two vertices.

    (c) three vertices.

2. Draw a tree with four vertices and three leaves.

3. Draw a disconnected graph such that $e = n - 1$.

4. Draw a tree to represent the possible outcomes of tossing three coins.

5. A tree with 100 vertices has how many edges?

6. A tree with n vertices is the smallest (in terms of edges) connected graph on n vertices. How many edges must the smallest connected graph on 14 vertices contain? Can you draw a simple example?

7. Which of the following graphs are trees? If not, why not?

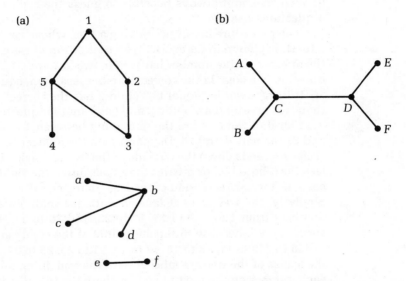

8. The following decision tree is constructed to locate a word in the sentence: "All trees are connected graphs without circuits." Describe the steps involved in locating the words:

    (a) circuits

    (b) are

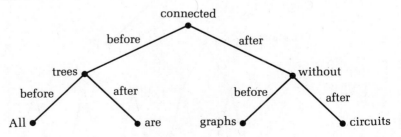

9. A *forest* is a graph that consists of a set of trees. Draw an example of a forest.

10. Can you find an analogous formula for the number of vertices and edges in a forest with three trees? In a forest with k trees?

3.2   *Games and Search I*

In this section, we introduce a method for locating files efficiently and adding new files as new accounts occur. We will illustrate this procedure with an example of a child's game.

A child's guessing game popular with children has two players, child 1 and child 2. Child 1 thinks of a number, and child 2 is to guess the number by asking as few questions as possible. If the number lies between 1 and 31 inclusive, is it always possible to guess the right number with at most 4 questions asked?

The procedure involves drawing a tree, whose vertices are labeled from 1 to 31 as shown in Figure 3.9. The root or top of the tree gets labeled with the number 16, the number halfway between 1 and 31. At that point the first question is asked: Is the correct number less than, equal to, or greater than 16. If the answer is "equal to," child 2 has the correct number. If it is "less than" or "greater than" child 2 must ask another question. The labels for the next level of the tree are the midpoints between 1 and 15 and between 15 and 31, namely 8 and 24. Depending on the answer to question 1, the child either proceeds down the left side of the tree and asks: Is the correct number less than, equal to, or greater than 8, or down the right side of the tree and asks if the correct number is less than, equal to, or greater than 24. Similarly, the tree is next labeled with the midpoints of the four sets of numbers from 1 to 7, 9 to 15, 17 to 23, and 25 to 31. At the next level, the vertices are labeled with the midpoints of the eight sets of numbers from 1 to 3, 5 to 7, 9 to 11, 13 to 15, 17 to 19, 21 to 23, 25 to 27, and 29 to 31. Finally the leaves of the tree are labeled with the remaining numbers so that below each number on the next to last level are the two numbers on either side of it numerically.

Figure 3.9

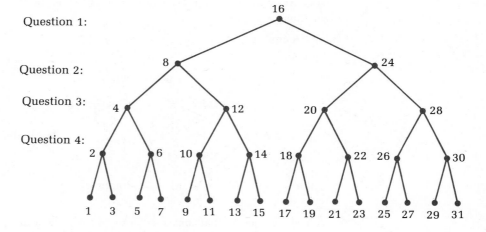

Each vertex of the tree is a decision point; either the correct number is less than, equal to, or greater than the number at that vertex. Even a wrong guess cuts the number of remaining possibilities in half. Therefore when searching for a number between 1 and 31, at most 4 questions have to be asked to arrive at the correct number.

The tree shown in Figure 3.9 and the one shown in Figure 3.1 are both examples of binary trees.

DEFINITIONS   A vertex, v, of a rooted tree is at **level k** if there are k edges on the unique path from the root to v. The root is set at level 0. All of the vertices adjacent to a vertex, u, and one level higher than the level of u, are called **children** of u. A **binary tree** is a rooted tree in which every vertex has either 0 or 2 children.

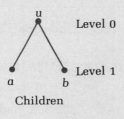

Binary trees have become essential to computer data organization and the ability to search for a particular file number or name. Suppose we have a list of file numbers and we want to set up a system so that we can find a particular file number quickly. As in the child's game, we can use a binary tree that has been prelabeled in a special way with these file numbers. We can also do it in such a way that new file numbers can be added at a later date without changing the whole tree.

We want to design (label) a **binary search tree** so that at each stage the following question will be asked: Is the file number less than, equal to, or greater than the file number at the vertex encountered? If the answer is "equal to," we would stop, having found the file. If the answer is "less than," we would proceed down the left side of the tree or subtree. If the answer is "greater than," we would proceed down the right side of the tree or subtree. If we do not know if a particular file number is present, then as a leaf is encountered, the question asked is: Is the file number we are searching for equal to the number on the leaf?

Before we begin we need to know how many vertices can exist in a binary tree with k levels. If a binary tree has only the root and two children, there are $1 + 2 = 3$ vertices. If each of these children has two children, there would be $1 + 2 + 4 = 7$ vertices, at levels 0, 1, and 2. In general, a binary tree with k levels can have as many as

$$1 + 2 + 4 + 8 + \cdots + 2^k = 1 + 2^1 + 2^2 + \cdots + 2^k = 2^{k+1} - 1$$

vertices. (In a later chapter, we will prove this equation.) Thus a binary tree with highest level 4 can have $2^5 - 1 = 31$ vertices, and a binary tree with highest level 5 can have as many as $2^6 - 1 = 63$ vertices.

EXAMPLE 1

We have the set of file numbers

$$S = \{100, 103, 105, 106, 110, 112, 114, 115, 116, 117, 120\}$$

We want to label a binary tree so that we can search for a particular file number from this set as fast as possible, by asking the least number of questions. ■

SEARCH ALGORITHM

STEP 1: Arrange the set of numbers in numerical increasing order and number them consecutively.

100	103	105	106	110	112	114	115	116	117	120
1	2	3	4	5	6	7	8	9	10	11

STEP 2: Of the numbers, 1, 3, 7, 15, . . . , $2^k - 1$, find the smallest number of this form greater than or equal to the total number of file numbers.

$$15 \geq 11 \quad \text{and} \quad 15 = 2^4 - 1$$

STEP 3: Label a tree as in the child's game with the numbers from 1 to 15 as shown in Figure 3.10.

Figure 3.10

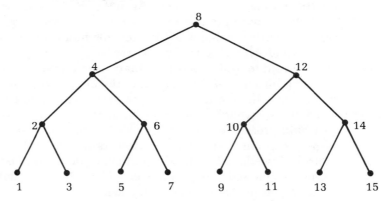

STEP 4: Redraw the tree with the file numbers replacing the numbers from 1 to 15 corresponding to the numbering in Step 1 (Figure 3.11). Move up any piece of the tree to replace those numbers not included.

To search the file for file number 116, we ask the following questions:

Is 116 <, or =, or > 115? > Proceed down to the right.
Is 116 <, or =, or > 117? < Proceed down to the left.
Is 116 <, or =, or > 116? = File found.

Figure 3.11

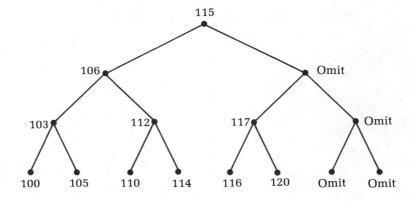

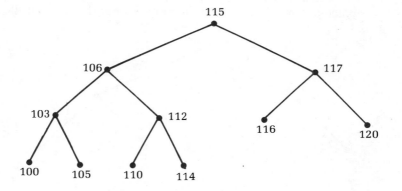

(See Aho, Hopcroft, and Ullman 1974 for a discussion of the efficiency of this search algorithm.)

EXAMPLE 2   Construct a binary search tree for the file numbers: $S = \{3, 8, 1, 10, 12\}$

STEP 1: 1,   3,   5,   8,   10,   12
         1   2   3   4   5   6

STEP 2: $2^3 - 1 = 7$ is closest to 6.

STEP 3:   Tree labeled with the numbers 1 to 7:

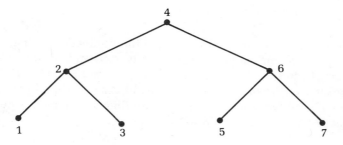

STEP 4:   Tree redrawn with the file numbers replacing the numbers 1 to 7:

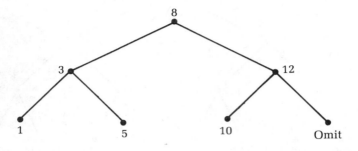

Choose any number greater than the largest file number to appear in place of "omit," in order to guarantee that the tree will be a binary tree.

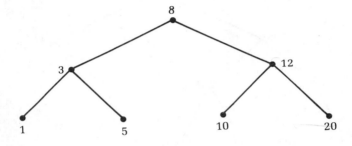

PRACTICE
EXAMPLE 1

Construct a binary search tree for the file numbers

$$S = \{25, 72, 31, 45, 64, 56, 18, 29, 54, 33, 49, 67\}$$

File numbers may correspond to patients in a doctor's office. As a new patient arrives, a new file number (any unused number) is assigned.

Suppose we want to insert a new file number, say 113, into our tree without completely reconstructing the whole tree. We can use the following **insert procedure**.

INSERT PROCEDURE

Search the tree in Figure 3.11 for the number 113. That number does not appear. When the leaf labeled 114 is encountered, the answer to the question: Is 113 less than, equal to, or greater than 114? is less than. A new subtree with 114 as root and left child 113 must be added. A right child must also be added, and it cannot be 115. Choose a nonexistent file number such as 114.1, shown in Figure 3.12.

Figure 3.12

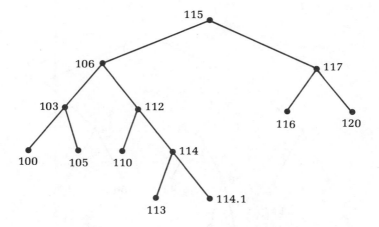

PRACTICE
EXAMPLE 2

Insert a file numbered 36 into the search tree of Practice Example 1.   ■

Trees were used in this section to facilitate efficient use of data, much as they were in the last section. In the next two sections, we use trees to model and solve very specific applied problems. In each case the structure and the properties of trees are used explicitly to determine the best solution to the problem.

CONCEPTS

level k	binary search tree
children	search algorithm
binary tree	insert procedure

SOLUTIONS TO PRACTICE EXAMPLES

1.

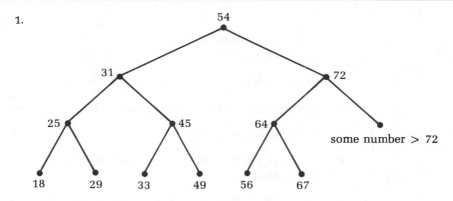

2.

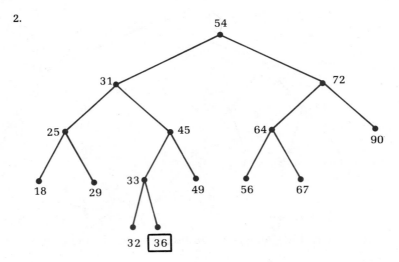

EXERCISES 3.2

1. Is the tree shown in Practice Example 1 a binary tree?

2. The leaves in the tree of Practice Example 1 are at what level?

3. Is the tree shown in Exercise 8 of Section 3.1 a binary tree? If not, why not?

4. In the child's guessing game, if the child asked you to guess a number between 1 and 63, how many questions of the form: "Is the number less than, equal to, or greater than?" would you need to ask?

5. How many numbers can you store in a binary tree with five levels?

6. In the child's guessing game, you are to guess a number between 1 and 7. Set up a binary tree to correspond to the questions you would ask in playing the game.

7. Use the tree in the previous exercise to help you label a tree to store the following set of file numbers: $S = \{324, 478, 213, 987, 387, 187, 921\}$.

8. Construct a binary search tree for the file numbers: 54, 89, 33, 26, 71, 46.

9. In the binary search tree constructed in Exercise 8, insert the file number 98.

10. In the binary search tree constructed in Exercise 8, insert the file number 17.

11. Construct a binary search tree for the file numbers: 8, 9, 2, 4, 27, 41, 23, 46, 32, 92, 67, 88, 34.

12. Insert the file number 58 into the search tree constructed for Exercise 11.

3.3   *Search II—One-way Streets*

It is desirable to decrease the amount of traffic congestion and pollution in New York or any other city. Given a network of all two-way streets, under what conditions is it possible to make each street one-way so that a person at one location can travel to any other location in the city? If it is possible, how can the assignment of street direction be made?

We can represent the street network of a city by a graph, G, whose vertices are the various locations in the city connected by two-way streets. There is an edge in G between two vertices a and b if location a is joined to location b by a two-way street. (See Boesh and Tindall 1980 for a solution to the traffic-flow problem if some of the streets are already one-way.) The traffic flow problem questions whether it is possible to assign a direction (**orientation**) to the edges of G so that one can always get from any point a to any other point b by a directed path from a to b. Once a direction is assigned to each edge of G, G becomes a directed graph.

As an example of a graph and orientations of the graph, consider the street network given by the graph G in Figure 3.13, and two possible orientations of G. In orientation (a), one can go from any vertex (location) to any other vertex (location) following the direction of the arrows. However, in orientation (b), a person located at vertex e is stuck there. He can go nowhere. A person at vertices d and f can only get to vertex e and then must remain there.

Figure 3.13

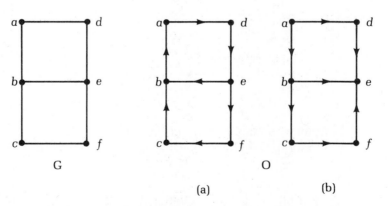

G   O

(a)   (b)

In 1939 Robbins provided the theorem that allows one to tell when a "proper" orientation exists.

DEFINITION   An orientation of a graph is **strongly connected** if for every two vertices a and b, there is a directed path from a to b and a directed path from b to a.

> DEFINITION An edge $\{u, v\}$ of a connected graph, G, is a **bridge** if $G - \{u, v\}$ is not connected.

In Figure 3.13, $O(a)$ is a strongly connected orientation, but $O(b)$ is not. The edge $\{u, v\}$ in the graph shown in Figure 3.14(a) is a bridge. Notice that once you cross the bridge following any orientation, it is not possible to get back to the other side. In using the term bridge, we must be careful not to infer more than the definition states. If there are two "bridges" over the same gap in the English-language sense, then neither is a bridge in the graph-theory sense, as shown in Figure 3.14(b).

Figure 3.14

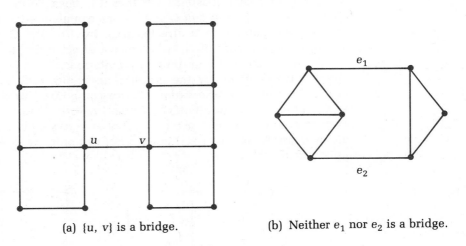

(a) $\{u, v\}$ is a bridge.   (b) Neither e_1 nor e_2 is a bridge.

> ROBBINS'S THEOREM A graph G has a strongly connected orientation if and only if G is connected and has no bridges.

Robbins's theorem tells us there is a one-way street assignment for connected bridgeless graphs, but it does not produce the assignment. We will now use a "depth-first search" procedure to find the orientation when one exists. The depth-first search procedure is highly efficient and is the basis for many computer programs. If the depth-first search procedure cannot be completed, and all the vertices cannot be labeled, then the original graph is not connected. Thus there cannot be a strongly connected orientation nor a one-way street assignment. We will illustrate the procedure using the graph in Figure 3.13.

DEPTH-FIRST SEARCH AND ONE-WAY STREET ASSIGNMENT ALGORITHM

STEP 1: Choose a vertex v, and label it ①(Figure 3.15).

Figure 3.15

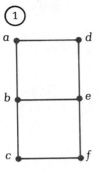

STEP 2: Choose a vertex adjacent to the previously labeled vertex and label it ②(Figure 3.16). Orient the edge from ① to ②.

Figure 3.16

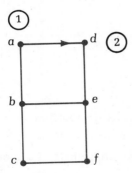

STEP 3: Continue to choose an unlabeled vertex adjacent to the previously labeled vertex ⓘ and label it ⓘ + 1 (Figure 3.17). Do this as long as possible. Orient the edge from ⓘ to ⓘ + 1

Figure 3.17

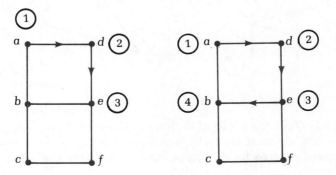

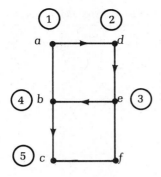

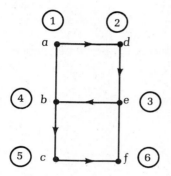

STEP 4: If there are no unlabeled vertices adjacent to the one previously labeled (i) yet there exist unlabeled vertices, back up to the last labeled vertex (j) with an unlabeled vertex adjacent to it. Label this unlabeled vertex $(i + 1)$ and orient the edge from (j) to $(i + 1)$

In our example, this step is unnecessary. Consider the graph shown in Figure 3.18 for an example of the use of Step 4.

Figure 3.18

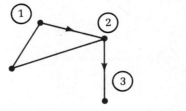

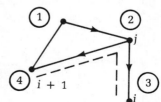

At this stage the edges of G that are oriented form a subgraph, which is a tree. Since each of the vertices of G are included in this subgraph, T is called a **spanning tree** for G. Figure 3.19 shows only the oriented edges of our example.

Figure 3.19

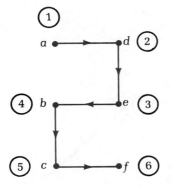

STEP 5:   All the vertices have number labels, and the edges of the spanning tree have been oriented. Orient all remaining edges from higher numbered vertex to lower numbered vertex as shown in Figure 3.20. (For a proof that this procedure produces a strongly connected orientation in a connected bridgeless graph, see Roberts 1976.)

Figure 3.20

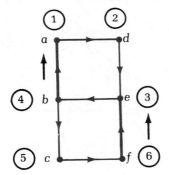

Let us apply the **depth-first search and one-way street assignment algorithm** to the graph shown in Figure 3.21.

Figure 3.21

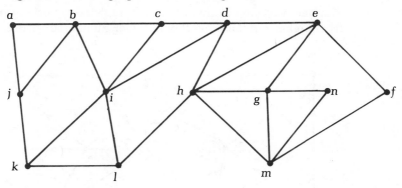

By starting with vertex a, the first three labeling steps can produce a tree subgraph as shown in Figure 3.22.

Figure 3.22

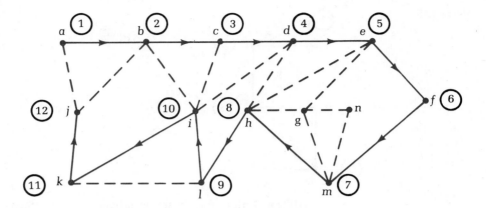

Now we have to use Step 4 and back up to vertex h, labeled ⑧, to label the remaining two vertices, g and n as ⑬ and ⑭, and get an oriented spanning tree (Figure 3.23).

Figure 3.23

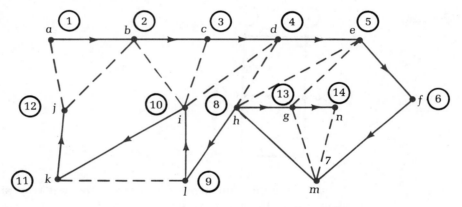

The one-way street orientation is completed by orienting the other edges from higher numbered vertex to lower numbered vertex, as in Figure 3.24.

Figure 3.24

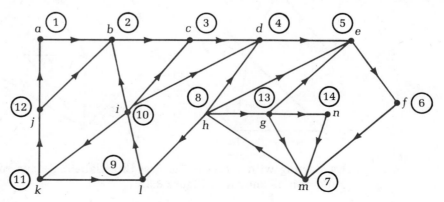

The depth-first search algorithm without the orientation portion of the steps is used to test, among other things, if a graph is connected, if a directed graph is strongly connected, or if a graph is two-colorable. The term "depth-first search" is used to indicate that the algorithm proceeds from the first labeled vertex as root of the spanning tree to a vertex at the highest level before backtracking.

PRACTICE EXAMPLE 1

Give a one-way street assignment to the street network given by the graph shown in Figure 3.25. ■

Figure 3.25

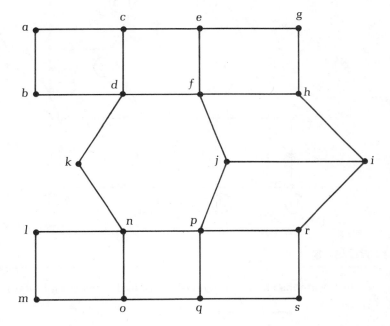

In this section, we developed a procedure to solve the traffic flow problem that constructed a spanning tree for the original graph. The properties of trees were not used explicitly in the algorithm, but they become part of the proof that the algorithm works. In the next section, a spanning tree is absolutely necessary to insure the least-cost aspect of the problem posed there.

CONCEPTS

orientation
strongly connected
bridge
depth-first search and one-way street assignment algorithm
spanning tree

SOLUTION TO PRACTICE EXAMPLE

1.
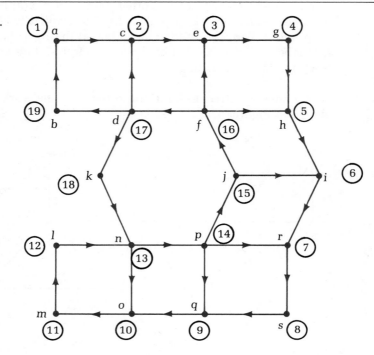

EXERCISES 3.3

In the graphs shown in Exercises 1–4, find all existing bridges.

1.
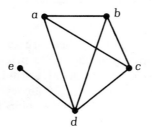

2.
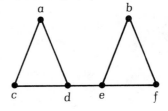

3.
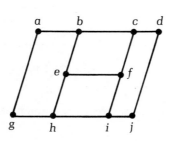

4.
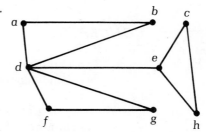

In the graphs shown in Exercises 5–10, find a one-way street assignment.

5.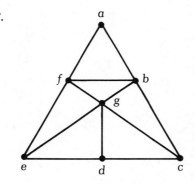

6.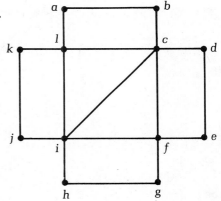

7.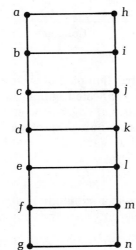

8.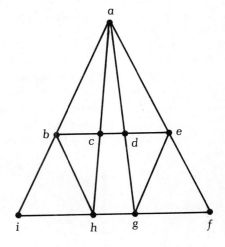

9.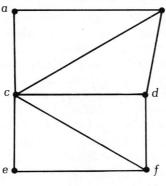

10.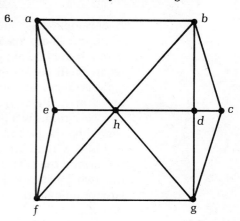

3.4 Minimum Spanning Trees

A developer has purchased a 25-square mile remote section of northern Vermont. There are no roads in the section, only a road leading to it. He wants to build a ski resort and condominium complex. The locations of the resort facilities and condominium units are fixed. Now he must decide the most economical way to put roads in the area so that people can go (not necessarily directly) from one location to another within the area.

We can draw a graph whose vertices are the locations in the area to be served by roads, and there is an edge between two locations if it is possible to build a road from one to the other. A weight assigned to each edge represents the cost in thousands of dollars of constructing a road between the two locations. Figure 3.26 shows a graph corresponding to the 25-square mile section of northern Vermont.

Figure 3.26

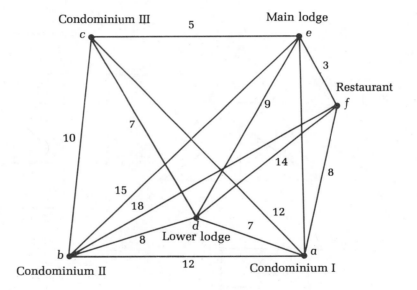

In order to find a road construction plan of least cost that will serve the whole area, we need to find a connected subgraph that includes all the vertices, and has the least number of edges to keep the total weight (cost) down. Thus, we are looking for a spanning tree of least total cost. Recall that a spanning tree of a graph includes each vertex and has one less edge than the number of vertices.

DEFINITION   A spanning tree is a **minimum spanning tree** if the sum of the weights on its edges is no larger than on any other spanning tree.

The algorithm used to find a minimum cost spanning tree in a graph is called greedy. We greedily choose the edges of the graph to build our tree that are of least weight, as long as they do not create a circuit. The algorithm described below is called Kruskal's algorithm after the man who developed this particular algorithm in 1956 and showed that it worked.

ALGORITHM TO FIND A MINIMUM SPANNING TREE IN A GRAPH

STEP 1:   List the edges of the graph by increasing weights.

$\{e, f\}$,	$\{c, e\}$,	$\{c, d\}$,	$\{d, a\}$,	$\{a, f\}$,	$\{d, b\}$,	$\{d, e\}$,
3	5	7	7	8	8	9

$\{b, c\}$,	$\{a, b\}$,	$\{a, c\}$,	$\{d, f\}$,	$\{b, e\}$,	$\{b, f\}$,
10	12	12	14	15	18

STEP 2:   Choose the first edge, the edge of least weight.

$$\{e, f\}$$

STEP 3:   Choose the next edge.

$$\{c, e\}$$

STEP 4:   Continue to choose the next edge in the list as long as it does not create a circuit. Step 4 will continue until $n - 1$ edges are chosen for an n vertex graph, thus creating a spanning tree. At the last step in Figure 3.27, the edge $\{a, f\}$ cannot be added, even though it occurs next in the list, since adding $\{a, f\}$ creates the circuit e-c-d-a-f-e. Instead $\{b, d\}$ is added.

Figure 3.27

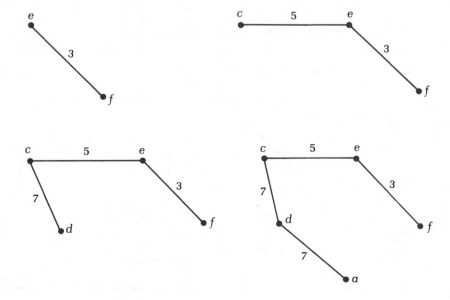

Figure 3.27

continued

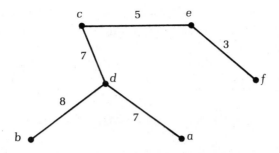

By giving a detailed explanation of Kruskal's algorithm, we do not mean to imply that it is the only algorithm for finding a minimum cost spanning tree. Prim developed an alternative algorithm in 1957 that is both greedy and grows a connected tree at each stage. Note that the spanning tree grown in the example given by Figure 3.27 is not connected at the end of Step 4. Both algorithms produce a minimum spanning tree of the same total weight, but not necessarily the same tree, especially when there are a number of edges with the same weight. To avoid confusion, in this section we will concentrate only on Kruskal's algorithm.

The U.S. Bureau of Standards needs to determine if a bimetallic object has a homogeneous composition. Given an object, a set of sample points are chosen, and the composition is measured at those sample points. We can construct a graph whose vertices are the sample points, and join two sample points with an edge if they are within 50 centimeters of each other. Assign a weight to each edge, a number between 0 and 1 inclusive, indicating the degree of similarity (according to a selected standard) of the composition of the two points. If the composition of two points is exactly alike, the weight is 0. If the composition of the two points is totally different, the weight is 1. The *homogeneity* of the object is the total weight of a minimum spanning tree for the corresponding graph. An object is completely homogeneous if the total weight is 0, and completely nonhomogeneous if the total

Figure 3.28

Bimetallic object

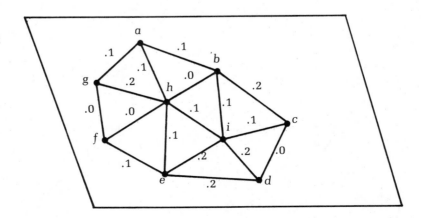

weight is $1(n - 1) = n - 1$ for n sample points. The Bureau of Standards rejects an object if the total weight is too large, say over $(n - 1)/4$ for n sample points.

Figure 3.28 gives a bimetallic object with its sample points, edges, and weights.

The listing of edges for Step 1 of the procedure for finding a minimum spanning tree is:

$\{b, h\}, \quad \{c, d\}, \quad \{h, f\}, \quad \{g, f\}, \quad \{a, g\}, \quad \{b, i\},$
$\quad .0 \qquad\quad .0 \qquad\quad .0 \qquad\quad .0 \qquad\quad .1 \qquad\quad .1$

$\{a, b\}, \quad \{i, c\}, \quad \{e, f\}, \quad \{h, e\}, \quad \{a, h\}, \quad \{h, i\},$
$\quad .1 \qquad\quad .1 \qquad\quad .1 \qquad\quad .1 \qquad\quad .1 \qquad\quad .1$

$\{e, d\}, \quad \{b, c\}, \quad \{i, d\}, \quad \{i, e\}, \quad \{g, h\}$
$\quad .2 \qquad\quad .2 \qquad\quad .2 \qquad\quad .2 \qquad\quad .2$

Therefore, we choose each of the .0 weight edges in order, since no circuits are created. The edges $\{a, g\}$ and $\{b, i\}$ are added next. The edge $\{a, b\}$ cannot be added since it would create a circuit, so the edges $\{i, c\}$ and $\{e, f\}$ are added next. Since we now have eight edges for a nine-vertex graph, we have a spanning tree and the procedure stops. Note that the resulting graph is connected. If a graph with n vertices has a subgraph with n vertices, $n - 1$ edges, and no circuits, the subgraph is connected and is a spanning tree. (For a proof, see Harary 1968.)

The resulting spanning tree, shown in Figure 3.29, has a total weight of .4. Since $(n - 1)/4 = (9 - 1)/2 = 2$, the object is not rejected.

Figure 3.29

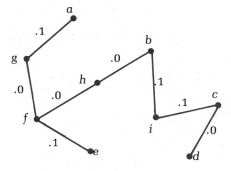

PRACTICE
EXAMPLE 1

The graph in Figure 3.30 corresponds to a telephone communications network. The weight on each edge is the distance between the two locations. If a message sent through the network must reach every location (not necessarily directly), what is the minimum distance the message travels, and what is the routing of the message?

Figure 3.30

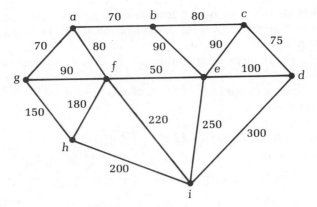

The methods and algorithms presented in this chapter are not the only problem-solving techniques that use trees, but they give a sample of the range of applications.

CONCEPTS

minimum spanning tree
minimum spanning tree algorithm

SOLUTION TO PRACTICE EXAMPLE

1.

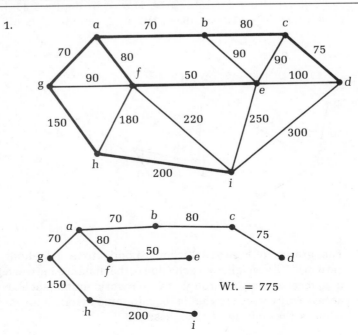

Wt. = 775

EXERCISES 3.4

Find a minimum spanning tree for each of the graphs shown in Exercises 1–8.

1.

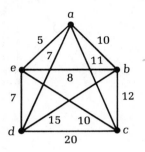

2.

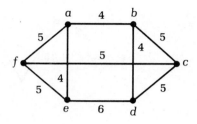

3.

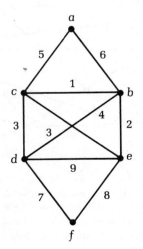

4.

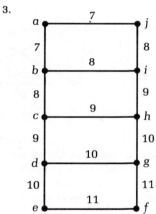

5.

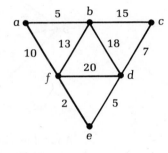

6.

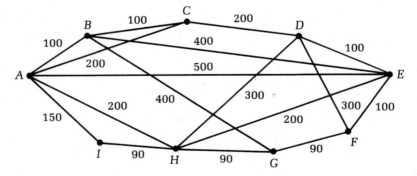

7.

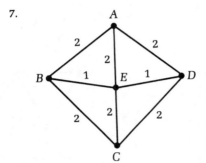

8.

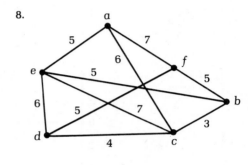

9. A pipeline can be constructed to take oil across the northern part of Canada. The various depots or connecting points for the oil are fixed by the Canadian government. The possible routes available are shown in the graph below, and the cost of construction is the weight of each edge. Find the minimum cost necessary to ship oil to each depot, by finding a minimum spanning tree for the graph.

10. In certain situations, it may be necessary to require a specific edge be used in a minimum spanning tree. In the example given of road construction in northern Vermont, there may be only one possible access road to the property and that road has to be considered part of the construction. Can you modify the minimum spanning tree algorithm to take this into account?

11. In the graph below, edge $\{a, b\}$ must be used in the spanning tree. Use the modification of Exercise 10 to find a minimum spanning tree with this requirement.

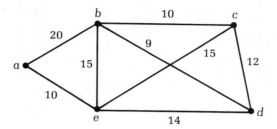

12. Is it possible to find a maximum spanning tree for a graph by changing Step 1 to a list of the edges in decreasing order by weight? Find a maximum spanning tree for the graph shown in Exercise 1. Can you think of any instances where it would be desirable to find a maximum spanning tree?

CHAPTER SUMMARY

A *tree* is a connected graph with no circuits. If a tree has n vertices then it has $n - 1$ edges. Every tree has at least one vertex of degree one, called a *leaf*.

In a *binary tree* every vertex has either 2 or 0 children. We use a binary tree to organize data so that files can be easily located and new files may be added. A *decision tree* is a binary tree.

A *spanning tree* for a graph, G, is a subgraph of G that is a tree and that contains all the vertices of G. We use the *minimum spanning tree algorithm* to find a spanning tree for a graph of least total weight (cost).

We use a *depth-first search* and *one-way street assignment algorithm* to find one-way orientation of the edges of a connected graph that has no bridges.

REVIEW EXERCISES FOR CHAPTER 3

1. Draw a tree with five vertices and three leaves.

2. How many edges does a tree with 53 vertices have?

3. Which of the following graphs are trees?
   (a)

(b)

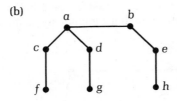

(c)

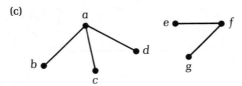

4. Draw a tree to represent the possible outcomes from rolling a pair of dice.

5. Draw a decision tree for ordering numbers a, b, c, and d if you already know that b is less than a.

6. How many numbers can you store in a binary tree with four levels? With six levels?

7. Is this figure a binary tree? At what level are the leaves?

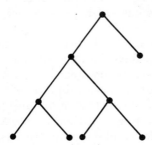

8. Construct a binary search tree for $S = \{32, 14, 8, 9, 25, 2, 19\}$.

9. Construct a binary search tree for
$$S = \{5, 22, 17, 31, 89, 42, 16, 10, 29, 35, 39, 42\}.$$

10. Insert the file number 50 into the search tree of Exercise 9.

11. Find a bridge, if one exists, in each of the following:

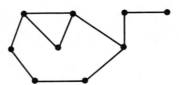

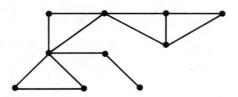

H

12.   Find a one-way street assignment for the following graph:

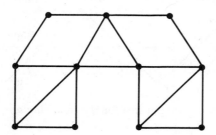

13.   Find a one-way street assignment for the following graph:

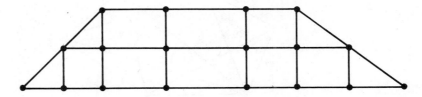

14.   Find a one-way street assignment for the following graph:

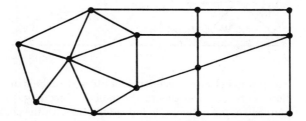

15.   How many streets would have to be closed for a one-way street assignment to be impossible for the graph in Exercise 14.

16.   Find a minimal spanning tree for the following graph:

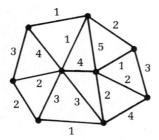

17.   Find a minimal spanning tree for the following graph:

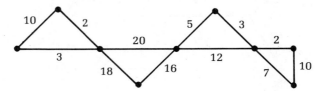

18.   Find a minimal spanning tree for the following graph:

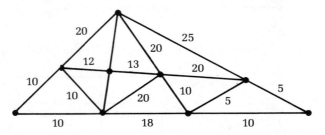

19.   The graph below represents computers at various branches of a large corporation. Vertex *A* represents the home office. Each of the computers can be
connected in a network as indicated and with the costs indicated at the edges.
Find a minimal spanning tree that will connect all of the computers.

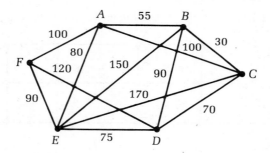

20.   Give an example of a situation where you might want to find a maximal
spanning tree. Find a maximal spanning tree for the graph in Exercise 19.

4 Counting

Counting goes back to the earliest, most primitive cultures, even those that had no symbols for numbers. In this chapter we present basic counting arguments and introduce probability theory. *Counting arguments* are general techniques designed to answer such questions as:

1. How many different computations are needed to solve a traveling salesman problem?
2. How many different ways are there to schedule the meetings for several different committees so that committees with members in common are not scheduled to meet at the same time?
3. How many different DNA chains of length less than four are possible?
4. How many different bets are possible in the state lottery?

In general, counting questions arise when you have a description of some set, the set of DNA chains of length less than four for example, and you want to know how many elements are in the set.

The counting rules presented in this chapter were originally formalized in the seventeenth century to solve probability problems. Today they form the basis for probability and statistics and are applied in a wide variety of settings, including computer science.

In Section 4.1 we introduce two basic counting rules: the product rule and the sum rule. We use the product rule to obtain a formula for permutations in Section 4.2 and a formula for combinations in Section 4.4. In Section 4.3 we use permutations to define a measure of voting power. This index is the probability that a voter is pivotal for the passage of some measure. The index is used when not all the participants have the same number of votes, such as in the United Nations Security Council, a stockholders' meeting, or the electoral college. The index shows that two people with different numbers of votes may have the same power, while a person with votes may have no power at all. We use counting arguments to compute probabilities in Section 4.5. The material on probability is continued in the next chapter where we present the basic theory of probability and give additional applications.

4.1 Sum and Product Rules—DNA Revisited

In this section we introduce two basic counting rules: the **product rule** and the **sum rule**. These rules are used to determine how long DNA chains have to be to encode all 20 basic amino acids. We derive a formula for the number of subsets of a set with N elements, and show that one-, two-, three-, and four-element sequences of dots and dashes are needed in Morse code to encode all 26 letters in the alphabet. The sum and product rules are used in Sections 4.2 and 4.4 to obtain additional rules for counting. Counting rules are used in the last section to compute probabilities.

EXAMPLE 1

How many different slates consisting of an endorsed candidate for governor and an endorsed candidate for lieutenant governor can be formed if the

Figure 4.1

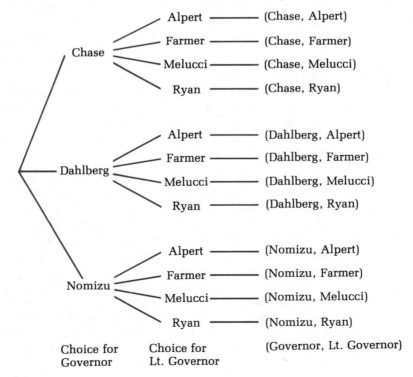

Alpert ——— (Chase, Alpert)
Farmer ——— (Chase, Farmer)
Chase
Melucci ——— (Chase, Melucci)
Ryan ——— (Chase, Ryan)

Alpert ——— (Dahlberg, Alpert)
Farmer ——— (Dahlberg, Farmer)
Dahlberg
Melucci ——— (Dahlberg, Melucci)
Ryan ——— (Dahlberg, Ryan)

Alpert ——— (Nomizu, Alpert)
Farmer ——— (Nomizu, Farmer)
Nomizu
Melucci ——— (Nomizu, Melucci)
Ryan ——— (Nomizu, Ryan)

Choice for   Choice for   (Governor, Lt. Governor)
Governor   Lt. Governor

candidates for governor are {Chase, Dahlberg, Nomizu} and the candidates for lieutenant governor are {Alpert, Farmer, Melucci, Ryan}? The tree diagram in Figure 4.1 gives a list of the possible slates. There are 12 slates. If you view the selection of a slate as filling in the two blanks below,

_____   _____
choice for   choice for
governor   lieutenant governor

then the number of slates equals

$$\left(\begin{array}{c}\text{number of ways to} \\ \text{fill in first blank}\end{array}\right) \times \left(\begin{array}{c}\text{number of ways to} \\ \text{fill in second blank}\end{array}\right) = 3 \times 4 = 12$$

If there are 5 candidates for governor and 4 candidates for lieutenant governor, then, using the following rule, there are $5 \times 4 = 20$ possible slates. ▪

> **PRODUCT RULE**   If there are B_1 ways to fill in a blank slot, and after filling in the first blank there are B_2 ways to fill in a second blank, then there are $B_1 \times B_2$ ways to fill in the two blanks.
>
> More generally, if there are B_1 ways to fill in a first blank, and after filling in the first blank there are B_2 ways to fill in a second blank, and after filling in the first two blanks there are B_3 ways to fill in a third blank and so on, then there are $B_1 \times B_2 \times B_3 \times B_4 \times \cdots \times B_k$ ways to fill in the first k blanks.

PRACTICE EXAMPLE 1   A complete meal at a restaurant consists of one of 3 appetizers, one of 4 main courses, and one of 10 desserts. How many different complete meals are there? ▪

Recall from Section 1.3, that a DNA chain is a sequence of the bases $B = \{\text{thymine} = T, \text{cytosine} = C, \text{adenine} = A, \text{guanine} = G\}$. From the product rule, it follows that there are $4 \times 4 = 4^2 = 16$ possible two-element DNA chains. They are:

Two-element DNA chains

TT	TC	TA	TG
CT	CC	CA	CG
AT	AC	AA	AG
GT	GC	GA	GG

Since there are 20 basic amino acids, we need longer than two-element DNA chains to encode the basic amino acids. By the product rule there are $4 \times 4 \times 4 \times 4^3 = 64$ possible three-element DNA chains. There are enough three-element chains to encode all 20 basic amino acids.

A pizza restaurant claims it has more than 150 different pizzas. Is their claim true if a pizza consists of a cheese pizza with some (or none) of the following toppings: extra cheese, extra sauce, sausage, mushroom, anchovies, pepperoni?

To find the number of different pizzas, imagine that the waiters in the restaurant take an order by putting check marks on an order form next to the toppings ordered by the customer.

Extra cheese ————	Mushrooms ————
Extra sauce ————	Anchovies ————
Sausage ————	Pepperoni ————

Order form

The number of different pizza orders is the number of ways to fill out the order form. Since there are two choices (no check mark; check mark) for each of the six blanks, there are $2 \times 2 \times 2 \times 2 \times 2 \times 2 = 2^6 = 64$ different pizzas. The restaurant's claim is false.   ∎

PRACTICE EXAMPLE 2   How many pizza toppings would a restaurant have to offer in order for there to be more than 150 different possible pizzas?   ∎

EXAMPLE 3   In this example we show that a set with N elements has 2^N subsets. First consider the problem of counting the subsets of $S = \{A, B, C, D, E\}$. A subset of S can be indicated by putting check marks over those elements in the subset. The subset $\{A, D\}$, for example, is given by:

$$\overset{\vee}{A}\ B\ C\ \overset{\vee}{D}\ E$$

(The empty set corresponds to no checks.) There are five blanks and two choices (no check, check) for each blank. By the product rule there are $2 \times 2 \times 2 \times 2 \times 2 = 2^5 = 32$ subsets of $S = \{A, B, C, D, E\}$.

A subset of an N-element set, P, is indicated by putting checks over the elements that are in the subset. There are two choices (no check, check) for each of the N elements. By the product rule, there are

$$\underbrace{2 \times 2 \times 2 \times \cdots \times 2 \times 2}_{N \text{ two's}} = 2^N$$

subsets of an N-element set, P.   ∎

EXAMPLE 4   In Morse code, letters are transmitted by sequences of dots (∗) and dashes (−). For example, E is ∗, T is −, A is ∗ −, N is − ∗, I is ∗ ∗, and M is − −. The set of one- and two-element sequences $S = \{∗, −, ∗ −, − ∗, ∗ ∗, − −\}$ encodes the letters {E, T, A, N, I, M} so some letters will need to be transmitted by sequences of length three or perhaps more. To see how long the sequences need to be, we start with the table below.

Length	Number of different sequences of dots and dashes
1	2
2	$2 \times 2 = 4$
3	$2 \times 2 \times 2 = 8$
4	$2 \times 2 \times 2 \times 2 = 16$

Figure 4.2

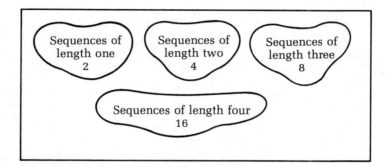

From the table or Venn diagram shown in Figure 4.2 we see:

$2 + 4 = 6$ is the number of one- and two-element sequences
$2 + 4 + 8 = 14$ is the number of one-, two-, and three-element sequences
$2 + 4 + 8 + 16 = 30$ is the number of one-, two-, three-, and four-element sequences

There are enough one-, two-, three-, and four-element sequences to encode all 26 letters of the alphabet. Indeed, Morse code uses all of the one-, two-, and three-element sequences and 12 of the 16 different four-element sequences to encode the letters of the alphabet.   ■

In counting the sequences of length one, two, three, and four we use the sum rule:

SUM RULE   For a collection of sets $\{A_1, A_2, \ldots, A_k\}$ with the property that no two of the sets have an element in common (i.e., $A_i \cap A_j = \varnothing$ for $i \neq j$) then $\#(A_1 \cup A_2 \cup \cdots \cup A_k) = \#(A_1) + \#(A_2) + \cdots + \#(A_k)$ where $\#(A_j)$ is the number of elements in the set A_j.

EXAMPLE 5   A restaurant offers three different kinds of meals. There are 15 different complete meals, two specialties of the house, and four specialties of the day.
    From the sum rule it follows that the restaurant offers $15 + 2 + 4 = 21$ different meals.   ■

PRACTICE
EXAMPLE 3   If a license plate consists of one letter followed by either a one-, two-, or three-digit number, how many different license plates are possible?   ■

In this section we have presented the product rule and the sum rule, fundamental rules for counting from which follow all other counting arguments in this chapter.

CONCEPTS

product rule
sum rule

SOLUTIONS TO PRACTICE EXAMPLES

1. The number of complete meals is the number of ways to fill in the blanks:

   _____   _____   _____
      appetizer   main course   dessert

   This is $3 \times 4 \times 10 = 120$ by the product rule.

2. If there are k toppings, then the number of different possible pizzas is 2^k.

$$2^6 = 64$$
$$2^7 = 128$$
$$2^8 = 256$$

   Thus the restaurant has to have 8 toppings in order to offer more than 150 different pizzas.

3. Using the product rule:

   number of license plates with one letter and one digit $= 26 \times 10 = 260$

   number of license plates with one letter and two digits $= 26 \times 10 \times 10 = 2600$

   number of license plates with one letter and three digits $= 26 \times 10 \times 10 \times 10 = 26,000$

   By the sum rule the number of different license plates $= 260 + 2600 + 26,000 = 28,860$.

EXERCISES 4.1

1. A convention will endorse one of five candidates for governor, one of six candidates for lieutenant governor, and one of three candidates for state treasurer. How many slates of endorsed candidates are possible?

2. A full dinner at a restaurant consists of one of 4 appetizers, one of 5 main courses, and one of 12 desserts. How many different complete dinners are there?

3. How many ways are there to fill out the answer sheet to a five-question test if the first three questions are to be answered true or false and the remaining two questions are to be answered *A*, *B*, or *C*?

4. How many ways are there to fill out the answer sheet to a five-question multiple-choice exam if each question is answered *A*, *B*, or *C*?

5. A ship with seven different signal flags can send a message by arranging three of the flags vertically on its flag mast. How many different messages are possible?

6. How many different license plates are there consisting of three letters followed by a three-digit number?

7. How many different ways are there to fill out the answer sheet to a 10-question test if each question is to be answered true or false?

8. A Social Security number has nine digits. How many different Social Security numbers are possible?

9. In Morse Code, each of the digits 0, 1, 2, 3, 4, 5, 6, 7, 8, 9 is encoded using a five-element sequence of dots and dashes. How many of the different five-element sequences of dots and dashes are *not* used to encode 0, 1, 2, 3, 4, 5, 6, 7, 8, 9?

10. A telephone number consists of a three-digit area code followed by a seven-digit number. How many different telephone numbers are there if the area code cannot begin with either 0 or 1, the second digit in the area code must be 0 or 1, and the seven-digit number after the area code cannot begin with 0?

11. The edges in the graph below represent main roads joining the vertices.
    (a) How many ways are there to get from Home to Granny's?
    (b) How many ways are there to get from Home to Granny's and back Home?

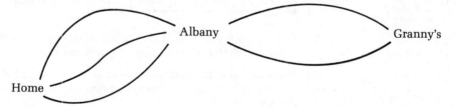

12. In the graph below, the vertices represent cities and the edges routes between the cities. In how many different ways can a person starting in Seattle visit each of the other cities once and return to Seattle?

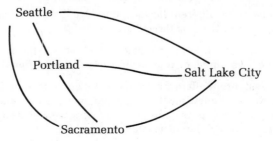

13. How many ways are there to put one of the letters M, W, F, by each of the vertices in the graph below so vertices joined by an edge have different letters next to them?

14. In a round-robin chess tournament each of five players will play each of the other players twice (once as black and once as white). How many games will be played?

15. A person getting ready to wash the kitchen floor has divided the floor into four areas and will wash first one area, then another, and so on until the four areas have been washed. How many different ways are there to wash the floor if area II cannot be washed last because there is no door?

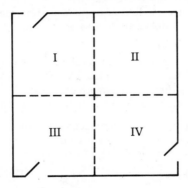

16. A town Rotary Club is deciding which (if any) of its five officers it will send to the international convention. How many different choices are there?

17. A delegation to the president is to consist of one of 100 senators or one of 435 members of the House of Representatives. How many different possible delegations are there?

18. In the computer language, BASIC, the name of a variable must either be a single letter or a letter followed by a one-digit number. How many different names for a variable are possible?

19. How many different license plates are there consisting of two letters followed by a one-, two-, or three-digit number?

20. How many different messages can a ship send by arranging on its flag mast one, two, three, or four of its eight different signal flags?

21. A restaurant offers 3 appetizers, 4 main dishes, and 10 desserts. A person can order a complete meal of appetizer, main course, and dessert; a dinner consisting of main course and either an appetizer or dessert; or just a main course. How many different meals are possible?

4.2 *Permutations*

If a committee chooses one of its members to be chairperson and one to be secretary, the choices can be given by listing first the name of the person selected to be chairperson and second the name of the person selected to be secretary. Such a list is called a permutation of two of the elements from the set of committee members. In general, an ordered arrangement of different elements from a set is called a **permutation**. Permutations were used by the Hindus as long ago as 1150 A.D.

In this section, we show how to use the product rule to count permutations. For example, if a committee of five people chooses first a chairperson and then a secretary, then there are five ways to make the first choice, four ways to make the second choice, and hence (by the product rule) 5 × 4 = 20 different ways to choose a chairperson and secretary.

Permutations are used in the next section to measure voting power and in Section 4.5 to compute probabilities.

EXAMPLE 1 Four teachers {Banchoff, Harris, Wiegand, Livingston} have been nominated for a teaching award. To help decide which teacher receives the award, students will fill in the ballot below.

———————————   ———————————
first choice   second choice
Ballot

The tree diagram in Figure 4.3 on page 150 shows all the different ways the ballot can be filled in. ∎

Each of the rankings shown in Figure 4.3—(B, H), (B, L), . . . , (W, H), (W, L)—is called a permutation of size 2 taken from the set {B, H, L, W}. An ordered arrangement of k of the elements from a set, S, is called a **permutation of size k taken from a set S**. The same elements arranged in a different order are considered to be different permutations. For example, (B, H) and (H, B) are different permutations of size 2 taken from {B, H, L, W}. We can use tree diagrams to make a list of all permutations of fixed size taken from a set, S.

PRACTICE EXAMPLE 1 Use a tree diagram to list all the permutations of size 2 taken from the set $S = \{A, B, C\}$. ∎

A permutation taken from a set S that includes all the elements of S is called a **permutation of the elements in a set S**. For example ABC, BAC, and CBA are permutations of the elements in $\{A, B, C\}$.

PRACTICE EXAMPLE 2 Use a tree diagram to list all the permutations of the elements in the set $S = \{E, H, L\}$. ∎

The product rule can be used to count the number of permutations of fixed size.

Figure 4.3

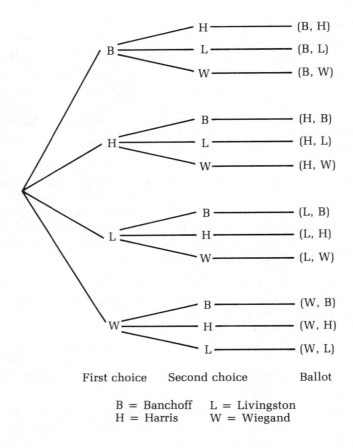

First choice   Second choice   Ballot

B = Banchoff   L = Livingston
H = Harris   W = Wiegand

EXAMPLE 2   How many permutations of size 3 can be taken from the set $\{A, B, C, D\}$?
One way to answer this question is to list the permutations using a tree diagram, as shown in Figure 4.4.

Another way to count permutations is to use the product rule. A permutation of size 3 taken from the set $S = \{A, B, C, D\}$ is given by filling in the three blanks:

     _____   _____   _____

       first element   second element   third element
        chosen   chosen   chosen

The number of permutations of size 3 taken from $S = \{A, B, C, D\}$ is the number of ways of filling in these blanks, which is

$$\begin{pmatrix} \text{number of} \\ \text{ways to fill in} \\ \text{first blank} \end{pmatrix} \times \begin{pmatrix} \text{number of} \\ \text{ways to fill in} \\ \text{second blank} \end{pmatrix} \times \begin{pmatrix} \text{number of} \\ \text{ways to fill in} \\ \text{third blank} \end{pmatrix} = 4 \times 3 \times 2 = 24$$

by the product rule.

Figure 4.4

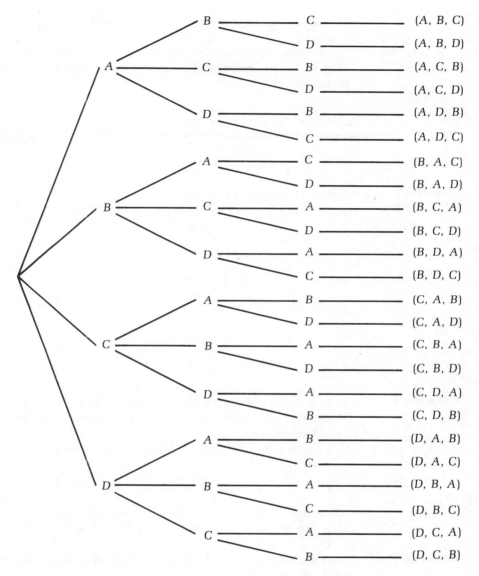

In general, the number of permutations of size k taken from a set, S, is the number of ways of filling in the k blanks

$$\underbrace{\qquad}_{\text{first element}} \quad \underbrace{\qquad}_{\text{second element}} \quad \cdots \quad \underbrace{\qquad}_{k^{\text{th}} \text{ element}}$$

Each time the number of choices is reduced by one.

$$\begin{pmatrix} \text{number of permutations of} \\ \text{size } k \text{ taken from} \\ \text{a set with } N \text{ elements} \end{pmatrix} = \underbrace{N \times (N-1) \times (N-2) \times \cdots}_{k \text{ terms}}$$

The factors in the product start with N and decrease by one until there are k terms.

Permutations arise frequently enough to justify using a special notation, $P(N, k)$, for the number of permutations of size k taken from a set with N elements.

$$P(N, k) = \underbrace{N \times (N - 1) \times (N - 2) \times \cdots \times (N - k + 1)}_{k \text{ terms}} = \left(\begin{array}{c} \text{number of permutations} \\ \text{of size } k \text{ taken from a set} \\ \text{with } N \text{ elements} \end{array} \right)$$

PRACTICE EXAMPLE 3

Complete the table below.

N	k	$P(N, k)$
3	2	$3 \times 2 = 6$
7	2	$7 \times 6 = 42$
10	3	$10 \times 9 \times 8 = 720$
6	4	$6 \times 5 \times 4 \times 3 = 360$
5	2	
6	2	
10	2	
6	3	
7	3	

EXAMPLE 3

In how many different ways can a committee choose one of its members to be chairperson and one of its members to be secretary if there are six people on the committee?

The number of different choices is the number of ways to fill in the slots:

$$\underline{\hspace{3cm}} \qquad \underline{\hspace{3cm}}$$
$$\text{chairperson} \qquad \text{secretary}$$

There are six ways to fill in the first slot and then five ways to fill the second slot. The number of choices is $P(6, 2) = 6 \times 5 = 30$. ■

EXAMPLE 4

How many ways are there to distribute four different free books among nine students, if

(a) no student gets more than one book?
(b) students can get more than one book?

The number of ways to distribute the books is the number of ways to fill in the slots:

$$\underline{\hspace{2cm}} \quad \underline{\hspace{2cm}} \quad \underline{\hspace{2cm}} \quad \underline{\hspace{2cm}}$$
$$\text{book 1} \qquad \text{book 2} \qquad \text{book 3} \qquad \text{book 4}$$

with the name of the student who gets the book.

If no student gets more than one book, then each slot must be filled with a different name, and the number of ways to fill the slots is $P(9, 4) = 9 \times 8 \times 7 \times 6 = 3024$.

If students can get more than one book, then there are nine ways to fill each of the slots, and the number of ways to distribute the books is $9 \times 9 \times 9 \times 9 = 6561$. ■

$P(N, N)$, the number of permutations of the elements in a set, S, with N elements, has its own special notation, $N!$, (read N factorial). For example $3! = 3 \times 2 \times 1 = 6$, $5! = 5 \times 4 \times 3 \times 2 \times 1 = 120$, and $8! = 8 \times 7 \times 6 \times 5 \times 4 \times 3 \times 2 \times 1 = 40{,}320$.

PRACTICE EXAMPLE 4

In how many different ways can four people be lined up for a picture? ■

In this section we used the product rule to derive a formula for counting permutations. Recall that in Section 2.3 we gave tables to indicate the length of time needed to solve a traveling salesman problem. In Exercise 30 you will see how to use counting rules to construct such tables.

Permutations are used in the next section to define a measure of voting power, in Section 4.4 to derive another counting rule, and in Section 4.5 to compute probabilities.

CONCEPTS

permutation of size k taken from a set S
permutation of the elements in a set S
$P(N, k)$

SOLUTIONS TO PRACTICE EXAMPLES

1.

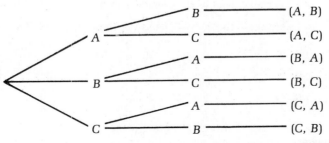

Permutations of size 2

2.

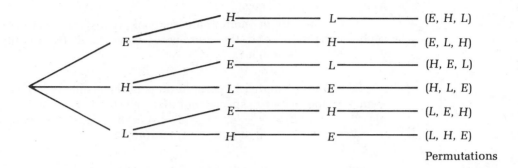

Permutations

3.

N	k	P(N, k)
5	2	5 × 4 = 20
6	2	6 × 5 = 30
10	2	10 × 9 = 90
6	3	6 × 5 × 4 = 120
7	3	7 × 6 × 5 = 210

4. P(4, 4) = 4! = 4 × 3 × 2 × 1 = 24

EXERCISES 4.2

In Exercises 1 through 6 use a tree diagram to make a list of:

1. The permutations of size 2 taken from $S = \{A, B, C\}$.

2. The permutations of size 2 taken from $S = \{A, B, C, D\}$.

3. The permutations of size 3 taken from $S = \{A, C, E, F\}$.

4. The permutations of the elements in $S = \{A, B\}$.

5. The permutations of the elements in $S = \{A, B, C\}$.

6. The permutations of the elements in $S = \{E, F, G, H\}$.

In Exercises 7 through 18, compute the number P(N, k).

7. P(3, 2)	10. P(2, 2) = 2!	13. P(7, 2)	16. P(10, 3)
8. P(4, 2)	11. P(4, 4) = 4!	14. P(7, 3)	17. P(9, 3)
9. P(4, 3)	12. P(6, 6) = 6!	15. P(10, 2)	18. P(9, 4)

In Exercises 19 through 26 find the numbers N and k so that the number P(N, k) answers the problem. Compute the number P(N, k) whenever you can.

19. In how many different ways can six people be lined up for a picture?

20. In how many ways can a committee choose one of its members to be chairperson and one its members to be secretary if the committee has

    (a) seven members?

    (b) twelve members?

    (c) N members?

21. In how many ways can a committee choose one of its members to be chairperson, one to be secretary, and one to be parliamentarian if the committee has

    (a) seven members?

    (b) twelve members?

    (c) N members?

22. The first-prize and second-prize winners in a lottery will be chosen by selecting two lottery tickets. The owner of the first ticket selected will win the second prize and the owner of the second ticket selected will win the first prize. In how many ways can first- and second-prize tickets be selected if

    (a) 10 tickets have been sold?

    (b) 50 tickets have been sold?

    (c) 100 tickets have been sold?

23. A consumer group will test the following computers: Compaq, IBM-PC, Epson QX-10, Kay Pro II, Apple IIe. The group will list their first, second, and third choice based on performance. How many different rating lists are possible?

24. How many different first-, second-, and third-place finishes are possible in a horse race with

    (a) nine horses?

    (b) ten horses?

    (c) thirteen horses?

25. A traveler who would like to visit New York, Paris, Brussels, Amsterdam, Copenhagen, Geneva, and Bonn has time to visit only three cities. The traveler will make an itinerary by choosing which city to visit first, which to visit second, and which to visit third. How many different itineraries are possible?

26. Six people are qualified to fill any of three available jobs. How many different ways are there to fill the jobs so each job is filled by a different person?

27. How many ways are there to distribute 7 different free books among 12 students, if

    (a) no student gets more than one book?

    (b) students can get more than one book?

28. In how many different ways can seven books be removed from a shelf, one book at a time?

29. A scrabble player has seven different letters.
    (a) How many different arrangements of four of the seven letters are possible?

(b) How long would it take the player to check all these possibilities to see which are words in the dictionary if it takes the player two seconds to check each arrangement of four of the seven letters?

30. An itinerary for a salesman who will visit each of five cities and then return home consists of a listing of which city to visit first, which to visit second, and so on.
    (a) How many different possible itineraries are there?
    (b) If it takes the salesman five seconds to write an itinerary, how long would it take (working 24 hours a day) to make a list of all possible itineraries?
    (c) How long would it take to list all the itineraries if there are 10 cities?

31. (a) In how many different ways can the nine players on a baseball team be lined up to bat?
    (b) How long would it take a person who writes down one batting order every five seconds, 24 hours a day, to make a list of all the different possible batting orders?

4.3   Voting Power

In this section we use permutations to define the **Shapley-Shubik power index**, which measures the influence a voter has on the passage of a motion. The index is used when not all the voters have the same number of votes, such as in the United Nations Security Council or in a stockholders' meeting.

The examples illustrate that voters with different numbers of votes may have the same power and people with votes may have no power at all.

EXAMPLE 1   Suppose there are four voters A, B, C, D, with 2, 1, 1, 1 votes, and three votes are needed to win. The first step in finding the indices of voting power is to list all the permutations of the voters.

ABCD	BACD	CABD	DABC
ABDC	BADC	CADB	DACB
ACBD	BCAD	CBAD	DBAC
ACDB	BCDA	CBDA	DBCA
ADBC	BDAC	CDAB	DCAB
ADCB	BDCA	CDBA	DCBA

Imagine that each permutation, read from left to right, gives the order in which voters join a coalition in favor of some proposal. Reading each permutation from left to right, circle the voter whose addition to the coalition gives the coalition just enough votes to pass the measure. This voter is called the **pivotal** member of the permutation. For the permutation BCDA, the pivotal member is D. The coalition BC has only two votes, not enough to win, while the coalition BCD has three votes, enough to win.

Circling the pivotal member of each permutation gives:

A$\textcircled{B}$CD	B$\textcircled{A}$CD	C$\textcircled{A}$BD	D$\textcircled{A}$BC
A$\textcircled{B}$DC	B$\textcircled{A}$DC	C$\textcircled{A}$DB	D$\textcircled{A}$CB
A$\textcircled{C}$BD	BC$\textcircled{A}$D	CB$\textcircled{A}$D	DB$\textcircled{A}$C
A$\textcircled{C}$DB	BC$\textcircled{D}$A	CB$\textcircled{D}$A	DB$\textcircled{C}$A
A$\textcircled{D}$BC	BD$\textcircled{A}$C	CD$\textcircled{A}$B	DC$\textcircled{A}$B
A$\textcircled{D}$CB	BD$\textcircled{C}$A	CD$\textcircled{B}$A	DC$\textcircled{B}$A

The *Shapley-Shubik power index* of a voter is defined by the formula:

SS (voter) =

$$\frac{\text{number of permutations in which the voter is pivotal (i.e., circled)}}{\text{number of permutations of the voters}}$$

The index of each of the voters is obtained by filling in the table below.

Voter	Number of times the voter is pivotal	Number of permutations of all the voters	Power index
A	12	24	$12 \div 24 = \frac{1}{2}$
B	4	24	$4 \div 24 = \frac{1}{6}$
C	4	24	$4 \div 24 = \frac{1}{6}$
D	4	24	$4 \div 24 = \frac{1}{6}$

Certain police courts that consist of three jurors and a judge operate with the system described in Example 1. *A* is the judge, *B*, *C*, and *D* are the jurors. The Shapley-Shubik indices show this system gives the judge three times as much power as any of the jurors (since $3 \times (\frac{1}{6}) = \frac{1}{2}$).

The steps to compute the Shapley-Shubik power index are:

1. List all permutations of the voters.
2. Circle the pivotal voter in each permutation.
3. SS (voter) = $\dfrac{\text{number of times the voter is pivotal}}{\text{number of permutations of the voters}}$

The Shapley-Shubik index of a voter is a number between 0 and 1. Voters with larger indices have more power. A voter with index 0 can never use his votes to influence the passage or defeat of a measure.

PRACTICE
EXAMPLE 1

Find the power indices of the voters A, B, and C if A has four votes, B has four votes, C has one vote, and five votes are needed to win.   ◼

PRACTICE
EXAMPLE 2

Find the power indices of the voters A, B, C, and D if A and B have four votes each, C and D have three votes each, and eight votes are needed to win.

◼

EXAMPLE 2

The Board of Supervisors for Nassau County, New York, in 1964 had six members with 31, 31, 28, 21, 2, and 2 votes. To pass a motion, 58 votes were needed. If we assume the three members with the fewest votes form a coalition, then we have essentially four voters A, B, C, and D with 31, 31, 28, and $25 = 21 + 2 + 2$ votes. To find the power indices of the voters, we start by listing the permutations of the voters A, B, C, D, and circling the pivotal voter in each permutation.

AⒷCD	BⒶCD	CⒶBD	DAⒷC
AⒷDC	BⒶDC	CⒶDB	DAⒸB
AⒸBD	BⒸAD	CⒷAD	DBⒶC
AⒸDB	BⒸDA	CⒷDA	DBⒸA
ADⒷC	BDⒶC	CDⒶB	DCⒶB
ADⒸB	BDⒸA	CDⒷA	DCⒷA

The power indices are:

Voter	Number of times the voter is pivotal	Number of permutations of all the voters	Power index
A	8	24	$8 \div 24 = 1/3$
B	8	24	$8 \div 24 = 1/3$
C	8	24	$8 \div 24 = 1/3$
D	0	24	$0 \div 24 = 0$

The coalition with 25 votes is never pivotal and hence has no power. The remaining members with 31, 31, and 28 votes share the voting power equally.

This example illustrates that people with votes may have no power, and that people with different numbers of votes may have the same power. Votes were distributed to members of the board of supervisors based on their districts' population under the assumption that this method for allotting votes gives power to members in proportion to the percentage of the population represented. However, the members with 21, 2, and 2 votes (representing 261,741 people) had no voting power.   ◼

PROPERTIES OF THE SHAPLEY-SHUBIK INDEX

1. Voters with the same number of votes have the same power.
2. The sum of all the power indices is 1.

These properties can be used to compute the power indices.

EXAMPLE 3   In the Australian government, each of the six states, New South Wales = N; Victoria = V; Queensland = Q; South Australia = S; Western Australia = W; Tasmania = T gets one vote; and the federal government = F gets three votes. Five votes are needed to win. There are $7! = 7 \times 6 \times 5 \times 4 \times 3 \times 2 \times 1 = 5040$ permutations of the elements in $\{N, V, Q, S, W, T, F\}$, so in this case listing the permutations is impractical. To find the Shapley-Shubik power indices, we begin by finding the index of the federal government. The federal government is pivotal in a permutation if it occurs in the third, fourth, or fifth slot. The number of permutations of the elements in $\{N, V, Q, S, W, T, F\}$ in which F occurs third is the number of ways of filling in the unfilled blanks.

$$\underline{}\ \underline{}\ \underset{1}{}\ \underset{2}{}\ \underset{3}{\text{F}}\ \underline{}\ \underline{}\ \underline{}\ \underline{}$$
$$1\quad 2\quad 3\quad 4\quad 5\quad 6\quad 7$$

with the letters $\{N, V, Q, S, W, T\}$. By the product rule, this is $6 \times 5 \times 4 \times 3 \times 2 \times 1 = 720$. Similarly there are 720 permutations in which F occurs fourth, and 720 permutations in which F occurs fifth. By the sum rule, there are $720 + 720 + 720 = 2160$ permutations in which F occurs either third, fourth, or fifth.

$$\text{SS (F)} = \frac{\text{number of permutations in which F is pivotal}}{\text{number of permutations of the voters}} = \frac{2160}{5040} = \frac{3 \times 720}{7 \times 720} = \frac{3}{7}$$

We can use the index properties given above to find the voting power of the states. The second property states that the sum of all the indices is 1. The index of the federal government is $\frac{3}{7}$, so the sum of the indices of the states is $1 - (\frac{3}{7}) = \frac{4}{7}$. Property one indicates that each of the six states has the same index, so the index of each state is $(\frac{1}{6}) \times (\frac{4}{7}) = \frac{2}{21}$.

Notice that since the ratio of the index of the federal government to the index of any state is $(\frac{9}{21}) \div (\frac{2}{21}) = \frac{9}{2}$, the federal government has four and one half times the voting power of any state. The corresponding ratio of votes, on the other hand, is only three to one. The federal government has more power than is indicated by the distribution of votes. ■

In this section we have defined the Shapley-Shubik index of voting power and computed the index in several examples. (For a discussion of this and other measures of voting power see Shapley 1981.)

CONCEPTS

Shapley-Shubik power index

SOLUTIONS TO PRACTICE EXAMPLES

1. $A\,Ⓑ\,C$ $B\,Ⓐ\,C$ $C\,Ⓐ\,B$

    $A\,Ⓒ\,B$ $B\,Ⓒ\,A$ $C\,Ⓑ\,A$

    $SS(A) = SS(B) = SS(C) = \frac{1}{3}$

2. $A\,Ⓑ\,CD$ $B\,Ⓐ\,CD$ $CA\,Ⓑ\,D$ $DA\,Ⓑ\,C$

    $A\,Ⓑ\,DC$ $B\,Ⓐ\,DC$ $CA\,Ⓓ\,B$ $DA\,Ⓒ\,B$

    $AC\,Ⓑ\,D$ $BC\,Ⓐ\,D$ $CB\,Ⓐ\,D$ $DB\,Ⓐ\,C$

    $AC\,Ⓓ\,B$ $BC\,Ⓓ\,A$ $CB\,Ⓓ\,A$ $DB\,Ⓒ\,A$

    $AD\,Ⓑ\,C$ $BD\,Ⓐ\,C$ $CD\,Ⓐ\,B$ $DC\,Ⓐ\,B$

    $AD\,Ⓒ\,B$ $BD\,Ⓒ\,A$ $CD\,Ⓑ\,A$ $DC\,Ⓑ\,A$

    $SS(A) = SS(B) = \frac{1}{3}$

    $SS(C) = SS(D) = \frac{1}{6}$

EXERCISES 4.3

In Exercises 1 through 21, find the Shapley-Shubik index of each voter.

1.

Voters	A	B	C
Number of votes	2	1	1

3 votes needed to win

2.

Voters	A	B	C
Number of votes	4	2	1

4 votes needed to win

3.

Voters	A	B	C
Number of votes	7	3	2

7 votes needed to win

4.

Voters	A	B	C
Number of votes	4	2	2

5 votes needed to win

5.

Voters	A	B	C
Number of votes	7	5	2

8 votes needed to win

6.

Voters	A	B	C
Number of votes	4	3	2

5 votes needed to win

7.

Voters	A	B	C
Number of votes	7	5	3

8 votes needed to win

8.

Voters	A	B	C	D
Number of votes	2	1	1	1

3 votes needed to win

9.

Voters	A	B	C	D
Number of votes	6	5	5	1

9 votes needed to win

10.

Voters	A	B	C	D
Number of votes	6	5	5	3

10 votes needed to win

11.

Voters	A	B	C	D
Number of votes	6	5	5	4

11 votes needed to win

12.

Voters	A	B	C	D
Number of votes	4	4	3	3

8 votes needed to win

13.

Voters	A	B	C	D
Number of votes	5	4	3	2

8 votes needed to win

14.

Voters	A	B	C	D
Number of votes	4	3	2	1

6 votes needed to win

15.

Voters	A	B	C	D
Number of votes	225	198	73	42

270 votes needed to win

A, B, C, and D represent the main parties in the 1983 Italian Chamber of Deputies.

16.

Voters	A	B	C	D
Number of votes	9	9	7	5

16 votes needed to win

A, B, and C are the members of the 1958 Nassau County Board of Supervisors with the most votes. D represents a coalition of the three members with the fewest votes.

17.

Voters	A	B	C	D	E
Number of votes	2	1	1	1	1

4 votes needed to win

18.

Voters	A	B	C	D	E
Number of votes	3	2	2	2	2

6 votes needed to win

19.

Voters	A	B	C	D	E
Number of votes	3	1	1	1	1

4 votes needed to win

20.

Voters	A	B	C	D	E
Number of votes	4	1	1	1	1

5 votes needed to win

21.

Voters	A	B	C	D	E	F
Number of votes	2	1	1	1	1	1

4 votes needed to win

4.4 Combinations

Suppose a committee chooses two of its members as a delegation to a national convention. Such a delegation is a two-element subset of the set of committee members. In general, a subset containing k of the elements from a set, S, is called a **combination of size k taken from set S**. Combinations were first formulated by the French mathematician, Pascal, in the 1640s.

In this section we give a formula for counting combinations, and we give examples that show how the product rule, sum rule, permutations, and combinations can be combined to solve a counting problem.

EXAMPLE 1

How many different school committees are possible if a committee consists of three of the candidates {Andrews = A, Cuskaden = C, Hance = H, Lakis = L, Murray = M}?

We begin by listing the $P(5, 3) = 5 \times 4 \times 3 = 60$ permutations of size 3 taken from the set {A, C, H, L, M}, as in Table 4.1.

TABLE 4.1

ACH	CAH	HAC	ALM	LAM	MAL
AHC	CHA	HCA	AML	LMA	MLA
ACL	CAL	LAC	CHL	HCL	LCH
ALC	CLA	LCA	CLH	HLC	LHC
ACM	CAM	MAC	CHM	HCM	MCH
AMC	CMA	MCA	CMH	HMC	MHC
AHL	HAL	LAH	CLM	LCM	MCL
ALH	HLA	LHA	CML	LMC	MLC
AHM	HAM	MAH	HLM	LHM	MHL
AMH	HMA	MHA	HML	LMH	MLH

Think of each of the 60 permutations as a listing of the members of the school committee in the order in which they were selected. We are only interested in who is on the committee, not the order in which they were

TABLE 4.2

Permutations of size 3 taken from {A, C, H, L, M}			Committees of size 3 taken from {A, C, H, L, M}
ACH	CAH	HAC	
AHC	CHA	HCA	{A, C, H}
ACL	CAL	LAC	
ALC	CLA	LCA	{A, C, L}
ACM	CAM	MAC	
AMC	CMA	MCA	{A, C, M}
AHL	HAL	LAH	
ALH	HLA	LHA	{A, H, L}
AHM	HAM	MAH	
AMH	HMA	MHA	{A, H, M}
ALM	LAM	MAL	
AML	LMA	MLA	{A, L, M}
CHL	HCL	LCH	
CLH	HLC	LHC	{C, H, L}
CHM	HCM	MCH	
CMH	HMC	MHC	{C, H, M}
CLM	LCM	MCL	
CML	LMC	MLC	{C, L, M}
HLM	LHM	MHL	
HML	LMH	MLH	{H, L, M}

selected. Thus permutations that list the same letters in a different order, ACH and CAH for example, correspond to the same committee. Grouping together the permutations that correspond to the same committee, we find there are 10 different school committees which are possible, as listed in Table 4.2. Each committee of three comes from six different permutations. The six permutations in the first two rows of the table, for example, are the six different ways to order the members of the committee $\{A, C, H\}$. In this example we have:

$$\begin{pmatrix} \text{number of committees of} \\ \text{size 3 taken from} \\ \{A, C, H, L, M\} \end{pmatrix} = \frac{\begin{pmatrix} \text{number of permutations of size} \\ \text{3 taken from } \{A, C, H, L, M\} \end{pmatrix}}{(\text{number of permutations of 3 elements})}$$

$$= \frac{P(5, 3)}{3!} = \frac{5 \times 4 \times 3}{3 \times 2 \times 1} = 10$$

Since a committee of three taken from $\{A, C, H, L, M\}$ is a three-element subset of $\{A, C, H, L, M\}$, we have shown there are 10 three-element subsets of $\{A, C, H, L, M\}$. A k-element subset of a set, S, is called a **combination of size k taken from the set S**. The symbol $C(N, k)$ is used for the number of combinations of size k taken from a set with N elements. We have:

$$\begin{pmatrix} \text{number of combinations} \\ \text{of size } k \text{ taken from a} \\ \text{set with } N \text{ elements} \end{pmatrix} = C(N, k) = \frac{P(N, k)}{k!}$$

$$= \frac{\begin{pmatrix} \text{number of permutations of size } k \\ \text{taken from a set with } N \text{ elements} \end{pmatrix}}{(\text{number of permutations of } k \text{ elements})}$$

$$= \frac{\overbrace{N(N-1)(N-2)\cdots(N-k+1)}^{k \text{ terms}}}{\underbrace{k(k-1)(k-2)\cdots 3 \times 2 \times 1}_{k \text{ terms}}}$$

PRACTICE EXAMPLE 1   (a) List (as in Table 4.2) all the permutations of size 2 taken from $\{A, B, C, D\}$ together with all the combinations of size 2 taken from $\{A, B, C, D\}$.

(b) Find the numbers:

1. C(4, 2).   3. C(6, 3).   5. C(7, 3).
2. C(5, 2).   4. C(7, 2).

■

Notice that the difference between a permutation and a combination is that in a permutation the order in which the elements are listed is important. In a combination, the same elements listed in a different order are the same combination. If you make a list of the restaurants in town that you like, the list is a combination. If you list these restaurants in order of preference, the list is a permutation.

EXAMPLE 2   A standard deck of cards contains 52 cards as pictured below. If a poker hand contains 5 cards and a bridge hand contains 13 cards,

(a) How many different poker hands are possible?
(b) How many different bridge hands are possible?

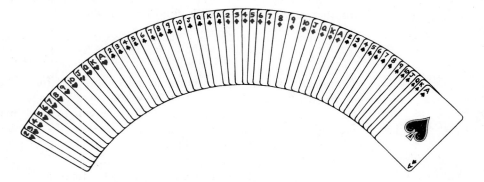

This is a problem in combinations since the same cards arranged in a different order are the same hand.

There are:

$$C(52, 5) = \frac{P(52, 5)}{5!} = \frac{(52)(51)(50)(49)(48)}{(5)(4)(3)(2)(1)}$$

$$= 2{,}598{,}960 \text{ (more than } 2\tfrac{1}{2} \text{ million) poker hands.}$$

There are:

$$C(52, 13) = \frac{P(52, 13)}{13!}$$

$$= \frac{(52)(51)(50)(49)(48)(47)(46)(45)(44)(43)(42)(41)(40)}{(13)(12)(11)(10)(9)(8)(7)(6)(5)(4)(3)(2)(1)}$$

$$= 635{,}013{,}559{,}600 \text{ (more than 635 billion) bridge hands.} \quad ■$$

The following examples show how different counting rules can be combined to solve a counting problem.

EXAMPLE 3 How many different committees are possible if a committee consists of 2 of 15 faculty and 4 of 10 students?

The number of committees is the number of ways to fill in the two blanks below.

_____   _____
faculty members   student members

There are $C(15, 2) = 105$ ways to choose the faculty members, and $C(10, 4) = 210$ ways to choose the student members. By the product rule there are $105 \times 210 = 22,050$ different committees. ∎

EXAMPLE 4 In how many ways can 12 different toys be given to 3 children if each child gets 4 toys.

The number of different ways to distribute toys to the children is the number of ways to fill in the blanks below.

_____   _____   _____
toys given to   toys given to   toys given to
first child   second child   third child

There are $C(12, 4) = 495$ ways to select the toys for the first child. This leaves 8 toys, so there are $C(8, 4) = 70$ ways to choose the toys for the second child. The remaining 4 toys are given to the third child. By the product rule there are $495 \times 70 \times 1 = 34,650$ different ways to distribute 12 toys among 3 children so that each child gets 4 toys. ∎

EXAMPLE 5 Of 10 computer chips, 3 will be selected for testing.

(a) How many different samples of three could be selected?

Suppose that 2 of the 10 chips are defective and 8 of the chips are good.

(b) How many of the samples contain only good chips?
(c) How many of the samples contain 2 good chips and 1 defective chip?
(d) How many of the samples contain one or more defective chips?

1. The number of different samples of size 3 is:

$$C(10, 3) = \frac{(10)(9)(8)}{(3)(2)(1)} = 120$$

2. The number of samples with only good chips is the number of samples of size 3 that can be taken from the eight good chips.

$$C(8, 3) = \frac{(8)(7)(6)}{(3)(2)(1)} = 56$$

3. To find the number of samples with 2 good chips and 1 defective chip, imagine the 10 chips are divided into 2 piles: a pile of good chips and

a pile of defective chips. Then using the product rule we have:

$$\begin{pmatrix} \text{number of samples of 3} \\ \text{containing 2 good chips} \\ \text{and 1 defective chip} \end{pmatrix} = \begin{pmatrix} \text{number of samples of} \\ \text{2 chips from the} \\ \text{pile of good chips} \end{pmatrix} \times \begin{pmatrix} \text{number of samples of} \\ \text{1 chip from the pile} \\ \text{of defective chips} \end{pmatrix}$$

$$= C(8, 2) \times C(2, 1) = 28 \times 2 = 56$$

Of the different possible samples 56 contain 2 good chips and 1 defective chip.

4. Samples with one or more defective chips can be counted in two different ways. A sample contains either only good chips or at least one defective chip, so we can use the sum rule to write:

$$\text{(number of samples)} = \begin{pmatrix} \text{number of samples with} \\ \text{only good chips} \end{pmatrix} + \begin{pmatrix} \text{number of samples with one} \\ \text{or more defective chips} \end{pmatrix}$$

Using the answers to (a) and (b) we get:

$$120 = 56 + \begin{pmatrix} \text{number of samples with one} \\ \text{or more defective chips} \end{pmatrix}$$

so

$$\begin{pmatrix} \text{number of samples with one} \\ \text{or more defective chips} \end{pmatrix} = 120 - 56 = 64$$

A second way to answer (d) is to use the sum rule to write:

$$\begin{pmatrix} \text{number of samples} \\ \text{with one or more} \\ \text{defective chips} \end{pmatrix} = \begin{pmatrix} \text{number of samples with} \\ \text{one defective chip} \\ \text{and two good chips} \end{pmatrix} + \begin{pmatrix} \text{number of samples with} \\ \text{two defective chips} \\ \text{and one good chip} \end{pmatrix}$$

$$= [C(8, 2) \times C(2, 1)] + [C(8, 1) \times C(2, 2)]$$

$$= [28 \times 2] + [8 \times 1] = 56 + 8 = 64 \qquad \blacksquare$$

In this section we presented a rule for counting combinations and gave examples to illustrate how counting rules can be combined to solve a counting problem.

Remember the criterion for determining whether a list is a combination or permutation. If the same elements listed in a different order give the same information, such as a list of people elected to the school board, then the list is a combination. If the same elements listed in different order yield a different result, such as a list of the president followed by the secretary of the school board, then the list is a permutation.

CONCEPTS

combinations of size k taken from a set S
$C(N, k)$

SOLUTION TO PRACTICE EXAMPLE

1. (a)

Permutations of size 2		Combinations of size 2
AB	BA	{A, B}
AC	CA	{A, C}
AD	DA	{A, D}
BC	BC	{B, C}
BD	DB	{B, D}
CD	DC	{C, D}

(b) 1. 6   2. 10   3. 20   4. 21   5. 35

EXERCISES 4.4

Find:

1. $C(3, 2)$.   4. $C(6, 2)$.   7. $C(10, 2)$.   10. $C(8, 4)$.
2. $C(4, 2)$.   5. $C(7, 3)$.   8. $C(9, 3)$.   11. $C(9, 4)$.
3. $C(5, 3)$.   6. $C(8, 2)$.   9. $C(8, 3)$.   12. $C(10, 4)$.

13. List the subsets of $S = \{A, B, C\}$ that have:

(a) 1 element.

(b) 2 elements.

(c) 3 elements.

14. List the subsets of $A = \{A, B, C, D\}$ that have:

(a) 1 element.

(b) 2 elements.

(c) 3 elements.

(d) 4 elements.

15. How many subsets of $S = \{A, B, C, D, E\}$ have:

(a) 1 element?

(b) 2 elements?

(c) 3 elements?

(d) 4 elements?

(e) 5 elements?

16. How many of the subsets of $S = \{A, B, C, D, E, F, G, H\}$ have:

(a) 3 elements?

(b) 4 elements?

(c) 6 elements?

17. How many different committees are possible if a committee consists of three of the people {Adams, Collins, Edwards, Jones, McDonald, West}?

18. If 10 people are running for the school committee and 4 will be elected, how many different school committees are possible?

19. How many different groups of three members can be selected from the student council to serve on the executive committee if the student council has

    (a) 7 members?

    (b) 12 members?

    (c) N members?

20. A town Rotary club wants to send a delegation consisting of two of the five officers to the international convention. How many different such delegations are possible?

21. Two grand-prizewinning lottery tickets will be chosen. How many different sets of two prizewinning tickets are possible if

    (a) 10 tickets were sold?

    (b) 50 tickets were sold?

    (c) 100 tickets were sold?

22. A quality control engineer will select 3 of 100 transistors for testing. How many different samples are possible?

23. A Chinese restaurant, the China Inn, offers a dinner special which consists of your choice of any four different main dishes. How many different dinner specials are possible if the China Inn has

    (a) 10 main dishes?

    (b) 30 main dishes?

    (c) 50 main dishes?

24. A library wants to buy enough language dictionaries so a person will be able to look up a word in Greek, Latin, French, German, Russian, or English and find its translation into any of the other languages. How many dictionaries does the library need if each of the dictionaries translates back and forth between two languages?

25. In how many different ways can a class of 10 students be split into 2 groups of 5 students each?

26. The Supreme Court has nine members. In how many different ways can the Court make a five-to-four decision?

27. How many different committees are possible if a committee is obtained by choosing 2 of 10 faculty and 3 of 22 students?

28. In how many ways can a panel of 12 jurors and 2 alternates be selected from a group of 25 people?

29. A new product team will contain three of six engineers, one of five marketing specialists, and one of three financial experts. How many different teams are possible?

30. In how many ways can six different books be given to three students, two books per student?

31. In how many ways can 10 different toys be given to 3 children if the youngest child gets four toys and the others get 3 each?

32. How many different ways are there to answer a 10-question test if each question is answered either true or false, 8 are answered correctly and 2 incorrectly?

33. How many different ways are there to fill out the answer sheet to a 10-question test if each question is answered *A*, *B*, or *C*; 7 questions are answered correctly, and 3 incorrectly?

34. How many different ways are there to arrange 3 red, 4 yellow, and 5 blue bulbs on a string of 12 light sockets where two arrangements are considered the same if they have the same colored bulbs in the same sockets?

35. There are 5 rotten apples in a crate of 25 apples. How many samples of 4 of the 25 apples contain

    (a) only good apples?

    (b) 3 good apples and 1 rotten apple?

    (c) one or more rotten apples?

36. How many of the 2,598,960 different poker hands contain

    (a) 5 diamonds?

    (b) 5 cards of the same suit (clubs, diamonds, hearts, or spades)?

37. The written test given by a motor vehicle department contains 10 questions. Eight or more of the questions must be answered correctly in order to pass.
    (a) How many different ways can the answer sheet be filled out if each question is answered either true or false?
    (b) How many different ways can the answer sheet be filled out so 8 or more questions are answered correctly?

38. The United Nations Security Council has 5 permanent members (China, France, Soviet Union, United Kingdom, and the United States) and 10 nonpermanent members. For a measure to pass the Security Council all permanent members and at least 4 of the nonpermanent members must vote for the measure.
    (a) Find the number of permutations of the members of the Security Council in which the United States is pivotal. (The definition of pivotal is given in Section 4.3.) To be pivotal the United States must be the ninth voter in the permutation. Such a permutation can be constructed in steps: first choose the members that will precede the United States in the permutation, then choose the order in which they appear in the permutation, then order the voters that follow the United States.
    (b) Find the Shapley-Shubik index of each permanent member of the Security Council.
    (c) Find the Shapley-Shubik index of each nonpermanent member.

4.5   *Probability*

In this section, we show how to compute probabilities and answer such questions as:

1. If you toss a coin three times, how likely is it that the coin lands heads up all three times?
2. Suppose 3 people from a 14-member company advisory committee are chosen at random to attend a conference in San Francisco. If 6 of the 14 committee members are officers of the company, how likely is it that all 3 members chosen to go to San Francisco are officers of the company?
3. A factory that makes calculators inspects them for defects by collecting the new calculators into lots of 10, choosing some of the lot for testing, and then passing the whole lot on for sale if all the calculators chosen passed the test. If 1 or more calculators fails the test, then all remaining calculators in the lot are tested. How many calculators should be selected from each lot for testing if the chances that a lot with 3 defective calculators passes inspection is to be less than 1 out of 10?

The **probability** of an event is the fraction of the time the event can be expected to occur. For example if a coin is tossed repeatedly, then the fraction of the time heads can be expected to occur is $\frac{1}{2}$. We say the probability of heads is $\frac{1}{2}$. We define probability and use counting rules from the other sections of this chapter to compute probabilities. In the next chapter, we present the fundamental principles of probability theory and give additional applications.

EXAMPLE 1

(a) If you toss a coin repeatedly then it is reasonable to expect that about half the time the coin will land heads up. We say the probability of heads is $\frac{1}{2}$.

(b) If you roll a six-sided die repeatedly then you can expect each of the six numbers, 1, 2, 3, 4, 5, 6, to land on top as frequently as any of the other numbers. Each one of the numbers occurs with probability $\frac{1}{6}$. For instance, the number 5 lands on top with probability $\frac{1}{6}$.

(c) An experiment consists of picking one card from a deck of 54 cards; 13 clubs, 13 diamonds, 13 hearts, 13 spades, and 2 jokers. Each time the experiment is done you expect that any one of the cards is as likely to be chosen as any of the others. We say each of the cards is picked with probability $\frac{1}{54}$. The probability of picking a jack, queen, or king is computed as follows. There are 4 jacks, 4 queens, and 4 kings in the deck of 54 cards, so the probability of picking one of these 12 face cards is $\frac{12}{54} = \frac{2}{9}$. ■

Before we can give a formula for computing probabilities, we need some terminology. Note that each part of Example 1 describes an experiment. In (a) the experiment is tossing a coin; in (b) the experiment is rolling a die; in

(c) the experiment is picking one of 54 cards. Recall from Section 1.3 that the set of different possible results of an experiment is called the **sample space**. The sample spaces in Example 1 are {Heads, Tails} in (a), {1, 2, 3, 4, 5, 6} in (b), and the set of 54 cards in (c). The subsets of the sample space are called **events**. For each subset E of the sample space we want a formula for the probability that the result of an experiment is one of the elements in E. In Example 1 we found the probabilities of the events: {Heads} in part (a), {1} in part (b), and E = the set of face cards in part (c).

DEFINITION   For S, a finite set, and E, any subset of S, the **probability of E**, denoted $P(E)$ is defined by

(1) $P(E) = \dfrac{\#(E)}{\#(S)}$ where $\#(E)$ = the number of elements in E
$\#(S)$ = the number of elements in S

S is the sample space and E is an event.

Equation (1) applies when each of the elements in S is as likely to occur as any of the others. In the next chapter, we show how to find probabilities when some of the elements in S are more likely to occur than others.

The probabilities in Example 1 are computed as follows:

(a) S = {Heads, Tails}
E = {Heads}
$$P(E) = \frac{\#(E)}{\#(S)} = \frac{\#(\{\text{Heads}\})}{\#(\{\text{Heads, Tails}\})} = \frac{1}{2}$$

(b) S = {1, 2, 3, 4, 5, 6}
E = {1}
$$P(E) = \frac{\#(E)}{\#(S)} = \frac{\#(\{1\})}{\#(\{1,\ 2,\ 3,\ 4,\ 5,\ 6\})} = \frac{1}{6}$$

(c) S = the set of cards in a 54-card deck
E = the set of face cards
$$P(E) = \frac{\#(E)}{\#(S)} = \frac{\text{number of face cards}}{\text{number of cards}} = \frac{12}{54} = \frac{2}{9}$$

The Shapley-Shubik index of a voter is the probability the voter is pivotal. Let S be the set of permutations of the voters and E the subset of S consisting of the permutations in which the voter is pivotal. The Shapley-Shubik index of the voter is:

$$\frac{\text{number of times the voter is pivotal}}{\text{number of permutations of the voters}} = \frac{\#(E)}{\#(S)} = P(E)$$

PRACTICE EXAMPLE 1   One card is picked from the cards ace, 2, 3, 4, 5, 6, 7, 8, 9, 10, jack, queen, and king of clubs. Find the probability that the card selected has an even number on it.   ■

If each of the elements in the sample space is as likely to occur as any of the others (as in Example 1 and in the practice example), and if the experiment is done repeatedly, then the fraction

$$\frac{\text{number of times the result of the experiment was an element of } E}{\text{number of times the experiment was performed}}$$

is close to the probability of E. As the experiment is repeated more and more often the difference between P(E) and this fraction generally becomes closer and closer to zero. For example, a computer simulated 1000 coin tosses with the following result.

Number of tosses	Number of heads	Number of heads/ Number of tosses	P{(heads)}
200	83	$\frac{83}{200} = .415$	.5
400	178	$\frac{178}{400} = .445$	.5
600	285	$\frac{285}{600} = .475$	.5
800	416	$\frac{416}{800} = .52$	.5
1000	517	$\frac{517}{1000} = .517$	.5

EXAMPLE 2   Of 10 people {Mr. Barker, Mrs. Heckman, Mr. McNabb, Mrs. Chase, Mr. Burnham, Mrs. Street, Mr. Street, Mrs. Raymond, Mrs. Gilmore, Mrs. Cenkl} 2 will be selected at random for jury duty. What is the probability that both people selected are women?

The sample space, S, is the set of combinations of size 2 taken from the set of 10 people. S has

$$C(10, 2) = \frac{10 \times 9}{2 \times 1} = 45$$

elements. The event, E, in which both people selected are women is the set of all combinations of size 2 taken from {Mrs. Heckman, Mrs. Chase, Mrs. Street, Mrs. Raymond, Mrs. Gilmore, Mrs. Cenkl}. E has

$$C(6, 2) = \frac{6 \times 5}{2 \times 1} = 15$$

elements. Thus

$$P(E) = \frac{\#(E)}{\#(S)} = \frac{15}{45} = \frac{1}{3}$$

PRACTICE EXAMPLE 2

An advisory committee to the president of a company has 14 members of which 6 are officers of the company. If 3 members of the committee are chosen at random to attend a conference in San Francisco, what is the probability that only officers of the company are selected?

Probability can be used in decision making.

EXAMPLE 3

Suppose that pocket calculators come off a production line in lots of 10. It is important to the manufacturer that the calculators it sells be in good working order. On the other hand thoroughly checking each calculator is too expensive. The quality control engineer has decided to test the same number of calculators out of each lot of 10. If all of the calculators tested are found to be in good working order, then the entire lot of 10 will be sold without further testing—otherwise each of the remaining calculators in the lot of 10 will be tested.

(a) If 2 calculators out of 10 are selected for testing, then what is the probability both calculators work if the lot of 10 contains 3 defective calculators?
(b) How many calculators should be selected from each lot of 10 in order for the probability of passing a lot with 3 defective calculators to be less than .1?

The sample space, S, is the set of combinations of size 2 taken from the lot of 10 calculators. S has

$$C(10, 2) = \frac{10 \times 9}{2 \times 1} = 45$$

elements. The subset, E, of S, consisting of samples containing only good calculators, has

$$C(7, 2) = \frac{7 \times 6}{2 \times 1} = 21$$

elements. The probability that a sample of 2 of the 10 calculators contains only good calculators is

$$P(E) = \frac{\#(E)}{\#(S)} = \frac{21}{45} = \frac{7}{15}$$

We use the table below to determine the smallest sample size for which the probability of passing a lot with three defectives is less than .1. The answer is five.

Number selected	Probability that only working calculators are selected
1	$\dfrac{C(7,\ 1)}{C(10,\ 1)} = .7$
2	$\dfrac{C(7,\ 2)}{C(10,\ 2)} = \dfrac{7 \times 6}{10 \times 9} = .467$
3	$\dfrac{C(7,\ 3)}{C(10,\ 3)} = \dfrac{7 \times 6 \times 5}{10 \times 9 \times 8} = .292$
4	$\dfrac{C(7,\ 4)}{C(10,\ 3)} = \dfrac{7 \times 6 \times 5 \times 4}{10 \times 9 \times 8 \times 7} = .167$
5	$\dfrac{C(7,\ 5)}{C(10,\ 5)} = \dfrac{7 \times 6 \times 5 \times 4 \times 3}{10 \times 9 \times 8 \times 7 \times 6} = .083 < .1$
6	$\dfrac{C(7,\ 6)}{C(10,\ 6)} = \dfrac{7 \times 6 \times 5 \times 4 \times 3 \times 2}{10 \times 9 \times 8 \times 7 \times 6 \times 5} = .033$
7	$\dfrac{C(7,\ 7)}{C(10,\ 7)} = \dfrac{7 \times 6 \times 5 \times 4 \times 3 \times 2 \times 1}{10 \times 9 \times 8 \times 7 \times 6 \times 5 \times 4} = .008$
8, 9, or 10	0

The following computation illustrates how the quotients in the table are simplified.

$$\frac{C(7,\ 3)}{C(10,\ 3)} = \frac{\dfrac{7 \times 6 \times 5}{3 \times 2 \times 1}}{\dfrac{10 \times 9 \times 8}{3 \times 2 \times 1}} = \left(\frac{7 \times 6 \times 5}{3 \times 2 \times 1}\right) \times \left(\frac{3 \times 2 \times 1}{10 \times 9 \times 8}\right)$$

$$= \frac{7 \times 6 \times 5}{10 \times 9 \times 8} \qquad \left(\text{recall } \frac{\dfrac{a}{b}}{\dfrac{c}{d}} = \frac{a}{b} \times \frac{d}{c}\right)$$

In general,

$$\frac{C(N,\ k)}{C(M,\ k)} = \frac{\dfrac{P(N,\ k)}{k!}}{\dfrac{P(M,\ k)}{k!}} = \frac{P(N,\ k)}{k!} \times \frac{k!}{P(M,\ k)} = \frac{P(N,\ k)}{P(M,\ k)}$$

The last line in the table is explained as follows. Each line of the table displays $P(E)$ where E is the set of samples of the specified size that contain only good calculators. Since there are just seven good calculators, any

sample of eight or more calculators contains at least one defective calculator. In this case $E = \varnothing$, $\#(E) = 0$, and so

$$P(E) = \frac{\#(E)}{\#(S)} = \frac{0}{\#(S)} = 0$$

A sample of size eight or more will never pass inspection.   ∎

There are events with probability 1. For example, suppose all 10
calculators in the lot are good, then every sample contains only good
calculators and hence passes inspection. If the sample size is 7, then

$E =$ samples of size 7 containing only good calculators

$=$ all samples of size 7

$= S$

and

$$P(E) = \frac{\#(E)}{\#(S)} = \frac{\#(S)}{\#(S)} = 1$$

> **THEOREM**   The probability of an event is always between 0 and 1.

Proof:

Let $S =$ sample space, let E be a subset of S, then

$$\varnothing \subseteq E \subseteq S$$

so

$$\#(\varnothing) \leq \#(E) \leq \#(S)$$

Dividing each term by $\#(S)$ we get:

$$\frac{0}{\#(S)} \leq \frac{\#(E)}{\#(S)} \leq \frac{\#(S)}{\#(S)}$$

$$0 \leq P(E) \leq 1$$

Sometimes it is easier to compute the probability that an event will *not*
happen than it is to compute the probability of the event itself. The formula
below can be used to find the probability of an event, E, when the probability that E will not happen is known. The formula says that the probability of an event will happen is one minus the probability it will not
happen.

Let E be a subset of S and denote by E' the complement of E in S. Then:

(2) $$P(E) = 1 - P(E')$$

The next example illustrates the use of this formula; its derivation follows the example.

EXAMPLE 4

For the situation in Example 3 what is the probability that a sample of 2 of the 10 calculators contains at least 1 defective calculator?

The sample space S = set of combinations of size 2 taken from the set of 10 calculators

E = combinations of size 2 containing at least 1 defective calculator

E' = combinations of size 2 that do not contain a defective calculator

From part (a) of Example 3, $P(E') = \frac{7}{15}$. Using Formula (2) we get

$$P(E) = 1 - P(E')$$

$$P(E) = 1 - \frac{7}{15}$$

$$P(E) = \frac{15 - 7}{15}$$

$$P(E) = \frac{8}{15}$$

Formula (2) is derived as follows:

$$\#(E) + \#(E') = \#(S)$$

since an element in S is in either E or E' but not both.

$$\frac{\#(E)}{\#(S)} + \frac{\#(E')}{\#(S)} = \frac{\#(S)}{\#(S)}$$

$$P(E) + P(E') = 1$$

so

$$P(E) = 1 - P(E')$$

EXAMPLE 5

Five people are chosen at random and asked which month of the year they were born. What is the probability that at least two people name the same month?

First we need to identify the sample space. Suppose the five people are {Alexander, Sarah, Richard, Mary, Nicholas}. The result of the experiment is a list which gives the birth month of each person. One possibility is:

April	June	December	May	August
Alexander	Sarah	Richard	Mary	Nicholas

The number of elements in the sample space is the number of ways to fill in the blanks, where each blank is filled by putting in one of 12 months.

| Alexander | Sarah | Richard | Mary | Nicholas |

By the product rule:

$$\#(S) = 12 \times 12 \times 12 \times 12 \times 12 = 248{,}832$$

The event, E, and its complement are described by:

E = the set of filled-in blanks in which at least one month is listed twice

E' = the set of filled-in blanks in which none of the months is listed more than once

$\#(E')$ = number of ways to fill in the blanks so no month occurs more than once

By the product rule:

$$\#(E') = 12 \times 11 \times 10 \times 9 \times 8 = 95{,}040$$

so

$$P(E') = \frac{\#(E')}{\#(S)} = \frac{95040}{248832} = .38194444$$

using Formula (2) we get

$$P(E) = 1 - P(E') = 1 - .38194444 = .61805556 \sim .62 \qquad \blacksquare$$

In this section we introduced probability and used the counting rules from other sections of the chapter to find probabilities. An introduction to the theory of probability and additional applications are given in the next chapter.

CONCEPTS

probability
sample space
event

SOLUTIONS TO PRACTICE EXAMPLES

1. $P(\text{even number}) = \dfrac{\#(\{2,\ 4,\ 6,\ 8,\ 10\})}{\#(\{\text{ace, 2, 3, 4, 5, 6, 7, 8, 9, 10, jack, queen, king}\})} = \dfrac{5}{13}$

2. $\dfrac{C(6,\ 3)}{C(14,\ 3)} = \dfrac{20}{364} = \dfrac{5}{91} = .055$

EXERCISES 4.5

1. For: $S = \{a, b, c, d, e\}$
   $E = \{a, b, c\}$
   $F = \{c, d, e\}$

   Find:

   (a) $P(E)$.   (c) $P(E')$.   (e) $P(E \cup F)$.
   (b) $P(F)$.   (d) $P(F')$.   (f) $P(E \cap F)$.

2. For: $S = \{1, 2, 3, 4, 5, 6, 7, 8, 9, 10\}$
   $E = \{1, 3, 5, 7\}$
   $F = \{3, 4, 5, 6, 7, 8\}$

   Find:

   (a) $P(E)$.   (c) $P(F)$.   (e) $P(E \cup F)$.
   (b) $P(S)$.   (d) $P(E \cap F)$.   (f) $P(F')$.

   In Exercises 3 and 4 list the elements in the sample space, list the elements in the event, E, whose probability answers the question, and compute the probability of E using the formula

   $$P(E) = \frac{\#(E)}{\#(S)}$$

3. A 12-sided die with faces numbered 1 through 12 is used in the game Dungeons and Dragons. If such a die is rolled, what is the probability that the number that lands on top is

   (a) the number 10?

   (b) the number 7?

   (c) an even number?

   (d) an odd number?

   (e) greater than 3?

   (f) greater than 8?

   (g) less than 6?

4. One card is selected from a 13-card pile that contains the ace, 2, 3, 4, 5, 6, 7, 8, 9, 10, jack, queen, king of hearts. What is the probability the card

   (a) is the ace?

   (b) has a number on it?

   (c) is a face card?

   If the ace, 2, 4, 6, 8, 10, and king of hearts are discarded from the deck of 13 heart cards and 2 cards are selected from the 6 remaining cards, then what is the probability that

   (d) both cards have numbers on them?

(e) neither card has a number on it?

(f) one card has a number on it and the other does not?

5. Let: $A = \{a, b, 1, 2, 3\}$

S = set of all combinations of size 2 taken from A

(a) List the elements in S. Find the probability of the following events:

(b) E = the combinations of size 2 containing two letters.

(c) F = the combinations of size 2 containing only numbers.

(d) G = the combinations of size 2 containing one letter and one number.

(e) H = the combinations of size 2 containing at least one letter.

6. Let: $A = \{a, b, c, 1, 2, 3, 4\}$

S = set of all combinations of size 3 taken from A

Find the probability of the following events:

(a) E = the combinations of size 3 containing only letters.

(b) F = the combinations of size 3 containing at least one number.

(c) G = the combinations of size 3 containing only numbers.

(d) H = the combinations of size 3 containing at least one letter.

7. A contestant on a T.V. game show can pick two of seven boxes. Two of the boxes have no prize in them. The remaining five boxes have prizes, one of which is the grand prize of a one-week vacation for four in Hawaii. What is the probability that the contestant

(a) does not win a prize?

(b) wins at least one prize?

(c) wins the vacation to Hawaii?

8. The French teacher has announced that on the next test, the students will be given 3 pages from the 10-page fourth chapter. To take the test the student picks one of the 3 given pages and translates that page.

(a) What is the probability that a student who has studied 4 of the 10 pages in Chapter 4 will not have studied any of the pages on the test?

(b) What is the probability that the student will have studied at least one of the pages on the test?

(c) How many pages would a student have to study in order for the probability that at least one of the pages on the test was studied to be greater than .9?

9. In the game of blackjack a two-card hand consisting of an ace and 10, jack, queen, or king is called blackjack and wins the game.

(a) What is the probability a player is dealt blackjack from a standard deck of 52 cards?

The cards used in one hand of the game are put aside when the hand is over, and a new hand is dealt from the deck of unused cards. Suppose that after several hands of blackjack the deck of unused cards contains two aces, two 3s, one 5, one 7, two 10s, and three queens.

(b) What is the probability a player is dealt blackjack from this deck of 11 cards?

(c) If the player is dealt the 5 and the 7 and asks for another card, then what is the probability that the card he receives is a 10 or a queen?

10. There are $C(52, 5) = 2,598,960$ different five-card poker hands. What is the probability that a five-card poker hand contains:

   (a) five cards of the same suit, for example the 2 of clubs, 3 of clubs, 5 of clubs, 10 of clubs, and the king of clubs? Such a hand is called a flush.

   (b) three of one kind and a pair, for example the 5 of clubs, 5 of hearts, 5 of diamonds, jack of clubs, and the jack of spades? Such a hand is called a full house. [Advice: Count the number of full houses using the product rule. Pick the rank of the "three of a kind" (5 in our example), then pick the three cards of that kind that are in the hand (5 of clubs, 5 of hearts, and 5 of diamonds in our example), then pick the rank of the pair (jack in our example), then pick the cards of that kind that are to be in the hand.]

   (c) three of a kind and the other two cards are not a pair—for example, the 8 of clubs, the 8 of spades, the 8 of hearts, the 2 of diamonds, and the jack of hearts?

11. Suppose four people get on an elevator that stops at seven different floors. Assuming each person is as likely to get off on one floor as any other floor, what is the probability that

   (a) they all get off on different floors?

   (b) at least two people get off on the same floor?

12. Five organizations have called the local convention center to reserve the banquet room. If each organization requested a day in June, what is the probability they all picked different days?

13. Suppose the person filling out the answer sheet to a 10-question true-false test has no idea which statements are true and which are false. What is the probability that the person gets 7 or more questions correct?

14. Anna, Alexander, and Benjamin are in a class of 30 students that will be split into 2 sections of 15 students each. If the teacher splits the class arbitrarily, then

   (a) what is the probability that Alexander and Benjamin will be in the same section?

   (b) what is the probability that Anna, Alexander, and Benjamin will be in the same section?

15. A box of 20 light bulbs contains 5 defective bulbs. If 4 bulbs are selected at random from the box, then

   (a) what is the probability that all 4 bulbs selected work?

   (b) what is the probability that at least one of the bulbs does not work?

16. A box of 20 light bulbs will be inspected by choosing some bulbs at random and testing the selected bulbs. If one or more of the selected bulbs fails to work the box fails the inspection and then every bulb in the box is tested. Otherwise the box passes inspection. What is the smallest number of bulbs that can be selected for testing if the probability that a box with 5 defective bulbs passes inspection is required to be less than .1?

17. Of the 50 tickets sold in a raffle 3 will be selected as prizewinning tickets. What is the probability a person wins one or more prizes if the person bought:

    (a) 1 ticket?

    (b) 4 tickets?

    (c) 10 tickets?

CHAPTER SUMMARY

In this chapter we presented the basic rules of counting and introduced probability. The product rule (Section 4.1) leads to the rules for counting permutations (Section 4.2) and for counting combinations (Section 4.4). These counting rules were applied in Section 4.3 to define a measure of voting power, and in Section 4.5 to compute probabilities.

In the next chapter, we develop the theory of probability and give additional applications. The counting rules of this chapter are applied to scheduling problems in Chapter 6 and in Chapter 10 to counting paths in a graph.

PRODUCT RULE   If there are B_1 ways to fill in a first blank, and after filling in the first blank there are B_2 ways to fill in a second blank, and after filling in the first two blanks there are B_3 ways to fill in a third blank and so on, then there are $B_1 \times B_2 \times B_3 \times \cdots \times B_k$ ways to fill in the first k blanks.

SUM RULE   For a collection of sets $\{A_1, A_2, \ldots, A_k\}$ with the property that no two of the sets have an element in common (i.e., $A_i \cap A_j = \emptyset$), then

$$\#(A_1 \cup A_2 \cup \cdots \cup A_k) = \#(A_1) + \#(A_2) + \cdots + \#(A_k)$$

PERMUTATION   An ordered list of different elements taken from some set. By the product rule the number of permutations of size k taken from a set with N elements is

$$P(N, k) = \underbrace{N \times (N - 1) \times (N - 2) \times \cdots \times (N - k + 1)}_{k \text{ factors}}$$

SHAPLEY-SHUBIK POWER INDEX   The power of a voter is defined to be the probability the voter is the pivotal element in a permutation of the voters.

COMBINATION   A combination of size k taken from a set, S, is a subset of S with k elements. The number of combinations of size k taken from a set with N elements is

$$C(N, k) = \frac{P(N, k)}{k!}$$

SAMPLE SPACE   The set of possible outcomes of an experiment.

EVENT   Any subset of the sample space.

PROBABILITY   The fraction of the time the event can be expected to occur. If each of the elements in the sample space is as likely to occur as any of the others, then the probability of an event, E, is

$$P(E) = \frac{\#(E)}{\#(S)}$$

REVIEW EXERCISES FOR CHAPTER 4

1. A full dinner at a restaurant consists of one of 5 appetizers, one of 6 main courses, and one of 20 desserts. How many different complete dinners are there?

2. How many different license plates are there consisting of three different letters followed by any three-digit number?

3. In the graph below, the vertices represent cities and the edges routes between cities. In how many different ways can a person starting at A visit each other city once and return to A?

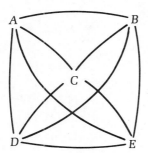

4. A newspaper is deciding which (if any) of its three available reporters to send to the scene of a local fire. How many different choices are there?

5. In a round-robin tennis tournament each of the eight players will play each other player once. How many matches will be played?

6. List the permutations of size 3 taken from $S = \{1, 2, 3, 4, 5\}$.

7. Find:

   (a) $P(4, 4)$ (b) $P(8, 3)$ (c) $P(8, 5)$

8. Suppose a person makes a bet in a lottery by choosing a four-digit number. Each digit must be taken from $\{1, 2, 3, 4, 5, 6, 7, 8, 9\}$ and no digit can be repeated. How many different bets are possible?

9. In how many ways can a committee choose one of its members to be chairperson and one of its members to be secretary if the committee has 11 members?

10. Five job candidates will be ranked. If no two candidates receive the same ranking, then how many different rankings are possible?

11. Find the Shapley-Shubik index of each voter if

Voters	A	B	C
Number of votes	5	3	4

7 votes are needed to win.

12. List the subsets of $S = \{1, 2, 3, 4, 5\}$ that have three elements.

13. Find:

   (a) $C(5, 3)$.   (b) $C(8, 3)$.   (c) $C(8, 5)$.

14. If 13 people are running for the school committee and 5 will be elected, then how many different school committees are possible?

15. A quality control engineer will select 3 of 25 transistors for testing. How many different samples are possible?

16. A box of 20 computer chips contains 3 defective chips. How many samples of 5 of the 20 chips contain exactly 1 defective chip?

17. How many of the samples in Exercise 16 contain:

   (a) no defective chips?

   (b) 2 defective chips?

   (c) 3 defective chips?

18. For:

   $S = \{a, b, c, d, e, f\}$
   $E = \{a, c, f\}$
   $F = \{a, b, c, e\}$

   Find:

   (a) $P(E)$.   (b) $P(F)$.   (c) $P(E')$.

   (d) $P(F')$.   (e) $P(E \cup F)$.   (f) $P(E \cap F)$.

19. A person filling out the answer sheet to a five-question true-false test guesses the answer to each question. What is the probability the person answers all the questions correctly?

20. A box of 15 computer disks contains 2 defective disks. If 3 disks are picked at random from the box, then what is the probability that both defective disks are among the 3 selected.

21. Two of 100 raffle tickets will be selected as prize-winning tickets. What is the probability that a person who bought 10 tickets will win at least one prize?

22. Three people are chosen at random and asked which month they were born. What is the probability that they were all born in different months?

5 *Probability*

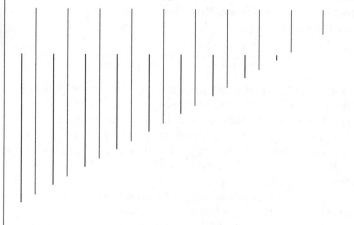

In this chapter, we present the basic principles of probability theory and give applications. In Section 5.1, we generalize the definition of probability given in Chapter 4 to include situations in which not all outcomes are equally likely. In Section 5.2, we show how probabilities can be used as evidence of a relationship between events. For example, the fact that the incidence of lung cancer is much higher among smokers than in the general population is used as evidence of a connection between smoking and lung cancer. In Section 5.3, we show how to compute probabilities to answer such questions as: What disease is causing the patient's symptoms? Who is most likely to be elected given the results of the latest poll?

In order to set a price for a policy, an insurance company needs to know the profit per policy at various selling prices. An oil company choosing among several drilling sites wants to know the profit it can expect to make at each of the sites. In Section 5.4, we show how to make such predictions.

The fundamental concepts of probability were developed in the middle of the seventeenth century by the famous mathematicians Pascal and Fermat. The problem that prompted Pascal and Fermat to begin their work is presented in Section 5.2.

5.1   *Probability Spaces*

In this section we review basic terms used in probability theory. We give

examples of probability spaces along with a formula relating probabilities of the union and intersection of two events to the probabilities of the events.

Recall that in Sections 1.3 and 4.5, we defined the **sample space**, S, of an experiment to be the set of different possible outcomes. A subset of S is called an **event**. An event that consists of a single element of S will be called a **simple event**. If the experiment is to choose three people and list the month each person was born, then the sample space is the set of ordered triples of months of the year.

April	July	June
first person	second person	third person

is an element of the sample space. Examples of events are: the set of triples in which all months are different, triples in which at least two of the months are the same, triples in which all three months are the same. The sets, {(April, July, June)} and {(December, October, February)} are simple events.

The basic question in probability theory is: given information about an experiment and a description of some event, E, find $P(E)$, the probability that the event E occurs.

Probabilities are assigned to events so that $P(E)$ represents the fraction of the time the event E can be expected to occur. If an event, E, has probability, $P(E) = .35$, and the experiment is repeated many times, then the fraction:

$$\frac{\text{number of times } E \text{ occurs}}{\text{number of times experiment is carried out}}$$

is expected to be close to .35. As the experiment is carried out more and more times the fraction of times E occurs is expected to get closer and closer to $P(E)$.

EXAMPLE 1

A spinner for a child's game is pictured in Figure 5.1. If we assume the spinner never stops on a line separating regions, then what is the probability the spinner stops in a region labeled:

(a) 1?
(b) 2?
(c) 3?
(d) 1 or 2?
(e) 3 or 2?
(f) 1 or 3?
(g) 1, 2, or 3?

The elements in the sample space are:

1 = spinner stops in a region labeled 1
2 = spinner stops in a region labeled 2
3 = spinner stops in a region labeled 3

Figure 5.1

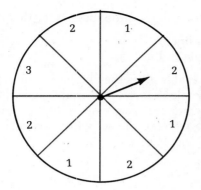

Since there are eight regions, each with the same area, we can assume the spinner stops in each region one-eighth of the time. There are three regions labeled 1 so the spinner is expected to stop in one of these three regions three-eighths of the time. $P(\{1\}) = \frac{3}{8}$.

Similarly,

$$P(\{2\}) = \frac{4}{8} = \frac{1}{2}$$

$$P(\{3\}) = \frac{1}{8}$$

$$P(\{1, 2\}) = \frac{7}{8}$$

since seven of the eight regions are labeled either 1 or 2. Similarly,

$$P(\{3, 2\}) = \frac{5}{8}$$

$$P(\{1, 3\}) = \frac{4}{8} = \frac{1}{2}$$

$$P(\{1, 2, 3\}) = \frac{8}{8} = 1$$

since we are assuming the spinner stops in one of the eight numbered regions. ■

EXAMPLE 2   The manager of a store counted the number of people in the checkout line at various times during the day and listed the results in the table below.

Number of people in line	0	1	2	3	More than 3, less than 10	Ten or more
Frequency	5	10	15	7	3	1

Based on this data what is the probability that there are:

(a) two or less people in line?
(b) more than three people in line?

The second row of the table gives the number of times the manager saw the specific number of people in line. For example the number 15 indicates that on 15 occasions the manager saw exactly two people in line.

For the sample space we take the set with elements:

0 = nobody in line
1 = one person in line
2 = two people in line
3 = three people in line
a = more than 3 and less than 10 people in line
b = ten or more people in line

(It might seem more natural to set the sample space equal to

$$\{0, 1, 2, 3, 4, 5, 6, 7 \ldots\}$$

but this does not correspond to the method used by the manager to record observations, and the table does not provide enough information to find the probabilities of all simple events.)

Recall that the probability of an event is the fraction of the time the event can be expected to occur. In this example we take the fraction of the time an event actually occurred as the fraction of the time the event can be expected to occur.

From the table we see that the manager made $5 + 10 + 15 + 7 + 3 + 1 = 41$ observations.

$$P(\{0, 1, 2\}) = \frac{5 + 10 + 15}{41} = \frac{30}{41}.$$

The answer to (a) is $\frac{30}{41}$.

$$P(\{a, b\}) = \frac{3 + 1}{41} = \frac{4}{41}$$

The answer to (b) is $\frac{4}{41}$.

In Examples 1 and 2 the probability of an event is a number greater than or equal to zero. In general, the probability of an event is the fraction of times the event can be expected to occur, and therefore, is greater than or equal to zero. Another observation that can be made from the examples is that the probability of an event, E, is the sum of the probabilities of the simple events contained in E. In Example 2, for instance,

$$P(\{0, 1, 2\}) = \frac{5 + 10 + 15}{41} = \frac{5}{41} + \frac{10}{41} + \frac{15}{41} = P(\{0\}) + P(\{1\}) + P(\{2\})$$

For the sample space, S, $P(S)$ is the fraction of the time S can be expected to occur and hence equals 1. Since $P(S)$ is the sum of the probabilities of all the simple events, it follows that:

$$1 = \text{sum of the probabilities of all the simple events}$$

DEFINITION Let S be a finite set and suppose each element, s, in S is assigned a number, $P(\{s\})$, so that

1. $P(\{s\}) \geq 0$ for each $s \in S$
2. The sum of all the numbers, $P(\{s\})$, for $s \in S$ equals 1.

Then S is called a finite **probability space**.

$P(\{s\})$ is called the probability of the simple event $\{s\}$.

$P(E)$ is defined to be the sum of the probabilities of the simple events in the subset E of S.

Examples 1 and 2 are examples of probability spaces. The set S and the probabilities of the simple events are:

For Example 1

$S = \{1, 2, 3\}$
$P(\{1\}) = \frac{3}{8}$
$P(\{2\}) = \frac{1}{2}$
$P(\{3\}) = \frac{1}{8}$

Note: $P(\{1\}) + P(\{2\}) + P(\{3\}) = \frac{3}{8} + \frac{1}{2} + \frac{1}{8} = \frac{3}{8} + \frac{4}{8} + \frac{1}{8} = \frac{8}{8} = 1.$

For Example 2

$S = \{0, 1, 2, 3, a, b\}$
$P(\{0\}) = \frac{5}{41}$
$P(\{1\}) = \frac{10}{41}$
$P(\{2\}) = \frac{15}{41}$
$P(\{3\}) = \frac{7}{41}$
$P(\{a\}) = \frac{3}{41}$
$P(\{b\}) = \frac{1}{41}$

Note: $P(\{0\}) + P(\{1\}) + P(\{2\}) + P(\{3\}) + P(\{a\}) + P(\{b\}) = \frac{5}{41} + \frac{10}{41} + \frac{15}{41} + \frac{7}{41} + \frac{3}{41} + \frac{1}{41} = \frac{41}{41} = 1.$

The examples of probability spaces in Section 4.5 have the property that the probabilities of the simple events are all equal. In this case, the probability space is called an **equiprobable probability space**. As we saw in Section 4.5, if the sample space, S, of an equiprobable probability space has N elements then the probability of each simple event is $1/N$, and the probability of an event, E, is the number of elements in E divided by the number of elements in S. If you look back at the probabilities computed in Examples

5.1 and 5.2, you will see that when the probability space is not equiprobable the probability of an event, E, cannot be computed as the number of elements in E divided by the number of elements in S.

EXAMPLE 3

Show that $S = \{s_1, s_2, s_3, s_4\}$ with $P(\{s_1\}) = \frac{1}{12}$, $P(\{s_2\}) = \frac{1}{6}$, $P(\{s_3\}) = \frac{1}{4}$, $P(\{s_4\}) = \frac{1}{2}$ is a probability space and find:

(a) $P(\{s_1, s_2\})$.
(b) $P(\{s_1, s_3\})$.
(c) $P(\{s_2, s_3\})$.
(d) $P(\{s_1, s_2, s_4\})$.

To show that a set, S, with given numbers, $P(\{s\})$, is a probability space we need to check conditions 1 and 2 in the definition of probability space. The given numbers $\frac{1}{12}, \frac{1}{6}, \frac{1}{4}$, and $\frac{1}{2}$ are each greater than or equal to zero so condition 1 is satisfied. To check condition 2, we add the probabilities of all simple events to see if the sum is one.

$$\frac{1}{12} + \frac{1}{6} + \frac{1}{4} + \frac{1}{2} = \frac{1}{12} + \frac{2}{12} + \frac{3}{12} + \frac{6}{12} = \frac{12}{12} = 1$$

Condition 2 is satisfied.

To answer (a) through (d) we add the probabilities of simple events.

(a) $P(\{s_1, s_2\}) = P(\{s_1\}) + P(\{s_2\}) = \frac{1}{12} + \frac{1}{6} = \frac{3}{12} = \frac{1}{4}$
(b) $P(\{s_1, s_3\}) = P(\{s_1\}) + P(\{s_3\})$
$\qquad = \frac{1}{12} + \frac{1}{4} = \frac{1}{12} + \frac{3}{12} = \frac{4}{12} = \frac{1}{3}$
(c) $P(\{s_2, s_3\}) = P(\{s_2\}) + P(\{s_3\}) = \frac{1}{6} + \frac{1}{4} = \frac{2}{12} + \frac{3}{12} = \frac{5}{12}$
(d) $P(\{s_1, s_2, s_4\}) = P(\{s_1\}) + P(\{s_2\}) + P(\{s_4\})$
$\qquad = \frac{1}{12} + \frac{1}{6} + \frac{1}{2} = \frac{1}{12} + \frac{2}{12} + \frac{6}{12} = \frac{9}{12} = \frac{3}{4}$ ■

PRACTICE EXAMPLE 1

Determine which of the following are probability spaces. For those that are probability spaces find $P(\{s_1, s_2\})$.

(a) $S = \{s_1, s_2, s_3\}$
$\quad P\{s_1\}) = \frac{1}{2}$
$\quad P\{s_2\}) = \frac{1}{3}$
$\quad P\{s_3\}) = \frac{1}{6}$

(c) $S = \{s_1, s_2, s_3\}$
$\quad P\{s_1\}) = \frac{7}{10}$
$\quad P\{s_2\}) = \frac{1}{5}$
$\quad P\{s_3\}) = \frac{1}{10}$

(b) $S = \{s_1, s_2, s_3\}$
$\quad P\{s_1\}) = \frac{7}{10}$
$\quad P\{s_2\}) = \frac{1}{5}$
$\quad P\{s_3\}) = \frac{1}{5}$ ■

EXAMPLE 4

A person approaching a traffic light will find the light is either red, yellow, or green. Construct a probability space corresponding to this situation if the light follows the cycle: red for 35 seconds, green for 45 seconds, yellow for 4 seconds. What is the probability that the light is either green or yellow?

The elements in the sample space are:

R = light is red
G = light is green
Y = light is yellow

We set the probability of each color equal to the fraction of the time the light is that color during one complete cycle of the light. The cycle time is $35 + 45 + 4 = 84$ seconds so the probability space is $S = \{R, G, Y\}$ with

$$P(\{R\}) = \frac{35}{84} = \frac{5}{12}$$

$$P(\{G\}) = \frac{45}{84} = \frac{15}{28}$$

$$P(\{Y\}) = \frac{4}{84} = \frac{1}{21}$$

$P(\text{light is either green or yellow}) = P(\{G, Y\})$

$$= P(\{G\}) + P(\{Y\}) = \frac{45}{84} + \frac{4}{84} = \frac{49}{84} = \frac{7}{12} \qquad ■$$

PRACTICE EXAMPLE 2

A bank has one customer line serviced by several tellers. At various times during the day the people waiting in line are counted. The table below gives the result.

Number of people in line	0	1	2	More than 2, less than 10	Ten or more
Frequency	3	2	5	20	8

(a) Use the table to construct a probability space. Give the sample space and the probability of each simple event.
(b) What is the probability there are more than two people waiting in line? ■

Frequently, the probability of an event can be computed in terms of other probabilities. If we know, for example, that some event does not occur 10% of the time, then we can say the event does occur 90% of the time and thus has probability .9. This principle, $P(E) = 1 - P(E')$, where E' denotes the complement of E, was used to compute probabilities in Examples 4 and 5 of Section 4.5. In the remainder of this section and in Sections 5.2 and 5.3, we show how to compute the probability of an event in terms of probabilities of related events.

EXAMPLE 5

A car repair shop knows from experience when someone calls to say a car will not start that 70% of the time the engine is flooded, 30% of the time the battery is weak, and 20% of the time neither one of these problems exists. What is the probability that a person calling to say their car will not start has both a flooded engine and a weak battery?

We will use a Venn diagram (see Chapter 1) to answer this question. The letters a, b, c, d in Figure 5.2 represent the probabilities of the regions. We will find the values for a, b, c, d.

Figure 5.2

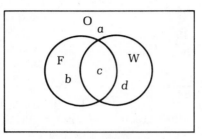

F = Flooded engine
W = Weak battery
O = Other

We are given:

$$P(F) = .7 = b + c$$
$$P(W) = .3 = c + d$$
$$P(O) = .2 = a$$

We are asked to find:

$$P(F \cap W) = c$$

Since 20% of the time the problem is neither a flooded engine nor a weak battery, the remaining 80% of the time either the engine is flooded or the battery is weak or both.

$$P(F \cup W) = .8 = b + c + d$$

Using $c + d = P(W) = .3$ we get $b = .5$

Using $b + c = P(F) = .7$ we get $d = .1$

From $b = .5$ and $b + c = .7$ we get $c = .2$

Figure 5.3 pictures this situation with the probabilities filled in. You should check that these numbers give the probabilities stated in the example: $P(F) = .7$, $P(W) = .3$, $P(O) = .2$.

Figure 5.3

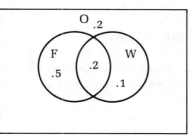

For the situation pictured in Figure 5.4, we have: $P(E) = a$, $P(E') = b$, and $a + b = 1$.

Figure 5.4

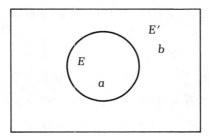

(1)	$P(E) = 1 - P(E')$

For the situation pictured in Figure 5.5, we have

Figure 5.5

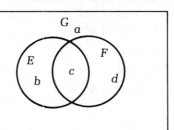

(2)	$P(E \cup F) = P(E) + P(F) - P(E \cap F)$

Since

$$P(E \cup F) = b + c + d$$
$$P(E) = b + c$$
$$P(F) = c + d$$

and

$$P(E \cap F) = c$$

Formulas (1) and (2) apply to all probability spaces. The problem in Example 5 can be solved using these formulas as follows.

We are given

$$P(O) = .2$$

$$P(F) = .7$$

$$P(W) = .3$$

and are asked to find $P(F \cap W)$. $O' = F \cup W$, so we can use formula (1) to find $P(F \cup W)$.

$$P(F \cup W) = P(O') = 1 - P(O) = 1 - .2 = .8$$

Now we use formula (2).

$$P(F \cup W) = P(F) + P(W) - P(F \cap W)$$

$$.8 = .7 + .3 - P(F \cap W)$$

so

$$P(F \cap W) = .7 + .3 - .8 = .2$$

as we found using a Venn diagram.

EXAMPLE 6   In a survey 45% of the people are under 40 years old, 30% are smokers, and 10% are both under 40 and smokers. Find the probability that a person selected at random from the survey is

(a) either a smoker or under 40.
(b) a nonsmoker and 40 or older.

The events are pictured in Figure 5.6.

Figure 5.6

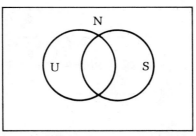

S = Smoker
U = Under 40
N = Nonsmoker and 40 or older

We are given

$$P(S) = .3$$

$$P(U) = .45$$

$$P(U \cap S) = .10$$

$$P(\text{smoker or under 40}) = P(S \cup U) = P(S) + P(U) - P(S \cap U)$$

$$= .3 + .45 - .1 = .65$$

and

$$P(\text{nonsmoker and 40 or older}) = P(N) = 1 - P(S \cup U)$$

$$= 1 - .65 = .35$$

The answer to (a) is .65. The answer to (b) is .35.

The Venn diagram with the probabilities filled in is pictured in Figure 5.7.

Figure 5.7

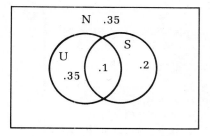

PRACTICE EXAMPLE 3

A car dealership conducted a survey of people inquiring about the dealer's new model van. Of the people surveyed, 50% had read a recent report on the van in *Consumer Reports*, 35% eventually bought a van, and 40% had neither read the report nor did they buy a van. What is the probability that a person selected at random from the survey read the *Consumer Reports* article and bought a van?

CONCEPTS

sample space
event
simple event
probability space
$P(E) = 1 - P(E')$
$P(E \cup F) = P(E) + P(F) - P(E \cap F)$

SOLUTIONS TO PRACTICE EXAMPLES

1. (a) $P(\{s_1\}) + P(\{s_2\}) + P(\{s_3\}) = (\frac{1}{2}) + (\frac{1}{3}) + (\frac{1}{6}) = 1$ and $P(\{s\}) \geq 0$ for each $s \in S$. This is a probability space. $P(\{s_1, s_2\}) = \frac{1}{2} + \frac{1}{3} = \frac{5}{6}$.

   (b) $P(\{s_1\}) + P(\{s_2\}) + P(\{s_3\}) = (\frac{7}{10}) + (\frac{1}{5}) + (\frac{1}{5}) = \frac{11}{10}$
   Condition 2 of the definition of probability space is not satisfied. This is *not* a probability space.

   (c) $P(\{s_1\}) + P(\{s_2\}) + P(\{s_3\}) = (\frac{7}{10}) + (\frac{1}{5}) + (\frac{1}{10}) = \frac{10}{10} = 1$ and $P(\{s\}) \geq 0$ for each $s \in S$. This is a probability space. $P(\{s_1, s_2\}) = \frac{7}{10} + \frac{1}{5} = \frac{9}{10}$.

2. (a) $S = \{0, 1, 2, a, b\}$
   0 = nobody waiting
   1 = one person waiting
   2 = two people waiting
   a = more than 2 and less than 10 people waiting
   b = 10 or more people waiting
   $P(\{0\}) = \frac{3}{38}$
   $P(\{1\}) = \frac{2}{38}$
   $P(\{2\}) = \frac{5}{38}$
   $P(\{a\}) = \frac{20}{38}$
   $P(\{b\}) = \frac{8}{38}$

   (b) P(more than two people waiting) $= P(\{a, b\}) = \frac{28}{38} = \frac{14}{19}$

3. Let R = read report,
   B = bought van

   Since $P((R \cup B)') = .4$, $P(R \cup B) = 1 - P((R \cup B)') = .6$
   $$P(R \cup B) = P(R) + P(B) - P(R \cap B)$$
   $$.6 = .5 + .35 - P(R \cap B)$$

   So, $P(R \cap B) = .25$.

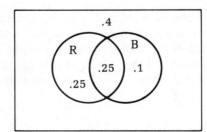

EXERCISES 5.1

In Exercises 1 through 5 decide whether the information defines a probability space.

1. $S = \{a, b, c\}$
   $P(\{a\}) = \frac{2}{5}$
   $P(\{b\}) = \frac{1}{2}$
   $P(\{c\}) = \frac{1}{10}$

2. $S = \{a, b, c, d\}$
   $P(\{a\}) = -\frac{1}{10}$
   $P(\{b\}) = \frac{1}{10}$
   $P(\{c\}) = \frac{1}{2}$
   $P(\{d\}) = \frac{1}{2}$

3. $S = \{a, b, c, d\}$
   $P(\{a\}) = \frac{1}{4}$
   $P(\{b\}) = \frac{1}{4}$
   $P(\{c\}) = \frac{1}{4}$
   $P(\{d\}) = \frac{1}{4}$

4. $S = \{1, 2, c, d\}$
    $P(\{1\}) = 0$
    $P(\{2\}) = \frac{1}{3}$
    $P(\{c\}) = \frac{3}{10}$
    $P(\{d\}) = \frac{2}{5}$

5. $S = \{1, 2, c, d, e\}$
    $P(\{1\}) = 0$
    $P(\{2\}) = \frac{1}{3}$
    $P(\{c\}) = \frac{1}{10}$
    $P(\{d\}) = \frac{2}{5}$
    $P(\{e\}) = \frac{1}{6}$

In Exercises 6, 7, and 8, you are given partial information about some probability space. Fill in the blanks.

6. $S = \{a, b, c\}$
    $P(\{a\}) = \frac{1}{2}$
    $P(\{b\}) = \frac{1}{3}$
    $P(\{c\}) = \_\_$
    $P(\{a, c\}) = \_\_$

7. $S = \{a, b, c, d\}$
    $P(\{a\}) = \frac{1}{12}$
    $P(\{c\}) = \frac{5}{12}$
    $P(\{a, b\}) = \frac{1}{4}$
    $P(\{b\}) = \_\_$
    $P(\{d\}) = \_\_$

8. $S = \{1, 2, a, b\}$
    $P(\{1\}) = \frac{1}{5}$
    $P(\{a\}) = \frac{1}{10}$
    $P(\{1, 2\}) = \frac{1}{2}$
    $P(\{2\}) = \_\_$
    $P(\{b\}) = \_\_$
    $P(\{1, 2, b\}) = \_\_$

In Exercises 9 through 12, information about probability spaces is given by a combination of a Venn diagram and equations. Put probabilities in each unnumbered region and fill in the blanks.

9.

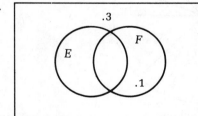

$P(F) = .5$
$P(E \cap F) = _____$

10.

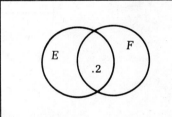

$P(E) = .5$
$P(F') = .4$
$P(E \cup F) = _____$
$P(F) = _____$

11.

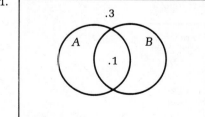

$P(A) = .3$
$P(B) = _____$

12.

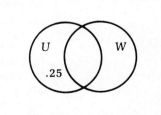

$P(U') = .65$
$P(W) = .45$
$P((U \cup W)') = _____$

13.   If $P(E) = P(F) = .5$ and $P(E \cup F) = .8$, then what is $P(E \cap F)$?

14.   If $P(E \cap F) = .3$, $P(E) = .6$, and $P(F) = .5$, then what is $P(E \cup F)$?

15.   If $P(A \cap V) = .2$, $P(A) = .5$, and $P(A \cup V) = .9$, then what is $P(V)$?

16.   A worker at a car wash counted the number of cars waiting in line to be washed at different times during the day. The table below gives the result.

Number in line	0	1	2	3, 4, or 5	More than 5
Frequency	10	15	9	8	0

(a) What is the probability there is more than one car waiting in line?
(b) What is the probability there are fewer than three cars waiting in line?

17.   The figure below pictures the spinner for a child's game.

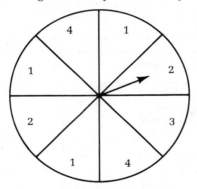

What is the probability the spinner stops when pointing to a region numbered 3 or 4?

18.   Testing of new tires produced at a certain plant shows that 2% of the tires are out of round, 5% have cracks, and 1% have both defects. If one of the tires tested is picked at random, then what is the probability the tire has neither of the defects?

19.   The table below gives the probability a customer's bill at a local supermarket is in the indicated range.

Amount	Probability
Less than $5	.01
$5 to $9.99	.18
$10 to $19.99	.20
$20 to $29.99	.20
$30 to $39.99	.30
$40 to $49.99	.03
$50 to $59.99	.03
$60 or more	.05

(a) What is the probability the bill is less than $30?

(b) What is the probability the bill is $30 or more?

20. The table below gives the results of a study of students taking both calculus and statistics.

		Statistics grade				
		A	B	C	D	F
	A	.05	.09	.01	0	0
Calculus	B	.10	.15	.02	0	0
grade	C	0	.05	.30	.03	.01
	D	0	.01	.06	.05	.01
	F	0	0	.01	.02	.03

The number .03 in row C, column D, of the table indicates 3% of students received a grade of C in calculus and a D in statistics. What is the probability a student gets:

(a) the same grade in both courses?

(b) a lower grade in statistics?

(c) an A in calculus?

21. The traffic light facing the main road into an intersection follows the cycle: green for 60 seconds, yellow for 5 seconds, red for 20 seconds. What is the probability that a driver approaching the intersection along the main road finds the light either green or yellow?

22. A driver approaches the traffic light described in Exercise 21 along the main road and sees the light is green. He decides to go ahead through the intersection whether the light changes or not. If it takes him seven seconds to get through the intersection, then what is the probability he makes it through the intersection before the light turns red?

23. A mathematics class has 35 students. Of these 25 are freshmen, 30 are business majors, and two are neither business majors nor freshmen. What is the probability a person picked at random from the class is a freshman not majoring in business? [Suggestion: Draw a Venn diagram with a circle for freshmen and a circle for business majors. Put numbers in each region corresponding to numbers of students. Divide each number by the total number of students (35) to get probabilities. Read the answer from the diagram.]

24. In a survey of customers at Grey's ice cream store, 87 people liked mocha chip, 35 liked double Dutch chocolate, and 20 liked peppermint. Nine people like both mocha chip and double Dutch chocolate, 7 liked double Dutch and peppermint, 8 liked peppermint and mocha chip, and 5 people liked all three flavors. Everyone surveyed liked at least one flavor.

(a) Draw a Venn diagram with one circle for each flavor.

(b) Fill in the regions with numbers corresponding to responses from the survey.

(c) How many people were surveyed?

(d) Fill in the regions with the corresponding probabilities.

(e) What is the probability a person surveyed likes one, but only one, flavor?

(f) What is the probability a person surveyed liked two of the flavors but not all three?

25. A survey of 50 women and 35 men who drink coffee found 33 people favored decaffeinated coffee and 23 women favored regular coffee. What is the probability a person selected at random from the survey favored regular coffee?

26. Scott Lakis and Janet Murray are on a nine-member board of directors from which four members will be chosen to constitute a planning committee. If the planning committee is chosen at random, then what is the probability the planning committee contains:

(a) neither of these two people?

(b) both Scott and Janet?

(c) one of the two people, but not both?

27. At a national convention, party rules require the credentials committee to have at least two men and at least two women. Suppose the committee will be chosen by selecting five people from a group of eight men and six women.

(a) If 5 people are chosen at random from the group of 14 people, then what is the probability the committee satisfies the rules?

(b) If the committee is chosen at random from among the committees that do satisfy the rules, then what is the probability that the committee has two men and three women?

5.2   *Conditional Probability and Independent Events*

Probabilities can be used to indicate whether two events are related. For example, the incidence of lung cancer is much higher among smokers than in the general population. This difference is used as evidence of a connection between smoking and lung cancer. A probability computed using a subset of the sample space in place of the whole sample space is called a **conditional probability**. The probability that one contracts lung cancer computed using only the set of smokers instead of the general population is an example of a conditional probability. If L represents contracts lung cancer and S represents smoker, then the conditional probability that a smoker gets lung cancer is written $P(L/S)$ and is read: the probability of L given S. If A and B are events and $P(A/B) \neq P(A)$, then this indicates a connection between A and B. The knowledge that the event B has occurred affects the probability that A will occur. On the other hand if $P(A/B) = P(A)$, then A and B are called **independent events**. In this section, we show how to calculate conditional probabilities, and how to compute $P(A \cap B)$ when the events A and B are independent of each other.

We begin with conditional probability.

EXAMPLE 1   In Lakewood 200 voters were asked:

1. Are you a registered Republican?
2. Do you support Garrahy, the Republican candidate for mayor?

The results are given in Figure 5.8, where G stands for Garrahy supporter and R stands for registered Republican.

Figure 5.8

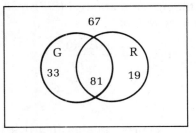

Find:

(a) $P(G)$ = fraction of people surveyed who support Garrahy.
(b) $P(G/R)$ = fraction of Republicans surveyed who support Garrahy.

Of the 200 people surveyed $81 + 33 = 114$ support Garrahy, so

$$P(G) = \frac{114}{200} = .57$$

Of the $81 + 19 = 100$ Republicans surveyed 81 support Garrahy so

$$P(G/R) = \frac{81}{81 + 19} = \frac{81}{100} = .81$$

The survey indicates support for Garrahy is stronger among Republicans than in the general population. ∎

We computed $P(G/R)$ from the Venn diagram in Figure 5.8 by taking the number in the region $G \cap R$ divided by the sum of the numbers in circle R. If we follow this procedure when the numbers in Figure 5.8 are replaced by probabilities (see Figure 5.9), then we still get $P(G/R)$.

Figure 5.9

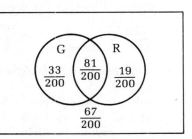

$$\frac{\dfrac{81}{200}}{\dfrac{81}{200} + \dfrac{19}{200}} = \left(\frac{81}{200}\right)\left(\frac{200}{81 + 19}\right) = \frac{81}{100} = .81 = P(G/R) = \frac{P(G \cap R)}{P(R)}$$

DEFINITION   The conditional probability, $P(E/F)$, read probability of E given F, is given by the equation:

(1) $$P(E/F) = \frac{P(E \cap F)}{P(F)}$$

EXAMPLE 2

A recent issue of *Consumer Reports* contains an article rating van-wagons. A car dealer wants to know whether people who read the report are more likely to buy its model of the van-wagon. Figure 5.10 illustrates the result of a survey of people inquiring about the dealer's van-wagon.

Figure 5.10

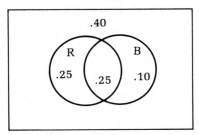

R = Read article in *Consumer Reports*
B = Bought the dealer's van–wagon

Find:

(a) $P(B)$.
(b) $P(B/R)$.

$$P(B) = .25 + .10 = .35$$

Thirty-five percent of those surveyed bought the dealer's van-wagon.

$$P(B/R) = \frac{P(B \cap R)}{P(R)} = \frac{.25}{.25 + .25} = \frac{.25}{.50} = .50$$

Fifty percent of the inquiries from people who had read the article resulted in sales.

The survey indicates people are more likely to buy the dealer's van-wagon if they have read the article. As a result, the dealer gives a copy of the *Consumer Reports* article to everyone inquiring about the van-wagon.

PRACTICE
EXAMPLE 1

The Venn diagram in Figure 5.11 gives the result of a survey designed to tell whether students who take a college algebra course do better in calculus.

Figure 5.11

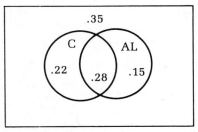

C = Student gets an A or B in calculus
AL = Student takes college algebra course

Find the probability that:

(a) a student gets an A or B in calculus.
(b) a student who takes the college algebra course gets an A or B in calculus.

Intuitively, two events, E and F, are considered independent if they have no influence on each other. For example if you flip a penny and a dime and set E = penny lands heads up, and F = dime lands tails up, then E and F are independent. Mathematically, events E and F are called independent if $P(E/F)$ equals $P(E)$. If we can assume E and F are independent, then $P(E \cap F)$ can be computed from $P(E)$ and $P(F)$, without knowning $P(E/F)$ or $P(F/E)$.

EXAMPLE 3

Mrs. Wilson visits two doctors, Dr. Johnson and Dr. Beekman, for a diagnosis. If Dr. Johnson correctly diagnoses diseases 92% of the time and Dr. Beekman 95% of the time, then (assuming that the doctors act independently of each other) what is the probability:

(a) both doctors correctly diagnose the disease?
(b) at least one of the two doctors gives a correct diagnosis?

Let

$$J = \text{Dr. Johnson gives a correct diagnosis}$$

$$B = \text{Dr. Beekman gives a correct diagnosis}$$

We are given

$$J \text{ and } B \text{ are independent}$$

$$P(J) = .92$$

$$P(B) = .95$$

and are asked to find:

(a) $P(J \cap B)$.
(b) $P(J \cup B)$.

To find $P(J \cap B)$ we use the independence of J and B, and the formula:

$$P(J/B) = \frac{P(J \cap B)}{P(B)}$$

$$.92 = P(J) = P(J/B) = \frac{P(J \cap B)}{P(B)} = \frac{P(J \cap B)}{.95}$$

Thus

$$P(J \cap B) = (.92)(.95) = .874.$$

Both doctors diagnose the disease correctly 87.4% of the time.

$$P(J \cup B) = P(J) + P(B) - P(J \cap B)$$

$$= .92 + .95 - .874$$

$$= .996$$

At least one of the two doctors gives the correct diagnosis 99.6% of the time.

We solved part (a) of Example 3 by first using the assumption that J and B are independent to replace $P(J/B)$ with $P(J)$ in the equation

$$P(J/B) = \frac{P(J \cap B)}{P(B)},$$

and then solving for $P(J \cap B)$.

In general, if E and F are independent, then

$$\frac{P(E \cap F)}{P(F)} = P(E/F) = P(E)$$

so

$$P(E \cap F) = P(E) P(F).$$

If E and F are *independent*, then

(2) $P(E \cap F) = P(E) P(F)$

EXAMPLE 4   Suppose a home fire alarm, the Safety Plus, sounds when there is a fire in 95 out of 100 cases. If two Safety Plus alarms are installed and act independently, then what is the probability at least one of the alarms sounds when there is a fire?

Let

$$I = \text{first alarm sounds}$$

$$II = \text{second alarm sounds}$$

I and II are independent so

$$P(I \cap II) = P(I) P(II) = (.95) (.95) = .9025$$

and

$$P(I \cup II) = P(I) + P(II) - P(I \cap II)$$

$$= .95 + .95 - .9025$$

$$= .9975 \qquad \blacksquare$$

PRACTICE EXAMPLE 2 The security check at a military base consists of a credentials check and a signature test. Suppose the probability of forged credentials passing the credentials check is .001, the probability of successfully forging a signature is .002, and the credentials check is independent of the signature test. What is the probability an unauthorized person passes both checks? $\blacksquare$

The formula $P(E \cap F) = (P(E) P(F))$ for independent events can be extended to any number of independent events.

If $E_1 \ldots E_k$ are independent events, then

$$(3) \qquad P(E_1 \cap E_2 \cap \cdots \cap E_k) = P(E_1) P(E_2) \cdots P(E_k)$$

EXAMPLE 5 For a certain home computer the probability that the monitor does not need repair during the first year is .99, the probability that the disk drive does not need repair during the first year is .95, and the probability that the remaining parts of the system do not need repair during the first year is .98. What is the probability the system does not need repair during the first year? Let

$$M = \text{Monitor does not need repair.}$$

$$D = \text{Disk drive does not need repair.}$$

$$O = \text{All other parts do not need repair.}$$

Assuming M, D, and O are independent,

$$P(M \cap D \cap O) = P(M) P(D) P(O) = (.99) (.95) (.98) = .92169 \qquad \blacksquare$$

PRACTICE
EXAMPLE 3   In the game of Monopoly, if you roll doubles three times in a row on a pair of dice, then you go to jail. What is the probability of rolling doubles three times in a row?   ■

    The original impetus for a systematic study of chance occurrences came from gambling. In 1654, Chevalier de Méré observed a game in which a player bet the house he could roll a single die four times without getting a six. Everyone knew this game favored the house. (See Exercise 17.) De Méré wondered how the odds changed when the single die is replaced by a pair of dice and a single occurrence of six with double sixes. Suppose you bet the house you will not roll double sixes. If you roll a pair of dice just once then you are likely to win. However the more times you roll the dice, the less likely you are to win. De Méré's question is: How many times must the dice be rolled in order to favor the house? You have the tools to answer De Méré's question (see Exercise 19).

    We end this section with a discussion of Bernoulli trials.

EXAMPLE 6   Suppose you roll a single die seven times.

(a) What is the probability a one lands on top on the first, fourth, and sixth rolls but not on any of the other rolls?
(b) What is the probability a one occurs on exactly three of the seven rolls?

    Let

$$S_i = \text{a one occurs on the } i\text{th roll}$$

$$F_i = \text{a one does not occur on the } i\text{th roll.}$$

    The event that one lands on top on the first, fourth, and sixth rolls, but not on any other roll is $S_1 \cap F_2 \cap F_3 \cap S_4 \cap F_5 \cap S_6 \cap F_7$. These are independent events so,

$$P(S_1 \cap F_2 \cap F_3 \cap S_4 \cap F_5 \cap S_6 \cap F_7) = \left(\frac{1}{6}\right)\left(\frac{5}{6}\right)\left(\frac{5}{6}\right)\left(\frac{1}{6}\right)\left(\frac{5}{6}\right)\left(\frac{1}{6}\right)\left(\frac{5}{6}\right)$$

$$= \frac{625}{279936}$$

$$= .0022327$$

    To answer (b) we indicate the result of seven throws by writing a word of length 7 in the letters S and F.

    SFFFSFS, for example, corresponds to a one occurring on the first, fifth, and seventh rolls but not on any of the other rolls. There are $C(7, 3) = 35$ words with three S's and four F's. As you can see from the computation used to answer part (a), each of these 35 words occurs with probability 625/279936. Thus the probability of rolling exactly three one's in seven rolls of the die is:

$$\frac{35(625)}{279936} = .0781429$$ ■

Rolling a die seven times and recording on each roll whether a one lands on top is an example of a sequence of Bernoulli trials.

> DEFINITION   A sequence of experiments is called a sequence of **Bernoulli trials** if
> 1. The outcomes of each trial are divided into two sets: S and F = S′. (S will be called success and F failure.)
> 2. $P(S)$ is the same for all trials.
> 3. The trials are independent.

For a sequence of Bernoulli trials the probability of exactly k successes in N trials is

(4) $P(k \text{ successes in } N \text{ trials}) = C(N, k)(P(S))^k (P(F))^{N-k}$

where $C(N, 0) = 1$.

EXAMPLE 7

Suppose 20% of the management trainees hired by the Dairy Food Corporation leave the company within five years, and the company has hired 10 new trainees. What is the probability that fewer than 3 of the new trainees leave the company within five years?

This is a Bernoulli trial with

$$S = \text{trainee leaves within five years}$$

$$F = \text{trainee does not leave within five years}$$

$$P(S) = .2$$

$$P(F) = .8$$

Applying formula (4) we get

$P(\text{none leave}) = C(10, 0)(.2)^0(.8)^{10} = (.8)^{10} = .1073742$

$P(\text{1 trainee leaves}) = C(10, 1)(.2)^1(.8)^9 = .2684355$

$P(\text{2 leave}) = C(10, 2)(.2)^2(.8)^8 = \dfrac{(10)9}{(2)1}(.2)^2(.8)^8 = .3019899$

$P(\text{fewer than 3 leave}) = .1073742 + .2684355 + .3019899 = .6777996$

**PRACTICE
EXAMPLE 4**

A printing press produces an average of 3 defective pages out of every 150. Find the probability that a 12-page pamphlet has

(a) no defective pages.
(b) fewer than 2 defective pages.

CONCEPTS

conditional probability
independent events
Bernoulli trials

SOLUTIONS TO PRACTICE EXAMPLES

1. (a) $P(C) = .22 + .28 = .5$

    (b) $P(C/AL) = \dfrac{P(C \cap AL)}{P(AL)} = \dfrac{.28}{.43} = .6512$

2. $(.001)(.002) = .000002$

3. The probability of rolling doubles on one throw of a pair of dice is $\frac{6}{36} = \frac{1}{6}$.
    $P(\text{doubles three times in a row}) = (\frac{1}{6})(\frac{1}{6})(\frac{1}{6}) = \frac{1}{216} = .00463$

4. This is a Bernoulli trial with

    $$S = \text{page is defective}$$
    $$F = \text{page is not defective}$$
    $$P(S) = \tfrac{3}{150} = .02$$
    $$P(F) = 1 - .02 = .98$$

    (a) $P(\text{no defective pages in 12-page pamphlet}) = C(12, 0)(.02)^0(.98)^{12}$
    $$= (.98)^{12} = .7847$$

    (b) $P(\text{fewer than two defective pages}) = P(\text{no defective pages}) + P(\text{1 defective page})$
    $$= .7847 + C(12, 1)(.02)^1(.98)^{11}$$
    $$= .9769$$

EXERCISES 5.2

1. If $P(F) = .8$ and $P(E \cap F) = .6$, then what is $P(E/F)$?

2. If $P(B) = .5$ and $P(A/B) = .2$, then what is $P(A \cap B)$?

3. The table below gives the result of testing a dollar-bill changer with 200 one-dollar bills, 50 of them counterfeit.

		Machine	
		A	R
Bill	L	118	32
	C	2	48

where

$$A = \text{Machine accepts the bill}$$
$$R = \text{Machine rejects the bill}$$
$$L = \text{The bill is legal}$$
$$C = \text{The bill is counterfeit}$$

Find:

(a) the probability that the machine accepts a counterfeit bill.

(b) P(L/A) = probability that a bill accepted by the machine is legal.

(c) P(A/L).

(d) P(C/R).

4. To test the effectiveness of a new drug, conventional treatment was given to 200 people and the new drug to another 200 people. The result is given in the table below.

	C	N
D	136	64
T	124	76

where

$$D = \text{Patient receives new drug}$$
$$T = \text{Patient receives conventional treatment}$$
$$C = \text{Patient is cured}$$
$$N = \text{Patient is not cured}$$

What is the probability that:

(a) a patient chosen at random from among the 400 is cured, P(C)?

(b) a patient given the new drug is cured, P(C/D)?

5. The owner of Jack's Antiques conducted a survey to see if people who come in and ask questions are more likely to make a purchase than the average customer. The results are pictured below in the Venn diagram.

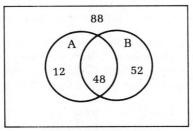

B = Buys something
A = Asks questions

(a) What is the probability that a person entering the store buys something?

(b) What is the probability a person who asks questions buys something?

(d) Is a person who asks questions more likely to buy something than the average person entering the store?

6. Are E and F independent if $P(E \cap F) = .2$, $P(E) = .3$, and $P(F) = .5$?

7. If E and F are independent, $P(E) = .6$, and $P(F) = .8$ then what is $P(E \cap F)$?

8. If E and F are independent, $P(E) = .9$, and $P(E \cap F) = .3$ then what is $P(F)$?

9. If E, F, and G are independent, $P(E) = .8$, $P(F) = .5$, and $P(G) = .6$, then what is $P(E \cap F \cap G)$?

10. A hospital has a backup electric generator for use when the electricity is out. If $P(\text{electricity is out}) = \frac{1}{500}$, $P(\text{backup generator fails}) = \frac{1}{20}$, and these events are independent, then what is the probability that the electricity is out and the backup generator fails?

11. A company makes two home burglar alarms—Home Alert and Home Security. The Home Alert System detects break-ins with probability .99. The Home Security system detects break-ins with probability .999 and costs twice as much as the Home Alert. A person is considering installing either two Home Alert systems that will act independently or one Home Security System. Which choice gives greater protection against burglars?

12. People seeking admission to a high security laboratory must pass a credentials check, voice pattern test, and handwriting check before being admitted. The probability of an unauthorized person passing the credentials check is .01, for the voice test the probability is .005, and for the handwriting test the probability is .04. Assuming the tests are independent, what is the probability an unauthorized person passes all tests?

13. Two machines, acting independently, test parts for defects. Both machines identify a defective part with probability .9. What is the probability that a defective part goes undetected through both machines?

14. A sales representative makes a sale in one out of every five calls.

(a) What is the probability the representative makes at least one sale in two calls? (Suggestion: find the probability of not making any sales and subtract this from one to get the probability of making at least one sale.)

(b) How many calls does the representative have to make in order for the probability of making at least one sale to be greater than one half?

15. A long-life light bulb has a probability .08 of burning out within the first 2000 hours of use. Suppose we want to light a corridor with long-life bulbs so that the probability of at least one of the lights lasting for 2000 hours is greater than .9999. If the light bulbs burn independently, how many bulbs are needed?

16. Suppose a coin is flipped three times.

(a) What is the probability the coin lands heads up all three times?

(b) If the coin lands heads up on the first two flips, then what is the probability it lands heads up on the third flip as well?

17. What is the probability that in four rolls of a die a six never occurs?

18. Suppose you bet that in four rolls of a pair of dice you will never roll double sixes. What is the probability that you win?

19. Suppose you roll a pair of dice several times. If a double six occurs on any roll, you lose. If double six does not occur on any of the rolls, you win.
    (a) Fill in the table:

Number of rolls of a pair of dice	Probability you win	Probability you lose
1		
10		
20		
30		

    (b) Using the answer to (a) as a starting point find the smallest number of times the dice have to be rolled in order for the probability of your losing to be greater than the probability of your winning.

20. Suppose that in a sequence of Bernoulli trials, $P(S) = .8$, $P(F) = .2$. Find the probability of:

    (a) no successes in three trials.

    (b) all successes in three trials.

    (c) exactly two successes in three trials.

21. Suppose that in a sequence of Bernoulli trials, $P(S) = \frac{3}{4}$, $P(F) = \frac{1}{4}$. Find the probability of:

    (a) exactly three successes in five trials.

    (b) more than three successes in five trials.

    (c) more than one success in five trials.

22. Five percent of the tapes produced by a machine are defective. What is the probability that a sample of three tapes contains

    (a) no defective tapes?

    (b) one defective tape?

    (c) two defective tapes?

    (d) three defective tapes?

23. One percent of the microchips produced by a company have defects. What is the probability that a sample of 25 microchips contains

    (a) fewer than three defective chips?

    (b) more than two defective chips?

24. Suppose 15 carrot seeds are planted and each seed has probability .8 of growing, .2 of dying. What is the probability that 13 or more of the seeds grow?

25. A person who answers true-false questions by guessing is correct with probability .5. What is the probability that a person who guesses the answer to each of 10 true-false questions gets 8 or more of them correct?

26. In a test for extrasensory perception four cards, one with a circle, one with a star, one with a cross, and one with a heart, are placed face down on a table. The person being tested is asked to point out the heart card. What is the probability that a person who just guesses each time can correctly point out the heart card in exactly 8 of 10 trials of this experiment?

27. The normal success rate for treatment of a certain disease is 50%. Dr. Calder developed a new treatment that is no more or less effective than the normal treatment. What is the probability that Dr. Calder's treatment is successful for

(a) 8 patients when the drug is tested on a group of 10 patients?

(b) more than 7 patients when the drug is tested on 10 patients?

(c) more than 15 patients when the drug is tested on a group of 20 patients?

28. Suppose that for each question on a test Sam has an 80% chance of answering the question correctly. What is the probability that on a 10-question test Sam answers

(a) 8 questions correctly?

(b) 9 questions correctly?

(c) all 10 questions correctly?

(d) 8 or more questions correctly?

29. Suppose that in Chicago 60% of the people favor a new housing bill and 40% are opposed. What is the probability that a random sample of five people in Chicago contains three or more people opposed to the bill?

30. A wine taster claims a 90% success rate in correctly naming the region a wine comes from after tasting the wine. To test this claim the taster is given 10 glasses of wine and asked to name the region corresponding to each wine. It is necessary to get 9 or more correct to pass the test. What is the probability the taster fails even though the claim of a 90% success rate is valid?

5.3   *Probability Trees—Bayes' Theorem*

In this section we introduce probability trees and show how they can be used to answer such questions as: What disease is causing the patients symptoms? Who is most likely to be elected given the results of the latest poll? What artist painted this picture? In Chapter 10 probability trees are combined with matrix theory to study Markov chains.

We begin with an example of a probability tree.

EXAMPLE 1   Of the tax returns submitted to the Internal Revenue Service, some are fraudulent, and some are audited. The numbers on the edges in Figure 5.12

are interpreted as follows:

.02 = P(A): 2% of the tax returns are audited

.98 = P(A'): 98% of the tax returns are not audited

.83 = P(F/A): 83% of the audited returns are fraudulent

.17 = P(F'/A): 17% of the audited returns are not fraudulent

.15 = P(F/A'): 15% of the returns not audited are fraudulent

.85 = P(F'/A'): 85% of the returns not audited are not fraudulent

Figure 5.12

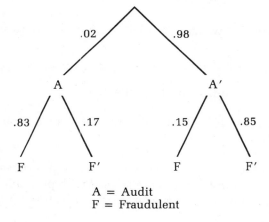

A = Audit
F = Fraudulent

The tree in Figure 5.12 is a probability tree. This tree is a rooted tree whose root is the unlabeled vertex. The product of the numbers along a path from the root to a leaf (vertex of degree one [see Section 3.1]) can also be interpreted as a probability. For example, the path from the root to A then to F gives the product (.02)(.83). This product is the probability of A $\cap$ F.

$$(.02)(.83) = P(A) P(F/A) = P(A) \frac{P(A \cap F)}{P(A)} = P(A \cap F) = .0166$$

Similarly,

$$(.02)(.17) = P(A \cap F') = .0034$$

$$(.98)(.15) = P(A' \cap F) = .147$$

$$(.98)(.85) = P(A' \cap F') = .833$$

Labeling the tree in Figure 5.12 with these products, we get the tree in Figure 5.13.

Figure 5.13

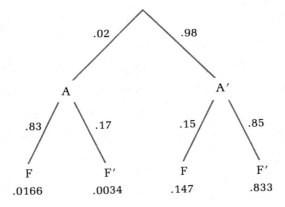

From Figure 5.13 we can find the percentage of returns that are fraudulent as follows:

$$P(F) = P(A \cap F) + P(A' \cap F) = .0166 + .147 = .1636$$

16.36% of the tax returns are fraudulent.

PRACTICE EXAMPLE 1

Use the numbers in Figure 5.13 to find the percentage of returns that are not fraudulent.

The tree in Figure 5.12 is a rooted tree. All the vertices but the root are labeled by events, and the edges are labeled with probabilities according to the scheme indicated in Figure 5.14. A tree with these properties is called a **probability tree**.

Figure 5.14

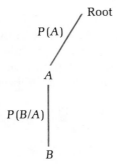

The next examples indicate general situations in which a probability tree can be used to compute probabilities.

EXAMPLE 2

A machine checks parts coming off a production line. Suppose 7% of the parts are defective, 93% are good, and the machine either accepts a part as good or rejects the part as defective. The machine correctly identifies a defective part 95% of the time and correctly identifies a good part 99% of the time. (Note: 5% of the defective parts are incorrectly accepted and 1% of the good parts are incorrectly rejected.) The probability tree in Figure 5.15 displays this information.

Figure 5.15

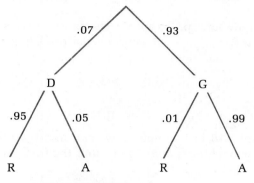

D = Part is defective
G = Part is good
R = Machine rejects the part
A = Machine accepts the part

Find:

(a) $P(A)$.
(b) $P(R)$.

STEP 1: Label each leaf with the product of the numbers on the edges of the path from the root to the leaf. This gives Figure 5.16.

Figure 5.16

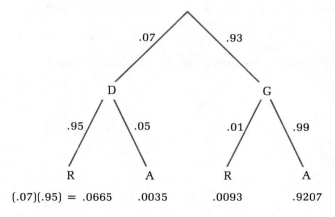

STEP 2: Find the probabilities of A and R using these products as follows:

$$P(A) = P(D \cap A) + P(G \cap A) = .0035 + .9207 = .9242$$

92.42% of the parts are accepted by the machine.

$$P(R) = P(D \cap R) + P(G \cap R) = .0665 + .0093 = .0758$$

7.58% of the parts are rejected by the machine. Note that since R = A′ we can also get the answer to (b) by subtracting .9242 from 1:

$$P(R) = 1 - P(A) = 1 - .9242 = .0758$$ ■

Next we show how probability trees can be used to find conditional probabilities. In Example 1, we can find the probability that a fraudulent return is audited from Figure 5.13.

$$P(\text{fraudulent return is audited}) = P(A/F) = \frac{P(A \cap F)}{P(F)} = \frac{.0166}{.0166 + .147}$$

$$= .1014669$$

From Figure 5.16 in Example 2, we can find the fraction of the parts accepted by the machine that are good, and the fraction that are defective.

$$P(G/A) = \frac{P(G \cap A)}{P(A)} = \frac{.9207}{.9207 + .0035} = .9962129$$

More than 99.6% of the parts accepted by the machine are good.

$$P(D/A) = \frac{P(D \cap A)}{P(A)} = \frac{.0035}{.9242} = .003787$$

Less than .4% of the parts accepted by the machine are defective.

PRACTICE EXAMPLE 2

At a certain plant the probability a worker makes an error is .1. Fifteen percent of the worker errors lead to accidents, the remaining 85% do not lead to accidents. The probability of an accident, given there is no worker error, is .01. Use this information to add probabilities to the tree in Figure 5.17. Find the probability of

(a) an accident.
(b) worker error given that an accident occurs.

Figure 5.17

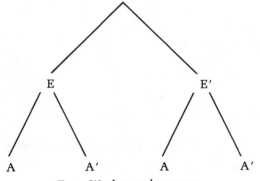

E = Worker makes error
E′ = No worker error
A = Accident
A′ = No accident

■

The next example illustrates how probability trees can help make a diagnosis.

EXAMPLE 3   People with a cold or the flu will have one of the combinations of symptoms FS = {fever, stuffed nose}, F = {fever}, S = {stuffed nose}. Use the probability tree in Figure 5.18 to find the probability that a person with a stuffed nose but no fever has a cold.

Figure 5.18

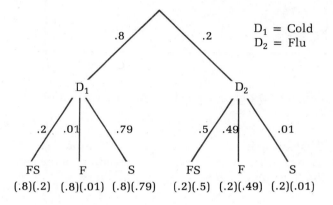

$$P(D_1/S) = \frac{P(D_1 \cap S)}{P(S)} = \frac{(.8)(.79)}{(.8)(.79) + (.2)(.01)} = \frac{.632}{.632 + .002} = \frac{.632}{.634} = .9968454$$

More than 99.6% of the people with symptoms of stuffed nose but no fever have a cold. ■

PRACTICE EXAMPLE 3   Use the probability tree in Figure 5.18 to find the probability that a person with only a fever has the flu. ■

If we replace each of the numbers in the above equation with its corresponding probability symbol (e.g., replace .8 with $P(D_1)$, .79 with $P(S/D_1)$, .2 with $P(D_2)$, and .01 with $P(S/D_2)$) then we get the following equation, a particular instance of Bayes' theorem.

$$P(D_1/S) = \frac{P(D_1)\, P(S/D_1)}{P(D_1)\, P(S/D_1) + P(D_2)\, P(S/D_2)}$$

Bayes' theorem, first published in 1763, computes the probability of a "cause" (flu or cold in Example 3) on the basis of the observed "effect" (the "effect" in Example 3 is the symptom, S). To state Bayes' theorem we need to define a partition of a set.

A collection $\{A_1, \cdots A_k\}$ of subsets of a set, S, is called a **partition** of S if each element of S is in exactly one of the sets A_j. In set notation:

$$A_1 \cup \cdots \cup A_k = S \qquad \text{and} \qquad A_i \cap A_j = \varnothing$$

whenever $i \neq j$.

Figure 5.19

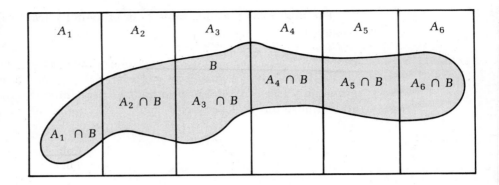

Figure 5.19 shows a set, S, and a partition of S,

$$S = A_1 \cup A_2 \cup A_3 \cup \cdots \cup A_k$$

If B is any subset of S, then the collection $\{A_1 \cap B, \cdots A_k \cap B\}$ is a partition of B. The probability of an event, B, is the sum of the probabilities of the outcomes in B so

(1) $$P(B) = P(A_1 \cap B) + \cdots + P(A_k \cap B)$$

In Example 3, the partition is the collection of diseases $\{D_1, D_2\}$, and the symptom, S, corresponds to the event, B, pictured in Figure 5.19.

> **BAYES' THEOREM** Let S be the sample space of a probability space and let $\{A_1, \cdots A_k\}$ be a partition of S. Then for any event, B, and any one of the events A_j, $P(A_j/B)$ satisfies
>
> (2) $$P(A_j/B) = \frac{P(A_j)P(B/A_j)}{P(A_1)P(B/A_1) + \cdots + P(A_k)P(B/A_k)}$$

A proof of Bayes' theorem is outlined in the exercises.

EXAMPLE 4   A company has plants in Pennsylvania, New Jersey, and Connecticut that produce 20%, 35%, and 45% of the company's output of TV sets. The percentages of output that are defective are $\frac{1}{2}$%, 1%, and 1.5%. Use Bayes' theorem to find the probability that a set that is found to be defective was made in the New Jersey plant.

The sample space, S, is the collection of TV sets made by the company. Let A_1, A_2, A_3, and D be the events:

$$A_1 = \text{set was made in Pennsylvania}$$

$$A_2 = \text{set was made in New Jersey}$$

$$A_3 = \text{set was made in Connecticut}$$

$$D = \text{set is defective}$$

Each TV set was made at one and only one of the three plants, so $\{A_1, A_2, A_3\}$ is a partition of the sample space. Substituting the values:

$$P(A_1) = .2 \qquad P(A_2) = .35 \qquad P(A_3) = .45$$

$$P(D/A_1) = .005 \qquad P(D/A_2) = .01 \qquad P(D/A_3) = .015$$

into the formula in Bayes' theorem gives:

$$P(A_2/D) = \frac{P(A_2)\,P(D/A_2)}{P(A_1)\,P(D/A_1) + P(A_2)\,P(D/A_2) + P(A_3)\,P(D/A_3)}$$

$$= \frac{(.35)(.01)}{(.2)(.005) + (.35)(.01) + (.45)(.015)}$$

$$= \frac{.0035}{.001 + .0035 + .00675} = \frac{.0035}{.01125} = .3111111$$

Roughly 31% of the defective sets were made in New Jersey.

As we have indicated in the examples, probability trees and Bayes' theorem can be used to assign probabilities to various possible causes or consequences of an event such as: Given the symptoms, what is the disease (cause)? Given the latest poll, who will be elected (consequence)? Bayes' theorem was used to investigate authorship of the *Federalist Papers* (Mosteller and Wallace 1964). Alexander Hamilton, John Jay, and James Madison published the *Federalist Papers* in 1787–88 under the pen name Publius. No assignment of specific papers to authors occurred until 1807, three years after Hamilton's death from a duel with Aaron Burr. There is general agreement as to the authors of 70 of the papers. Of the remaining 15 papers, 3 appear to be joint works. The remaining 12 were examined by Mosteller and Wallace. The political content of a Federalist paper is not considered convincing proof of authorship since the purpose of the *Federalist Papers* was not to present the authors' views, but to persuade the voters in New York State they should ratify the Constitution. Mosteller and Wallace used a Bayes' model to assign a probability of authorship to each of the three possible authors for each of the 12 papers. The conclusion they reached is that it is extremely likely that Madison wrote all of the disputed papers. The weakest evidence is for paper number 55 for which their model assigns a probability of .987 to Madison's authorship.

CONCEPTS

probability trees
Bayes' theorem

SOLUTIONS TO PRACTICE EXAMPLES

1. $P(F') = .0034 + .833 = .8364$

2. (a) $P(A) = .015 + .009 = .024$
    (b) $P(E/A) = (.015)/(.024) = .625$

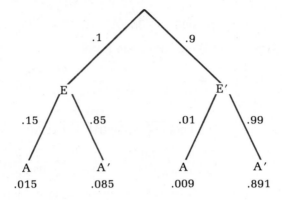

3. $P(F/S_2) = \dfrac{.098}{.008 + .098} = \dfrac{.098}{.106} = .9245$

EXERCISES 5.3

Use the probability tree in Figure 5.20 to do Exercises 1 through 6.

Figure 5.20

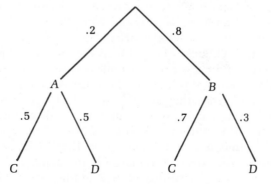

Find:

1. $P(C)$.
2. $P(D)$.
3. $P(A/C)$.
4. $P(B/C)$.
5. $P(A/D)$.
6. $P(B/D)$.

Use the probability tree in Figure 5.21 to do Exercises 7 through 15.

Figure 5.21

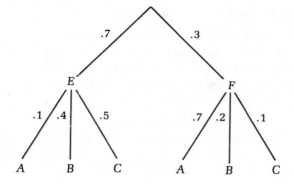

Find:

7. $P(A)$.

8. $P(B)$.

9. $P(C)$.

10. $P(E/B)$.

11. $P(F/A)$.

12. $P(E/C)$.

13. $P(F/B)$.

14. $P(E/A)$.

15. $P(F/C)$.

16. A machine checks parts coming off a production line for defects. Ten percent of the parts coming off the line are defective. The machine checks each part and either rejects the part as defective or accepts the part as good. The machine correctly rejects 80% of the defective parts and correctly accepts 99% of the good parts.

(a) What fraction of the parts are accepted by the machine?

(b) What fraction of the parts accepted by the machine are defective?

17. All shirts made by a clothing company are inspected by hand before being sold. Ninety-eight percent of the shirts given to the inspectors have no defects. The remaining 2% have some defect. The inspectors correctly identify 70% of the defective shirts. A good shirt always passes inspection. Find:

(a) the fraction of shirts that pass inspection.

(b) the probability that a shirt that passes inspection has a defect.

18. A screening test for tuberculosis has the following properties: 20% of those taking the test have tuberculosis; the remaining 80% do not have tuberculosis; 90% of those with tuberculosis have a positive reaction to the test (the test indicates they have tuberculosis); 75% of those who do not have tuberculosis have a negative reaction to the test. Find the probability that a person

(a) has a positive reaction to the test.

(b) has tuberculosis given they have a positive reaction to the test.

(c) has tuberculosis given they have a negative reaction to the test.

19. People with a positive reaction to the screening test for tuberculosis described in Exercise 18 take a more thorough diagnostic test. Suppose that half the people who take the diagnostic test have tuberculosis and half do not. The diagnostic test correctly detects tuberculosis in 98% of the patients who have tuberculosis and correctly finds no tuberculosis in 99% of the patients who

have no tuberculosis. Find the probability that

(a) the results of the diagnostic test are correct.

(b) a person has tuberculosis given the diagnostic test indicates he has tuberculosis.

(c) a person does not have tuberculosis given the diagnostic test indicates he does not have tuberculosis.

20. At a certain plant the probability a worker makes an error is .1. Half the time worker error leads to an accident, half the time it does not. The probability of an accident given there is no worker error is .01. Find the probability of worker error given that an accident has occurred.

21. A company drilling for oil finds oil 10% of the time and fails to find oil the other 90% of the time. While drilling, the company finds a special rock formation below the surface. From past experience, it is known that when there is oil 70% of the time this rock formation is also present. When there is no oil this rock formation occurs only 20% of the time. What is the probability of finding oil given that the rock formation is present?

22. To test a new lie detector for accuracy, people are asked to sometimes tell the truth and sometimes lie. Suppose that 90% of the lies were correctly identified as lies by the machine and 4% of the true statements were incorrectly identified by the machine as lies. Assuming that people taking the lie detector test lie half the time, what is the probability that

(a) a person is lying given the machine indicates a lie?

(b) a person is telling the truth given the machine indicates the truth?

23. A poll was made of 100 Democrats, 100 Republicans, and 100 Independents in order to project a winner in the race for district representative. The results are given in the table below.

	R	D	I
Andrews	15	90	48
Wilson	85	10	52

Thirty percent of the voters in the district are Democrats, 50% are Republicans, and 20% are Independents. Based on the poll and distribution of voters by party, who will win the election?

24. To test the reliability of a new calculus placement test, students were given the test before taking calculus. All students who took the test then took calculus. Eighty percent of the students passed calculus. Of those who passed calculus, 99% passed the placement test. Of those who failed calculus, 5% passed the placement test. Find the probability that

(a) a person who passes the placement test passes calculus.

(b) a person who fails the placement test fails calculus.

25. A placement test is given to all freshmen who sign up for calculus. People who fail the placement test must take an algebra course before going on to calculus. Suppose 98% of those who pass the test also pass calculus, while 90% of those who fail the placement test pass calculus after taking algebra. If 80% of those taking the placement test pass the test, then

    (a) what fraction pass calculus when they take the course?
    (b) what is the probability that someone who fails calculus also failed the placement test and hence took an algebra course first?

26. In the probability tree in the figure below the D's represent diseases and the S's are symptoms.

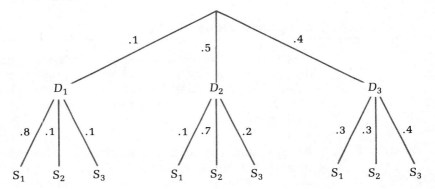

    Find:

    (a) $P(D_1/S_1)$.
    (b) $P(D_2/S_2)$.
    (c) $P(D_3/S_3)$.

27. One of two coins is picked at random. One coin is fair, the other has two heads. The selected coin is flipped and lands heads up each time. Find the probability the coin is the two-headed coin if the coin was flipped

    (a) once.
    (b) three times.
    (c) five times.

28. Each of three identical chests has two drawers. One chest has a penny in each drawer, one chest has a nickel in each drawer, and the third chest has a penny in one drawer and a nickel in the other. A chest is selected at random and a drawer of the chest opened. If the opened drawer has a penny in it, then what is the probability the chest selected is the one with a penny in each drawer?

29. In this exercise you will prove Bayes' theorem. The assumptions are

    (a) S is the sample space of a probability space.
    (b) $\{A_1 \cdots A_k\}$ is a partition of S.
    (c) B is an event (a subset of S).

Let A_j be any one of the sets in the partition $\{A_1 \cdots A_k\}$, prove

$$P(A_j/B) = \frac{P(A_j)\,P(B/A_j)}{P(A_1)\,P(B/A_1) + \cdots + P(A_k)\,P(B/A_k)}$$

by starting with the equation

$$P(A_j/B) = \frac{P(A_j \cap B)}{P(B)}$$

and then changing the right-hand side. First, use Equation (1) of this section, and then the formula $P(E \cap F) = P(E)\,P(F/E)$.

5.4   Expected Value

In order to set a price for a policy, an insurance company needs to predict the profit per policy at various selling prices. An oil company choosing among several drilling sites wants to know the profit it can expect to make at each of these sites. In this section we will show how to make such predictions.

EXAMPLE 1

At most airports there is a machine or desk where you can buy flight insurance. Suppose a $100,000 policy costs $1 and there are 27 deaths for every 10 million passengers. On the average, how much can the insurance company expect to make for each policy it sells?

The company makes $1 when no death occurs. If death occurs, then the company takes in $1 and pays out $100,000 for a loss of $99,999. For every 10 million policies sold the company can expect to take in one dollar, 9,999,973 times and lose $99,999, 27 times. The result is a gain of ($1)(9,999,973) + (−$99,999)(27) = $7,300,000 for 10 million policies. Dividing by 10 million gives an average expected gain of $.73 per policy. ∎

EXAMPLE 2

The $100,000 Give Away has one grand prize of $100,000 and 99 prizes of $100 each. If the Give Away sends letters to one million people, how much can you expect to gain by responding?

If you win the $100,000 prize your gain is the prize money minus the cost of the stamp you used to find out whether you are a winner. If a stamp costs $.22, then the net gain in this case is $99,999.78. If you win one of the $100 prizes your gain is $99.78. If you do not win a prize, then you have lost the price of a stamp. The gain is − $.22. The expected gain from responding can be found by multiplying each possible gain by the probability that the gain occurs and taking the sum of these products. As illustrated in Table 5.1, you can expect to lose an average of slightly more than $.11 every time you respond to a promotion like the Give Away. If a large group of people share both the expense of sending entries to the contest and the winnings, then the group should expect to pay about $.11 for each entry the group sends in.

TABLE 5.1

Gain	Probability	Product
99,999.78	1/1,000,000	.0999997
99.78	99/1,000,000	.0098782
−.22	(999,900)/1,000,000	−.219978

Total = −.1101001

Examples 1 and 2 are special cases of the general situation where you are given a probability space, a function (gain) defined on the sample space, and you are asked to find the expected average of the function (gain). The insurance company in Example 1 expects an average of $.73 per policy sold. People responding to promotions like the Give Away described in Example 2 can expect to lose an average of slightly more than $.11 per response.

A function, X, with a sample space as domain and the set of real numbers as codomain is called a **random variable**. The expected average of X is called the **expected value** of X and is denoted $E(X)$. In Example 2 we computed the expected value by multiplying each of the possible values by the probability that value occurs and then adding the products. Table 5.2 illustrates this method applied to Example 1.

TABLE 5.2

Gain	Probability	Product
1	(9,999,973)/10,000,000	.9999973
−99,999	27/10,000,000	−.2699973

$(1)(P(1) + (−99,999)P(−99,999) = .73$

The expected value of a random variable on a finite sample space is defined as follows:

DEFINITION   If X is a random variable, then $E(X)$, the **expected value of X**, is computed by multiplying each of the possible values of X by the probability that that value occurs and then taking the sum of these products. In other words, if $v_1, v_2, \ldots, v_n$ is the set of possible values of X, then

$$E(X) = v_1 P(v_1) + v_2 P(v_2) + \cdots + v_n P(v_n)$$

where $P(v_i)$ is the probability that the value v_i occurs.

EXAMPLE 3   The table below gives the values of a random variable, X, and the probability that each value occurs. Find the expected value of X.

TABLE 5.3

X	Probability
1	.1
2	.5
−5	.4

Multiplying each value of X by the probability that value occurs and then adding the products gives the table below.

TABLE 5.4

X	Probability	Product
1	.1	0.1
2	.5	1.0
−5	.4	−2.0

$E(X) = 1(.1) + 2(.5) + (−5)(.4) = −0.9$

PRACTICE
EXAMPLE 1

Find the expected value of the random variable, X, described in Table 5.5.

TABLE 5.5

X	Probability
100	.3
10	.2
−50	.5

EXAMPLE 4

An architect is deciding whether to enter the competition for the design of a new community center. The cost of drawing up and submitting preliminary plans is $1000. If the architect wins the contract, the net gain is $100,000 minus the $1000 preparation costs. If the architect enters the competition, the probability of winning the contract is .2. What is the expected value (gain) if the architect enters the contest?

TABLE 5.6

Gain	Probability	Product
99,000	.2	19,800
−1,000	.8	−800

$99,000(.2) + (−1,000)(.8) = \$19,000 =$ expected value (gain)

From Table 5.6 it follows that the architect can expect an average gain of $19,000 per entry when entering such competitions.

PRACTICE EXAMPLE 2

A dollar-bill changer returns $.95 change for each dollar the machine accepts. If the bill is legal, then the operators of the machine gain $1.00 − $.95 = $.05. If the bill is counterfeit, the operators lose 95 cents. What is the expected gain per transaction if 1% of the bills changed are counterfeit? ■

Expected value can be useful in making decisions. An insurance company, such as in Example 1, wants to predict the average gain on a policy sold at various prices in order to set the price of the policy. The expected gain from responding to a giveaway such as in Example 2 can help you decide whether or not you want to respond. The architect in Example 3 can use the expected gain from entering the competition to help decide whether to enter the competition. The next examples provide more illustrations of the use of expected value in decision making.

EXAMPLE 5

A lawyer is deciding how to bill a client for an up-coming suit. The lawyer could charge a flat fee of $8000 or take a percentage of the amount awarded to the client. If the case is lost and the bill is based on percentage, then the lawyer receives no money which can be considered to be a loss of $8000. If the case is won, the lawyer's percentage amounts to $25,000. Suppose the probability of winning the case is .6.

(a) What is the expected gain for the lawyer when the bill is based on a percentage of the settlement?
(b) Which method of billing gives the lawyer the higher expected gain?

The expected gain when the bill is based on a percentage of the settlement is computed in Table 5.7.

TABLE 5.7

Gain	Probability	Product
25,000	.6	15,000
− 8,000	.4	− 3,200

$11,800 expected gain

The expected gain when the bill is based on a percentage is $11,800. This is more than the $8000 flat fee and hence gives the higher of the two expected gains. ■

PRACTICE EXAMPLE 3

An oil company wants to decide which of two sites to drill. If site *A* is drilled, the probability of finding oil is .2. In this case the profit for the company is $40 million. If no oil is found on site *A*, the company loses $5 million. If site *B* is drilled, the probability of finding oil is .1. If oil is found on site *B*, the company's profit is $90 million. If no oil is found on site *B*, the company loses $7 million. Which site has the larger expected profit? ■

EXAMPLE 6   Rent-A-Wreck, a local car-rental agency, is deciding how many cars it should have in order to make as large a profit as possible. The agency's profit on a rented car is $11 per day. If a car is not rented, the cost to the company is $10 a day. The table below gives the daily demand for the agency's cars.

Number of cars requested	5	6	7	8	9
Probability	.1	.2	.2	.2	.3

The company presently has seven cars. Find the expected daily profit if the agency has seven cars, eight cars, or nine cars. Can Rent-A-Wreck increase its profit by buying more cars?

The tables below give the computations of the expected daily profit for seven cars, eight cars, and nine cars.

Seven cars

Number of cars rented	Profit	Probability	Product
5	55 — 20	.1	3.5
6	66 — 10	.2	11.2
7	77	.7	53.9

$68.6 = expected daily profit

Eight cars

Number of cars rented	Profit	Probability	Product
5	55 — 30	.1	2.5
6	66 — 20	.2	9.2
7	77 — 10	.2	13.4
8	88	.5	44

$69.10 = expected daily profit

Nine cars

Number of cars rented	Profit	Probability	Product
5	55 — 40	.1	1.5
6	66 — 30	.2	7.2
7	77 — 20	.2	11.4
8	88 — 10	.2	15.6
9	99	.3	29.7

$65.4 = expected daily profit

The highest expected daily profit is $69.10 for eight cars so the agency can increase its daily profit by buying one more car. ■

Expected value can be used to predict the average winnings from a betting system. Below we outline a system that can be used in gambling casinos. In Example 7 we see what happens when the system is used to play roulette.

1. If you win the first game, quit.
2. If you lose the first game, increase the amount bet on the second game so that if you win the second game you can quit having won more than you lost.
3. If you win a game, quit.
4. Whenever you lose a game, continue to play. Each time increase the amount bet so that if you win you can quit having won more than you lost.
5. If you run out of money or want to bet more than the house limit, then you will have to quit.

As we shall see this system is generally disastrous for the player and quite profitable for the casino.

EXAMPLE 7

Suppose you have $1500 to bet, the house limit on a single bet is $1000, and you use the system outlined above to play roulette. Start with a $10 bet, bet on red each time, and increase the amount bet so that when you win, the amount you win minus your losses will be $10. In roulette if you bet on a color and win, the amount bet is the amount won. For example if you bet $10 and win, you get your $10 back and an additional $10 in winnings. What is the expected value of your winnings?

The first step is to see how many times you can play the game if you lose every bet.

TABLE 5.8

Game	Bet	Total losses after game
1	10	10
2	20	30
3	40	70
4	80	150
5	160	310
6	320	630
7	640	1270
8	1280	2550

Notice in Table 5.8 that each bet is $10 more than the total losses up to that point. This betting system is often called "doubling up" since the next bet is always twice the previous bet.

From Table 5.8 it follows that if you lose the first seven games then the eighth game requires a bet of $1280, which is more than the limit and also more than you have available to bet. Thus, if you lose seven games you have to quit.

The possible gains are $10, which occurs if you win any of the first seven games, and $-$1270, which occurs if you lose seven games.

The next step is to find the probability of losing the first seven games. Of the 38 slots on a roulette wheel 18 are red. So the probability of losing when you bet red is

$$\frac{20}{38} = \frac{10}{19}$$

Each game is independent of the others so the probability of losing seven games in a row is

$$\left(\frac{10}{19}\right)^7 = .0111873$$

The probability of winning one of the first seven games is $1 - .0111873 = .9888127$. The expected winnings are computed in Table 5.9.

TABLE 5.9

Winnings	Probability	Product
10	.9888127	9.8881271
$-$1270	.0111872	$-$14.207871

$-$4.3197439 = expected winnings

You can expect to lose more than four dollars every time you play this system.

In Chapter 12 we use matrices to compute the expected value of playing certain games.

CONCEPTS

expected value
random variable

SOLUTIONS TO PRACTICE EXAMPLES

1.

X	Probability	Product
100	.3	30
10	.2	2
− 50	.5	− 25

$$7 = E(X)$$

2.

Gain	Probability	Product
.05	.99	.0495
− .95	.01	− .0095
		.04

The expected gain is 4 cents per transaction.

3. Site *A*

Gain	Probability	Product
40	.2	8
− 5	.8	− 4
		4 million

Site *B*

Gain	Probability	Product
90	.1	9
− 7	.9	− 6.3
		2.7 million

Site *A* has the larger expected profit.

EXERCISES 5.4

In Exercises 1 through 4 find the expected value of the random variable, X.

1.

X	Probability
10	.8
− 20	.2

2.

X	Probability
1,000	.9
− 10,000	.1

3.

X	Probability
10	.2
20	.5
− 100	.3

4.

X	Probability
5	.2
3	.7
− 4	.1

5. A sanitation company bids for contracts in area towns. Each bid costs the company $500. If the bid is successful, the company's profit is $40,000 minus the cost of the bid. What is the expected profit per bid if 20% of the company's bids are successful?

6. An appliance repair shop sells maintenance contracts for refrigerators at a price of $50 a year. Suppose the average cost to the shop for repairing a broken refrigerator is $250 and the probability a refrigerator needs repair is .1. What is the repair shop's expected profit per policy?

7. An architect is deciding whether to enter the competition to design a new school building. If the contract is awarded, the architect's profit is $50,000 minus the $1200 cost of entering the competition. If the probability of getting the contract is .1, then what is the architect's expected profit?

8. A car insurance company sells one-year policies for $150. The average claim is $1000 and the probability a policyholder makes a claim is .08. What is the company's expected gain per policy?

9. A person who takes out a one-year life insurance policy for $10,000 pays $100 for the insurance. What is the expected gain per policy for the insurance company if the probability the person lives out the year is .995?

10. As a Christmas promotion, a mail-order company sends a $5 holiday gift to its regular customers. The certificate is good for $5 toward the customer's next purchase (before January 1). From past experience the company knows that 20% of the customers will not place an order. The company considers this a $1 loss in revenue due to the cost of printing and mailing the gift. The certificate is used by 60% of the customers, who buy what they would have bought without the certificate. The company considers this a $6 loss in revenue: $5 for the gift and $1 for the cost of sending the certificate. The remaining 20% of the customers purchase an average of $100 more merchandise than they would have without the certificate. The company considers this a $94 increase in revenue. What is the company's expected revenue per holiday gift?

11. A local supermarket loses an average of $600 a week to theft. If security measures are implemented, then the weekly loss is given by:

Loss	Probability
500	.01
400	.04
300	.35
200	.30
100	.25
0	.05

(a) What is the expected loss after the security measures are implemented?

(b) If the security measures cost $200 a week, then how much money is saved per week by implementing the security measures?

12. Diane flips a coin until she gets two heads in a row and then bets Kathy she will get heads on the next flip. If heads lands up, then Diane wins two dollars, if not she loses one dollar. What are Diane's expected winnings per game?

13. As part of a game show, the contestant gets to pick one of four boxes. Two of the boxes contain $1 each. One box contains a $100 prize, and one box contains a grand prize of $5000. What are the contestant's expected winnings per game?

14. A lottery has fifty $10 prizes, fifty $100 prizes, and a $1000 first prize. If 10,000 tickets are sold at $1 each, then what is the expected gain from buying a ticket?

15. Suppose you pay four dollars to roll a die, and you receive, in dollars, the amount you roll. If you roll a six for example, then you get six dollars, for a profit of two dollars. What is the expected profit per play of this game?

16. An oil company is deciding which of two sites to drill. If oil is found on the first site, the company's profit is $100 million. If no oil is found on the first site, then the company loses $10 million. If oil is found on the second site, the company's profit is $50 million. If no oil is found on the second site, the company loses $5 million. The probability of finding oil is .1 on the first site and .2 on the second site. Which site has the larger expected profit?

17. The Rent-All company rents TV sets on a monthly basis. The company has 14 sets and is deciding whether to buy more. The monthly profit from a rented set is $20. The company loses $5 per set each month a set goes unrented. The demand for sets is given by:

Number of sets that can be rented	14	15	16	17
Probability	.2	.3	.3	.2

What number of sets should the company own in order to obtain the largest expected monthly profit on TV rentals?

18. An inventor has spent $5000 designing a new car-suspension system which he hopes to sell to a car manufacturer for $100,000. He can try to sell his design directly to the manufacturer or hire an engineering consulting firm to help him with his presentation to the manufacturer. The probability he can sell the design on his own is .1. If he hires the consulting firm, then the probability of success is .4. The consultant's fee is $3000. Which strategy yields the higher expected profit?

19. In this exercise you find the expected winnings from using the doubling-up betting system in a fair game. Suppose the game is tossing a coin. If you call the toss correctly, you win the amount bet. Suppose you start with a dollar bet. Double the bet each time until you win once or lose five times in a row. What are the expected winnings?

CHAPTER SUMMARY

In this chapter we have presented the basic principles of probability theory and given applications. Probability theory is used in Chapter 10 to study Markov chains and in Chapter 12 in the presentation of game theory.

The *conditional probability* of E given F is

$$P(E/F) = \frac{P(E \cap F)}{P(F)}$$

The events E and F are called *independent* if $P(E/F) = P(E)$.

Expected value: The expected value of a random variable, X, is computed by multiplying each of the possible values of X times the probability that that value occurs and then taking the sum of these products. If v_1, $v_2, \ldots, v_n$ is the set of possible values of X, then:

$$E(X) = v_1 P(v_1) + v_2 P(v_2) + \cdots + v_n P(v_n)$$

The following formulas are used to compute probabilities:

$$P(E) = 1 - P(E')$$

$$P(E \cup F) = P(E) + P(F) - P(E \cap F)$$

$$P(E \cap F) = P(F) \, P(E/F)$$

If E and F are independent, then $P(E \cap F) = P(E) \, P(F)$.

The probability of k successes in a sequence of N Bernoulli trials is

$$C(N, K)(P(S))^k (P(F))^{N-k}$$

where $P(S)$ is the probability of success in one trial and $P(F)$ is the probability of failure.

REVIEW EXERCISES FOR CHAPTER 5

In Exercises 1 through 3 decide whether the information defines a probability space.

1. $S = \{a, b, c\}$
    $P(\{a\}) = \frac{2}{3}$
    $P(\{b\}) = \frac{1}{6}$
    $P(\{c\}) = \frac{1}{12}$

2. $S = \{a, b, c, d\}$
    $P(\{a\}) = \frac{1}{2}$
    $P(\{b\}) = \frac{1}{4}$
    $P(\{c\}) = \frac{1}{8}$
    $P(\{d\}) = \frac{1}{8}$

3. $S = \{a, b, c, d\}$
    $P(\{a\}) = \frac{1}{3}$
    $P(\{b\}) = \frac{1}{4}$
    $P(\{c\}) = \frac{1}{4}$
    $P(\{d\}) = \frac{1}{6}$

4. $S = \{1, 2, a, b\}$ is the sample space of a probability space with $P(\{1\}) = \frac{1}{2}$, $P(\{a\}) = \frac{1}{10}$, and $P(\{1, 2\}) = \frac{3}{10}$. Find $P(\{2\})$ and $P(\{b\})$.

5. (a) Put probabilities in the unnumbered regions of the Venn diagram below, if $P(A) = .5$

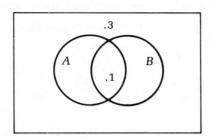

(b) Find $P(B)$ and $P(B/A)$. Are B and A independent events?

6. If $P(A \cap B) = .3$, $P(B) = .5$, and $P(A \cup B) = .7$, then what is $P(A)$? Are A and B independent events?

7. If E and F are independent events, $P(E) = .5$, and $P(E \cap F) = .4$, then what is $P(F)$?

8. To test the effectiveness of a new drug, conventional treatment was given to 500 people and the new drug to another 500 people. The result is given in the table below.

	C	N
D	410	90
T	398	102

where

$$D = \text{Patient receives new drug}$$
$$T = \text{Patient receives conventional treatment}$$
$$C = \text{Patient is cured}$$
$$N = \text{Patient is not cured}$$

What is the probability that

(a) a patient given the new drug is cured?

(b) a patient is cured?

(c) a patient who is cured received the new drug?

9. Suppose a company's security system can detect an intruder 95% of the time, and a second system that detects an intruder with probability .9 is installed. If the two systems act independently, then what is the probability an intruder goes undetected by both systems?

10. Suppose that for each question on a history test Mary has a 90% chance of answering the question correctly. What is the probability that on a 10-question test Mary answers 9 or 10 questions correctly?

11. Suppose that 55% of the people in a large town are in favor of a new zoning law and 45% are opposed. What is the probability that a random sample of four people contains three or more people opposed to the new zoning law?

Use the probability tree below to find the probabilities asked for in Exercises 12 through 19.

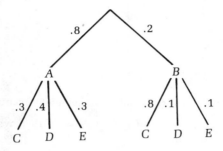

12. P(C).	15. P(A/C).	18. P(A/E).
13. P(D).	16. P(B/C).	19. P(B/E).
14. P(E).	17. P(A/D).	

20. A company drilling for oil finds oil 10% of the time. While drilling, the company finds a special rock formation below the surface. From past experience, the company knows that when there is oil, 80% of the time the rock formation is also present, and when there is no oil, this rock formation occurs only 30% of the time. What is the probability of finding oil given that the rock formation is present?

21. All the suits made by a clothing company are inspected by hand before being sold, and 95% of them have no defects. The inspectors correctly identify 80% of the suits that have some defect. A suit without defects always passes inspection. Find

(a) the percentage of suits that pass inspection.

(b) the probability that a suit that passes inspection has a defect.

22. The random variable, X, takes on the value 10 with probability .3, the value −20 with probability .5, and the value 100 with probability .2. What is the expected value of X?

23. A computer store sells maintenance contracts for $200 per year. Suppose the average cost to the store for repairing a computer is $500 and, on the average, 20% of the computers covered by the maintenance contract are brought in for repair sometime during the year. How much profit can the store expect to make on each contract?

24. A person who takes out a one-year life insurance policy for $50,000 pays $200. What is the expected gain per policy for the insurance company if the probability the person lives out the year is .998?

25. A local toy store loses an average of $500 a week to theft. If security measures are implemented, then the weekly loss is given by:

Loss	Probability
500	.01
400	.10
300	.20
200	.40
100	.27
0	.02

(a) What is the expected loss per week after the security measures are implemented?

(b) If the security measures cost $150 per week to implement, then how much money is saved per week by implementing the security measures?

Relations and Functions

6

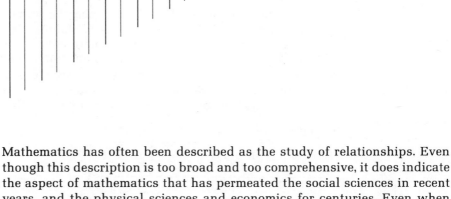

Mathematics has often been described as the study of relationships. Even though this description is too broad and too comprehensive, it does indicate the aspect of mathematics that has permeated the social sciences in recent years, and the physical sciences and economics for centuries. Even when relationships cannot be made precise in quantitative ways, mathematics is used to establish some order to these relationships. In this chapter, we look at combining sets in a way different from those described in Chapter 1, this time as the cartesian product of two sets. We define a *relation* to be any subset of a cartesian product.

Relations can be classified as to specific types. Probably the most familiar kind of relation is a function. Leibnitz first introduced the word *function* in 1694 to denote any quantity connected with a curve. This definition was much too restrictive and was modified by Bernoulli, in 1718, to be any expression made up of variables and constants, and by Dirichlet, in the first half of the nineteenth century, to involve a rule or correspondence relating variables. Cantor at the end of the nineteenth century extended the definition of function to embrace relationships between any two types of sets *A* and *B*, not just sets of numbers.

Relations often involve the cartesian product of a set with itself. Among a set of people we may talk about the relation of being "the brother of," among a set of students of "having the same class schedule," among a set of voting members of an organization of "having the same preference for candidates." We often want to use relations to better organize data so that it can be processed faster and more systematically. A type of relation called an *equivalence relation* allows us to reduce the amount of data to be processed, and the type of relation called a *partial order* allows us to process data more systematically, both important in today's computer-based world.

In this chapter the reader is asked to look closely at various types of relations, and to understand how each is used in analyzing problems in such fields as business, economics, psychology, political sciences, and biology. It is hoped that with these skills the reader will be able to look at his own problems, now and in the future, and be able to apply these techniques to make them more manageable.

6.1   *Relations*

Table 6.1 indicates a relationship between the years from 1985 to 1989 and the billions of dollars projected as the budget deficit for those years. This relationship could be expressed more concisely as the set of pairs {(1985, 207), (1986, 219), (1987, 224), (1988, 207), (1989, 198)}. The first member of each pair is a year, and the second member is a number expressing billions of dollars of deficit in that year. Notice that the number 207 is a second member twice, corresponding to both 1985 and 1988.

TABLE 6.1   **The Incredible Shrinking Deficit**

Final year	Budget deficit (in billions of dollars)	% GNP
1985	207	3.5
1986	219	2.7
1987	224	2.1
1988	207	1.1
1989	198	.3

Data: Office of Management and Budget, Council of Economic Awareness, Treasury Dept.

Similarly we could look at the relationships between years from 1985 to 1989 and the percent the projected deficit is of the projected Gross National Product. Now the set of pairs would be [(1985, 3.5), (1986, 2.7), (1987, 2.1), (1988, 1.1), (1989, .3)].

Figure 6.1

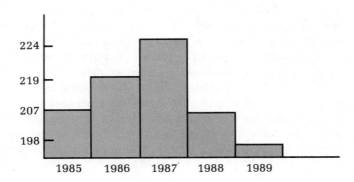

The relationship between years and projected deficit was presented in a table and by a set of ordered pairs. It can also be shown by various kinds of graphs. The bar graph is popular in business and would look like that shown in Figure 6.1 for this data. Using the last digit of the year, the pairs could be plotted on a graph such as those in Figure 6.2, with the x-axis corresponding to the year and the y-axis corresponding to the projected deficit in billions of dollars, or the x-axis corresponding to the year and the y-axis corresponding to projected percent of GNP.

Figure 6.2

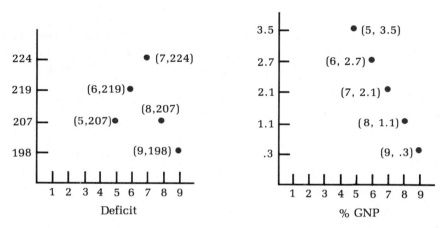

Tables, graphs, and sets of ordered pairs, are all methods of indicating the relationship between years and deficit.

Psychologists and advertisers often perform paired comparison experiments to determine a person's preference for a set of alternatives or brands. The person is asked to consider each pair of alternatives and choose one over the other. The results of this type of experiment produce a preference relation such that for every pair of alternatives, a and b, either a is preferred to b, denoted (a, b) or b is preferred to a, denoted (b, a).

EXAMPLE 1

A group of people are asked their preference in a paired comparison experiment of four brands of coffee. If more than 50% prefer coffee x to coffee y then the group is said to prefer coffee x to coffee y. The directed graph in Figure 6.3 represents the preference relation for brands of coffee. There is a directed edge from one coffee to another if the first coffee is preferred to the second.

Figure 6.3

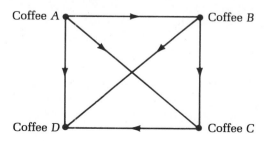

As a set of pairs, the relation can be written as [(*A*, *B*), (*C*, *D*), (*A*, *D*), (*B*, *D*), (*C*, *D*)]. (This relation could have been used to determine a ranking of brands using the condorcet criterion for preference orders as in Section 1.4.)

In Chapter 1 we looked at various ways of combining two sets, namely the union of two sets and the intersection of two sets. We can formally define a relation by first defining another way of combining two sets.

> DEFINITION   For any sets *A* and *B*, the **cartesian product** of *A* and *B* is the set of all ordered pairs such that the first element of each pair is an element of *A* and the second element of each pair is an element of *B*.

We denote the cartesian product of *A* and *B* by $A \times B$, and sometimes refer to it as the *cross product* of *A* and *B*. The set of pairs in the cartesian coordinate system is merely the cartesian product of the real numbers with the real numbers. Each point is a pair of real numbers.

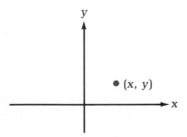

In our example given in Table 6.1 we could have: $A = $ [1985, 1986, 1987, 1988, 1989] and $B = $ [207, 224, 198, 219]. $A \times B = $ (1985, 207), (1986, 207), (1987, 207), (1988, 207), (1989, 207), (1985, 224), (1986, 224), (1987, 224), (1988, 224), (1989, 224), (1985, 198), (1986, 198), (1987, 198), (1988, 198), (1989, 198), (1985, 219), (1986, 219), (1987, 219), (1988, 219), (1989, 219).

> DEFINITION   Given two sets *A* and *B* (not necessarily distinct) a **relation** from *A* to *B* is a subset of $A \times B$. Thus if *R* is a relation from *A* to *B* then $R \subseteq A \times B$.

EXAMPLE 2   *A* is a set of applicants {Jones, Smith, Barry, Warner} and *B* is a set of jobs {purchasing agent, marketing director, accountant, salesperson}. *R* is the relation of "being qualified for." These relations can be depicted by exhibiting the sets A and B and directed edges between applicants qualified for specific jobs as indicated by the directed graph in Figure 6.4. R is therefore the set of ordered pairs $\{(J, PA), (S, S), (B, MD), (B, S), (W, PA), (W, A)\} \subseteq A \times B$.

Figure 6.4

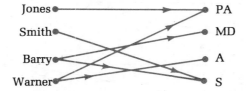

In Section 2.4 we tried to find a particular kind of relation in assignment problems, called a matching.

Sometimes we talk about **relations on a set**, S, where the relation is from S to S. If $S = \{1, 2, 3, 4\}$ then the $\leq$ relation on S is the set of ordered pairs $\{(1, 2), (1, 3), (1, 4), (2, 3), (2, 4), (3, 4), (1, 1), (2, 2), (3, 3), (4, 4)\} \subseteq S \times S$.

Figure 6.5

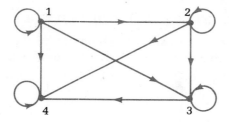

Note that the directed graph for this relation shown in Figure 6.5 contains edges from a vertex to itself, called a **loop**.

PRACTICE EXAMPLE 1

Draw the directed graph corresponding to the relation: $\{(1, 1), (1, 2), (2, 1), (3, 4), (4, 4)\} \subseteq \{1, 2, 3, 4\} \times \{1, 2, 3, 4\}$.

TABLE 6.2

C	Colter Bay Village	***
Ja	Jackson Lake Lodge	****
Je	Jenny Lake Lodge	***
M	Moose Head Ranch	***
T	Triangle X Ranch	**
L	Lost Creek Ranch	****
H	Hatchet	**

Table 6.2 gives the ratings of resorts in the Jackson Hole, Wyoming, area from the 1984 *Mobil Travel Guide*. We can analyze this data by using the relation "is preferred to" to obtain the preference graph shown in Figure 6.6. One resort is preferred to another if it has more stars in the

rating than the other. In other words the ordered pairs are: (L, Je), (Ja, Je), (L, C), (Ja, C), (L, M), (Ja, M), (L, T), (Ja, T), (L, H), (Ja, H), (C, T), (C, H), (Je, T), (Je, H), (M, T), and (M, H).

Figure 6.6

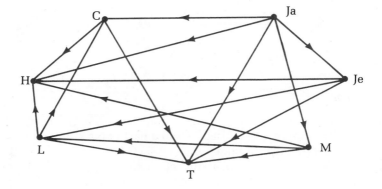

PRACTICE EXAMPLE 2

(a) Describe in words the relation:

$$\{(1, 2), (2, 4), (3, 6)\} \subseteq \{1, 2, 3\} \times \{1, 2, 3, 4, 5, 6\}$$

(b) Write the set of ordered pairs corresponding to the relation given by Table 6.3. The relation is a subset of which possible cartesian product?

TABLE 6.3   Saab 1984 Price List

900 3-door	$11,110
900 4-door	$11,420
900S 3-door	$13,850
900S 4-door	$14,310
900Turbo 3-door	$16,940
900Turbo 4-door	$17,400

EXAMPLE 3

A large doctors' office needs to organize its files for the various insurance programs of its patients. Two patients' records will be filed together (are related) if these two patients belong to the same insurance program and have the same first initial of their last name. Using the product rule for counting given in Chapter 4, if there are 10 insurance programs and 26 letters of the alphabet, the office needs 260 file compartments. If S is the set of patients, then this relation can be described in set notation as $R = \{(a, b) \in S \times S \mid a$ and b have the same insurance program and have the same first initial of their last name$\}$.

As a preview of the next few sections, we will look closely at some of the properties of this relation R. Each patient may be related to many other patients. For example there may be 10 patients who have a last name starting with S and who belong to the Blue Shield program. In other words there is not a unique correspondence between patients. But this relation does allow the office to divide up its files into subsets that do not overlap and whose union is the total set of files. If patient A has the same last initial and belongs to the same insurance program as patient B, and patient B has the same last initial and belongs to the same insurance program as patient C, then patient A and patient C have the same last initial and belong to the same insurance program.

In the next section we look at relations (subsets of $A \times B$), called *functions*, that pair each element in A with one and only one element of B.

CONCEPTS

relation
cartesian product

SOLUTIONS TO PRACTICE EXAMPLES

1.

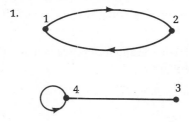

2.   (a) $R = \{(a, b) \mid a \text{ is half of } b\}$
     (b) 1. $\{(900 \text{ 3-door}, 11{,}110), (900 \text{ 4-door}, 11{,}420),$
         $(900S \text{ 3-door}, 13{,}850), (900S \text{ 4-door}, 14{,}310),$
         $(900\text{Turbo 3-door}, 16{,}940), (900\text{Turbo 4-door}, 17{,}400)\}$
         2. $A = \{\text{models of Saab}\}$, $B = \text{real numbers}$, $R \subseteq A \times B$.

EXERCISES 6.1

1. Find the cartesian product $A \times B$ for each of the following.

    (a) $A = \{1, 2\}$ and $B = \{3, 4\}$
    (b) $A = \{1, 2\}$ and $B = \{1, 2\}$
    (c) $A = \{1\}$ and $B = \{1, 2\}$
    (d) $A = \{1, 2\}$ and $B = \{1\}$

2. What is the cartesian product of the empty set with any set?

3. If A is a set of shirts a man owns and B is a set of pants he owns, what is an interpretation of the cartesian product of A with B?

4. Describe in words the relations given by the following set of ordered pairs.

   (a) {(1, 1), (2, 4), (3, 9), (4, 16)}

   (b) {(a, A), (b, B), (c, C), (d, D)}

   (c) {(Reagan, Bush), (Carter, Mondale), (Nixon, Agnew)}

5. The table below gives the percent of equity expenditure in Latin America of four U.S. banks. Using the abbreviations given, write the set of ordered pairs relating percent to bank.

	Bank	% Expenditure
CM	Chase Manhattan	1.98
C	Citicorp	1.95
BA	Bank of America	1.64
MG	Morgan Guaranty	1.36

6. Draw the directed graph corresponding to the relation:
$$R = \{(1, 1), (2, 2), (3, 3), (4, 4), (4, 3), (1, 2), (3, 2)\}$$

7. Draw the directed graph corresponding to the relation: $R = \{(a, b) \mid a \geq b\}$ on $S = \{1, 3, 5, 7\}$.

8. The following is the preference graph for brands of margarine. Write the corresponding set of ordered pairs.

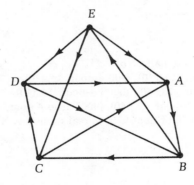

9. The following table provides the price list for Commodore Computer disk drives. Give three other ways of describing the relation between drive and price.

Drive	Price
1541 Disk Drive	$249
MSD Dual Disk Drive	649
MSD Single Disk Drive	349
9050 Drive	979

6.2   *Functions—Input-Output*

SEER, the seasonal energy efficiency ratio, is the measure of how efficiently a central air conditioning unit works. SEER ranges between 1 and 14. The annual cost, C, of operating a unit is computed by assuming a cooling capacity of 36,000 BTUs, a cooling season of 1500 hours, and a cost of electricity of $.05 a kilowatt hour. This can be expressed as:

$$C = (36,000/\text{SEER})(1500/1000)(.05) = 2700/\text{SEER}$$

Thus for a SEER of 6, we have $C = 2700/6 = \$450$, for a SEER of 8, we have $C = 2700/8 = \$337.50$, and for a SEER of 10, we have $C = 2700/10 = \$270$.

This relationship between SEER rating and cost is a subset of the cartesian product of the set $A = 1, 2, 3, \ldots, 14$ and the positive real numbers. Thus the pairs (6, 450), (8, 337.50), and (10, 270) are some of the pairs in this relation. This SEER-cost relation is an example of a particular type of relation called a function.

> DEFINITION   A **function** from a set A to a set B is a relation from A to B in which each element of set A is paired with one and only one element of set B. The set of first members, A, is called the **domain** of the function. The set of second members is called the **range**, and the set B is called the **codomain**. The range is a subset of the codomain.

In the previous example, the domain is the set of possible SEER values from 1 to 14, and the codomain is the set of positive real numbers. The range is the set of 14 values of the cost function computed for the SEER numbers between 1 and 14 inclusive, $\{2700, 1350, 900, 675, 540, 450, 385.71, 337.50, 300, 270, 245.45, 225, 207.69, 192.86\}$.

VHF television channels must be assigned to the 12 stations in New England. To prevent interference two stations must get different channel numbers if they are within 100 miles of one another. Only channel numbers between 2 and 12 may be used. The relation that pairs each station with a channel must be a function since no station may be assigned two channels and each station must get a channel assigned to it. Figure 6.7 shows the actual channel assignment in use in New England.

The techniques of Section 2.1 can be used to find the least number of channels needed to be assigned. Section 6.3 applies these techniques to this problem.

Figure 6.7 shows a way of representing functions with the domain on the left, the codomain on the right, and the correspondence given by arrows from the members of A to the members of B.

The relation $F_1 = \{(1985, 207), (1986, 219), (1987, 224), (1988, 207), (1989, 198)\}$ of Table 6.1 relating projected deficit to years is also a function, as is the one relating percent of GNP to years, $F_2 = \{(1985, 3.5), (1986, 2.7), (1987, 2.1), (1988, 1.1), (1989, .3)\}$. Note that in F_2, each element of the range corresponds to only one element in the domain. In F_1, 207 corresponds to two different elements, 1985 and 1988, in the domain.

Figure 6.7

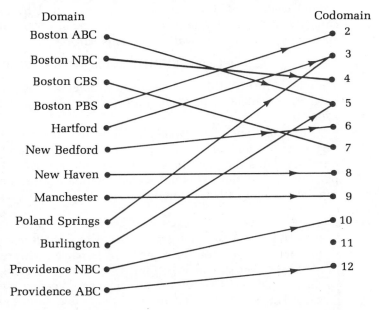

DEFINITION   A function from A to B is **one-to-one** if each element in the range corresponds to only one element in the domain.

Thus, F_2 is a one-to-one function, whereas F_1 is not. In the channel assignment example illustrated in Figure 6.7, the function is not one-to-one, since Boston ABC and Burlington are both paired with channel 5.

DEFINITION   A function F from A to B is **onto** if the range of F is the same as the codomain.

Thus if $B = \{207, 224, 219, 198\}$ then F_1 is an onto function, but if $B = \{\text{the real numbers}\}$, it is not. The channel assignment function is not onto, since no station is assigned channel 11.

So far we have specified relations and functions by sets and ordered pairs, by directed graphs (showing the correspondence with arrows), and by a table. One example, the SEER example, illustrates a function specified by an equation; another example of a function is pictured with a bar graph, and on an x–y coordinate system. The x values correspond to the numbers in the domain, and the y values correspond to the numbers in the range. Now let us focus our attention on functions specified by equations, and the corresponding x–y coordinate system graphs.

In the SEER example, if we let the domain, A, be the set of possible SEER values from 1 to 14, and the codomain, B, be the set of positive real numbers, then the function can be described by the equation: $y = 2700/x$, where $x \in A$ and $y \in B$. This type of equation is familiar to all who have had some algebra. The x is called the **independent variable**, or *input*, and the y is called the **dependent variable**, or *output*. In applications it is often more useful to define functions with equations that are more suggestive of their purpose, and to distinguish equations that determine functions from those that do not. Therefore, the equation, $y = 2700/x$ can be written in **functional notation** as $C(x) = 2700/x$. $C(x)$ denotes the cost for SEER value x, and is called the **image** of x under the function C. x values are assigned from the domain, and the $C(x)$ values must be in the codomain.

For any element x in the domain of the function f, the symbol $f(x)$ denotes the element in the range of f paired with x. The ordered pair $(x, f(x))$ belongs to the function f. x is called the **input**; $f(x)$ is called the **output**.

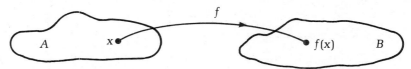

Let us look at examples of functions and nonfunctions, and various ways of specifying functions. Let $\mathscr{R}$ denote the set of real numbers, and $\mathscr{N}$ denote the set of natural numbers 1, 2, 3, ...

EXAMPLE 1

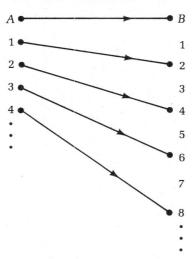

Equation:

$$y = 2x \text{ with } A = B = \mathscr{N}$$

Functional equation:

$$f(x) = 2x \text{ with } A = B = \mathscr{N}$$

x–y coordinate system graph:

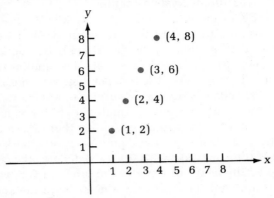

This is a function that is one-to-one, but not onto, since nothing in *A* corresponds to the odd number 3 in *B*.

EXAMPLE 2

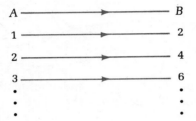

Equation:

$$y = 2x, \text{ with } A = \mathcal{N} \text{ and } B = 2, 4, 6, \ldots$$

Functional equation:

$$f(x) = 2x, \text{ with } A = \mathcal{N} \text{ and } B = 2, 4, 6$$

x–y coordinate graph:

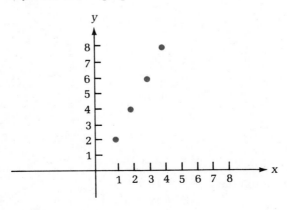

This function is both one-to-one and onto.

Notice that Examples 1 and 2 are almost the same functions, only the codomain has changed.

EXAMPLE 3

$$\{(x, y) \mid x^2 + y^2 = 2 \text{ and } A = B = \mathscr{R}\}$$

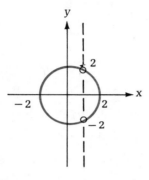

This is not a function for two reasons. There does not exist a $y \in B$ for $x = 3 \in A$. Also if $x = 1$, then $y = +1$ and -1. There is not a unique y value for each x value.

Example 3 illustrates the **vertical line test**: if any vertical line cuts the graph in two or more distinct points, the graph is not the graph of a function.

EXAMPLE 4

$$\{(x, y) \mid y = x^2 \text{ and } A = B = \mathscr{R}\}$$
$$f(x) = x^2$$

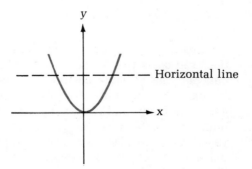

This is a function since given any real number, we can square it to get another unique real number. This function is not onto, because there is nothing in A that corresponds to any negative number. It is not one-to-one since $+1$ and -1 are both paired with 1.

The above example demonstrates the **horizontal line test**: if any horizontal line crosses the graph of a function in two or more points, then the function is not one-to-one.

PRACTICE EXAMPLE 1
Indicate if each of the following is a function, if it is one-to-one, and if it is onto.

1. $A \longrightarrow B$ 2. $A \longrightarrow B$ 3. $A \longrightarrow B$

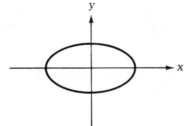

4. $\{(x, y) \mid y = 3x + 2 \text{ and } A = B = \mathscr{R}\}$

5. $\{(x, y) \mid x^2 = y^2 = 9 \text{ and } A = B = \mathscr{R}\}$

6. $\{(x, y) \mid y = \sqrt{x} \text{ and } A = \text{positive } \mathscr{R} \text{ and } B = \mathscr{R}\}$

7.

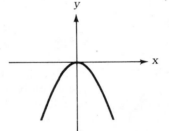

$A = B = \mathscr{R}$

8.

$A = B = \mathscr{R}$

9. $f(x) = x^2 + 5$
$A = \mathscr{R}, B = \mathscr{R}+$

Costs of operating a manufacturing business fall into two categories, the **fixed costs** that must be paid whether any items are manufactured or not, and the **variable costs** that depend on the number of items manufactured. For example if an airline company each year must repay $236 million in loans, and has to pay $160 million for items such as salaries and building maintenance, then the company's total fixed cost is $236 + 160 = \$396$ million. It also costs the company an average of $20 per passenger ticket or a total of $20 \times$ (number of passengers) in variable costs. Therefore if x is the number of passenger tickets, the **cost function** can be written as $C(x) = 20x + 396,000,000$. If 5 million tickets are sold, the cost is:

$$C(5,000,000) = 20(5,000,000) + 396,000,000 = 406,000,000$$

Profit for the company per year is the difference between revenue (sales) and cost. If the airline takes in an average of $140 a ticket, the revenue function is $R(x) = 140x$, where x is the number of tickets sold. Therefore, the profit function is the revenue function minus the cost function:

$$P(x) = R(x) - C(x) = 140x - (20x + 396,000,000)$$

$$= 140x - 20x - 396,000,000 = 120x - 396,000,000$$

Therefore, if 5 million tickets are sold, the profit is:

$$C(5,000,000) = 140(5,000,000) - 396,000,000 = 204,000,000$$

PRACTICE EXAMPLE 2

It costs $10 to produce each game disk for the ABC computer and $575 in fixed costs per week. If x disks are produced, write the cost function, f, of producing x disks per week. If each disk sells for $30, and all that are produced can be sold, write the revenue and profit functions for x disks per week. ■

In the first 100 days that the Apple Macintosh was on the market, 70,000 Macintosh computers were sold (*Personal Computing*, July 1984). If sales continue at the same rate, we can write a function representing sales per day. $70,000/100 = 700$ are sold per day. If x is the number of days, then the sales function is $S(x) = 700x$. In a year, or 365 days, $S(365) = 700(365) = 255,500$ will be sold. The yearly sales function can be written as $Y(x) = 255,500x$, where x is now the number of years.

PRACTICE EXAMPLE 3

The temperature in Celsius is $\frac{5}{9}$ of the difference between the Farenheit reading and $32°$. If x is the Farenheit temperature, write a function to compute the Celsius temperature. ■

Computers can be thought of as large function machines. The set of possible input values is the domain, and the set of output values is the range. The program gives the correspondence or pairing. For example if we want to compute the average of 10 numbers, we can write a program to compute the sum of the 10 numbers and divide this sum by 10. If we represent the 10 input numbers by $x_1, x_2, x_3, \ldots, x_{10}$, then the program will compute values of the function

$$M(x_1, x_2, x_3, \ldots, x_{10}) = \frac{x_1 + x_2 + x_3 + \cdots + x_{10}}{10}$$

and output these values. The domain may be the set of natural numbers, and the range will be a subset of the set of real numbers. In this example there is not just one independent variable, but 10 independent variables, each representing a number to be averaged. M is said to be a **function of several variables**. What will the computer printout for the following input values: 13, 56, 45, 78, 98, 42, 39, 67, 16, 91? More complicated programs may involve more than one function, and these functions are combined to give a single output.

PRACTICE
EXAMPLE **4**

Let $C(x_1, x_2) = 3x_1 + 4x_2 + 100$ be a function of two variables, representing the cost of manufacturing x_1 items of product 1 and x_2 items of product 2. Complete Table 6.3 below.

TABLE 6.3

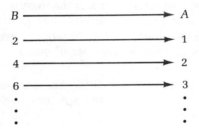

x_1	x_2	$C(x_1, x_2)$
10	20	
50	10	
60	9	
8	30	
15	15	

Sometimes the sets can be switched so that B becomes the domain, A the codomain, with the correspondence reversed, and the set of ordered pairs is still a function. If we reverse the sets and the correspondence shown in the figure in Example 2 we get the following:

$$B \longrightarrow A$$

$$2 \longrightarrow 1$$

$$4 \longrightarrow 2$$

$$6 \longrightarrow 3$$

$$\vdots \qquad\qquad \vdots$$

We still have a function, called the **inverse function**. Since $f(x) = 2x$, it is easy to see that the inverse function, denoted f^{-1}, is $f^{-1}(x) = \frac{1}{2}x$.

DEFINITION   If f is a function from A to B that is one-to-one and onto, then the **inverse function** exists, and is denoted by:

$$f^{-1} = \{(b, a) \mid (a, b) \in f\}$$

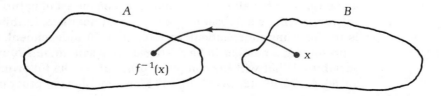

In Example 1, reversing the correspondence does not produce a function, since the odd numbers will have nothing paired with them. You will recall that this function was not onto.

Many of the functions depicted as a table have inverse functions. For example F_2 as shown in Table 6.1 has an inverse function as shown in Figure 6.8.

Figure 6.8

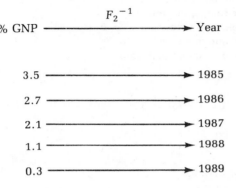

$$F_2^{-1}$$

% GNP $\longrightarrow$ Year

3.5 $\longrightarrow$ 1985

2.7 $\longrightarrow$ 1986

2.1 $\longrightarrow$ 1987

1.1 $\longrightarrow$ 1988

0.3 $\longrightarrow$ 1989

However, F_1 of Table 6.1 does not have an inverse. The years 1985 and 1988 are both paired with 207, so that when the correspondence is reversed, 207 is paired with more than one date. As we discussed earlier F_1 is not a one-to-one function, so no inverse function is possible.

PRACTICE EXAMPLE 5

Which of the functions in Practice Example 1 have inverses?

In this section we have discussed functions, properties of functions, and relations that are not functions. In the next section we look at the set of polynomial functions in one variable, functions of the form:

$$f(x) = a_0 + a_1 x + a_2 x^2 + \cdots + a_n x^n$$

CONCEPTS

function	dependent variable
domain	vertical line test
codomain	horizontal line test
range	fixed costs
functional notation	variable costs
image	cost function
one-to-one $(1-1)$	function of several variables
onto	inverse function
independent variable	

SOLUTIONS TO PRACTICE EXAMPLES

1. 1. function, one-to-one, onto
    2. function, one-to-one, not onto
    3. function, onto, not one-to-one
    4. function, one-to-one, onto
    5. not a function, no value for x = 1
    6. function, one-to-one, not onto
    7. not a function, two values for x = 0
    8. function, not one-to-one, not onto
    9. function, not one-to-one, not onto

2. $C(x) = 10x + 575$
    $R(x) = 30x$
    $P(x) = 30x - (10x + 575) = 30x - 10x - 575 = 20x - 575$

3. $C(x) = \dfrac{5}{9}(x - 32)$

4.

x_1	x_2	$C(x_1, x_2)$
10	20	210
50	10	290
60	9	316
8	30	244
15	15	205

5. The functions that have inverses are those that are one-to-one and onto: 1 and 4.

EXERCISES 6.2

1. $P(x) = 120x - 6000$ is the profit function for producing x items. Find $P(x)$ for each of the following values of x:
    (a) ·x = 10
    (b) x = 20
    (c) x = 50
    (d) x = 100
    (e) x = 1000

2. In Exercise 1, how many items must the company produce before a profit is made?

In Exercises 3 through 14 indicate if each is a function, one-to-one, and onto:

3. $A \longrightarrow B$ 4. $A \longrightarrow B$ 5. $A \longrightarrow B$

1 $\longrightarrow$ a	$a \longrightarrow$ 1	0 $\longrightarrow$ @
2	b	#
3	$c \longrightarrow$ 3	%

6. $\{(a, b) \mid a = b \text{ and } A = B = \mathcal{N}\}$

7. $\{(a, b) \mid a^2 = b^2 \text{ and } A = B = \mathcal{N}\}$

8. $\{(a, b) \mid 2a = b \text{ and } A = B = \mathcal{N}\}$

9. $\{(x, y) \mid y = x^3 \text{ and } A = B = \mathcal{N}\}$

10.

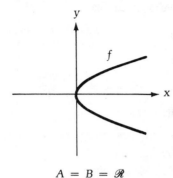

$A = B = \mathcal{R}$

11.

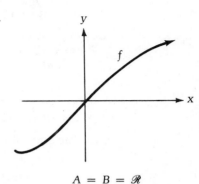

$A = B = \mathcal{R}$

12. $\{(1, 1), (1, 2), (2, 2)\}\ A = B = \{1, 2\}$

13. $\{(a, b), (b, c), (c, d)\}\ A = B = \{a, b, c, d\}$

14. $\{(10, \$50), (20, \$100), (30, \$50)\}$ where $A = \{10, 20, 30\}$ and $B = \{\$50, \$100\}$

15. Of those that are functions in Exercises 3 through 14, which have inverses? If the inverse exists, describe it.

16. It costs \$25 to produce each ABC Walkman and fixed costs are \$1800 a month. Write the monthly cost function.

17. Each ABC Walkman sells for \$48. If x Walkmans can be sold, what is the revenue function and what is the profit function?

18. The cost of producing x_1 pairs of shoes and x_2 handbags is given by the function:

$$C(x_1, x_2) = 15x_1 + 20x_2 + 1000$$

Complete the following table:

x_1	x_2	$C(x_1, x_2)$
8	6	
15	9	
50	20	
100	50	

19. In Exercise 18, the domain of $C(x_1, x_2)$ is $\{(x_1, x_2)\ x_1 \in \mathcal{N}, x_2 \in \mathcal{N}\}$. What is the range?

20. For $f(x) = 1/x$ to be a function, what number must be excluded from the domain?

21.   If $C(x) = \begin{cases} 1000 & x \le 100 \\ 10x & x > 100 \end{cases}$

find $C(0)$, $C(50)$, $C(100)$, and $C(300)$.

22.   A health insurance company pays 80% of all medical bills after the first $150. If x is the total amount of medical bills, write a function to represent the amount paid by the insurance company.

23.   Let a be the age of a child, and MA his mental age as measured on standardized tests. IQ can be written as a function of the two variables, a and MA, as follows:

$$IQ(a, MA) = \frac{100MA}{a}$$

Find IQ(10, 12) and IQ(15, 15).

*24.   The State of New Jersey charges income tax as follows:

2% of taxable income on taxable income less than or equal to $20,000

2.5% on taxable income over $20,000

Write a function, $T(x)$ for the amount of New Jersey income tax to be paid on a taxable income of x. How much would a person pay on a taxable income of $35,000?

6.3   *Polynomial Functions—Coloring Revisited*

The cost, revenue, and product functions of the last section are examples of polynomial functions in one variable. The computation of the average is a polynomial function in 10 variables. In this section we look at specific types of polynomial functions and use a special polynomial function to count the number of colorings of a graph.

Linear functions, functions that can be expressed as $f(x) = ax + b$, where a and b are constants, will be used extensively in the remaining chapters of this book. If both the domain and codomain of these functions is the set of real numbers then linear functions are precisely those functions that when graphed in the cartesian coordinate system yield a straight line. You probably remember from algebra and geometry that although two points determine a straight line, teachers insisted that you plot a third as a checkpoint. If we know we have a linear function (equation) it suffices to consider just two points.

Suppose we make the assumption that the points (pairs), (5, 3.5) and (7, 2.1) of the relation between year and percent of GNP in Table 6.1 lie on a straight line. (They determine a linear function.) Can we write the function, and then check to see if the other pairs (points) satisfy the function?

*denotes more challenging problem.

Figure 6.9

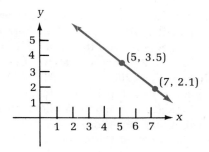

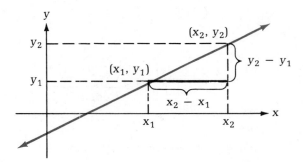

DEFINITION   For any two points on a line, the **slope** of the line is:

$$\frac{\text{change in the y coordinates}}{\text{change in the x coordinates}} = \frac{y_2 - y_1}{x_2 - x_1}$$

Figure 6.10

The straight line containing (5, 3.5) and (7, 2.1) has slope

$$\frac{3.5 - 2.1}{5 - 7} = \frac{1.4}{-2} = -.7$$

Since this is true for any pair of points on the line through (5, 3.5) and (7, 2.1), even an arbitrary point (x, y), the slope is also given by:

$$\frac{3.5 - y}{5 - x}$$

Since it is the same straight line, the slopes must be equal, so

$$\frac{3.5 - y}{5 - x} = -.7 \quad \text{or} \quad 3.5 - y = -.7(5 - x)$$
$$3.5 - y = -3.5 + .7x$$
$$7 = y + .7x$$
$$y = 7 - .7x$$

Considering only the two pairs (5, 3.5) and (7, 2.1) we can write the percent of GNP as a linear function $G(x) = 7 - .7x$ where x is the last digit of the year. Does the function represent *all* the data? If $x = 6$, corresponding to 1986, $G(6) = 7 - 4.2 = 2.8$, not quite 2.7, but close. If $x = 9$ corresponding to 1989, $G(9) = 7 - .7(9) = 7 - 6.3 = .7$, a bit farther off. Therefore, this function is not linear, but it sometimes suffices to approximate it by a linear one. It looked fairly close as sketched in Figure 6.2.

We defined linear functions as those that could be written as $f(x) = ax + b$, and now have defined the slope of a line in terms of two points. The student should observe in the last example that the slope of $-.7$ is the coefficient a of x in the final function. This is not coincidental, for suppose we have two points (x_1, y_1) and (x_2, y_2). The equation of the line containing them can be computed as before by finding two representatives of the slope and setting them equal to one another:

$$\frac{y_2 - y_1}{x_2 - x_1} = \frac{y - y_1}{x - x_1}$$

If we simplify we get

$$\left(\frac{y_2 - y_1}{x_2 - x_1}\right) x - \left(\frac{y_2 - y_1}{x_2 - x_1}\right) x_1 = y - y_1$$

For

$$y = \underbrace{\left(\frac{y_2 - y_1}{x_2 - x_1}\right)}_{\substack{\text{Constant } a \\ = \text{ slope}}} x \underbrace{- \left(\frac{y_2 - y_1}{x_2 - x_1}\right) x_1 + y_1}_{\text{Constant } b}$$

or

$$y = mx + b, \text{ where } m = \text{ the slope } = \frac{y_2 - y_1}{x_2 - x_1}$$

PRACTICE EXAMPLE 1

Write the linear function that describes the cost of producing x items if it costs \$1500 to produce 100 items and \$2500 to produce 200 items. ■

Recall from the last section that we said that the cost of producing x items is the sum of the variable costs and fixed costs. The fixed costs represent the amount that must be spent even if no items are produced, or, equivalently, the point (0, fixed cost) satisfies the function. If we are graphing the function, this point corresponds to the point where the graph of the function crosses the y-axis.

DEFINITION   The **y-intercept** of a function $f(x)$ is the point where the graph of the function crosses the y-axis, the point $(0, f(0))$. The **x-intercept** of a function $f(x)$ is the point(s) where the graph of the function crosses the x-axis, the point $(f^{-1}(0), 0)$ when the inverse function exists. (See Sections 9.1 and 9.2.)

In the general linear function $f(x) = ax + b$, a is the slope of the line and $(0, b)$ is the y-intercept, since $f(0) = b$. The x-intercept can be computed by solving the equation $0 = ax + b$, to get $x = -b/a$, or an x-intercept of $(-b/a, 0)$, and there is only one x-intercept.

Linear functions do not have to be written in function notation in order to compute the x and y intercepts. For example, if it requires 3 hours to produce a camera and 4 hours to produce a radio and there is 100 hours of manufacturing time, then if x is the number of cameras produced and y is the number of radios produced, we can write a linear equation to represent the total hours worked, $3x + 4y = 100$. One can solve for y as a function of x and get

$$3x + 4y = 100$$

$$4y = 100 - 3x$$

$$y = 25 - \left(\frac{3}{4}\right)x$$

If we simply want to draw the straight line representing this function (see Figure 6.12), this is unnecessary. If $x = 0$, then

$$3(0) + 4y = 100$$

$$4y = 100$$

$$y = 25$$

so the y-intercept is $(0, 25)$.

If $y = 0$, then

$$3x + 4(0) = 100$$

$$3x = 100$$

$$x = \frac{100}{3},$$

so the x-intercept is $(\frac{100}{3}, 0)$.

Figure 6.11

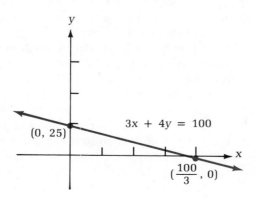

EXAMPLE 1   A real estate agent gets a commission of 5% on the sale of each house, but the agent must pay $200 for membership in a multiple-listing service and $100 for newspaper advertising even if he does not sell any houses. He must also pay 1% of the selling price of each house to the brokerage firm. We can write the linear function that describes the agent's income in terms of the total selling price of his houses, x.

$$I(x) = .05x - 100 - 50 - .01x$$

$$I(x) = .04x - 150$$

The slope of the line representing this function is .04, the place where it crosses the y-axis, the y-intercept, is $(0, -150)$, and the place where it crosses the x-axis, the x-intercept, is $(3750, 0)$, since

$$0 = .04x - 150$$

$$150 = .04x$$

$$15000 = 4x$$

$$3750 = x$$

The agent must pay $150 even if he sells no houses, and a total sale of $3750 produces $0 income.

In Chapter 9 we will graph straight lines almost exclusively by finding the x and y intercepts and plotting these two points.

PRACTICE   Find the x and y intercepts for $2x + 5y = 10$.
EXAMPLE 2

In linear functions the highest power of the variables is one. A **quadratic function** is a function that can be expressed in the form

$$F(x) = ax^2 + bx + c$$

where a, b, and c are constants, $a \neq 0$. Therefore in a quadratic function the highest power of the independent variable is 2, and it appears to that power.

After extensive analysis, a market research company determined that the demand for a personal computer is related to the price of the computer and can be given by the function: $D(p) = 32000 - 4p$, where p represents price. The revenue from selling computers is the price times the quantity, thus the revenue function can be written as $R(p) = p(32000 - 4p) = 32000p - 4p^2$. If the price is p, the demand function tells us the quantity sold will be $32000 - 4p$. The revenue function is a quadratic function in terms of p. Usually the price is limited so that the domain of the function will include only positive numbers, and those for which there will be a positive demand. $0 < p < 8000$. Notice that 8000 is the value of p for which $D(p) = 0$, the p-intercept of the demand function.

EXAMPLE 2

An economist for the Reagan administration claims that public concern for the budget deficit is unfounded, and that by 1991 we will have a negative budget deficit. Therefore, we will have a surplus at that time. To support his theory, he claims that the budget deficit function is quadratic and is given by $B(x) = -17x^2 + 102x + 71$, where x is the number of years from 1984. He says that all of his statistics and analysis has allowed him to compute this function. Does Table 6.1, given at the beginning of this chapter, indicating projected budget deficit, support his claim?

The table indicates that in 1987, the projected deficit is $224 billion. The year 1987 is three years from 1984, thus we need to compute $B(3)$.

$$B(3) = -17(3)^2 + 102(3) + 71$$
$$= -17(9) + 306 + 71$$
$$= -153 + 377$$
$$= 224$$

The year 1987 with projected deficit of $224 billion clearly substantiates his claim, but what about the other years? The year 1988 corresponds to $x = 4$:

$$B(4) = -17(4)^2 + 102(4) + 71$$
$$= -272 + 408 + 71$$
$$= 207$$

The figure of $207 billion agrees with the table. However, $B(2) = 207$, compared to 219 in the table; $B(1) = 156$, compared to 207, and $B(5) = 156$, compared to 198. If the advisor uses only the years 1987 and 1988, he can substantiate his claim, but not otherwise. If his audience believes the function $B(x) = -17x^2 + 102x + 71$ represents the projected deficit, then in 1991, the budget deficit would be a negative amount, as claimed.

$$B(7) = -17(7)^2 + 102(7) + 71$$
$$= -833 + 714 + 71$$
$$= -48 \text{ billion}$$

EXAMPLE 3

In families where genes for sickle-cell anemia are present it is important to calculate the probability of producing affected children. Suppose a couple wants to have two children, and the probability from a single mating for this couple that they will have a child with sickle-cell anemia is p. Since the birth of each child is independent of preceding children, the probability of having exactly one child with sickle-cell anemia can be expressed as a quadratic function (see Section 5.2):

$$P(p) = C(2, 1)p(1 - p) = 2(p)(1 - p) = 2p - 2p^2$$

Thus, if $p = \frac{1}{4}$, $P(\frac{1}{4}) = 2(\frac{1}{4})(\frac{3}{4}) = \frac{3}{8}$.

Note that this is the same probability that you would have computed had you used the product and sum rules of Chapter 4.

$$P = \left(\frac{1}{4}\right)\left(\frac{3}{4}\right) + \left(\frac{3}{4}\right)\left(\frac{1}{4}\right) = 2\left(\frac{3}{16}\right) = \frac{3}{8}.$$

If the couple wishes to determine the probability that exactly one of four anticipated children will have sickle-cell anemia, then the function is still a polynomial function, but not quadratic. The function is now

$$P(p) = C(4, 1)(p)(1 - p)^3 = 4p(1 - p)^3$$ ■

PRACTICE EXAMPLE 3

Evaluate the quadratic probability function above for $p = \frac{1}{2}$ and $p = \frac{1}{8}$. Evaluate the fourth degree probability function for the same values. ■

Suppose G is a graph and we want to count the number of ways of coloring (see Section 2.1) G with four colors. We can represent that number by function $P_G(x)$. For example, if G is the graph shown in Figure 6.12, the number of ways of coloring G with two colors is given by $P_G(2) = 2 \times 1 \times 1 = 2$, by the product rule. There are two choices for vertex a, after coloring a there is one choice for vertex b since it must be of a different color, and one for vertex c since its color must be different from b's. Similarly $P_G(3) = 3 \times 2 \times 2 = 12$. Generally, $P_G(x) = x(x - 1)(x - 1) = x(x - 1)$ for G as shown in Figure 6.12.

Figure 6.12

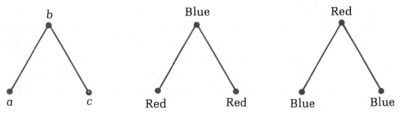

If G is the graph shown in Figure 6.13, then

$$P_G(x) = x(x - 1)(x - 2)(x - 3)$$

since there are x choices for coloring a, then one less, or $x - 1$ choices for coloring b since b is adjacent to a, then $x - 2$ for coloring c since c is adjacent to a and b, and last, $x - 3$ choices for coloring d since d is adjacent to each of the other three. The student should observe that we must have $x \geq 4$ for $P_G(x)$ to be positive, so at least four colors are used to color the graph in Figure 6.13.

Figure 6.13

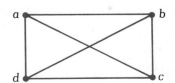

The graph coloring problem is directly related to coloring maps as was pointed out in Section 2.1. Birkhoff in 1912 showed that $P_G(x)$, is always a polynomial function where G corresponds to a map, and, with Lewis in 1946, showed that for all G, $P_G(x)$ is a polynomial. $P_G(x)$ is called the **chromatic polynomial** for the graph G.

Let us return to the channel assignment function given in Section 6.2. How many ways are there of assigning the 11 numbered channels to TV stations in New England so that the stations less than 100 miles apart receive different numbers?

Figure 6.14

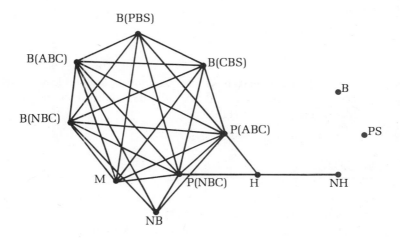

In Figure 6.14, an edge joins two stations if the stations are less than 100 miles apart. If we start with a Boston station, then each must get a different channel, and each different from the two Providence channels, so we have $11 \times 10 \times 9 \times 8 \times 7 \times 6$ choices for these six stations. Similarly Manchester and New Bedford must get a different channel from Boston and Providence as they are less than 100 miles apart. Thus we have $11 \times 10 \times 9 \times 8 \times 7 \times 6 \times 5 \times 4$ at this point, or more generally $x(x - 1)(x - 2)(x - 3)(x - 4)(x - 5)(x - 6)(x - 7)$. Burlington and Poland Springs are not within 100 miles of any place else so they can be assigned any one of the 11 channels. Hartford must be different from the two Providence stations, thus nine choices remain for Hartford. New Haven must be different from Hartford, thus 10 choices are possible for New Haven. Therefore the number of ways the 11 stations can be assigned is $(11 \times 10 \times 9 \times 8 \times 7 \times 6 \times 5 \times 4)(11)(11)(9)(10)$ or more generally for the graph corresponding to the stations and the distance between them:

$$P_G(x) = (x)(x - 1)(x - 2)(x - 3)(x - 4)(x - 5)(x - 6)(x - 7)(x)(x)(x - 2)(x - 1)$$

$$P_G(x) = x^3(x - 1)^2(x - 2)^2(x - 3)(x - 4)(x - 5)(x - 6)(x - 7)$$

PRACTICE
EXAMPLE **4** Compute the chromatic polynomial for the graph shown below. How many
ways are there to color the graph using four colors?

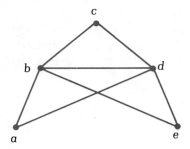

In the next section we look at another special kind of relation, called an
equivalence relation, and we consider such problems as finding the right
blood donor or the right car.

CONCEPTS

linear function	x-intercept
slope	quadratic function
y-intercept	chromatic polynomial

SOLUTIONS TO PRACTICE EXAMPLES

1. Points (100, 1500) and (200, 2500)

$$\frac{2500 - 1500}{200 - 100} = \frac{y - 1500}{x - 100}$$

$$1000(x - 100) = 100(y - 1500)$$

$$10x - 1000 = y - 1500$$

$$10x + 500 = y$$

2. $2x + 5y = 10$. Intercepts are (0, 2) and (5, 0).

3. $P(p) = 2p - 2p^2$

$P\left(\frac{1}{2}\right) = \frac{1}{2}$, and $P\left(\frac{1}{8}\right) = \frac{7}{32}$

$P(p) = 4p(1 - p)^3$

$P\left(\frac{1}{2}\right) = \frac{1}{4}$ and $P\left(\frac{1}{8}\right) = \frac{343}{1024}$

4. $P_G(x) = x(x - 1)(x - 2)^3$

    $P_G(3) = 6$ and $P_G(4) = 96$

    x choices for a, then only $x - 1$ choices for b, and $x - 2$ choices for c, d, and e.

EXERCISES 6.3

For Exercises 1 through 5, find the equation of the straight line through each of the following pairs of points:

1. (200, 30) and (500, 10)

2. (15, 5) and (5, 10)

3. (1000, 100) and (100, 1000)

4. (10, 25) and (20, 35)

5. (120, 10) and (100, 8)

6. It costs $1500 to produce 100 shirts and $2000 to produce 200 shirts. Write the linear cost equation where x is the number of shirts produced and y is the cost to produce the shirts.

7. It requires 8 men to lay 75 miles of asphalt, and it requires 10 men to lay 100 miles of asphalt. Write a linear equation where x is the number of men and y is the number of miles of asphalt.

8. A liquor company produces whiskey that requires 4 machine hours to bottle one bottle and bourbon that requires 3 machine hours to bottle one bottle. There are 20,000 machine hours used. Let x denote the number of bottles of whiskey and y denote the number of bottles of bourbon. Write a linear equation to represent the machine hours.

9–11. Find the intercepts in the equations derived in Exercises 6 through 8.

12. Which of the following are linear equations?

    (a) $2x - y = 10$

    (b) $x^2 + y = 5$

    (c) $3x_1 + 4x_2 = 10$

    (d) $3x_1^2 - 4x_2^2 = 10$

    (e) $p(p + 1) = 100$

    *(f) $pq = 4$

13. The cost of removing x pounds of pollutant from water is $C(x) = .2x^2 + 1000$. Find $C(0)$ and $C(100)$.

14. The table below represents data relating net income and stock price:

Net income (in thousands)	Stock price
$106	$29
51	23
34	16
11	13

An analyst claims that stock prices, p, are related to net income, n, by the equation $16n + 1059 = 95p$. Does the table substantiate that claim?

15. Can you find another equation for the table above, using pairs (51, 23) and (11, 13)?

16. How many ways are there to color the graph shown with three colors? With four colors?

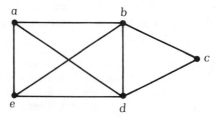

17. What is the chromatic polynomial for the graph below?

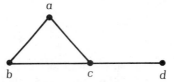

6.4   *Equivalence Relations—How to Cut up the Pie*

In this section we look at another special type of relation on a set, called an equivalence relation. Computer technology has allowed us to store increasingly large amounts of data, retrieve bits of data quickly, and manipulate the data. Even the largest computers cannot store every piece of information in the world, much less call forth a particular item at a moment's notice. Therefore, we need ways of classifying information so that we can work with representatives of each class, rather than whole classes.

EXAMPLE 1   Let S be the set of people in Massachusetts who have been blood typed, and R be the relation of having the same blood type. As shown in Figure 6.15, the set S is divided into pieces (classes) according to blood type by the relation *R*. A person who enters Massachusetts General Hospital needs blood and is blood typed as A+. Rather than look at all the people in Massachusetts that have been blood typed, it suffices to look at the piece (class) of *S* with blood type A+, and to choose one representative from this piece to donate blood.

Figure 6.15

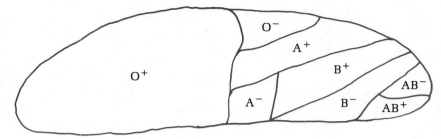

EXAMPLE 2

The Pontiac dealers in New York State want to know which dealers in the state have which models of 1986 Pontiac cars in case a customer wants a model that the local dealer does not have. Let *S* be the set of 1986 Pontiac cars located on dealer lots in New York State. Two cars in *S* are in the relation *P* if they are the same model. All dealers have computers that allow them to type in the model of the 1986 Pontiac that they want, and the computer should produce a list of the dealers with that model. The relation *P* divides the set of 1986 Pontiac cars on New York State dealers' lots into classes based on model, as illustrated by Figure 6.16, and this information can be fed into the computer. Once the computer has produced the list of dealers that have the particular model, an appropriate car can be found by choosing any one of the dealers from the list and negotiating a trade.

Figure 6.16

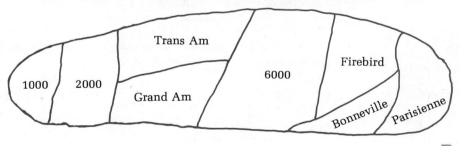

EXAMPLE 3

Sequences of 0's and 1's can be used to encode information. For example, 1 can denote that a switch is on (electric current can flow), 0 can denote that a switch is off (electric current cannot flow). Suppose we have a set of three switches, as in a light that has three separate control switches (one on the lamp and two wall switches). We can list the eight different possibilities for this sequence of three switches in the set:

$$S = \{000, 100, 010, 001, 110, 101, 011, 111\}$$

and define a relation T on S by relating two sequences if they have the same number of 1's. Now the set S can be divided into pieces, each piece representing a certain number of "on" switches in the sequences in that piece (see Figure 6.17). If a person wants only one "on" switch, he chooses a sequence from the piece labeled II.

Figure 6.17

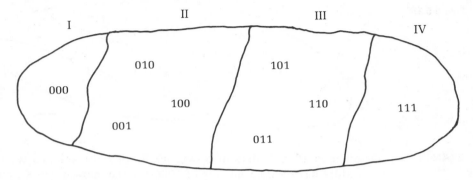

Problems of this type frequently arise in electric circuit design, where 1 indicates that a "gate" is open and 0 indicates that a "gate" is closed.

Each of these three examples is an example of an equivalence relation, since each has the three properties defined below.

DEFINITION   A relation R on a set S is **reflexive** if for all $a \in S$, $(a, a) \in R$. (Everything is related to itself.)

The directed graph representing reflexive relations, as shown in Figure 6.18, has a loop at each vertex.

Figure 6.18

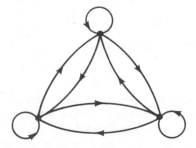

In Example 1 a person always has the same blood type as oneself. In Example 2 a car is the same model as itself, and in Example 3 a sequence of 0's and 1's has the same number of 1's as itself. In Example 3 of

Section 6.1, a person has the same insurance company and same last initial as oneself. Each of these relations are reflexive relations. On the other hand, the relation of being "the father of" on the set of people at a family reunion is not a reflexive relation, since one cannot be one's own father.

> **DEFINITION**   A relation R on a set S is **symmetric** if for all a and b in S, if $(a, b) \in R$ then $(b, a) \in R$. (If a is related to b then b is related to a.)

The directed graph of a symmetric relation is such that if one edge exists going one direction between two vertices, then there exists a second edge going in the opposite direction, as in Figure 6.18.

In Example 1 if a has the same blood type as b, then b has the same blood type as a. In Example 2 if car a is the same model as car b, then car b is the same model as car a. And in Example 3 if sequence a has the same number of 1's as sequence b, then sequence b has the same number of 1's as sequence a. Therefore, each of these examples is an example of a symmetric relation, as is the relation involving patients in a doctor's office in Section 6.1. On the other hand, the relation of being "the brother of" on a set of people that includes brothers and sisters is not a symmetric relation. John may be the brother of Mary, but Mary is not the brother of John.

The third property of an equivalence relation is usually the hardest one to check.

> **DEFINITION**   A relation R in a set S is **transitive** if for all a, b, and c in S, if $(a, b) \in R$, and $(b, c) \in R$, then $(a, c) \in R$. (If a is related to b, and b is related to c, then a is related to c.)

The directed graph shown in Figure 6.18 represents a transitive relation. For example $(1, 2) \in R$, $(2, 3) \in R$, and $(1, 3) \in R$. If person a has the same blood type as person b, who in turn has the same blood type as person c, then a and c have the same blood type. Similarly if the model of car a is the same as the model of car b, and the model of car b is the same as the model of car c, then the model of car a is the same as the model of car c. Also if a sequence of 0's and 1's, call it a, has the same number of 1's as another sequence of 0's and 1's, b, and b has the same number of 1's as a third sequence, c, then a and c have the same number of 1's. Therefore, each of these three examples is an example of a transitive relation. We noted in Section 6.1 that the relation on patients in a doctor's office was transitive. However, the relation of "is the mother of" on a set of people at a family reunion is not transitive since if a is the mother of b and b is the mother of c, a is not the mother of c, but is the grandmother of c.

> DEFINITION   A relation R on a set S is an **equivalence relation** if R is reflexive, symmetric, and transitive.

The name equivalence relation comes from the fact that equality is the prototype equivalence relation. Transitivity can be translated as "things equal to the same thing are equal to each other."

An equivalence relation R on a set S divides the set into subsets, called **equivalence classes**, such that the union of all the classes is the whole set, and such that the intersection of any two classes is the empty set.

> DEFINITION   Let R be an equivalence relation on set S. If $a \in S$, then the **equivalence class of a**, denoted C_a, is:
>
> $$C_a = \{b \mid b \in S \text{ and } (a, b) \in R\}$$

In our first three examples the classes are: various blood types for Example 1, the models of 1986 Pontiac cars for Example 2, and the four classes denoted by I, II, III, IV in Figure 6.17, corresponding to 0, 1, 2, or 3 ones in a sequence.

Different equivalence relations on the same set create different equivalence classes. For example if S is the set of 1986 Pontiac cars on dealers' lots in New York State, the relation of "being on the same lot" would divide the set into many more and different classes than the relation of "being the same model as."

Once an equivalence relation divides the set into equivalence classes, one representative of each class can be chosen to work with, rather than having to look at each member of the set individually. In our examples one person can be chosen from class A+ to give blood, one dealer of a particular model Pontiac car can be chosen to negotiate a trade, one sequence with just one 1 in it can be chosen to be sure that the light is on, not off. Each member of a class will have the same characteristic as every other member of the class.

PRACTICE EXAMPLE 1

Tell whether each of the following relations is an equivalence relation; if not, why not. If it is an equivalence relation tell what the equivalence classes are.

1. $S = \{0, 1, 2, 3\}$ and $R = \{(a, b) \mid a \leq b\}$.
2. S is the set of NFL football players and R is the relation of "being on the same team."
3. $S = \{0, 1, 00, 01, 10, 11, 000, 001, 010, 100, 110, 101, 011, 111\}$ and $R = \{(a, b) \mid a$ and b have the same number of digits in their respective sequences (the same length sequence)$\}$.

4. S is the lovers' triangle of John, Mary, and Peter. $R = \{$(John, Mary), (Mary, John), (Mary, Peter), (Peter, Mary)$\}$.

In this section we considered equivalence relations—relations that are reflexive, symmetric, and transitive. In the next section we look at relations that are reflexive and transitive, but not symmetric.

CONCEPTS

reflexive	equivalence relation
symmetric	equivalence classes
transitive	equivalence class of a

SOLUTIONS TO PRACTICE EXAMPLES

1. (1) $S = \{0, 1, 2, 3\}$ and $R = \{(a, b) \mid a \leq b\}$. It is not an equivalence relation because it is not symmetric.
    (2) $S = \{$NFL football players$\}$ and $R = $ "being on the same team as." It is an equivalence relation; the equivalence classes are the teams.
    (3) $S = \{0, 1, 00, \ldots, 111\}$ and $R = \{(a, b) \mid$ length of $a = $ length of $b\}$. It is an equivalence relation, and the equivalence classes are: $C_1 = \{0, 1\}$, $C_2 = \{00, 01, 10, 11\}$, and $C_3 = \{000, 001, 010, 100, 110, 101, 011, 111\}$.
    (4) It is not an equivalence relation—it is not reflexive and not transitive.

EXERCISES 6.4

In each of the Exercises 1 through 14, indicate if the relation is an equivalence relation; if not, why not.

1. $R = \{(1, 1), (1, 3), (3, 3), (3, 1)\}$.

2. $R = \{(a, b), (b, c), (c, d), (a, d), (a, c), (b, d)\}$.

3. $R = \{(3, 4), (4, 3), (5, 6), (6, 5), (3, 3), (4, 4), (5, 5), (6, 6)\}$.

4. $R = \{(\#, \$), (\#, \#), (\%, \%), (\$, \$)\}$.

5. $R = \{(1, 1), (2, 2), (3, 3), (1, 2), (3, 2)\}$.

    $S = $ set of books in the bookstore
6. $R = \{(a, b) \mid$ book a costs more than book $b\}$.

7. $R = \{(a, b) \mid$ book a has the same number of pages as book $b\}$.

8. $R = \{(a, b) \mid$ book a and book b are for the same course$\}$.

    $S = $ set of people in Ohio
9. $R = \{(a, b) \mid a$ and b own the same computer$\}$.

10. $R = \{(a, b) \mid a$ and b have the same last name$\}$.

11. $R = \{(a, b) \mid a$ is older than $b\}$.

12. $R = \{(a, b) \mid a$ is a relative of $b\}$.

S = set of squares

13. $R = \{(a, b) \mid a$ and b have the same area$\}$.

14. $R = \{(a, b) \mid$ the length of side of a is the same as the length of the side of $b\}$.

15. In each of Exercises 1 through 14, if R is an equivalence relation, describe the equivalence classes.

In Exercises 16 through 21 each directed graph corresponds to a relation. Which correspond to equivalence relations? Which do not? Why not?

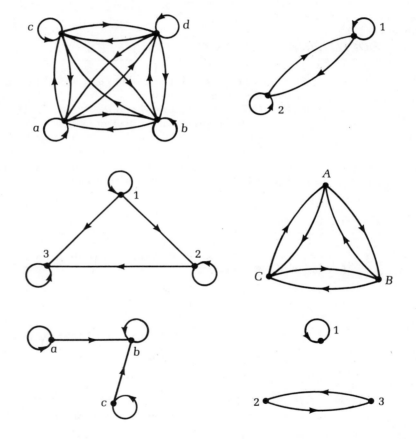

22. $S = \mathcal{N}$, E is the even numbers, and O is the odd numbers. Define an equivalence relation on S so that E and O are the equivalence classes.

23. $S = \{$registered voters$\}$, $A = \{$registered Republicans$\}$, $B = \{$registered Democrats$\}$, $C = \{$no party affiliation$\}$. Describe an equivalence relation on S such that A, B, and C are the equivalence classes.

6.5   Order Relations

In the last section, we looked at relations on a set, called equivalence relations, that allowed us to divide the set into pieces, or classes, so that we could choose a representative from each class and work with only these representatives, instead of the whole class. In other words we grouped like things together. In this section we will look at properties of relations on a set that accentuate differences and allow us to arrange, or order, the set in different ways.

EXAMPLE 1   A computer is given a set of file numbers corresponding to invoices for a particular manufacturing firm. The numbers are not given in any particular order. The firm would like to have the file numbers arranged in numerical order from highest (most recent) to lowest (oldest). ▪

EXAMPLE 2   Four people are left in an international horseshoes tournament. Because each contestant is so talented, the tournament committee decides to have each person play each other person, and not to allow ties. Using this method, is it always possible to determine a winner and a ranking of the four players? If so, how? ▪

EXAMPLE 3   In computing the amount of federal income tax a person owes, the accountant usually has to complete many forms. Unfortunately some of the forms or parts of forms must be completed before others. It would save the accountant considerable time if the forms and parts of forms were organized in the order in which each had to be completed. Can this be done? ▪

EXAMPLE 4   A group of four people are asked to visit five restaurants and to indicate if they like the restaurant or do not like the restaurant. When all the data is collected, the researcher would like to list the people and the restaurants on a line, so that each person likes all the restaurants that follow him or her on the line and dislikes all the restaurants that precede him or her on the line. ▪

Each of these examples illustrates an application of various types of "order" relations on a set. Before we look at these examples in detail, we need to define some additional properties of relations.

> DEFINITION   A relation R on a set S is **antisymmetric** if for all a and b in S, if $(a, b) \in R$ and $(b, a) \in R$, then $a = b$.

The relation less than or equal to on the set $S = \{0, 1, 2, 3\}$ is antisymmetric, for if $a \leq b$ and $b \leq a$ then $a = b$. The relation less than is also antisymmetric because we never have $a < b$ and $b < a$. Each of the four examples of equivalence relations in the last section were not anti-symmetric, since we always had a class with more than one element.

> DEFINITION   A relation R on a set S is **complete** (sometimes called **strongly complete**) if for all a and b in S, either $(a, b) \in R$ or $(b, a) \in R$.

Notice that a relation that is complete must be reflexive, since all pairs (a, a) must be in R.

The set S of file numbers given to the computer in Example 1 is related by the greater than or equal to relation, which is an antisymmetric and complete relation on S. A property of inequalities states that if $a \geq b$ and $b \geq c$ then $a \geq c$, thus greater than or equal to is also a transitive relation. These properties are sufficient to order the set in descending (or ascending) order, in other words, in a line. Even sets that do not contain numbers can be ordered in a straight line if the relation on the set is antisymmetric, transitive, and complete.

> DEFINITION   A relation R on a set S is a **linear order** if R is anti-symmetric, transitive, and complete.

Various computer algorithms (programs) exist that will put the file numbers in ascending linear order, including Quicksort, Mergesort, and Heapsort. Bubblesort is an easy, but not very efficient, way to order the file numbers in ascending order. Compare the last number with the number before it, moving it ahead of the number if it is smaller than it. Continue comparisons moving down the list from right to left, until the smallest number is in the first place. Repeat this procedure, so that the second number is in the second place, and so on. For example sort 10, 3, 9, 5, 8, 7:

$$
\left.
\begin{array}{l}
10, 3, 9, 5, 8, 7 \\
10, 3, 9, 5, 7, 8 \\
10, 3, 5, 9, 7, 8 \\
3, 10, 5, 9, 7, 8
\end{array}
\right\} \text{ to get 3 in the first place}
$$

$$
\left.
\begin{array}{l}
3, 10, 5, 7, 9, 8 \\
3, 10, 5, 7, 8, 9 \\
3, 5, 10, 7, 8, 9
\end{array}
\right\} \text{ to get 5 in the second place}
$$

$$
\left.
\begin{array}{l}
3, 5, 7, 10, 8, 9 \\
3, 5, 7, 8, 10, 9 \\
3, 5, 7, 8, 9, 10
\end{array}
\right\} \text{ to get 7 in the third place}
$$

Recall from Chapter 3 that we could also use a decision tree to sort this set of numbers.

PRACTICE EXAMPLE 1

Determine which of the following relations is a linear order:

1. $S = \{A, A-, B, B+, B-, C+, C, C-, F\}$; R is the relation of "being a better than or equal grade"
2. $S = \{$students in History 101$\}$; R is the relation of having the same professor

Let S be the set of four finalists in the horseshoe tournament of Example 2, and R be the relation of "beats." Assume that the players play until someone wins (no ties). This relation R is antisymmetric, but it is not complete, since it is not reflexive. A player cannot beat onself.

Our horseshoe game is a tournament according to *Webster's* dictionary, which defines a *tournament* as a game in which competitors play a series of contests. However since we want to define a tournament more rigorously so that each player must play each other player until one or the other wins (no ties), we will use the graph theoretical definition of a tournament.

> DEFINITION   A directed graph is a **tournament** if for all vertices a and b, $a \neq b$, (a, b) is a directed edge, or (b, a) is a directed edge, but not both.

Thus a tournament corresponds to an antisymmetric relation that is almost complete. The reflexive pairs are not required. Mathematicians studied tournaments to answer questions about determining winners.

In a tournament, we can associate with each player a **score**, namely, the number of players that the player beats. In any graph, the score of a vertex, v, is the number of vertices, u, such that there is an edge from v to u (the outdegree of v). For example consider the tournament shown in Figure 6.19. The player with the maximum score, namely player C, is declared the winner.

Figure 6.19

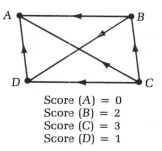

Score $(A) = 0$
Score $(B) = 2$
Score $(C) = 3$
Score $(D) = 1$

A famous theorem of Landau states: In a tournament, if player (vertex) v has maximum score, then for all other players (vertices) u, either v beats u or player v beats a player w, who in turn beats u.

Landau discovered this theorem while studying the pecking order of chickens. Every chicken is pecked by a "king" chicken or is pecked by a chicken that is pecked by a king chicken.

Not only can we find the player(s) with the maximum score in many tournaments, but we can determine when the scores will produce a ranking of the players.

Not all tournaments are transitive (correspond to transitive relations). Figure 6.20(a) gives a transitive tournament, but Figure 6.20(b) gives a nontransitive tournament.

Figure 6.20

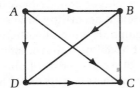 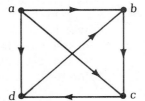

THEOREM   A tournament has a unique hamiltonian path if and only if the corresponding relation is transitive. Moreover, the unique hamiltonian path can be found by choosing vertices in decreasing order of their scores.

Thus, if a tournament is transitive, we can find not only a winner, but a complete ranking of players. We are able to get a linear type of ordering even when the relation is not reflexive.

A trivial example of a tournament is the greater than relation on the set $S = \{0, 1, 2, 3, 4, 5\}$. What is the score of each element here?

Figure 6.21 represents the results of a paired comparison experiment, where each of a group of 21 individuals was asked his or her preference for one brand of TV over another. The group is said to prefer one over the other if more than half have that preference.

Figure 6.21

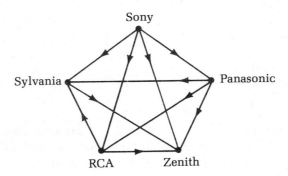

To get a ranking of the brands of TV:

STEP 1:   Compute the score of each brand:

score(Sony) = 4
score(Sylvania) = 1
score(Panasonic) = 3
score(RCA) = 2
score(Zenith) = 0

STEP 2:   Rank the brands by arranging the scores in descending order:

4 — Sony
3 — Panasonic
2 — RCA
1 — Sylvania
0 — Zenith

The theorem not only gives the conditions required for a ranking to exist in a tournament, but also tells when the corresponding relation is transitive (sometimes a difficult task otherwise). Simply compute the set of scores and see if the set is the set of integers from 0 to $n - 1$, where n is the number of vertices. The hamiltonian path will be $u_1, u_2, \ldots, u_n$, where score$(u_1) = n - 1$, score$(u_2) = n - 2, \ldots,$ score$(u_k) = n - k, \ldots,$ score$(u_n) = 0$. (See Moon 1968 for a proof.)

PRACTICE EXAMPLE 2

The results of a paired comparison experiment for brands of coffee were given in Section 6.1. Does there exist a "best" brand and a ranking of the brands? What is this ranking?

In the income tax problem of Example 3, we are looking for some way to order the forms where a linear ordering is not initially given. The relation of "must precede or is the same form as" on the set of income tax forms or parts of forms is not complete, thus it is not a linear order and is not a tournament. It is a reflexive and transitive relation as well as an antisymmetric relation.

> DEFINITION   A relation R on a set S is a **partial order** if R is reflexive, antisymmetric, and transitive.

The relation "must precede or is the same as" on the set of income tax forms or parts of forms in Example 3 is therefore a partial order. Every linear order is a partial order, but not vice versa.

Relations that are partial orders have the advantage that they can be pictured as a graph, not just as a directed graph. The graph of a partial order, called a **Hasse diagram**, culls out the essential parts of the directed graph. Since partial orders are reflexive, the loops at each vertex are suppressed, and since a partial order is also antisymmetric, an edge rather than a directed edge is included between two paired vertices. To indicate direction, vertex a is positioned below vertex b if $(a, b) \in R$. If $(a, b) \in R$, a will be below b, and if $(b, c) \in R$, b will be below c; thus there will be a path from a up to c, and the need to include an edge between a and c is eliminated. Figure 6.22 gives the Hasse diagram for the income tax forms in Example 3.

Figure 6.22

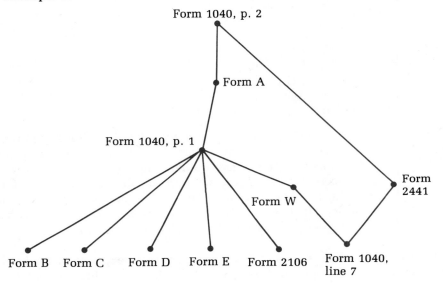

In order to answer the question originally posed in Example 3, we want to find a linear order of forms that contains all of the pairs of the partial order relation. Since the Hasse diagram includes vertices positioned above or below others, the diagram can be considered to have levels. Level 0 consists of all vertices that no vertex precedes. Level 1 consists of all vertices preceded by vertices in at most one step. Level k consists of vertices preceded by vertices along a longest upward path with k edges. To construct the linear order, simply list the vertices by level—all those at level 0, followed by all those at level 1, etc. (This procedure is often called *topological sorting.*) The linear order of forms in our income tax example is:

B, C, D, E, 2106, line 7, W, 2441, page 1, A, page 2

Levels: 0   1   2   3   4

Hasse diagrams of partially ordered sets representing precedence relations are called *PERT networks.*

**PRACTICE
EXAMPLE 3**

Let $S = \{1, 2, 3, 4, 5, 6\}$ and $R = \{(1, 1), (1, 2), (1, 3), (1, 4), (1, 5), (1, 6), (2, 2), (2, 4), (2, 6), (3, 3), (3, 6), (4, 4), (5, 5), (6, 6)\}$. Is R a partial order? Draw the Hasse diagram for R. Can you describe the relation R in words? ■

The restaurant evaluation problem posed in Example 4 asks if there exists a listing (ordering) of people and restaurants, such that each person in the list likes the restaurants that follow him or her in the list and dislikes the restaurants that precede him or her in the list. We could say each restaurant is liked by those people preceding it in the list and disliked by those people following it in the list. We can define a relation, R, from the set of people, S, to the set of restaurants, T, where (a, b) is in R if $a \in S$ and $b \in T$ and a likes b. $R \subseteq S \times T$. If we want R to be a relation *on* a set, then we could view R as a relation from $S \cup T$ to $S \cup T$. Now $R \subseteq (S \cup T) \times (S \cup T)$. Either way, R is not reflexive, not transitive, and not complete, but is antisymmetric. Therefore this relation does not fall into any of our previous categories.

The basic techniques for creating lists with two different sets interlocked in this way is called **Guttman scaling**. Guttman originally used this technique during World War II to investigate such diverse topics as enlisted men's attitudes toward officers and fear symptoms in combat. It is used in educational testing with sets of individuals and test items. An individual answers every question correctly that follows him or her in the list and answers every question incorrectly that precedes him or her in the list. If a Guttman scale exists for the data, one of the questions is given to another person, and if that person answers it correctly, it can be predicted that that person will answer all of the questions following it on the scale correctly.

The procedure for determining if a Guttman scale exists for a set of data, and that for actually constructing the scale are the same. In 1983 techniques of graph theory were applied to the construction of Guttman scales. We apply this procedure to a hypothetical set of data for the restaurant problem:

STEP 1: Construct a graph as follows (Figure 6.23). The vertex set is $V = S \cup T$, and $\{a, b\}$ is an edge if a and b are both in S, or $a \in S$ and $b \in T$ and a likes b.

Figure 6.23

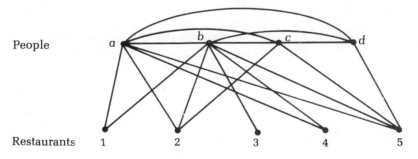

People

a   b   c   d

Restaurants   1   2   3   4   5

STEP 2: If there is a Guttman scale, then there is a vertex (person) that is adjacent to all others (maybe more than one), or a vertex (restaurant) (maybe more than one) that is adjacent to no others. Choose such a vertex to be first on your list. In this example, choose b.

STEP 3: Remove the chosen vertex, b, and all adjacent edges, from the graph. If a Guttman scale exists, there will again be a vertex adjacent to all others, or a vertex adjacent to no others. Choose such a vertex to be next on your list. In this example choose 3.

Repeat steps 2 and 3 until two vertices remain.

STEP 4: Two vertices remain, say x and y.

1. If $\{x, y\} \notin E$ and x is a subject and y is an item, choose y then x.
2. If $\{x, y\} \in E$ and both are subjects, choose x, then y.
3. If $\{x, y\} \in E$ and x is a subject and y is an item, choose x then y.

The resulting list will be a Guttman scale for the data. If you cannot continue at any stage, then no Guttman scale is possible. Figure 6.24 shows Steps 2–4 of the procedure applied to the restaurant problem.

Figure 6.24

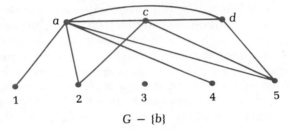

$G - \{b\}$

Choose vertex 3, then vertex a:

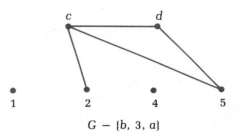

$G - \{b, 3, a\}$

Choose vertex 1 and vertex 4:

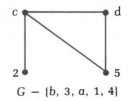

$G - \{b, 3, a, 1, 4\}$

Choose vertex c:

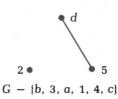

$G - \{b, 3, a, 1, 4, c\}$

Choose vertex 2:

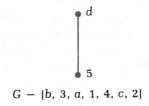

$$G - \{b, 3, a, 1, 4, c, 2\}$$

$\{d, 5\} \in E$. d is subject, 5 is item. Choose vertex d, then vertex 5. The Guttman scale is:

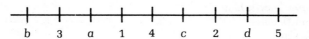

b 3 a 1 4 c 2 d 5

EXAMPLE 5

Four trial questions for the SAT exam are posed to four students, and their correct responses are recorded in Table 6.4.

TABLE 6.4

		Questions			
		1	2	3	4
	A	C		C	
Students	B		C		C
	D	C	C		C
	E		C	C	C

The graph constructed in Step 1 of the procedure for finding a Guttman scale is shown in Figure 6.25. Step 2 cannot be carried out, because there is no vertex adjacent to all others, nor a vertex adjacent to no others. Therefore no Guttman scale exists for this data.

Figure 6.25

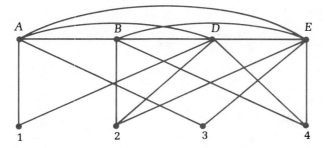

PRACTICE
EXAMPLE 4

In eight civil rights cases presented to the U.S. Supreme Court in 1961, the nine judges voted the liberal side of eight cases as shown in Table 6.5. L means liberal side. Those judges who voted exactly alike on the eight cases are grouped together, as are cases for which the votes were the same. Can the judges and the cases be arranged in a list so that each judge voted the liberal side of each case that follows him in the list, and did not vote the liberal side of each case that precedes him in the list?

TABLE 6.5

| | Cases | | |
	1, 2, 3, 7, 8, 4	5	6
Warren and Brennan	L L		L
Frankfurter and Harlan	L		
Black and Douglas	L L	L	L
Whittaker and Clark			
Stewart	L		L

CONCEPTS

antisymmetric

complete (strongly complete)

linear order

tournament

score

partial order

Hasse diagram

Guttman scaling

SOLUTIONS TO PRACTICE EXAMPLES

1. (1) Yes.
   (2) No because it is not symmetric.

2. score(A) = 3, score(B) = 2, score(C) = 1, score(D) = 0. Yes, the ranking is A–B–C–D, and A is best.

3. Yes it is a partial order.

Hasse diagram

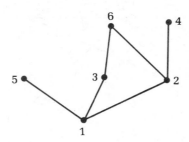

R is the relation "a divides b" on the set.
$S = \{1, 2, 3, 4, 5, 6\}$.

4.

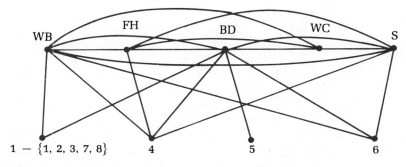

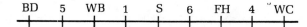

$1 - \{1, 2, 3, 7, 8\}$ 4   5   6

Guttman scale is:

BD   5   WB   1   S   6   FH   4   ¨WC

EXERCISES 6.5

1–21.   For each of the exercises 1 through 21 of Exercise 6.4, indicate if the relation R is a:

(a) linear order.

(b) partial order.

22.   Recall that the power set of a set A is the set of all subsets of A. Let $A = \{1, 2, 3\}$.

(a) Find the power set of A, denoted $\mathscr{P}(A)$.

(b) Let $S = \mathscr{P}(A)$ and R be the subset relation. $T_1 R T_2$ if $T_1 \subseteq T_2$. Write out R.

(c) Show that R is a partial order on S.

(d) Draw the Hasse diagram.

In each of the tournaments illustrated in Exercises 23 through 25, find the score of each individual, a hamiltonian path if one exists, and a winner.

23.

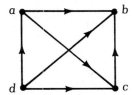

24.

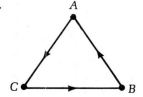

25.

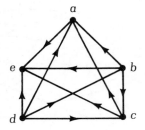

26. The following directed graph corresponds to a relation on $S = \{0, 1, 2, 3, 4, 5\}$. Use the scores to determine if the relation is transitive.

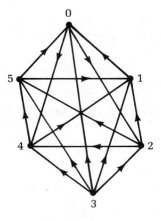

27. The following data represent agreement by individuals with key issues in a local election. A denotes agree. Construct a Guttman scale for this data.

		Issues				
		1	2	3	4	5
	P_1	A	A		A	A
	P_2	A	A		A	
Individuals	P_3					
	P_4	A	A		A	
	P_5		A			

28. Is the score sequence just another way of doing a borda count to get a ranking? (See Chapter 1.4.) Discuss.

29. A bicycle manufacturer must include a set of instructions for putting the bicycle together. There are six parts that must be assembled. The following Hasse diagram illustrates those parts that must be assembled before other parts. The manufacturer wants to number the parts from 1 to 6 in the order the customer can put them together. Find such a numbering.

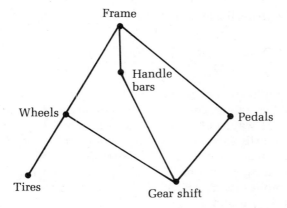

CHAPTER SUMMARY

In this chapter we defined a *relation* as the subset of a *cartesian product* of two sets (not necessarily distinct). We showed that relations can be described by tables, charts, coordinate system graphs, and directed graphs.

A *function* is a particular kind of relation, or subset of $A \times B$, where the first members may not be repeated, and each member of A appears as a first member in the relation. If a relation is depicted by an x–y coordinate system graph, then the *vertical line test* can be used to check if it is a function. A function from A to B is *onto* if the *range* of the function is all of B. A function from A to B is *one-to-one* if each element of the range corresponds to only one element of the *domain*. If a function is depicted with an x–y coordinate system graph, then the *horizontal line test* can be used to check if it is one-to-one.

Functions are a useful way of describing such relationships as those that determine cost, sales, revenue, and profit. A *cost function* is made up of two parts, the variable part or *variable costs*, which depend on the quantity produced, and the *fixed costs*, which are incurred even if nothing is produced.

When a function, f, is one-to-one and onto from A to B, we can reverse the pairs in the relation and get the *inverse function*, f^{-1}, from B to A. For example, it is often useful to think of both price as a function of demand, and demand as a function of price. One function is the inverse of the other.

In Section 6.3, we discussed various types of polynomial functions that can be expressed as:

$$f(x) = a_0 + a_1 x + a_2 x^2 + \cdots + a_n x^n, \quad a_n \neq 0$$

When $a_i = 0$ for all $i \geq 2$ and $a_1 \neq 0$, f is called a *linear function*, and when $a_i = 0$ for all $i \geq 3$ and $a_2 \neq 0$, f is called a *quadratic function*. We can graph linear functions in the x–y coordinate system by finding the x- and y-intercepts, points where the graph crosses the x and y axes. We can most easily write linear equations given two points by using the slope equation:

$$m = \frac{y_2 - y_1}{x_2 - x_1} = \frac{y - y_1}{x - x_1}$$

As an application of polynomial functions we computed the chromatic polynomial for graphs. The *chromatic polynomial* of a graph G, $P_G(x)$, counts the number of ways of coloring G with x colors.

In the fourth section we looked at another special kind of relation, called an *equivalence relation*. A relation $R \subseteq S \times S$ is *reflexive* if for all $a \in S$, $(a, a) \in R$. A relation $R \subseteq S \times S$ is *symmetric* if for all $a, b \in S$, $(a, b) \in R$ implies $(b, a) \in R$. A relation $R \subseteq S \times S$ is *transitive* if for all $a, b, c \in S$, $(a, b) \in R$ and $(b, c) \in R$ implies $(a, c) \in R$. An equivalence relation is reflexive, symmetric, and transitive. We used equivalence relations to find representatives of equivalent elements of a set, called *equivalence classes*.

A relation $R \subseteq S \times S$ is *antisymmetric* if for all $a, b \in S$, (a, b) in R and (b, a) in R implies $a = b$. A *partial order* is a reflexive, antisymmetric, and transitive relation. A relation $R \subseteq S \times S$ is *complete* if for all $a, b \in S$, either $(a, b) \in R$ or $(b, a) \in R$. A complete partial order is a *linear order*. We showed how to get a linear order that contains a partial order. If the relation is complete then it is a *tournament*, and a ranking of players is possible if there is a hamiltonian path (if the relation is transitive). We also showed how to use the properties of a relation to construct a *Guttman scale*.

REVIEW EXERCISES FOR CHAPTER 6

1. Draw the directed graph corresponding to the relation $R = \{(1, 1), (1, 2), (3, 1), (2, 3), (3, 3)\}$.

2. Write the set of ordered pairs for the relation described by the following directed graph:

3. Write the set of ordered pairs for the relation described in the following table:

Price	Demand
$50	1500
$52	1000
$54	800
$60	500

4. Find the cartesian product of $A = \{a, b, c\}$ and $B = \{1, 2\}$.

5. $C(x) = 200x + 560$ is the cost function for producing x items. Find $C(x)$ for x = 0, 10, 15, and 20.

In Exercises 6 through 8 indicate if each is a function, one-to-one, and onto:

6. $A \longrightarrow B$

7. $A = B = \mathscr{R}$

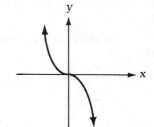

8. $\{(x, y \mid y = x - 1\}$

$A = B = \mathscr{R}$

9. A shirt sells for $16; it costs $8 to produce, plus fixed costs of $1000. Write a linear cost function, revenue function, and profit function.

10. Find the equation of the straight line through (100, 50) and (250, 100).

11. It requires 10 accountants to process 100 tax returns and 15 accountants to process 180 tax returns. Write a linear equation with x as the number of tax returns and y as the number of accountants.

12. The cost of storing x tons of hazardous waste is $C(x) = .1x^2 - x + 1000$. Find $C(0)$, $C(10)$, and $C(100)$.

13. How many ways are there to color the graph shown with three colors? With four colors?

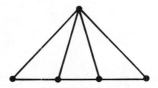

Indicate if the relation given in Exercises 14 through 19 is an equivalence relation, partial order, or linear order. If not, why not?

14. $S = \{A, B, C\}$. $R = \{(A, A), (A, B), (A, C), (B, B), (C, C), (B, A), (C, A)\}$.

15. $S = \{$Massachusetts tax returns filed$\}$.
    $R = \{(a, b) \mid$ return a and return b indicate the same net tax$\}$.

16. $S = \{a, b, c\}$, $R = \{(a, b), (a, c), (b, c), (a, a), (b, b), (c, c)\}$.

17. $S = \{1, 2, 3, 4\}$. $R = \{(1, 1), (1, 2), (3, 4), (4, 4)\}$.

18. $S = \{$students graduating from Hudson High School$\}$.
    $R = \{(a, b) \mid a$ has a higher or equal class rank than $b\}$.

19. $S = \{$students in Accounting I$\}$.
     $R = \{(a, b) \mid a$ and b have the same professor$\}$.

20. $S = \{$students applying for jobs with IBM, Kodak, Xerox$\}$
     $A = \{$students applying for jobs with IBM$\}$
     $B = \{$students applying for jobs with Kodak$\}$
     $C = \{$students applying for jobs with Xerox$\}$

     Describe an equivalence relation on S such that A, B, and C are the equivalence classes.

21. Is the following directed graph the graph of an equivalence relation? If not, why not?

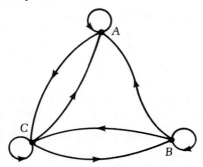

22. Find the score of each player in the following tournament. Find a hamiltonian path if one exists.

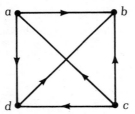

23. Draw the Hasse diagram for the partial order defined on $S = \{00, 01, 10, 11\}$ by $R = \{(a, b)$ number of zeroes of $a \leq$ number of zeroes of $b\}$. Find a linear order that contains the partial order.

Mathematics of Finance

7

In this chapter, we show how to answer such questions as: How much money must a company invest in order to have $100,000 two years from now to modernize a warehouse? How much money must a state lottery deposit into an account in order to pay out $50,000 a year for 20 years to the winner of their million dollar prize? How much will a couple have 20 years from now if they deposit $2000 each year into a retirement account? How much money can you borrow if you can afford to pay back the loan with payments of $200 a month?

In Section 7.1, we treat the situation in which one deposit is made. In Section 7.2, we show how to find future balances when regular deposits or withdrawals are made. Mortgages and installment loans are covered in Section 7.3.

7.1 Savings Accounts—Compound Interest

In most accounts, **interest** is periodically added to the balance, and this new balance is then used to compute the interest for the next period. This procedure for computing the interest is called **compounding the interest**. In this section we show how to compute the balance in an account in which the interest is compounded. You will also learn how to compute the amount of money that must be deposited now in order to have a specified amount in the future.

The formula:

(1)   interest = (balance) × (interest rate in decimal form)

is used to compute the interest earned on an account. For example, if the balance is $1000 and the **interest rate** is five percent (.05) **per year** then the interest for one year is computed by substituting:

$$interest = (balance) \times (interest\ rate)$$

$$= 1000 \times .05$$

$$= 50$$

The interest earned on $1000 at five percent for one year is $50.

EXAMPLE 1   If $1000 is deposited in a bank account that earns interest at the rate of six percent per year:

(a) What is the interest earned during the first year?
(b) What is the balance at the end of the first year?

The interest is found by applying formula (1):

$$interest = (1000) \times (.06) = \$60$$

The balance at the end of one year is obtained by adding the interest to the balance at the beginning of the year:

$$\$1000 + \$60 = \$1060 = balance\ at\ the\ end\ of\ one\ year$$

In general,

(2)   balance = (previous balance) + (interest)

EXAMPLE 2   If $1060 is on deposit in an account that earns interest at the rate of six percent per year:

(a) What is the interest earned in one year?
(b) What is the balance at the end of one year?

By formula (1):

$$interest = (1060) \times (.06) = \$63.60$$

By substituting into formula (2):

$$balance = \$1060 + \$63.60 = \$1,123.60$$

PRACTICE EXAMPLE 1 $600 is deposited in an account that earns interest at the rate of eight percent per year.

(a) What is the interest earned in one year?
(b) What is the balance at the end of one year?

If the interest is computed periodically and added to the balance (as in savings and other types of accounts), then we say the interest is **compounded**. The length of time between computations of the interest is called the **interest period**. If $1000 is deposited in an account that earns interest at the rate of six percent per year, and the bank adds the interest to the balance at the end of each year, then we say the interest rate is six percent per year compounded yearly. The interest period is one year. Example 1 shows that the balance at the end of one year is $1060 and the balance at the end of two years is $1,123.60 according to Example 2.

If an account earns interest at the rate of eight percent per year compounded quarterly, then interest is added to the balance four times a year. The interest period is three months. The amount of interest is computed using formula (1), where the interest rate is the rate of interest for the three-month interest period = .08/4 = .02.

If interest is compounded once or more a year then:

$$(3) \qquad \left(\begin{matrix} \text{interest rate per} \\ \text{interest period} \end{matrix}\right) = \frac{\text{yearly interest rate}}{\begin{matrix} \text{number of times a year} \\ \text{interest is compounded} \end{matrix}}$$

For example, if an account earns interest at the rate of eight percent per year compounded quarterly (four times a year) then the **interest rate per interest period** is .08/4 = .02.

EXAMPLE 3

$1000 is deposited in an account that earns interest at the rate of six percent per year compounded twice a year. What is the balance at the end of the first interest period?

By formula (3) the interest rate for each six-month interest period is .06/2 = .03. So the interest earned during the first interest period is:

$$(\text{balance}) \times (\text{interest rate}) = (1000) \times (.03) = 30$$

The balance at the end of the first interest period is:

$$(\text{previous balance}) + (\text{interest}) = \$1000 + \$30 = \$1030 \qquad ■$$

PRACTICE EXAMPLE 2

$2000 is deposited into an account that earns interest at the rate of eight percent per year compounded four times a year.

(a) What is the interest period?
(b) What is the balance at the end of the first interest period?   ■

Next we give a formula for computing the balance at the end of each of several consecutive interest periods.

Let

i = interest rate per interest period in decimal form

B_k = balance at the end of k interest periods

Then from formulas (1) and (2) we get:

$$\begin{pmatrix} \text{interest earned} \\ \text{during } (k+1)\text{st} \\ \text{interest period} \end{pmatrix} = B_k \times (i)$$

and

$$B_{k+1} = B_k + (B_k \times i) = B_k(1 + i)$$

---

(4) $B_{k+1} = B_k(1 + i)$ i = interest rate per interest period
B_k = balance at the end of k interest
periods

Formula (4) says the balance at the end of an interest period is obtained by multiplying the balance at the start of the interest period times one plus the interest rate per interest period.

EXAMPLE 4

$5000 is deposited in an account that earns eight percent interest compounded twice a year. What is the balance at the end of:

(a) six months?
(b) one year?
(c) 18 months?
(d) two years?

(a) From formula (3) we get

$$\begin{pmatrix} \text{interest rate per} \\ \text{interest period} \end{pmatrix} = \frac{\text{yearly interest rate}}{\text{number of times a year interest is compounded}}$$

$$= \frac{.08}{2}$$

$$= .04$$

B_0 = balance at the end of zero interest periods

= initial deposit

= $5000

B_1 = balance at the end of one interest period

= balance at the end of six months

= $B_0(1 + i)$

= $(5000)(1.04)$

= $5200

(b) B_2 = balance at the end of two interest periods

   = balance at the end of one year

   = $B_1(1 + i)$

   = $(5200)(1.04)$

   = $5408

(c) B_3 = balance at the end of three interest periods

   = balance at the end of 18 months

   = $B_2(1 + i)$

   = $(5408)(1.04)$

   = $5,624.32

(d) B_4 = balance at the end of four interest periods

   = balance at the end of two years

   = $B_3(1 + i)$

   = $(5,624.32)(1.04)$

   = $5,849.29

The following formula can be used to compute the balance at the end of k interest periods without having to first find the balance at the end of each prior interest period.

$$B_k = B_0 \underbrace{(1 + i)(1 + i) \cdots (1 + i)}_{k}$$

(5) $$B_k = B_0(1 + i)^k$$

where

i = interest rate per interest period

B_0 = initial balance

k = number of interest periods

B_k = balance at the end of k interest periods

EXAMPLE 5

$3000 is deposited in an account that earns interest at the rate of eight percent per year compounded monthly. What is the balance at the end of two years?

By formula (3) the monthly interest rate is:

$$i = \text{interest rate per interest period} = \frac{.08}{12} = .006667$$

Since interest is compounded 12 times a year, the balance at the end of two years is the balance at the end of the twenty-fourth interest period. Using formula (5) we get

$$\text{balance at the end of two years} = B_{24} = B_0(1 + i)^{24}$$

$$= (3000)(1.006667)^{24}$$

$$= (3000)(1.1728879)$$

$$= 3518.6637$$

The balance at the end of two years is $3,518.66. ∎

PRACTICE EXAMPLE 3

$4000 is deposited in an account that earns interest at the rate of 10% per year compounded quarterly (four times a year). What is the balance at the end of nine months? ∎

Formula (5), $B_k = B_0(1 + i)^k$, can be used to determine how much must be deposited now in order to have a specified amount in the future.

EXAMPLE 6

How much should be deposited now into an account that earns interest at the rate of 10% per year compounded twice a year in order for the balance to be $8000 three years from now?

Use formula (5) with

$$i = \frac{.10}{2} = .05$$

$$k = 6 \qquad \text{since three years from now is at the end}$$
$$\text{of the sixth interest period}$$

$$B_6 = 8000 = \text{balance at the end of the sixth interest period}$$

This gives

$$8000 = B_0(1 + i)^6$$

$$8000 = B_0(1.05)^6$$

$$8000 = B_0(1.3400956)$$

$$\frac{8000}{1.3400956} = B_0$$

$$5969.72 = B_0$$

Thus, $5,969.72 deposited now in an account that earns interest at the rate of 10% per year compounded twice a year will produce a balance of $8000 in three years. ∎

PRACTICE EXAMPLE 4

How much should be deposited now in an account that earns interest at the rate of 10% per year compounded yearly in order for the balance to be $12,000 four years from now? ∎

In the next section we examine how the balance changes in an interest-earning account when regular deposits or withdrawals are made.

CONCEPTS

interest
interest period
interest rate per year
interest rate per interest period
compound interest

SOLUTIONS TO PRACTICE EXAMPLES

1. (a) interest $= 600 \times (.08) = \$48$
    (b) balance $= 600 + 48 = \$648$

2. (a) interest period is three months
    (b) balance $= 2000 \times (.08) + 2000 = 160 + 2000 = \$2160$

3. $B_3 = 4000(1.025)^3 = \$4307.56$

4. $12,000 = B_0(1.1)^4$
    $12,000 = B_0(1.4641)$
    $\dfrac{12000}{1.4641} = \$8,196.16 = B_0$

EXERCISES 7.1

In Exercises 1 through 4 find the interest at the end of one year.

Initial balance	Yearly interest rate
1. $1000	6%
2. $500	10%
3. $800	8%
4. $2000	11%

In Exercises 5 through 8 find:

(a) the interest at the end of one year.

(b) the balance at the end of one year.

Initial balance	Yearly interest rate
5. $2000	10%
6. $800	7%
7. $1000	9%
8. $1200	8%

In Exercises 9 through 12 find:

(a) the interest period,

(b) the interest rate per interest period,

for an account that earns

9.   6% per year compounded quarterly (four times a year).

10. 10% per year compounded monthly.

11. 12% per year compounded semiannually (two times a year).

12. 8% per year compounded yearly.

In Exercises 13 through 16 find the balance at the end of the first interest period in an account with:

	Initial balance	Yearly interest rate	Interest period
13.	$1000	8%	3 months
14.	$1100	10%	6 months
15.	$600	7%	1 month
16.	$15,000	12%	1 year

In Exercises 17 through 24 find the balance as indicated in the last column.

	Initial balance	Yearly interest rate	Interest period	Find the balance at the end of
17.	$500	8%	3 months	3 years
18.	$700	10%	6 months	1 year
19.	$10,000	12%	1 year	5 years
20.	$300	4%	1 month	2 years
21.	$800	5%	3 months	1 year
22.	$50,000	14%	1 month	6 months
23.	$12,000	13%	6 months	2 years
24.	$1,000,000	14%	1 month	2 years

25. Find the balance at the end of two years if $1000 is deposited in an account that earns 12% interest per year compounded

(a) yearly.

(b) semiannually.

(c) quarterly.

(d) monthly.

(e) weekly.

In Exercises 26 through 33 find the amount that should be deposited now in order to have the amount in the first column.

Desired amount	in	Yearly interest rate	Interest period
26. $5000	3 years	9%	1 year
27. $1000	1 year	8%	1 month
28. $100	1 year	5%	1 month
29. $10,000	10 years	9%	1 year
30. $100,000	30 years	12%	1 year
31. $100,000	30 years	12%	1 month
32. $30,000	10 years	10%	1 year
33. $20,000	20 years	8%	1 month

34. Suppose $10 was deposited in the year 1900 in an account that earns interest at the rate of six percent per year. What will be the balance in the year 2000 if the interest is compounded

(a) yearly?

(b) semiannually?

(c) monthly?

35. Suppose one dollar was deposited in the year 1776 in an account that earns interest at the rate of eight percent per year. What was the balance in 1976 if interest was compounded

(a) yearly?

(b) semiannually?

(c) monthly?

7.2   Annuities and Sinking Funds—Accumulating Capital

If a deposit is made into an interest-earning account, the balance after the deposit has been made is the sum of the previous balance, the interest earned by the previous balance, and the deposit. In this section we show how to find the balance from one deposit to the next and we give a formula for computing the balance after several deposits have been made.

EXAMPLE 1   Suppose $20 is deposited at the end of each month in a payroll savings account that earns interest at the rate of six percent per year compounded monthly. If the present balance is $500, what will be the balance at the end of

(a) one month?
(b) two months?

To find the balance in one month use:

(1) balance after deposit = (previous balance) + (interest) + (deposit)

The interest per month is computed by:

(2)   interest = (previous balance) × (interest rate per month)

$$= \text{(previous balance)} \times \left(\frac{.06}{12}\right)$$

The balance at the end of the month is:

$$\text{balance} = (500) + (500)\left(\frac{.06}{12}\right) + 20$$

$$= 500 + 2.5 + 20$$

$$= \$522.50$$

Similarly the balance at the end of two months is:

$$\text{balance} = (522.50) + (522.5)\left(\frac{.06}{12}\right) + 20$$

$$= (522.50) + 2.61 + 20$$

$$= \$545.11$$

A sequence of regular deposits made into an account is called an **annuity**. If the interest period in the account is the same as the period between deposits, then the annuity is called a **regular annuity**. Let

$$B_0 = \text{original balance}$$

$$i = \text{interest rate per interest period}$$

$$B_k = \text{balance after } k \text{ interest periods}$$

$$C = \text{amount of the regular deposits}$$

Substituting these symbols into formulas (1) and (2) we get

$$B_{k+1} = B_k + \text{(interest)} + C$$

$$\text{(interest)} = B_k(i)$$

These equations combined to give:

(3) $B_{k+1} = B_k(1 + i) + C$

where

$$C = \text{amount of regular deposit}$$

$$k = \text{number of interest periods}$$

$$i = \text{interest rate per interest period}$$

$$B_k = \text{balance after } k \text{ interest periods}$$

**PRACTICE
EXAMPLE 1**

$1000 is deposited each year in an annuity that earns interest at the rate of 10% per year compounded yearly. If the balance now is $5000 what will be the balance at the end of:

(a) one year?
(b) two years?
(c) three years?

Formula (3) also applies when money is withdrawn regularly from an account. Set C equal to the amount withdrawn written as a negative number. For example, if $20 is withdrawn each month from the account described in Example 1, then formula (3) becomes:

$$B_{k+1} = B_k\left(1 + \frac{.06}{12}\right) - 20$$

yielding the month-by-month balances, as long as there is money in the account.

EXAMPLE 2

$1000 is withdrawn each year from an account that earns interest at the rate of 10% per year compounded yearly. If the balance is now $5000 what will be the balance at the end of:

(a) one year?
(b) two years?
(c) three years?

Formula (3) with $C = -1000$ and $i = .1$ is:

$$B_{k+1} = B_k(1.1) - 1000$$

Using this formula and starting with $B_0 = \$5000 =$ balance now, we get:

$$
\begin{aligned}
\text{Balance at the end of one year} = B_1 &= B_0(1.1) - 1000 \\
&= (5000)(1.1) - 1000 \\
&= 5500 - 1000 \\
&= \$4500 \\
\text{Balance at the end of two years} = B_2 &= B_1(1.1) - 1000 \\
&= (4500)(1.1) - 1000 \\
&= (4950) - 1000 \\
&= \$3950 \\
\text{Balance at the end of three years} = B_3 &= B_2(1.1) - 1000 \\
&= (3950)(1.1) - 1000 \\
&= 4345 - 1000 \\
&= 3345
\end{aligned}
$$

Continue the year-by-year balance computation in Example 2 until the balance drops below $1000. What does this say about the number of yearly $1000 withdrawals that can be taken from the account?   ■

The formula below can be used to compute the balance at the end of k interest periods, without having to first find the balance at the end of each previous interest period.

(4)
$$B_k = \left(B_0 + \frac{C}{i} \right)(1 + i)^k - \frac{C}{i}$$

where

C = amount of deposit

i = interest rate per interest period

k = number of interest periods = number of deposits

B_k = balance after k interest periods

B_0 = initial balance

The derivation of formula (4) is given in the next chapter.

EXAMPLE 3

$8000 is the present balance in an annuity that earns interest at the rate of nine percent per year compounded yearly. If a deposit of $1000 is added to the account at the end of each of the next five years, what will be the balance at the end of five years?

Using formula (4) with

C = $1000 = amount of deposit

B_0 = $8000 = initial deposit

i = .09 = interest rate per interest period

we get

B_5 = balance at the end of five interest periods

= balance at the end of five years

$$= \left((8000) + \frac{1000}{.09} \right)(1.09)^5 - \frac{1000}{.09}$$

$= (8000 + 11{,}111.11)(1.538624) - 11{,}111.11$

$= (19{,}111.11)(1.538624) - 11{,}111.11$

$= 29{,}404.81 - 11{,}111.11$

$= \$18{,}293.70$

We can test the accuracy of formula (4) by using formula (3) to list the year-by-year balances for the next five years.

$$B_0 = \$8000$$

$$B_1 = (8000)(1.09) + 1000 = \$9720$$

$$B_2 = (9720)(1.09) + 1000 = \$11{,}594.80$$

$$B_3 = (11{,}594.80)(1.09) + 1000 = 13{,}638.33$$

$$B_4 = (13{,}638.33)(1.09) + 1000 = 15{,}865.78$$

$$B_5 = (15{,}865.78)(1.09) + 1000 = 18{,}293.70$$

Formula (4) gives a method for computing the balance after five years without having to first find the balance at the end of each previous year.

PRACTICE EXAMPLE 3

$20,000 is the present balance in an annuity that earns interest at the rate of 12% per year compounded monthly. If $300 is deposited into the account at the end of each month, what will be the balance four months from now?

Formula (4) can be used when regular withdrawals from an account are made. In this case C is the negative of the amount withdrawn and the formula applies as long as the balance remains positive.

EXAMPLE 4

$5000 is the present balance in an account that earns interest at the rate of nine percent per year compounded monthly. If $300 is withdrawn from the account at the end of each month, what will be the balance seven months from now?

Using formula (4) with

$$C = -300 = \text{negative of the amount withdrawn}$$

$$i = \frac{.09}{12} = .0075$$

$$B_0 = \$5000$$

we get

$$B_7 = \text{balance after seven interest periods}$$

$$= \text{balance after seven months}$$

$$= \left(B_0 + \frac{C}{i} \right)(1 + i)^7 - \frac{C}{i}$$

$$= \left(5000 + \frac{(-300)}{.0075} \right)(1.0075)^7 - \frac{(-300)}{.0075}$$

$$= (5000 - 40{,}000)(1.0536961) + 40{,}000$$

$$= (-35{,}000)(1.0536961) + 40{,}000$$

$$= -36{,}879.36 + 40{,}000$$

$$= \$3{,}120.64$$

Alternatively we can use formula (3) to obtain a table of month-by-month balances.

$B_0 = 5000 =$ present balance

$B_1 = 5000(1.0075) - 300 = 4,737.50 =$ balance after one month

$B_2 = (4,737.50)(1.0075) - 300 = 4,473.03 =$ balance after two months

$B_3 = (4,473.03)(1.0075) - 300 = 4,206.58 =$ balance after three months

$B_4 = (4,206.58)(1.0075) - 300 = 3,938.13 =$ balance after four months

$B_5 = (3,938.13)(1.0075) - 300 = 3,667.67 =$ balance after five months

$B_6 = (3,667.67)(1.0075) - 300 = 3,395.18 =$ balance after six months

$B_7 = (3,395.18)(1.0075) - 300 = 3,120.64 =$ balance after seven months   ∎

If all but one of the numbers C, i, B_k, B_0 in formula (4) are known, then the formula can be used to find the unknown number.

EXAMPLE 5   A state lottery offers a prize of \$500,000 paid at the rate of \$50,000 a year for 10 years. The state can invest money at 11% per year compounded yearly. How much should be deposited into the account if the first payment is due one year from now?
We use formula (4) with

$i = .11$

$C = -50,000 =$ negative of the amount of the regular withdrawals

$B_0 =$ unknown

$B_{10} = 0 =$ balance after 10 payments

$$0 = \left(B_0 + \frac{-50,000}{.11}\right)(1.11)^{10} - \frac{-50,000}{.11}$$

$$0 = (B_0 - 454,545.45)(2.839421) + 454,545.45$$

$$0 = (2.839421)B_0 - 1,290,645.9 + 454,545.45$$

$$0 = (2.839421)B_0 - 836,100.45$$

$$836,100.45 = (2.839421)B_0$$

$$\frac{836,100.45}{2.839421} = B_0$$

$$294,461.60 = B_0$$

If the state lottery deposits \$294,461.60 into the account, then there will be just enough to pay out \$50,000 each year for 10 years. ∎

EXAMPLE 6

A couple wants to open an annuity account to pay for their young daughter's college education. They will put enough money aside each year so that when the payments for college begin, there will be just enough in the account to make four yearly withdrawals of \$12,000 each. How much must be in the annuity at the beginning of the payment period if the annuity earns interest at the rate of nine percent per year compounded yearly?

In this example we are given

$C = -12{,}000$ since there are regular withdrawals of \$12,000 each

$i = .09 =$ interest rate per interest period

$B_4 = 0 =$ balance at the end of four interest periods corresponding to the four years that withdrawals from the account will be used for college expenses

$B_0 = ?$

Substituting the given information into formula (4) we get

$$B_4 = \left(B_0 + \frac{C}{i}\right)(1 + i)^4 - \frac{C}{i}$$

$$0 = \left(B_0 + \frac{(-12{,}000)}{.09}\right)(1.09)^4 - \frac{(-12{,}000)}{.09}$$

$$0 = (B_0 - 133{,}333.33)(1.4115816) + 133{,}333.33$$

$$0 = (1.4115816)B_0 - (133{,}333.33)(1.4115816) + 133{,}333.33$$

$$0 = (1.4115816)B_0 - 188{,}210.88 + 133{,}333.33$$

$$0 = (1.4115816)B_0 - 54{,}877.55$$

So,

$$(1.4115816)B_0 = 54{,}877.55$$

$$B_0 = \frac{54{,}877.55}{1.4115816}$$

$$B_0 = 38{,}876.64$$

\$38,876.64 must be in the account at the beginning of the payment period in order to be able to make four yearly withdrawals of \$12,000 each. ∎

An annuity whose purpose is to produce a specified sum in the future, is called a **sinking fund**.

EXAMPLE 7

A couple plans to start a sinking fund. They will make yearly deposits into an account that earns nine percent per year compounded yearly in order to have a balance of $39,000 15 years from now. If the first deposit is made now, how much should the yearly deposits be?

In this example we have

$$C = \text{unknown}$$

$$i = .09 = \text{interest rate per period}$$

$$B_{15} = 39,000 = \text{balance at the end of 15 years}$$

$$B_0 = \text{initial deposit} = C$$

Substituting into formula (4) gives

$$B_k = \left(B_0 + \frac{C}{i} \right)(1 + i)^k - \frac{C}{i}$$

$$B_{15} = \left(B_0 + \frac{C}{i} \right)(1 + i)^{15} - \frac{C}{i}$$

$$39,000 = \left(C + \frac{C}{.09} \right)(1.09)^{15} - \frac{C}{.09}$$

$$39,000 = \frac{(.09C + C)}{.09}(1.09)^{15} - \frac{C}{.09}$$

$$39,000 = \frac{C(1.09)(1.09)^{15}}{.09} - \frac{C}{.09}$$

$$39,000(.09) = C(1.09)^{16} - C$$

$$39,000(.09) = C[(1.09)^{16} - 1]$$

$$3510 = C(2.9703059)$$

$$\frac{3510}{2.9703059} = C$$

$$1,181.70 = C$$

The couple should make yearly deposits of $1,181.70, in order to have $39,000 15 years from now.

PRACTICE
EXAMPLE 4   How much should be deposited monthly in a sinking fund in order to have $1,200 one year from now if the interest is five percent per year compounded monthly, the first payment is made now, and the last payment one year from now?

CONCEPTS

annuity
regular annuity
sinking fund

SOLUTIONS TO PRACTICE EXAMPLES

1. (a) $B_1 = 5000(1.1) + 1000 = 6500$
   (b) $B_2 = B_1(1.1) + 1000 = 8150$
   (c) $B_3 = B_2(1.1) + 1000 = 9965$

2. $B_4 = (3345)(1.1) - 1000 = 2,679.50$
   $B_5 = (2,679.50)(1.1) - 1000 = 1,947.45$
   $B_6 = (1,947.45)(1.1) - 1000 = 1,142.20$
   $B_7 = (1,142.20)(1.1) - 1000 = 256.41$

   Seven yearly withdrawals of \$1000 each can be made. After the seventh with-
   drawal, the balance is \$256.41.

3. $B_k = \left(B_0 + \dfrac{C}{i}\right)(1 + i)^k - \dfrac{C}{i}$

   $B_4 = \left(20,000 + \dfrac{300}{.01}\right)(1.01)^4 - \dfrac{300}{.01}$

   $B_4 = 50,000(1.040604) - 30,000 = 22,030.20$

4. $B_k = \left(B_0 + \dfrac{C}{i}\right)(1 + i)^k - \dfrac{C}{i}$

   $1200 = \left(C + \dfrac{C}{.0041888}\right)(1.0041666)^{12} - \dfrac{C}{.0041666}$

   Multiply by .0041666

   $$5 = [(.0041666)C + C](1.0041666)^{12} - C$$
   $$5 = [(1.0041666)^{13} - 1]C$$
   $$5 = (0.0555417)C$$
   $$\frac{5}{0.0555417} = C = 90.02$$

EXERCISES 7.2

In Exercises 1 through 8 use formulas (1) and (2) to find:

(a) the interest earned during one interest period.

(b) the balance after the deposit is made at the end of the interest period.

	Initial balance	Yearly interest rate	Interest period	Deposit
1.	\$500	9%	1 month	\$20
2.	\$10,000	11%	6 months	\$1000
3.	\$350	6%	1 month	\$25
4.	\$1200	8%	3 months	\$100
5.	\$800	7%	1 month	\$50
6.	\$20,000	14%	6 months	\$1200

7.	$1000	10%	12 months	$100
8.	$50,000	14%	1 month	$1500

In Exercises 9 through 12 use formulas (1) and (2) to find:

(a) the interest earned during one interest period.

(b) the balance after the withdrawal is made at the end of the interest period.

Initial balance	Yearly interest rate	Interest period	Withdrawal
9. $10,000	12%	1 month	$5000
10. $8000	10%	1 year	$1000
11. $7000	8%	6 months	$150
12. $6000	12%	3 months	$500

In Exercises 13 through 20 use formula (3) to find the balance in the annuity at the end of each of the next three interest periods (see the last part of Example 3).

Initial balance	Yearly interest rate	Interest period	Deposit
13. $100	5%	1 month	$20
14. $500	6%	6 months	$50
15. $1000	7%	1 month	$100
16. $750	6%	1 month	$30
17. $351	7%	1 month	$50
18. $10,000	8%	6 months	$150
19. $278	6%	1 month	$30
20. $12,000	10%	1 year	$175

In Exercises 21 through 24 use formula (3) to find the balance at the end of each of the next three interest periods. The withdrawals are made at the end of each interest period.

Initial balance	Yearly interest rate	Interest period	Withdrawal
21. $400	5%	1 year	$100
22. $1000	8%	1 month	$150
23. $500	10%	6 months	$75
24. $1000	7%	3 months	$200

In Exercises 25 through 32 use formula (4) to find the balance in the annuity.

Initial balance	Yearly interest rate	Interest period	Regular deposits	Find the balance at the end of
25. $500	12%	1 year	$100	2 years
26. $1000	6%	1 month	$50	1 year
27. $2000	10%	6 months	$100	2 years

28.	$10,000	14%	1 year	$500	4 years
29.	$750	7%	1 month	$100	2 years
30.	$950	5%	1 month	$100	6 months
31.	$593	8%	1 month	$75	8 months
32.	$50,000	14%	6 months	$1000	5 years

In Exercises 33 through 36 use formula (4) to find the balance.

	Initial balance	Yearly interest rate	Interest period	Regular withdrawals	Find the balance at the end of
33.	$10,000	12%	1 year	$1000	3 years
34.	$10,000	11%	6 months	$500	3 years
35.	$1000	8%	3 months	$100	1 year
36.	$3000	5%	1 week	$200	12 weeks

37. A professional athlete deposits $25,000 in an annuity at the end of each year for seven years. If the account earns 10% interest per year compounded yearly, what is the balance after the last deposit?

38. A person has just opened an IRA (individual retirement account) with an initial deposit of $2000. He plans to deposit $2000 at the end of each year until he retires (including a $2000 deposit at the end of the last year he works). Find the balance in the annuity when he retires if the account earns interest at the rate of 12% per year compounded yearly and he retires after:

   (a) 10 years.

   (b) 20 years.

   (c) 30 years.

39. A city sold bonds to finance renovation of city hall. When the bonds mature 10 years from now the city will need $2 million to pay the people who bought the bonds. In order to pay this debt, the city will establish a sinking fund and make regular deposits, one deposit every six months, into an account that earns interest at the rate of eight percent per year compounded twice a year. If the city makes the first deposit now and the last deposit 10 years from now, what must be the amount of each deposit in order for the balance to be $2 million at the end of 10 years?

40. A car dealership wants to build a new showroom and service center in five years. The dealership will make regular deposits into a sinking fund at the end of each year for the next five years in order to accumulate the necessary capital. The fund earns interest at the rate of 10% per year compounded yearly. Find the amount of each deposit if the capital required in five years is:

   (a) $500,000.

   (b) $1 million.

41. A couple planning for their retirement have just opened an IRA with a deposit of $3500. They want to make yearly deposits so that when they retire, the balance in the account will be $1 million. If the account earns interest at the

rate of 12% per year compounded yearly, how much should the yearly deposits be if the couple makes its first yearly deposit one year from now and its last yearly deposit

(a) 30 years from now?

(b) 35 years from now?

42. What lump sum deposited today at nine percent compounded twice a year would permit withdrawals of $1000 at the end of each six-month period for five years if the balance in the account after the last withdrawal is to be 0?

43. A state lottery offers a grand prize of $1 million paid at the rate of $50,000 at the end of each year for 20 years. The state can invest money at 12% per year compounded yearly. How much should be deposited into the account if the first $50,000 payment is due one year from now?

44. A couple have decided to use a tuition payment plan to pay $7000 for their daughter's college expenses this year. The college expenses are paid in 10 equal monthly installments of $700 each. The first installment and a $40 processing fee are due now. To finance the remaining nine payments of $700 each, the couple will deposit a lump sum now in an account that earns interest at the rate of six percent per year compounded monthly. How much should the lump sum deposit be in order to be able to withdraw $700 at the end of each of the next nine months and have a balance of 0 after the last withdrawal?

7.3 Amortization Tables—Installment Loans

Loans that are paid off by paying a certain amount at regular times are called **installment loans**. Car loans and home mortgages are installment loans. Part of each payment is used to pay interest. The remainder of the payment is used to reduce the principal. In this section, we show how to make a table that lists how much of each payment is used for interest and how much is used to reduce the amount owed (called the **remaining principal**). We will show how to find the principal after a number of payments have been made and how to find the amount of the regular payments.

Suppose a person has taken out a loan for $15,000, at 12% interest per year compounded monthly, with monthly payments of $200. The first monthly payment of $200 is credited according to the following steps.

STEP 1: Compute the **interest due**.

(1)   interest due = principal × interest rate per month

$$= 15{,}000 \times \left(\frac{.12}{12}\right)$$

$$= 15{,}000 \times .01$$

$$= 150$$

$150 of the payment is used to pay interest.

STEP 2:   Subtract the interest from the payment. The result is the amount by which the principal is reduced, called the **principal payment**.

(2)
$$\text{principal payment} = \text{payment} - \text{interest}$$
$$= 200 \quad - 150$$
$$= 50$$

STEP 3:   Subtract the principal payment from the principal. The result is the remaining principal owed.

(3)
$$\begin{pmatrix} \text{remaining} \\ \text{principal} \end{pmatrix} = \begin{pmatrix} \text{principal} \\ \text{before payment} \end{pmatrix} - \begin{pmatrix} \text{principal} \\ \text{payment} \end{pmatrix}$$
$$= 15{,}000 \quad - 50$$
$$= 14{,}950$$

In this example $150 of the payment was used to pay interest. The remaining $50 of the payment was used to reduce the principal.

A table that lists the interest, the principal payment, and the remaining principal after each of several payments is called an **amortization schedule**. An amortization schedule can be constructed by following the three steps above for each of the payments included on the schedule.

EXAMPLE 1   Make an amortization schedule for the first 12 payments of $200 on a loan of $15,000 at 12% per year compounded monthly. What is the total interest paid in the first year?

The amortization schedule is constructed by starting with a principal of $15,000 and using formulas (1), (2), and (3).

Payment	Interest	Principal payment	Remaining principal
0	0	0	15,000
1	150	50	14,950
2	149.50	50.50	14,899.50
3	149.00	51.00	14,848.50
4	148.49	51.51	14,796.99
5	147.97	52.03	14,744.96
6	147.45	52.55	14,692.41
7	146.92	53.08	14,639.33
8	146.39	53.61	14,585.72
9	145.86	54.14	14,531.58
10	145.32	54.68	14,476.90
11	144.77	55.23	14,421.67
12	144.22	55.78	14,365.89
Total	1,765.89	634.11	

The interest on an installment loan can be listed as an itemized deduction on Schedule A of your federal income tax.

The interest charges on the amortization schedule above were obtained by rounding off the numbers obtained from formula (1) to the nearest penny. One-half cent is rounded up to the next highest penny. For example,

Interest	in line	is rounded to
(14,848.50) × (.01) = 148.485	4	148.49
(14,796.99) × (.01) = 147.9699	5	147.97
(14,692.41) × (.01) = 146.9241	7	146.92

PRACTICE EXAMPLE 1

The table below is part of an amortization schedule for a loan of $5000 at 14% compounded monthly, with monthly payments of $170.89. Fill in the missing lines, for the third, fourth, seventeenth, eighteenth, and thirty-first payments.

Payment	Interest	Principal payment	Remaining principal
0	0	0	5000
1	58.33	112.56	4887.44
2	57.02	113.87	4773.57
3	____	____	____
4	____	____	____
:			
:			
15	38.49	132.4	3166.54
16	36.94	133.95	3032.59
17	____	____	____
18	____	____	____
:			
:			
30	13.33	157.56	984.64
31	____	____	____

Note that in the schedule in Example 1, the amount of interest due decreases each month, since the remaining principal decreases.

Formula (4) below can be used to find the principal after several payments have been made without having to find the principal after each previous payment. The formula can also be used to find the amount of the regular payments. Formula (4) is derived in Chapter 8.

(4)
$$P_k = \left(P_0 - \frac{M}{i}\right)(1 + i)^k + \frac{M}{i}$$

where

$$P_k = \text{principal after } k \text{ payments have been made}$$
$$M = \text{the amount of the monthly payment}$$
$$i = \text{the interest rate per month}$$

EXAMPLE 2

Use formula (4) to find the principal after:

(a) 3 payments of \$310.53 each on a loan for 20,000 at 14% per year.
(b) 5 payments of \$166.53 each on a loan for 7000 at 15% per year.
(c) 10 payments of \$45.21 each on a loan for \$1200 at 21% per year.

(a) $P_k = \left(P_0 - \dfrac{M}{i}\right)(1 + i)^k + \dfrac{M}{i}$ with

$$P_0 = 20,000$$
$$M = 310.53$$
$$i = \frac{.14}{12} = .011666$$

gives

$$P_3 = \left(20,000 - \frac{310.53}{.011666}\right)(1 + i)^3 + \frac{310.53}{.011666}$$

$$P_3 = (20,000 - 26,617.009)(1.0354097) + 26,617.009$$

$$P_3 = (-6617.009)(1.0354097) + 26,617.009$$

$$P_3 = -6851.3153 + 26,617.009$$

$$P_3 = 19,765.694$$

Principal after three payments is \$19,765.69.

(b) Substituting the values:

$$P_0 = 7000$$
$$i = \frac{.15}{12} = .0125$$
$$M = 166.53$$

into formula (4) we get

$$P_5 = \left(7000 - \frac{166.53}{.0125}\right)(1.0125)^5 + \frac{166.53}{.0125}$$

$$P_5 = (7000 - 13,322.4)(1.0125)^5 + 13,322.4$$

$$P_5 = (-6,322.4)(1.0640822) + 13,322.4$$

$$P_5 = 6,727.5533 + 13,322.4$$

$$P_5 = 6,594.8467$$

The principal after five payments is $6,594.85.

(c) Substituting the values:

$$P_0 = 1200$$

$$i = \frac{.21}{12} = .0175$$

$$M = 45.21$$

into formula (4) we get

$$P_{10} = \left(1200 - \frac{45.21}{.0175}\right)(1.0175)^{10} + \frac{45.21}{.0175}$$

$$P_{10} = (1200 - 2,583.4286)(1.0175)^{10} + 2,583.4286$$

$$P_{10} = (-1,383.4286)(1.1894445) + 2,583.4286$$

$$P_{10} = -1,645.5115 + 2,583.4286$$

$$P_{10} = 937.91706$$

The principal after 10 payments is $937.92.

Formula (4) can also be used to find the monthly payment.

EXAMPLE 3   Find the monthly payment on a loan of $6000 at 14% for three years. We have

$$P_0 = 6000$$

$$M = ?$$

$$i = \frac{.14}{12} = .011666$$

$$P_{36} = \text{principal after 36 payments}$$
$$= \text{principal after three years} = 0$$

Substituting these values into formula (4) with $k = 36$, we get

$$0 = \left(6000 - \frac{M}{.011666}\right)(1.011666)^{36} + \frac{M}{.011666}$$

Multiply both sides of the equation by .011666:

$$0 = [(6000)(.011666) - M](1.011666)^{36} + M$$

$$0 = (69.996 - M)(1.51823) + M$$

$$0 = (69.996)(1.51823) - M(1.51825) + M$$

$$0 = 106.27003 + M(1 - 1.51825)$$

$$M(1.51825 - 1) = 106.27003$$

$$M = \frac{106.27003}{.51825} = 205.05553$$

The monthly payment is $205.06. ■

PRACTICE
EXAMPLE 2

Find the monthly payment on a loan of $1000 for one year at 12%. ■

Formula (4) can also be used to find the amount of money that one can afford to borrow.

EXAMPLE 4

The credit union where Mark works offers used-car loans at 14% for three years, and new-car loans at 12% for four years. If Mark can afford monthly payments of $200, then:

(a) how much can he afford to pay for a used car?
(b) how much can he afford to pay for a new car if a new-car loan requires a down payment of 20% of the sticker price, and Mark has $2000 available for the down payment?

(a) For a used-car loan we have

$$P_0 = ?$$

$$M = 200$$

$$i = \frac{.14}{12} = .011666$$

$$P_{36} = \text{principal after 36 payments}$$
$$= \text{principal after three years} = 0$$

Substituting into formula (4), we get

$$0 = \left(P_0 - \frac{200}{.011666}\right)(1.011666)^{36} + \frac{200}{.011666}$$

$$0 = [P_0(.011666) - 200](1.011666)^{36} + 200$$

$$0 = P_0(.011666)(1.011666)^{36} - 200(1.011666)^{36} + 200$$

$$0 = (.0177116)P_0 - 303.646 + 200$$

$$0 = (.0177116)P_0 - 103.646$$

$$103.646 = (.0177116)P_0$$

$$P_0 = 5,851.8708$$

Mark can afford to borrow $5,851.87 for a used car.

(b) There are two restrictions on the amount of money Mark can afford to pay for a new car.

1. The required down payment of 20% of the sticker price cannot be more than $2000.
2. The remaining 80% of the sticker price cannot require monthly payments of more than $200.

If we let S = sticker price of a new car, then using only the condition on the down payment gives

$$.2S = 2000$$

$$S = 10,000$$

as the largest possible sticker price.

The next step is to use formula (4) to find out how much money Mark can afford to borrow at 12% for four years. We have

$$P_0 = ?$$

$$i = \frac{.12}{12} = .01$$

$$M = 200$$

$$P_{48} = \text{principal after four years} = 0$$

Substituting into formula (4) we get:

$$0 = \left(P_0 - \frac{200}{.01}\right)(1.01)^{48} + \frac{200}{.01}$$

$$0 = (P_0 - 20,000)(1.612226) + 20,000$$

$$0 = (1.612226)P_0 - 32,244.52 + 20,000$$

$$(1.612226)P_0 = 12,244.52$$

$$P_0 = 7,594.7913$$

Mark can afford to borrow up to $7,594.79 to finance 80% of the sticker price. So using the condition on the remainder, the sticker price cannot be more than

$$.8S = 7,594.79$$

$$S = 9,493.49$$

We have found that the condition on the down payment restricts the sticker price to $10,000 or less, and Mark's ability to make monthly payments restricts the sticker price to $9,493.49 or less. Thus Mark can afford to buy a new car with a sticker price of $9,493.49 or less. ∎

In the next chapter we use equations, such as those used in this chapter to compute balances in an account, to model radioactive decay, population growth, heating and cooling, and the spread of information and disease.

CONCEPTS

installment loan
interest due
principal payment
remaining principal
amortization schedule

SOLUTIONS TO PRACTICE EXAMPLES

1.

Payment	Interest	Principal payment	Remaining principal
3	55.69	144.31	4629.26
4	54.01	145.99	4483.27
:	:	:	:
17	35.38	164.62	2867.97
18	33.46	166.54	2701.43
:	:	:	:
31	11.49	188.51	796.13

2. $P_k = \left(P_0 - \dfrac{M}{i}\right)(1 + i)^k + \dfrac{M}{i}$ $0 = \left(1000 - \dfrac{M}{.01}\right)(1.01)^{12} + \dfrac{M}{.01}$

Multiply by .01.

$$0 = [(1000)(.01) - M](1.01)^{12} + M$$

$$0 = (10 - M)(1.126825) + M$$

$$0 = 11.26825 - (1.126825)M + M$$

$$0 = 11.26825 - (.126825)M$$

$$\frac{11.26825}{.126825} = 88.848807 = M$$

Monthly payment is $88.85.

EXERCISES 7.3

In Exercises 1 through 4, fill in the blank lines in the amortization schedule.

1. For a loan of $5000 at 14% interest for three years with monthly payments of $170.89.

Payment	Interest	Principal payment	Remaining principal
0	0	0	5000
1	58.33	112.56	4887.44
2	____	____	____
3	55.69	115.20	4658.37

2. For a loan of $1000 at 21% interest for two years with monthly payments of $51.39.

Payment	Interest	Principal payment	Remaining principal
13	9.66	41.73	510.05
14	8.93	42.46	467.59
15	_____	_____	_____
16	_____	_____	_____

3. For a loan of $50,000 at 14% interest for 20 years with monthly payments of $621.76.

Payment	Interest	Principal payment	Remaining principal
0	0	0	50,000
1	583.33	38.43	49,961.57
2	582.89	38.87	49,922.70
3	_____	_____	_____
:			
:			
169	352.03	269.73	29,904.47
170	348.89	272.87	29,631.60
171	_____	_____	_____

4. For a loan of $80,000 at 13% interest for 30 years with monthly payments of $884.96.

Payment	Interest	Principal payment	Remaining principal
0	0	0	80,000
1	866.67	18.29	79,981.71
2	866.47	18.49	79,963.22
3	_____	_____	_____
:			
:			
109	826.39	58.57	76,223.50
110	_____	_____	_____
:			
:			
229	671.54	213.42	61,775.11
230	_____	_____	_____

In Exercises 5 and 6 fill in the blank lines in the amortization schedule, find the total interest and the principal payment for the year.

5. For the second year of a loan of $5000 at 14% interest for three years with monthly payments of $170.89.

Payment	Interest	Principal payment	Remaining principal
13	41.52	129.37	3429.82
14	40.01	130.88	3298.94
15	_____	_____	_____
16	36.94	133.95	3032.59
17	35.38	133.51	2807.08
18	_____	_____	_____
19	32.20	138.69	2621.30
20	30.58	140.31	2480.99
21	28.94	141.95	2339.04
22	27.29	143.60	2195.44
23	25.61	145.28	2050.16
24	_____	_____	_____

6. For the twentieth year of a loan of $80,000 at 13% interest for 30 years with monthly payments of $884.96.

Payment	Interest	Principal payment	Remaining principal
229	671.54	213.42	61,775.11
230	669.23	215.73	61,559.38
231	_____	_____	_____
232	664.53	220.43	61,120.88
233	662.14	222.82	60,898.06
234	659.73	225.23	60,672.83
235	657.29	227.67	60,445.15
236	_____	_____	_____
237	652.33	232.63	59,982.39
238	649.81	235.15	59,747.24
239	647.26	237.70	59,509.54
240	_____	_____	_____

In Exercises 7 through 10, use formula (4) to find the remaining principal:

7. After 12 payments of $100 each on a loan for $7000 at 15% interest.

8. After six payments of $150 each on a loan for $10,000 at 12% interest.

9. After 12 payments of $300 each on a loan for $25,000 at 13% interest.

10. After 120 payments of $600 each on a loan for $50,000 at 14% interest.

In Exercises 11 through 14, find the monthly payment for a loan of:

11. $1000 at 15% for one year.

12. $10,000 at 12% for five years.

13. $25,000 at 11% for eight years.

14. $75,000 at 15% for 25 years.

In Exercises 15 through 18 find the amount that can be borrowed if

	Monthly payments	Yearly interest rate	for
15.	$60	21%	3 years
16.	$150	18%	4 years
17.	$800	14%	10 years
18.	$300	17%	5 years

19. How much can a couple afford to pay for a new car if they can pay $250 a month on a four-year loan at 13% interest and they have $2,500 for the required down payment of 20% of the sticker price?

20. How much can Pete afford to pay for a new car if he can pay $300 a month on a four-year loan at 13% and has $3000 for the down payment of 20% of the sticker price?

21. How much can a couple spend for a new house if they can afford to pay $800 a month for a mortgage at 12% per year for:

(a) 20 years?

(b) 30 years?

22. How much can a couple spend on a new house if they can afford to pay $1000 a month for a mortgage at 12% per year for:

(a) 20 years?

(b) 30 years?

In this section we have used formula (4) with M = monthly payment and i = interest rate per month. The formula:

$$P_k = \left(P_0 - \frac{M}{i} \right)(1 + i)^k + \frac{M}{i}$$

also applies for other than one-month payment periods by setting:

P_0 = original principal

M = amount of the regular payment

i = interest rate for the period between payments

P_k = remaining principal after k payments

Use formula (4) with the above meanings of P_0, M, i, and P_k to solve Exercises 23 through 26.

23. A company has opened a new store representing an investment of $490,000. The company paid $60,000 as a down payment and agreed to pay off the remaining balance in quarterly payments over eight years at 12% compounded quarterly. Find the amount of the quarterly payments.

24. A law firm took out a 15-year mortgage 10 years ago for $110,000 at 7% interest with annual payments.
    (a) What is the amount of yearly payments?
    (b) What is the remaining principal if the firm has made 10 payments?

25. An accounting firm pays $3500 for a new printer for its computer. To pay for the printer the firm has taken out a loan at 10% compounded annually with yearly payments for four years.
    (a) Find the amount of the yearly payments.
    (b) Write the amortization schedule for the loan.

26. To open a new office a company spent $14,000 on furniture, $50,000 on equipment, and $10,000 on a lease for the office space. The company paid $7000 down and took out a loan with semiannual payments for seven years at 12% compounded semiannually.
    (a) Find the amount of the semiannual payments.
    (b) Write the amortization schedule for the first two years of the loan.

CHAPTER SUMMARY

If an initial deposit is made into an account that earns *compound interest*, then the balance after $k + 1$ *interest periods* can be found using the two formulas below.

$$\left(\begin{matrix} interest\ rate\ per \\ interest\ period \end{matrix} \right) = \frac{yearly\ interest\ rate}{number\ of\ times\ a\ year\ interest\ is\ compounded}$$

$$B_{k+1} = B_k(1 + i) \qquad i = \text{interest rate per interest period}$$

$$k = \text{number of interest periods}$$

$$B_k = \text{balance at the end of } k \text{ interest periods}$$

and $B_{k+1} = B_0(1 + i)^{k+1}$ $\qquad B_0 = \text{initial balance}$

The following two formulas give the balances in an account when regular deposits or withdrawals are made.

$$B_{k+1} = B_k(1 + i) + C$$

where

$i = \text{interest rate per interest period}$

$k = \text{number of interest periods} = \text{number of deposits (withdrawals)}$

$B_k = \text{balance after } k \text{ deposits (withdrawals)}$

$$C = \text{amount of the regular deposits or the negative of the}$$
$$\text{amount of the regular withdrawals}$$

$$B_{k+1} = \left(B_0 + \frac{C}{i}\right)(1 + i)^{k+1} - \frac{C}{i} \qquad B_0 = \text{balance before any deposits or withdrawals are made}$$

The following three formulas are used to write an *amortization schedule.*

$$(\textit{interest due}) = \left(\begin{array}{c}\text{principal} \\ \text{before payment}\end{array}\right) \times \left(\begin{array}{c}\text{interest rate} \\ \text{per payment period}\end{array}\right)$$

$$\textit{principal payment} = \textit{payment} - \textit{interest}$$

$$\left(\begin{array}{c}\textit{remaining} \\ \textit{principal}\end{array}\right) = \left(\begin{array}{c}\text{principal} \\ \text{before payment}\end{array}\right) - \left(\begin{array}{c}\text{principal} \\ \text{payment}\end{array}\right)$$

The remaining principal after payments of an *installment loan* is given by:

$$P_k = \left(P_0 - \frac{M}{i}\right)(1 + i)^k + \frac{M}{i}$$

where

$$P_k = \text{principal after } k \text{ payments}$$
$$M = \text{amount of each payment}$$
$$i = \text{interest rate per payment period}$$

REVIEW EXERCISES FOR CHAPTER 7

In Exercises 1 through 3, find the balance at the end of each of the first two interest periods.

Initial balance	Yearly interest rate	Interest period
1. $1000	12%	1 month
2. $500	10%	6 months
3. $700	8%	3 months

In Exercises 4 through 6 find the balance as indicated in the last column.

Initial balance	Yearly interest rate	Interest period	Find the balance at the end of
4. $500	8%	3 months	1 year
5. $1200	10%	6 months	3 years
6. $2000	12%	1 year	6 years

7. To help pay for their children's education, a couple plans to make a deposit into an account in order to have $12,000 10 years from now. How much should the couple deposit if the account earns interest at the rate of 12% per year compounded quarterly?

8. Suppose $100 is deposited at the end of each month into an account that earns interest at the rate of 10% per year compounded monthly. List the balance immediately after each of the first three deposits.

9. Suppose $50 is withdrawn each month from an account that earns interest at the rate eight percent per year compounded monthly. How much is left in the account after three withdrawals if the balance before the first withdrawal is $500?

10. What is the balance in an annuity after 20 yearly deposits of $2000 each, if the account earns interest at the rate of 12% per year compounded yearly?

11. A couple wants to have $1 million when they retire. They have just opened an IRA with a deposit of $3500. If the account earns interest at the rate of 11% per year and the couple makes 30 deposits beginning one year from now, then how much should the yearly deposits be?

12. A company wants to set up a sinking fund to pay for a new warehouse in five years. How much are the yearly deposits if the company will make five yearly deposits of the same amount, the account earns interest at the rate of nine percent per year compounded yearly, and the warehouse costs $700,000?

13. What lump sum deposited today at seven percent compounded quarterly would permit 10 quarterly withdrawals of $800 each, if the first withdrawal occurs three months from now?

14. The table below is part of an amortization schedule for a loan of $4000 at 15% compounded monthly, with monthly payments of $138.66. Fill in the missing lines for the second, twelfth, twenty-third, and twenty-fourth payments.

Payment	Interest	Principal payment	Remaining principal
1	50.00	88.66	3911.34
2	____	____	____
:			
11	38.27	100.39	2961.44
12	____	____	____
:			
22	23.57	115.09	1770.80
23	____	____	____
24	____	____	____

15. The table below is part of an amortization schedule for a loan of $80,000 at 12% compounded monthly, with monthly payments of $880.87. Fill in the missing lines for the second, twelfth, one hundred twenty-first, one hundred eighty-first, two hundred thirty-ninth, and two hundred fortieth payments.

Payment	Interest	Principal payment	Remaining principal
1	800.00	80.87	79,919.13
2	_____	_____	_____
:			
11	790.65	90.22	78,974.36
12	_____	_____	_____
:			
120	616.61	264.26	61,396.75
121	_____	_____	_____
:			
180	400.79	480.08	39,598.89
181	_____	_____	_____
:			
238	25.89	854.98	1,734.49
239	_____	_____	_____
240	_____	_____	_____

16. What is the remaining principal after the first two monthly payments of $310.53 on a loan for $20,000 at 14% per year?

17. What is the remaining principal after the first 12 monthly payments of $166.53 each on a loan for $7000 at 15% per year? How much of the first year's payments are used to pay interest?

18. Find the monthly payment on a loan for $3000 at 15% for two years.

19. Find the monthly payment on a loan for $60,000 at 12% interest for 20 years?

20. How much can Mary afford to pay for a computer if she can pay $150 a month on a two-year loan at 15% interest?

21. How much can a couple spend for a new house if they can afford to pay $700 a month for a mortage at 13% per year for 25 years and they have $15,000 for the required down payment of 20% of the selling price?

22. Five years ago a local supermarket financed the modernization of its store by taking out a loan for $100,000 at 10% per year for 10 years with quarterly payments. How much are the quarterly payments and how much does the supermarket owe after making the twentieth payment?

8 Difference Equations

Radioactive decay, population growth, heating, cooling, learning curves, and the spread of information and disease are examples of situations that are modeled by difference equations. A difference equation reduces the computation of later terms in a sequence (the sequence might be a sequence of temperatures, population sizes, or bank balances) to the computation of earlier terms in the sequence. For example, if an account earns 7% interest compounded yearly, then the terms, B_0, B_1, B_2, ... , B_k, B_{k+1}, ... in the sequence of yearly balances are related by the difference equation $B_{k+1} = B_k(1.07)$. This equation reduces the computation of the balance at the end of any year to the computation of the balance at the end of the previous year. Traditionally, equations that relate later terms in a sequence to the preceding terms are called difference equations. Today, difference equations are viewed as a particular kind of relation, called a recurrence relation.

In Section 8.1, we discuss difference equations and give examples. In Section 8.2, we show how to answer such questions as:

1. If the population of a country of 25 million continues to increase at the rate of two percent a year, what will be the population five years from now?
2. How old are the paintings in the caves at Lascaux, France?
3. How long will it take a cup of hot coffee to cool to within 10° of room temperature?

In Section 8.3, we derive solutions of difference equations using the method of iteration. These solutions are used in Section 8.2 of this chapter and throughout chapter 7 (see formula (5), Section 7.1; formula (4), Section 7.2; and formula (4), Section 7.3). Recurrence relations and difference equations that are more complicated than those presented here are often solved using a computer and a recursive algorithm (an algorithm that contains a procedure or routine that invokes itself).

8.1   *Introduction to Difference Equations—The Tower of Hanoi*

Suppose $5000 is deposited in an account that earns eight percent interest compounded twice a year. Then interest is added to the balance at the end of six-month periods and we get a **sequence** of balances.

$$B_0 = \text{initial balance} = \$5000$$

$$B_1 = \text{balance at the end of the first six-month period}$$

$$B_2 = \text{balance at the end of the second six-month period}$$

$$\vdots$$

$$B_k = \text{balance at the end of } k \text{ six-month periods}$$

$$B_{k+1} = \text{balance at the end of the } (k + 1) \text{ six-month periods}$$

$$\vdots$$

If a cup of hot coffee is left in a room to cool, then we can record the temperature of the coffee at the end of each minute and write down the sequence of readings.

$$T_0 = \text{initial temperature}$$

$$T_1 = \text{temperature at the end of one minute}$$

$$T_2 = \text{temperature at the end of two minutes}$$

$$\vdots$$

$$T_k = \text{temperature at the end of } k \text{ minutes}$$

$$T_{k+1} = \text{temperature at the end of } k + 1 \text{ minutes}$$

$$\vdots$$

The balances in the account described above are related by the difference equation $B_{k+1} = B_k(1.04)$ (see Example 4, Section 7.1). This difference equation gives the balance after $k + 1$ interest periods directly from the previous balance. In general, an equation that gives each number of a sequence in terms of preceding numbers is called a **difference equation** or

recurrence relation. The following equations are difference equations:

1. $A_k = A_{k-1} + A_{k-2}$
2. $A_k = 2A_{k-1}$
3. $b_k = 2b_{k-1} + 1$
4. $B_k = (1.1)B_{k-1}$
5. $B_k = (1.1)B_{k-1} + 100$

PRACTICE EXAMPLE 1

Which one of the difference equations 1 through 5 corresponds to the sequence 1, 2, 4, 8, 16, 32, 64, . . . ?

In this section we show how to use a difference equation to compute some of the numbers in a sequence, and we give examples in which a difference equation is a natural way to find the numbers in a sequence.

EXAMPLE 1

A cup of coffee left in a room will cool to room temperature. Suppose the temperature of the coffee is originally 180° and changes according to the difference equation:

(1) $T_k = .95T_{k-1} + 4$ where T_k = temperature of the coffee k minutes after being set in the room to cool

Find the temperatures T_1, T_2, T_3, and T_4.

$$T_0 = \text{temperature after 0 minutes} = 180°$$

Using the difference equation (1) above, we get:

$$T_1 = (.95)(180) + 4 = 171 + 4 = 175$$

$$T_2 = (.95)(175) + 4 = 166.25 + 4 = 170.25$$

$$T_3 = (.95)(170.25) + 4 = 161.74 + 4 = 165.74$$

and

$$T_4 = (.95)(165.74) + 4 = 157.45 + 4 = 161.45$$

PRACTICE EXAMPLE 2

How long does it take the coffee described in Example 1 to cool below 150°?

EXAMPLE 2

Find the numbers a_4, a_5, a_6 in the sequence a_1, a_2, a_3, . . . , with

(a) $a_1 = a_2 = 1$

(b) $a_k = a_{k-1} + a_{k-2}$

We are given

$$a_1 = 1$$

$$a_2 = 1$$

To find a_3 we use the difference equation (b) with k replaced by 3.

$$a_3 = a_{3-1} + a_{3-2}$$
$$= a_2 + a_1$$
$$= 1 + 1$$
$$= 2$$

Similarly,

$$a_4 = a_3 + a_2 = 2 + 1 = 3$$
$$a_5 = a_4 + a_3 = 3 + 2 = 5$$
$$a_6 = a_5 + a_4 = 5 + 3 = 8$$

Note that in order to find a_3 using the formula $a_3 = a_2 + a_1$ it is necessary to know a_2 and a_1. $a_1 = a_2 = 1$ is called an initial condition for the difference equation $a_k = a_{k-1} + a_{k-2}$. In general, the number (or numbers) in a sequence that must be given in order to use the difference equation to compute the remaining numbers in the sequence is called an **initial condition**. The initial condition in Example 1 is $T_0 = 180$, which provides enough information to compute T_1, then T_2, and then T_3.

PRACTICE EXAMPLE 3

Find the numbers a_3, a_4, a_5, and a_6 in the sequence a_1, a_2, . . . with difference equation $a_k = a_{k-1} + a_{k-2}$ and initial condition $a_1 = 2$, $a_2 = 6$.

The sequence in Example 2 is called the Fibonacci sequence after Leonardo de Pisa, better known as Fibonacci, who posed the following problem in 1202.

If we start with one pair of newborn rabbits of opposite sex, then how many pairs of rabbits are there at the end of one month, two months, three months, four months, and so on, if we assume:

1. It takes a newborn rabbit two months to mature into an adult rabbit.
2. A pair of adult rabbits of opposite sex each month produces one pair of newborn rabbits also of opposite sex.
3. The rabbits never die.

The first step is to find the number of pairs of rabbits at the end of each of the first few months and see if the computation suggests a pattern that can be used to predict the number of pairs of rabbits at the end of the following months.

At the end of the first month there is still one pair of newborn rabbits.

In the second month the pair of rabbits matures into a pair of adult rabbits (assumption 1). Therefore, at the end of two months there is one pair of adult rabbits.

During the third month the pair of adult rabbits produces (by assumption 2) a pair of newborn rabbits. Since the rabbits never die (assumption 3), there will be two pairs of rabbits (one adult pair, one newborn pair) at the end of the third month.

This situation is pictured in the tree diagram in Figure 8.1.

Figure 8.1

End of
first month   End of
second month   End of
third month

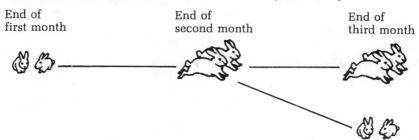

Using the following steps, we can extend the tree diagram to include the end of the fourth month. From assumptions 2 and 3 the adult pair of rabbits continues to live and produces a pair of newborn rabbits. So the adult pair of rabbits at the end of the third month contributes an adult pair of rabbits and a newborn pair of rabbits at the end of the fourth month. Schematically,

Figure 8.2

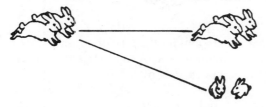

From assumption 1, the pair of rabbits that is newborn during the third month will mature during the fourth month and be adults at the end of the fourth month. Schematically, we have:

Figure 8.3

Adding these branches to the tree diagram in Figure 8.1 gives the tree diagram in Figure 8.4.

Figure 8.4

End of
first month   End of
second month   End of
third month   End of
fourth month

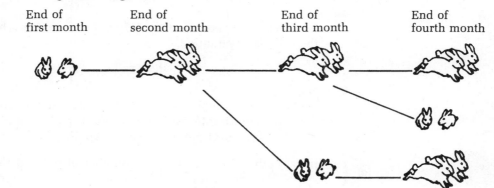

In general,

(a) Each adult pair present at the end of a month counts as an adult pair and a newborn pair at the end of the next month (assumptions 2 and 3).

Figure 8.5

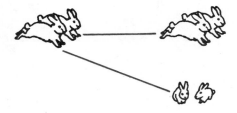

(b) Each newborn pair present at the end of a month matures during the next month and counts as an adult pair at the end of the next month (assumption 1).

Figure 8.6

PRACTICE EXAMPLE 4

Use (a) and (b) above to extend the tree diagram in Figure 8.4 to include the fifth month. In your diagram, use A to represent an adult pair of rabbits and N to represent a newborn pair of rabbits. ■

If we set b_k = number of pairs of rabbits at the end of the kth month, then from Figure 8.4 we have

$$b_1 = 1$$
$$b_2 = 1$$
$$b_3 = 2$$
$$b_4 = 3$$

and from Practice Example 4 it follows that $b_5 = 5$. Notice that the first few numbers in this sequence are the same as those in the sequence of Example 2.

The next step is to show that the sequence of numbers b_1, b_2, b_3, . . . satisfies the difference equation:

$$b_k = b_{k-1} + b_{k-2}$$

Can you see why?

The tree diagram in Figure 8.4 suggests we divide the pairs of rabbits at the end of each month into two groups—adult pairs and newborn pairs—and count the number of pairs in each group. From (a) and (b) we have:

(c) $\left(\begin{array}{c}\text{number of adult pairs at the} \\ \text{end of the } k\text{th month}\end{array}\right) = \left(\begin{array}{c}\text{number of pairs at the end} \\ \text{of the } (k-1)\text{st month}\end{array}\right)$

(d) $\begin{pmatrix} \text{number of newborn pairs} \\ \text{at the end of the } k\text{th month} \end{pmatrix} = \begin{pmatrix} \text{number of adult pairs at the} \\ \text{end of the } (k - 1)\text{st month} \end{pmatrix}$

$= \begin{pmatrix} \text{number of pairs at the} \\ \text{end of the } (k - 2)\text{nd month} \end{pmatrix}$

The difference equation $b_k = b_{k-1} + b_{k-2}$ is derived from (c) and (d) as follows.

$b_k = $ (number of pairs at the end of the kth month)

$= \begin{pmatrix} \text{number of adult pairs at} \\ \text{the end of the } k\text{th month} \end{pmatrix} + \begin{pmatrix} \text{number of newborn pairs at} \\ \text{the end of the } k\text{th month} \end{pmatrix}$

$= b_{k-1} + \begin{pmatrix} \text{number of adult pairs at the} \\ \text{end of the } (k - 1)\text{st month} \end{pmatrix}$

$= b_{k-1} + \begin{pmatrix} \text{number of pairs at the end} \\ \text{of the } (k - 2)\text{nd month} \end{pmatrix}$

$= b_{k-1} + b_{k-2}$

Thus the sequence $b_1, b_2, b_3 \ldots$, which gives the number of pairs of rabbits at the end of each month, satisfies the initial condition $b_1 = b_2 = 1$ and the difference equation $b_k = b_{k-1} + b_{k-2}$. The first ten numbers in this sequence are:

$$b_1 = 1$$
$$b_2 = 1$$
$$b_3 = 2$$
$$b_4 = 2 + 1 = 3$$
$$b_5 = 3 + 2 = 5$$
$$b_6 = 5 + 3 = 8$$
$$b_7 = 8 + 5 = 13$$
$$b_8 = 13 + 8 = 21$$
$$b_9 = 21 + 13 = 34$$
$$b_{10} = 34 + 21 = 55$$

The numbers in the Fibonacci sequence are called **Fibonacci numbers**. These numbers occur surprisingly often in nature. Phyllotaxis is a field of botany that studies such phenomena as the arrangement of leaves around the stem, scales on a cone, florets on a flower, or whorls (shapes arranged in a circle) on a pineapple. In some trees, like the elm or basswood, the leaves along a branch seem to occur alternately on opposite sides and we say the elm has $\frac{1}{2}$-phyllotaxis. An apple tree and a rosebush have a leaf every 144 degrees around the branch, or five leaves for every two turns around the branch $[5(144°) = 2(360°)]$. The apple tree and rosebush are said to have $\frac{2}{5}$-phyllotaxis. The pear and poplar tree have $\frac{3}{8}$-phyllotaxis. You probably have noticed that the ratios used to describe the phyllotaxis are ratios of Fibonacci numbers. There is no known explanation for why Fibonacci numbers arise in phyllotaxis (see Adler 1977).

EXAMPLE 3

Find the numbers C_2, C_3, C_4, and C_5 in the sequence $C_1, C_2, \ldots$ with initial condition $C_1 = 1$ and difference equation $C_k = 2C_{k-1} + 1$.

$$C_1 = 1 \quad \text{(given)}$$
$$C_2 = 2C_1 + 1 \quad \text{(from the difference equation)}$$
$$= 2(1) + 1$$
$$= 3$$
$$C_3 = 2C_2 + 1 = 2(3) + 1 = 6 + 1 = 7$$
$$C_4 = 2C_3 + 1 = 2(7) + 1 = 14 + 1 = 15$$
$$C_5 = 2C_4 + 1 = 2(15) + 1 = 30 + 1 = 31$$

Each of the numbers $C_1 = 1$, $C_2 = 3$, $C_3 = 7$, $C_4 = 15$, and $C_5 = 31$ is one less than a power of two.

$$C_1 = 1 = 2^1 - 1$$
$$C_2 = 3 = 2^2 - 1$$
$$C_3 = 7 = 2^3 - 1$$
$$C_4 = 15 = 2^4 - 1$$
$$C_5 = 31 = 2^5 - 1$$

You will show in Exercise 3 of Section 8.3 that

(2) if $C_1 = 1$ and $C_k = 2C_{k-1} + 1$ then $C_k = 2^k - 1$ for $k = 1, 2, 3, \ldots$

The sequence of numbers in Example 3 is associated with an ancient legend called the **Tower of Hanoi puzzle**. This puzzle resembles a child's stacking toy that can be bought today.

In the Great Temple of Benares there is a large brass slab on which there are three diamond needles, each a cubit high, and as thick as the body of a bee. At the beginning of the world, God placed 64 gold disks with holes in their centers on one of these needles, the largest resting on the brass slab, and the others decreasing in size to the top. Day and night, the priests transfer the disks from needle to needle, one disk at a time, one each second, and so that any disk moved is placed on either a free needle, or on a larger disk (see Dewdney 1984).

As the legend goes, when all 64 disks are on another needle, the temple will crumble, and the world will come to an end. How long will it take the priests to move all 64 disks to another needle?

We will solve this puzzle by considering the problem when there are one disk, two disks, three disks, and so on.

Figure 8.7

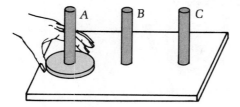

Let M_k = number of moves needed in order to transfer k disks from one needle to another. If there is one disk on needle A as in Figure 8.7 then the disk can be moved to either B or C in one move so

$$M_1 = 1$$

The two disks pictured in Figure 8.8 can be moved to needle C in three moves.

Figure 8.8

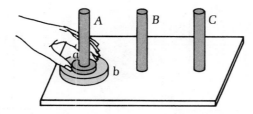

Move disk a to needle B as shown in Figure 8.9.

Figure 8.9

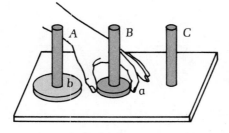

Move disk b to needle C (Figure 8.10).

Figure 8.10

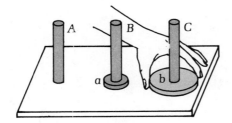

Move disk a to needle C (Figure 8.11).

Figure 8.11

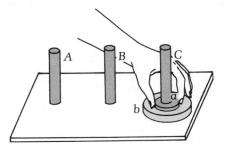

Two disks stacked on a needle can be transferred to another needle in three moves.

$$M_2 = 3$$

Three disks can be transferred from needle A to needle C as follows:

STEP 1   Transfer disks a and b to needle B. This takes three moves as pictured in Figure 8.12.

Figure 8.12

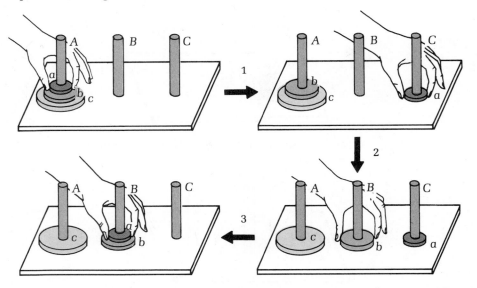

STEP 2   Transfer disk c to needle C. This takes one move as shown in Figure 8.13.

Figure 8.13

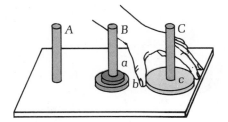

STEP 3   Transfer disks a and b to needle C. This is the same as the preceding problem of moving two disks and hence takes three moves (move disk a to needle A, move disk b to needle C, then move disk a to needle C).

The total number of moves is $3 + 1 + 3 = 7$, so $M_3 = 7$.

PRACTICE EXAMPLE 5   How many moves are needed to transfer four disks on needle A to another needle?

In general, k disks can be transferred from needle A to needle C by carrying out the following steps:

1. Transfer the top $(k - 1)$ disks from needle A to needle B.
2. Transfer the remaining disk on needle A to needle C.
3. Transfer the $(k - 1)$ disks on needle B to needle C.

If you had difficulty with Practice Example 5, try it again using these three steps.

We get a difference equation for the sequence M_1, M_2, M_3, . . . by counting the number of moves needed to carry out the transfers in the three steps above.

Steps	Number of moves needed
1. Transfer the top $(k - 1)$ disks from needle A to needle B.	M_{k-1}
2. Transfer the remaining disk on needle A to needle C.	1
3. Transfer the $(k - 1)$ disks on needle B to needle C.	M_{k-1}
Total	$M_k = 2M_{k-1} + 1$

The sequence M_1, M_2, . . . has $M_1 = 1$, satisfies the difference equation $M_k = 2M_{k-1} + 1$, and hence is the same as the sequence C_1, C_2, . . . in Example 3. From statement (2) we have:

$$(3) \qquad M_k = 2^k - 1$$

for $k = 1, 2, 3, 4, ...$

The answer to the Tower of Hanoi puzzle is that it will take $2^{64} - 1 = 1.8446744 \times 10^{19}$ seconds, which is about 586,146,827,560 years, to transfer 64 disks from one needle to another. (The article in *Scientific American*, Dewdney 1984, includes an alternative solution to the Tower of Hanoi puzzle and discusses a similar Chinese rings puzzle.)

In this section, we gave examples of difference equations and showed how to use them to compute terms in the sequence. In the next section, we use difference equations to model radioactive decay, population growth, heating and cooling, and show how to compute terms in the sequence using the solution of the difference equation.

CONCEPTS

difference equation
recurrence relation
Fibonacci sequence
Tower of Hanoi puzzle

SOLUTIONS TO PRACTICE EXAMPLES

1. The difference equation $A_k = 2A_{k-1}$ corresponds to the sequence 1, 2, 4, 8, 16, 32, 64, ...

2. Using the difference equation: $T_k = .95T_{k-1} + 4$, and $T_4 = 161.45$, we get:

$$T_5 = 157.3775$$
$$T_6 = 153.50863$$
$$T_7 = 149.83319$$
$$T_8 = 146.34153$$

It takes seven minutes for the coffee to cool below 150°.

3. $a_1 = 2$
$a_2 = 6$
$a_3 = a_2 + a_1 = 8$
$a_4 = a_3 + a_2 = 14$
$a_5 = a_4 + a_3 = 22$
$a_6 = a_5 + a_4 = 36$

4.

End of first month	End of second month	End of third month	End of fourth month	End of fifth month

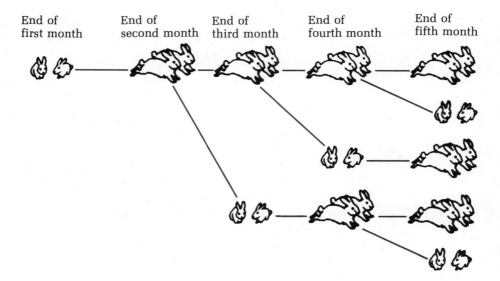

5. Suppose the four disks, from smallest to largest, are a, b, c, d. These disks can be moved from needle A to needle B in 15 moves as follows.

1. Move the disks a, b, c from needle A to needle C following the steps pictured in Figures 8.12 and 8.13. This takes $M_3 = 7$ moves.
2. Move disk d to needle B. This takes 1 move.
3. Move disks a, b, c from needle C to needle B in $M_3 = 7$ moves.

EXERCISES 8.1

In Exercises 1 through 10 find the third, fourth, and fifth numbers in the sequence.

1. (a) initial condition $a_1 = 3$
   (b) difference equation $a_k = 2a_{k-1} + 1$

2. (a) initial condition $b_1 = 4$
   (b) difference equation $b_k = 2b_{k-1} + 1$

3. (a) initial condition $a_1 = 2$, $a_2 = 4$
   (b) difference equation $a_k = a_{k-1} + a_{k-2}$

4. (a) initial condition $a_1 = 3$, $a_2 = 6$
   (b) difference equation $a_k = a_{k-1} + a_{k-2}$

5. (a) initial condition $c_1 = 1$
   (b) difference equation $c_k = c_{k-1} + k$

6. (a) initial condition $b_1 = 3$
   (b) difference equation $b_k = b_{k-1} + 1$

7. (a) initial condition $d_1 = 64$
   (b) difference equation $d_k = (\frac{1}{2})d_{k-1}$

8. (a) initial condition $a_1 = 2$
   (b) difference equation $a_k = a_{k-1}(3 - a_{k-1})$

9. (a) initial condition $a_1 = 1$
   (b) difference equation $a_k = a_{k-1}(3 - a_{k-1})$

10. (a) initial equation $a_1 = 1$
    (b) difference equation $a_k = a_{k-1}(3 - a_{k-1}) + 1$

11. If a glass of lemonade at 35°F warms to room temperature according to the difference equation:

$$T_k = \frac{8}{9} T_{k-1} + \frac{80}{9}$$

where T_k = temperature of the lemonade after k minutes. Then find the temperature after:
(a) one minute.
(b) two minutes.

12. Suppose the flu spreads through the town according to the formula:

$$A_k = A_{k-1}(1 - A_{k-1}) + A_{k-1}$$

where A_k = fraction of people in town who will have been exposed to the flu k days from now. If $A_0 = .1$, then find the fraction of people who will have been exposed to the flu:
(a) one day from now.
(b) two days from now.
(c) three days from now.
(d) four days from now.

13. Suppose 100 mgs of a radioactive substance decays so that at the end of each year the amount remaining is 90% of the amount present at the beginning of the year.
  Let A_k = amount of radioactive material remaining after k years.
(a) Find A_0
(b) Find a difference equation for the sequence $A_0, A_1, A_2, \ldots$.
(c) Find the amount of radioactive material remaining after

  (i) one year.

  (ii) two years.

  (iii) three years.

14. The ancient Greeks attributed special characteristics to certain numbers. Some numbers are male, some female, some are square, and some are triangular. In this exercise we ask you to find a difference equation for the sequence of triangular numbers. A number is called *triangular* if it is the total number of dots in a triangular array such as:

1st triangular number	2nd triangular number	3rd triangular number	4th triangular number
.	. .	. . . . .	. . . .
1	3	6	10

(a) Find the fifth and sixth triangular numbers.
(b) Let A_k = kth triangular number.

From above we have

$$A_1 = 1$$
$$A_2 = 3$$
$$A_3 = 6$$
$$A_4 = 10$$

Find a difference equation for the sequence $A_1, A_2, \ldots$.

15. According to legend, when King Shirham of India offered to reward his Grand Vizier, Sissa Ben Dahir, for inventing the game of chess, the Grand Vizier requested one grain of wheat for the first square on a chess board, two grains for the second square, four grains for the third square, eight for the fourth square, and so on.

(a) How many grains of wheat were requested for the

   (i) fifth square?

   (ii) sixth square?

(b) Find an expression for the number of grains of wheat requested for the kth square.

Let s_k = the total number of grains of wheat requested for the first k squares.

(c) Find:

   (i) s_1.

   (ii) s_2.

   (iii) s_3.

   (iv) s_4.

   (v) s_5.

(d) Find a difference equation for the sequence $s_1, s_2, s_3, \ldots$.

(e) There are 64 squares on a chess board. What is the total number of grains of wheat requested by the Grand Vizier? (Compare your answer to (c) with the first few numbers in the sequence of Example 2.)

*16. Straight lines (of infinite length) in a plane are said to be in general position if no two lines are parallel and no three lines intersect at the same point. Let r_k = number of regions in the plane determined by k lines in general position. Since one line divides the plane into two regions, $r_1 = 2$.

(a) Find (by drawing pictures):

   (i) r_2.

   (ii) r_3.

   (iii) r_4.

   (iv) r_5.

(b) If $(k - 1)$ lines in general position have been drawn, then how many additional regions are created by adding one more line, also in general position? (Note the new line divides each of the regions it intersects into two regions.)

(c) Find a difference equation for the sequence $r_1, r_2, r_3, r_4, \ldots$.

(d) Use your answer to (c) to find:

   (i) r_6.

   (ii) r_7.

   (iii) r_8.

   (iv) r_9.

   (v) r_{10}.

*17. Let $C_k = \dfrac{k(k + 1)}{2}$ for $k = 1, 2, 3, 4, 5, 6, \ldots$.

(a) Show that the sequence $c_1, c_2, c_3, \ldots$ satisfies the difference equation $c_{k+1} = c_k + (k + 1)$.

(b) Find a solution for:

   (i) The difference equation in Exercise 14.

   (ii) The difference equation in Exercise 16.

8.2   Applications—Radioactive Decay, Newton's Law of Cooling

In this section we give applications of difference equations to radioactive decay, population growth, spread of information and disease, and heating and cooling, and show how to compute increased costs based on inflation. We will use the following equations to compute numbers in a sequence without having to first find all the preceding numbers in the sequence.

> If x_0, x_1, x_2, . . . is a sequence satisfying a difference equation of the form:
>
> (1) $$x_k = ax_{k-1} + b$$
>
> then the numbers in the sequence can be computed using the equation:
>
> (2) $$x_k = \frac{b}{1-a} + \left(x_0 - \frac{b}{1-a}\right)a^k \qquad \text{when } a \neq 1$$

We will show in the next section how equation (2) can be derived from equation (1).

In the first example, we use the difference equation $x_k = ax_{k-1}$ to compute increased costs due to inflation.

EXAMPLE 1

If a college education cost \$50,000, and the cost continues to increase each year by four percent of the previous year's cost, then how much will a college education cost 18 years from now?

Let x_k be the cost k years from now. We have

$$x_0 = 50{,}000$$

$$\text{(yearly increase in cost)} = (.04)\text{(previous year's cost)}$$

$$(x_k - x_{k-1}) = (.04)x_{k-1}$$

$$x_k = (1.04)x_{k-1}$$

Using equation (2) with

$$x_0 = 50{,}000$$

$$a = 1.04$$

$$b = 0$$

we get $x_k = (50{,}000)(1.04)^k$.

The cost 18 years from now is

$$x_{18} = (50{,}000)(1.04)^{18}$$

$$= (50{,}000)(2.0258165)$$

$$= 101{,}290.83$$

If the cost of a college education increases by four percent each year, then in 18 years the cost will be more than $100,000. ■

PRACTICE
EXAMPLE 1

Suppose the value of a $65,000 house increases each year by five percent. How much will the house be worth 10 years from now? ■

Radioactive decay occurs over time periods of fixed length so that if x_k = amount of radioactive material remaining after k time periods, then the sequence x_0, x_1, x_2, ... satisfies a difference equation of the form $x_k = ax_{k-1}$. The value of a depends on the particular radioactive material.

EXAMPLE 2

A radioactive material decays so that $x_k = (.99)x_{k-1}$ where x_k = amount of material remaining after k years. If there are presently 20 units of the material, how much will be left at the end of

(a) 1 year?
(b) 5 years?
(c) 10 years?

The sequence of numbers x_0, x_1, x_2, ... satisfies the difference equation $x_k = (.99)x_{k-1}$ with initial condition $x_0 = 20$ = amount remaining after 0 years.

Using equation (2) with

$$x_0 = 20$$

$$a = .99$$

$$b = 0$$

we get

$$x_k = 0 + (20 - 0)(.99)^k$$

$$x_k = 20(.99)^k$$

$$x_1 = 20(.99)^1 = 19.8$$

There are 19.8 units remaining after one year.

$$x_5 = (20)(.99)^5 = (20)(.951) = 19.02$$

There are 19.02 units remaining at the end of five years.

$$x_{10} = (20)(.99)^{10} = (20)(.904382) = 18.087642$$

Rounding to the nearest hundredth of a unit, we conclude there will be 18.09 units at the end of 10 years. ■

PRACTICE
EXAMPLE 2

A radioactive substance is decaying so that at the end of each day the amount remaining is one half of the amount present one day earlier.

Let x_k = amount remaining at the end of k days and suppose there are presently 256 mgs.

(a) Find a difference equation for the sequence $x_0, x_1, \ldots$.
(b) How much of the 256 mg sample will remain after five days?   ■

Different radioactive materials have been used to estimate the age of ancient objects. The most commonly used is radioactive carbon. In the atmosphere, and in all living things, the ratio of radioactive carbon, C^{14}, to nonradioactive carbon, C^{12}, is one part C^{14} for every 10^{12} parts C^{12}. When an object dies, the C^{14} decays, but the amount of C^{12} does not change. By measuring the ratio of C^{14} to C^{12} in an object to be dated (for example, a bone fragment) you can estimate the amount of C^{14} that has decayed and hence the object's age.

EXAMPLE 3   Radioactive carbon, C^{14}, decays so that at the end of a 5000-year period the amount of C^{14} remaining is .5444256 times the amount present at the beginning of the period.

(a) A fossil contains 100 units of radioactive carbon. Find the amount of radioactive carbon remaining at the end of:

  (i) 5000 years.
  (ii) 10,000 years.
  (iii) 15,000 years.
  (iv) 20,000 years.

(b) Use the answer to (a) to estimate the age of a fossil that contained 100 units of radioactive carbon when alive and presently contains 16 units of radioactive carbon.

Let x_k = amount of radioactive carbon remaining after k time periods of 5000 years each. Then

$$x_0 = 100$$

$$x_k = (.5444256)x_{k-1}.$$

Using equation (2) with

$$a = .5444256$$

$$b = 0$$

$$x_0 = 100$$

we get $x_k = 100(.5444256)^k$ = amount remaining after k time periods of 5000 years each. So,

  (i) $x_1 = 100(.5444256) = 54.44256$
     or   54.44 units remain at the end of 5000 years.
  (ii) $x_2 = 100(.5444256)^2 = 100(.2963992) = 29.63992$
     or   29.64 units remain at the end of 10,000 years.

(iii) $x_3 = 100(.5444256)^3 = 100(.1613673)$
   or   16.14 units remain at the end of 15,000 years.
(iv) $x_4 = 100(.5444256)^4 = 100(.0878525) = 8.78525$
   or   8.79 units remain at the end of 20,000 years.

From the answer to (iii), it follows that the fossil is slightly more than 15,000 years old.

Carbon dating was used to estimate the paintings in the Lascaux Caves in France to be 15,500 years old.

The difference equation $x_k = ax_{k-1}$ can also be used to model **population growth**. For example a population of E. Coli bacteria in the body can double its size every two hours. In this case if $x_k =$ number of bacteria after k time periods of two hours each, then the sequence $x_0, x_1. \ldots$ satisfies the difference equation $x_k = 2x_{k-1}$.

EXAMPLE 4   In a certain country the population increases each year by an amount equal to two percent of the population at the beginning of the year.

(a) Find a difference equation for the population size.
(b) If the current population is 25 million what will be the population five years from now?

From the description above we have

$$\begin{pmatrix} \text{population increase} \\ \text{during the } k\text{th year} \end{pmatrix} = .02 \begin{pmatrix} \text{population at the end} \\ \text{of the } (k-1)\text{st year} \end{pmatrix}$$

Setting $x_k =$ population in millions of people after k years we get

$$(x_k - x_{k-1}) = .02x_{k-1}$$

$$x_k = x_{k-1} + .02x_{k-1}$$

$$x_k = (1 + .02)x_{k-1}$$

$$x_k = (1.02)x_{k-1}$$

Using equation (2) with

$$a = 1.02$$

$$b = 0$$

$$x_0 = 25$$

gives

$$x_k = 25(1.02)^k$$

The population five years from now will be

$$x_5 = 25(1.02)^5 = 25(1.1040808)$$

$$= 27.60202 \text{ million people}$$

EXAMPLE 5   Newton's law of cooling says that over time periods of fixed length the change in the temperature of an object is proportional to the difference between the temperature of the object at the beginning of the time period and the room temperature. For example if a cup of coffee at 180°F is placed in a room whose temperature is 80°F and cools to 175°F in one minute, then we can use Newton's law of cooling to find:

(a) a difference equation for the temperature of the coffee.
(b) the temperature of the coffee after 20 minutes.

NEWTON'S LAW OF COOLING

$$(3) \quad \begin{pmatrix} \text{change in} \\ \text{temperature over} \\ \text{one time period} \end{pmatrix} = A \begin{pmatrix} \text{temperature at the} \\ \text{beginning of the} \\ \text{time period} \end{pmatrix} - \begin{pmatrix} \text{room} \\ \text{temperature} \end{pmatrix}$$

If x_k = temperature of the coffee after k minutes, then:

$$x_k - x_{k-1} = A(x_{k-1} - 80)$$

We are given that $x_0 = 180$ and $x_1 = 175$. Substituting these values in

$$x_1 - x_0 = A(x_0 - 80)$$

gives

$$(75 - 180) = A(180 - 80)$$

$$-5 = A(100)$$

$$-.05 = A$$

Substituting $A = -.05$ into equation (3) gives

$$x_k - x_{k-1} = (-.05)(x_{k-1} - 80)$$

Now solve for x_k.

$$x_k = x_{k-1} + (-.05)(x_{k-1} - 80)$$

$$= x_{k-1} + (-.05)x_{k-1} + (-.05)(-80)$$

$$= [1 + (-.05)]x_{k-1} + 4$$

$$x_k = (.95)x_{k-1} + 4$$

A difference equation for the minute-by-minute temperatures of the coffee is:

$$x_k = (.95)x_{k-1} + 4$$

Using equation (2) with

$$a = .95$$

$$b = 4$$

$$x_0 = 180$$

gives

$$x_k = \frac{4}{1 - .95} + \left(180 - \frac{4}{1 - .95}\right)(.95)^k$$

$$= 80 + (180 - 80)(.95)^k$$

$$= 80 + (100)(.95)^k$$

The temperature of the coffee after 20 minutes is:

$$x_{20} = 80 + (100)(.95)^{20}$$

$$= 80 + (100)(.3584859)$$

$$= 80 + 35.84859$$

$$= 115.84859°F$$

Therefore to the nearest one hundredth of a degree the temperature after 20 minutes is 115.85°F.

PRACTICE EXAMPLE 3

A glass of lemonade placed in a room warms from 40°F to 42°F in one minute. If the room temperature is 90°F:

(a) Find the difference equation for the temperature of the lemonade.
(b) Use equation (2) to find the temperature of the lemonade after 10 minutes.

EXAMPLE 6

A **model for the spread of information and disease** is obtained by assuming that over time periods of fixed length the number of people newly exposed to the information or disease is proportional to the number of people not yet exposed at the beginning of the time period. If x_k = number of people exposed after k time periods and P = number of people in the entire population, then:

$$\begin{pmatrix} \text{number of people newly} \\ \text{exposed during the} \\ k\text{th time period} \end{pmatrix} = A \begin{pmatrix} \text{number of people} \\ \text{not exposed after} \\ k - 1 \text{ time periods} \end{pmatrix}$$

(4) $$(x_k - x_{k-1}) = A(P - x_{k-1})$$

The flu is spreading through a campus of 5000 students. If 1000 students have presently been exposed to the flu, and this number will grow to 1500 tomorrow, then how many students will have been exposed to the flu one week from now?

Let x_k = number of students exposed k days from now. Substituting

$$x_0 = 1000$$

$$x_1 = 1500$$

$$P = 5000$$

into equation (4) gives

$$(1500 - 1000) = A(5000 - 1000)$$

$$500 = A(4000)$$

$$\frac{500}{4000} = A$$

$$.125 = A$$

Replacing A in equation (4) with .125 we get:

$$x_k - x_{k-1} = .125(5000 - x_{k-1})$$

Solve for x_k:

$$x_k = x_{k-1} + .125(5000 - x_{k-1})$$

$$= x_{k-1} + .125(5000) - .125 x_{k-1}$$

$$= (1 - .125) x_{k-1} + 625$$

$$x_k = .875 x_{k-1} + 625$$

This is a difference equation for the number of students exposed k days from now.

Now use the equation (2) with

$$a = .875$$

$$b = 625$$

$$x_0 = 1000$$

$$x_k = \frac{625}{.125} + \left(1000 - \frac{625}{.125}\right)(.875)^k$$

$$= 5000 + (-4000)(.875)^k$$

The number of students who will have been exposed one week from now will be:

$$x_7 = 5000 + (-4000)(.875)^7$$

$$= 5000 - 4000(.3926959)$$

$$= 5000 - 1,570.7836$$

$$= 3,429.2164$$

This model predicts that 3429 students will have been exposed one week from now. ◼

The next example illustrates how to find the numbers a and b in the difference equation, $x_k = a x_{k-1} + b$, from the first three numbers in the sequence. Equation (2) can then be used to find any of the other numbers in the sequence.

EXAMPLE 7

$x_0 = 1$, $x_1 = 3$, $x_2 = 7$, are the first three terms in a sequence x_0, x_1, x_2, x_3 ... that satisfies a difference equation of the form $x_k = ax_{k-1} + b$. Find the difference equation.

Assuming that $x_k = ax_{k-1} + b$ for some values of a and b we have

$$x_1 = ax_0 + b$$

$$x_2 = ax_1 + b$$

Replace x_0 with 1, x_1 with 3, and x_2 with 7 to get

(5) $3 = a(1) + b$

(6) $7 = a(3) + b$

Now subtract equation (5) from equation (6).

$$(7 - 3) = [a(3) - a(1)] + (b - b)$$

$$4 = 2a$$

So $a = 2$, and the difference equation must be:

$$x_k = 2x_{k-1} + b \text{ for some number } b$$

To find b, replace a with the number 2 in equation (5).

$$3 = 2(1) + b$$

$$3 = 2 + b$$

$$1 = b$$

The difference equation is $x_k = 2x_{k-1} + 1$.

The technique used in Example 7 to find a difference equation of the form $x_k = ax_{k-1} + b$, given the first three terms x_0, x_1, and x_2, is:

1. Substitute the values for x_0, x_1, and x_2 into the equations:

$$x_1 = ax_0 + b$$

$$x_2 = ax_1 + b$$

2. Find the numbers a and b (see Section 9.2).

The difference equation is $x_k = ax_{k-1} + b$.

In Example 7 the given numbers are $x_0 = 1$, $x_1 = 3$, $x_2 = 7$.

Step 1 is to write the equations $3 = a(1) + b$
$7 = a(3) + b$

Step 2 is to solve the equations in step 1 for the numbers a and b. In Example 7 the solution is $a = 2$, $b = 1$.

Step 3 is the difference equation $x_k = 2x_{k-1} + 1$.

PRACTICE
EXAMPLE 4 Suppose that over the last three years the cost of a particular item has risen from \$3000 to \$3500 to the present price of \$4250. Use a difference equation of the form $x_k = ax_{k-1} + b$ to predict the cost of the item next year. ▪

In this section, we used difference equations of the form $x_k = ax_{k-1} + b$ to model radioactive decay, population growth, cooling, the spread of information and disease, and the rise in cost due to inflation. Equation (2) was used to compute terms in a sequence that satisfies a difference equation of the form $x_k = ax_{k-1} + b$. In the next section, we present a general method, the method of iteration, for solving difference equations and use the method to derive equation (2) from equation (1).

CONCEPTS

radioactive decay
carbon dating
population growth
Newton's law of cooling

model for the spread of information and disease
finding the difference equation from the first
   three numbers in the sequence

SOLUTIONS TO PRACTICE EXAMPLES

1. $x_0 = 65,000$ and

$$(x_{k-1} - x_{k-2}) = (.05)x_{k-1}$$

so

$$x_k = (1.05)x_{k-1}$$

Using equation (2) with

$$x_0 = 65,000$$
$$a = 1.05$$
$$b = 0$$

we get

the value of the house in 10 years $= x_{10}$
$$= (65,000)(1.05)^{10}$$
$$= (65,000)(1.6288946)$$
$$= \$105,878.15$$

2. (a) $x_k = \dfrac{1}{2} x_{k-1}$

   (b) Use equation (2) with $a = \frac{1}{2}$, $b = 0$, and $x_0 = 256$.

$$x_k = 256 \left(\frac{1}{2}\right)^k$$

$$x_5 = 256 \left(\frac{1}{2}\right)^5 = \frac{256}{32} = 8 \text{ mgs}$$

3. (a) From equation (3):

$$x_k - x_{k-1} = A(x_{k-1} - 90)$$

The first step is to find the value of A.

$$x_1 - x_0 = A(x_0 - 90)$$

$$42 - 40 = A(40 - 90)$$

$$2 = A(-50)$$

$$A = \frac{-2}{50} = -.04$$

$$(x_k - x_{k-1}) = -.04(x_{k-1} - 90)$$

$$x_k = x_{k-1} - .04 x_{k-1} + 3.6$$

$$x_k = .96 x_{k-1} + 3.6$$

Use equation (2) with

$$a = .96$$

$$b = 3.6$$

$$x_0 = 40$$

Then

$$\frac{b}{1-a} = \frac{3.6}{1-.96} = 90$$

and

$$x_k = 90 + (40 - 90)(.96)^k$$

$$x_k = 90 - 50(.96)^k$$

$$x_{10} = 56.76°F \text{ (to the nearest one hundredth of a degree)}$$

4. $x_0 = 3000$
$x_1 = 3500$
$x_2 = 4250$

$$3500 = a(3000) + b$$

$$4250 = a(3500) + b$$

$$(4250 - 3500) = a(3500 - 3000) + (b - b)$$

$$750 = a(500)$$

$$1.5 = a$$

$$3500 = (1.5)(3000) + b$$

$$b = -1000$$

The difference equation is:

$$x_k = 1.5 x_{k-1} - 1000$$

The predicted cost of the item next year is:

$$x_3 = (1.5)(4250) - 1000$$

$$x_3 = \$5375$$

EXERCISES 8.2

In Exercises 1 through 6 use equation (2) to find the solution.

1. Difference equation $x_k = 2x_{k-1} + 1$ with initial condition $x_0 = 4$.

2. Difference equation $x_k = 2x_{k-1} + 3$ with initial condition $x_0 = 4$.

3. Difference equation $x_k = (.1)x_{k-1} + 2$ with initial condition $x_0 = 3$.

4. Difference equation $x_k - x_{k-1} = 10(50 - x_{k-1})$ with initial condition $x_0 = 20$.

5. Difference equation $x_k - x_{k-1} = 2(100 - x_{k-1})$ with initial condition $x_0 = 50$.

6. Difference equation $x_k - x_{k-1} = 7(19 - x_{k-1})$ with initial condition $x_0 = 9$.

In Exercises 7, 8, and 9 find a difference equation of the form $x_k = ax_{k-1} + b$ so that the numbers given in the problem are the first three terms in a sequence satisfying your difference equation.

7. $x_0 = 1$, $x_1 = 4$, $x_2 = 13$.

8. $x_0 = 128$, $x_1 = 56$, $x_2 = 20$.

9. $x_0 = 100$, $x_1 = 83$, $x_2 = 69.4$.

10. If the current model of a car costs \$10,000 and the cost increases each year by three percent, then how much will the car cost four years from now?

11. Suppose a company's sales increase by five percent over each of the next three years. What will be the company's sales three years from now if the current sales are 50,000 items?

12. The Consumer Price Index (CPI) computed by the Department of Labor, Bureau of Statistics, measures the average change in prices over time. The CPI is based on prices of food, clothing, shelter, fuels, transportation, medical costs, and the other goods and services that people buy for day-to-day living. From 1980 to 1984 the CPI rose on the average 5.3% each year. If the CPI continues to increase at this rate, then how much would a person have to earn in 1990 in order to have the same purchasing power as someone who earned \$40,000 in 1980?

13. A radioactive material decays so that $x_k = (.9)x_{k-1}$ where $x_k =$ amount of material remaining after k years. If there are presently 100 units of the radioactive material, how much will be left after:

    (a) 1 year?

    (b) 3 years?

    (c) 15 years?

14. Uranium has been used to date rocks. It takes 4.5 billion years for half the uranium in a sample to decay. How old is a rock that presently contains one eighth as much uranium as when the rock was formed?

15. It takes 1660 years for one half of the radium in a sample to decay. Estimate the age of an object that contained 10 units of radium when new and presently contains three tenths of a unit of uranium.

16. An island contaminated by nuclear fallout has 10 times the acceptable level of strontium 90. How many years will it take before the level of strontium 90 is acceptable if the amount of strontium 90 remaining in a sample is 78% of the amount present 10 years earlier?

17. In a city with current population of 80,000, the population increases each year by two percent taking into account births and deaths. In addition 1000 more people move out of the city each year than move into the city. Find a difference equation for x_k, the population in the city k years from now.

18. Over the last three years the population of a city has gone from 60,000 to 59,000 to 58,200. Use a difference equation of the form $x_k = ax_{k-1} + b$ to predict the population next year.

19. A cup of coffee placed in a room cools from 160°F to 150°F in one minute. If the room temperature is 65°F find a difference equation for T_k = temperature of the coffee after k minutes.

20. A glass of lemonade placed in a room warms from 34°F to 40°F in three minutes. If the temperature of the room is 90°F then what is the temperature of the lemonade nine minutes after being left in the room?

21. Use formula (2) to show that a sequence satisfying the difference equation $x_k - x_{k-1} = A(R - x_{k-1})$ has the solution:

$$x_k = R + (x_0 - R)(1 - A)^k$$

22. A hard-boiled egg is left standing in a room to cool. Originally the temperature of the egg is 155°F. After one minute the temperature is 146°F, and after two minutes it is 137.9°F.
    (a) Find a difference equation for T_k, the temperature of the egg after k minutes (see Example 7).
    (b) Use equation (2) to write the solution of this difference equation.
    (c) Use the result of Exercise 21 to find the temperature of the room.

23. Suppose that beginning at noon on a certain day, local radio and television stations start broadcasting an important news item. Assume the number of people learning the news each hour is 70% of the people who had not heard the news at the beginning of the hour, and the town has a population of 100,000.
    (a) Find a difference equation for x_k, the number of people who have heard the news after k hours.
    (b) How many people will have heard the news by three o'clock in the afternoon?

24. Glucose is being given to a patient at the rate of 50 mgs per minute. Let x_k be the amount of glucose in the blood after k minutes and suppose that each minute the body absorbs three percent of the glucose present at the beginning of the minute. Thus each minute the amount of glucose in the blood is increased by the 50 mg injection and reduced by absorption into the body. Find a difference equation for x_k.

25. The atmospheric pressure at sea level is 14.7 pounds per square inch. At any elevation an increase in altitude of one mile results in a decrease in the atmospheric pressure of 20% of the pressure at that elevation. Find a dif-

ference equation for x_k, the atmospheric pressure k miles above sea level. What is the atmospheric pressure two miles above sea level?

26. In certain learning situations the amount of material that can be learned each hour is proportional to the amount yet to be learned at the beginning of the hour. If a student can learn 3 of 12 units of information in the first hour, find a difference equation for x_k, the amount of information the student can learn in k hours.

27. Over the past three years a company's sales have risen from 100,000 units to 150,000 units, to 225,000 units. Assume the yearly sales satisfy a difference equation of the form $x_k = ax_{k-1} + b$ and predict the amount of sales next year.

8.3 Solving Difference Equations by Iteration

In this section we give a general method for solving difference equations, the **method of iteration**. The method of iteration is used to show that the difference equation:

(1) $$x_k = ax_{k-1} + b$$

has solution:

(2) $$x_k = \frac{b}{1-a} + \left(x_0 - \frac{b}{1-a}\right)a^k$$

provided $a \neq 1$, as indicated in the beginning of Section 8.2.

We used equation (2) often in the previous section. In Example 1 and in the first two exercises, you will see how equation (2) leads to formulas used in Chapter 7.

To solve a difference equation by iteration, write the initial condition and then repeatedly substitute into the difference equation to obtain successive terms in the sequence. For example if $x_0 = 3$ and $x_k = 2x_{k-1}$ then starting with the initial condition and repeatedly substituting into the difference equation gives:

$$x_0 = 3$$
$$x_1 = 2x_0 = 2(3)$$
$$x_2 = 2x_1 = 2[(2)3] = 2^2(3)$$
$$x_3 = 2x_2 = 2[2^2(3)] = 2^3(3)$$
$$x_4 = 2x_3 = 2[2^3(3)] = 2^4(3)$$
$$\vdots$$
$$x_k = 2^k(3)$$

The solution to $x_k = 2x_{k-1}$, $x_0 = 3$ is $x_k = 2^k(3)$.

In general, the solution to $x_k = ax_{k-1}$ is obtained using the method of iteration as follows.

$$x_0$$

$$x_1 = ax_0$$

$$x_2 = ax_1 = a[(a)x_0] = a^2(x_0)$$

$$x_3 = ax_2 = a[a^2(x_0)] = a^3(x_0)$$

$$x_4 = ax_3 = a[a^3(x_0)] = a^4(x_0)$$

$$\cdot$$
$$\cdot$$
$$\cdot$$

$$x_k = a^k(x_0)$$

The solution to $x_k = ax_{k-1}$, is $x_k = a^k(x_0)$.

PRACTICE EXAMPLE 1

Use the method of iteration to solve the difference equation $x_k = x_{k-1} + b$.

◼

To solve the difference equation $x_k = ax_{k-1} + b$ with $a \neq 1$, we will need the formula:

(3) $1 + a + a^2 + a^3 + a^4 + a^5 + \cdots + a^k = \dfrac{1 - a^{k+1}}{1 - a}$ $(a \neq 1)$

This formula says, for instance, that

$$1 + 3 + 3^2 + 3^3 = \frac{1 - 3^4}{1 - 3}$$

We can verify the formula in this instance by computing each side.

Left side	*Right side*
$1 + 3 + 3^2 + 3^3$	$\dfrac{1 - 3^4}{1 - 3}$
$1 + 3 + 9 + 27$	$\dfrac{1 - 81}{1 - 3}$
$13 + 27$	$\dfrac{-80}{-2}$
40	40

THEOREM 1

$$1 + a + a^2 + \cdots + a^k = \frac{1 - a^{k+1}}{1 - a}$$

for $a \neq 1$ and $k > 0$.

Proof:

Set: $s_k = 1 + a + a^2 + \cdots + a^k$

Then: $a(s_k) = a(1 + a + a^2 + \cdots + a^k)$

$$= a + a^2 + a^3 + \cdots + a^k + a^{k+1}$$

Subtracting the second equation from the first gives:

$$s_k - a(s_k) = (1 + a + a^2 + \cdots + a^k) - (a + a^2 + \cdots + a^k + a^{k+1})$$

$$= 1 + (a - a) + (a^2 - a^2) + \cdots + (a^k - a^k) - a^{k+1}$$

$$s_k - a(s_k) = 1 - a^{k+1}$$

$$(1 - a)s_k = 1 - a^{k+1}$$

$$s_k = \frac{1 - a^{k+1}}{1 - a} \qquad \text{provided } a \neq 1$$

THEOREM 2   The solution to $x_k = ax_{k-1} + b$ is:

$$x_k = \frac{b}{1 - a} + \left(x_0 - \frac{b}{1 - a}\right)a^k \qquad \text{provided } a \neq 1$$

Proof:

$$x_1 = ax_0 + b$$

$$x_2 = ax_1 + b = a(ax_0 + b) + b = a^2x_0 + ab + b$$

$$= a^2x_0 + (a + 1)b$$

$$x_3 = ax_2 + b = a(a^2x_0 + ab + b) + b = a^3x_0 + a^2b + ab + b$$

$$= a^3x_0 + (a^2 + a + 1)b$$

$$x_4 = ax_3 + b = a(a^3x_0 + a^2b + ab + b)$$

$$= a^4x_0 + a^3b + a^2b + ab + b$$

$$= a^4x_0 + (a^3 + a^2 + a + 1)b$$

$$\vdots$$

$$x_k = a^kx_0 + a^{k-1}b + a^{k-2}b + \cdots + a^2b + ab + b$$

This last formula is simplified using Theorem 1:

$$x_k = a^k x_0 + (a^{k-1} + a^{k-2} + \cdots + a^2 + a + 1)b$$

$$x_k = a^k x_0 + \left(\frac{1 - a^k}{1 - a}\right)b$$

$$x_k = a^k x_0 + \frac{b}{1 - a} - \frac{a^k b}{1 - a}$$

$$x_k = \frac{b}{1 - a} + x_0 a^k - \left(\frac{b}{1 - a}\right)a^k$$

or, as claimed:

$$x_k = \frac{b}{1 - a} + \left(x_0 - \frac{b}{1 - a}\right)a^k$$

Recall from Section 7.3 that each monthly payment on an installment loan is credited by carrying out the steps:

1. Compute interest due.

interest due = (principal before payment) × (interest rate per month)

2. Subtract the interest due from the payment. The difference is the amount by which the principal is reduced, called the principal payment.

principal payment = payment − interest due

3. Subtract the principal payment from the principal before payment. The difference is the remaining principal owed.

$$\begin{pmatrix} \text{remaining} \\ \text{principal} \end{pmatrix} = \begin{pmatrix} \text{principal before} \\ \text{payment} \end{pmatrix} - \begin{pmatrix} \text{principal} \\ \text{payment} \end{pmatrix}$$

EXAMPLE 1   Find a difference equation for P_k, the remaining principal after k payments with monthly payments, M, and monthly interest rate, i. Write the solution to this difference equation.

Substituting P_k, M, and i into Step 1, then 2, then 3 gives:

1. Interest due = iP_{k-1}

2. Principal payment = M − interest due
   $$= M - iP_{k-1}$$

3. $P_k = P_{k-1} - (M - iP_{k-1})$
   $$= P_{k-1} - M + iP_{k-1}$$
   $$P_k = (1 + i)P_{k-1} - M$$

Apply Theorem 2 with

$$a = 1 + i$$

$$b = -M$$

$$x_k = P_k$$

$$P_k = \frac{-M}{1 - (1 + i)} + \left(P_0 - \frac{(-M)}{1 - (1 + i)}\right)(1 + i)^k$$

$$P_k = \frac{M}{i} + \left(P_0 - \frac{M}{i}\right)(1 + i)^k$$

This is formula (4) in Section 7.3.

CONCEPT

method of iteration

SOLUTION TO PRACTICE EXAMPLE

1. x_0

$x_1 = x_0 + b$

$x_2 = x_1 + b = (x_0 + b) + b = x_0 + 2b$

$x_3 = x_2 + b = (x_0 + 2b) + b = x_0 + 3b$

$x_4 = x_3 + b = (x_0 + 3b) + b = x_0 + 4b$

.
.
.

$x_k = x_0 + kb$

EXERCISES 8.3

1. Find the solution to the difference equation:

$$B_k = B_{k-1}(1 + i)$$

This equation was used in Section 7.1 where B_0 is the initial balance in an account that earns compound interest. B_k is the balance after k interest periods and i is the interest rate per interest period.

2. Find the solution to the difference equation:

$$B_k = B_{k-1}(1 + i) + C$$

This equation was used in Section 7.2 where B_0 is the initial balance in an account that earns compound interest and regular deposits are made into the account. B_k is the balance after k interest periods. The interest rate per interest period is i, and C is the amount of deposit made at the end of each interest period.

3. Show that if $C_1 = 1$ and $C_k = 2C_{k-1} + 1$, then $C_k = 2^k - 1$ for $k = 1, 2, 3, \ldots$.

4. Recall from Section 3.2 that adding a new level to a binary search tree doubles the leaves.

(a) Find a difference equation for the number of leaves in the full binary search tree with k levels, $k = 1, 2, 3, \ldots$.

(b) What is the solution to the difference equation in part (a)?

(c) Find a difference equation for the largest number of files in a binary search tree with k levels.

(d) What is the solution to the difference equation in part (c)?

(e) How many levels must be in a binary search tree in order for the tree to be large enough to store 127 files?

In Exercises 5 through 10 find the sum.

5. $1 + 2 + 2^2 + 2^3 + \cdots + 2^6$

6. $1 + \dfrac{1}{2} + \left(\dfrac{1}{2}\right)^2 + \cdots + \left(\dfrac{1}{2}\right)^6$

7. $1 + 10 + (10)^2 + (10)^3$

8. $1 + \dfrac{1}{3} + \left(\dfrac{1}{3}\right)^2 + \left(\dfrac{1}{3}\right)^3 + \cdots + \left(\dfrac{1}{3}\right)^6$

9. $3 + \dfrac{3}{2} + \dfrac{3}{4} + \dfrac{3}{8} + \dfrac{3}{16} + \dfrac{3}{32} + \dfrac{3}{64} + \dfrac{3}{127}$

10. $2 + \dfrac{2}{3} + \dfrac{2}{9} + \dfrac{2}{27} + \dfrac{2}{81} + \dfrac{2}{243} + \dfrac{2}{729} + \dfrac{2}{2187}$

11. A sequence of the form $r, ra, ra^2, ra^3, ra^4, ra^5, \ldots, ra^k$ with $r \neq 0$ and $a \neq 1$ is called a geometric series.

(a) Use theorem 1 to find a formula for the sum:

$$r + ra + ra^2 + ra^3 + ra^4 + \cdots + ra^k = ?$$

(b) Use your answer to (a) to find the sum:

$$2 + \dfrac{2}{3} + 2\left(\dfrac{1}{3}\right)^2 + 2\left(\dfrac{1}{3}\right)^3 + \cdots + 2\left(\dfrac{1}{3}\right)^7$$

12. Use theorem 1 and a calculator to fill in the table below where S_k is the sum:

$$S_k = \left(\dfrac{1}{2}\right) + \left(\dfrac{1}{2}\right)^2 + \left(\dfrac{1}{2}\right)^3 + \left(\dfrac{1}{2}\right)^4 + \cdots + \left(\dfrac{1}{2}\right)^k$$

k	S_k
1	
2	
3	
8	
10	
50	
100	

What happens to these sums as the value of k gets larger?

CHAPTER SUMMARY

In this chapter we introduced *difference equations* and used them to model *radioactive decay, population growth, heating, cooling,* and the *spread of information and disease*. The mathematics of finance in Chapter 7 gives additional situations described by difference equations. All of these situations are modeled by a difference equation of the form:

(1) $$x_k = ax_{k-1} + b$$

In Section 8.3, we showed the solution to (1) is:

(2) $$x_k = \frac{b}{1-a} + \left(x_0 - \frac{b}{1-a}\right)a^k$$

provided $a \neq 1$. If $b = 0$, then equation (2) simplifies to:

(3) $$x_k = x_0 a^k$$

If $a = 1$, then equation (1) has the form $x_k = x_{k-1} + b$, and the solution is:

(4) $$x_k = x_0 + kb$$

Notice in equation (1) that x_k is given in terms of the preceding number, x_{k-1}. In the difference equation for the *Fibonacci sequence*:

(5) $$x_k = x_{k-1} + x_{k-2}$$

x_k is given in terms of the two preceding numbers, x_{k-1} and x_{k-2}. Difference equations such as (5) that involve three or more of the numbers in the sequence arise often but are generally more difficult to solve than equation (1). Terms in such sequences are often found using a computer. (Techniques for solving general types of difference equations, including the Fibonacci sequence, are described in Roberts 1984 along with applications.)

REVIEW EXERCISES FOR CHAPTER 8

1. For the third, fourth, and fifth numbers in the sequence satisfying the difference equation $a_k = 2a_{k-1} + a_{k-2}$ with initial condition $a_1 = 1$ and $a_2 = 3$.

2. Last year a company's profit increased by eight percent. Suppose the profit continues to increase by eight percent each year for the next two years. If the current yearly profit is $120,000 then what will be the yearly profit two years from now?

3. A radioactive material decays so that the amount remaining at the end of a 10-year period is 80% of the amount present at the beginning of the period. What fraction of the original amount remains after 30 years? How many ten-year periods are necessary before the amount remaining is less than one-fourth the original amount?

4. Estimate the age of a skull fragment that contains 8.8% of the C^{14} present when the animal was alive. Recall that radioactive carbon, C^{14}, decays so that at the end of a 5,000-year period the amount remaining is .5444256 times the amount present at the beginning of the period.

5. If the population of a city of 50,000 declines at the rate of three percent per year for each of the next three years, then what will be the population three years from now?

6. A glass of soda warms from $36°$ to $40°$ in one minute, and the temperature of the room is $76°$.
   (a) Use Newton's law of cooling to find a difference equation for the sequence of temperatures of the soda where $x_0 = 36$, $x_1 = 40$, ...
   (b) Write the solution of this difference equation.
   (c) Find x_{10}.

7. $x_0 = 2$, $x_1 = 4$, $x_2 = 8$, are the first three numbers in a sequence that satisfies a difference equation of the form $x_k = ax_{k-1} + b$. Find the difference equation.

8. Over the last three years a company's profits have risen from 3 million to 3.5 million and then to 4.25 million. Assume the yearly profits satisfy a difference equation of the form $x_k = ax_{k-1} + b$ and predict the yearly profits for the next two years.

9. Use the method of iteration to solve the difference equation:
$$x_k = x_{k-1} + 2 \qquad \text{with } x_0 = 1$$

10. Find the sum:
$$2 + 1 + \frac{1}{2} + \frac{1}{4} + \frac{1}{8} + \cdots + \frac{1}{128}$$

11. Show the sequence $x_k = k(k-1)/2$ satisfies the difference equation:
$$x_{k+1} = x_k + k \qquad \text{with } x_0 = 0$$
Use the answer to find the sum:
$$1 + 2 + 3 + 4 + 5 + 6 + \cdots + 95 + 96 + 97 + 98 + 99 + 100$$

12. Find a difference equation for the sequence x_1, x_2, x_3, . . . , x_k where x_k is the number of different ways to pair up $2k$ people for k tennis matches. Find x_1, x_2, x_3.

Linear Programming—A Geometrical Approach

9

Management science is the term commonly used to describe applications of quantitative tools (mathematical tools) to the solutions of problems that managers must solve. A manager may be the head of a large corporation, a military leader, a shipping magnate, or anyone who must make decisions. The decisions may concern such questions as the quantities of items to be produced or shipped or the number of people to be assigned to various jobs. Even an experimental psychologist can be considered a manager when he must decide the numbers of various colored mice to be used in an experiment.

The roots of management science can be traced to earliest times, but it was not until World War II and the period immediately following that it was recognized as a separate discipline, and one of great importance. Economists and military and political leaders all recognized that many of the problems that they were trying to solve involved optimizing (either maximizing or minimizing) some quantity—cost, profit, manpower, or gross national product. In 1947, Dantzig studied "programming in a linear structure," now called linear programming, and, to solve such problems, invented the simplex method. The advent of the computer allowed this method to be applied to solving real-world problems. The first problems to be solved using the Dantzig simplex method, which brought together the seemingly different military and economic problems under one heading, involved transporting goods from one set of locations to another set of locations.

In Chapter 11, we will develop the simplex method for solving linear programming problems. In this chapter, we will develop the geometrical basis for the simplex method. To accomplish this we need to be able to graph straight lines, solve systems of equations, and graph systems of inequalities. To solve real-world problems using linear programming techniques, we must be able to translate the problems into mathematical terms: a system of constraints and a function to be maximized or minimized.

9.1   *Graphing Linear Equations*

In Section 6.2, we started our study of linear equations. In this section, we will discuss *graphing straight lines* in more detail and will undertake graphing more than one linear equation at a time.

As was stated in Chapter 6, the easiest way to graph a linear equation is to find two points that satisfy the equation, plot them, and draw the line between the two. Most of the time, the easiest two points to find and plot are the two intercepts—the x-intercept and the y-intercept. The **x-intercept** is the point where the line crosses the x-axis; therefore, the x-intercept is the point where $y = 0$. The **y-intercept** is the point where the line crosses the y-axis; therefore, the y-intercept is the point where $x = 0$.

As an example, consider the linear equation $3x + 4y = 12$. To find the x-intercept, set $y = 0$, and solve for x.

$$3x + 4(0) = 12$$
$$3x = 12$$
$$x = 4$$

The x-intercept is the point (4, 0).

To find the y-intercept, set $x = 0$, and solve for y.

$$3(0) + 4y = 12$$
$$4y = 12$$
$$y = 3$$

The y-intercept is the point (0, 3).

To graph the equation $3x + 4y = 12$, plot the points (4, 0) and (0, 3) and draw the line between the two points. Label the line with its equation. See Figure 9.1.

Figure 9.1

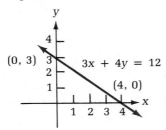

In setting up our linear programming problems, most of our equations will have variable terms on one side of the equation and the constant term on the other side of the equation, as in $3x + 4y = 12$. Since we may want to use more than two variables, we will often use subscripts to indicate the variables. For example, we could use x_1 and x_2 instead of x and y. Only the names of the axes are changed. The graph shown in Figure 9.1 is the same as that shown in Figure 9.2. Of course, as we increase the number of variables, graphing linear equations becomes more difficult. We cannot even attempt it for more than three variables.

Figure 9.2

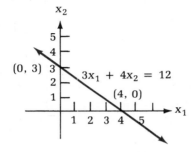

PRACTICE
EXAMPLE 1

Find the intercepts and graph the linear equation

$$2x_1 + 7x_2 = 28$$

If the line passes through $(0, 0)$, then the x-intercept and the y-intercept are exactly the same point. The x-intercept is $(0, 0)$, and the y-intercept is $(0, 0)$. For example, consider the equation $x - y = 0$. The point $(0, 0)$ is both the x-intercept and the y-intercept. Therefore, to graph this straight line, we need to choose another value for x, different from 0, and compute the corresponding y-value to get a second point. Let $x = 2$. Then $x - y = 0$ becomes $2 - y = 0$ or $2 = y$. Our second point is $(2, 2)$, and the graph is as shown in Figure 9.3.

Figure 9.3

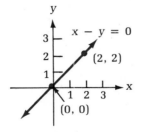

If a straight line is parallel to either axis, there will be only one intercept. This occurs in equations where only one variable appears—for example, the equation $x = 4$ has no y-intercept. If we substitute $x = 0$, we get a contradiction, $0 = 4$. For any value of y, including $y = 0$, $x = 4$, thus the x-intercept is $(4, 0)$. For any other value of y, say $y = 2$, x is also 4. Thus, a second point is (4, 2). As shown in Figure 9.4, the graph of $x = 4$ is a straight line parallel to the y-axis and four units to the right.

Figure 9.4

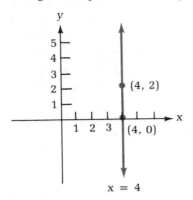

Similarly, if only the second variable, y, appears in the equation, the graph is a straight line with only one intercept, the y-intercept. For example, consider the equation $y = 7$. If $y = 0$, then we get $0 = 7$, a contradiction. If $x = 0$, or any other value, we get $y = 7$. Therefore the y-intercept is the point (0, 7). To get a second point, choose any other value for x, say $x = 2$, and y is still equal to 7. A second point is (2, 7). As shown in Figure 9.5, the graph $y = 7$ is a straight line parallel to the x-axis and seven units above it.

Figure 9.5

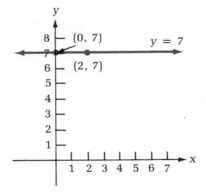

PRACTICE
EXAMPLE **2**

Graph the linear equations:

(a) $x_1 + x_2 = 0$

(b) $x_1 = 5$

(c) $x_2 = 4$

Often, we will want to graph more than one linear equation on the same set of axes. If the straight lines cross one another, and we are able to read their points of intersection, we will do so. The student should be aware that most of the time the graphing is not precise enough to actually identify these points exactly. In the next section, we will show how to find points of intersection algebraically.

EXAMPLE 1

$$2x_1 + 5x_2 = 10$$

$$x_1 + x_2 = 4$$

Graph each equation separately, but on the same set of axes, as shown in Figure 9.6.

Line 1: $\qquad\qquad\qquad 2x_1 + 5x_2 = 10$

If $x_1 = 0$, then:

$$2(0) + 5x_2 = 10$$

$$5x_2 = 10$$

$$x_2 = 2$$

The x_2-intercept is (0, 2).
If $x_2 = 0$, then:

$$2x_1 + 5(0) = 10$$

$$2x_1 = 10$$

$$x_1 = 5$$

The x_1-intercept is (5, 0).

Figure 9.6

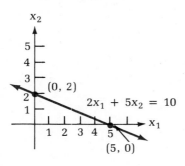

Line 2: $\qquad\qquad\qquad x_1 + x_2 = 4$

If $x_1 = 0$ then:

$$0 + x_2 = 4$$

$$x_2 = 4$$

The x_2-intercept is (0, 4).
If $x_2 = 0$ then:

$$x_1 + 0 = 4$$

$$x_1 = 4$$

The x_1-intercept is (4, 0).

Figure 9.7

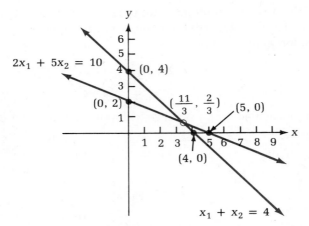

Figure 9.7 shows the graphs of the two equations on the same set of axes. If you are very careful, you will see that the lines cross at the point $(\frac{11}{3}, \frac{2}{3})$. To check that the point $(\frac{11}{3}, \frac{2}{3})$ is the point of intersection, substitute $\frac{11}{3}$ for x_1 and $\frac{2}{3}$ for x_2 in each of the two equations and check for equality. You will need some other method to find the point if your guess is incorrect.

EXAMPLE 2

$$x_1 - x_2 = 3$$
$$3x_1 + x_2 = 9$$

Line 1: $\qquad\qquad\qquad\qquad x_1 - x_2 = 3$

If $x_2 = 0$, then:

$$x_1 - 0 = 3$$
$$x_1 = 3$$

The x_1-intercept is $(3, 0)$.

If $x_1 = 0$, then:

$$0 - x_2 = 3$$
$$-x_2 = 3$$
$$x_2 = -3$$

The x_2-intercept is $(0, -3)$.

Line 2: $\qquad\qquad\qquad\qquad 3x_1 + x_2 = 9$

If $x_1 = 0$, then:

$$3(0) + x_2 = 9$$
$$x_2 = 9$$

The x_2-intercept is $(0, 9)$.

If $x_2 = 0$, then:

$$3x_1 + 0 = 9$$
$$3x_1 = 9$$
$$x_1 = 3$$

The x_1-intercept is (3, 0).

Figure 9.8

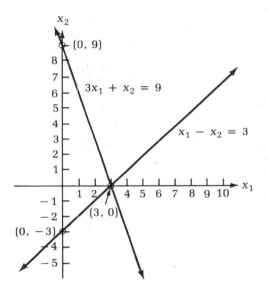

This time it is easy to see where the lines cross (Figure 9.8), since (3, 0) is the x_1-intercept for both equations. No further computations are necessary.

PRACTICE EXAMPLE 3

Graph the equations $2x_1 + 7x_2 = 28$ and $x_1 + 2x_2 = 0$ on the same set of axes.

In this section, we reviewed graphing sets of straight lines on the same coordinate axes. In the next section we investigate ways of finding the points of intersection of the straight lines by solving systems of equations.

CONCEPTS

graphing straight lines
x-intercept
y-intercept

SOLUTIONS TO PRACTICE EXAMPLES

1. $2x_1 + 7x_2 = 28$. The intercepts are $(0, 4)$ and $(14, 0)$.

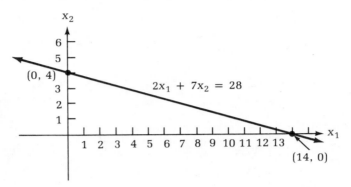

2. (a) $x_1 + x_2 = 0$. The intercept is $(0, 0)$. The second point is $(3, -3)$.

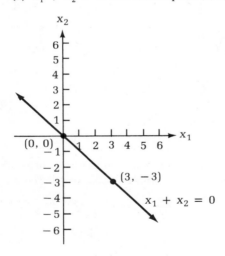

   (b) $x_1 = 5$. The intercept is $(5, 0)$. The second point is $(5, 2)$.

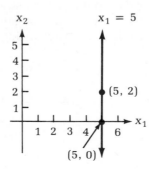

(c) $x_2 = 4$. The intercept is (0, 4). The second point is (2, 4).

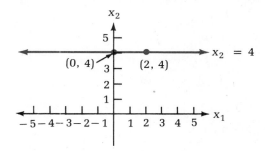

3. $2x_1 + 7x_2 = 28$ $x_1 + 2x_2 = 0$

     Intercepts   *Intercept*

    (0, 4), (14, 0)   (0, 0)

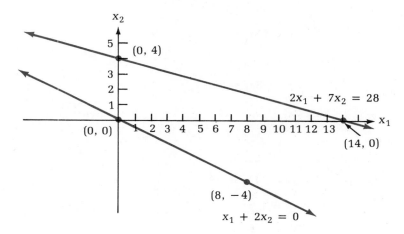

EXERCISES 9.1

Find the intercepts and graph of each of the following.

1. $2x_1 + 3x_2 = 6$

2. $x_1 - x_2 = 2$

3. $5x_1 + 3x_2 = 15$

4. $3x_1 - 4x_2 = 12$

5. $x_1 + 4x_2 = 8$

6. $7x_1 - x_2 = 14$

Graph each of the following.

7. $x_1 = 7$

8. $x_2 = -6$

9. $x_1 = 1$

10. $x_2 = 4$

11. $x_1 - x_2 = 0$

12. $2x_1 + 3x_2 = 0$

Graph the following pairs of equations on the same set of axes. If possible, read the point corresponding to the intersection of the straight lines.

13. $2x_1 + 3x_2 = 6$

$x_1 - x_2 = 2$

14. $x_1 = 7$

$x_1 + 4x_2 = 8$

15. $x_1 - x_2 = 0$

$5x_1 + 3x_2 = 15$

16. $7x_1 - x_2 = 14$

$x_1 = 4$

17. $2x_1 + 3x_2 = 15$

$3x_1 - 4x_2 = 12$

18. $x_1 = 3$

$x_2 = -6$

9.2   *Algebraic Solutions to Systems of Linear Equations*

In the last section, we saw how it is possible to graph each of the equations in a set (system) of linear equations on the same set of axes, and to attempt to find the point(s) of intersection of the lines. The point where two lines cross corresponds to the simultaneous solution of the two equations. However, unless the lines cross at integer valued points, it is almost impossible to read accurately the coordinates of the point(s) of intersection. Even when the lines cross at integer-valued points, the equations would have to be graphed on graph paper to insure accuracy. In this section, we look at two methods for solving a system of linear equations. The choice of which method to use will largely depend on the equations themselves, and the student's preference. We will concentrate on solving systems of two linear equations in two variables and will include a few examples of three linear equations in two variables. In Chapter 10 methods will be presented in a different format for solving systems of equations with more than two variables.

The following examples illustrate the kind of problems we will solve in this section.

EXAMPLE 1   An accounting firm has $3850 that must be spent on four new portable computers. They are considering the Commodore computer that costs $900 and the Apple computer that costs $1150. How many of each brand of computer should the firm buy?

EXAMPLE 2   An insurance agent sells 100 whole-life policies and 20 more term than straight-life policies. The agent's commission totals $55,000, based on $300 for each whole-life policy sold, $500 for each straight-life policy sold, and $375 for each term policy sold. How many of each type of policy does the agent sell?

EXAMPLE 3   A woman has $300 to spend. Slacks cost $32 a pair and blouses cost $28 each. She needs an equal number of blouses and slacks. How many of each should she buy so that she spends all her money?

A **system of equations** is a set of equations, each in the same set of variables. The **solution set** for a system of equations in two variables is the set $\{(x_1, x_2) \mid x_1 \text{ and } x_2 \text{ simultaneously satisfy each of the equations in the system}\}$. For example, if we have the system of equations:

$$x_1 - x_2 = 4$$

$$2x_1 + x_2 = 2$$

then the solution set is $\{(2, -2)\}$, since $2 - (-2) = 4$ and $2(2) + (-2) = 2$. The solution set for the system:

$$x_1 + x_2 = 2$$

$$3x_1 + 3x_2 = 6$$

is an infinite set, and can be written in the form $\{(a, 2 - a) \mid a \text{ is any real number}\}$. The pairs that satisfy the first equation in the system are exactly the same pairs that satisfy the second. The solution set is the set of points on the one straight line.

The solution set for a system of equations in k variables is the set $\{(x_1, x_2, \ldots, x_k) \mid x_1, x_2, \ldots, x_k \text{ simultaneously satisfy each of the equations in the system}\}$.

METHOD I ADDITION

The object of Method I in solving systems of equations is to modify the equations so that when they are added, the number of variables is decreased. The following rules can be applied without changing the solution set for the system of equations:

1. Any equation may be multiplied by any nonzero number. For example, $x_1 + x_2 = 3$, $5x_1 + 5x_2 = 15$, $-x_1 - x_2 = -3$, and $\frac{1}{2}x_1 + \frac{1}{2}x_2 = \frac{3}{2}$ are all equivalent in determining solution sets.

2. Any two equations may be added. For example,

$$x_1 + x_2 = 3$$
$$x_1 - x_2 = 4$$
$$\oplus \quad \overline{\qquad 2x_1 = 7}$$

and

$$2x_1 + x_2 = 2$$
$$5x_1 + 3x_2 = 1$$
$$\oplus \quad \overline{7x_1 + 4x_2 = 3}$$

3. Rules 1 and 2 can be combined in any way. For example, consider the system:

$$2x_1 + x_2 = 2$$
$$5x_1 + 3x_2 = 1$$

Apply rule 1 to the first equation by multiplying the equation by (-3).

$$(-3)(2x_1 + x_2 = 2) = -6x_1 - 3x_2 = -6.$$

Apply rule 2 and add this new equation to the second equation:

$$-6x_1 - 3x_2 = -6$$
$$5x_1 + 3x_2 = 1$$
$$\oplus \quad \overline{-x_1 = -5 \text{ or } x_1 = 5}$$

Note that we have solved for one of the variables in our system of equations. To solve for the other variable, we need only to substitute 5 for x_1 in any of the equations in the system.

$$2(5) + x_2 = 2$$
$$10 + x_2 = 2$$
$$x_2 = -8$$

Thus, the solution set is $\{(5, -8)\}$.

In this example of the use of rule 1, -3 was chosen as the number by which to multiply the first equation to assure ourselves that when we add the two equations the x_2 variable will vanish. Similarly, if the first equation is multiplied by 5 to get $10x_1 + 5x_2 = 10$, the second equation multiplied by -2 to get $-10x_1 - 6x_2 = -2$, and the resulting equations are added, we will have:

$$10x_1 + 5x_2 = 10$$
$$\underline{-10x_1 - 6x_2 = -2}$$
$$-x_2 = 8$$

or
$$x_2 = -8$$

This time the variable x_1 was eliminated. The essential part of Method I is thus deciding what to multiply the equations by so that one of the variables is eliminated when the equations are added.

The following are the steps of Method I applied to the general system of two equations:

(1)
$$ax_1 + bx_2 = c$$

(2)
$$dx_1 + ex_2 = f$$

STEP 1: To eliminate x_1, multiply equation 1 by d and equation 2 by $(-a)$.

$$adx_1 + bdx_2 = cd$$
$$\underline{-adx_1 - aex_2 = -af}$$

STEP 2: Add. $bdx_2 - aex_2 = cd - af$

STEP 3: Solve for x_2. $(bd - ae)x_2 = cd - af$

$$x_2 = \frac{cd - af}{bd - ae}$$

If x_2 has also been eliminated, along with x_1, then a unique solution does not exist. Either the solution set is the empty set—when the equations are added no variables remain and a nonzero number appears on the right, or the solution set is an infinite set—the two equations are essentially the same equation. We will see examples of each of these later.

STEP 4: Substitute the solution for x_2 computed in Step 3 into equation 1, and solve for x_1.

Let us look at Example 1. We first have to set up the equations comprising the system of equations. The question posed in Example 1 is: How many of each brand of computer should the firm buy? Let x_1 denote the number of Commodore computers to be purchased, and x_2 denote the number of Apple computers to be purchased. Since the firm requires four new computers, one of the equations is $x_1 + x_2 = 4$. Each Commodore costs \$900 and each Apple costs \$1150. Thus, the total cost is $900x_1 + 1150x_2$. Since the firm must spend \$3850, the second equation is $900x_1 + 1150x_2 = 3850$. We now have a system of equations:

$$x_1 + x_2 = 4$$

$$900x_1 + 1150x_2 = 3850$$

To solve this system of equations, apply Method I.

STEP 1: Multiply $x_1 + x_2 = 4$ by 900 and $900x_1 + 1150x_2 = 3850$ by -1, to get:

$$900x_1 + 900x_2 = 3600$$

$$-900x_1 - 1150x_2 = -3850$$

STEP 2: Add. $\oplus$ $\qquad -250x_2 = -250$

STEP 3: Solve for x_2. $\qquad x_2 = -250/-250 = 1$

STEP 4: Solve for x_1 by substituting in equation 1 the value for x_2.

$$x_1 + 1 = 4$$

$$x_1 = 3$$

To check the solution, substitute $x_1 = 3$ and $x_2 = 1$ in each equation and check for equality:

$$3 + 1 = 4 \quad \checkmark$$

$$900(3) + 1150(1) = 2700 + 1150 = 3850. \quad \checkmark$$

The solution set is $\{(3, 1)\}$, or the firm should purchase three Commodores and one Apple.

Example 2 poses the question: How many of each type of insurance policy did the agent sell? Let x_1 denote the number of straight-life policies sold and x_2 denote the number of term policies sold. We know 100 whole-life policies were sold, and we know that 20 more term than straight-life policies were sold, so $x_2 = x_1 + 20$.

The total commission is computed as follows: \$300 for each whole-life policy, or a total of 300(100), \$500 for each straight-life policy, or a total of $500x_1$, and \$375 for each term policy, or a total of $375x_2$. Thus, the total commission of \$55,000 can be written as $300(100) + 500x_1 + 375x_2 = 55,000$. The system of equations can be written in simplified form as:

$$-x_1 + x_2 = 20$$

$$500x_1 + 375x_2 = 25,000$$

Apply Method I:

STEP 1: Multiply $-x_1 + x_2 = 20$ by 500 and $500x_1 + 375x_2 = 2500$ by 1 (unchanged).

STEP 2: Add the resulting equations:

$$-500x_1 + 500x_2 = 10{,}000$$
$$500x_1 + 375x_2 = 25{,}000$$
$$875x_2 = 35{,}000$$

STEP 3: Solve for x_2:

$$x_2 = 35{,}000/875 = 40$$

STEP 4: Solve for x_1 by substituting $x_2 = 40$ in equation 1.

$$-x_1 + 40 = 20$$
$$-x_1 = -20$$
$$x_1 = 20$$

The solution set is $\{(20, 40)\}$. The agent sold 100 whole-life policies, 20 straight-life policies, and 40 term policies.

PRACTICE EXAMPLE 1

Use Method I to solve the system of equations:

$$2x_1 + 3x_2 = 65$$
$$3x_1 + 4x_2 = 90$$

If we try Method I on the system of equations:

$$x_1 + x_2 = 3$$
$$x_1 + x_2 = 5$$

we would get

$$x_1 + x_2 = 3$$
$$\oplus \quad -x_1 - x_2 = -5$$
$$\overline{\qquad 0 = -2}$$

which is a contradiction. Therefore the solution set is the empty set. The corresponding lines are parallel; there is no intersection.

Similarly, if Method I is applied to the system of equations:

$$2x_1 - x_2 = 3$$
$$-4x_1 + 2x_2 = -6$$

we get

$$-8x_1 + 4x_2 = -12$$
$$\oplus \quad 8x_1 - 4x_2 = 12$$
$$\overline{\qquad 0 = 0}$$

Since it is always true that $0 = 0$, we have an infinite solution set. The two equations represent exactly the same line. The solution set is the set of points on the line.

METHOD II SUBSTITUTION

In our solution of the system of equations in Example 2, we put each equation in the form $ax_1 + bx_2 = c$, even though the first equation was written as $x_2 = x_1 + 20$. When one of the equations in a system of equations has one variable expressed in terms of the other variable(s), it is often easier to apply Method 2—substitution. As we outline the steps, we will apply this method to the system of equations of Example 2.

STEP 1:   Choose an equation where one variable is expressed in terms of the other variable. (If no equation has this form, Method II can be applied by choosing an equation and solving for one variable in terms of the other.)

$$x_2 = x_1 + 20$$

STEP 2:   Substitute the expression for the one variable in the other equation(s).

$$500x_1 + 375x_2 = 25{,}000$$
$$500x_1 + 375(x_1 + 20) = 25{,}000$$

STEP 3:   Solve the resulting equation in one variable.

$$500x_1 + 375x_1 + 7500 = 25{,}000$$
$$875x_1 + 7500 = 25{,}000$$
$$875x_1 = 175{,}000$$
$$x_1 = \frac{17{,}500}{875} = 20$$

STEP 4:   Substitute back in the original expression to find the other variable.

$$x_2 = x_1 + 20$$
$$x_2 = 20 + 20 = 40$$

In Example 3 we want to determine how many blouses and slacks should be purchased. Let x_1 be the number of slacks, and x_2 be the number of blouses. An equal number of each must be purchased. Thus, $x_1 = x_2$.

Slacks cost \$32 a pair, and blouses cost \$28 each, for a total cost of $32x_1 + 28x_2$. Since \$300 must be spent, $32x_1 + 28x_2 = 300$. Therefore, the system of equations is:

$$x_1 = x_2$$
$$32x_1 + 28x_2 = 300$$

Applying Method 2.

STEP 1:

$$x_1 = x_2$$

Express one variable in terms of the other.

STEP 2:   Substitute the expression.

$$32x_1 + 28x_2 = 300$$
$$32(x_2) + 28x_2 = 300$$

STEP 3:   Solve for x_2.

$$60x_2 = 300$$
$$x_2 = \frac{300}{60} = 5$$

STEP 4:   Substitute back.

$$x_1 = x_2 = 5$$

The solution set is $\{(5, 5)\}$. Thus, she must buy five blouses and five pairs of slacks.

In summary, the procedure to use in setting up a system of equations is shown in the following box.

---

1. Read the problem and determine the question being asked.
2. Let $x_1, x_2, \ldots, x_n$ stand for each of the unknowns in the question.
3. Read the problem again and summarize the data.
4. Write an equation to represent each of the pieces of data.
5. Read the problem again to be sure nothing was missed.
6. Write the system of equations and decide on a method for solving.

EXAMPLE 4

A car dealership makes a profit of $3000 on each full-size car it sells, and $2000 on each small car it sells. Its profit for the month of May is $210,000. The dealership sells twice as many small cars as full-size cars. How many of each size car did the dealership sell in May?

1. Question: How many full-size cars and how many small cars were sold?
2. Let x_1 = the number of full-size cars and x_2 = the number of small cars sold.

3. Data summary: Twice as many small cars as full-size cars. Profit is 3000 per full-size and 2000 per small car. Total profit is 210,000.
4. $x_2 = 2x_1$ represents the first piece of data. $3000x_1 + 2000x_2 = 210,000$ represents the second piece of data.
5. Rereading the problem shows no data has been missed.
6. The system of equations is:

$$x_2 = 2x_1$$

$$3000x_1 + 2000x_2 = 210,000.$$

PRACTICE EXAMPLE 2

Solve the system of equations in Example 4 above.

In this section we learned two methods of solving systems of linear equations in two variables. We applied these methods to solve problems that first had to be formulated as a system of linear equations. In the next section we look at systems of inequalities and find the solution sets for these systems.

CONCEPTS

Method I—Addition
Method II—Substitution

SOLUTIONS TO PRACTICE EXAMPLES

1. $2x_1 + 3x_2 = 65$

$3x_1 + 4x_2 = 90$

$3(2x_1 + 3x_2 = 65)$ $6x_1 + 9x_2 = 195$

$-2(3x_1 + 4x_2 = 90)$ $-6x_1 - 8x_2 = -180$

Add: $x_2 = 15$

Substitute: $2x_1 + 3(15) = 65$

Solve: $2x_1 = 65 - 45$

$2x_1 = 20$

$x_1 = 10$

The solution set is $\{(10, 15)\}$.

2. Use Method II.

$$x_2 = 2x_1$$

$$3000x_1 + 2000x_2 = 210,000$$

Substitute the first equation in the second equation:

$$3000x_1 + 2000(2x_1) = 210,000$$

$$3000x_1 + 4000x_1 = 210,000$$

$$7000x_1 = 210,000$$

$$x_1 = \frac{210,000}{7000} = 30$$

Substitute back:

$$x_2 = 2x_1 = 2(30) = 60$$

Solution set is $\{(30, 60)\}$, or 30 full-size cars and 60 small cars were sold in May.

EXERCISES 9.2

Solve each of the following systems of equations:

1. $x_1 + 2x_2 = 38$

   $3x_1 + x_2 = 39$

2. $x_1 + x_2 = 650$

   $5x_1 + 2x_2 = 1900$

3. $5x_1 + 8x_2 = 105$

   $6x_1 + 4x_2 = 70$

4. $7x_1 + 3x_2 = 850$

   $2x_1 + 5x_2 = 450$

5. $3x_1 - 5x_2 = 16$

   $x_1 + 4x_2 = 28$

6. $3x_1 = x_2$

   $2x_1 + x_2 = 60$

7. $x_1 = 5x_2 + 10$

   $2x_1 + 3x_2 = 39$

8. $7x_1 + x_2 = 21$

   $7x_1 = 2x_2$

9. An experimental psychologist had to perform twice as many rat experiments as mouse experiments. Each rat experiment used five rats and each mouse experiment used eight mice. A total of 90 mice and rats were used. How many rat experiments and how many mouse experiments were performed?

10. A person wants to consume exactly 2000 calories a day from two food groups A and B. One ounce of food group A contains 50 calories, and one ounce of food group B contains 80 calories. The person also wishes to consume 520 mgs of Vitamin C. Each ounce from food group A contributes 10 mgs of Vitamin C, and each ounce of food group B contributes 22 mgs of Vitamin C. How many ounces of each food group must be consumed?

11. A production company has 10 working hours that must be used for two tasks. Task 1 requires three hours per unit and task 2 requires four hours per unit. It costs $1000 to perform each unit of task 1 and $1500 to perform each unit of task 2. There is $3500 to be used for the two tasks. How many units of task 1 and how many units of task 2 can be performed?

12. The cost function for manufacturing x units of a commodity is given by $C = 100x + 2000$, and the revenue function is given by $R = 200x$. The *break-even point* is where cost is equal to revenue. Thus the break-even point is the intersection of the straight lines $y = 100x + 2000$ and $y = 200x$, or the solution set of the system of equations:

$$y = 100x + 2000$$

$$y = 200x$$

Find the break-even point.

Find the break-even point in each of the following:

13. $C = 1.50x + 225$

$R = 2.50x$

14. $C = 1200x + 2500$

$R = 2000x$

15. $C = .5x + 75$

$R = 3.5x$

9.3   *Graphing Linear Inequalities*

We have described linear equations as equations of the form $ax + by = c$, or $ax_1 + bx_1 = c$. If we replace the $=$ sign with $<$, $>$, $\leq$, or $\geq$, we have a **linear inequality**. Recall that $<$ stands for less than, $>$ for greater than, $\leq$ for less than or equal to, and $\geq$ for greater than or equal to. The **solution set** for a system of linear inequalities is the set of values of the variables that satisfy each of the inequalities in the system. The **graph of a linear inequality** is the set of points that satisfy the inequality.

As an example, consider the inequality $x_1 \geq 3$. Since x_2 is arbitrary in the inequality, all the points to the right of the line $x_1 = 3$ and on the line $x_1 = 3$ are points that satisfy the inequality, as shown in Figure 9.9.

Figure 9.9

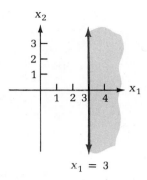

$x_1 = 3$

The line $x_1 = 3$ divides the coordinate system (plane) into three parts, the points to the left of the line, the points to the right of the line, and the points on the line. Two of these sets of points comprise the graph of the inequality $x_1 \geq 3$, the points on the line, and the points to the right of the line.

In general, a line $ax + by = c$ in the plane divides the plane into three parts:

$$\{(x, y) \mid ax + by = c\}$$
$$\{(x, y) \mid ax + by < c\}$$
$$\{(x, y) \mid ax + by > c\}$$

This fact makes it easy to graph linear inequalities.

PROCEDURE FOR GRAPHING INEQUALITIES

STEP 1:   Graph the corresponding linear equation to get a line.

STEP 2:   Select a point not on the line. ((0, 0) is often easiest.)

STEP 3:   Test the point in the linear inequality. If the point satisfies the inequality, shade the side of the line that includes the point.

If the point does not satisfy the inequality, shade the side of the line that does not contain the point.

If the inequality is $\leq$ or $\geq$, include the line by hashing the line ++++++.

EXAMPLE 1

$$2x_1 + 3x_2 > 6$$

STEP 1:   Graph the straight line $2x_1 + 3x_2 = 6$ (Figure 9.10). The x_1-intercept is where $x_2 = 0$. Thus, $2x_1 = 6$ or $x_1 = 3$, and the x_1-intercept is (3, 0).

The x_2-intercept is where $x_2 = 0$. Thus, $3x_2 = 6$ or $x_2 = 2$, and the x_2-intercept is (0, 2).

STEP 2:   Choose a point not on the line. (0, 0).

Figure 9.10

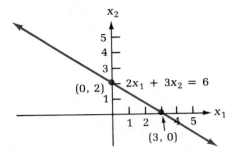

STEP 3: Test the point in the inequality $2x_1 + 3x_2 > 6$.

$$2(0) + 3(0) = 0 \not> 6.$$

The point $(0, 0)$ does not satisfy the inequality; thus, the points not on the same side as $(0, 0)$ should be shaded, as shown in Figure 9.11.

Figure 9.11

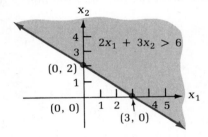

EXAMPLE 2 $\qquad\qquad\qquad x_1 - x_2 \leq 5$

STEP 1: Graph the line $x_1 - x_2 = 5$ (Figure 9.12). The intercepts are $(0, -5)$, and $(5, 0)$.

Figure 9.12

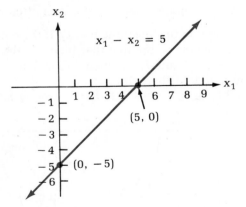

STEP 2: Choose a point not on the line. $(0, 0)$

STEP 3: Test $(0, 0)$ in $x_1 - x_2 \leq 5$.

$$0 - 0 \leq 5.$$

Shade the side of the line that includes (0, 0). Hash the line, since the inequality is $\leq$ as shown in Figure 9.13.

Figure 9.13

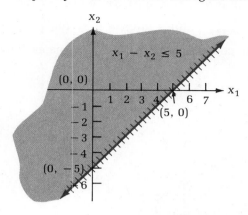

PRACTICE EXAMPLE 1

Graph the inequality $x_1 + 2x_2 \leq 8$.

EXAMPLE 3

A firm has a total of 100 machine-hours available to work on two products. Each unit of product A requires three machine-hours, and each unit of product B requires five machine-hours. If x_1 is the number of units of product A, and x_2 is the number of units of product B, product A uses $3x_1$ machine-hours and product B uses $5x_2$ machine-hours. Since there are 100 machine-hours available, the firm can use less than or equal to 100 machine-hours. We have the following inequality:

$$3x_1 + 5x_2 \leq 100$$

The points in the graph of the inequality are the pairs of numbers that represent the number of units of products A and B that can be constructed in the amount of time available.

STEP 1: Graph $3x_1 + 5x_2 = 100$ (Figure 9.14). The intercepts are (0, 20) and $(33\frac{1}{3}, 0)$.

Figure 9.14

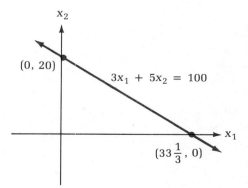

STEP 2:   Choose a point not on the line. (0, 0).

STEP 3:   Test (0, 0) in the inequality $3x_1 + 5x_2 \leq 100$.

$$3(0) + 5(0) = 0 \leq 100$$

Shade the portion containing (0, 0). Hash the line as shown in Figure 9.15.

Figure 9.15

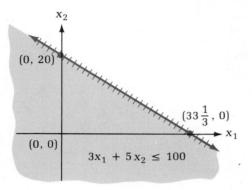

As in Section 9.1, we often want to construct a *graph of systems of inequalities*—more than one inequality on the same set of axes. We can do this by graphing each inequality separately, being careful to shade the inequalities so that we can distinguish which is which. The solution set to the system of inequalities is the intersection of the solution sets of each linear inequality.

EXAMPLE 4   Graph the system

$$x_1 + x_2 \leq 4$$
$$2x_1 + x_2 \leq 6$$

The intercepts for $x_1 + x_2 = 4$ are (4, 0) and (0, 4). Test (0, 0) in the inequality $x_1 + x_2 \leq 4$.

$$0 + 0 \leq 4$$

Shade the portion containing the point (0, 0). Hash the line as shown in Figure 9.16.

Figure 9.16

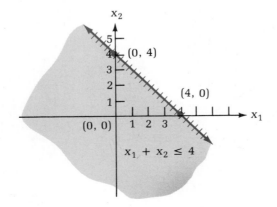

The intercepts for $2x_1 + x_2 = 6$ are $(0, 6)$ and $(3, 0)$. Test $(0, 0)$ in the inequality $2x_1 + x_2 \leq 6$. Satisfied. Shade differently from the previous line, the portion containing $(0, 0)$. Hash the line as shown in Figure 9.17.

Figure 9.17

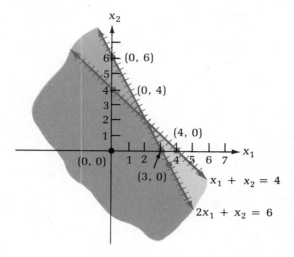

The solution set of the system of linear inequalities is the region that has been shaded darker as shown in Figure 9.18.

Figure 9.18

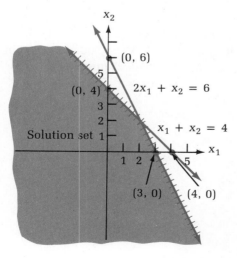

EXAMPLE 5   The firm in Example 3 has at most $5000 that can be spent on each product. Each unit of product A costs $200 to construct, and each unit of product B costs $100 to construct. If x_1 is the number of units of product A, and x_2 is the number of units of product B, the cost inequality is

$$200x_1 + 100x_2 \leq 5000.$$

We can graph the system of inequalities:

$$3x_1 + 5x_2 \leq 100$$

$$200x_1 + 100x_2 \leq 5000$$

We have already graphed $3x_1 + 5x_2 \leq 100$ as pictured in Figure 9.19.

Figure 9.19

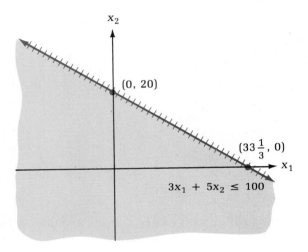

Graph the equation $200x_1 + 100x_2 = 5000$, with intercepts $(25, 0)$ and $(0, 50)$. Test $(0, 0)$ in $200x_1 + 100x_2 \leq 5000$. Shade the area containing $(0, 0)$ and hash the line as shown in Figure 9.20.

Figure 9.20

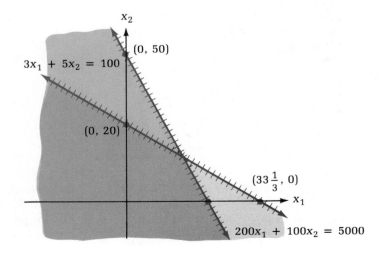

The solution set is the darker shaded area shown in Figure 9.21.

Figure 9.21

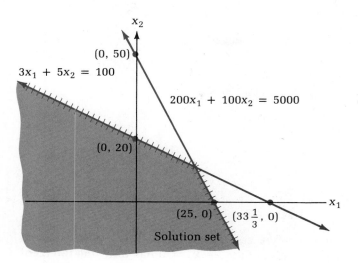

As we shall see in the next section, problems of this form have the implicit requirement that each of the variables not be negative. We cannot produce a negative quantity of a product. Thus, $x_1 \geq 0$ and $x_2 \geq 0$. This actually makes graphing easier, since it allows us to restrict our attention to the first quadrant, and the graph in Figure 9.21 becomes as shown in Figure 9.22.

Figure 9.22

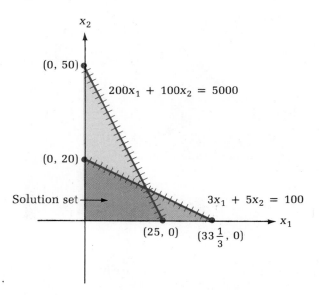

PRACTICE EXAMPLE 2

Graph the system:

$$x_1 + 2x_2 \leq 8$$

$$3x_1 + x_2 \leq 12$$

EXAMPLE 6

Graph the system:

$$x_1 - x_2 \geq 0$$

$$3x_1 + 5x_2 \geq 15$$

$$x_1 \geq 0$$

$$x_2 \geq 0$$

Note that we can restrict our attention to the first quadrant. The line corresponding to $x_1 - x_2 = 0$ has only one intercept, $(0, 0)$, but the point $(2, 2)$ can be used as an additional point. Since $(0, 0)$ is a point on the line we need to choose another point not on the line to test in the inequality, say $(4, 1)$. $4 - 1 \geq 0$, so the area including $(4, 1)$ is shaded, and the line is hashed as in Figure 9.23.

Figure 9.23

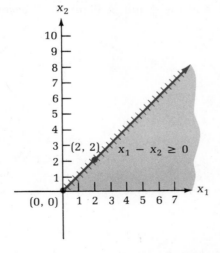

The intercepts for $3x_1 + 5x_2 = 15$ are $(0, 3)$ and $(5, 0)$. The point $(0, 0)$ does not satisfy the inequality $3x_1 + 5x_2 \geq 15$, so the area not including $(0, 0)$ is shaded in Figure 9.24 for the second inequality.

Figure 9.24

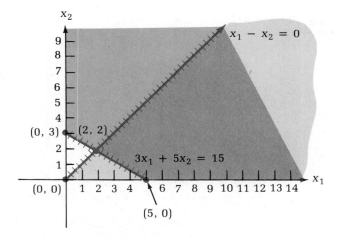

The solution set for the system of inequalities is therefore the darker shaded area shown in Figure 9.25.

Figure 9.25

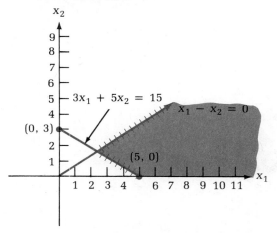

In this section we graphed inequalities and systems of inequalities in two variables. We found the solution set for a system of inequalities to be a region in the plane. In the next section we will use systems of inequalities as part of a linear program in order to maximize or minimize linear functions. In that section we will be primarily interested in setting up the system of inequalities and the function to be maximized or minimized, and in the last section we will actually solve the problems.

CONCEPTS

inequality
graph of a linear inequality
graph of systems of inequalities

SOLUTIONS TO PRACTICE EXAMPLES

1. $x_1 + 2x_2 \leq 8$

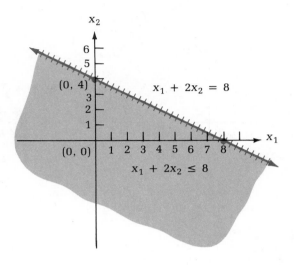

2. $x_1 + 2x_2 \leq 8$
     $3x_1 + x_2 \leq 12$

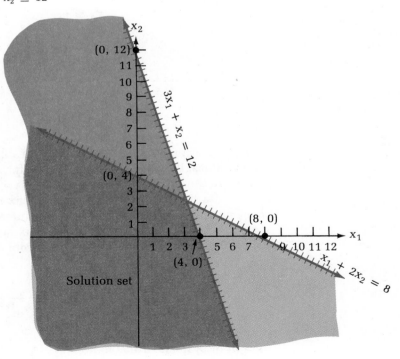

EXERCISES 9.3

Graph each of the following inequalities:

1. $x_1 - x_2 \leq 4$

2. $2x_1 + 5x_2 \geq 20$

3. $3x_1 - 4x_2 < 12$

4. $x_1 \geq x_2$

5. $100x_1 + 300x_2 \leq 900$

6. $25x_1 + 50x_2 < 75$

7. $10x_1 + 2x_2 < 10$

8. $x_1 + x_2 \leq 7$

Graph each of the following systems of inequalities. Identify the solution set in each case.

9. $x_1 + x_2 \leq 7$

$3x_1 + 7x_2 \leq 21$

10. $2x_1 + 5x_2 \geq 20$

$5x_1 + 2x_2 \geq 10$

11. $x_1 \leq 3$

$x_1 + x_2 \leq 8$

12. $100x_1 + 300x_2 \leq 900$

$200x_1 + 400x_2 \leq 1000$

$x_1 \geq 0$

$x_2 \geq 0$

13. $x_1 \geq 5$

$2x_1 + x_2 \leq 20$

$x_1 + 3x_2 \leq 18$

14. $x_1 \leq 6$

$x_2 \geq 4$

$x_1 + 2x_2 \leq 8$

Write inequalities to express what is stated in each of the following. Be sure to label what your variables represent. Graph each of the resulting inequalities.

15. An investment firm has $100,000 to invest in two stocks, A and B. Stock A sells for $42 a share and stock B sells for $28 a share. Not all the money need be invested.

16. Product a requires two pounds of aluminum per unit and product b requires three pounds of aluminum per unit. There are 900 pounds of aluminum available.

17. Each ounce of food group A contains 1.0 mgs of iron, and each ounce of food B contains 1.5 mgs of iron. The minimum daily requirement for iron is 10 mgs.

18. It costs $5000 a day to ship oil through pipeline A and $4000 a day to ship oil through pipeline B. The company has 100 days to ship the oil, and oil can be shipped through only one pipeline a day. They also have at most $200,000 to be spent on the shipping. (Hint: This is a system of inequalities.)

9.4   Linear Programming—Problem Formulation

In Examples 3 and 5 of the last section, we considered a firm that had $5000 and 100 machine-hours available for the manufacture of two products. Each unit of product A required three machine-hours and $200 to construct, and each unit of product B required five machine-hours and $100 to construct. By letting x_1 be the number of units of product A and x_2 be the number of units of product B, we developed a system of linear inequalities that must be satisfied by x_1 and x_2, namely:

$$3x_1 + 5x_2 \leq 100$$
$$200x_1 + 100x_2 \leq 5000$$
$$x_1 \geq 0$$
$$x_2 \geq 0$$

At this stage, we have a set of linear inequalities—a part of what we will call a linear program. If we also have a linear function in the same variables as are used in the inequalities that we want to maximize or minimize, we will have a complete linear program.

Suppose in this example we want to maximize the profit of the firm, and we know that each unit of product A contributes $75 to profit and each unit of product B contributes $45 to profit. The profit function can be written as:

$$P(x_1, x_2) = 75x_1 + 45x_2$$

To summarize, we want to maximize:

$$P(x_1, x_2) = 75x_1 + 45x_2$$

subject to:

$$3x_1 + 5x_2 \leq 100$$
$$200x_1 + 100x_2 \leq 5000$$
$$x_1 \geq 0$$
$$x_2 \geq 0$$

We have constructed a linear program to represent the information about the manufacturing concern.

> DEFINITION A **linear program** consists of a linear function that is to be maximized or minimized, called the **objective function**, and a system of linear inequalities, called **constraints**. The constraints that require the variables to be greater than or equal to 0 are called **nonnegativity constraints**.

> DEFINITION A **solution to a linear program** is a point (values for the variables) that satisfies the constraints and yields the maximum (minimum) value when substituted in the objective function.

In the next section and in Chapter 11, we will show how to find a solution to a linear program when it exists (not all linear programs have solutions). In this section we will concentrate on setting up linear programs, for example:

$$\text{minimize: } C(x_1, x_2) = 100x_1 + 200x_2 \qquad \text{objective function}$$

$$\text{subject to: } \left.\begin{array}{r} 2x_1 + 5x_2 \leq 80 \\ 3x_1 + 10x_2 \leq 30 \\ x_1 \geq 0 \\ x_2 \geq 0 \end{array}\right\} \quad \text{constraints}$$

Henceforth we will abbreviate maximize as max and minimize as min and will not write "subject to" each time.

The first linear program involves a transportation problem.

EXAMPLE 1

A company has a warehouse and two terminals. The company manager must decide how many items should be shipped to each terminal so that the total cost is minimized. There is a total supply of 1000 units in the warehouse, and a demand for 400 units at each terminal. It costs $10 to ship each unit to terminal A and $12 to ship each unit to terminal B.

The objective function is a minimization function. The company wants to minimize the total cost. Let x_1 be the number of units shipped to terminal A and x_2 be the number of units shipped to terminal B. The objective function is then:

$$\min C(x_1, x_2) = 10x_1 + 12x_2$$

The constraints are given by the supply and the demand.

$$x_1 + x_2 \leq 1000 \qquad \text{supply at warehouse}$$

$$x_1 \geq 400 \qquad \text{demand at terminal } A$$

$$x_2 \geq 400 \qquad \text{demand at terminal } B$$

No nonnegativity constraints are needed because of the demand constraints. The complete linear program is:

$$\min C(x_1, x_2) = 10x_1 + 12x_2$$

$$x_1 + x_2 \leq 1000$$

$$x_1 \geq 400$$

$$x_2 \geq 400$$

The general transportation problem involves n warehouses and m terminals. Let x_{ij} denote the number of units to be shipped from warehouse i to terminal j, and c_{ij} denote the cost of shipping one unit from warehouse i to terminal j. If d_k is the demand at terminal k and s_l is the supply at warehouse l, then we have m demand constraints and n supply constraints. The objective function for this linear program has nm variables. The general transportation linear program is:

$$\min C(x_{11}, x_{12}, \ldots, x_{nm}) = c_{11}x_{11} + c_{12}x_{12} + \cdots + c_{nm}x_{nm}$$

$$x_{11} + x_{21} + \cdots + x_{n1} \geq d_1$$

$$x_{12} + x_{22} + \cdots + x_{n2} \geq d_2$$

$$\vdots$$

$$x_{1m} + x_{2m} + \cdots + x_{nm} \geq d_m$$

$$x_{11} + x_{12} + \cdots + x_{1m} \leq s_1$$

$$x_{21} + x_{22} + \cdots + x_{2m} \leq s_2$$

$$\vdots$$

$$x_{n1} + x_{n2} + \cdots + x_{nm} \leq s_n$$

$$x_{ij} \geq 0$$

EXAMPLE 2   A family has just inherited \$100,000 after taxes in the settlement of an estate. They want to invest their money so as to maximize their return at the end of the year. They can invest some money in a money market account at 10% annual interest, some in stocks that pay \$3.60 a share per quarter and sell for \$52 a share, and some in a mutual fund that guarantees 10.5% annual interest. The contributions to the mutual fund are limited to \$50,000, and the amount put in a money market account is limited to $40,000. At least 20% of the money must be invested in stocks. How should the money be invested?

The same procedure used in setting up a system of equations in Section 9.2 should be applied in setting up linear programs.

1. Question asked: How should the money be invested?
2. Let x_1 be the amount invested in a money market account, x_2 be the amount invested in stocks, and x_3 be the amount invested in the mutual fund.
3. Data: $100,000 total money
   money market account pays 10%
   stocks pay 3.60 per share per quarter
   stocks sell for $52 a share
   mutual fund pays 10.5%
   invest for one year
   mutual fund limited to $50,000
   money market account limited to $40,000
   stocks must be at least 20% of $100,000
4. Write constraints and objective function.

The return is computed as follows: 10% on money market account, or $.10x_1$; 10.5% on mutual funds, or $.105x_3$; and $3.60 four times a year on stocks that cost $52 a share, or $4(3.60)(x_2/52)$.

$$\max P(x_1, x_2, x_3) = \underbrace{.10x_1}_{\text{mma}} + \underbrace{4(3.60)(x_2/52)}_{\text{stocks}} + \underbrace{.105x_3}_{\text{mf}}$$

$x_1 + x_2 + x_3 \leq 100{,}000$	total money
$x_1 \leq 40{,}000$	money market constraint
$x_3 \leq 50{,}000$	mutual fund constraint
$x_2 \geq .20(100{,}000)$	stock constraint
$x_1 \geq 0$	
$x_3 \geq 0$	

EXAMPLE 3

A family has two cars. The first one gets 20 miles to the gallon, and the second one gets 25 miles to the gallon of gas. The car that gets 20 miles to the gallon uses unleaded fuel that sells for $1.12 a gallon, whereas the one that gets 25 miles to the gallon uses super unleaded fuel that sells for $1.25 a gallon. They want to maximize the total miles driven, but they have only $800 to spend on gas. They must drive at least 200 miles. How many miles should be driven with each car?

1. Question: How many miles should be driven with each car?
2. Let x_1 be the number of miles driven with the first car and x_2 be the number of miles driven with the second car.

3. Data: first car gets 20 mpg
second car gets 25 mpg
fuel for first costs $1.12 per gal.
fuel for second costs $1.25 per gal.
$800 to spend on gas
200 miles minimum total

4. Objective function and constraints:

$$\max M(x_1, x_2) = x_1 + x_2 \quad \text{total miles}$$

Note that the number of gallons used is the number of miles driven divided by the number of miles per gallon. Thus, if x_1 miles are driven by the first car, then $x_1/20$ is the number of gallons used. Similarly, if x_2 is the number of miles driven by the second car, then $x_2/25$ is the number of gallons used by the second car. Therefore the cost of the gas and the total amount of money available gives a cost constraint:

$$1.12 \left(\frac{x_1}{20}\right) + 1.25 \left(\frac{x_2}{25}\right) \leq 800$$

The total number of miles driven must be at least 200; thus we have the constraint:

$$x_1 + x_2 \geq 200$$

The linear program for this problem is:

$$\max M(x_1, x_2) = x_1 + x_2$$

$$1.12 \left(\frac{x_1}{20}\right) + 1.25 \left(\frac{x_2}{25}\right) \leq 800$$

$$x_1 + x_2 \geq 200$$

$$x_1 \geq 0$$

$$x_2 \geq 0$$

EXAMPLE 4   A bottling company bottles regular cola and caffeine-free cola. There are 20,000 machine-minutes available for bottling. It requires three machine-minutes and costs $.30 to bottle a bottle of regular cola and four machine minutes and $.20 to bottle the caffeine-free cola. The company has $1200 available for bottling. A bottle of regular cola sells for $.60 and a bottle of caffeine-free cola sells for $.54. How many bottles of each type of cola should be bottled to maximize the revenue, assuming all that is bottled can be sold?

1. Question: How many bottles of each type should be bottled?
2. Let x_1 be the number of bottles of regular cola bottled and x_2 be the number of bottles of caffeine-free cola bottled.

3. Data: Table format

	Regular cola	Caffeine-free	Available
	x_1	x_2	
Machine-minutes	3	4	20,000
Cost	.30	.20	1200
Revenue	.60	.54	

4. Objective function: to maximize revenue derived from $.60x_1$ and $.54x_2$.

$$\max R(x_1, x_2) = .60x_1 + .54x_2$$

constraints: machine minutes: $3x_1 + 4x_2 \leq 20,000$

cost: $.30x_1 + .20x_2 \leq 1200$

Notice that when the table of data is arranged with the variables as column headings, each row of the table corresponds to a constraint or the objective function. Therefore the linear program for this problem is:

$$\max R(x_1, x_2) = .60x_1 + 54x_2$$

$$3x_1 + 4x_2 \leq 20,000$$

$$.30x_1 + .20x_2 \leq 1200$$

$$x_1 \geq 0$$

$$x_2 \geq 0$$

EXAMPLE 5   The Color Camera Company manufactures only two kinds of cameras, an instamatic, and a disc camera. Each instamatic camera contributes $12 to profit and each disc camera contributes $9 to profit. The distribution center requires at least 250 instamatic cameras and 375 disc cameras. Each camera requires the times listed in the table below in the various departments.

	Instamatic	Disc
Manufacture of parts	$\frac{1}{2}$ hr.	$\frac{3}{4}$ hr.
Assembly	1 hr.	1 hr.
Inspection-packaging	$\frac{1}{4}$ hr.	$\frac{1}{2}$ hr.

The manufacturing department has 550 hours available, the assembly department has 850 hours available, and the inspection-packaging department has 350 hours available. How many of each type of camera should the company produce to maximize profit, assuming that they can sell all they produce?

1. Question: How many instamatic cameras and how many disc cameras should be produced?

2. Let x_1 be the number of instamatic cameras produced, and x_2 be the number of disc cameras produced.
3. Data: Table

	Instamatic	Disc	Available
	x_1	x_2	
Manufacture	$\frac{1}{2}$	$\frac{3}{4}$	550
Assembly	1	1	850
Packaging	$\frac{1}{4}$	$\frac{1}{2}$	350
Minimum needed:	250		
		375	
Profit	$12	$9	

4. The objective function can be read from the last line of the table and the constraints from the middle lines of the table.

$$\max P(x_1, x_2) = 12x_1 + 9x_2$$

$$\tfrac{1}{2}x_1 + \tfrac{3}{4}x_2 \leq 550$$

$$1x_1 + 1x_2 \leq 850$$

$$\tfrac{1}{4}x_1 + \tfrac{1}{2}x_2 \leq 350$$

$$x_1 \geq 250$$

$$x_2 \geq 375$$

PRACTICE EXAMPLE 1

Set up a linear program to solve the following problem. A company makes three types of toasters: a toaster oven that contributes $10 per toaster to profit; a four-slice toaster that contributes $8 per toaster to profit; and a two-slice toaster that contributes $4 per toaster to profit. Each type of toaster must pass through three processes as shown in the table below.

	Toaster oven	Four-slice	Two-slice
Manufacture	15 mins.	12 mins.	8 mins.
Assembly	5 mins.	4 mins.	3 mins.
Packaging	4 mins.	4 mins.	3 mins.

The manufacturing department has 1200 mins. available per day; the assembly department has 600 mins. available per day; and the packaging department has 480 mins. available per day. How many of each type of toaster should be manufactured to maximize the profit per day?

EXAMPLE 6

A cereal is to be manufactured containing only wheat and oats. At least 2000 lbs. of cereal must be manufactured. Only 1200 lbs. of oats is available. Wheat costs $4 per lb., and oats costs $3 per lb. Regulations require that at least 20% of the total be wheat and at least 10% of the total be oats. How many pounds of each grain should be used to minimize cost?

1. Question: How many pounds of wheat and oats should be used?
2. Let x_1 be the number of pounds of wheat and x_2 be the number of pounds of oats to be used.
3. Data: at least 2000 lbs. total
   no more than 1200 lbs. oats
   wheat at least 20% of total
   oats at least 10% of total
   wheat costs $4 per lb.
   oats cost $3 per lb.
4. The objective function minimizes the total cost:

$$\min C(x_1, x_2) = 4x_1 + 3x_2$$

Constraints: total: $x_1 + x_2 \geq 2000$

total oats: $x_2 \leq 1200$

wheat at least 20% of total of $x_1 + x_2$:

$$x_1 \geq .20(x_1 + x_2)$$

oats at least 10% of total of $x_1 + x_2$:

$$x_2 \geq .10(x_1 + x_2)$$

The last two constraints can be simplified:

wheat: $x_1 \geq .2x_1 + .2x_2$

$$.8x_1 \geq .2x_2$$

$$.8x_1 - .2x_2 \geq 0$$

oats: $x_2 \geq .1x_1 + .1x_2$

$$.9x_2 \geq .1x_1$$

$$.9x_2 - .1x_1 \geq 0$$

Therefore the linear program can be written as:

$$\min C(x_1, x_2) = 4x_1 + 3x_2$$

$$x_1 + x_2 \geq 2000$$

$$x_2 \leq 1200$$

$$.8x_1 - .2x_2 \geq 0$$

$$.9x_2 - .1x_1 \geq 0$$

$$x_1 \geq 0$$

$$x_2 \geq 0$$

In this section we set up linear programs consisting of an objective function and a system of inequalities called constraints. In the next section we find solutions to problems written as linear programs.

CONCEPTS

linear program
objective function
constraints
nonnegativity constraints

SOLUTION TO PRACTICE EXAMPLE

1. Table:

	Toaster oven	Four-slice	Two-slice	Available
	x_1	x_2	x_3	
Manufacture	15	12	8	1200
Assembly	5	4	3	600
Packaging	4	4	3	480
Profit	10	8	4	

$$\max P(x_1, x_2, x_3) = 10x_1 + 8x_2 + 4x_3$$
$$15x_1 + 12x_2 + 8x_3 \leq 1200$$
$$5x_1 + 4x_2 + 3x_3 \leq 600$$
$$4x_1 + 4x_2 + 3x_3 \leq 480$$
$$x_1 \geq 0$$
$$x_2 \geq 0$$
$$x_3 \geq 0$$

EXERCISES 9.4

Set up a linear program to solve each of the following problems.

1. A contractor builds two types of homes, a colonial that requires 300 days to build and costs $40,000 in capital, and a ranch house that requires 180 days to build and $30,000 in capital. The contractor has 18,000 days available and $3,600,000 in capital to build houses. The profit earned is $15,000 per colonial home and $10,000 per ranch house. How many of each house should the contractor build to maximize profit?

2. A company has to ship 10,000 barrels of oil to a site across the country. It has two pipeline routes possible. The first route can take a maximum of 5,000 barrels of oil. It costs $1 and 15 days to ship a barrel of oil through the first route, whereas it costs $2 and 10 days to ship a barrel of oil through the second route. The company has $16,000 to meet shipping costs. How much oil should be sent through each route to minimize the number of days required?

3. A zoologist conducts two types of experiments with lizards. An experiment of type 1 requires three brown lizards and one gray lizard, whereas an experiment of type 2 requires one brown lizard and two gray lizards. Each experiment of type 1 earns one point toward the zoologist's research, and each experiment of type 2 earns two points. There are 60 brown lizards and 40 gray lizards available. How many experiments of each type should be performed to maximize the total points earned?

4. A farmer can grow alfalfa and corn. The profit made is $200 a ton on alfalfa and $250 a ton on corn. Corn requires three hours a ton to harvest, and alfalfa requires two hours a ton to harvest. Each requires an hour a ton to plant. The planting time available is 400 hours, and the harvesting time available is 900 hours. How much of each should the farmer plant to maximize the profit?

5. A manufacturer wishes to produce two types of jewelry that are each part gold and part platinum. The table below gives the jewelry requirements:

	Bracelet	Pin	Available
Gold	10	5	100 g
Platinum	6	8	96 g
Profit	$12	$8	

How many bracelets and how many pins should be manufactured to maximize profit?

6. Registration for transfer students at a big university requires processing in three departments. The time required in each department is different for freshmen, other undergraduates, and graduate students, as the table indicates:

	Freshmen	Undergraduates	Graduates	Available
Advisor	20	15	10	4800 mins.
Sign-up	5	5	8	1500 mins.
Payment	10	5	5	2500 mins.

How many students of each type should be processed to maximize the overall total number of students?

7. A hospital is trying to set up a three-day weekend work shift schedule for nurses. The requirements are that at least as many nurses be scheduled as

shown below:

	7–3	3–11	11–7
Day 1	4	4	3
Day 2	3	3	2
Day 3	5	4	3

There are a total of 50 nurses available and no nurse may work more than one shift in the weekend. The value to patients of a nurse on the 7–3 shift is 10, whereas the value to patients of a nurse on the 3–11 shift is 8, and on the 11–7 shift is 5. The higher the number, the higher the value. How many nurses should be assigned to each of the nine shifts to maximize patient value? (Hint: There are nine variables here.)

8. A company has two warehouses and two terminals. It costs $10 a ton to ship from warehouse 1 to terminal 1, $12 a ton to ship from warehouse 1 to terminal 2, $15 a ton to ship from warehouse 2 to terminal 1, and $8 a ton to ship from warehouse 2 to terminal 2. Each warehouse has a supply of 200 tons. The demand at terminal 1 is for 150 tons, and the demand at warehouse 2 is for 180 tons. How much should be shipped between each terminal and each warehouse to minimize the total cost?

9. A firm wishes to buy printers to go with its microcomputers. The letter-quality printers have a speed of 55 characters per second and cost $1500 each. The matrix-dot printers have a speed of 250 characters per second and cost $750 each. The firm needs at least three letter-quality printers and has $19,500 to spend on the printers. How many of each type should be purchased to maximize the speed?

10. A leather goods factory manufactures five styles of handbags, whose profit contributions are $30, $40, $45, $25, and $60, per dozen, respectively (Bradley, Hax, Magnanti 1977). The products must pass through four work centers in which the working-hours available are: clicking (700), paring (600), stitching (400), and finishing (900). Hourly requirements for each dozen handbags are:

Style	Click	Pare	Stitch	Finish
341	3	8	2	6
262	4	3	1	0
43	2	2	0	2
784	2	1	3	4
5-A	5	4	4	3

To prevent adding to inventory levels already on hand, the production manager has reviewed the weekly sales forecasts and has specified that no more than 100, 50, 90, 70, and 30 dozen of each style, respectively, may be produced. Each handbag is made from five materials as specified in the table, which also gives the total of each material available. (Numbers are given per dozen.)

Style	Leather	Fabric	Backing	Lining	Acces.
341	0	1	4	2	3
262	4	0	7	4	4
43	5	7	6	2	0
784	6	4	1	1	2
5-A	2	3	3	0	4
Total avail.	300	400	1000	900	1600

Devise next week's manufacturing schedule to maximize profit.

9.5   *Linear Programming—Geometrical Solutions*

In the last section, we formulated many problems as linear programs. In this section we develop one approach to finding a solution to linear programs with two variables. Since this approach involves graphing, it is difficult to apply it to programs with three variables, and impossible to apply it to programs with more than three variables. In Chapter 11 we develop the simplex method for finding solutions to linear programs with an arbitrary number of variables. The simplex method is more complicated than the geometrical method and does not provide the insight into the nature of the problems that the geometrical method provides.

EXAMPLE 1   Find a solution to the linear program that was the intoductory example in Section 9.4:

$$\max P(x_1, x_2) = 75x_1 + 45x_2$$

$$3x_1 + 5x_2 \leq 100$$

$$200x_1 + 100x_2 \leq 5000$$

$$x_1 \geq 0$$

$$x_2 \geq 0$$

Since a solution to the linear program is a point (x_1, x_2) that must satisfy the constraints of the linear program, we need to find the solution set for the system of inequalities that is the set of constraints. These are the points that are feasible as solutions to the linear program.

> DEFINITION   The solution set for the system of constraints in a linear program is called the **feasible set** or **feasible region**.

The feasible set can be found by graphing the system of inequalities as in Figure 9.26 (in the same manner as in Figure 9.25 in Section 9.3).

Figure 9.26

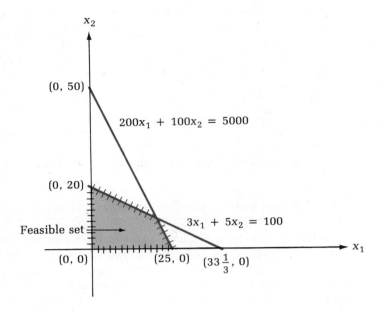

The boundary of the feasible region in the graph is shown with hashed lines. Note that the feasible region has the shape of a polygon. In this case, the boundary contains portions of two axes and portions of two straight lines. The corners of this polygon are easily computed—three of them can be read directly from the graph: $(0, 0)$, $(25, 0)$, and $(0, 20)$. (*Notice the importance of labeling the intercepts on your graph when drawing straight lines.*) The fourth point is the point where the two lines intersect and is the solution to the system of equations:

$$3x_1 + 5x_2 = 100$$

$$200x_1 + 100x_2 = 5000$$

This system can be simplified to:

$$3x_1 + 5x_2 = 100$$

$$2x_1 + x_2 = 50$$

by multiplying the second equation by $\frac{1}{100}$. Applying the method of addition we can compute the solution:

$$2(3x_1 + 5x_2 = 100) \qquad 6x_1 + 10x_2 = 200$$

$$-3(2x_1 + x_2 = 50) \qquad \underline{-6x_1 - 3x_2 = -150}$$

$$\oplus \qquad \qquad 7x_2 = 50$$

$$x_2 = \frac{50}{7}$$

$$3x_1 + 5\left(\frac{50}{7}\right) = 100$$

$$3x_1 + \frac{250}{7} = 100$$

$$3x_1 = 100 - \frac{250}{7} = \frac{700}{7} - \frac{250}{7} = \frac{450}{7}.$$

$$x_1 = \frac{450}{21} = \frac{150}{7}$$

The solution set for these two equations is $\{(\frac{150}{7}, \frac{50}{7})\}$ or approximately $\{(21.43, 7.14)\}$.

Our goal is to make $P = 75x_1 + 45x_2$ as large as possible, using only points in the feasible region. A few trial examples are shown in the table below:

x_1	x_2	$P = 75x_1 + 45x_2$
5	5	$75(5) + 45(5) = 375 + 225 = 600$
25	0	$75(25) + 45(0) = 1875$
0	20	$75(0) + 45(20) = 900$
20	5	$75(20) + 45(5) = 1500 + 225 = 1725$
21.43	7.14	$75(21.43) + 45(7.14) = 1928.55$

From the sample of points we tried, (21.43, 7.14) yielded the highest value of P, but maybe we did not try the "best" point. The feasible region has infinitely many points.

Figure 9.27

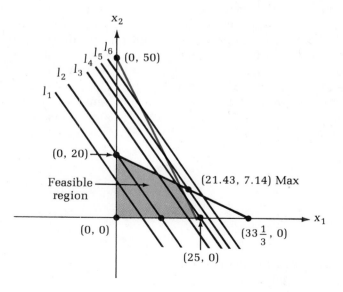

Each value of P determines a straight line. Thus, $75x_1 + 45x_2 = 600$ is one straight line, l_1 in Figure 9.27; $75x_1 + 45x_2 = 900$, call it l_2; $75x_1 + 45x_2 = 1725$, call it l_3; $75x_1 + 45x_2 = 1875$, call it l_4; $75x_1 + 45x_2 = 1928.55$, call it l_5. The line l_6 or $75x_1 + 45x_2 = 2000$ does not touch the feasible region, but nevertheless is a line corresponding to a value of P.

Each of the lines l_1 through l_5 intersects the feasible set. The set of lines l_1 through l_6 is a set of parallel lines, each with slope $-\frac{75}{45} = -\frac{5}{3}$. Therefore, of the set of all possible lines with slope $-\frac{5}{3}$, we are looking for the one "farthest out" that includes at least one feasible point. The line for this problem is l_5, which contains the corner point (21.43, 7.14). The solution to this linear program is (21.43, 7.14), with a maximum value for P of \$1928.55 as shown in the table above. In other words, the manufacturing firm should construct 21.43 units of product A and 7.14 units of product B to maximize profit. ◼

Be careful. Sometimes it is not possible to construct fractional parts. However, a unit may actually be 100 or 1000 items, in which case rounding to integer values would not destroy the optimality. More will be said about this at the end of Chapter 11.

How closely are the constraints satisfied in this problem? We will use the fractional solution here.

constraint 1: $\quad 3\left(\dfrac{150}{7}\right) + 5\left(\dfrac{50}{7}\right) = \dfrac{450}{7} + \dfrac{250}{7} = 100$

constraint 2: $\quad 200\left(\dfrac{150}{7}\right) + 100\left(\dfrac{50}{7}\right) = \dfrac{30,000}{7} + \dfrac{5000}{7} = 5000$

They are satisfied exactly. This is not surprising, since this solution was the solution to the system of equations corresponding to the two constraints. This will not always be the case, as our next example illustrates.

Suppose in the previous example, the profit from product A falls to \$40 per unit, and the profit from product B rises to \$80 a unit. The constraints are still the same. Is it still more profitable to produce 21.43 units of product A and 7.14 units of product B?

The graph of the feasible region remains the same, and the profit function becomes $P(x_1, x_2) = 40x_1 + 80x_2$. Thus, we are looking at parallel lines, each with slope $-\frac{40}{80} = -\frac{1}{2}$. A sample of such lines is shown in Figure 9.28.

$l_1: \quad 40x_1 + 80x_2 = 1000$

$l_2: \quad 40x_1 + 80x_2 = 1200$

$l_3: \quad 40x_1 + 80x_2 = 1428.4$

$l_4: \quad 40x_1 + 80x_2 = 1600$

If you carefully move the lines out, the last point of the feasible region hit is (0, 20), again a corner point. Thus, now the firm should manufacture only product B in the quantity of 20 units, for a maximum profit of \$1600.

Figure 9.28

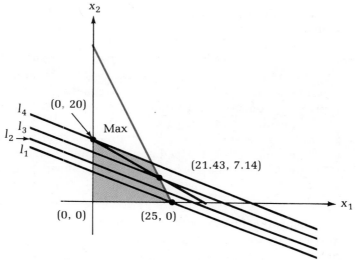

Consider constraint (2) for the point (0, 20):

$$200(0) + 100(20) = 2000 < 5000$$

In other words, there is a slack of $3000 in the cost constraint, whereas constraint (1) is satisfied exactly.

To avoid having to draw these parallel lines each time we want to solve a linear program, we can use the theory of linear programming to find solutions. Before stating the fundamental theorem of linear programming we need the following definition:

DEFINITION   A set of points in the plane is **bounded** if it is contained in some circle centered at the origin, otherwise it is **unbounded**.

Figure 9.29(a) gives an example of a bounded set, and Figure 9.29(b) gives an example of an unbounded set.

Figure 9.29

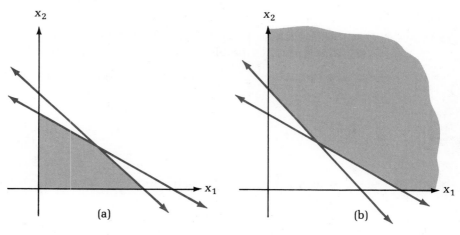

We state the following theorem without proof. (For a proof, see Simmons 1972.)

FUNDAMENTAL THEOREM OF LINEAR PROGRAMMING   If the feasible set for a linear program is bounded, then the objective function attains its maximum and minimum value (not necessarily unique) at a corner point of the feasible region.

If the feasible region is unbounded, then the maximum and/or minimum is either attained at a corner point or the maximum and/or minimum does not exist (can become arbitrarily large or small).

Using the fundamental theorem, we can find a solution to a linear program by the geometrical method.

GEOMETRICAL METHOD

STEP 1:   Graph the constraints to get the feasible set.

STEP 2:   Determine the corner points of the feasible set.

STEP 3:   Substitute each corner point in the objective function to get a value.

STEP 4:   Select the largest of the values if the objective function is to be maximized, and the smallest of the values if the objective function is to be minimized. If the feasible set is bounded, then the solution to the linear program is the point(s) corresponding to the largest (smallest) value.

EXAMPLE 2

We will now apply the geometrical method to the linear program of the transportation problem in Example 1 in Section 9.4.

$$\min C(x_1, x_2) = 10x_1 + 12x_2$$

$$x_1 + x_2 \leq 1000$$

$$x_1 \geq 400$$

$$x_2 \geq 400$$

STEP 1:   Graph the constraints to determine the feasible region (Figure 9.30).

Figure 9.30

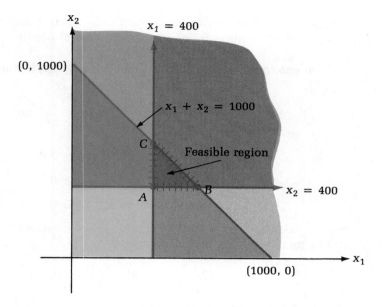

STEP 2:   Compute the corner points. They are labeled on the graph as A, B, and C.

A has coordinates (400, 400) since it is the point where the line $x_1 = 400$ and the line $x_2 = 400$ cross.

B has coordinates (600, 400) since it is the point where the line $x_2 = 400$ and the line $x_1 + x_2 = 1000$ cross.

$$x_1 + 400 = 1000$$

$$x_1 = 600$$

C has coordinates (400, 600) since it is the point where the line $x_1 = 400$ and the line $x_1 + x_2 = 1000$ cross.

$$400 + x_2 = 1000$$

$$x_2 = 600$$

STEP 3:   Substitute in objective function:

Corner points	$C = 10x_1 + 12x_2$
(400, 400)	$10(400) + 12(400) =$ 8,800 min
(400, 600)	$10(400) + 12(600) = 11,200$
(600, 400)	$10(600) + 12(400) = 10,800$

STEP 4:   The point corresponding to the minimum value is (400, 400). Since the feasible set is bounded, this is the solution, with minimum value 8800.

Therefore 400 units should be shipped to terminal A and 400 units should be shipped to terminal B, for a minimum cost of \$8800.   ▪

EXAMPLE 3

We will use the geometrical method to solve Example 3 of Section 9.4:

$$\max T(x_1, x_2) = x_1 + x_2$$

$$1.12 \left(\frac{x_1}{20} \right) + 1.25 \left(\frac{x_2}{25} \right) \le 800$$

$$x_1 + x_2 \ge 200$$

$$x_1 \ge 0$$

$$x_2 \ge 0$$

STEP 1:   Graph the constraints (Figure 9.31). First, simplify the first constraint by multiplying it by 100 to get

$$112 \left(\frac{x_1}{20} \right) + 125 \left(\frac{x_2}{25} \right) \le 80{,}000$$

then by 100 to eliminate fractions:

$$560 x_1 + 500 x_2 \le 8{,}000{,}000$$

$$56 x_1 + 50 x_2 \le 800{,}000$$

Figure 9.31

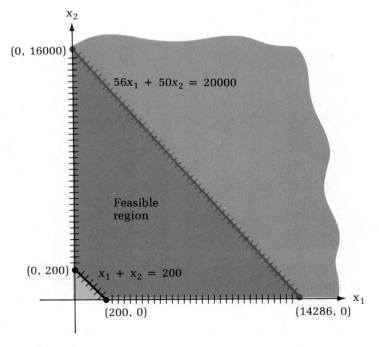

Note that the feasible region is contained between the two lines.

STEP 2:   Compute the corner points: This is easy, since they are the intercepts: (200, 0), (0, 200), (14286, 0), and (0, 16000).

STEP 3:   Compute the values of T at the corner points:

Corner points	$T = x_1 + x_2$
(200, 0)	200
(0, 200)	200
(14,286, 0)	14,286
(0, 16,000)	16,000 max

The maximum occurs at (0, 16000). Since the feasible region is bounded, this point is the solution to the linear program. Only the second car should be driven. It should be driven 16,000, the maximum number of miles. ■

PRACTICE EXAMPLE 1   Find a solution to the linear program given in Example 4 of Section 9.4. ■

EXAMPLE 4   Find a solution to the problem presented in Example 5 of Section 9.4:

$$\max P(x_1, x_2) = 12x_1 + 9x_2$$

$$\frac{x_1}{2} + \frac{3x_2}{4} \leq 550$$

$$x_1 + x_2 \leq 850$$

$$\frac{x_1}{4} + \frac{x_2}{2} \leq 350$$

$$x_1 \geq 250$$

$$x_2 \geq 375$$

STEP 1:   Graph the constraints (first simplify them) as shown in Figure 9.32.

$$\left(\frac{x_1}{2} + \frac{3x_2}{4} \leq 550\right) \times 4 = (2x_1 + 3x_2 \leq 2200)$$

$$\left(\frac{x_1}{4} + \frac{x_2}{2} \leq 350\right) \times 4 = (x_1 + 2x_2 \leq 1400)$$

Be careful graphing the three constraints so that you will be able to determine which lines are intersecting, and where.

Figure 9.32

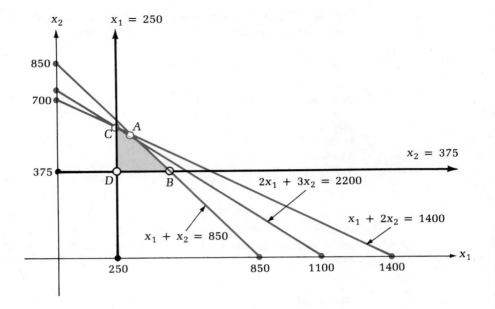

STEP 2:   Compute the corner points of the feasible region. One of the corner points, D, is easily found: $(250, 375)$. The other three corner points correspond to the solution of the following three systems of equations:

1. $2x_1 + 3x_2 = 2200$
   $x_1 + x_2 = 850$
2. $2x_1 + 3x_2 = 2200$
   $x_1 = 250$
3. $x_1 + x_2 = 850$
   $x_2 = 375$

To solve the first system, multiply its second equation by -2, and add:

$$2x_1 + 3x_2 = 2200$$
$$-2x_1 - 2x_2 = -1700$$
$$\oplus \overline{ x_2 = 500}$$
$$x_1 + 500 = 850$$
$$x_1 = 350$$

The solution set is $\{(350, 500)\}$, point A.

To solve the second system, multiply its second equation by -2 and add:

$$2x_1 + 3x_2 = 2200$$
$$-2x_1 = -500$$
$$\oplus \overline{ 3x_2 = 1700}$$
$$x_2 = 566.67$$

The solution set is $\{(250, 566.67)\}$, point C.

To solve the third system, multiply its second equation by -1 and add:

$$x_1 + x_2 = 850$$
$$-x_2 = -375$$
$$\oplus \qquad x_1 = 475$$

The solution set is $\{(475, 375)\}$, point B.

STEP 3:   Substitute the corner points into the objective function:

Corner points	$P = 12x_1 + 9x_2$
(250, 375)	6375
(475, 375)	9075 max
(250, 566.67)	8100
(350, 500)	8700

STEP 4:   The largest value is 9075; therefore the solution to the linear program is (475, 375)) with value of 9075. The company should produce 475 instamatic cameras and 375 disc cameras for a maximum profit of $9075.

EXAMPLE 5

As our last example, consider the following linear program:

$$\max P(x_1, x_2) = x_1 + 3x_2$$
$$x_1 \leq 4$$
$$x_2 \geq 6$$
$$x_1 \geq 0$$

The graph is as shown in Figure 9.33. Note that the feasible region is unbounded.

Figure 9.33

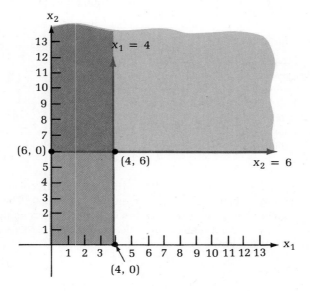

The corner points are (0, 6) and (4, 6), with corresponding P values of 18 and 22, respectively. Neither of these is a maximum, since x_2 can become increasingly larger, forcing P to be larger. For example if x_2 is 100, and x_1 is 4, then P is 304. There is *no* solution to this linear program.   ■

CONCEPTS

feasible set or feasible region
fundamental theorem of linear programming
geometrical method

SOLUTION TO PRACTICE EXAMPLE

1. Graph:

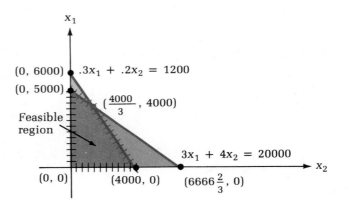

Corner points	$R = .6x_1 + .54x_2$
(0, 0)	0
(4000, 0)	2400
(0, 5000)	2700
($\frac{4000}{3}$, 4000)	2960 max

The company should bottle $\frac{4000}{3}$ bottles of regular cola and 4000 bottles of caffeine-free cola for a maximum revenue of \$2960. These results help the bottling company only if they deal in lot sizes that are multiples of three since one cannot bottle a fraction of a bottle. Rounding to (1333, 4000) will give a good approximation, however, and is still in the feasible region.

EXERCISES 9.5

Solve each of the following linear programming problems:

1. max $P = x_1 + 2x_2$

    $x_1 + 2x_2 \leq 4$

    $x_1 + x_2 \leq 3$

    $x_1 \geq 0, x_2 \geq 0$

2. max $P = 2x_1 + x_2$

    $x_1 + 2x_2 \leq 4$

    $x_1 + x_2 \leq 3$

    $x_1 \geq 0, x_2 \geq 0$

3. min $C = 3x_1 + 4x_2$

    $x_1 + x_2 \geq 5$

    $2x_1 + 5x_2 \geq 10$

    $x_1 \geq 0, x_2 \geq 0$

4. min $T = 2x_1 - x_2$

    $x_1 \geq 5$

    $x_2 \geq 6$

    $x_1 + x_2 \leq 10$

5. max $A = 30x_1 + 40x_2$

    $2x_1 + x_2 \leq 10$

    $x_1 + x_2 \leq 6$

    $x_1 + 2x_2 \leq 14$

    $x_1 \geq 0, x_2 \geq 0$

6. max $P = 100x_1 + 200x_2$

    $30x_1 + 10x_2 \leq 210$

    $x_1 + x_2 \leq 9$

    $10x_1 + 30x_2 \leq 210$

    $x_1 \geq 0, x_2 \geq 0$

7. Example 6 of Section 9.4.

8–13.   Exercises 1–5, and 9 of Exercises 9.4.

CHAPTER SUMMARY

This chapter has concentrated on solving problems that involve maximizing or minimizing a function, subject to a set of conditions expressed as inequalities, or *constraints*. To solve the problem using the *geometrical method*, the problem must be written in a particular format, called a *linear program*, shown here in two variables:

$$\max P = 3x_1 + 4x_2 \qquad \text{objective function}$$

$$2x_1 + 5x_2 \leq 10$$

$$4x_1 + x_2 \leq 8 \qquad \text{constraints}$$

$$x_1 \geq 0$$

$$x_2 \geq 0$$

The first step of the geometrical method is to *graph the system of inequalities* to find the *feasible region*. In order to graph an inequality it is first necessary to graph the corresponding equation by computing the intercepts. The intercepts for each of the equations help identify the corner points of the feasible region. The remaining corner points of the feasible region are computed by solving pairs of the equations to get the points of intersection of the lines that bound the feasible region.

Once the corner points of the feasible region are computed, these points are substituted (one at a time) into the objective function to determine which point yields the largest value (maximization problems) or smallest value (minimization problems). The *fundamental theorem of linear programming* tells us that the maximum and minimum will occur at one of these points if the feasible region is bounded. Therefore, we have found the solution to the problem.

REVIEW EXERCISES FOR CHAPTER 9

1. Graph the straight line $2x_1 + 3x_2 = 12$.

2. Write the equation of the straight line with intercepts $(0, 5)$ and $(2, 0)$.

3. Find the intercepts and graph the equation of the line $3x_1 - 4x_2 = 0$.

4. Graph $x_1 + x_2 = 6$ and $2x_1 + 3x_2 = 12$ on the same set of axes. Find the point of intersection.

In Exercises 5 through 8, solve the systems of equations.

5. $3x_1 - 4x_2 = 15$

    $x_1 + x_2 = 6$

6. $2x_1 - x_2 = 10$

   $3x_1 + 5x_2 = 29$

7. $7x_1 - x_2 = 15$

   $x_2 = x_1 + 1$

8. $5x_1 + 4x_2 = 16$

   $3x_1 - 2x_2 = 15$

9. Sketch the graph of the inequality:

$$x_1 + 3x_2 \leq 9$$

10. Sketch the graph of the inequality:

$$5x_1 - 3x_2 \geq 21$$

11. Sketch the graph of the inequality:

$$2x_1 - x_2 \geq 0$$

12. Sketch the graph of the following system of inequalities on the same axes, and indicate the solution for the system:

$$x_1 + x_2 \leq 8$$

$$2x_1 + 5x_2 \leq 30$$

13. Sketch the graph of the following system of inequalities on the same axes, and indicate the solution for the system:

$$x_1 \geq x_2$$

$$6x_1 + 5x_2 \leq 30$$

In Exercises 14 through 17, set up linear programs to solve each of the problems. Do not solve.

14. A manufacturing company must dispose of 4000 tons of toxic wastes each year. There are two waste disposal plants available. Plant A can take at most 2500 tons, and plant B can take at most 1800 tons. It costs $50 a ton to ship to plant A and $60 a ton to ship to plant B. How much should be shipped to each plant to minimize the total cost?

15. A manufacturer produces two types of educational software, Aristotle and Socrates. Each piece of software requires development and production, and sells for a fixed price as indicated in the table. The company has determined that it can sell no more than 2000 Aristotles and 3000 Socrates. How many of each should be produced to maximize sales revenue?

	Aristotle	Socrates	Available
Development hrs/disk	1	1	3000
Production hrs/disk	1	2	4000
Selling price/disk	$15	$20	

16.   A tennis-racquet manufacturer makes two kinds of racquets, the deluxe and the standard models. Using the information below, how many of each type of racquet should be produced to maximize the profit?

Per racquet	Standard	Deluxe	Available
Manufacturing	1	$\frac{1}{2}$	20
Finishing	$\frac{1}{2}$	$\frac{1}{2}$	16
Profit	$30	$20	

17.   Horses that are ridden often need a diet rich in protein and minerals. Every 50 lbs of sweet feed provides 64 ozs of protein and 14 ozs of minerals, whereas 50 lbs of "short" feed provides 58 ozs of protein and 18 ozs of minerals. A stable manager buys 50,000 lbs of feed a month. It costs $8 a 50-lb bag of sweet feed and $7 a bag for "short" feed. How much of each type should be bought to minimize total cost if at least 60,000 ozs of protein and at least 15,000 ozs of minerals are needed. (Be careful, one of the constraints is an equality. And do, not forget to change ounces to pounds.)

18–21.   Solve each of the problems in Exercises 14 through 17.

Matrices

10

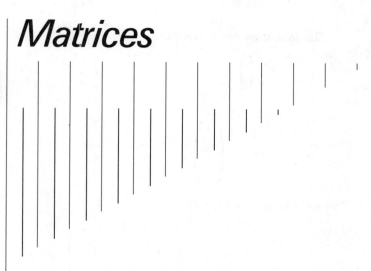

This chapter provides an introduction to matrices and their applications. Matrices are used to model, and hence predict, changes over time (Section 10.3), solve systems of linear equations (Sections 10.4, 10.5, and 10.6), solve optimization problems (Section 10.4), and model the relationship between input and output in economies and large businesses (Section 10.6). The terminology used in working with matrices is presented in Section 10.1. Addition, subtraction, and multiplication of matrices are covered in Section 10.2. The algorithm given in the next chapter for solving linear programs uses the techniques presented in Sections 10.4 and 10.5.

The mathematical study of matrices began with the work of the English mathematicians Arthur Cayley (1821–95) and James Sylvester (1814–97). Matrices are a natural way to organize and manipulate data to solve problems. Recently, as computers have made it possible to handle ever larger amounts of information, the use of matrices has taken on increasing importance in management and other areas of business. In this chapter you are introduced to the basic techniques used in this setting.

10.1 Matrices, Relations, and Graphs

In this section, we introduce the terminology of matrices and show how various kinds of information such as graphs, relations, and systems of **419** linear equations can be written as matrices.

> DEFINITION A **matrix** is a rectangular array enclosed by parentheses.

The following are matrices.

$$\begin{pmatrix} 1 & 2 \\ 3 & -1 \end{pmatrix} \quad (4 \quad 1 \quad 7) \quad \begin{pmatrix} 1 \\ 3 \\ 8 \end{pmatrix} \quad \begin{pmatrix} 1 & 2 & -1 \\ 3 & 5 & 7 \end{pmatrix}$$

$$\begin{pmatrix} a & b \\ c & d \end{pmatrix} \quad \begin{pmatrix} x \\ y \\ z \end{pmatrix}$$

The following is not a matrix.

$$\begin{pmatrix} & & 1 & \\ & 1 & 2 & 1 \\ 1 & 3 & 3 & 1 \end{pmatrix}$$

A matrix consists of **rows** and **columns**. For

$$A = \begin{pmatrix} 1 & -1 & 2 & 1 \\ 3 & 0 & 1 & 0 \\ 2 & -1 & 5 & 6 \end{pmatrix}$$

first row of $A = R_1(A) = (1 \quad -1 \quad 2 \quad 1)$

second row of $A = R_2(A) = (3 \quad 0 \quad 1 \quad 0)$

third row of $A = R_3(A) = (2 \quad -1 \quad 5 \quad 6)$

The columns of A are:

first column $= C_1(A) = \begin{pmatrix} 1 \\ 3 \\ 2 \end{pmatrix}$ second column $= C_2(A) = \begin{pmatrix} -1 \\ 0 \\ -1 \end{pmatrix}$

third column $= C_3(A) = \begin{pmatrix} 2 \\ 1 \\ 5 \end{pmatrix}$ fourth column $= C_4(A) = \begin{pmatrix} 1 \\ 0 \\ 6 \end{pmatrix}$

The (i, j)-entry, $A_{i,j}$, in a matrix, A, is the **entry** that is in both the ith row and the jth column of the matrix.

For

$$A = \begin{pmatrix} 7 & 8 & 9 \\ -2 & 4 & -3 \end{pmatrix}$$

(1, 1)-entry $= A_{1,1} =$ entry in the first row and the first column of $A = 7$

(1, 3)-entry $= A_{1,3} =$ entry in the first row and the third column of $A = 9$

(1, 2)-entry $= A_{1,2} = 8$

(2, 1)-entry $= A_{2,1} = -2$

$A_{1,1} = 7 \qquad A_{1,2} = 8 \qquad A_{1,3} = 9$

$A_{2,1} = -2 \qquad A_{2,2} = 4 \qquad A_{2,3} = -3$

PRACTICE
EXAMPLE 1

For

$$A = \begin{pmatrix} 1 & 2 \\ 3 & -1 \\ 4 & 7 \end{pmatrix}$$

write:

(a) the first row of A
(b) $R_3(A)$
(c) the second column of A
(d) $C_1(A)$
(e) (1, 2)-entry
(f) $A_{2,1}$
(g) (3, 2)-entry

The table below represents a shipping schedule between two factories, A and B, and two terminals, S and T.

		Terminals	
		S	T
Factories	A	100	200
	B	150	75

The table can be expressed as a matrix:

$$\begin{pmatrix} 100 & 200 \\ 150 & 75 \end{pmatrix}$$

Each row in the matrix represents the number of units shipped out of each factory and each column represents the number of units shipped into each terminal. The (i, j)-entry is the number of units shipped from the ith factory to the jth terminal. Thus the (2, 1)-entry, 150, means 150 units are shipped from the second factory, B, to the first terminal, S.

A matrix can be used to represent the coefficients and constant terms of a system of equations. For example:

$$4x_1 + 3x_2 = 7$$

$$5x_1 + 2x_2 = 5$$

can be written in "shorthand" matrix notation as:

$$\begin{pmatrix} 4 & 3 & 7 \\ 5 & 2 & 5 \end{pmatrix}$$

where each row represents an equation. The first and second columns correspond to coefficients of the first and second variables and the third column corresponds to the constants. This matrix notation for systems of equations is used in Section 10.4 where we give a systematic method for solving systems of linear equations.

An important property used in describing matrices is the size of a matrix. A matrix with p rows and q columns has **size p by q**. Thus a matrix with two rows and three columns has size 2 by 3.

$$\begin{pmatrix} 100 & 200 \\ 150 & 75 \end{pmatrix} \text{ has size 2 by 2.} \qquad \begin{pmatrix} 4 & 3 & 7 \\ 5 & 2 & 5 \end{pmatrix} \text{ has size 2 by 3.}$$

$$\begin{pmatrix} 2 & 6 \\ 5 & 7 \\ 8 & 3 \end{pmatrix} \text{ has size 3 by 2.} \qquad \begin{pmatrix} 2 & 1 & 5 & 4 \\ 5 & 1 & 8 & 3 \\ 2 & 5 & 7 & 6 \end{pmatrix} \text{ has size 3 by 4.}$$

A matrix with only one row is called a **row matrix**, and a matrix with only one column is called a **column matrix**. $(1 \quad 2 \quad -5)$ is a row matrix and

$$\begin{pmatrix} 5 \\ 3 \\ 2 \end{pmatrix}$$

is a column matrix.

Two matrices A and B are called **equal** if they have the same size, and corresponding entries are equal, that is $A_{i,j} = B_{i,j}$ for all i and j. For example, if

$$A = \begin{pmatrix} 1 & 2 \\ 3 & 5 \end{pmatrix}$$

and

$$B = \begin{pmatrix} 1 & 2 \\ 3 & 7 \end{pmatrix}$$

then $5 = A_{2,2} \neq B_{2,2} = 7$ so $A \neq B$.

We gave a procedure above for writing a system of equations in matrix form. Other types of information, relations and graphs for example, can also be written in matrix form. Recall from Chapter 6 that a relation on a set $S = \{s_1, s_2, s_3 \ldots, s_n\}$ is a set, R, of pairs of elements from S. For example $R = \{(1, 1), (2, 2), (3, 3), (4, 4), (1, 2), (3, 2), (4, 3)\}$ is a relation on $S = \{1, 2, 3, 4\}$. The **matrix, A, of a relation** is defined by setting:

$$A_{i,j} = \begin{cases} 1 \text{ if } (s_i, s_j) \in R \\ 0 \text{ if } (s_i, s_j) \notin R \end{cases}$$

The matrix corresponding to the relation R is:

$$\begin{pmatrix} 1 & 1 & 0 & 0 \\ 0 & 1 & 0 & 0 \\ 0 & 1 & 1 & 0 \\ 0 & 0 & 1 & 1 \end{pmatrix}$$

PRACTICE EXAMPLE 2

Write the matrix corresponding to the relation $R = \{(1, 2), (3, 4), (1, 4), (2, 1), (2, 4), (3, 1), (4, 1), (4, 3)\}$. ∎

Graphs can be input into a computer using matrices. The **incidence** (or adjacency) **matrix of a graph** with vertices $\{v_1, v_2, \ldots, v_n\}$ is defined by setting:

$$A_{i,j} = \begin{cases} 1 \text{ if there is an edge joining } v_i \text{ and } v_j \\ 0 \text{ if there is not an edge joining } v_i \text{ and } v_j \end{cases}$$

For example, the incidence matrix of the graph in Figure 10.1 is:

$$\begin{pmatrix} 0 & 1 & 0 \\ 1 & 0 & 1 \\ 0 & 1 & 0 \end{pmatrix}$$

Figure 10.1

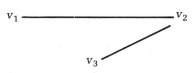

PRACTICE EXAMPLE 3

Find the incidence matrix of the graph in Figure 10.2.

Figure 10.2

$v_1 \underline{\hspace{1.5cm}} v_2 \qquad\qquad v_3 \underline{\hspace{1.5cm}} v_4$ ∎

Another way to associate a matrix to a graph is to have the entries in the matrix correspond to the number of edges joining vertices. The **edge** matrix, A, **of a graph** is defined by setting $A_{i,j}$ = the number of edges joining v_i and v_j. For example, the edge matrix corresponding to the graph in Figure 10.3 is:

$$\begin{pmatrix} 1 & 1 & 0 \\ 1 & 0 & 2 \\ 0 & 2 & 0 \end{pmatrix}$$

Figure 10.3

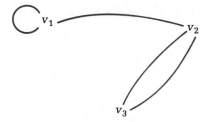

PRACTICE EXAMPLE 4

(a) Find the edge matrix of the graph in Figure 10.4.

Figure 10.4

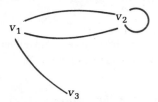

(b) Find the edge matrix of the graph in Figure 10.5.

Figure 10.5

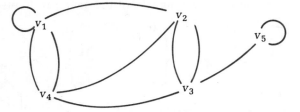

If the edges are directed, then the edge matrix counts the number of edges directed from one vertex to another. The entries are defined by: $A_{i,j}$ = the number of edges directed from v_i to v_j. The edge matrix of the graph in Figure 10.6 is:

$$\begin{pmatrix} 0 & 2 & 0 & 0 \\ 0 & 0 & 1 & 1 \\ 1 & 0 & 0 & 0 \\ 0 & 1 & 0 & 0 \end{pmatrix}$$

Figure 10.6

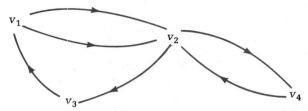

If the graph in Figure 10.6 is an airline chart of direct flights between cities, then each row represents the flights out of some city and each column represents the flights into some city. The entries give the number of nonstop flights from one city to another.

In this section we introduced the terminology of matrices and gave examples to show how various types of information (relations, graphs, and systems of linear equations) can be written as matrices. The procedure used in this section for writing a system of linear equations as a matrix is used in Section 10.4 where we give a general method for solving systems of linear equations. In the next section we show how to add, subtract, and multiply matrices.

CONCEPTS

matrix	entry	incidence matrix of a graph
row	size	edge matrix of a graph
column	matrix corresponding to a relation	equality of matrices

SOLUTIONS TO PRACTICE EXAMPLES

1. (a) $(1 \quad 2)$ (b) $(4 \quad 7)$ (c) $\begin{pmatrix} 2 \\ -1 \\ 7 \end{pmatrix}$ (d) $\begin{pmatrix} 1 \\ 3 \\ 4 \end{pmatrix}$

(e) 2 (f) 3 (g) 7

2. $\begin{pmatrix} 0 & 1 & 0 & 1 \\ 1 & 0 & 0 & 1 \\ 1 & 0 & 0 & 1 \\ 1 & 0 & 1 & 0 \end{pmatrix}$
3. $\begin{pmatrix} 0 & 1 & 0 & 0 \\ 1 & 0 & 0 & 0 \\ 0 & 0 & 0 & 1 \\ 0 & 0 & 1 & 0 \end{pmatrix}$

4. (a) $\begin{pmatrix} 0 & 2 & 1 \\ 2 & 1 & 0 \\ 1 & 0 & 0 \end{pmatrix}$ (b) $\begin{pmatrix} 1 & 1 & 0 & 2 & 0 \\ 1 & 0 & 2 & 1 & 0 \\ 0 & 2 & 0 & 1 & 1 \\ 2 & 1 & 1 & 0 & 0 \\ 0 & 0 & 1 & 0 & 1 \end{pmatrix}$

EXERCISES 10.1

1. For:

$$A = \begin{pmatrix} 1 & 3 & 5 \\ 2 & 4 & 2 \end{pmatrix}$$

   find:

   (a) $R_1(A)$ (b) $C_2(A)$

   (c) $A_{1,3}$ (d) the (2,1)-entry

2. For:

$$A = \begin{pmatrix} 0 & 1 & 5 \\ 3 & 2 & -1 \\ 7 & 4 & 8 \end{pmatrix}$$

   find:

   (a) $R_2(A)$ (b) $C_3(A)$

   (c) $A_{2,1}$ (d) the (1, 2)-entry

3. For:

$$A = \begin{pmatrix} 1 & -1 \\ 4 & 5 \\ 3 & -2 \end{pmatrix}$$

   find:

   (a) $R_3(A)$ (b) $C_1(A)$

   (c) $A_{2,1}$ (d) the (3, 2)-entry

4. Write the matrix, A, whose rows are $R_1(A) = (1 \quad 0 \quad 1)$, $R_2(A) = (2 \quad 1 \quad -4)$, and $R_3(A) = (5 \quad -1 \quad 7)$.

5. Write the matrix whose columns are

$$C_1(A) = \begin{pmatrix} 2 \\ 0 \\ 7 \end{pmatrix} \quad C_2(A) = \begin{pmatrix} 4 \\ -1 \\ 2 \end{pmatrix} \quad C_3(A) = \begin{pmatrix} 4 \\ 5 \\ 3 \end{pmatrix} \quad C_4(A) = \begin{pmatrix} 1 \\ -1 \\ 2 \end{pmatrix}$$

6. The Cinema Center has four cinemas: I, II, III, and IV. At a Sunday matinee cinema I had 225 children, 110 students, and 50 adults; cinema II had 75 children, 180 students, and 225 adults; cinema III had 280 children, 85 students, and 110 adults; cinema IV had no children, 250 students, and 225 adults. Put this information in a matrix whose rows correspond to the cinemas.

In Exercises 7 and 8 write the matrix corresponding to the given relation.

7. $R = \{(1, 1), (1, 2), (1, 3), (2, 3), (2, 4), (3, 4), (4, 4)\}$.

8. $R = \{(a, b) : a < b\} \subseteq \{1, 2, 3, 4\} \times \{1, 2, 3, 4\}$.

9. Find the incidence matrix of the graph:

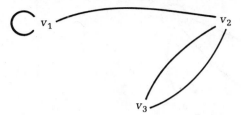

10. Find the incidence matrix of the graph:

11. Find the edge matrix of the graph:

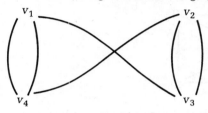

12. Find the edge matrix of the graph:

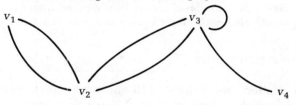

13. Draw a graph (undirected edges) with edge matrix:

$$\begin{pmatrix} 1 & 0 & 2 \\ 0 & 0 & 1 \\ 2 & 1 & 1 \end{pmatrix}$$

14. Find the edge matrix of the directed graph:

15. Find the edge matrix of the directed graph:

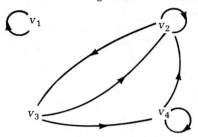

16. Draw a directed graph whose edge matrix is:

$$\begin{pmatrix} 1 & 2 \\ 0 & 1 \end{pmatrix}$$

17. The graph below is the graph of a tournament (see Section 6.5).

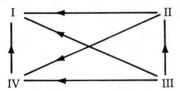

(a) Write the edge matrix corresponding to this graph.
(b) A player's score in a tournament is the number of players he or she beats. How can each player's score be computed from the matrix of the tournament? Find each player's score in the tournament above.

10.2 Matrix Arithmetic

In this section, we define addition, subtraction, and multiplication of matrices, and show how systems of linear equations correspond to a single matrix equation. Matrix arithmetic is used in the next section to model changes in certain types of situations called Markov chains and in Section 10.6 to model the relationship between input and output in an economy or large corporation.

MATRIX ADDITION AND SUBTRACTION

Suppose the matrices:

$$\begin{array}{cc} & S \qquad T \\ \begin{array}{c} A \\ B \end{array} & \begin{pmatrix} 100 & 200 \\ 150 & 75 \end{pmatrix} \end{array} \quad \text{and} \quad \begin{array}{cc} & S \qquad T \\ \begin{array}{c} A \\ B \end{array} & \begin{pmatrix} 250 & 100 \\ 100 & 93 \end{pmatrix} \end{array}$$

first week   second week

represent the number of units shipped from two factories, A and B, to two terminals, S and T, during each of two weeks. We get a matrix representing the total number of units shipped during the two-week period by adding the corresponding entries in the matrices.

$$\begin{pmatrix} 100 & 200 \\ 150 & 75 \end{pmatrix} + \begin{pmatrix} 250 & 100 \\ 100 & 93 \end{pmatrix} = \begin{pmatrix} 100 + 250 & 200 + 100 \\ 150 + 100 & 75 + 93 \end{pmatrix} = \begin{pmatrix} 350 & 300 \\ 250 & 168 \end{pmatrix}$$

first week   second week   total

> **DEFINITION** The **sum** (difference) of two matrices A and B of the same size is the matrix whose entries are the sums (differences) of the corresponding entries in A and B.
>
> $$(A + B)_{i,j} = A_{i,j} + B_{i,j}$$
>
> and
>
> $$(A - B)_{i,j} = A_{i,j} - B_{i,j}$$
>
> If A and B are not the same size, then $A + B$ and $A - B$ are not defined.

EXAMPLE 1

(a) $\begin{pmatrix} 1 & 3 & -1 \\ 2 & 4 & 5 \end{pmatrix} + \begin{pmatrix} 6 & 1 & 3 \\ 7 & 3 & 2 \end{pmatrix} = \begin{pmatrix} 1 + 6 & 3 + 1 & -1 + 3 \\ 2 + 7 & 4 + 3 & 5 + 2 \end{pmatrix} = \begin{pmatrix} 7 & 4 & 2 \\ 9 & 7 & 7 \end{pmatrix}$

(b) $\begin{pmatrix} -2 & 8 \\ 7 & 2 \\ -1 & 8 \end{pmatrix} + \begin{pmatrix} 7 & 9 \\ -3 & 0 \\ 8 & -5 \end{pmatrix} = \begin{pmatrix} -2 + 7 & 8 + 9 \\ 7 + (-3) & 2 + 0 \\ -1 + 8 & 8 + (-5) \end{pmatrix} = \begin{pmatrix} 5 & 17 \\ 4 & 2 \\ 7 & 3 \end{pmatrix}$

(c) $\begin{pmatrix} 1 & 3 & -1 \\ 2 & 4 & 5 \end{pmatrix} - \begin{pmatrix} 6 & 1 & 3 \\ 7 & 3 & 2 \end{pmatrix} = \begin{pmatrix} 1 - 6 & 3 - 1 & -1 - 3 \\ 2 - 7 & 4 - 3 & 5 - 2 \end{pmatrix} = \begin{pmatrix} -5 & 2 & -4 \\ -5 & 1 & 3 \end{pmatrix}$

PRACTICE EXAMPLE 1

Find:

(a) $\begin{pmatrix} 1 & 2 \\ 3 & 7 \end{pmatrix} + \begin{pmatrix} 1 & 7 \\ 3 & 2 \end{pmatrix}$

(b) $\begin{pmatrix} 0 & 5 & 1 \\ 8 & 0 & 3 \end{pmatrix} - \begin{pmatrix} 1 & 3 & 0 \\ 4 & 0 & 2 \end{pmatrix}$

(c) $\begin{pmatrix} 1 \\ 3 \end{pmatrix} + \begin{pmatrix} 2 \\ 5 \end{pmatrix}$

(d) $(1 \quad 3 \quad 7) - (1 \quad 2 \quad 3)$

(e) $(7) + (5)$

(f) $(6) - (2)$

PROPERTIES OF ADDITION AND SUBTRACTION

Matrix addition and subtraction have the following properties in common with addition and subtraction of numbers.

1. $A + B = B + A$

2. $(A + B) + C = A + (B + C)$

3. $A + 0 = A$

4. $A - A = 0$

where 0 denotes a matrix all of whose entries are the number zero.

The following example illustrates properties 1 through 4.

EXAMPLE 2   For:

$$A = \begin{pmatrix} 1 & 2 \\ -3 & 4 \end{pmatrix}, \qquad B = \begin{pmatrix} 0 & 3 \\ 5 & -2 \end{pmatrix}, \qquad C = \begin{pmatrix} -1 & 5 \\ 2 & 3 \end{pmatrix}$$

find:

1. (a) $A + B$ 2. (a) $(A + B) + C$ 3. $A + 0$ 4. $A - A$

   (b) $B + A$ (b) $A + (B + C)$

1. (a) $A + B = \begin{pmatrix} 1 & 2 \\ -3 & 4 \end{pmatrix} + \begin{pmatrix} 0 & 3 \\ 5 & -2 \end{pmatrix}$

$$= \begin{pmatrix} 1 + 0 & 2 + 3 \\ -3 + 5 & 4 + (-2) \end{pmatrix} = \begin{pmatrix} 1 & 5 \\ 2 & 2 \end{pmatrix}$$

   (b) $B + A = \begin{pmatrix} 0 & 3 \\ 5 & -2 \end{pmatrix} + \begin{pmatrix} 1 & 2 \\ -3 & 4 \end{pmatrix}$

$$= \begin{pmatrix} 0 + 1 & 3 + 2 \\ 5 + (-3) & -2 + 4 \end{pmatrix} = \begin{pmatrix} 1 & 5 \\ 2 & 2 \end{pmatrix}$$

Note: $A + B = B + A$.

2. (a) The parentheses enclosing $A + B$ in the expression $(A + B) + C$ indicate the expression is to be calculated by first finding $A + B$ and then adding C to it.

$$A + B = \begin{pmatrix} 1 & 5 \\ 2 & 2 \end{pmatrix}$$

$$(A + B) + C = \begin{pmatrix} 1 & 5 \\ 2 & 2 \end{pmatrix} + \begin{pmatrix} -1 & 5 \\ 2 & 3 \end{pmatrix} = \begin{pmatrix} 0 & 10 \\ 4 & 5 \end{pmatrix}$$

(b) $A + (B + C)$ is computed by first finding $B + C$ and then adding A.

$$B + C = \begin{pmatrix} 0 & 3 \\ 5 & -2 \end{pmatrix} + \begin{pmatrix} -1 & 5 \\ 2 & 3 \end{pmatrix} = \begin{pmatrix} -1 & 8 \\ 7 & 1 \end{pmatrix}$$

$$A + (B + C) = \begin{pmatrix} 1 & 2 \\ -3 & 4 \end{pmatrix} + \begin{pmatrix} -1 & 8 \\ 7 & 1 \end{pmatrix} = \begin{pmatrix} 0 & 10 \\ 4 & 5 \end{pmatrix}$$

Note: $(A + B) + C = A + (B + C)$.

3. $A + 0 = \begin{pmatrix} 1 & 2 \\ -3 & 4 \end{pmatrix} + \begin{pmatrix} 0 & 0 \\ 0 & 0 \end{pmatrix} = \begin{pmatrix} 1 & 2 \\ -3 & 4 \end{pmatrix}$. So $A + 0 = A$.

4. $A - A = \begin{pmatrix} 1 & 2 \\ -3 & 4 \end{pmatrix} - \begin{pmatrix} 1 & 2 \\ -3 & 4 \end{pmatrix}$

$$= \begin{pmatrix} 1 - 1 & 2 - 2 \\ -3 - (-3) & 4 - 4 \end{pmatrix} = \begin{pmatrix} 0 & 0 \\ 0 & 0 \end{pmatrix}. \text{ So } A - A = 0.$$

■

MATRIX MULTIPLICATION

The product of a row and column is a matrix with one entry. In **matrix multiplication**, the matrix product: (row) $\times$ (column), is computed by multiplying each entry in the row matrix times the corresponding entry in the column matrix and then adding all the products. In general, the entries in the product, AB, of matrices A and B are given by the products; (a row of A) $\times$ (a column of B). An example will illustrate the definition of the product: (row) $\times$ (column).

EXAMPLE 3

A factory has three production lines: I, II, and III. Line I produces 50 items per hour, II produces 40 items per hour, and III produces 60 items per hour. Find the total production for the week if I runs for 30 hours during the week, II runs for 20 hours, and III runs for 40 hours.

Figure 10.7

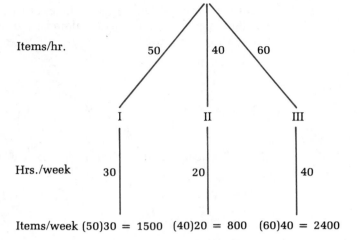

Items/hr. 50 40 60

I II III

Hrs./week 30 20 40

Items/week (50)30 = 1500 (40)20 = 800 (60)40 = 2400

The total production can be computed from the tree in Figure 10.7. The numbers along the bottom give the output of each production line. Thus, the total production is 1500 + 800 + 2400 = 4700 items. If the hourly production is written as a row matrix, and a column matrix is used to represent the number of hours each line runs during the week, then the matrix product: (row) × (column) is:

$$\begin{matrix} \text{I} & \text{II} & \text{III} \\ (50 & 40 & 60) \end{matrix} \quad \begin{matrix} \text{I} \\ \text{II} \\ \text{III} \end{matrix} \begin{pmatrix} 30 \\ 20 \\ 40 \end{pmatrix} = (50)30 + (40)20 + (60)40 = 4700$$

and hence represents the total production.

The computation above can arise in a variety of situations. If the row represents the number of each of three items: I, II, and III, sold, and the column represents the cost per item, then the product: (row) × (column), is the total revenue. If the row represents the number of units shipped from a factory to each of three stores: I, II, and III, and the column represents shipping cost per item, then the product, (row) × (column), represents the total shipping cost. ■

DEFINITION For:
$$A = (a_1, a_2, \ldots, a_n) \quad \text{and} \quad B = \begin{pmatrix} b_1 \\ b_2 \\ . \\ . \\ . \\ b_n \end{pmatrix}$$

the **product** AB is the 1-by-1 matrix with entry:

$$a_1b_1 + a_2b_2 + \cdots + a_nb_n$$

The product: (row) $\times$ (column), is not defined unless the number of entries in the row is the same as the number of entries in the column.

EXAMPLE 4

(a) $(1 \quad 5) \begin{pmatrix} -2 \\ 3 \end{pmatrix} = [1(-2) + 5(3)] = [-2 + 15] = [13]$

(b) $(4 \quad 1 \quad 7) \begin{pmatrix} 2 \\ 0 \\ 3 \end{pmatrix} = [4(2) + 1(0) + 7(3)] = [8 + 0 + 21] = [29]$

(c) $(2 \quad 6 \quad -4 \quad 5) \begin{pmatrix} 2 \\ -1 \\ 3 \\ 7 \end{pmatrix} = [2(2) + 6(-1) + (-4)(3) + 5(7)]$

$$= [4 - 6 - 12 + 35] = [21]$$

(d) $(1 \quad 3 \quad 2) \begin{pmatrix} 8 \\ 5 \\ -4 \end{pmatrix} = [1(8) + 3(5) + 2(-4)] = [15]$

PRACTICE
EXAMPLE 2

Find:

(a) $(1 \quad 2) \begin{pmatrix} 3 \\ 1 \end{pmatrix}$

(d) $(1 \quad 0 \quad 1) \begin{pmatrix} 2 \\ 3 \\ 4 \end{pmatrix}$

(b) $(2 \quad -1) \begin{pmatrix} 3 \\ 4 \end{pmatrix}$

(e) $(1 \quad 3 \quad 5 \quad 2) \begin{pmatrix} 4 \\ 1 \\ -2 \\ 3 \end{pmatrix}$

(c) $(1 \quad 3 \quad 5) \begin{pmatrix} 2 \\ -1 \\ 0 \end{pmatrix}$

Note: in the special case $A = (a_1)$, $B = (b_1)$, the entry in the product AB is the usual product $a_1 b_1$ of the numbers a_1 and b_1. For example if $A = (3)$ and $B = (5)$ then $AB = (15)$. ■

EXAMPLE 5

Recall from Section 5.4 that the expected value, $E(X)$, is computed by multiplying each of the possible values of X times the probability that that value occurs and then adding the products. For example, if the random variable has value 5 with probability .1, value -2 with probability .2 and value 11 with probability .7, then $E(X) = 5(.1) + (-2)(.2) + 11(.7) = 7.8$. If R is the row matrix listing the possible values of X, $R = (5 \quad -2 \quad 11)$, and C is the column matrix that lists the corresponding probabilities of these values,

$$C = \begin{pmatrix} .1 \\ .2 \\ .7 \end{pmatrix}$$

then the entry in the product RC is $E(X)$, the expected value of X.

$$RC = (5 \quad -2 \quad 11) \begin{pmatrix} .1 \\ .2 \\ .7 \end{pmatrix} = (7.8) = (E(X))$$

■

In general, the entries in the product, AB, of matrices A and B are given by the products of the rows of A with the columns of B. The (i, j)-entry of AB is given by the product of the ith row of A with the jth column of B.

EXAMPLE 6

A company has two factories, each with three production lines: I, II, and III. The matrix below represents the hourly production of the lines.

$$\begin{array}{ccccc} & & \text{I} & \text{II} & \text{III} \\ \text{Factories} & 1 & \begin{pmatrix} 50 & 40 & 60 \\ 30 & 50 & 55 \end{pmatrix} \\ & 2 & \end{array}$$

The following matrix represents the number of hours per week each line is run during a two-week period.

$$\begin{array}{ccc} & \text{Week} & \\ & 1 & 2 \\ \text{I} & \begin{pmatrix} 30 & 40 \\ 20 & 10 \\ 40 & 30 \end{pmatrix} \\ \text{II} & \\ \text{III} & \end{array}$$

As in Example 3, the product: (row of A) $\times$ (column of B), represents the output of one of the factories during one of the weeks. The company's production is represented by the matrix whose (i, j) entry is given by the product of the ith row of A with the jth column of B.

$$\begin{pmatrix} 50 & 40 & 60 \\ 30 & 50 & 55 \end{pmatrix} \begin{pmatrix} 30 & 40 \\ 20 & 10 \\ 40 & 30 \end{pmatrix}$$

$$= \left(\begin{array}{c|c} (50)30 + (40)20 + (60)40 & (50)40 + (40)10 + (60)30 \\ \hline (30)30 + (50)20 + (55)40 & (30)40 + (50)10 + (55)30 \end{array} \right)$$

$$= \text{Factory} \begin{array}{cc} & \text{Week} \\ & \begin{array}{cc} 1 & 2 \end{array} \\ \begin{array}{c} 1 \\ 2 \end{array} & \begin{pmatrix} 4700 & 4200 \\ 4100 & 3350 \end{pmatrix} \end{array}$$

■

> **DEFINITION**   If A is a p-by-q matrix and B is an r-by-s matrix and $q = r$, then the **product matrix**, AB, is the p-by-s matrix whose (i, j) entry is determined by multiplying $R_i(A)$ by $C_j(B)$.
>   The product AB is defined only when the number of entries in each row of A equals the number of entries in each column of B.

The number of rows in AB is the number of rows in A, and the number of columns of AB is the number of columns in B. For example, if A is a 2-by-3 matrix and B is a 3-by-5 matrix, then AB is a 2-by-5 matrix.

$$\begin{array}{cc} (2 \text{ by } 3) & (3 \text{ by } 5) \\ \underbrace{\hspace{3cm}} \\ AB \text{ defined} \\ \underbrace{\hspace{5cm}}_{\text{size of } AB} \end{array}$$

EXAMPLE 7

1. Tell whether each product is defined. If so what is the size of the product?

   (a) $(1 \quad 2) \begin{pmatrix} 2 & -1 \\ 4 & 3 \end{pmatrix}$

   (c) $\begin{pmatrix} 1 & 3 & -1 \\ 2 & 0 & 5 \end{pmatrix} \begin{pmatrix} 5 & 3 & 2 \\ -1 & 1 & 3 \\ 2 & 0 & 7 \end{pmatrix}$

   (b) $(1 \quad 3 \quad -1) \begin{pmatrix} 5 & 3 & 2 \\ -1 & 1 & 3 \\ 2 & 0 & 7 \end{pmatrix}$

   (d) $\begin{pmatrix} 1 & 3 & -1 \\ 2 & 0 & 5 \end{pmatrix} \begin{pmatrix} 5 & 3 & 2 \\ -1 & 1 & 3 \end{pmatrix}$

2. Compute each of the products in (1) that is defined.

Solutions

1. (a) The product: (1-by-2 matrix) × (2-by-2 matrix) is defined and has size 1 by 2.
   (b) The product: (1-by-3 matrix) × (3-by-3 matrix) is defined and has size 1 by 3.
   (c) The product: (2-by-3 matrix) × (3-by-3 matrix) is defined and has size 2 by 3.
   (d) The product: (2-by-3 matrix) × (2-by-3 matrix) is not defined.

2. (a) For:

$$A = (1 \quad 2) \quad \text{and} \quad B = \begin{pmatrix} 2 & -1 \\ 3 & 4 \end{pmatrix}$$

$$(AB)_{1,1} = \text{(first row of } A) \times \text{(first column of } B)$$

$$= (1 \quad 2) \begin{pmatrix} 2 \\ 4 \end{pmatrix} = 2 + 8 = 10$$

$$(AB)_{1,2} = \text{(first row of } A) \times \text{(second column of } B)$$

$$= (1 \quad 2) \begin{pmatrix} -1 \\ 3 \end{pmatrix} = 5$$

so

$$AB = (10 \quad 5)$$

(b) $$(1 \quad 3 \quad -1) \begin{pmatrix} 5 & 3 & 2 \\ -1 & 1 & 3 \\ 2 & 0 & 7 \end{pmatrix} = (0 \quad 6 \quad 4)$$

since

$$(1 \quad 3 \quad -1) \begin{pmatrix} 5 \\ -1 \\ 2 \end{pmatrix} = 5 - 3 - 2 = 0;$$

$$(1 \quad 3 \quad -1) \begin{pmatrix} 3 \\ 1 \\ 0 \end{pmatrix} = 3 + 3 = 6;$$

$$(1 \quad 3 \quad -1) \begin{pmatrix} 2 \\ 3 \\ 7 \end{pmatrix} = 4$$

(c)
$$\begin{pmatrix} 1 & 3 & -1 \\ 2 & 0 & 5 \end{pmatrix} \begin{pmatrix} 5 & 3 & 2 \\ -1 & 1 & 3 \\ 2 & 0 & 7 \end{pmatrix}$$

$$= \left(\begin{array}{c|c|c} (1)5 + 3(-1) + (-1)2 & (1)3 + (3)1 + (-1)0 & (1)2 + (3)3 + (-1)7 \\ \hline (2)5 + 0(-1) + \quad (5)2 & (2)3 + 0(1) + \quad (5)0 & (2)2 + (0)3 + \quad (5)7 \end{array} \right)$$

$$= \begin{pmatrix} 0 & 6 & 4 \\ 20 & 6 & 39 \end{pmatrix}$$ ∎

The product AB can be found as follows: compute the product of the first row of A with each column of B. The result is the first row of AB. Next compute the product of the second row of A with each column of B. This gives the second row of AB. Continue until all rows of A have been used.

PRACTICE EXAMPLE 3 Which of the products below is defined? Compute the products that are defined.

(a) $\begin{pmatrix} 1 & 2 & 3 \\ 0 & 1 & 2 \end{pmatrix} \begin{pmatrix} 1 & 3 & 0 \\ 2 & 1 & 5 \end{pmatrix}$

(d) $\begin{pmatrix} 1 & 0 \\ 0 & 1 \end{pmatrix} \begin{pmatrix} 1 & 2 \\ 5 & 7 \end{pmatrix}$

(b) $\begin{pmatrix} 1 & 2 & 3 \\ 0 & 1 & 2 \\ 0 & 2 & -1 \end{pmatrix} \begin{pmatrix} 1 & 3 & 0 & 1 \\ 2 & 1 & 5 & 0 \\ 0 & 2 & -1 & 3 \end{pmatrix}$

(e) $\begin{pmatrix} 1 & 2 & 5 \\ 3 & 1 & 2 \\ 4 & 1 & 6 \\ 6 & 2 & 7 \end{pmatrix} \begin{pmatrix} 1 & 0 & 0 \\ 0 & 1 & 0 \\ 0 & 0 & 1 \end{pmatrix}$

(c) $\begin{pmatrix} 1 & 2 \\ 0 & 1 \\ -1 & 4 \end{pmatrix} \begin{pmatrix} 1 \\ 2 \end{pmatrix}$

(f) $\begin{pmatrix} 5 & 3 \\ 2 & 7 \end{pmatrix} \begin{pmatrix} 1 & 0 \\ 0 & 1 \end{pmatrix}$ ∎

EXAMPLE 8 The following matrices:

	Reg.	Unleaded	Super Unleaded
Mon.	260	320	180
$A =$ Tue.	220	300	170
Wed.	250	310	200

Gallons sold

		Revenue/gal.	Profit/gal.
	Reg.	1.05	.10
$B =$	U	1.10	.12
	S-U	1.15	.14

give the sales, selling price, and profit information for a local gas station on the Monday, Tuesday, and Wednesday of a particular week. For example, the (2, 1) entry, 220, in matrix A indicates that on Tuesday the station sold 220 gallons of regular gas. The entries in the third row of B indicate the station charges \$1.15 for a gallon of super unleaded gas and makes a profit of \$.14 on each gallon of super unleaded it sells.

Find the product, AB, and interpret the entries.

$$AB = \begin{pmatrix} 260(1.05) + 320(1.10) + 180(1.15) & 260(.10) + 320(.12) + 180(.14) \\ 220(1.05) + 300(1.10) + 170(1.15) & 220(.10) + 300(.12) + 170(.14) \\ 250(1.05) + 310(1.10) + 200(1.15) & 250(.10) + 310(.12) + 200(.14) \end{pmatrix}$$

$$\begin{array}{c} \\ \text{Mon.} \\ \text{Tue.} \\ \text{Wed.} \end{array} \begin{matrix} \text{Revenue} & \text{Profit} \\ \begin{pmatrix} 832 & 89.60 \\ 756.50 & 81.80 \\ 833.50 & 90.20 \end{pmatrix} \end{matrix}$$

The first column of AB lists the total revenue from selling gas for each of the three days. The second column of AB lists the profit from the sale of gas for each of the days.

Note that when doing applied problems, in order to multiply a matrix A times a matrix B, not only must the number of columns of A equal the number of rows of B, but also the labels of the columns of A must be the same as the labels of the rows of B. In this example, these labels are the types of gasoline. ∎

Matrices with the same number of rows as columns are called **square matrices**. The square matrices:

(1)
$$\begin{pmatrix} 1 & 0 \\ 0 & 1 \end{pmatrix} \qquad \begin{pmatrix} 1 & 0 & 0 \\ 0 & 1 & 0 \\ 0 & 0 & 1 \end{pmatrix} \qquad \begin{pmatrix} 1 & 0 & 0 & 0 \\ 0 & 1 & 0 & 0 \\ 0 & 0 & 1 & 0 \\ 0 & 0 & 0 & 1 \end{pmatrix}$$

etc. are called **identity matrices**. A square matrix is an identity matrix if each of the entries $A_{i,i}$ is equal to one and the entries $A_{i,j}$ are zero when $i \neq j$. Identity matrices play a role in matrix arithmetic that is similar to that of the number one in ordinary arithmetic. For example, if I is an identity matrix then $AI = A$ and $IB = B$ as you saw in parts (d), (e), and (f) of Practice Example 3.

PROPERTIES OF MULTIPLICATION AND ADDITION

Matrix multiplication and addition have the following properties in common with multiplication and addition of numbers.

1. $(AB)C = A(BC)$

2. $A(B + C) = AB + AC$

3. $(A + B)C = AC + BC$

4. $A0 = 0$

5. $0B = 0$

6. $AI = A$

7. $IB = B$

where I denotes an identity matrix and 0 denotes a matrix all of whose entries are the number zero.

For numbers a and b the product ab is the same as the product ba (5×2 is the same as 2×5). For matrices A and B the product AB is, in general, *not* the same as the product BA (see Exercises 16, 17, 18, and 19).

Next we show how a **system of linear equations corresponds to a matrix equation**. This correspondence is used in Section 10.6 to solve systems of linear equations and study input-output models. If for a product: (row) $\times$ (column), the entries in the row are constants and the entries in the column are variables, then the product has the form $a_1 x_1 + \cdots + a_n x_n$. For example:

$$(1 \quad 3 \quad 5) \begin{pmatrix} x_1 \\ x_2 \\ x_3 \end{pmatrix} = (x_1 + 3x_2 + 5x_3)$$

The matrix equation:

$$(1 \quad 3 \quad 5) \begin{pmatrix} x_1 \\ x_2 \\ x_3 \end{pmatrix} = (7)$$

corresponds to the linear equation $x_1 + 3x_2 + 5x_3 = 7$. Adding a row on the left and on the far right corresponds to adding a new equation in the variables, x_1, x_2, x_3. For example:

$$\begin{pmatrix} 1 & 3 & 5 \\ 2 & 1 & 7 \end{pmatrix} \begin{pmatrix} x_1 \\ x_2 \\ x_3 \end{pmatrix} = \begin{pmatrix} 7 \\ 6 \end{pmatrix}$$

corresponds to the system:

$$x_1 + 3x_2 + 5x_3 = 7$$

$$2x_1 + x_2 + 7x_3 = 6$$

In general, if A is a matrix of constants, X is a column of variables, and b is a column of constants, then the matrix equation, $AX = b$, corresponds to a system of linear equations. The number of equations must be the number of rows of A, and the number of variables must be the number of columns of A. A is called the **coefficient matrix** of the system of equations.

EXAMPLE 9   For each matrix equation find the corresponding system of linear equations.

(a) $\begin{pmatrix} 2 & 13 \\ 1 & 7 \end{pmatrix} \begin{pmatrix} x_1 \\ x_2 \end{pmatrix} = \begin{pmatrix} 5 \\ 11 \end{pmatrix}$

(b) $\begin{pmatrix} 2 & 1 & 7 \\ 3 & 2 & 4 \\ 5 & -1 & 6 \end{pmatrix} \begin{pmatrix} x_1 \\ x_2 \\ x_3 \end{pmatrix} = \begin{pmatrix} 8 \\ 9 \\ -4 \end{pmatrix}$

(a)

$$\begin{pmatrix} 2 & 13 \\ 1 & 7 \end{pmatrix} \begin{pmatrix} x_1 \\ x_2 \end{pmatrix} = \begin{pmatrix} 2x_1 + 13x_2 \\ x_1 + 7x_2 \end{pmatrix}$$

Replacing

$$\begin{pmatrix} 2 & 13 \\ 1 & 7 \end{pmatrix} \begin{pmatrix} x_1 \\ x_2 \end{pmatrix} \quad \text{with} \quad \begin{pmatrix} 2x_1 + 13x_2 \\ x_1 + 7x_2 \end{pmatrix}$$

gives

$$\begin{pmatrix} 2x_1 + 13x_2 \\ x_1 + 7x_2 \end{pmatrix} = \begin{pmatrix} 5 \\ 11 \end{pmatrix}$$

which is the same as the system of equations:

$$2x_1 + 13x_2 = 5$$

$$x_1 + 7x_2 = 11$$

(b) By the same procedure the matrix equation

$$\begin{pmatrix} 2 & 1 & 7 \\ 3 & 2 & 4 \\ 5 & -1 & 6 \end{pmatrix} \begin{pmatrix} x_1 \\ x_2 \\ x_3 \end{pmatrix} = \begin{pmatrix} 8 \\ 9 \\ -4 \end{pmatrix}$$

corresponds to the system of equations:

$$2x_1 + x_2 + 7x_3 = 8$$
$$3x_1 + 2x_2 + 4x_3 = 9$$
$$5x_1 - x_2 + 6x_3 = -4$$

■

PRACTICE EXAMPLE 4

(a) Find the system of equations corresponding to the matrix equation:

$$\begin{pmatrix} 2 & 3 \\ 5 & 7 \end{pmatrix} \begin{pmatrix} x_1 \\ x_2 \end{pmatrix} = \begin{pmatrix} 4 \\ 6 \end{pmatrix}$$

(b) Find the matrix equation corresponding to the given system of equations. What is the coefficient matrix of this system of equations?

$$3x_1 + 7x_2 = 5$$
$$2x_1 + 6x_2 = 7$$

■

In this section, we defined matrix addition, subtraction, and multiplication and showed that systems of linear equations correspond to a single matrix equation. In the next section, we use matrix multiplication to model changes in a system over time.

CONCEPTS

matrix addition and subtraction
matrix multiplication
square matrices
identity matrices
a system of linear equations corresponds to a matrix equation

SOLUTIONS TO PRACTICE EXAMPLES

1. (a) $\begin{pmatrix} 2 & 9 \\ 6 & 9 \end{pmatrix}$ (d) $(0 \quad 1 \quad 4)$

   (b) $\begin{pmatrix} -1 & 2 & 1 \\ 4 & 0 & 1 \end{pmatrix}$ (e) (12)

   (c) $\begin{pmatrix} 3 \\ 8 \end{pmatrix}$ (f) (4)

2. (a) $(1(3) + 2(1)) = (5)$ (d) (6)

   (b) (2) (e) $(4 + 3 - 10 + 6) = (3)$

   (c) (-1)

3. (a) The product is not defined. (d) $\begin{pmatrix} 1 & 2 \\ 5 & 7 \end{pmatrix}$

(b) $\begin{pmatrix} 5 & 11 & 7 & 10 \\ 2 & 5 & 3 & 6 \\ 4 & 0 & 11 & -3 \end{pmatrix}$ (e) $\begin{pmatrix} 1 & 2 & 5 \\ 3 & 1 & 2 \\ 4 & 1 & 6 \\ 6 & 2 & 7 \end{pmatrix}$

(c) $\begin{pmatrix} 5 \\ 2 \\ 7 \end{pmatrix}$ (f) $\begin{pmatrix} 5 & 3 \\ 2 & 7 \end{pmatrix}$

4. (a) $2x_1 + 3x_2 = 4$
       $5x_1 + 7x_2 = 6$

   (b) The matrix equation is: $\begin{pmatrix} 3 & 7 \\ 2 & 6 \end{pmatrix}\begin{pmatrix} x_1 \\ x_2 \end{pmatrix} = \begin{pmatrix} 5 \\ 7 \end{pmatrix}$

   The coefficient matrix is: $\begin{pmatrix} 3 & 7 \\ 2 & 6 \end{pmatrix}$

EXERCISES 10.2

In Exercises 1 through 6 find the indicated sum or difference.

1. $\begin{pmatrix} 1 & 2 \\ -1 & 4 \end{pmatrix} + \begin{pmatrix} 5 & 1 \\ 3 & 7 \end{pmatrix}$ 2. $(1 \quad 5 \quad -1) - (1 \quad -2 \quad 0)$

3. $\begin{pmatrix} 0 \\ 1 \\ -10 \end{pmatrix} + \begin{pmatrix} 12 \\ 1 \\ 3 \end{pmatrix}$ 4. $\begin{pmatrix} 1 & 2 & 7 \\ -1 & 0 & 2 \end{pmatrix} + \begin{pmatrix} 3 & 0 & 1 \\ 2 & 1 & 0 \end{pmatrix}$

5. $\begin{pmatrix} 1 & 2 \\ -1 & 3 \\ 0 & 4 \end{pmatrix} - \begin{pmatrix} 1 & 1 \\ 0 & 2 \\ 1 & 3 \end{pmatrix}$ 6. $\begin{pmatrix} 1 & 3 & 5 \\ 2 & 4 & 6 \end{pmatrix} - \begin{pmatrix} 5 & 2 & 3 \\ 1 & 2 & 1 \end{pmatrix}$

In Exercises 7 through 25 find the product

7. $(1 \quad 2)\begin{pmatrix} 3 \\ 5 \end{pmatrix}$ 8. $(2 \quad 3)\begin{pmatrix} -1 \\ 5 \end{pmatrix}$ 9. $(1 \quad 2 \quad 3)\begin{pmatrix} 5 \\ 1 \\ 6 \end{pmatrix}$

10. $(1 \quad 0 \quad -1) \begin{pmatrix} 7 \\ 10 \\ 5 \end{pmatrix}$

11. $(1 \quad 2 \quad 5 \quad -3) \begin{pmatrix} 7 \\ 8 \\ -4 \\ -1 \end{pmatrix}$

12. $\begin{pmatrix} 1 & 2 \\ 2 & 3 \end{pmatrix} \begin{pmatrix} 3 & -1 \\ 5 & 5 \end{pmatrix}$

13. $\begin{pmatrix} 1 & 2 \\ 2 & 3 \end{pmatrix} \begin{pmatrix} 1 \\ 1 \end{pmatrix}$

14. $\begin{pmatrix} 4 & 1 & 7 \\ -1 & 2 & 5 \\ 3 & 0 & 1 \end{pmatrix} \begin{pmatrix} 5 \\ 1 \\ -1 \end{pmatrix}$

15. $\begin{pmatrix} 1 \\ 2 \end{pmatrix} (3 \quad 4)$

16. $\begin{pmatrix} 1 & 2 \\ 3 & 4 \end{pmatrix} \begin{pmatrix} 2 & -3 \\ 5 & 6 \end{pmatrix}$

17. $\begin{pmatrix} 2 & -3 \\ 5 & 6 \end{pmatrix} \begin{pmatrix} 1 & 2 \\ 3 & 4 \end{pmatrix}$

18. $\begin{pmatrix} 2 & 3 \\ 6 & 9 \end{pmatrix} \begin{pmatrix} 3 & -6 \\ -2 & 4 \end{pmatrix}$

19. $\begin{pmatrix} 3 & -6 \\ -2 & 4 \end{pmatrix} \begin{pmatrix} 2 & 3 \\ 6 & 9 \end{pmatrix}$

20. $\begin{pmatrix} 3 & -6 \\ 7 & 9 \end{pmatrix} \begin{pmatrix} 1 & 0 \\ 0 & 1 \end{pmatrix}$

21. $\begin{pmatrix} 1 & 0 \\ 0 & 1 \end{pmatrix} \begin{pmatrix} 3 & -6 \\ 7 & 9 \end{pmatrix}$

22. $\begin{pmatrix} 1 & 0 & 0 \\ 0 & 1 & 0 \\ 0 & 0 & 1 \end{pmatrix} \begin{pmatrix} 7 \\ 8 \\ 9 \end{pmatrix}$

23. $(5 \quad -1 \quad 2) \begin{pmatrix} 1 & 0 & 0 \\ 0 & 1 & 0 \\ 0 & 0 & 1 \end{pmatrix}$

24. $\begin{pmatrix} 2 & 5 \\ 1 & 3 \end{pmatrix} \begin{pmatrix} 3 & -5 \\ -1 & 2 \end{pmatrix}$

25. $\begin{pmatrix} 3 & -1 & -1 \\ -4 & 2 & 1 \\ -1 & 0 & 1 \end{pmatrix} \begin{pmatrix} 2 & 1 & 1 \\ 3 & 2 & 1 \\ 2 & 1 & 2 \end{pmatrix}$

In Exercises 26 through 30, find $A^2 = AA$

26. $A = \begin{pmatrix} -1 & 3 \\ 2 & 4 \end{pmatrix}$

27. $A = \begin{pmatrix} 0 & 1 \\ 1 & 0 \end{pmatrix}$

28. $A = \begin{pmatrix} 1 & 0 \\ 0 & 1 \end{pmatrix}$

29. $A = \begin{pmatrix} 1 & 1 \\ 1 & 1 \end{pmatrix}$

30. $A = \begin{pmatrix} 1 & 0 & 1 \\ 2 & 1 & 0 \\ 3 & 1 & 5 \end{pmatrix}$

In Exercises 31 through 34 find the system of linear equations corresponding to the given matrix equation.

31. $\begin{pmatrix} 1 & 2 \\ 4 & -3 \end{pmatrix} \begin{pmatrix} x_1 \\ x_2 \end{pmatrix} = \begin{pmatrix} 7 \\ 5 \end{pmatrix}$ 32. $\begin{pmatrix} 10 & -8 \\ 3 & 1 \end{pmatrix} \begin{pmatrix} x_1 \\ x_2 \end{pmatrix} = \begin{pmatrix} 0 \\ 0 \end{pmatrix}$

33. $\begin{pmatrix} 1 & 2 & -1 \\ 3 & 5 & -2 \end{pmatrix} \begin{pmatrix} x_1 \\ x_2 \\ x_3 \end{pmatrix} = \begin{pmatrix} 0 \\ 1 \end{pmatrix}$ 34. $\begin{pmatrix} 1 & 3 & 4 \\ 5 & 0 & 1 \\ 1 & 1 & 1 \end{pmatrix} \begin{pmatrix} x_1 \\ x_2 \\ x_3 \end{pmatrix} = \begin{pmatrix} 5 \\ 3 \\ -10 \end{pmatrix}$

In Exercises 35 through 38 find the matrix equation corresponding to the given system of linear equations. Find the coefficient matrix in each case.

35. $x_1 + x_2 = 4$ 36. $x_1 - x_2 = 5$ 37. $x_1 + x_2 - x_3 = 0$

 $2x_1 - 3x_2 = 11$ $2x_1 + 3x_2 = 7$ $2x_1 - x_2 + 3x_3 = 4$

 $3x_1 + x_2 - 5x_3 = 63$

38. $x_1 - x_2 + 4x_3 = 11$

 $2x_1 + 3x_2 - 5x_3 = 0$

39. A store buys 70 shirts from a warehouse at a cost of $5 each, 100 pairs of pants at $9 each, and 50 pairs of socks at $2 each. Write the store's purchase as a row matrix. List the costs per item in a column matrix and interpret the product of the row matrix with the column matrix.

40. The Cinema Center has four cinemas: I, II, III, and IV. The admission price is $2 for children, $3 for students, and $5 for adults. At a Sunday matinee cinema I had 225 children, 110 students, and 50 adults; cinema II had 75 children, 180 students, and 225 adults; cinema III had 280 children, 85 students, and 110 adults; cinema IV had no children, 250 students, and 225 adults. Display this information in matrix form and use matrix multiplication to find the amount of money taken in by each of the four cinemas.

41. Suppose we make the following assumptions about beetles. (See the article by H. Bernadelli in J. Burma Res. Soc. *31* 1941, 1–18.)

1. A beetle lives, at most, three years.

2. Beetles reproduce only in their third year.

3. Fifty percent of the beetles born in one year survive into the next year.

4. Of the beetles who survive into their second year, 70% survive into their third year.

5. On the average, four new beetles are produced for each beetle who survives into its third year.

Denote by a_k, b_k, and c_k the number of beetles of ages 1, 2, and 3 alive k years from now and set P_k equal to the population matrix $(a_k \quad b_k \quad c_k)$

(a) Find a matrix A with the property that $P_k A = P_{k+1}$
(b) Use the result in (a) to show that:

$$(a_{k+3} \quad b_{k+3} \quad c_{k+3}) = (1.4 a_k \quad 1.4 b_k \quad 1.4 c_k)$$

42. In the graph below, there is an edge from city a to city b if there is a nonstop flight from a to b.

   (a) Use a tree to find the number of one-stop flights from Chicago to each city. Represent the number of one-stop flights from Chicago in a row matrix.
   (b) Find the edge matrix, A, of the graph.
   (c) Compute the product $A^2 = AA$. (The first row of A^2 should be the row matrix in your answer to (a). In general, the (i, j)-entry in the square, A^2, of the edge matrix of a graph is the number of paths from the ith vertex to the jth vertex consisting of two edges.)

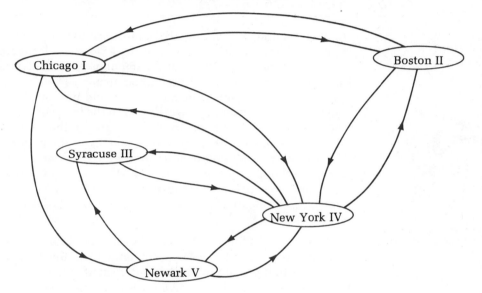

A relation, R, is called a dominance relation on a set $S = \{s_1, s_2, \ldots, s_n\}$ (of individuals) if:

1. $(s_i, s_i) \notin R$ for all i.

2. For each pair of different numbers, i and j, between 1 and n either (s_i, s_j) is in R or (s_j, s_i) is in R, but *not* both.

(Graphs of dominance relations were called tournaments in Section 6.5.)

   If (s_i, s_j) is in R, we say that individual s_i *dominates* s_j. If s_i dominates s_j and s_j dominates s_k, then we say there is a *two-stage* dominance of s_i over s_k.

   Finally, the *power* of s_i is defined to be the total number of one- and two-stage dominances that individual i can exert. Equivalently, the power of s_i is the sum of the entries in the ith row of the matrix $A + A^2$.

   The matrices A in Exercises 43 and 44 are the matrices of dominance relations. In each case find:

(a) A^2.

(b) $A + A^2$.

(c) the power of each individual.

43. $A = \begin{pmatrix} 0 & 1 & 1 \\ 0 & 0 & 1 \\ 0 & 0 & 0 \end{pmatrix}$

44. $A = \begin{pmatrix} 0 & 1 & 1 & 1 \\ 0 & 0 & 1 & 0 \\ 0 & 0 & 0 & 1 \\ 0 & 1 & 0 & 0 \end{pmatrix}$

10.3   Markov Chains—Transition Matrices

In this section, we use matrix multiplication to model the way certain systems change over time. Suppose, for example, a local grocery store, Ted's, recently started an advertising campaign to attract new customers and improved its service to help retain customers. The manager of Ted's would like to know how much the advertising and improved service will help the business over the next few weeks and in the long run. If we can assume that the week-to-week change in Ted's share of the market (the fraction of shoppers who shop at Ted's) depends only on the previous week's share of the market and not on the situation two weeks ago or even farther back in time, then this is an example of a **Markov chain**. After describing more situations that can be viewed as Markov chains we will show how to use matrix multiplication to answer the manager's question.

EXAMPLE 1   Commuters to Philadelphia can be divided into two groups: those who commute by car, and those who commute by public transportation. Suppose each year that 5% of the car commuters switch to public transportation (the remaining 95% of the car commuters continue to commute by car) and 10% of the commuters using public transportation switch to cars (the remaining 90% continue to use public transportation). ■

EXAMPLE 2   To see how well mice can learn, 300 mice are run repeatedly through the maze in Figure 10.8.

Figure 10.8

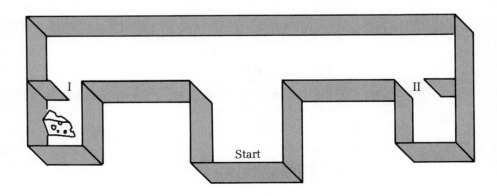

A mouse is placed at the start and then removed from the maze after entering either room I or room II. A mouse entering room I is rewarded with cheese. A mouse entering room II receives no reward. Suppose that when the experiment is run repeatedly, 80% of the mice that ended in room I the last time end in room I again and the remaining 20% end in room II. Of the mice that ended in room II last time, 60% end in room I the next time and 40% end in room II the next time.   ■

EXAMPLE 3   A taxi company in Chicago divides its territory into three regions: I = inner city, II = airport, III = suburbs. The table below gives the fractions (in decimal form) of the fares picked up in one region that are dropped in any other region:

		Dropped in region		
		I	II	III
Picked up in region	I	.80	.15	.05
	II	.90	.01	.09
	III	.15	.25	.60

■

In each of these examples one can ask: How does the situation change from one time to the next? For example, suppose that this year 80% of the commuters to Philadelphia commute by public transportation and 20% by car, then what fraction of the commuters will commute by public transportation one year from now, two years from now, and so on? The next example shows how the answer can be found by multiplying matrices.

EXAMPLE 4   Suppose in Example 1 that at the beginning of this year, 80% of the commuters commute by car and 20% commute by public transportation. Find the percentages of commuters who will commute by car and by public transportation at the beginning of next year.

The tree in Figure 10.9 displays the given information, where C stands for car and P for public transportation.

Figure 10.9

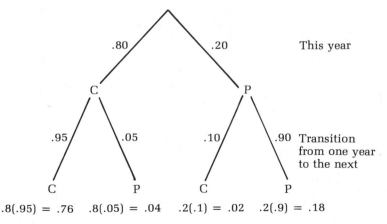

The product of the fraction of commuters who commute by car this year with the fraction of this year's commuters who commute by car again next year gives the fraction of commuters who commute by car both this year and next year. Thus,

.8(.95) = percentage of commuters who commute by car both this year and next year

.8(.05) = percentage of all commuters who commute by car at the beginning of this year and by public transportation at the beginning of next year

.2(.1) = percentage of commuters who commute by public transportation at the beginning of this year and by car at the beginning of next year

.2(.9) = percentage of all commuters who commute by public transportation at the beginning of this year and at the beginning of next year

The percentage, in decimal form, of commuters who commute by car at the beginning of next year is:

$$(.80)(.95) + (.20)(.10) = .76 + .02 = .78$$

The percentage of commuters who commute by public transportation at the beginning of next year is:

$$(.80)(.05) + (.20)(.90) = .4 + .18 = .22$$

Thus at the beginning of next year 78% of the commuters will commute by car and 22% will commute by public transportation. ∎

The numbers on the tree in Figure 10.9 are probabilities. For example .80 is the probability a commuter commutes by car this year, .05 is the conditional probability that a commuter commutes by public transportation next year given that he commutes by car this year. The interpretation of the numbers along the bottom row of Figure 10.9 follows from the general probability formula: $P(E \cap F) = P(F) P(E/F)$ given in Section 5.2. Thus .80(.05) is the probability a commuter commutes by car this year and by public transportation next year.

The sums of products can conveniently be written as the entries in the matrix product below:

$$\text{this year} \quad \begin{array}{cc} C & P \\ (.80 & .20) \end{array} \quad \begin{array}{c} C \\ P \end{array} \begin{pmatrix} C & P \\ .95 & .05 \\ .10 & .90 \end{pmatrix} = \begin{array}{cc} C & P \\ (.78 & .22) \end{array} \quad \text{next year}$$

year to year
transition

The matrix:

$$
\begin{array}{c@{\quad}c}
 & \begin{array}{cc} \text{C} & \text{P} \end{array} \\
\begin{array}{c} \text{C} \\ \text{P} \end{array} &
\left(\begin{array}{cc} .95 & .05 \\ .10 & .90 \end{array} \right)
\end{array}
$$

is called the **transition matrix** of the Markov chain. The matrices:

$$
\begin{array}{cc}
\begin{array}{cc} \text{C} & \text{P} \end{array} & \begin{array}{cc} \text{C} & \text{P} \end{array} \\
(.80 \quad .20) \quad \text{and} & (.78 \quad .22)
\end{array}
$$

are called **distribution matrices**. The distribution of commuters into those that commute by car and those that commute by public transportation at the beginning of this year is (.80 .20). The corresponding distribution at the beginning of next year is (.78 .22). More formal definitions of Markov chain, transition matrix, and distribution matrix are given later in this section.

Example 4 illustrates the general property that the product: (distribution matrix)(transition matrix) is the next distribution matrix.

EXAMPLE 5   Suppose that the first time the mice go through the maze in Example 2, half end in room I and half end in room II. What percentage of the mice end in room I and what percentage end in room II the second time the mice go through the maze?

The tree is:

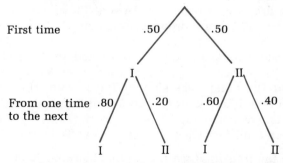

First time

From one time to the next

The numbers on the top edges are the entries in the first distribution matrix.

$$
\begin{array}{cc}
 & \begin{array}{cc} \text{I} & \text{II} \end{array} \\
\text{first time through the maze} \quad D(1) = & (.50 \quad .50)
\end{array}
$$

The numbers on the bottom edges are the entries in the transition matrix:

$$
\text{transition matrix} \qquad
\begin{array}{c@{\quad}c}
 & \begin{array}{cc} \text{I} & \text{II} \end{array} \\
\begin{array}{c} \text{I} \\ \text{II} \end{array} &
\left(\begin{array}{cc} .80 & .20 \\ .60 & .40 \end{array} \right)
\end{array}
$$

As we saw in Example 4, the product: (distribution matrix)(transition matrix), is the next distribution matrix so:

$$
\begin{array}{cc}
\text{I} & \text{II} \\
(.50 & .50)
\end{array}
\begin{pmatrix}
.80 & .20 \\
.60 & .40
\end{pmatrix}
=
\begin{array}{cc}
\text{I} & \text{II} \\
(.70 & .30)
\end{array}
$$

is the distribution matrix for the second trial of the experiment. The second time through the maze 70% of the mice end in room I and 30% end in room II.   ■

EXAMPLE 6

Suppose in Example 3 that 50% of the taxis drop their first fare of the day in region I, 40% drop their first fare in region II, and 10% drop their first fare in region III. For each of the three regions find the percentage of taxis that drop off their second fare of the day in that region.

The product:

$$
\begin{array}{ccc}
\text{I} & \text{II} & \text{III} \\
(.50 & .40 & .10)
\end{array}
\begin{pmatrix}
.80 & .15 & .05 \\
.90 & .01 & .09 \\
.15 & .25 & .60
\end{pmatrix}
=
\begin{array}{ccc}
\text{I} & \text{II} & \text{III} \\
(.775 & .104 & .121)
\end{array}
$$

is the distribution of the second-fare drop-off regions. Of the second fares, 77.5% are dropped in region I, 10.4% of the second fares are dropped in region II, and 12.1% are dropped in region III.   ■

PRACTICE EXAMPLE 1

A local grocery store, Ted's, recently started an advertising campaign and improved its service. Suppose that each week 85% of the shoppers who shopped at Ted's last week shop at Ted's again this week (the remaining 15% shop at a different store) and 5% of the shoppers who did not shop at Ted's last week shop at Ted's this week (95% of the shoppers who did not shop at Ted's last week do not shop at Ted's this week either).

(a) Write the transition matrix for this Markov chain.
(b) If 20% of the shoppers in town shop at Ted's this week, then what percentage of shoppers will shop at Ted's next week?   ■

The situations described in Examples 1, 2, and 3 are experiments that can be repeated. The possible outcomes of a particular experiment are called **states**. The states in Example 1 are: commutes by car, commutes by public transportation. The states in Example 2 are: mouse ends in room I, mouse ends in room II. The states in Example 3 are the three drop-off regions.

The entries in the transition matrix are the probabilities of going from one state to another. For example, the (2, 1) entry, .6, in the transition matrix of Example 5 is the probability that a mouse that ended in room II last time will end in room I the next time. The (1, 1) entry, .95, in the transition matrix of Example 4 is the probability that a person who commutes by car one year will commute by car the next year. If the probabilities of going from one state to another do not change during repeated trials of the experiment, then the process is called a **Markov chain**.

The transition matrix, T, of a Markov chain with states $S_1 \cdots S_n$ is the N by N matrix with:

$T_{i,j}$ = probability of state S_j on the next trial given that the state was S_i on the last trial.

The distribution matrix, $D(k)$, for the kth trial of the experiment is the row matrix with:

$(D(k))_{1,j}$ = probability of the state S_j on the kth trial.

The computation in Example 4 illustrates the general result:

(1) $$D(k)\,T = D(k + 1)$$

Equation 1 says that multiplication by the transition matrix takes the distribution on the kth trial and produces the distribution on the $(k + 1)$st trial.

PRACTICE EXAMPLE 2

$$
\begin{array}{cc}
\quad S_1 & \quad S_2 \\
D(1) = (.60 & .40)
\end{array}
$$

is the distribution matrix for the first trial of a Markov chain with transition matrix:

$$
T = \begin{array}{c} \\ S_1 \\ S_2 \end{array}
\begin{array}{c}
\quad S_1 \quad\quad S_2 \\
\begin{pmatrix} .90 & .10 \\ .30 & .70 \end{pmatrix}
\end{array}
$$

Find:

(a) $D(2) = D(1)\,T$
(b) $D(3) = D(2)\,T$
(c) $D(4) = D(3)\,T$

PRACTICE EXAMPLE 3

A town has two competing evening local news shows: one on channel 7 and one on channel 11. The people who watch the news every evening are divided into two groups: those who watch channel 7 and those who watch channel 11. Seventy percent of those who watch channel 7 one night watch channel 7 the next night, the remaining 30% watch channel 11 the next night. Twenty percent of those who watch channel 11 one night watch channel 7 the next night, the remaining 80% watch channel 11 the next night. Suppose a survey shows that 60% of the people who watch the news every night watched the channel 7 news last night and 40% watched channel 11. What percentage of the regular news watchers watch channel 7 and what percentage watch channel 11

(a) tonight?
(b) tomorrow night?
(c) the night after tomorrow night?   ■

   There are two basic questions one can ask about a Markov chain. The first question is: Given the distribution matrix corresponding to some trial of the experiment how do you find the distribution matrix corresponding to the next trial of the experiment? This question is answered by Equation 1. The second question is: What happens eventually? To illustrate the type of answer this question might have we list succeeding distributions for the Markov chain in Examples 2 and 5.
   The transition matrix is:

$$T = \begin{array}{c} \\ \text{I} \\ \text{II} \end{array} \begin{array}{cc} \text{I} & \text{II} \\ \begin{pmatrix} .8 & .2 \\ .6 & .4 \end{pmatrix} \end{array}$$

If $D(1) = (.5 \quad .5)$ then (rounded to four decimal places):

$$D(2) = (.7 \qquad .3)$$
$$D(3) = (.74 \qquad .26)$$
$$D(4) = (.748 \qquad .252)$$
$$D(5) = (.7496 \qquad .2504)$$
$$D(6) = (.7499 \qquad .2501)$$
$$D(7) = (.75 \qquad .25)$$
$$D(8) = (.75 \qquad .25)$$
$$D(9) = (.75 \qquad .25)$$
$$D(k) = (.75 \qquad .25) \text{ for } k > 9$$

   The list of distributions indicates that if the first time through the maze half the mice end in room I and the other half in room II, then by the seventh time through the maze 75% of the mice find the cheese in room I and 25% end in room II without any cheese. These percentages remain unchanged for the eighth and all following times the mice are put in the maze. In this sense the mice "learn" where the cheese is. Eventually 75% of the mice end in room I and 25% in room II.

The following two lists, together with the one above, indicate that the eventual behavior of the mice is unrelated to what they do the first time through the maze. If all the mice end in room I the first time through the maze, then (rounded to four decimal places):

$$D(1) = (1 \qquad 0)$$
$$D(2) = (.8 \qquad .2)$$
$$D(3) = (.76 \qquad .24)$$
$$D(4) = (.752 \qquad .248)$$
$$D(5) = (.7504 \qquad .2496)$$
$$D(6) = (.7501 \qquad .2499)$$
$$D(7) = (.7500 \qquad .2500)$$
$$D(k) = (.7500 \qquad .2500) \text{ for } k > 7$$

If all the mice end in room II the first time through the maze, then (rounded to four decimal places):

$$D(1) = (0 \qquad 1)$$
$$D(2) = (.6000 \qquad .40000)$$
$$D(3) = (.7200 \qquad .2800)$$
$$D(4) = (.7440 \qquad .2560)$$
$$D(5) = (.7488 \qquad .2512)$$
$$D(6) = (.7498 \qquad .2502)$$
$$D(7) = (.7500 \qquad .2500)$$
$$D(k) = (.7500 \qquad .2500) \text{ for } k > 7$$

These lists of succeeding distributions for the Markov chain in Examples 2 and 5 indicate that no matter what the starting distribution, eventually 75% of the mice end in room I and 25% in room II. In other words, no matter what the initial distribution for the Markov chain in examples 2 and 5, succeeding distributions approach the distribution (.75   .25).

As the lists above indicate, the particular distribution $D = (.75 \quad .25)$ has the property that if D is the distribution matrix for some time the mice are sent through the maze, then D is the distribution matrix for all the following times the mice are sent through the maze. It follows from equation (1) that $DT = D$. A distribution that satisfies the equation $DT = D$ is called a **steady state distribution** for the Markov chain with transition matrix T.

The following theorem describes the eventual behavior of a typical Markov chain such as illustrated in the discussion above.

THEOREM If each entry in the transition matrix T of a Markov chain is a nonzero number, then:

1. There is one and only one distribution D with $DT = D$. There is a steady state distribution and it is unique.
2. For any distribution $D(1)$ the succeeding distributions:

$$D(2) = D(1) T$$

$$D(3) = D(2) T$$

$$D(4) = D(3) T$$

$$\vdots$$

$$D(k + 1) = D(k) T$$

approach the steady state distribution D.

In Exercises 23 and 24 you will see that statements 1 and 2 of the theorem may not be true if the transition matrix has entries that are zero. A proof of the theorem in the case where there are two states is outlined in Exercises 25 and 26.

Next we show how to find the steady state distribution of a Markov chain with two states. If $(x \quad y)$ is a distribution matrix, then x represents the fraction in the first state and y represents the fraction in the second state. Thus $x + y = 1$ and $(x \quad y) = (x \quad 1 - x)$. If $D = (x \quad 1 - x)$ is the steady state distribution of a Markov chain with transition matrix:

$$T = \begin{pmatrix} a & b \\ c & d \end{pmatrix}$$

then the condition, $DT = D$, can be written:

$$(x \quad 1 - x) \begin{pmatrix} a & b \\ c & d \end{pmatrix} = (x \quad 1 - x)$$

The product DT is $(ax + c[1 - x] \quad bx + d[1 - x])$. Setting DT equal to D gives two equations.

$$ax + c[1 - x] = x \quad \text{and} \quad bx + d[1 - x] = 1 - x$$

The steady state can be found by solving either one of these equations for x.

EXAMPLE 7 Find the steady state distribution of commuters:

$$\begin{array}{cc} C & P \end{array}$$

$$D = (x \quad y)$$

for the Markov chain in Example 1, where C represents commutes by car and P commutes by public transportation.

The transition matrix is:

$$T = \begin{array}{c} \\ C \\ P \end{array} \begin{array}{cc} C & P \\ \begin{pmatrix} .95 & .05 \\ .10 & .90 \end{pmatrix} \end{array}$$

In this case the equation $DT = D$ is:

$$(x \quad 1 - x) \begin{pmatrix} .95 & .05 \\ .10 & .90 \end{pmatrix} = (x \quad 1 - x)$$

This matrix equation corresponds to the two equations:

$$.95x + (.10)(1 - x) = x; \qquad (.05)\,x + .90(1 - x) = 1 - x$$

We need only one of these equations to find x.

$$.95x + (.10)(1 - x) = x$$

$$.95x + .10 - .10x = x$$

$$.85x + .10 = x$$

$$.10 = x - .85x$$

$$.10 = 1x - .85x$$

$$.10 = (1 - .85)\,x$$

$$.10 = .15x$$

$$\frac{.10}{.15} = x$$

$$x = \frac{10}{15} = \frac{2}{3}$$

$$x = \frac{2}{3} \text{ so } 1 - x = \frac{1}{3}$$

$D = (\tfrac{2}{3} \quad \tfrac{1}{3})$ is the steady state distribution. If at the beginning of some year two-thirds of the commuters commute by car and the remaining one-third by public transportation, then at the beginning of each of the following years two-thirds of the commuters commute by car and one-third commute by public transportation. From statement 2 of the theorem it follows that no matter what the present distribution of commuters, eventually two-thirds of the commuters will commute by car and one-third by public transportation. If as in Example 4, $D(1) = (.80 \quad .20)$ then (to four decimal places):

$$D(1) = (.8 \quad .2)$$
$$D(10) = (.6975 \quad .3025)$$
$$D(20) = (.6727 \quad .3273)$$
$$D(30) = (.6679 \quad .3321)$$
$$D(40) = (.6669 \quad .3331)$$
$$D(50) = (.6667 \quad .3333)$$
$$D(k) = (.6667 \quad .3333) \text{ for } k > 50$$

In this case, the distributions approach the steady state distribution more slowly than is the case for the Markov chain in Example 2. ■

PRACTICE EXAMPLE 4

Find the steady state distribution matrix for the Markov chain with transition matrix:

$$T = \begin{array}{c} \\ \text{I} \\ \text{II} \end{array} \begin{array}{cc} \text{I} & \text{II} \\ \begin{pmatrix} .7 & .3 \\ .1 & .9 \end{pmatrix} \end{array}$$

■

The next example illustrates the technique for finding the steady state matrix of a Markov chain with three states.

EXAMPLE 8

Find the steady state distribution for the Markov chain with the transition matrix:

$$T = \begin{array}{c} \\ \text{I} \\ \text{II} \\ \text{III} \end{array} \begin{array}{ccc} \text{I} & \text{II} & \text{III} \\ \begin{pmatrix} .8 & .15 & .05 \\ .9 & .01 & .09 \\ .15 & .25 & .60 \end{pmatrix} \end{array}$$

Suppose $D = (x, y, z)$ is the steady state distribution. Since $x + y + z = 1$, we can replace z with $1 - x - y$. The equation

$$DT = D$$

$$(x \quad y \quad 1 - x - y) \begin{pmatrix} .8 & .15 & .05 \\ .9 & .01 & .09 \\ .15 & .25 & .60 \end{pmatrix} = (x \quad y \quad 1 - x - y)$$

corresponds to the three equations:

$$.8x + .9y + .15(1 - x - y) = x$$
$$.15x + .01y + .25(1 - x - y) = y$$
$$.05x + .09y + .60(1 - x - y) = 1 - x - y$$

To find x and y we need only the first two equations. The equation .8x + .9y + .15(1 − x − y) simplifies to 7x − 15y = 3, and the equation .15x + .01y + .25(1 − x − y) simplifies to 10x + 124y = 25. We solve this system of two equations by the addition method described in Chapter 9.

$$-10(7x - 15y = 3)$$
$$7(10x + 124y = 25)$$

gives

$$-70x + 150y = -30$$
$$70x + 868y = 175$$
$$\overline{\qquad\qquad\qquad}$$
$$1018y = 145$$

so y = 145/1018.

Substituting this value for y into either 7x − 15y = 3 or 10x + 124y = 25 and solving for x gives the value x = 747/1018. z = 1 − x − y so z = 126/1018.

The steady state distribution for the Markov chain with transition matrix:

$$T = \begin{pmatrix} .8 & .15 & .05 \\ .9 & .01 & .09 \\ .15 & .25 & .60 \end{pmatrix}$$

is D = (747/1018 145/1018 126/1018) ∼ (.7338 .1424 .1238). ■

In this section we have combined matrix multiplication and probability theory to model the changes over time given by a Markov chain. In Example 8, we saw that the problem of finding the steady state distribution for a Markov chain with three states reduces to the problem of solving two linear equations in two unknowns. In general, the problem of finding the steady state distribution for a Markov chain with N states reduces to solving a system of N − 1 linear equations in N − 1 unknowns. In the next two sections, we use matrices to give a systematic procedure for finding solutions to any number of equations in any number of unknowns.

CONCEPTS

Markov chain
states
transition matrix

distribution matrix
steady state distribution

SOLUTIONS TO PRACTICE EXAMPLES

1. (a) The transition matrix is:

$$
\begin{array}{c c}
 & \begin{array}{c c} \text{T} & \text{A} \end{array} \\
\begin{array}{c} \text{T} \\ \text{A} \end{array} &
\begin{pmatrix} .85 & .15 \\ .05 & .95 \end{pmatrix}
\end{array}
$$

where T denotes: shops at Ted's
and A denotes: shops at another store.

(b)
$$
\begin{array}{cc} \text{T} & \text{A} \end{array} \quad\quad
\begin{array}{c c} \text{T} & \text{A} \end{array}
$$

$$
\begin{array}{cc} (.2 & .8) \end{array} \quad
\begin{array}{c} \text{T} \\ \text{A} \end{array}
\begin{pmatrix} .85 & .15 \\ .05 & .95 \end{pmatrix} =
\begin{array}{c c} \text{T} & \text{A} \\ (.21 & .79) \end{array}
$$

21% of the shoppers will shop at Ted's next week.

2. (a) $D(2) = D(1)\,T = (.6 \quad .4)\begin{pmatrix} .9 & .1 \\ .3 & .7 \end{pmatrix} = (.66 \quad .34)$

(b) $D(3) = D(2)\,T = (.66 \quad .34)\begin{pmatrix} .9 & .1 \\ .3 & .7 \end{pmatrix} = (.696 \quad .304)$

(c) $D(4) = D(3)\,T = (.696 \quad .304)\begin{pmatrix} .9 & .1 \\ .3 & .7 \end{pmatrix} = (.7176 \quad .2824)$

3.

$$
\begin{array}{c c} \text{ch 7} & \text{ch 11} \end{array} \quad\quad\quad
\begin{array}{c c} \text{ch 7} & \text{ch 11} \end{array}
$$

$$
D(1) = (.6 \quad .4) \quad\quad
T = \begin{array}{c} \text{ch 7} \\ \text{ch 11} \end{array}
\begin{pmatrix} .7 & .3 \\ .2 & .8 \end{pmatrix}
$$

(a) $(.6 \quad .4)\begin{pmatrix} .7 & .3 \\ .2 & .8 \end{pmatrix} = (.5 \quad .5)$ *answer: 50%*

(b) $(.5 \quad .5)\begin{pmatrix} .7 & .3 \\ .2 & .8 \end{pmatrix} = (.45 \quad .55)$ *answer: 55%*

(c) $(.45 \quad .55)\begin{pmatrix} .7 & .3 \\ .2 & .8 \end{pmatrix} = (.425 \quad .575)$ *answer: 57.5%*

4. If:

$$
(x \quad 1-x)\begin{pmatrix} .7 & .3 \\ .1 & .9 \end{pmatrix} = (x \quad 1-x)
$$

then $.7x + .1(1-x) = x.$
This equation has solution $x = \frac{1}{4}$.
The steady state distribution is $(\frac{1}{4} \quad \frac{3}{4})$.

EXERCISES 10.3

In Exercises 1 through 6 find:

(a) $D(2)$.

(b) $D(3)$.

(c) $D(4)$.

1. $D(1) = (.4 \quad .6), \quad T = \begin{pmatrix} .8 & .2 \\ .7 & .3 \end{pmatrix}$

2. $D(1) = (.5 \quad .5), \quad T = \begin{pmatrix} .6 & .4 \\ .3 & .7 \end{pmatrix}$

3. $D(1) = (1 \quad 0), \quad T = \begin{pmatrix} .1 & .9 \\ .3 & .7 \end{pmatrix}$

4. $D(1) = (.7 \quad .3), \quad T = \begin{pmatrix} .9 & .1 \\ .2 & .8 \end{pmatrix}$

5. $D(1) = (.3 \quad .3 \quad .4), \quad T = \begin{pmatrix} .2 & .6 & .2 \\ .7 & .2 & .1 \\ .1 & .1 & .8 \end{pmatrix}$

6. $D(1) = (.5 \quad .1 \quad .4), \quad T = \begin{pmatrix} .8 & .1 & .1 \\ .2 & .8 & .0 \\ .2 & .1 & .7 \end{pmatrix}$

In Exercises 7 through 16 find the steady state distribution for the Markov chain with transition matrix T.

7. In Exercise 1.   8. In Exercise 2.   9. In Exercise 3.

10. In Exercise 4.   11. In Exercise 5.   12. In Exercise 6.

13. $T = \begin{pmatrix} .75 & .25 \\ .1 & .9 \end{pmatrix}$ 14. $T = \begin{pmatrix} .85 & .15 \\ .05 & .95 \end{pmatrix}$

15. $T = \begin{pmatrix} .98 & .02 \\ .20 & .80 \end{pmatrix}$ 16. $T = \begin{pmatrix} .9 & .1 \\ .1 & .9 \end{pmatrix}$

17. Commuters to a city are divided into those who commute by car and those who commute by public transportation. Suppose that each year 3% of the car commuters switch to public transportation (the remaining 97% continue to commute by car) and each year 12% of those using public transportation

switch to commuting by car (the remaining 88% continue to use public transportation).

(a) Write the transition matrix for this Markov chain.

(b) Suppose that 90% of the commuters presently commute by car. Find the percentage of commuters who commute by car:

(i)   one year from now.

(ii) two years from now.

(iii) three years from now.

18. Mice are run repeatedly through the maze in Figure 10.8 of this section. Suppose that of the mice who ended in room I, 90% will end in room I again and of the mice who ended in room II last time 50% will end in room II again next time.

(a) Write a transition matrix for this Markov chain.

Suppose that the first time through the maze half the mice end in room I and half in room II. Find the percentage of mice that end in room I and that end in room II:

(b) on the second trial.
(c) on the third trial.
(d) on the fourth trial.
(e) in the long run.

19. Suppose for the city of Detroit that each year 10% of those living in the city move to the suburbs and 5% of those living in the suburbs move into the city.

(a) Write a transition matrix for this Markov chain.

Suppose 40% of the people in the area presently live in the city and 60% live in the suburbs. Find the percentages of people in each region:

(b) one year from now.
(c) two years from now.
(d) in the long run.

20. There are two competing restaurants, Colton's and Alfredo's, in a shopping center. Presently 40% of the people who regularly eat at one or the other of the restaurants eat at Colton's. Colton's advertising and service have recently improved so that each day 88% of the people eating at Colton's will eat there again the next day and 13% of those eating at Alfredo's one day will eat at Colton's the next day.

(a) Write a transition matrix for this Markov chain.
(b) Find the steady state distribution.
(c) Assuming the present distribution is:

$$\begin{array}{cc} \text{Colton's} & \text{Alfredo's} \\ D(0) = (.40 & .60) \end{array}$$

How long will it be before at least half the people are eating at Colton's?

21. Space probes contain equipment to diagnose and correct misalignment of the probe. If the system is aligned one minute, then 95% of the time the system is aligned the next minute. Five percent of the time the system is not aligned the next minute. If the system is not aligned one minute, then 35% of the time the system will be aligned the next minute, and 65% of the time it will continue to be not aligned the next minute.

    (a) Write a transition matrix for this Markov chain.
    (b) In the long run, what percentage of the time is the system aligned?

22. A state legislature is debating a bill that requires a two-thirds majority to pass. Each day the debate continues without a vote, 3% of the legislators in favor of the bill change their minds and 3% of those against the bill change their minds. Presently, 70% of the legislators are for the bill and 30% are against the bill.

    (a) Write a transition matrix for the Markov chain with states F = for the bill; A = against the bill.
    (b) List in a table the percentage of votes for the bill if the vote is held one day from now, two days from now, and so on, up to six days from now. Will the bill pass or fail if the vote is held six days from now?
    (c) Based on your answers to (b), does the percentage of voters for the bill decrease each day?
    (d) Find the steady state distribution.

23. Find all the steady state distributions for the Markov chain with transition matrix:

    (a) $\begin{pmatrix} 0 & 1 \\ 1 & 0 \end{pmatrix}$ (b) $\begin{pmatrix} 1 & 0 \\ 0 & 1 \end{pmatrix}$

24. Give an example to show statement 2 of the theorem in this section is false when applied to the transition matrix:

$$T = \begin{pmatrix} 0 & 1 \\ 1 & 0 \end{pmatrix}$$

Why does this not contradict the theorem?

In Exercises 25 and 26 use the notation:

$$T = \begin{pmatrix} a & 1-a \\ b & 1-b \end{pmatrix}$$

with:

$$0 < a < 1$$
$$0 < b < 1$$

for the transition matrix of a Markov chain with two states and:

$$D = (x \quad 1-x) \quad \text{with} \quad 0 < x < 1$$

for the distribution matrices.

25. Show that if each entry in T is nonzero, then there is one and only one distribution D with $DT = D$. Write the entries in D in terms of a and b.

26. Use the theory of difference equations in Section 8.3 to prove statement 2 of the theorem in this section as follows: Let T be the transition matrix of a Markov chain with two states.

   (a) Given a number x_0 with $0 < x_0 < 1$ denote by $x_1, x_2, x_3, \ldots, x_k, x_{k+1}$ the numbers defined by:

   $$(x_0 \quad 1 - x_0)\,T = (x_1 \quad 1 - x_1)$$
   $$(x_1 \quad 1 - x_1)\,T = (x_2 \quad 1 - x_2)$$
   $$\cdot$$
   $$\cdot$$
   $$\cdot$$
   $$(x_k \quad 1 - x_k)\,T = (x_{k+1} \quad 1 - x_{k+1})$$

   Find a difference equation for the sequence $x_0, x_1, x_2, \ldots$
   (b) Find the solution of this difference equation.
   (c) Show that if each entry in T is nonzero, then for any distribution $D(0) = (x_0 \quad 1 - x_0)$ the succeeding distributions:

   $$D(0)\,T = D(1)$$
   $$D(1)\,T = D(2)$$
   $$\cdot$$
   $$\cdot$$
   $$\cdot$$
   $$D(k)\,T = D(k + 1)$$

   approach the steady state distribution found in Exercise 25. (You will need the fact that if r is a number with $-1 < r < 1$, then powers of r: $r^1, r^2, r^3, \ldots, r^k$, r^{k+1} approach zero.)

10.4   Gauss-Jordan Elimination: Systems with a Unique Solution

In this section and the next, we give a general method, Gauss-Jordan elimination, for solving systems of linear equations. Systems of linear equations arise in business, science, and engineering. In Chapter 9 you saw that solving a system of two equations in two unknowns is an important step in solving linear programs in two variables. In the previous section, we saw that finding the steady state distribution of a Markov chain reduces to finding the solution of a system of linear equations. In this section, we use the method of addition to solve systems that have one and only one solution. In the next section, we use Gauss-Jordan elimination to find the solutions to systems of linear equations that have more than one solution, and give applications. The steps in Gauss-Jordan elimination are used in Section 10.6 to solve matrix equations and in Chapter 11 to find solutions for linear programs.

The goal of Gauss-Jordan elimination is to transform a given system of linear equations into a much simpler form without changing the sólutions. For example, we will use Gauss-Jordan elimination in Example 2 to transform the system:

System 1

$$x_1 + 2x_2 - x_3 = -4$$
$$x_1 - x_2 + 2x_3 = 14$$
$$2x_1 + 2x_2 - x_3 = -1$$

to the system:

System 2

$$x_1 = 3$$
$$x_2 = -1$$
$$x_3 = 5$$

Hence $x_1 = 3$, $x_2 = -1$, $x_3 = 5$ is the solution to the equations in System 1. The steps used to get from System 1 to System 2 are given in Example 2.

Recall from Section 9.2 the following rules for changing a system of equations without changing the solutions.

1. Multiply an equation by a nonzero number.
2. Add two equations.
3. Any combination of 1 and 2.

We add one more rule:

4. Change the order of the equations.

The steps in **Gauss-Jordan elimination** are: first, using only rules 1 through 4 eliminate the first variable from all but the first equation. Then eliminate the second variable from all but the second equation. Continue to eliminate variables one at a time. After as many variables have been eliminated as is possible, solve the resulting system of equations. This gives the solution(s) to the original system of equations.

We will use the method of Section 10.1 for writing a system of equations in matrix form. This shortens the amount of writing needed. The matrix corresponding to a system of equations is called the **augmented matrix** of the system. For example, the system of linear equations:

$$2x_1 + 3x_2 = 13$$
$$5x_1 + 7x_2 = 2$$

has augmented matrix:

$$\begin{pmatrix} 2 & 3 & | & 13 \\ 5 & 7 & | & 2 \end{pmatrix}$$

EXAMPLE 1   Solve:

$$2x_1 + 3x_2 = 1$$
$$5x_1 + 7x_2 = 1$$

by Gauss-Jordan elimination. The augmented matrix is:

$$\begin{pmatrix} 2 & 3 & | & 1 \\ 5 & 7 & | & 1 \end{pmatrix}$$

We will use the notation E_i for equation i, r_i for row i.

STEP 1:   Eliminate x_1 from all but the first equation.

Equations	Matrix

$$2x_1 + 3x_2 = 1 \qquad \begin{pmatrix} 2 & 3 & | & 1 \\ 5 & 7 & | & 1 \end{pmatrix}$$
$$5x_1 + 7x_2 = 1$$

x_1 can be eliminated from the second equation by adding 5 times equation one to (-2) times equation two. This corresponds to replacing the second row of the augmented matrix with the sum of 5 times row one and (-2) times row 2.

$$\begin{array}{ll} 5E_1 & 10x_1 + 15x_2 = 5 \\ -2E_2 & -10x_1 - 14x_2 = -2 \\ \hline 5E_1 - 2E_2 & x_2 = 3 \end{array}$$

$$5r_1 - 2r_2 \begin{pmatrix} 2 & 3 & | & 1 \\ 5(2) - 2(5) & 5(3) - 2(7) & | & 5(1) - 2(1) \end{pmatrix}$$

$$\|$$

$$\begin{pmatrix} 2 & 3 & | & 1 \\ 0 & 1 & | & 3 \end{pmatrix}$$

STEP 2:   Eliminate x_2 from all but the second equation.

$$2x_1 + 3x_2 = 1$$
$$x_2 = 3$$

$$\begin{array}{ll} E_1 & 2x_1 + 3x_2 = 1 \\ -3E_2 & -3x_2 = -9 \\ \hline E_1 - 3E_2 & 2x_1 = -8 \end{array}$$

$$r_1 - 3r_2 \begin{pmatrix} 2 - 3(0) & 3 - 3(1) & | & 1 - 3(3) \\ 0 & 1 & | & 3 \end{pmatrix}$$

$$\|$$

$$\begin{pmatrix} 2 & 0 & | & -8 \\ 0 & 1 & | & 3 \end{pmatrix}$$

STEP 3:   Solve for x_1 and x_2.

$$2x_1 = -8$$

$$x_2 = 3$$

$(1/2)\,E_1 \qquad x_1 = -4$

$$x_2 = 3$$

$(1/2)\,r_1 \begin{pmatrix} 1 & 0 & \bigm| & -4 \\ 0 & 1 & \bigm| & 3 \end{pmatrix}$

The solution is $x_1 = -4$, $x_2 = 3$. ■

Notice in Example 1 that each of the operations on equations corresponds to an operation on the rows of an augmented matrix. The rules 1 through 4 correspond to the following operations on the rows of a matrix.

ROW OPERATIONS

1. Multiply a row by a nonzero number.
2. Add two rows.
3. Any combination of 1 and 2.
4. Change the order of the rows.

Note: In using these operations to change the rows of a matrix, a combination of rows must replace one of the rows used in the combination. For example $r_1 + 3r_2$ can replace either row one or row two but not row three.

Notice that the solution in Example 1 is easily read from the final augmented matrix because the final matrix contains an identity matrix.

GAUSS-JORDAN ELIMINATION APPLIED TO AN AUGMENTED MATRIX
Using only row operations 1 through 4 transform the given augmented matrix $(A\,|\,b)$ to an augmented matrix of the form $(I\,|\,b')$ where I is an identity matrix.

EXAMPLE 2   Solve by Gauss-Jordan elimination

$$x_1 + 2x_2 - x_3 = -4$$

$$x_1 - x_2 + 2x_3 = 14$$

$$2x_1 + 2x_2 - x_3 = -1$$

The augmented matrix is:

$$\left(\begin{array}{ccc|c} 1 & 2 & -1 & -4 \\ 1 & -1 & 2 & 14 \\ 2 & 2 & -1 & -1 \end{array}\right)$$

STEP 1: Apply row operations 1 through 4 to change the first column to the first column of an identity matrix.

$$\begin{pmatrix} 1 \\ 0 \\ 0 \end{pmatrix}$$

$$\begin{array}{l} \text{want } 1 \longrightarrow \\ \text{want } 0 \longrightarrow \\ \text{want } 0 \longrightarrow \end{array}\left(\begin{array}{ccc|c} 1 & 2 & -1 & -4 \\ 1 & -1 & 2 & 14 \\ 2 & 2 & -1 & -1 \end{array}\right)$$

$$\begin{array}{l} \\ r_2 - r_1 \\ r_3 - 2r_1 \end{array}\left(\begin{array}{ccc|c} 1 & 2 & -1 & -4 \\ 1-1 & -1-2 & 2-(-1) & 14-(-4) \\ 2-2(1) & 2-2(2) & -1-2(-1) & -1-2(-4) \end{array}\right) \text{row 1 ok}$$

$$\parallel$$

$$\left(\begin{array}{ccc|c} 1 & 2 & -1 & -4 \\ 0 & -3 & 3 & 18 \\ 0 & -2 & 1 & 7 \end{array}\right)$$

STEP 2: We want the second column to be the second column of an identity matrix.

$$\begin{pmatrix} 0 \\ 1 \\ 0 \end{pmatrix}$$

$$\left(\begin{array}{ccc|c} 1 & 2 \text{ (want 0)} & -1 & -4 \\ 0 & -3 \text{ (want 1)} & 3 & 18 \\ 0 & -2 \text{ (want 0)} & 1 & 7 \end{array}\right)$$

First we replace -3 with 1.

$$-(1/3)\,r_2 \left(\begin{array}{ccc|c} 1 & 2 \text{ (want 0)} & -1 & -4 \\ 0 & 1 & -1 & -6 \\ 0 & -2 \text{ (want 0)} & 1 & 7 \end{array}\right)$$

Now apply row operations so that the new second column is:

$$\begin{pmatrix} 0 \\ 1 \\ 0 \end{pmatrix}$$

$$\begin{matrix} r_1 - 2r_2 \\ \\ r_3 + 2r_2 \end{matrix} \begin{pmatrix} 1 - 2(0) & 2 - 2(1) & -1 - 2(-1) & | & -4 - 2(-6) \\ 0 & 1 & -1 & | & -6 \\ 0 + 2(0) & -2 + 2(1) & 1 + 2(-1) & | & 7 + 2(-6) \end{pmatrix}$$

$$||$$

$$\begin{pmatrix} 1 & 0 & 1 & | & 8 \\ 0 & 1 & -1 & | & -6 \\ 0 & 0 & -1 & | & -5 \end{pmatrix}$$

Note: You might have been tempted to add rows 1 and 3 to get a 0 in the (3, 2) entry, but that would have destroyed the first column of the identity as the first column. You could, however, have added rows 1 and 3 to get the 0 in the (1, 2) entry. There is *no one* sequence of row operations.

STEP 3:   We want the third column to be the third column of the identity matrix:

$$\begin{pmatrix} 0 \\ 0 \\ 1 \end{pmatrix}$$

$$\begin{pmatrix} 1 & 0 & 1 \text{ (want 0)} & | & 8 \\ 0 & 1 & -1 \text{ (want 0)} & | & -6 \\ 0 & 0 & -1 \text{ (want 1)} & | & -5 \end{pmatrix}$$

$$\begin{matrix} r_1 + r_3 \\ r_2 - r_3 \\ -r_3 \end{matrix} \begin{pmatrix} 1 & 0 & 1 + (-1) & | & 8 + (-5) \\ 0 & 1 & -1 - (-1) & | & -6 - (-5) \\ 0 & 0 & 1 & | & 5 \end{pmatrix}$$

$$||$$

$$\begin{pmatrix} 1 & 0 & 0 & | & 3 \\ 0 & 1 & 0 & | & -1 \\ 0 & 0 & 1 & | & 5 \end{pmatrix}$$

Find the solution to the original system of equations by writing the equations corresponding to the last augmented matrix.

$$x_1 = 3$$
$$x_2 = -1$$
$$x_3 = 5$$

We can check the answer by substituting these values for the variables in the original system of equations.

$$x_1 + 2x_2 - x_3 = -4 \qquad 3 + 2(-1) - 5 = -4$$
$$x_1 - x_2 + 2x_3 = 14 \qquad 3 - (-1) + 2(5) = 14$$
$$2x_1 + 2x_2 - x_3 = -1 \qquad 2(3) + 2(-1) - 5 = -1 \qquad ∎$$

EXAMPLE 3

A dietician wants to combine three foods: I, II, and III, to make a meal with 44 units of vitamin A, 55 units of vitamin B, and 48 units of vitamin C. The table below gives the vitamin content in units per ounce for each food. How many ounces of each food should be in the meal?

	I	II	III
Vitamin A	1	2	3
Vitamin B	2	1	4
Vitamin C	2	5	1

If we set:

$$x_1 = \text{number of ounces of I in the meal}$$
$$x_2 = \text{number of ounces of II in the meal}$$
$$x_3 = \text{number of ounces of III in the meal}$$

then the answer to the problem is given by the solution to:

$$x_1 + 2x_2 + 3x_3 = 44$$
$$2x_1 + x_2 + 4x_3 = 55$$
$$2x_1 + 5x_2 + x_3 = 48$$

The augmented matrix is:

$$\begin{pmatrix} 1 & 2 & 3 & | & 44 \\ 2 & 1 & 4 & | & 55 \\ 2 & 5 & 1 & | & 48 \end{pmatrix}$$

STEP 1: We want the first column to be the first column of the identity:

$$\begin{pmatrix} 1 \\ 0 \\ 0 \end{pmatrix}$$

$$\begin{array}{l} \text{want 1} \longrightarrow \\ \text{want 0} \longrightarrow \\ \text{want 0} \longrightarrow \end{array} \begin{pmatrix} 1 & 2 & 3 & \bigm| & 44 \\ 2 & 1 & 4 & \bigm| & 55 \\ 2 & 5 & 1 & \bigm| & 48 \end{pmatrix}$$

$$\begin{array}{l} \\ 2r_1 - r_2 \\ r_3 - r_2 \end{array} \begin{pmatrix} 1 & 2 & 3 & \bigm| & 44 \\ 2(1) - 2 & 2(2) - 1 & 2(3) - 4 & \bigm| & 2(44) - 55 \\ 2 - 2 & 5 - 1 & 1 - 4 & \bigm| & 48 - 55 \end{pmatrix} \quad \text{row 1 ok}$$

$$\|$$

$$\begin{pmatrix} 1 & 2 & 3 & \bigm| & 44 \\ 0 & 3 & 2 & \bigm| & 33 \\ 0 & 4 & -3 & \bigm| & -7 \end{pmatrix}$$

STEP 2: We want the second column to be the second column of the identity:

$$\begin{pmatrix} 0 \\ 1 \\ 0 \end{pmatrix}$$

$$\begin{pmatrix} 1 & 2 \,(\text{want } 0) & 3 & \bigm| & 44 \\ 0 & 3 \,(\text{want } 1) & 2 & \bigm| & 33 \\ 0 & 4 \,(\text{want } 0) & -3 & \bigm| & -7 \end{pmatrix}$$

We do this in two steps.

$$r_3 - r_2 \begin{pmatrix} 1 & 2 & 3 & \bigm| & 44 \\ 0 & 4 - 3 & -3 - 2 & \bigm| & -7 - 33 \\ 0 & 4 & -3 & \bigm| & -7 \end{pmatrix}$$

$$\|$$

$$\begin{pmatrix} 1 & 2 \,(\text{want } 0) & 3 & \bigm| & 44 \\ 0 & 1 & -5 & \bigm| & -40 \\ 0 & 4 \,(\text{want } 0) & -3 & \bigm| & -7 \end{pmatrix}$$

$$r_1 - 2r_2 \begin{pmatrix} 1 - 0 & 2 - 2(1) & 3 - 2(-5) & 44 - 2(-40) \\ 0 & 1 & -5 & -40 \\ 0 & 4 - 4(1) & -3 - 4(-5) & -7 - 4(-40) \end{pmatrix}$$

$$\|$$

$$\begin{pmatrix} 1 & 0 & 13 & 124 \\ 0 & 1 & -5 & -40 \\ 0 & 0 & 17 & 153 \end{pmatrix}$$

STEP 3: We want the third column to be the third column of the identity:

$$\begin{pmatrix} 0 \\ 0 \\ 1 \end{pmatrix}$$

$$\begin{pmatrix} 1 & 0 & 13 \text{ (want 0)} & 124 \\ 0 & 1 & -5 \text{ (want 0)} & -40 \\ 0 & 0 & 17 \text{ (want 1)} & 153 \end{pmatrix}$$

$$r_3/17 \begin{pmatrix} 1 & 0 & 13 \text{ (want 0)} & 124 \\ 0 & 1 & -5 \text{ (want 0)} & -40 \\ 0 & 0 & 1 & 9 \end{pmatrix}$$

$$\begin{matrix} r_1 - 13r_3 \\ r_2 + 5r_3 \end{matrix} \begin{pmatrix} 1 & 0 & 13 - 13(1) & 124 - 13(9) \\ 0 & 1 & -5 + 5(1) & -40 + 5(9) \\ 0 & 0 & 1 & 9 \end{pmatrix}$$

$$\|$$

$$\begin{pmatrix} 1 & 0 & 0 & 7 \\ 0 & 1 & 0 & 5 \\ 0 & 0 & 1 & 9 \end{pmatrix}$$

STEP 4: The solution to the system of equations is:

$$x_1 = 7$$
$$x_2 = 5$$
$$x_3 = 9$$

The meal should have seven ounces of food I, five ounces of food II, and nine ounces of food III. ■

PRACTICE EXAMPLE 1   Solve by Gauss-Jordan elimination:

(a) $x_1 + 2x_2 = 1$ (b) $x_1 + 2x_2 + x_3 = 7$

$3x_1 + 5x_2 = 1$ $2x_1 + 7x_2 + 5x_3 = 26$

$x_1 + 5x_2 + 5x_3 = 18$ ■

PRACTICE EXAMPLE 2   A shirt manufacturer makes women's, men's, and children's shirts. Production of a shirt is done in three steps: cutting, sewing, and inspection. The table gives the number of minutes needed to carry out each step.

Time in minutes

	Women's shirt	Men's shirt	Child's shirt
Cutting	4	3	2
Sewing	5	4	4
Inspection	1	1	1

The total labor time available each week for cutting is 8,200 minutes, for sewing 11,800 minutes, and for inspection 2,700 minutes. How many shirts of each kind should be made in a week if all the available labor time is to be used?   ■

In this section, we have introduced Gauss-Jordan elimination, and used this method to solve systems of linear equations that have a unique solution. In the next section, we show how the method applies to systems of linear equations that have an infinite number of solutions, and give applications.

CONCEPTS

Gauss-Jordan elimination
augmented matrix
row operations

SOLUTIONS TO PRACTICE EXAMPLES

1. (a)
$$\begin{pmatrix} 1 & 2 & | & 1 \\ 3 & 5 & | & 1 \end{pmatrix}$$

$$\Downarrow$$

$$3r_1 - r_2 \begin{pmatrix} 1 & 2 & | & 1 \\ 3(1) - 3 & 3(2) - 5 & | & 3(1) - 1 \end{pmatrix}$$

$$\|$$

$$\begin{pmatrix} 1 & 2 & | & 1 \\ 0 & 1 & | & 2 \end{pmatrix}$$

$$\Downarrow$$

$$r_1 - 2r_2 \begin{pmatrix} 1 & 2 - 2(1) & | & 1 - 2(2) \\ 0 & 1 & | & 2 \end{pmatrix}$$

$$\|$$

$$\begin{pmatrix} 1 & 0 & | & -3 \\ 0 & 1 & | & 2 \end{pmatrix} \qquad \text{solution: } x_1 = -3 \\ x_2 = 2$$

(b)

$$\begin{pmatrix} 1 & 2 & 1 & | & 7 \\ 2 & 7 & 5 & | & 26 \\ 1 & 5 & 5 & | & 18 \end{pmatrix}$$

$$\Downarrow$$

$$\begin{matrix} \\ r_2 - 2r_1 \\ r_3 - r_1 \end{matrix} \begin{pmatrix} 1 & 2 & 1 & | & 7 \\ 2 - 2(1) & 7 - 2(2) & 5 - 2(1) & | & 26 - 2(7) \\ 1 - 1 & 5 - 2 & 5 - 1 & | & 18 - 7 \end{pmatrix}$$

$$\|$$

$$\begin{pmatrix} 1 & 2 & 1 & | & 7 \\ 0 & 3 & 3 & | & 12 \\ 0 & 3 & 4 & | & 11 \end{pmatrix}$$

$$\Downarrow$$

$$r_2/3 \begin{pmatrix} 1 & 2 & 1 & | & 7 \\ 0 & 1 & 1 & | & 4 \\ 0 & 3 & 4 & | & 11 \end{pmatrix}$$

$$\Downarrow$$

$$\begin{matrix} r_1 - 2r_2 \\ \\ r_3 - 3r_2 \end{matrix} \begin{pmatrix} 1 - 2(0) & 2 - 2(1) & 1 - 2(1) & | & 7 - 2(4) \\ 0 & 1 & 1 & | & 4 \\ 0 & 3 - 3(1) & 4 - 3(1) & | & 11 - 3(4) \end{pmatrix}$$

$$\|$$

$$\begin{pmatrix} 1 & 0 & -1 & | & -1 \\ 0 & 1 & 1 & | & 4 \\ 0 & 0 & 1 & | & -1 \end{pmatrix}$$

$$\Downarrow$$

$$\begin{matrix} r_1 + r_3 \\ r_2 - r_3 \end{matrix} \begin{pmatrix} 1 & 0 & 0 & | & -2 \\ 0 & 1 & 0 & | & 5 \\ 0 & 0 & 1 & | & -1 \end{pmatrix}$$

The solution is:

$$x_1 = -2$$
$$x_2 = 5$$
$$x_3 = -1$$

2. Let:

$$x_1 = \text{number of women's shirts made}$$
$$x_2 = \text{number of men's shirts made}$$
$$x_3 = \text{number of children's shirts made}$$

The system of equations is:

$$4x_1 + 3x_2 + 2x_3 = 8{,}200$$
$$5x_1 + 4x_2 + 4x_3 = 11{,}800$$
$$x_1 + x_2 + x_3 = 2{,}700$$

The augmented matrix is:

$$\begin{pmatrix} 4 & 3 & 2 & | & 8{,}200 \\ 5 & 4 & 4 & | & 11{,}800 \\ 1 & 1 & 1 & | & 2{,}700 \end{pmatrix}$$

The system of equations is solved by applying the following row operations: First interchange rows one and three. This gives:

$$\begin{pmatrix} 1 & 1 & 1 & | & 2{,}700 \\ 5 & 4 & 4 & | & 11{,}800 \\ 4 & 3 & 2 & | & 8{,}200 \end{pmatrix}$$

The next step is:

$$\begin{matrix} \\ 5r_1 - r_2 \\ 4r_1 - r_3 \end{matrix} \begin{pmatrix} 1 & 1 & 1 & | & 2700 \\ 0 & 1 & 1 & | & 1700 \\ 0 & 1 & 2 & | & 2600 \end{pmatrix}$$

Now work on the second column.

$$r_1 - r_2 \begin{pmatrix} 1 & 0 & 0 & | & 1000 \\ 0 & 1 & 1 & | & 1700 \\ r_3 - r_2 & 0 & 0 & 1 & | & 900 \end{pmatrix}$$

The last step is:

$$r_2 - r_3 \begin{pmatrix} 1 & 0 & 0 & | & 1000 \\ 0 & 1 & 0 & | & 800 \\ 0 & 0 & 1 & | & 900 \end{pmatrix}$$

The solution to the system of equations is:

$$x_1 = 1000$$
$$x_2 = 800$$
$$x_3 = 900$$

The only way to use all the labor time available in one week is to make 1000 women's shirts, 800 men's shirts, and 900 children's shirts.

EXERCISES 10.4

In Exercises 1 through 5 fill in the blank rows.

1.
$$\begin{pmatrix} 1 & 2 & 1 \\ 3 & 4 & 4 \end{pmatrix}$$
$$\Downarrow$$
$$3r_1 - r_2 \begin{pmatrix} 1 & 2 & 1 \\ & & \end{pmatrix}$$

2.
$$\begin{pmatrix} 5 & -1 & 4 \\ 2 & -2 & 3 \end{pmatrix}$$
$$\Downarrow$$
$$r_1 - 2r_2 \begin{pmatrix} & & \\ 2 & -2 & 3 \end{pmatrix}$$

3.
$$\begin{pmatrix} 1 & -1 & 1 & 3 \\ 2 & 4 & 5 & -2 \\ -1 & 4 & 8 & 0 \end{pmatrix}$$
$$\Downarrow$$
$$\begin{matrix} r_2 - 2r_1 \\ r_1 + r_3 \end{matrix} \begin{pmatrix} 1 & -1 & 1 & 3 \\ & & & \\ & & & \end{pmatrix}$$

4.
$$\begin{pmatrix} 1 & -2 & 4 & 1 \\ 0 & 3 & 4 & 0 \\ 0 & 2 & 3 & 1 \end{pmatrix}$$
$$\Downarrow$$
$$\begin{matrix} r_1 + r_3 \\ r_2 - r_3 \end{matrix} \begin{pmatrix} & & & \\ & & & \\ 0 & 2 & 3 & 1 \end{pmatrix}$$

5.
$$\begin{pmatrix} 3 & 1 & 4 & 0 \\ 2 & 0 & 5 & 7 \\ 5 & -1 & 7 & 8 \end{pmatrix}$$

$$\begin{matrix} r_1 - r_2 \\ 2r_1 - 3r_2 \\ 5r_1 - 3r_3 \end{matrix} \Downarrow \begin{pmatrix} & & & \\ & & & \\ & & & \end{pmatrix}$$

Solve Exercises 6 through 24 by Gauss-Jordan elimination.

6. $x_1 - x_2 = 5$
   $x_1 + x_2 = 9$

7. $3x_1 + 4x_2 = 5$
   $5x_1 + 7x_2 = 8$

8. $900x_1 + 1150x_2 = 3850$
   $x_1 + x_2 = 4$

9. $500x_1 + 375x_2 = 25000$
   $-x_1 + x_2 = 20$

10. $7x_1 + 5x_2 = 22$
    $x_1 - x_2 = 4$

11. $x_1 + 2x_2 - 3x_3 = 15$
    $x_2 + x_3 = 4$
    $2x_1 + x_2 + x_3 = 8$

12. $x_1 - x_2 + x_3 = 0$
    $2x_2 + x_3 = -2$
    $3x_2 - 5x_3 = 23$

13. $x_1 + x_2 - 4x_3 = 0$
    $x_2 - x_3 = 5$
    $3x_2 - 4x_3 = 13$

14. $x_1 + x_2 + x_3 = 9$
    $5x_2 - 3x_3 = 9$
    $3x_2 + 7x_3 = 23$

15. $2x_1 + x_2 + 2x_3 = 28$
    $x_2 + x_3 = 12$
    $3x_1 + x_2 + x_3 = 21$

16. $x_1 + 2x_2 + x_3 = 4$
    $x_1 + 2x_2 + 3x_3 = 2$
    $x_1 + x_2 - x_3 = 2$

17. $x_1 - 2x_2 + 3x_3 = 7$
    $x_1 - 4x_2 - x_3 = 1$
    $x_1 - 4x_2 + 4x_3 = 11$

18. $x_1 + 2x_2 - x_3 = 10$
    $3x_1 + x_2 - 8x_3 = 15$
    $5x_1 + 2x_2 + 3x_3 = 10$

19. $5x_1 - x_2 + x_3 = 27$
    $2x_1 + x_2 - 2x_3 = 27$
    $7x_1 + x_2 + x_3 = 47$

20. $5x_1 + 3x_2 - 2x_3 = 13$
    $2x_1 + 4x_2 - x_3 = 19$
    $7x_1 + 6x_2 - 6x_3 = 24$

21. A dietician wants to combine two foods, I and II, to make a meal containing 1800 calories and 81 units of vitamin C. Each ounce of food I contains 150 calories and 10 units of vitamin C. Each ounce of food II contains 300 calories and 7 units of vitamin C. How many ounces of each food should be in the meal?

22. A company makes three kinds of chairs, C = captain's chair, S = straight back chair, R = rocking chair. Each chair is sanded, stained, and varnished. Each day there are 588 minutes of labor available for sanding, 705 minutes available for staining, and 1110 minutes available for varnishing. The table below gives the time in minutes to process each kind of chair. If all the available labor time is to be used each day, then how many chairs of each kind should be made each day?

	C	R	S
Sand	5	10	8
Stain	10	15	5
Varnish	15	20	10

23. Find numbers a, b, and c so that the polynomial $p(x) = ax^2 + bx + c$ satisfies $p(1) = 6$, $p(2) = 19$, and $p(3) = 38$.

24. Find numbers a, b, and c so that the polynomial $p(x) = ax^2 + bx + c$ satisfies $p(1) = 8$, $p(3) = 60$, and $p(5) = 168$. What is $p(2)$ for this polynomial?

25. In June 1984, the Office of Management and Budget, Council of Economic Awareness, Treasury Department projected the federal deficit will be 207 billion dollars at the end of 1985, 219 billion dollars at the end of 1986, and 224 billion dollars at the end of 1987. Find a polynomial of the form $p(x) = ax^2 + bx + c$ with $p(0) = 207$, $p(1) = 219$, and $p(2) = 224$. Use the polynomial to predict the federal deficit at the end of 1988.

10.5   Gauss-Jordan Elimination: Systems with More than One Solution

In this section, we show how the method of Gauss-Jordan elimination applies to systems of linear equations that do not have a unique solution and give applications.

Recall from the previous section that in Gauss-Jordan elimination, the augmented matrix, $(A|b)$, of a system of linear equations is transformed using the row operations 1 through 4:

1. Multiply a row by a nonzero number.
2. Add two rows.
3. Any combination of 1 and 2.
4. Change the order of the rows.

The goal is to transform the original augmented matrix, $(A|b)$, to an augmented matrix whose corresponding system of equations is much simpler to solve. Since row operations do not change the solutions, the original system of equations and the simpler system have the same solutions. In the previous section, each augmented matrix was transformed by row operations to an augmented matrix of the form $(I|b')$. In this section, we give examples where the matrix of coefficients, A, cannot be transformed to an identity matrix. In this case it is important to know when to stop using row operations. The following steps give the most general description of the method of Gauss-Jordan elimination. Step 2 indicates the objective to be obtained by row operations and hence when to stop the process of changing the rows. This method applies to any number of linear equations in any number of unknowns.

GAUSS-JORDAN ELIMINATION

1. Write the augmented matrix for the given system of linear equations.
2. Use row operations to transform the augmented matrix to a matrix in which:
   (a) The leftmost nonzero entry in each row is the number 1.
   (b) Each column that contains such a 1 has all other entries in the column equal to 0.
   (c) Any row consisting entirely of zeroes is below any row that has nonzero entries.
   (d) The leftmost 1 in any row is to the right of any leftmost 1 that occurs in a previous row.
3. Solve the system of equations corresponding to the augmented matrix found in Step 2.

A matrix with properties 2(a) through 2(d) is called **reduced**. The conditions (a) and (b) correspond to conditions on the system of equations. For example, (a) says that the first variable occurring in any equation occurs with coefficient 1. Condition (b) says that a variable that is the first variable occurring in some equation does not occur in any of the other equations. A matrix satisfying conditions (a) and (b) can be transformed to a reduced matrix simply by changing the order of the rows.

It is always possible to use row operations to transform a matrix to a reduced matrix. While there is no one sequence of row operations for reducing a given matrix, the final reduced matrix depends only on the original matrix and not on the steps used to reduce it.

The following example illustrates the method of Gauss-Jordan elimination applied to a system with more than one solution.

EXAMPLE 1   Solve by Gauss-Jordan elimination:

$$x_1 + x_2 - 3x_3 = -3$$
$$2x_1 + x_2 - 4x_3 = -1$$
$$3x_1 - 2x_2 + x_3 = 16$$

The augmented matrix is:

$$\begin{pmatrix} 1 & 1 & -3 & | & -3 \\ 2 & 1 & -4 & | & -1 \\ 3 & -2 & 1 & | & 16 \end{pmatrix}$$

STEP 1:   We want the first column to be the first column of an identity:

$$\begin{pmatrix} 1 \\ 0 \\ 0 \end{pmatrix}$$

$$\begin{matrix} \\ 2r_1 - r_2 \\ (1/5)(3r_1 - r_3) \end{matrix} \begin{pmatrix} 1 & 1 & -3 & | & -3 \\ 0 & 1 & -2 & | & -5 \\ 0 & 1 & -2 & | & -5 \end{pmatrix}$$

STEP 2:   We want the second column to be the second column of an identity:

$$\begin{pmatrix} 0 \\ 1 \\ 0 \end{pmatrix}$$

$$\begin{matrix} r_1 - r_2 \\ \\ r_2 - r_3 \end{matrix} \begin{pmatrix} 1 & 0 & -1 & | & 2 \\ 0 & 1 & -2 & | & -5 \\ 0 & 0 & 0 & | & 0 \end{pmatrix}$$

This last matrix is reduced so the process of simplifying the equations by applying row operations to an augmented matrix is complete. The next step is to write and then solve the system of equations corresponding to the reduced matrix.

The equation corresponding to the third row, $0x_1 + 0x_2 + 0x_3 = 0$, is satisfied for *all* values of x_1, x_2, and x_3 and hence places no restriction on the values of x_1, x_2, and x_3. The equations corresponding to the first two rows are:

$$x_1 - x_3 = 2$$
$$x_2 - 2x_3 = -5$$

Solving for x_1 and x_2 we get:

$$x_1 = 2 + x_3$$
$$x_2 = -5 + 2x_3$$

This system of equations has one solution for each value of x_3, for example:

if $x_3 = 0$, then: if $x_3 = 1$, then: if $x_3 = 7$, then:

$$x_1 = 2 \qquad\qquad x_1 = 3 \qquad\qquad x_1 = 9$$

$$x_2 = -5 \qquad\qquad x_2 = -3 \qquad\qquad x_2 = 9$$

$$x_3 = 0 \qquad\qquad x_3 = 1 \qquad\qquad x_3 = 7$$

Therefore the system:

$$x_1 + x_2 - 3x_3 = -3$$
$$2x_1 + x_2 - 4x_3 = -1$$
$$3x_1 - 2x_2 + x_3 = 16$$

has an infinite number of solutions, one for each choice of value for x_3. Given a value for x_3 the values of x_1 and x_2 are given by:

$$x_1 = 2 + x_3$$
$$x_2 = -5 + 2x_3$$

PRACTICE EXAMPLE 1

Solve by Gauss-Jordan elimination:

$$2x_1 + 5x_2 + 3x_3 = 50$$
$$3x_1 + 7x_2 + x_3 = 48$$
$$5x_1 + 13x_2 + 11x_3 = 152$$

EXAMPLE 2

A company with two warehouses received orders from three stores for TV sets. Figure 10.10 shows the number of sets available for shipping from the warehouses and the numbers of sets ordered from the stores.

Figure 10.10

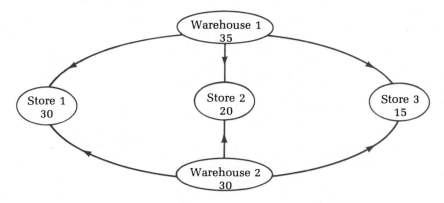

How many sets should be shipped from each warehouse to each store in order to fill the orders?

Let x_{ij} = the number of sets shipped from warehouse i to store j. Then:

(1) $\qquad x_{11} + x_{21} = 30 \qquad$ (30 sets are shipped to store 1)

(2) $\qquad x_{12} + x_{22} = 20 \qquad$ (20 sets are shipped to store 2)

(3) $\qquad x_{13} + x_{23} = 15 \qquad$ (15 sets are shipped to store 3)

Notice that the number of sets ordered is the same as the number of sets available for shipping. Hence all sets will be shipped out of each warehouse. This gives two more equations.

(4) $\quad x_{11} + x_{12} + x_{13} = 35 \qquad$ (35 sets are shipped from warehouse 1)

(5) $\quad x_{21} + x_{22} + x_{23} = 30 \qquad$ (30 sets are shipped from warehouse 2)

The augmented matrix corresponding to the system of equations is:

x_{11}	x_{12}	x_{13}	x_{21}	x_{22}	x_{23}	constants
1	0	0	1	0	0	30
0	1	0	0	1	0	20
0	0	1	0	0	1	15
1	1	1	0	0	0	35
0	0	0	1	1	1	30

Notice this matrix is not reduced. While the leftmost nonzero entry in each row is the number 1, their columns have other entries that are nonzero. The matrix is transformed to a matrix whose first three columns are the first three columns of an identity matrix as follows.

$$r_4 - (r_3 - r_2 - r_1) \begin{pmatrix} 1 & 0 & 0 & 1 & 0 & 0 & | & 30 \\ 0 & 1 & 0 & 0 & 1 & 0 & | & 20 \\ 0 & 0 & 1 & 0 & 0 & 1 & | & 15 \\ 0 & 0 & 0 & -1 & -1 & -1 & | & -30 \\ 0 & 0 & 0 & 1 & 1 & 1 & | & 30 \end{pmatrix}$$

The final step is:

$$\begin{matrix} r_4 + r_1 \\ \\ \\ -r_4 \\ r_4 + r_5 \end{matrix} \begin{pmatrix} 1 & 0 & 0 & 0 & -1 & -1 & | & 0 \\ 0 & 1 & 0 & 0 & 1 & 0 & | & 20 \\ 0 & 0 & 1 & 0 & 0 & 1 & | & 15 \\ 0 & 0 & 0 & 1 & 1 & 1 & | & 30 \\ 0 & 0 & 0 & 0 & 0 & 0 & | & 0 \end{pmatrix}$$

The corresponding system of equations is:

$$x_{11} - x_{22} - x_{23} = 0$$
$$x_{12} + x_{22} \qquad\quad = 20$$
$$x_{13} + \qquad\quad x_{23} = 15$$
$$x_{21} + x_{22} + x_{23} = 30$$

Solve each equation for the first variable occurring in the equation.

(1) $\qquad\qquad\qquad x_{11} = x_{22} + x_{23}$

(2) $\qquad\qquad\qquad x_{12} = 20 - x_{22}$

(3) $\qquad\qquad\qquad x_{13} = 15 - x_{23}$

(4) $\qquad\qquad\qquad x_{21} = 30 - x_{22} - x_{23}$

Equations (1) through (4) are instructions for writing out a shipping schedule once values for x_{22} and x_{23} have been chosen. If, for example, $x_{22} = 10$ and $x_{23} = 7$, then:

$$x_{11} = 10 + 7 = 17$$
$$x_{12} = 20 - 10 = 10$$
$$x_{13} = 15 - 7 = 8$$
$$x_{21} = 30 - 10 = 13$$

This gives the shipping schedule pictured in Figure 10.11, where the numbers on the edges indicate the number of TV sets shipped.

Figure 10.11

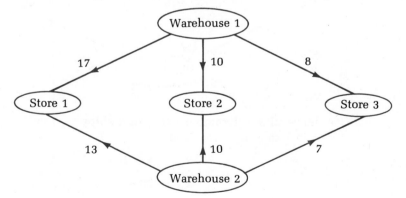

Any choice of values for x_{22} and x_{23} gives a solution to the original system of equations (1) through (4). To obtain a shipping schedule, x_{22} and x_{23} have to be chosen so that all the variables are whole numbers, 0, 1, 2, 3, 4, etc. ∎

Notice that when Gauss-Jordan elimination is applied to a system of equations with more than one solution, the reduced matrix can be used to divide the variables into two sets: the variables that correspond to a column of an identity matrix, called **basic variables**, and the remaining variables, called **nonbasic variables**. In Example 2, the basic variables are x_{11}, x_{12}, x_{13}, and x_{21}, and the nonbasic variables are x_{22} and x_{23}. Solving the equations corresponding to a reduced matrix gives an equation for each basic variable in terms of nonbasic variables. Any choice of values for the nonbasic variables gives a solution to the original system of equations. In Chapter 11, we will use the distinction between basic and nonbasic variables to get an algorithm that solves linear programs.

In Example 3, we show that if a system of equations has more than one solution, then it is possible to use the results of Gauss-Jordan elimination to select an optimal solution—for example, one that maximizes profit or minimizes cost.

EXAMPLE 3

The numbers on the edges in Figure 10.12 give the cost of shipping one TV along that edge route for the shipping problem described in Example 2.

Figure 10.12

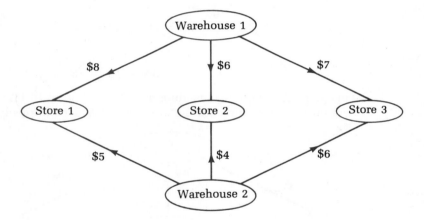

Use the results of Example 2 to find a shipping schedule of least cost.

From Example 2, we have:

(1) $$x_{11} = x_{22} + x_{23}$$

(2) $$x_{12} = 20 - x_{22}$$

(3) $$x_{13} = 15 - x_{23}$$

(4) $$x_{21} = 30 - x_{22} - x_{23}$$

where x_{ij} denotes the number of sets shipped from warehouse i to store j. Equations (1) through (4) can be used to find a shipping schedule of least cost as follows:

The total shipping cost is obtained by multiplying the amount shipped along a route times the cost of shipping one set along that route and then adding the products. This gives the following formula for the total cost.

$$\text{total cost} = 8x_{11} + 6x_{12} + 7x_{13} + 5x_{21} + 4x_{22} + 6x_{23}$$

By using equations (1) through (4) we can reduce the number of variables in the equation for cost from six to two.

$$\text{total cost} = 8(x_{22} + x_{23}) + 6(20 - x_{22}) + 7(15 - x_{23})$$
$$+ 5(30 - x_{22} - x_{23}) + 4x_{22} + 6x_{23}$$
$$= 375 + x_{22} + 2x_{23}$$

Hence the smallest shipping cost is obtained by choosing $x_{22} + 2x_{23}$ as small as possible. Since x_{22} and x_{23} are numbers of sets to be shipped, the smallest value for $x_{22} + 2x_{23}$ is obtained by choosing x_{22} and x_{23} to be zero. Substituting $x_{22} = x_{23} = 0$ into equations (1) through (4) gives the shipping schedule of least cost indicated in Figure 10.13.

Figure 10.13

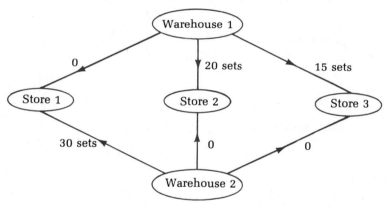

The numbers on the edges in Figure 10.13 give the number of sets shipped along each route in the shipping schedule of least cost. The total shipping cost is $6(20) + 7(15) + 5(30) = \$375$. ∎

PRACTICE EXAMPLE 2

A nutritionist wants to know how many ounces of each of four foods F_1, F_2, F_3, and F_4 should be mixed in order to provide 25 units of vitamin C, 55 units of calcium, and 441 units of iron. The table gives the number of units per ounce in each food.

	F_1	F_2	F_3	F_4
Vitamin C	2	3	1	2
Calcium	5	7	2	2
Iron	38	57	19	4

(a) Write a system of equations corresponding to the requirements; one equation for the vitamin C requirement, one for the calcium requirement, and one for the iron requirement.

(b) Apply Gauss-Jordan elimination to this system of equations and find a mixture that satisfies the requirements.

(c) Suppose each ounce of F_1 contains 185 calories, each ounce of F_2 contains 110 calories, each ounce of F_3 contains 150 calories, and each ounce of F_4 contains 200 calories. Find a mixture of the foods that has the required amount of vitamin C, calcium, and iron and the fewest possible calories. ■

Example 4 illustrates what happens when Gauss-Jordan elimination is applied to a system of equations with no solutions.

EXAMPLE **4**   Solve by Gauss-Jordan elimination:

$$x_1 + x_2 - x_3 = 5$$
$$2x_1 - x_2 + 4x_3 = 1$$
$$5x_1 + 2x_2 + x_3 = 3$$

The augmented matrix is:

$$\begin{pmatrix} 1 & 1 & -1 & | & 5 \\ 2 & -1 & 4 & | & 1 \\ 5 & 2 & 1 & | & 3 \end{pmatrix}$$

STEP 1:   Change the first column to:

$$\begin{pmatrix} 1 \\ 0 \\ 0 \end{pmatrix}$$

$$\begin{array}{c} \\ (1/3)(2r_1 - r_2) \\ 5r_1 - r_3 \end{array} \begin{pmatrix} 1 & 1 & -1 & | & 5 \\ 0 & 1 & -2 & | & 3 \\ 0 & 3 & -6 & | & 22 \end{pmatrix}$$

STEP 2:   Change the second column to:

$$\begin{pmatrix} 0 \\ 1 \\ 0 \end{pmatrix}$$

$$\begin{array}{c} r_1 - r_2 \\ \\ r_3 - 3r_2 \end{array} \begin{pmatrix} 1 & 0 & 1 & | & 2 \\ 0 & 1 & -2 & | & 3 \\ 0 & 0 & 0 & | & 13 \end{pmatrix}$$

The equation corresponding to the last row in the augmented matrix is $0x_1 + 0x_2 + 0x_3 = 13$. For any choice of values for x_1, x_2, and x_3, the sum $0x_1 + 0x_2 + 0x_3$ is equal to zero, not 13; so the equation $0x_1 + 0x_2 + 0x_3 = 13$ has no solutions. Row operations 1 through 4 do not change the solutions. So there are no solutions to the original system:

$$x_1 + x_2 - x_3 = 5$$
$$2x_1 - x_2 + 4x_3 = 1$$
$$5x_1 + 2x_2 + x_3 = 3$$

If, when applying row operations to an augmented matrix $(A\,|\,b)$, you obtain a row of 0's followed by a nonzero number in the last column, then there is no solution to the system of equations with augmented matrix $(A\,|\,b)$.

In the last two sections, we have described the method of Gauss-Jordan elimination and used it to solve systems of linear equations. In Example 3 and in Practice Example 2, we showed that the results of Gauss-Jordan elimination can be used to solve linear optimization problems. In these examples the method of Gauss-Jordan elimination reduces the optimization problem to a linear program involving only the nonbasic variables. Row operations and the correspondence between systems of linear equations and augmented matrices are fundamental to the algorithm for solving linear programs in the next chapter and to solving matrix equations in the next section.

Gauss-Jordan elimination is a modification by the French mathematician, Camille Jordan (1838–1922), of the original elimination method invented by Carl Friedrich Gauss (1777–1855). Gauss's method is to eliminate the first variable from the second and all following equations, then eliminate the second variable from the third and all following equations and so on, to obtain a system of equations in which each equation has fewer variables than the one preceding it. The system of equations is then solved by "back substitution." First solve the equation with the fewest variables. Substitute the solution into the preceding equation. Solve this equation. Continue to solve and substitute working back to the equation with the largest number of variables. These changes in the system of equations can be carried out using row operations on the corresponding augmented matrices. The end result is the same reduced matrix obtained by working on the columns from left to right as we did in all the examples in this section and the last. Thus, the two methods obtain the same reduced matrix but by a different sequence of row operations. With a little practice, you should be able to use either method. The original method of Gauss requires fewer computations than Gauss-Jordan elimination and is the most efficient matrix elimination procedure for use on computers.

CONCEPTS

> reduced
> basic variables
> nonbasic variables

SOLUTIONS TO PRACTICE EXAMPLES

1. The augmented matrix is:

$$\begin{pmatrix} 2 & 5 & 3 & \bigm| & 50 \\ 3 & 7 & 1 & \bigm| & 48 \\ 5 & 13 & 11 & \bigm| & 152 \end{pmatrix}$$

The system of equations is solved by carrying out the following row operations. Replace row one with $r_2 - r_1$. Then replace row two with $r_2 - 3r_1$ and row three with $r_3 - 5r_1$. This gives:

$$\begin{pmatrix} 1 & 2 & -2 & \bigm| & -2 \\ 0 & 1 & 7 & \bigm| & 54 \\ 0 & 3 & 21 & \bigm| & 162 \end{pmatrix}$$

The last step is:

$$\begin{matrix} r_1 - 2r_2 \\ \\ r_3 - 3r_2 \end{matrix} \begin{pmatrix} 1 & 0 & -16 & \bigm| & -110 \\ 0 & 1 & 7 & \bigm| & 54 \\ 0 & 0 & 0 & \bigm| & 0 \end{pmatrix}$$

The augmented matrix corresponds to the equations:

$$x_1 - 16x_3 = -110$$
$$x_2 + 7x_3 = 54$$

Hence:

(a) $x_1 = 16x_3 - 110$
(b) $x_2 = 54 - 7x_3$

and the original system of linear equations has an infinite number of solutions, one for each choice of value for x_3. The values of x_1 and x_2 are determined by equations (a) and (b).

2. (a) If:

$$x_1 = \text{number of units of food } F_1 \text{ in the mixture}$$
$$x_2 = \text{number of units of food } F_2 \text{ in the mixture}$$
$$x_3 = \text{number of units of food } F_3 \text{ in the mixture}$$

and

$$x_4 = \text{number of units of food } F_4 \text{ in the mixture}$$

then the system of equations corresponding to the requirements is:

$$2x_1 + 3x_2 + x_3 + 2x_4 = 25 \quad \text{(vitamin C)}$$

$$5x_1 + 7x_2 + 2x_3 + 2x_4 = 55 \quad \text{(calcium)}$$

$$38x_1 + 57x_2 + 19x_3 + 4x_4 = 441 \quad \text{(iron)}$$

(b) The augmented matrix is:

$$\begin{pmatrix} 2 & 3 & 1 & 2 & | & 25 \\ 5 & 7 & 2 & 2 & | & 55 \\ 38 & 57 & 19 & 4 & | & 441 \end{pmatrix}$$

The system of equations is solved using the following row operations. Replace row one with $r_2 - 2r_1$, then replace row two with $r_2 - 5r_1$, and row three with $r_3 - 38r_1$. This gives:

$$\begin{pmatrix} 1 & 1 & 0 & -2 & | & 5 \\ 0 & 2 & 2 & 12 & | & 30 \\ 0 & 19 & 19 & 80 & | & 251 \end{pmatrix}$$

Next replace row two with $r_2/2$; then replace row one with $r_1 - r_2$ and row three with $19r_2 - r_3$. This gives:

$$\begin{pmatrix} 1 & 0 & -1 & -8 & | & -10 \\ 0 & 1 & 1 & 6 & | & 15 \\ 0 & 0 & 0 & 34 & | & 34 \end{pmatrix}$$

Now divide row three by 34; replace row one with $r_1 + 8r_3$ and row two with $r_2 - 6r_3$. This gives:

$$\begin{pmatrix} 1 & 0 & -1 & 0 & | & -2 \\ 0 & 1 & 1 & 0 & | & 9 \\ 0 & 0 & 0 & 1 & | & 1 \end{pmatrix}$$

Write the equations and solve for x_1, x_2, and x_4.

(i) $x_1 = -2 + x_3$
(ii) $x_2 = 9 - x_3$
(iii) $x_4 = 1$

A mixture is obtained by choosing a value for x_3 and then substituting into (i) and (ii) to find the amount of the other foods that should be added. Notice that the value of x_3 must be chosen so that the resulting values of x_1 and x_2 are greater than or equal to 0. (You cannot mix in -2 ounces of food F_1). If we choose x_3 to be 9, then $x_1 = 7$, $x_2 = 0$, $x_3 = 9$, and $x_4 = 1$. One of the possible mixtures is:

7 ozs of food F_1

0 ozs of food F_2

9 ozs of food F_3

1 oz of food F_4

(c) The total number of calories in a mixture is:

$$185x_1 + 110x_2 + 150x_3 + 200x_4$$

Substituting into (i), (ii), and (iii) gives:

$$185(x_3 - 2) + 110(9 - x_3) + 150x_3 + 200(1) = 820 + 225x_3$$

The mixture with the least number of calories is obtained by choosing the smallest possible value for x_3. From equation (i) it follows that the smallest possible value for $x_3 = 2$. (Note x_1 must be greater than or equal to 0.) Thus the mixture with the smallest number of calories is:

0 ozs of food F_1

7 ozs of food F_2

2 ozs of food F_3

1 oz of food F_4

The total number of calories in this mixture is:

$$820 + 225(2) = 1270$$

EXERCISES 10.5

In Exercises 1 through 10, solve the given system of equations by Gauss-Jordan elimination.

1. $2x_1 + 3x_2 + x_3 = 11$

   $3x_1 + 4x_2 + 2x_3 = 15$

2. $5x_1 + 2x_2 + 15x_3 = 39$

   $7x_1 + 3x_2 + 21x_3 = 52$

3. $3x_1 + x_2 + 7x_3 = 14$

   $4x_1 + x_2 + 9x_3 = 17$

   $9x_1 + 4x_2 + 22x_3 = 47$

4. $x_1 + 4x_2 + 2x_3 = 9$

   $7x_1 + x_2 + 14x_3 = 36$

   $3x_1 + 2x_2 + 6x_3 = 21$

5. $x_1 + x_2 + x_3 = 1$

   $2x_1 - x_2 + x_3 = 7$

   $5x_1 + 2x_2 + 4x_3 = 10$

6. $x_1 + x_2 + x_3 = 1$

   $2x_1 - x_2 + x_3 = 7$

   $5x_1 + 2x_2 + 4x_3 = 8$

7. $x_1 - x_2 + 2x_3 = 3$

   $3x_1 - 4x_2 + x_3 = 1$

   $5x_1 - 6x_2 + 5x_3 = 7$

8. $x_1 - x_2 + 2x_3 = 2$

   $3x_1 - 4x_2 + x_3 = 1$

   $5x_1 - 6x_2 + 5x_3 = 7$

9. $x_1 + 2x_2 + x_3 + x_4 = 12$

   $2x_1 + 3x_2 + x_3 + x_4 = 17$

   $5x_1 + x_2 + 3x_3 - 4x_4 = 11$

10. $x_1 + 3x_2 + x_3 + x_4 = 3$

    $2x_1 + x_2 - 3x_3 + 2x_4 = 1$

    $-1x_1 + 4x_2 + 6x_3 - x_4 = 4$

11. The table below gives the number of units of vitamin A, vitamin C, and calcium in each ounce of three different foods, F_1, F_2, and F_3.

	F_1	F_2	F_3
Vitamin A	10	20	80
Vitamin C	30	10	90
Calcium	225	250	1200

(a) Find a mixture of these three foods that contains 280 units of vitamin A, 390 units of vitamin C, and 4500 units of iron.

(b) Find the least expensive mixture that satisfies the requirements in part (a) if F_1 costs $.11 an ounce, F_2 costs $.13 an ounce and:

(i) F_3 costs $.62 an ounce.

(ii) F_3 costs $.60 an ounce.

12. A truck is to be loaded with three different types of containers. The first type weighs 300 lbs and takes up 15 cubic ft of space. The second type of container weighs 100 lbs and occupies 20 cubic ft. The third type of container weighs 700 lbs and occupies 50 cubic ft. The truck has a capacity of 9500 lbs and 1000 cubic ft. How many containers of each type should be loaded into the truck in order to fill the truck to capacity and carry as many containers of the third type as possible?

13. A company makes sofas, chairs, tables, and desks. Production is done in three steps: carpentry work, assembly, and finishing. The following table gives the number of minutes needed to carry out these steps.

	Sofa	Chair	Table	Desk
Carpentry	120	60	60	60
Assembly	180	60	120	120
Finishing	60	30	45	60

The total labor time available each week is 30,000 min of carpentry time, 51,000 min of assembly time, and 19,500 min for finishing. A production schedule is a list that specifies how many products of each kind are to be made.
(a) Find a weekly production schedule that uses all the available labor time.
(b) Suppose the profit is $100 for a sofa, $30 for a chair, $55 for a table, and $30 for a desk. Find a weekly production schedule that uses all available labor time and maximizes the profit.

14. A company has two plants that produce both washers and dryers. Each plant can make up to a total of 525 appliances a day. The company wants to make 600 washers and 450 dryers a day. Let:

x_1 = number of washers to be made at the first plant

x_2 = number of dryers to be made at the first plant

x_3 = number of washers to be made at the second plant

x_4 = number of dryers to be made at the second plant

(a) Replace each statement below with a corresponding equation.

525 appliances are made at the first plant

525 appliances are made at the second plant

600 washers are made

450 dryers are made

(b) Solve the system of equations in part (a).
(c) If it costs the company $104 to make a washer and $88 to make a dryer at the first plant, and $92 to make a washer and $80 to make a dryer at the second plant, then how many washers and how many dryers should be made each day at each plant in order for the total cost to be as small as possible?

15. A company with two warehouses has received orders for videotape machines from three stores. The figure below gives the number of machines available in

the warehouses, the number of machines ordered, and the shipping costs per machine. Find a shipping schedule of least cost.

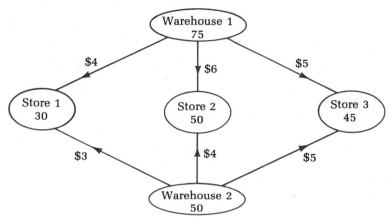

10.6   *Inverses—Leontief Input-Output Models*

In this section, we show how row operations are used to find the inverse, A^{-1}, of a matrix, A. The **inverse of a matrix** is the analogue in matrix arithmetic of the reciprocal of a number and is used to solve matrix equations of the form $BX = C$ for the matrix X. We use matrix inverses to show how the demand (or change in demand) for a product affects production in other directly and indirectly related areas. Such models, called **input-output models**, have been used to study the interrelationships between divisions within companies and between industries within countries.

The inverse of the number 5 is:

$$(5)^{-1} = \frac{1}{5} = .2$$

The inverse of 5 has the property:

$$(5)(5)^{-1} = (5)^{-1}(5) = 1$$

since

$$5(.2) = (.2)(5) = 1$$

In general, the inverse of a number, a, is the number b that satisfies $ab = ba = 1$. The inverse of a matrix, A, is defined similarly.

DEFINITION   The inverse of an n-by-n matrix, A, is a square matrix B that satisfies:

$$AB = BA = I$$

where I denotes the n-by-n identity matrix. The inverse of A is denoted by A^{-1}.

The inverse of:

$$A = \begin{pmatrix} 2 & 1 \\ 3 & 4 \end{pmatrix}$$

is the matrix:

$$\begin{pmatrix} .8 & -.2 \\ -.6 & .4 \end{pmatrix} = A^{-1}$$

since:

$$\begin{pmatrix} 2 & 1 \\ 3 & 4 \end{pmatrix} \begin{pmatrix} .8 & -.2 \\ -.6 & .4 \end{pmatrix} = \begin{pmatrix} 1 & 0 \\ 0 & 1 \end{pmatrix}$$

and:

$$\begin{pmatrix} .8 & -.2 \\ -.6 & .4 \end{pmatrix} \begin{pmatrix} 2 & 1 \\ 3 & 4 \end{pmatrix} = \begin{pmatrix} 1 & 0 \\ 0 & 1 \end{pmatrix}$$

Only square matrices have inverses. The condition that AB and BA be defined and equal implies that A and B are square matrices of the same size. If A is an n-by-n square matrix, then $(A|I)$ denotes the n-by-$2n$ matrix whose first n columns are the columns of A and whose last n columns are the columns of the n-by-n identity. $(I|A)$ is defined similarly.

PROCEDURE FOR FINDING INVERSES

To find the inverse of a matrix A, use the row operations 1 through 4 (Section 10.4) to transform the matrix $(A|I)$ to a matrix of the form $(I|B)$. B is the inverse of A.

To see why this procedure works, consider the problem of finding the inverse of:

$$\begin{pmatrix} 1 & 3 \\ 2 & 4 \end{pmatrix}$$

If:

$$\begin{pmatrix} b_{11} & b_{12} \\ b_{21} & b_{22} \end{pmatrix}$$

is the inverse, then the matrix equation:

$$\begin{pmatrix} 1 & 3 \\ 2 & 4 \end{pmatrix} \begin{pmatrix} b_{11} & b_{12} \\ b_{21} & b_{22} \end{pmatrix} = \begin{pmatrix} 1 & 0 \\ 0 & 1 \end{pmatrix}$$

corresponds to the two systems of equations:

$$b_{11} + 3b_{21} = 1$$
$$2b_{11} + 4b_{21} = 0$$

and

$$b_{12} + 3b_{22} = 0$$
$$2b_{12} + 4b_{22} = 1$$

These can be solved by applying row operations to the augmented matrices:

$$\begin{pmatrix} 1 & 3 & | & 1 \\ 2 & 4 & | & 0 \end{pmatrix} \quad \text{and} \quad \begin{pmatrix} 1 & 3 & | & 0 \\ 2 & 4 & | & 1 \end{pmatrix}$$

The technique described above for finding the inverse amounts to solving both these systems at one time by applying row operations to:

$$\begin{pmatrix} 1 & 3 & | & 1 & 0 \\ 2 & 4 & | & 0 & 1 \end{pmatrix}$$

EXAMPLE 1

Find the inverse of:

$$A = \begin{pmatrix} 1 & 3 \\ 2 & 4 \end{pmatrix}$$

According to the procedure, if we use row operations to transform:

$$\begin{pmatrix} 1 & 3 & | & 1 & 0 \\ 2 & 4 & | & 0 & 1 \end{pmatrix}$$

into an augmented matrix of the form:

$$\begin{pmatrix} 1 & 0 & | & b_{11} & b_{12} \\ 0 & 1 & | & b_{21} & b_{22} \end{pmatrix}$$

then:

$$A^{-1} = \begin{pmatrix} b_{11} & b_{12} \\ b_{21} & b_{22} \end{pmatrix}$$

We want to apply row operations to:

$$\begin{pmatrix} 1 & 3 & | & 1 & 0 \\ 2 & 4 & | & 0 & 1 \end{pmatrix}$$

to replace the first two columns of the matrix with the first two columns of the 2-by-2 identity. The first step is to replace the first column with the first column of the identity.

$$2r_1 - r_2 \begin{pmatrix} 1 & 3 & | & 1 & 0 \\ 0 & 2 & | & 2 & -1 \end{pmatrix}$$

$$(1/2)\, r_2 \begin{pmatrix} 1 & 3 & | & 1 & 0 \\ 0 & 1 & | & 1 & -\dfrac{1}{2} \end{pmatrix}$$

$$r_1 - 3r_2 \begin{pmatrix} 1 & 0 & | & -2 & \dfrac{3}{2} \\ 0 & 1 & | & 1 & -\dfrac{1}{2} \end{pmatrix}$$

We can check that:

$$\begin{pmatrix} -2 & \dfrac{3}{2} \\ 1 & -\dfrac{1}{2} \end{pmatrix}$$

is the inverse of:

$$\begin{pmatrix} 1 & 3 \\ 2 & 4 \end{pmatrix}$$

by computing the products:

$$\begin{pmatrix} 1 & 3 \\ 2 & 4 \end{pmatrix}\begin{pmatrix} -2 & \dfrac{3}{2} \\ 1 & -\dfrac{1}{2} \end{pmatrix}$$

and:

$$\begin{pmatrix} -2 & \dfrac{3}{2} \\ 1 & -\dfrac{1}{2} \end{pmatrix}\begin{pmatrix} 1 & 3 \\ 2 & 4 \end{pmatrix}$$

to verify these products are the 2-by-2 identity.

$$\begin{pmatrix} 1 & 3 \\ 2 & 4 \end{pmatrix} \begin{pmatrix} -2 & \dfrac{3}{2} \\ 1 & -\dfrac{1}{2} \end{pmatrix} = \begin{pmatrix} -2+3 & \dfrac{3}{2}+3\left(-\dfrac{1}{2}\right) \\ 2(-2)+4 & 2\left(\dfrac{3}{2}\right)+4\left(-\dfrac{1}{2}\right) \end{pmatrix} \begin{pmatrix} 1 & 0 \\ 0 & 1 \end{pmatrix}$$

$$\begin{pmatrix} -2 & \dfrac{3}{2} \\ 1 & -\dfrac{1}{2} \end{pmatrix} \begin{pmatrix} 1 & 3 \\ 2 & 4 \end{pmatrix} = \begin{pmatrix} -2+\left(\dfrac{3}{2}\right)2 & -2(3)+\left(\dfrac{3}{2}\right)4 \\ 1+\left(-\dfrac{1}{2}\right)2 & 3+\left(-\dfrac{1}{2}\right)4 \end{pmatrix} = \begin{pmatrix} 1 & 0 \\ 0 & 1 \end{pmatrix}$$

■

It turns out that for square matrices A and B, if either of the products AB or BA is an identity matrix, then so is the other. Thus to check the answer in Example 1, it would have been enough to compute just one of the products.

$$\begin{pmatrix} 1 & 3 \\ 2 & 4 \end{pmatrix} \begin{pmatrix} -2 & \dfrac{3}{2} \\ 1 & -\dfrac{1}{2} \end{pmatrix} \; ; \qquad \begin{pmatrix} -2 & \dfrac{3}{2} \\ 1 & -\dfrac{1}{2} \end{pmatrix} \begin{pmatrix} 1 & 3 \\ 2 & 4 \end{pmatrix}$$

EXAMPLE 2 Find the inverse of the matrix:

$$A = \begin{pmatrix} 1 & 0 & 2 \\ 0 & 1 & 1 \\ 1 & 1 & 4 \end{pmatrix}$$

Applying row operations to:

$$\left(\begin{array}{ccc|ccc} 1 & 0 & 2 & 1 & 0 & 0 \\ 0 & 1 & 1 & 0 & 1 & 0 \\ 1 & 1 & 4 & 0 & 0 & 1 \end{array}\right)$$

we get:

$$\begin{array}{c} \\ \\ r_3 - r_1 \end{array} \left(\begin{array}{ccc|ccc} 1 & 0 & 2 & 1 & 0 & 0 \\ 0 & 1 & 1 & 0 & 1 & 0 \\ 0 & 1 & 2 & -1 & 0 & 1 \end{array}\right)$$

$$
\begin{array}{c}
\\
\\
r_3 - r_2
\end{array}
\left(
\begin{array}{ccc|ccc}
1 & 0 & 2 & 1 & 0 & 0 \\
0 & 1 & 1 & 0 & 1 & 0 \\
0 & 0 & 1 & -1 & -1 & 1
\end{array}
\right)
$$

$$
\begin{array}{c}
r_1 - 2r_3 \\
r_2 - r_3 \\
\\
\end{array}
\left(
\begin{array}{ccc|ccc}
1 & 0 & 0 & 3 & 2 & -2 \\
0 & 1 & 0 & 1 & 2 & -1 \\
0 & 0 & 1 & -1 & -1 & 1
\end{array}
\right)
$$

We check that:

$$
\begin{pmatrix}
1 & 0 & 2 \\
0 & 1 & 1 \\
1 & 1 & 4
\end{pmatrix}^{-1}
=
\begin{pmatrix}
3 & 2 & -2 \\
1 & 2 & -1 \\
-1 & -1 & 1
\end{pmatrix}
$$

by computing:

$$
\begin{pmatrix}
1 & 0 & 2 \\
0 & 1 & 1 \\
1 & 1 & 4
\end{pmatrix}
\begin{pmatrix}
3 & 2 & -2 \\
1 & 2 & -1 \\
-1 & -1 & 1
\end{pmatrix}
$$

$$
=
\begin{pmatrix}
3 - 2 & 2 - 2 & -2 + 2 \\
1 + (-1) & 2 - 1 & -1 + 1 \\
3 + 1 - 4 & 2 + 2 - 4 & -2 - 1 + 4
\end{pmatrix}
=
\begin{pmatrix}
1 & 0 & 0 \\
0 & 1 & 0 \\
0 & 0 & 1
\end{pmatrix}
$$

■

PRACTICE EXAMPLE 1

Find the inverse of each of the following matrices:

(a) $\begin{pmatrix} 1 & 4 \\ 3 & 16 \end{pmatrix}$
 (b) $\begin{pmatrix} 1 & 2 & 1 \\ 3 & 7 & 4 \\ 5 & 6 & 0 \end{pmatrix}$ ■

Inverses can be used to solve matrix equations.

THEOREM 1   If B has an inverse, then the equation $BX = C$ has solution $X = B^{-1}C$.

To show this is true we need to verify that if X is replaced by $B^{-1}C$ then BX equals C.

$$BX = B(B^{-1}C)$$
$$= (BB^{-1})C$$
$$= IC$$
$$= C$$

EXAMPLE 3   Use theorem 1 to solve the matrix equations:

$$\begin{pmatrix} 1 & 3 \\ 2 & 4 \end{pmatrix}\begin{pmatrix} x_1 \\ x_2 \end{pmatrix} = \begin{pmatrix} 5 \\ 8 \end{pmatrix} \qquad \begin{pmatrix} 1 & 3 \\ 2 & 4 \end{pmatrix}\begin{pmatrix} y_1 \\ y_2 \end{pmatrix} = \begin{pmatrix} -1 \\ 10 \end{pmatrix}$$

From theorem 1 it follows that the solutions are given by:

$$\begin{pmatrix} x_1 \\ x_2 \end{pmatrix} = \begin{pmatrix} 1 & 3 \\ 2 & 4 \end{pmatrix}^{-1}\begin{pmatrix} 5 \\ 8 \end{pmatrix} \qquad \begin{pmatrix} y_1 \\ y_2 \end{pmatrix} = \begin{pmatrix} 1 & 3 \\ 2 & 4 \end{pmatrix}^{-1}\begin{pmatrix} -1 \\ 10 \end{pmatrix}$$

From Example 1:

$$\begin{pmatrix} 1 & 3 \\ 2 & 4 \end{pmatrix}^{-1} = \begin{pmatrix} -2 & \dfrac{3}{2} \\ 1 & -\dfrac{1}{2} \end{pmatrix}$$

so:

$$\begin{pmatrix} x_1 \\ x_2 \end{pmatrix} = \begin{pmatrix} -2 & \dfrac{3}{2} \\ 1 & -\dfrac{1}{2} \end{pmatrix}\begin{pmatrix} 5 \\ 8 \end{pmatrix} \qquad \begin{pmatrix} y_1 \\ y_2 \end{pmatrix} = \begin{pmatrix} -2 & \dfrac{3}{2} \\ 1 & -\dfrac{1}{2} \end{pmatrix}\begin{pmatrix} -1 \\ 10 \end{pmatrix}$$

$$\begin{pmatrix} x_1 \\ x_2 \end{pmatrix} = \begin{pmatrix} 2 \\ 1 \end{pmatrix} \qquad\qquad \begin{pmatrix} y_1 \\ y_2 \end{pmatrix} = \begin{pmatrix} 17 \\ -6 \end{pmatrix}$$

Notice that in Example 3, we solved two systems of linear equations:

$$x_1 + 3x_2 = 5 \qquad \text{and} \qquad x_1 + 3x_2 = -1$$
$$2x_1 + 4x_2 = 8 \qquad\qquad\qquad 2x_1 + 4x_2 = 10$$

using the inverse of the matrix of coefficients:

$$\begin{pmatrix} 1 & 3 \\ 2 & 4 \end{pmatrix}$$

Theorem 1 gives an effective way to solve systems of linear equations when the coefficients of the variables remain fixed and the constants change, as in Example 3.

PRACTICE
EXAMPLE 2

Use the theorem above to solve:

(a) $\begin{pmatrix} 1 & 0 & 2 \\ 0 & 1 & 1 \\ 1 & 1 & 4 \end{pmatrix} \begin{pmatrix} x_1 \\ x_2 \\ x_3 \end{pmatrix} = \begin{pmatrix} 2 \\ -1 \\ 3 \end{pmatrix}$ (b) $\begin{pmatrix} 1 & 0 & 2 \\ 0 & 1 & 1 \\ 1 & 1 & 4 \end{pmatrix} \begin{pmatrix} y_1 \\ y_2 \\ y_3 \end{pmatrix} = \begin{pmatrix} 3 \\ 1 \\ 1 \end{pmatrix}$ ■

The next example illustrates that if A cannot be converted to I by row operations, then A does not have an inverse.

EXAMPLE 4

Show the matrix:

$$A = \begin{pmatrix} 1 & 3 \\ 2 & 6 \end{pmatrix}$$

does not have an inverse.

Applying the procedure for finding A^{-1} to:

$$A = \begin{pmatrix} 1 & 3 \\ 2 & 6 \end{pmatrix}$$

we get:

$$\begin{pmatrix} 1 & 3 & | & 1 & 0 \\ 2 & 6 & | & 0 & 1 \end{pmatrix}$$

$$2r_1 - r_2 \begin{pmatrix} 1 & 3 & | & 1 & 0 \\ 0 & 0 & | & 2 & -1 \end{pmatrix}$$

So:

$$\begin{pmatrix} 1 & 3 & | & 1 & 0 \\ 2 & 6 & | & 0 & 1 \end{pmatrix}$$

cannot be transformed to:

$$\begin{pmatrix} 1 & 0 & | & b_{11} & b_{12} \\ 0 & 1 & | & b_{21} & b_{22} \end{pmatrix}$$

using row operations. We can see that A has no inverse as follows. If A has an inverse, then the first column of A^{-1}, $C_1(A^{-1})$, is a solution to the system of equations with augmented matrix:

$$\begin{pmatrix} 1 & 3 & | & 1 \\ 2 & 6 & | & 0 \end{pmatrix}$$

but this can be converted to:

$$\left(\begin{array}{cc|c} 1 & 3 & 1 \\ 0 & 0 & 2 \end{array}\right)$$

which has no solution. Hence there is no inverse for:

$$\begin{pmatrix} 1 & 3 \\ 2 & 6 \end{pmatrix}$$

In the rest of this section we will use the following formula to compute inverses of 2-by-2 matrices.

FORMULA FOR THE INVERSE OF A 2-BY-2 MATRIX

$$\begin{pmatrix} a & b \\ c & d \end{pmatrix}^{-1} = \begin{pmatrix} d/D & -b/D \\ -c/D & a/D \end{pmatrix}$$

where: $D = ad - bc$. If $D = ad - bc = 0$ then:

$$\begin{pmatrix} a & b \\ c & d \end{pmatrix}$$

has no inverse.

**PRACTICE
EXAMPLE 3**

Use the formula above to find the inverse (if there is one) of:

(a) $\begin{pmatrix} 1 & 3 \\ 2 & 4 \end{pmatrix}$

(b) $\begin{pmatrix} 1 & 4 \\ 3 & 16 \end{pmatrix}$

(c) $\begin{pmatrix} 1 & 3 \\ 2 & 6 \end{pmatrix}$

Compare your answers with those in Example 1, Practice Example 1(a) of Section 10.6, and Example 4.

The number $D = ad - bc$ is called the **determinant** of:

$$\begin{pmatrix} a & b \\ c & d \end{pmatrix}$$

There are corresponding formulas for the determinant and for the inverse of 3-by-3, 4-by-4 matrices, and so on. For these larger matrices the computations involved in using the determinant to compute the inverse can be impractically complicated and lead to large round-off errors. Generally, Gauss-Jordan elimination is quicker and more accurate.

Matrix inverses arise naturally in input-output models. These models are used to predict how the demand (or change in demand) for a product affects production in other directly and indirectly related areas. A change in demand for computers, for example, affects companies that make such related products as monitors, printers, microchips, and computer disks. These changes affect companies that produce supplies for the makers of monitors, printers, and so on. The objective of an input-output model is to predict the total effect on each industry or company resulting from a change in demand.

At the end of World War II input-output modeling of the U.S. economy accurately predicted a postwar shortage of steel. At the time, many economists anticipated that the switch from a wartime to peacetime economy would lead to a surplus of steel. Input-output analysis was invented by the Harvard economist Wassily Leontief, who presented his theory in 1936. However, because of the large number of computations needed to apply the theory (inverting a matrix with 100 rows and columns, for example), it was not until the late 1940s and early 1950s that computations related to the American economy were obtained with the help of a computer. In 1973, Leontief was awarded the Nobel Prize for his creation of input-output analysis. (See *Scientific American*, April 1965, Vol. 212, No. 4, 25–35, as well as Leontief 1966.)

The first step toward understanding input-output models is to see the connection between output and demand given by matrix multiplication.

EXAMPLE 5   Some companies, Texas Instruments for example, make both microchips and computers. The microchip division supplies chips to the computer division, and the computer division supplies itself and the microchip division with the computers they need to run their divisions. Suppose each dollar's worth of output from the computer division requires $.25 worth of input from the microchip division and $.03 worth of input from the computer division. Suppose each dollar's worth of output from the microchip division requires $.02 worth of output from the computer division. How much total output will be required from each division to meet an expected demand next year for $100 million worth of the company's computers and $50 million worth of the company's microchips? Here demand refers to the dollar value of sales outside the company and does not include any of the company's output that is used within the company. The **input-output graph** in Figure 10.14 pictures the given information.

Figure 10.14

Input-output
graph

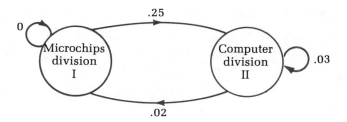

We can construct a matrix, A, from the input-output graph by setting $A_{i,j}$ = number on the directed edge from division i to division j. A is called the **input-output matrix**:

$$
\begin{array}{cc}
& \begin{array}{cc} \text{I} & \text{II} \end{array} \\
\begin{array}{c} \text{I} \\ \text{II} \end{array} & \left(\begin{array}{cc} 0 & .25 \\ .02 & .03 \end{array} \right)
\end{array}
$$

Let x_1 = dollar value of the total output of the microchip division for the year, and x_2 = dollar value of the total output of the computer division.

The amount of the **total output** sold outside the company is called the **final demand**. We have been given

$$
\text{final demand} = D = \left(\begin{array}{c} 50 \\ 100 \end{array} \right) \quad \begin{array}{l} \text{microchips} \\ \text{computers} \end{array}
$$

and are asked to find

$$
\text{total output} = X = \left(\begin{array}{c} x_1 \\ x_2 \end{array} \right) \quad \begin{array}{l} \text{microchips} \\ \text{computers} \end{array}
$$

We can add the unknowns, x_1 and x_2, to the input-output graph to obtain the **output flow graph** of Figure 10.15.

Figure 10.15

Output flow
graph

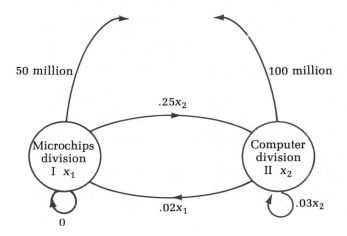

The number $.25x_2$ on the edge from I to II is interpreted as follows.

$$.25x_2 = \begin{pmatrix} \text{amount of output from I} \\ \text{needed to produce \$1 worth} \\ \text{of output from II} \end{pmatrix} \times \begin{pmatrix} \text{Amount of total} \\ \text{output from II} \end{pmatrix}$$

$$= \text{amount of total output from I used by II}$$

Similarly,

$$.03x_2 = \text{amount of total output from II used by II}$$

$$.02x_1 = \text{amount of total output from II used by I}$$

Hence,

$$\begin{pmatrix} .25x_2 \\ .02x_1 + .03x_2 \end{pmatrix} = \begin{pmatrix} \text{amount of output from I used within the company} \\ \text{amount of output from II used within the company} \end{pmatrix}$$

$$= \text{amount of each division's output consumed within the company}$$

Hence,

$$\underset{A}{\begin{pmatrix} 0 & .25 \\ .02 & .03 \end{pmatrix}} \underset{X}{\begin{pmatrix} x_1 \\ x_2 \end{pmatrix}} = \text{amount of each division's output consumed within the company}$$

Each division's output is equal to the amount consumed within the company plus the division's final demand. Hence the matrix equation:

$$X = AX + D$$

relates

$$X = \text{total output}$$

$$D = \text{final demand}$$

$$A = \text{input-output matrix}$$

This equation can be solved for D as follows.

$$X = AX + D$$

$$X - AX = D$$

The equation $X - AX = D$ computes the final demand if the total output is known.

In this example we are given the final demand:

$$D = \begin{pmatrix} 50 \\ 100 \end{pmatrix}$$

and want to find the total output X. The equation $X - AX = D$ is solved for X as follows.

$$X - AX = D$$

$$IX - AX = D$$

$$(I - A)X = D$$

So,

$$X = (I - A)^{-1}D$$

The equation $X = (I - A)^{-1}D$ computes the total output if the demand is known.

In this example,

$$A = \begin{pmatrix} 0 & .25 \\ .02 & .03 \end{pmatrix}$$

$$(I - A) = \begin{pmatrix} 1 & 0 \\ 0 & 1 \end{pmatrix} - \begin{pmatrix} 0 & .25 \\ .02 & .03 \end{pmatrix} = \begin{pmatrix} 1 - 0 & 0 - .25 \\ 0 - .02 & 1 - .03 \end{pmatrix}$$

$$= \begin{pmatrix} 1 & -.25 \\ -.02 & .97 \end{pmatrix}$$

Using the formula:

$$\begin{pmatrix} a & b \\ c & d \end{pmatrix}^{-1} = \begin{pmatrix} d/D & -b/D \\ -c/D & a/D \end{pmatrix}, \qquad D = ad - bc$$

we get $D = 1(.97) - (-.25)(-.02) = .97 - .005 = .965$, so:

$$(I - A)^{-1} = \begin{pmatrix} 1 & -.25 \\ -.02 & .97 \end{pmatrix}^{-1} = \begin{pmatrix} \dfrac{.97}{.965} & \dfrac{.25}{.965} \\ \dfrac{.02}{.965} & \dfrac{1}{.965} \end{pmatrix}$$

$$D = \begin{pmatrix} 50 \\ 100 \end{pmatrix} \quad \begin{array}{l} \text{final demand for the company's microchips} \\ \text{final demand for the company's computers} \end{array}$$

$$(I - A)^{-1}D = \begin{pmatrix} \dfrac{.97}{.965} & \dfrac{.25}{.965} \\ \dfrac{.02}{.965} & \dfrac{1}{.965} \end{pmatrix} \begin{pmatrix} 50 \\ 100 \end{pmatrix} = \begin{pmatrix} 76.1658 \\ 104.6632 \end{pmatrix}$$

(numbers rounded to four decimal places)

The microchip division needs to produce $76.1658 million worth of microchips and the computer division needs to produce $104.6632 million worth of computers in order for the company to meet a demand for $50 million worth of the company's microchips and $100 million worth of the company's computers.   ■

Suppose the input-output graph of a company with two divisions is the graph in Figure 10.16.

Figure 10.16

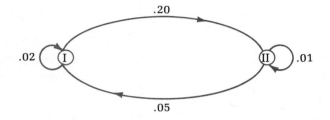

Find:

(a) The input-output matrix A.

Use

$$X = \begin{pmatrix} 200 \\ 150 \end{pmatrix} \begin{matrix} \text{total output of I} \\ \text{total output of II} \end{matrix}$$

Find:

(b) AX.
(c) $X - AX$.
(d) Interpret your answers to (b) and (c).
(e) Make a table that lists for each division the amount of total output consumed within the company, the amount sold outside the company, and the division's total output.   ■

If

$$A = \begin{pmatrix} 0 & .4 \\ .3 & .2 \end{pmatrix} \quad \text{and} \quad D = \begin{pmatrix} 102 \\ 170 \end{pmatrix}$$

find:

(a) $I - A$.
(b) $(I - A)^{-1}$.
(c) $(I - A)^{-1}D$.
(d) If A is an input-output matrix and D is the final demand, then what is the interpretation of $(I - A)^{-1}D$?   ■

In the equation $(I - A)^{-1}D = X$ the demand, D, can be replaced by a change in demand, ΔD; and the total output, X, can be replaced by a change in total output, ΔX. If the demand goes from D_1 to D_2, and the output goes from X_1 to X_2, then:

$$(I - A)^{-1})(\Delta D) = \Delta X$$

where:

$$\Delta D = D_2 - D_1$$
$$\Delta X = X_2 - X_1$$

EXAMPLE 6   Suppose the company described in Example 5 predicts a change in demand of:

$$\Delta D = \begin{pmatrix} 5 \\ -3 \end{pmatrix} \qquad \text{change in demand for company's microchips}$$
$$\text{change in demand for company's computers}$$

where the numbers indicate millions of dollars. Find the corresponding change in each division's total output.

Use the equation:

$$(I - A)^{-1}(\Delta D) = \Delta X$$

with:

$$(I - A)^{-1} = \begin{pmatrix} \dfrac{.97}{.965} & \dfrac{.25}{.965} \\ \dfrac{.02}{.965} & \dfrac{1}{.965} \end{pmatrix}$$

from Example 5 and with:

$$\Delta D = \begin{pmatrix} 5 \\ -3 \end{pmatrix}$$

$$\begin{pmatrix} \dfrac{.97}{.965} & \dfrac{.25}{.965} \\ \dfrac{.02}{.965} & \dfrac{1}{.965} \end{pmatrix} \begin{pmatrix} 5 \\ -3 \end{pmatrix} = \begin{pmatrix} 4.2487 \\ -3.0052 \end{pmatrix} \qquad \begin{matrix} \text{change in output of microchips} \\ \text{change in output of computers} \end{matrix}$$

$$= \Delta X$$

The entries in ΔX are rounded to four decimal places and indicate millions of dollars. Can you explain why an increase in output of $4.2487 million worth of microchips might be enough to meet an increase in demand of $5 million?   ∎

In this section, we showed how to find the inverse of a matrix, in general using row operations, and, in the 2-by-2 case, using determinants. The inverse of a matrix is used to solve systems of linear equations (theorem 1).

In input-output analysis, the matrix equations:

$$(I - A)^{-1}D = X \quad \text{and} \quad (I - A)^{-1}(\Delta D) = \Delta X$$

are used to find the total output, X, needed to meet a given demand, D, and to predict how a change in demand, ΔD, results in a change in total output, ΔX.

CONCEPTS

inverse of a matrix
determinant
input-output models
input-output graph

input-output matrix
output flow graph
total output
final demand

SOLUTIONS TO PRACTICE EXAMPLES

1. (a) $\begin{pmatrix} 1 & 4 \\ 3 & 16 \end{pmatrix}^{-1} = \begin{pmatrix} 4 & -1 \\ -\dfrac{3}{4} & \dfrac{1}{4} \end{pmatrix}$ (b) $\begin{pmatrix} 1 & 2 & 1 \\ 3 & 7 & 4 \\ 5 & 6 & 0 \end{pmatrix}^{-1} = \begin{pmatrix} 24 & -6 & -1 \\ -20 & 5 & 1 \\ 17 & -4 & -1 \end{pmatrix}$

2. From Example 2:

$$\begin{pmatrix} 1 & 0 & 2 \\ 0 & 1 & 1 \\ 1 & 1 & 4 \end{pmatrix}^{-1} = \begin{pmatrix} 3 & 2 & -2 \\ 1 & 2 & -1 \\ -1 & -1 & 1 \end{pmatrix}$$

(a) $\begin{pmatrix} x_1 \\ x_2 \\ x_3 \end{pmatrix} = \begin{pmatrix} 3 & 2 & -2 \\ 1 & 2 & -1 \\ -1 & -1 & 1 \end{pmatrix} \begin{pmatrix} 2 \\ -1 \\ 3 \end{pmatrix} = \begin{pmatrix} -2 \\ -3 \\ 2 \end{pmatrix}$

(b) $\begin{pmatrix} y_1 \\ y_2 \\ y_3 \end{pmatrix} = \begin{pmatrix} 3 & 2 & -2 \\ 1 & 2 & -1 \\ -1 & -1 & 1 \end{pmatrix} \begin{pmatrix} 3 \\ 1 \\ 1 \end{pmatrix} = \begin{pmatrix} 9 \\ 4 \\ -3 \end{pmatrix}$

3. (a) $D = 4 - 6 = -2;$ $\begin{pmatrix} 1 & 3 \\ 2 & 4 \end{pmatrix}^{-1} = \begin{pmatrix} -2 & \dfrac{3}{2} \\ 1 & -\dfrac{1}{2} \end{pmatrix}$

(b) $D = 16 - 12 = 4;$ $\begin{pmatrix} 1 & 4 \\ 3 & 16 \end{pmatrix}^{-1} = \begin{pmatrix} 4 & -1 \\ -\dfrac{3}{4} & \dfrac{1}{4} \end{pmatrix}$

(c) This has no inverse, since $D = 6 - 6 = 0$.

4. (a) $A = \begin{pmatrix} .02 & .20 \\ .05 & .01 \end{pmatrix}$

(b) $AX = \begin{pmatrix} 34 \\ 11.5 \end{pmatrix}$

(c) $X - AX = \begin{pmatrix} 200 \\ 150 \end{pmatrix} - \begin{pmatrix} 34 \\ 11.5 \end{pmatrix} = \begin{pmatrix} 166 \\ 138.5 \end{pmatrix}$

(d) $\begin{pmatrix} 34 \\ 11.5 \end{pmatrix}$ amount of division I's output consumed within the company

            amount of division II's output consumed within the company

$\begin{pmatrix} 166 \\ 138.5 \end{pmatrix}$ division I's final demand

            division II's final demand

Division	Amount consumed within company	Amount sold outside company	Total output
I	34	166	200
II	11.5	138.5	150

5. (a) $I - A = \begin{pmatrix} 1 & -.4 \\ -.3 & .8 \end{pmatrix}$

(b) $D = .8 - .12 = .68;$ $(I - A)^{-1} = \begin{pmatrix} \dfrac{.8}{.68} & \dfrac{.4}{.68} \\ \dfrac{.3}{.68} & \dfrac{1}{.68} \end{pmatrix}$

(c) $(I - A)^{-1}D = \begin{pmatrix} \dfrac{.8}{.68} & \dfrac{.4}{.68} \\ \dfrac{.3}{.68} & \dfrac{1}{.68} \end{pmatrix} \begin{pmatrix} 102 \\ 170 \end{pmatrix} = \begin{pmatrix} 220 \\ 295 \end{pmatrix}$

(d) $\begin{pmatrix} 220 \\ 295 \end{pmatrix}$ is the total output needed to meet the final demand $\begin{pmatrix} 102 \\ 170 \end{pmatrix}$

EXERCISES 10.6

In Exercises 1 through 10 use row operations to find the inverse (if it exists) of the given matrix.

1. $\begin{pmatrix} 1 & 2 \\ 5 & 9 \end{pmatrix}$ 2. $\begin{pmatrix} 2 & 3 \\ 4 & 7 \end{pmatrix}$ 3. $\begin{pmatrix} 3 & 2 \\ 7 & 5 \end{pmatrix}$ 4. $\begin{pmatrix} 3 & 2 \\ 9 & 6 \end{pmatrix}$

5. $\begin{pmatrix} 1 & 1 & 0 \\ 0 & 1 & 2 \\ 1 & 1 & 1 \end{pmatrix}$ 6. $\begin{pmatrix} 1 & 2 & 3 \\ 2 & 5 & 10 \\ 1 & 2 & 4 \end{pmatrix}$ 7. $\begin{pmatrix} 1 & 2 & 1 \\ 1 & 3 & 2 \\ 0 & 2 & 1 \end{pmatrix}$

8. $\begin{pmatrix} 1 & 1 & 2 \\ 2 & 3 & 4 \\ 1 & 3 & 3 \end{pmatrix}$ 9. $\begin{pmatrix} 1 & 2 & 1 & 3 \\ 0 & 1 & 2 & 0 \\ 1 & 2 & 2 & 6 \\ 0 & 0 & 1 & 4 \end{pmatrix}$

10. $\begin{pmatrix} 2 & 2 & 1 & 0 \\ 2 & 2 & 1 & 1 \\ 1 & 2 & 1 & 0 \\ 1 & 1 & 1 & 1 \end{pmatrix}$

11. Use the answer to Exercise 1 to solve the matrix equations:

(a) $\begin{pmatrix} 1 & 2 \\ 5 & 9 \end{pmatrix}\begin{pmatrix} x_1 \\ x_2 \end{pmatrix} = \begin{pmatrix} -1 \\ 7 \end{pmatrix}$ (b) $\begin{pmatrix} 1 & 2 \\ 5 & 9 \end{pmatrix}\begin{pmatrix} x_1 \\ x_2 \end{pmatrix} = \begin{pmatrix} 3 \\ 5 \end{pmatrix}$

12. Use the answer to Exercise 3 to solve the matrix equations:

(a) $\begin{pmatrix} 3 & 2 \\ 7 & 5 \end{pmatrix}\begin{pmatrix} x_1 \\ x_2 \end{pmatrix} = \begin{pmatrix} 12 \\ 8 \end{pmatrix}$ (b) $\begin{pmatrix} 3 & 2 \\ 7 & 5 \end{pmatrix}\begin{pmatrix} x_1 \\ x_2 \end{pmatrix} = \begin{pmatrix} 9 \\ -1 \end{pmatrix}$

(c) $\begin{pmatrix} 3 & 2 \\ 7 & 5 \end{pmatrix}\begin{pmatrix} x_1 \\ x_2 \end{pmatrix} = \begin{pmatrix} 0 \\ 5 \end{pmatrix}$

13. Use the answer to Exercise 5 to solve the matrix equations:

(a) $\begin{pmatrix} 1 & 1 & 0 \\ 0 & 1 & 2 \\ 1 & 1 & 1 \end{pmatrix}\begin{pmatrix} x_1 \\ x_2 \\ x_3 \end{pmatrix} = \begin{pmatrix} 1 \\ -1 \\ 2 \end{pmatrix}$ (b) $\begin{pmatrix} 1 & 1 & 0 \\ 0 & 1 & 2 \\ 1 & 1 & 1 \end{pmatrix}\begin{pmatrix} x_1 \\ x_2 \\ x_3 \end{pmatrix} = \begin{pmatrix} 2 \\ 1 \\ 0 \end{pmatrix}$

14. Use the answer to Exercise 7 to solve the matrix equations:

(a) $\begin{pmatrix} 1 & 2 & 1 \\ 1 & 3 & 2 \\ 0 & 2 & 1 \end{pmatrix} \begin{pmatrix} x_1 \\ x_2 \\ x_3 \end{pmatrix} = \begin{pmatrix} 0 \\ 1 \\ 3 \end{pmatrix}$ (b) $\begin{pmatrix} 1 & 2 & 1 \\ 1 & 3 & 2 \\ 0 & 2 & 1 \end{pmatrix} \begin{pmatrix} x_1 \\ x_2 \\ x_3 \end{pmatrix} = \begin{pmatrix} 1 \\ 0 \\ 7 \end{pmatrix}$

(c) $\begin{pmatrix} 1 & 2 & 1 \\ 1 & 3 & 2 \\ 0 & 2 & 1 \end{pmatrix} \begin{pmatrix} x_1 \\ x_2 \\ x_3 \end{pmatrix} = \begin{pmatrix} 1 \\ 1 \\ 1 \end{pmatrix}$

15. Show that

$$\begin{pmatrix} a & b \\ c & d \end{pmatrix}^{-1} = \begin{pmatrix} d/D & -b/D \\ -c/D & a/D \end{pmatrix}$$

if $D = ad - bc$ is nonzero, by showing:

$$\begin{pmatrix} a & b \\ c & d \end{pmatrix} \begin{pmatrix} d/D & -b/D \\ -c/D & a/D \end{pmatrix} = \begin{pmatrix} 1 & 0 \\ 0 & 1 \end{pmatrix}$$

In Exercises 16 through 19 find $I - A$ and then use the formula in Exercise 15 to find $(I - A)^{-1}$ for the given matrix A. (Round the entries in your answer to four decimal places.)

16. $A = \begin{pmatrix} 0 & .20 \\ .40 & 0 \end{pmatrix}$ 17. $A = \begin{pmatrix} .30 & .10 \\ .20 & .02 \end{pmatrix}$

18. $A = \begin{pmatrix} .01 & .50 \\ .20 & .03 \end{pmatrix}$ 19. $A = \begin{pmatrix} .02 & .50 \\ .10 & .05 \end{pmatrix}$

In Exercises 20 through 23 the given graph is the input-output graph of divisions within a company and the given matrix X is the total output.

(a) On each edge directed from i to j put the amount of the total output of i used by j.
(b) On the edge directed from i out of the company put the amount of the total output from i not used within the company. (This is final demand.)
(c) Use the answer to (a) to find a matrix whose entries are the amount of each division's total output consumed within the company.
(d) Use the answer to (b) to find a matrix whose entries give each division's final demand.
(e) Find the input-output matrix, A.
(f) Compute AX.
(g) Compute $X - AX$.

20. $X = \begin{pmatrix} 100 \\ 250 \end{pmatrix} \begin{matrix} I \\ II \end{matrix}$

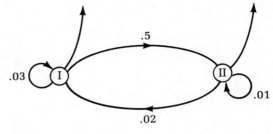

21. $X = \begin{pmatrix} 100 \\ 500 \end{pmatrix} \begin{matrix} I \\ II \end{matrix}$

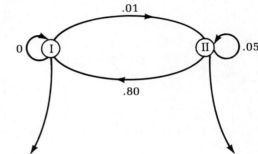

22. $X = \begin{pmatrix} 100 \\ 200 \\ 500 \end{pmatrix} \begin{matrix} I \\ II \\ III \end{matrix}$

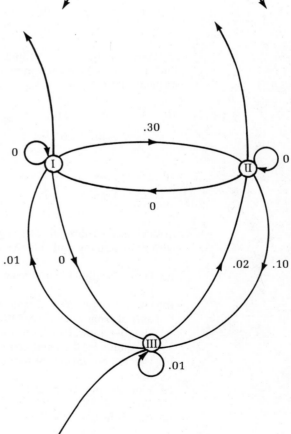

23. $X = \begin{pmatrix} 1,000 \\ 300 \\ 200 \end{pmatrix} \begin{matrix} I \\ II \\ III \end{matrix}$

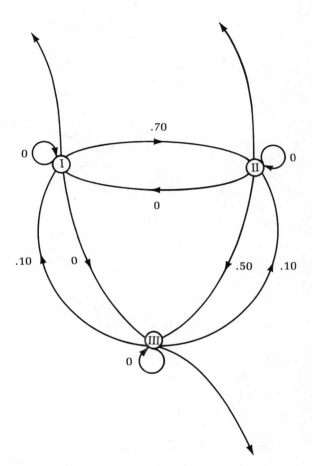

24. Suppose the graph below is the input-output graph for the auto and rubber industries.

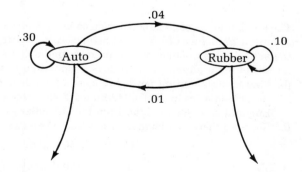

(a) What total output is necessary to meet a final demand for $12 billion worth of autos and $8 billion worth of rubber?

(b) How would a drop of $1 billion in the demand for autos change the total output of rubber?

25. Suppose the graph below is the input-output graph for the auto and steel industries.

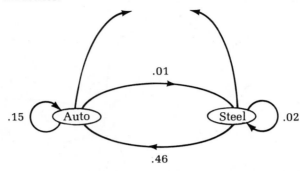

(a) What total output is necessary to meet a final demand for $50 billion worth of autos and $100 billion worth of steel?
(b) How would an increase of $10 billion in the demand for autos change the total output of steel?

26. A company has subsidiaries in the United States, England, and France. The subsidiaries purchase goods and services from each other as given in the input-output graph below.

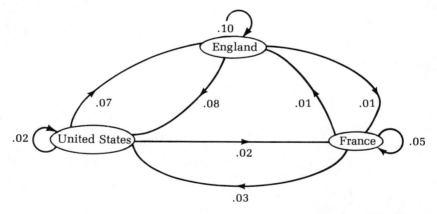

The number on an edge directed from country A to country B gives the amount of output (in dollars) from the subsidiaries in country A needed in order for the subsidiaries in country B to produce one dollar's worth of output.

(a) Write the input-output matrix corresponding to this input-output graph.
(b) Find the total output needed to meet a final demand for $700 million from the subsidiaries in the United States, $500 million from the subsidiaries in England, and $600 million from the subsidiaries in France.
(c) Suppose there is a change in demand given by:

$$\Delta D = \begin{pmatrix} 50 \\ -10 \\ 0 \end{pmatrix} \begin{matrix} \text{U.S.} \\ \text{England} \\ \text{France} \end{matrix}$$

where the entries represent millions of dollars. What change in total output is needed to meet this change in demand?

27. A simplified input-output model for the 1963 British economy can be obtained by dividing the economy into three segments (See Bergman 1970.):

N nonmetals

M metals

E energy and services

The resulting input-output matrix is:

$$
\begin{array}{c}
 & \begin{array}{ccc} N & M & E \end{array} \\
\begin{array}{c} N \\ M \\ E \end{array} &
\begin{pmatrix}
.18 & .10 & .41 \\
.07 & .20 & .11 \\
.13 & .14 & .32
\end{pmatrix}
\end{array}
$$

(a) Suppose the final demand in millions of British pounds is:

$$
D = \begin{pmatrix} 10 \\ 6 \\ 15 \end{pmatrix} \begin{array}{c} N \\ M \\ E \end{array}
$$

What total output is needed to meet this demand?

(b) What change in total output results from a change in demand of:

$$
\Delta D = \begin{pmatrix} 1 \\ -.5 \\ 1.5 \end{pmatrix}
$$

28. A simplified input-output model of the 1958 Israeli economy has input-output matrix:

$$
\begin{array}{c}
 & \begin{array}{ccc} A & M & E \end{array} \\
\begin{array}{c} A \\ M \\ E \end{array} &
\begin{pmatrix}
.293 & 0 & 0 \\
.014 & .207 & .017 \\
.044 & .010 & .216
\end{pmatrix}
\end{array}
$$

where A represents agriculture, M manufacturing, and E represents energy. (See Leontief 1966.) Find the total output needed to meet the final demand:

$$
D = \begin{pmatrix} 138{,}213 \\ 17{,}597 \\ 1{,}786 \end{pmatrix} \begin{array}{c} A \\ M \\ E \end{array}
$$

where the numbers are thousands of Israeli pounds.

CHAPTER SUMMARY

In this chapter, we have provided an introduction to *matrix* theory and given applications. Matrices are used to model changes over time (Section 10.3), to solve systems of linear equations (Sections 10.4, 10.5, and 10.6), and to model the interrelationship between final demand and total output (Section 10.6).

The terminology used in working with matrices is presented in Section 10.1, along with matrix descriptions of *relations* and *graphs*.

In Section 10.2, we defined *addition, subtraction, and multiplication of matrices*. Recall that for

$$A = (a_1, a_2, \ldots, a_n) \quad \text{and} \quad B = \begin{pmatrix} b_1 \\ b_2 \\ \cdot \\ \cdot \\ \cdot \\ b_n \end{pmatrix}$$

the product AB is the 1-by-1 matrix with entry:

$$a_1 b_1 + a_2 b_2 + \cdots + a_n b_n$$

In general, if A is a p-by-q matrix and B is a r-by-s matrix and $q = r$, then the product AB is the p-by-s matrix whose (i, j) entry is the entry in the product $R_i(A) C_j(B)$.

The study of *Markov chains* in Section 10.3 illustrates the use of matrix multiplication to model changes over time. A Markov chain is a repeated experiment with outcomes $S_1, S_2, \ldots, S_n$ with the property that the probabilities: $T_{i,j}$ = probability of state S_j on the next trial given that the state was S_i on the last trial, do not change from trial to trial.

The matrix, T, is called the *transition matrix* of the Markov chain and the matrices: $(D(k))_{1,j}$ = probability of the state S_j on the kth trial, are called *distribution matrices*. The formula:

$$D(k) T = D(k + 1)$$

is used to compute successive distribution matrices. *Steady state distributions*, D, for a Markov chain are found by solving the matrix equation $DT = D$ for D.

Sections 10.4 and 10.5 show that the solutions to any system of linear equations can be found through *Gauss-Jordan elimination*. The procedure is as follows:

1. Write the augmented matrix for the given system of linear equations.
2. Use row operations to transform the *augmented matrix* to a matrix in which:
   (a) The leftmost nonzero entry in each row is the number 1.
   (b) Each column that contains such a 1 has all other entries in the column equal to 0.
   (c) Any row consisting entirely of zeroes is below any row that has nonzero entries.
   (d) The leftmost 1 in any row is to the right of any leftmost 1 that occurs in a previous row.

3. Solve the system of equations corresponding to the augmented matrix found in Step 2.

Recall that the *row operations* are:

1. Multiply a row by a nonzero number.
2. Add two rows.
3. Any combination of 1 and 2.
4. Change the order of the rows.

In Section 10.5, we gave some examples to illustrate how the results of Gauss-Jordan elimination can be used to solve linear optimization problems.

In Section 10.6, we showed how to find the *inverse of a matrix* using row operations and applied inverses to model the interrelationship between input and output in large companies or economies.

The inverse of a matrix, A, is obtained by using row operations to transform the matrix $(A|I)$ to a matrix of the form $(I|B)$. If this transformation can be done, then B is the inverse of A. If the transformation cannot be done, then A does not have an inverse.

Let:

$$A = \text{the input-output matrix for some economy}$$

$$D = \text{final demand}$$

$$X = \text{total output}$$

$$\Delta D = \text{change in final demand}$$

$$\Delta X = \text{change in total output}$$

The equation:

$$(I - A)^{-1}D = X$$

computes the total output, X, needed to meet a given demand D; and the equation:

$$(I - A)^{-1}(\Delta D) = \Delta X$$

computes the change in total output, ΔX, needed to meet a given change in total demand, ΔD.

REVIEW EXERCISES FOR CHAPTER 10

1. For:

$$A = \begin{pmatrix} 1 & 3 & 2 \\ 4 & 5 & 8 \end{pmatrix}$$

write:

(a) the first row of A.

(b) the second column of A.

(c) $R_2(A)$.   (d) $C_1(A)$.   (e) the (2, 3) entry.

2. Write the matrix corresponding to the relation:
$$R = \{(1, 2), (2, 3), (2, 4), (1, 4), (1, 3)\}.$$

3. Write the incidence matrix of the graph:

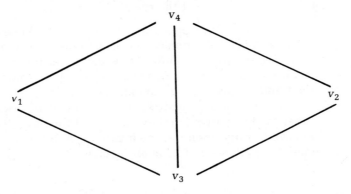

4. Draw the graph with edge matrix:
$$\begin{pmatrix} 0 & 1 & 0 & 0 & 1 \\ 1 & 0 & 0 & 0 & 1 \\ 0 & 0 & 0 & 1 & 1 \\ 0 & 0 & 1 & 0 & 1 \\ 1 & 1 & 1 & 1 & 0 \end{pmatrix}$$

5. On Monday and Tuesday of a particular week a gas station sold 160 gallons of regular gas, 200 gallons of unleaded gas, and 220 gallons of super unleaded gas on Monday; and 120 gallons of regular, 150 gallons of unleaded, and 100 gallons of super unleaded on Tuesday.
    (a) Write this information in a matrix with one column listing Monday's sales of gas and a second column for Tuesday's sales of gas.
    (b) What is the total number of gallons sold on Monday?
    (c) How much unleaded gas was sold during the two-day period?

6. Find the indicated sum or difference.

(a) $\begin{pmatrix} 1 & -1 \\ 3 & 4 \end{pmatrix} + \begin{pmatrix} 1 & 3 \\ 2 & -2 \end{pmatrix}$

(b) $\begin{pmatrix} 1 & 3 & 2 \\ 4 & 1 & 5 \end{pmatrix} - \begin{pmatrix} 0 & 1 & 2 \\ 4 & 1 & 5 \end{pmatrix}$

7. Find the products.

(a) $\begin{pmatrix} 1 & 2 & 5 \end{pmatrix} \begin{pmatrix} 3 \\ 1 \\ 2 \end{pmatrix}$

(b) $\begin{pmatrix} 2 & 5 \end{pmatrix} \begin{pmatrix} -1 \\ 3 \end{pmatrix}$

8. Find the products.

(a) $\begin{pmatrix} 3 & 5 & 4 \\ 2 & 6 & 1 \end{pmatrix} \begin{pmatrix} 2 & 3 \\ 4 & 2 \\ 1 & -1 \end{pmatrix}$

(b) $\begin{pmatrix} 1 & 0 & -1 \\ 1 & 1 & 1 \\ 0 & 1 & 0 \end{pmatrix} \begin{pmatrix} 3 & 0 & 6 \\ 4 & 1 & 5 \\ -2 & 0 & 7 \end{pmatrix}$

9. Write the system of linear equations corresponding to:

(a) $\begin{pmatrix} 2 & 5 \\ -1 & 4 \end{pmatrix} \begin{pmatrix} x_1 \\ x_2 \end{pmatrix} = \begin{pmatrix} 7 \\ 9 \end{pmatrix}$

(b) $\begin{pmatrix} 3 & 1 & 4 \\ 1 & 2 & 5 \\ -1 & 3 & 7 \end{pmatrix} \begin{pmatrix} x_1 \\ x_2 \\ x_3 \end{pmatrix} = \begin{pmatrix} 1 \\ -1 \\ 3 \end{pmatrix}$

10. A warehouse receives orders from three stores. The first store orders 100 shirts, 50 pairs of pants, and 30 jackets. The second store orders 300 shirts, 150 pairs of pants, and 30 jackets. The third store orders 200 shirts, 100 pairs of pants, and 80 jackets. The warehouse charges $5 for a shirt, $10 for a pair of pants, and $20 for a jacket.
    (a) Write a matrix which has one row for each store and whose entries give the number of each type of item ordered by each store.
    (b) Write the amounts charged by the warehouse as a column.
    (c) Find the product of the two matrices and interpret the entries in the product.

11. Find the distribution matrices $D(2)$ and $D(3)$ for the Markov chain with transition matrix:

$$T = \begin{pmatrix} .8 & .2 \\ .7 & .3 \end{pmatrix}$$

if $D(1) = (.5 \quad .5)$.

12. Find the distribution matrix, $D(2)$, for the Markov chain with transition matrix:

$$T = \begin{pmatrix} .3 & .2 & .5 \\ .1 & .6 & .3 \\ .2 & .3 & .5 \end{pmatrix}$$

if $D(1) = (.4 \quad .5 \quad .1)$.

13. Find the steady state distribution for the Markov chain with transition matrix:

$$T = \begin{pmatrix} .9 & .1 \\ .4 & .6 \end{pmatrix}$$

14. Suppose that in a certain city 92% of the commuters who commute by car one year continue to commute by car the next year and 2% of the commuters who commute by public transportation one year commute by car the next year.
    (a) Write the transition matrix for this Markov chain.
    (b) If 30% of the commuters presently commute by car, then what percentage of commuters will commute by car next year?
    (c) Find the steady state distribution.
    (d) In the long run what percentage of commuters will commute by car?

15. A fast-food restaurant has added a new item to its menu. A survey shows that 30% of those ordering the new item last time will order the item again next time, while 50% of those who did not order the item last time will order the new item the next time they are in the restaurant.
    (a) Find the transition matrix for this Markov chain, with states N = orders new item; D = does not order new item.
    (b) Find the steady state distribution for this Markov chain.
    (c) The restaurant has decided it will drop the new item from the menu unless 30% or more of the customers will order the new item. Use your answer to part (b) to predict whether the new item will be dropped.

In Exercises 16 through 18, solve the given system of equations.

16. $3x_1 + 2x_2 + 5x_3 = 36$

    $10x_1 + 7x_2 + 2x_3 = 83$

    $4x_1 + x_2 + 3x_3 = 25$

17. $2x_1 + 3x_2 + 5x_3 = 11$

    $3x_1 + 5x_2 + 8x_3 = 18$

    $6x_1 + 2x_2 + 8x_3 = 12$

18. $5x_1 + 2x_1 + 16x_3 = 9$

    $2x_1 + x_2 + 7x_3 = 5$

    $3x_1 + x_2 + 9x_3 = 5$

19. The table below gives the number of units of vitamin A, iron, and vitamin C in each ounce of three foods: F_1, F_2, F_3.

	F_1	F_2	F_3
Vitamin A	10	7	13
Iron	30	20	20
Vitamin C	100	85	115

Find a mixture of the three foods that contains exactly 135 units of vitamin A, 400 units of iron, and 1425 units of vitamin C.

20. Suppose that the costs of the foods F_1, F_2, and F_3 of Exercise 19 are $.42 for an ounce of F_1, $.35 per ounce for F_2, and $.45 per ounce for F_3. Find a mixture of the three foods that satisfies the requirements in Exercise 19 for vitamin A, iron, and vitamin C at the smallest possible cost.

In Exercises 21 and 22, use row operations to find the inverse of the given matrix.

21. $\begin{pmatrix} 2 & 5 \\ 3 & 7 \end{pmatrix}$

22. $\begin{pmatrix} 3 & 5 & 6 \\ 2 & 5 & 6 \\ 4 & 1 & 1 \end{pmatrix}$

23. Use your answer to Exercise 21 to solve:

(a) $2x_1 + 5x_2 = 1$ (b) $2x_1 + 5x_2 = 7$ (c) $2x_1 + 5x_2 = 3$

   $\ 3x_1 + 7x_2 = 4$ $\ 3x_1 + 7x_2 = -1$ $\ 3x_1 + 7x_2 = 2$

24. Use your answer to Exercise 22 to solve:

(a) $3x_1 + 5x_2 + 6x_3 = 1$ (b) $3x_1 + 5x_2 + 6x_3 = 2$

   $\ 2x_1 + 5x_2 + 6x_3 = 3$ $\ 2x_1 + 5x_2 + 6x_3 = 0$

   $\ 4x_1 + x_2 + x_3 = 5$ $\ 4x_1 + x_2 + x_3 = 9$

25. A utility company produces electricity and natural gas. To produce $1 worth of electricity the company uses $.20 worth of its electricity and $.02 worth of natural gas. To produce $1 worth of natural gas the company uses $.15 worth of its electricity and $.25 worth of its natural gas.

(a) Write the input-output matrix.

(b) Find the total output required each month to meet a final demand for $100 million worth of electricity and $10 million worth of natural gas.

(c) Suppose the monthly demand for electricity increases to $103 million and the demand for natural gas drops to $9 million per month. How does this change the total output?

Linear Programming–The Simplex Algorithm

11

At the beginning of Chapter 9, we described the development of linear programming immediately following World War II. It was at that time that Dantzig developed an algorithm called the *simplex algorithm*, to find solutions to linear programs. During the 1970s public attention was focused on linear programming for two reasons. In 1975, L. V. Kantorovich and T. C. Koopmans, contemporaries of Dantzig, were awarded the Nobel Prize in economics for their work in linear programming, particularly as it applied to optimum allocation problems. (There is no Nobel Prize awarded in mathematics.) At the end of the decade, a Russian mathematician, L. G. Kachian, discovered a new algorithm to find solutions to linear programs. Theoretically, Kachian's algorithm was "better" than the simplex algorithm, because the time necessary to run it can be given by a polynomial in the size of the input. In practice, however, the simplex algorithm performs well and is not nearly as complicated. Typical problems with 100 variables and 100 constraints can be solved in seconds with a computer.

In this chapter we systematically develop the simplex algorithm and indicate its relationship to the graphical method developed in Chapter 9. Initially, solutions are found to linear programs whose objective function is to be maximized, but in Section 11.3 we show how we can use the principle of duality to solve minimization problems. The economic interpretation of dual variables of a linear program is discussed at length.

The authors realize that even the simplex algorithm is difficult to apply by hand to linear programs with more than three variables. Since almost

every computer on the market today has software available to implement the simplex algorithm, the fourth section is devoted to analyzing the output provided by such a computer program. Sensitivity analysis is discussed in this context, so that the student is better able to interpret the results.

11.1 Simplex Algorithm—Getting Started—Pivoting

In this section we use some of the techniques of the last chapter to develop a procedure for finding solutions to linear programs. The **simplex algorithm** is a method of finding and checking corner points of the feasible region, even when there are more than two variables and the feasible region cannot be graphed. In particular, as the algorithm finds each successive corner point, the value of the objective function improves, getting closer to the optimum each time. Because each corner point found improves the value of the objective function, not all corner points need to be considered.

The simplex algorithm requires that linear programs be set up in a standard form.

> DEFINITION A linear program is in **standard maximum form** (SMF) if the objective function is a function to be maximized, each of the constraints (except the nonnegativity constraints) is in the form $a_1x_1 + a_2x_2 + \cdots + a_nx_n \leq b$, and each of the variables is constrained to be nonnegative.

The requirement that the constraints be in a specific form is not as strong as it might seem—any linear inequality can be converted to the form $a_1x_1 + a_2x_2 + \cdots + a_nx_n \leq b$. For example, the constraint: $x_1 + x_2 \geq 200$ is the same as the constraint $-x_1 - x_2 \leq -200$, just by multiplying by -1. The constraint $x_1 + x_2 = 5$ is the same as the pair of constraints:

$$x_1 + x_2 \leq 5$$

$$x_1 + x_2 \geq 5$$

which is the same as the pair of constraints:

$$x_1 + x_2 \leq 5$$

$$-x_1 - x_2 \leq -5$$

PRACTICE EXAMPLE 1

Write the following constraints as constraints for a linear program in standard maximum form:

(a) $5x_1 + 7x_2 \geq 3500$

(b) $3x_1 + 9x_2 = 54$

(c) $4x_1 \leq 5x_2 + 1$

(d) $x_1 \geq 2x_2 + 6$

We developed matrix methods (Gauss-Jordan elimination) in the last chapter to solve systems of equations. Once we put the constraints of a linear program in standard maximum form, we want to add new variables to each inequality to make each into an equation.

DEFINITION   A **slack variable** is a nonnegative variable, s, that added to an inequality of the form:

$$a_1 x_1 + a_2 x_2 + \cdots + a_n x_n \le b$$

creates the equation:

$$a_1 x_1 + a_2 x_2 + \cdots + a_n x_n + s = b$$

In other words, $s = b - a_1 x_1 - a_2 x_2 - \cdots - a_n x_n$. s is the amount left over when the values of $x_1, x_2, \ldots, x_n$ are substituted in the left side of the constraint. s is always nonnegative, otherwise $x_1, x_2, \ldots, x_n$ would not have satisfied the inequality.

For example, in a problem in Chapter 9 we had the constraint $3x_1 + 5x_2 \le 100$, representing machine-hours. If we introduce the slack variable s, we have the equation: $3x_1 + 5x_2 + s = 100$. If $x_1 = 0$ and $x_2 = 0$, then $s = 100$. If $x_1 = 25$ and $x_2 = 0$, then $s = 100 - 3(25) = 25$; there are 25 machine-hours left over. If $x_1 = 0$ and $x_2 = 20$, then $s = 100 - 5(20) = 0$; there are no machine-hours left over. The value of the slack variable depends on the values of the variables x_1 and x_2.

We add one slack variable for each constraint in the linear program. Once the constraints have been converted to equations with the addition of slack variables, each constant of the equation must be made nonnegative. For example, the equation $-x_1 + x_2 + s = -5$ must be written as

$$x_1 - x_2 - s = 5$$

Now that all of the constraints, except for the nonnegativity constraints, are converted to equations, the objective function has to be written so that all the variables including the variable to be maximized are on the left side of the equal sign. For example, if the objective function is $P = 40x_1 + 80x_2$, then it is written as $-40x_1 - 80x_2 + P = 0$. Now, we have a system of equations corresponding to the constraints and the objective function.

SETTING UP A LINEAR PROGRAM FOR THE SIMPLEX ALGORITHM

1. Write the linear program in SMF:

$$\max P = c_1 x_1 + c_2 x_2 + \cdots + c_n x_n$$

$$\text{constraints: } a_1 x_1 + a_2 x_2 + \cdots + a_n x_n \le b$$

$$x_1 \ge 0, x_2 \ge 0, \ldots, x_n \ge 0$$

2. Introduce a slack variable for each constraint to create an equation:

$$a_1x_1 + a_2x_2 + \cdots + a_nx_n + s = b$$

3. If $b \leq 0$ then multiply the equation by -1.
4. Write the objective function with all variables to the left of the equal sign:

$$-c_1x_1 - c_2x_2 - \cdots - c_nx_n + P = 0$$

5. Write the augmented matrix for the system of equations formed from 2–4 above. Call it the **first tableau**. Use headings for the columns to keep track of the variables.

EXAMPLE 1

$$\max P = 40x_1 + 80x_2$$

$$3x_1 + 5x_2 \leq 100$$

$$200x_1 + 100x_2 \leq 5000$$

$$x_1 \geq 0, \ x_2 \geq 0$$

Introduce slack variables:

$$3x_1 + 5x_2 + s_1 = 100$$

$$200x_1 + 100x_2 + s_2 = 5000$$

Write the objective function in proper form:

$$-40x_1 - 80x_2 + P = 0.$$

The augmented matrix for the system of equations is:

x_1	x_2	s_1	s_2	P	constants
3	5	1	0	0	100
200	100	0	1	0	5000
-40	-80	0	0	1	0

We can rephrase our linear programming problem as follows. Among all the solutions to the system of equations:

$$3x_1 + 5x_2 + s_1 = 100$$

$$200x_1 + 100x_2 + s_2 = 5000$$

$$-40x_1 - 80x_2 + P = 0$$

we want a solution such that $x_1 \geq 0$, $x_2 \geq 0$, $s_1 \geq 0$, $s_2 \geq 0$, and P is as large as possible.

Note that the system of equations has infinitely many solutions. Given any pair of values for x_1 and x_2, we get a triple of values for s_1, s_2, and P. If x_1 and x_2 are both 0, $s_1 = 100$, $s_2 = 5000$, and $P = 0$. But, if $x_1 = 0$ and $x_2 = 20$, then $s_1 = 0$ and $s_2 = 5000 - 2000 = 3000$, and $P = 80(20) = 1600$.

There are two types of variables in this system of equations, the variables x_1 and x_2 that we started with and the variables s_1, s_2, and P that can be determined from the values of x_1 and x_2.

Observe that the columns corresponding to this second group of variables, s_1, s_2, and P, form the 3×3 identity matrix. These variables, corresponding to columns of the identity matrix, are called **basic variables**, or variables in the *basis*. The other variables are called **nonbasic variables**. Any solution to the linear program that results from setting the nonbasic variables equal to 0 is called a **basic solution**. If all of the variables in the basic solution, except the variable to be maximized, are nonnegative, then it is called a **basic feasible solution**.

Recall from the last chapter that if we have a matrix that contains the columns of the identity matrix, and that resulted from applying row operations to an augmented matrix of a system of equations, we can read the solution immediately from the last column. For example:

$$\begin{pmatrix} 0 & 0 & 1 & 4 \\ 1 & 0 & 0 & 5 \\ 0 & 1 & 0 & 2 \end{pmatrix}$$

indicates a solution of $x_1 = 5$, $x_2 = 2$, and $x_3 = 4$. The x_1-column has a 1 in the second row, whose last entry is 5, the x_2-column has a 1 in the last row, whose last entry is 2, and the x_3-column has a 1 in the first row, whose last entry is 4.

Therefore, from our initial tableau, if $x_1 = 0$ and $x_2 = 0$, we can concentrate on the columns corresponding to the identity matrix:

$$\begin{array}{cccc} s_1 & s_2 & P & \text{constants} \\ \begin{pmatrix} 1 & 0 & 0 & 100 \\ 0 & 1 & 0 & 5000 \\ 0 & 0 & 1 & 0 \end{pmatrix} \end{array}$$

We will get one member of the solution set for the linear program: $x_1 = 0$, $x_2 = 0$, $s_1 = 100$, $s_2 = 5000$, and $P = 0$. The basic variables here are s_1, s_2, and P, and the solution is a basic feasible solution.

EXAMPLE 2

$$\max P = 12x_1 + 9x_2$$

$$x_1 + x_2 \le 850$$

$$2x_1 + 3x_2 \le 2200$$

$$x_1 + 2x_2 \leq 1400$$

$$x_1 \geq 0, x_2 \geq 0$$

Introduce slack variables for each constraint:

$$x_1 + x_2 + s_1 = 850$$

$$2x_1 + 3x_2 + s_2 = 2200$$

$$x_1 + 2x_2 + s_3 = 1400$$

Write the objective function in proper form:

$$-12x_1 - 9x_2 + P = 0.$$

Set up the first tableau (augmented matrix of coefficients):

$$
\begin{array}{ccccccc}
x_1 & x_2 & s_1 & s_2 & s_3 & P & \text{constants} \\
\end{array}
$$

$$
\begin{pmatrix}
1 & 1 & 1 & 0 & 0 & 0 & 850 \\
2 & 3 & 0 & 1 & 0 & 0 & 2200 \\
1 & 2 & 0 & 0 & 1 & 0 & 1400 \\
-12 & -9 & 0 & 0 & 0 & 1 & 0
\end{pmatrix}
$$

One member of the solution set for the system of equations is $x_1 = 0$, $x_2 = 0$, $s_1 = 850$, $s_2 = 2200$, $s_3 = 1400$, and $P = 0$, and can be read from the submatrix:

$$
\begin{pmatrix}
1 & 0 & 0 & 0 & 850 \\
0 & 1 & 0 & 0 & 2200 \\
0 & 0 & 1 & 0 & 1400 \\
0 & 0 & 0 & 1 & 0
\end{pmatrix}
$$

Note that $x_1 = 0$ and $x_2 = 0$ correspond to a corner point of the feasible set of constraints (see Figure 9.32). ■

In the last chapter, we learned how to apply basic row operations to the augmented matrix corresponding to a system of equations to find a solution to the system of equations. These operations allowed us to transform the matrix into an equivalent matrix (in terms of solutions to the system) with columns of the identity matrix.

Suppose we apply some elementary row operations to the first tableau (matrix) in an attempt to get a column of the identity matrix in place of the first column.

want		x_1	x_2	s_1	s_2	s_3	P	constants
1 $\longrightarrow$		1	1	1	0	0	0	850
0 $\longrightarrow$		2	3	0	1	0	0	2200
0 $\longrightarrow$		1	2	0	0	1	0	1400
0 $\longrightarrow$		-12	-9	0	0	0	1	0

To get a 0 in the first entry of row 2, multiply row 1 by -2, and add it to row 2 as indicated $(-2r_1 + r_2)$. Row 2 becomes:

$$-2 + 2 \quad -2 + 3 \quad -2 + 0 \quad 0 + 1 \quad 0 + 0 \quad 0 + 0 \quad -2(850) + 2200$$

$$0 \qquad\quad 1 \qquad\quad -2 \qquad\quad 1 \qquad\quad 0 \qquad\quad 0 \qquad\quad 500$$

To get a 0 in the first entry of row 3, multiply row 1 by -1, and add it to row 3 $(-r_1 + r_3)$.

$$-1 + 1 \quad -1 + 2 \quad -1 + 0 \quad 0 + 0 \quad 0 + 1 \quad 0 + 0 \quad -850 + 1400$$

$$0 \qquad\quad 1 \qquad\quad -1 \qquad\quad 0 \qquad\quad 1 \qquad\quad 0 \qquad\quad 550$$

To get a 0 in the first entry of row 4, multiply row 1 by 12 and add it to row 4 $(12r_1 + r_4)$.

$$12 - 12 \quad 12 - 9 \quad 12 + 0 \quad 0 + 0 \quad 0 + 0 \quad 0 + 1 \quad 12(850) + 0$$

$$0 \qquad\quad 3 \qquad\quad 12 \qquad\quad 0 \qquad\quad 0 \qquad\quad 1 \qquad\quad 10{,}200$$

The resulting matrix, or new tableau, with the row operations indicated is:

	x_1	x_2	s_1	s_2	s_3	P	constants
	1	1	1	0	0	0	850
$-2r_1 + r_2$	0	1	-2	1	0	0	500
$-r_1 + r_3$	0	1	-1	0	1	0	550
$12r_1 + r_4$	0	3	12	0	0	1	10,200

The columns corresponding to the identity columns are now x_1, s_2, s_3, and P, which are basic variables, while x_2 and s_1 are nonbasic variables. If $x_2 = 0$ and $s_1 = 0$, we get another member of the solution set for the system of equations, by reading the submatrix:

x_1	s_2	s_3	P	constants
1	0	0	0	850
0	1	0	0	500
0	0	1	0	550
0	0	0	1	10,200

When $x_2 = 0$ and $s_1 = 0$, $x_1 = 850$, $s_2 = 500$, $s_3 = 550$, and $P = 10{,}200$.

The changes we made in the first tableau to get the second tableau involved replacing the first column with the column of the identity matrix. The succession of row operations used to accomplish this is called *pivoting*. The entry of our matrix that we want to become the 1 of the identity column is called the *pivot entry* or **pivot element**. In the next section, we shall see how to choose the pivot entry so that we continue to get solutions and so that the value of the objective function is improved.

As another example of the pivoting process, we will return to the first tableau in Example 1.

$$
\begin{array}{cccccc}
x_1 & x_2 & s_1 & s_2 & P & \text{constants} \\
\end{array}
$$

$$
\begin{pmatrix}
3 & 5 & 1 & 0 & 0 & 100 \\
200 & \boxed{100} & 0 & 1 & 0 & 5000 \\
-40 & -80 & 0 & 0 & 1 & 0
\end{pmatrix}
$$

Suppose we want to make the x_2-column become the identity column $0-1-0$. We are now pivoting on the $(2, 2)$-entry as circled in the tableau.

Since we want the 100 to become 1, row 2 is divided by 100. We want the 5 to become a 0, so row 2 is multiplied by $\frac{-5}{100}$ and added to row 1. Similarly, we want the -80 to become 0, so row 2 is multiplied by $\frac{80}{100}$ and added to row 3.

$$
\begin{array}{cccccc}
& x_1 & x_2 & s_1 & s_2 & P & \text{constants} \\
\end{array}
$$

$$
\begin{array}{c}
\frac{-5}{100}r_2 + r_1 \\[2mm]
r_2/100 \\[2mm]
\frac{80}{100}r_2 + r_3
\end{array}
\begin{pmatrix}
-7 & 0 & 1 & -.05 & 0 & -150 \\
2 & 1 & 0 & .01 & 0 & 50 \\
120 & 0 & 0 & .8 & 1 & 4000
\end{pmatrix}
$$

If x_1 and s_2 are set equal to 0, we get $x_2 = 50$, $s_1 = -150$, and $P = 4000$. This is not a member of the solution set, since all variables, including the slack variables, are supposed to be nonnegative. Pivoting on the $(2, 2)$-entry *did not* yield a feasible solution.

Suppose, instead, we pivot on the $(1, 2)$-entry, which is 5. We want to make the second column become $1-0-0$. We divide row 1 by 5 to get a 1 in the first position. Take -20 times row 1 and add it to row 2 to get a 0 in the next position, and take 16 times row 1 and add it to row 3 to get a 0 in the last position.

$$
\begin{array}{cccccc}
& x_1 & x_2 & s_1 & s_2 & P & \text{constants} \\
\end{array}
$$

$$
\begin{array}{c}
\dfrac{r_1}{5} \\[2mm]
-20r_1 + r_2 \\[2mm]
16r_1 + r_3
\end{array}
\begin{pmatrix}
.6 & 1 & .2 & 0 & 0 & 20 \\
140 & 0 & -20 & 1 & 0 & 3000 \\
8 & 0 & 16 & 0 & 1 & 1600
\end{pmatrix}
$$

Setting $x_1 = 0$ and $s_1 = 0$, we get $x_2 = 20$, $s_2 = 3000$, and $P = 1600$. Thus, $x_1 = 0$, $x_2 = 20$, $s_1 = 0$, $s_2 = 3000$, and $P = 1600$ is a member of the solution set of the system of equations. $(0, 20)$ is also a corner point of the feasible region for the linear program.

PRACTICE EXAMPLE 2

Write the following linear program in SMF, add slack variables, and set up the first tableau:

$$\max T = 3x_1 + 2x_2$$
$$x_1 + x_2 \le 5$$
$$x_1 + 2x_2 \le 8$$
$$x_1 \ge 0, \, x_2 \ge 0$$

EXAMPLE 3

$$\max T = x_1 + 2x_2$$
$$x_1 \ge 3$$
$$x_2 \le 5$$
$$2x_1 + x_2 \le 14$$
$$x_1 \ge 0, \, x_2 \ge 0$$

Convert the program to SMF by rewriting $x_1 \ge 3$ as $-x_1 \le -3$. Add slack variables to get the system of equations:

$$-x_1 + s_1 = -3$$
$$x_2 + s_2 = 5$$
$$2x_1 + x_2 + s_3 = 14$$
$$-x_1 - 2x_2 + T = 0 \qquad \text{objective function}$$

Write the system so that all constants are nonnegative:

$$x_1 - s_1 = 3$$
$$x_2 + s_2 = 5$$
$$2x_1 + x_2 + s_3 = 14$$
$$-x_1 - 2x_2 + T = 0$$

Set up the first tableau:

x_1	x_2	s_1	s_2	s_3	T	constants
1	0	-1	0	0	0	3
0	1	0	1	0	0	5
2	1	0	0	1	0	14
-1	-2	0	0	0	1	0

If $x_1 = 0$ and $x_2 = 0$, we have the solution $s_1 = -3$, $s_2 = 5$, $s_3 = 14$, and $T = 0$. However, this solution is not feasible, since each variable must be nonnegative. Suppose we pivot on the (1, 1)-entry, 1. In other words, we want to make the first column look like the column $1-0-0-0$.

row operations	x_1	x_2	s_1	s_2	s_3	T	constants
	1	0	-1	0	0	0	3
	0	1	0	1	0	0	5
$-2r_1 + r_3$	0	1	2	0	1	0	8
$r_1 + r_4$	0	-2	-1	0	0	1	3

The basic variables are x_1, s_2, s_3, and T. Setting $x_2 = 0$ and $s_1 = 0$, we get $x_1 = 3$, $s_2 = 5$, $s_3 = 8$, and $T = 3$. The solution $x_1 = 3$ and $x_2 = 0$ is a feasible solution. However, as we will see when we finish this example in the next section, this solution does not produce the maximum value of T. Try applying the geometrical method to get the solution. ■

In this section we learned how to put a maximization problem in a form to apply the simplex algorithm. We introduced slack variables and created the first tableau. We used row operations to transform one tableau into another. In the next section we will determine which entry of the matrix to pivot on to get to the optimal solution (if one exists). We will complete the simplex algorithm, obtaining a solution to the problem.

CONCEPTS

simplex algorithm
standard maximum form
slack variable
first tableau
basic variables

nonbasic variables
basic solution
basic feasible solution
pivot element

SOLUTIONS TO PRACTICE EXAMPLES

1. (a) $-5x_1 - 7x_2 \leq -3500$

   (b) $3x_1 + 9x_2 \leq 54$

   $-3x_1 - 9x_2 \leq -54$

   (c) $4x_1 - 5x_2 \leq 1$

   (d) $-x_1 + 2x_2 \leq -6$

2. max $T = 3x_1 + 2x_2$

$$\left.\begin{array}{r} x_1 + x_2 \leq 5 \\ x_1 + 2x_2 \leq 8 \\ x_1 \geq 0, \; x_2 \geq 0 \end{array}\right\} \text{ in SMF}$$

$x_1 + x_2 + s_1 = 5$

$x_1 + 2x_2 + s_2 = 8$

$-3x_1 - 2x_2 + T = 0$

x_1	x_2	s_1	s_2	T	constants
1	1	1	0	0	5
1	2	0	1	0	8
-3	-2	0	0	1	0

EXERCISES 11.1

Write each of the following constraints as constraints for a linear program in SMF.

1. $10x_1 + 7x_2 \geq 25$

2. $x_1 \geq 6$

3. $4x_1 + 5x_2 = 10$

4. $2x_1 \geq 3x_2 + 15$

5. $12 \leq x_1 + x_2$

Convert each of the following linear programs to SMF.

6. max $P = 3x_1 + 9x_2$

   $x_1 + x_2 \geq 5$

   $2x_1 - 3x_2 \leq 7$

   $x_1 \geq 4, \; x_2 \geq 0$

7. max $S = 2x_1 + 7x_2$

   $2x_1 + 3x_2 \leq 10$

   $x_1 - x_2 \geq 5$

   $6 \leq -x_1 + 5x_2$

   $x_1 \geq 0, \; x_2 \geq 0$

8. max $T = x_1 + x_2 + x_3$

   $x_1 + 2x_2 + 3x_3 \geq 4$

   $2x_1 + 3x_2 + x_3 \leq 15$

$$x_1 \geq x_2 + x_3$$
$$x_1 \geq 0, x_2 \geq 0, x_3 \geq 0$$

For each of the following linear programs introduce the slack variables and set up the first tableau.

9. Program of Exercise 6

10. Program of Exercise 7

11. Program of Exercise 8

12. max $P = 2x_1 - x_2$

$$x_1 + x_2 \leq 6$$
$$2x_1 + x_2 \leq 9$$
$$3x_1 + 4x_2 \leq 20$$
$$x_1 \geq 0, x_2 \geq 0$$

13. max $W = x_1 + x_2 + x_3$

$$2x_1 + x_2 \leq 4$$
$$x_2 + 3x_3 \leq 7$$
$$x_1 + x_3 \leq 6$$
$$x_1 \geq 0, x_2 \geq 0, x_3 \geq 0$$

14. max $P = 5x_1 + 10x_2$

$$x_1 + 3x_2 \leq 9$$
$$2x_1 \geq x_2$$
$$x_1 \geq 0, x_2 \geq 0$$

15. Set up the linear program and the first tableau for the following problem.

The Corner Meat Market sells two grades of hamburger, a 90% lean and an 80% lean. A pound of 90%-lean hamburger sells for $1.59 and a pound of 80% lean sells for $1.39. The butcher has 1000 pounds of pure beef and 200 pounds of pure fat to make each type. How many pounds of each type should be ground up to maximize revenue?

11.2 Simplex Algorithm—Finding the Optimum

In the last section, we learned how to take a maximization linear program, put it in the proper form for the simplex algorithm, introduce slack variables, and create the first tableau (matrix). We also saw how we could use row operations to convert the first tableau into another tableau by changing the set of basic variables. This process is called pivoting. Unfortunately, we did not know what entry of the matrix to pivot on to improve the value of the objective function.

In this section, we will not only determine which entry of a tableau is the "best" pivot entry, but we will be able to tell when we reach the maximum, if one exists, and to determine when no maximum exists.

First we will consider the geometry of the simplex method. Suppose we have a feasible region as shown in Figure 11.1 with corner points labeled A, B, C, D, and E. Assume that the linear program had three major constraints, one determining the line containing BC, one determining the line containing CD, and the third determining the line containing DE. Thus, we would have introduced three slack variables, s_1, s_2, and s_3. The initial tableau would have three basic variables, s_1, s_2, and s_3, with values equal to the three constants of the constraints, and two nonbasic variables x_1 and x_2, each set equal to 0. In terms of the feasible region, the values of x_1 and x_2 determine the corner point A $(0, 0)$.

Figure 11.1

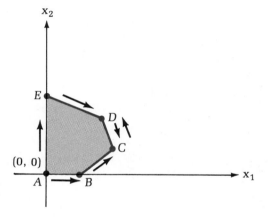

We want to pivot to increase the value of the objective function by increasing the value of x_1 and/or x_2. In particular, we want to move out to another corner point of the feasible region. If B is the corner point we get to in the next pivot, x_1 will be a basic variable and x_2 will be a nonbasic variable. x_2 and one of the slack variables will be set equal to 0. Similarly, if E is the next point then x_1 will be a nonbasic variable and x_2 will be a basic variable.

Which way do we move about the feasible region, so that we use the least number of pivots, or tableaus? If we knew that E or D produces the maximum, then we would pivot on an entry in the x_2-column so that we would get to E next. If either B or C produces the maximum, we want to go to B second and thus would pivot on an entry in the x_1-column. But we do not know a priori where the maximum occurs. We need a procedure for determining the order of the pivots, or the order of the tableaus. We also need to know when to stop. If B is the point that produces the maximum, we do not want to pivot again and go past it.

Note that even though we have only drawn feasible regions in the plane (two-dimensional space), the feasible region for a k-variable linear program is the analogue of a polygon, called a *polytope*, in k-dimensional space. This polytope has corner points, and the simplex method systematically visits its corner points until the maximum is found.

The first tableau does not necessarily reflect a starting corner point of the feasible region. In our example the feasible region had $(0, 0)$ as a corner point, and the first tableau started at that point. However, in Example 3 of the last section, setting $x_1 = 0$ and $x_2 = 0$ produced a negative slack variable, contradicting the nonnegativity constraints. Therefore, $(0, 0)$ for that linear program was not a corner point of the feasible region. We had to pivot at least once to get a starting corner point. In our example, we pivoted once to get to the point $(3, 0)$. Figure 11.2 shows the feasible region for this example. Note that $(0, 0)$ is not a corner point, but $(3, 0)$ is a corner point.

Figure 11.2

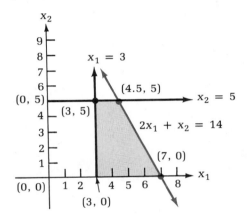

In choosing an entry of a tableau to pivot on, we want to increase the value of the objective function while still maintaining feasibility. In other words, we want to increase the value of the objective function, but not pivot to a point outside of the feasible region.

To increase the value of the objective function, we want to increase the variable that contributes most in the computation of the objective function. Recall that the objective function is written so that the x_i variables and the function letter, say P, are to the left of the equal sign. In Example 1 of Section 11.1, $P = 40x_1 + 80x_2$ is recorded in the last row of the first tableau as $-40x_1 - 80x_2 + P = 0$. Each unit of x_2 contributes \$80 to profit, whereas each unit of x_1 contributes only \$40 to profit. We would therefore like to increase x_2 as much as possible to increase the profit as much as possible. The pivot entry comes from the column, called the pivot column, in the tableau corresponding to the most negative number in the last row. If no entry in the last row is negative, excluding the last entry, then you have found the maximum. This pivot column will be converted to a column of the identity matrix, so the variable corresponding to this column becomes a basic variable. This variable is said *to enter the basis*.

The **pivot element** is the entry of the pivot column that is converted to 1. We determine which entry is the pivot element by taking the ratios of the constant column entries to the pivot column entries, all but the bottom row, and choosing the smallest nonnegative ratio. We disregard any 0 entries in the pivot column since division by zero is undefined. The minimum ratio choice guarantees that we will not add more of any variable to the solution than is feasible.

EXAMPLE 1

The first tableau for our system of equations is shown with the pivot column circled, and the ratios computed to the side.

$$
\begin{array}{cccccc}
x_1 & x_2 & s_1 & s_2 & P & \text{constants} \\
\left(\begin{array}{cccccc}
3 & \textcircled{5} & 1 & 0 & 0 & 100 \\
200 & 100 & 0 & 1 & 0 & 5000 \\
-40 & -80 & 0 & 0 & 1 & 0
\end{array}\right)
\end{array}
\qquad
\begin{array}{l}
\text{ratios} \\[6pt]
\dfrac{100}{5} = 20 \ \text{smallest} \\[10pt]
\dfrac{5000}{100} = 50
\end{array}
$$

Since the ratio $\frac{100}{5} = 20$ is the smallest of the set $\{\frac{100}{5}, \frac{5000}{100}\}$, and comes from the first row, the first row becomes the **pivot row**. The (1, 2)-entry is the pivot element. In other words, the x_2-column will be transformed to the identity column $1-0-0$, the existing s_1-column. The x_2 variable becomes a basic variable and the s_1 variable becomes a nonbasic variable. We say x_2 enters the basis and s_1 leaves the basis.

To keep track of the variables in the basis (the basic variables) we will label the rows of the tableau to the right to record this information. In so doing we will be able to read off the values of the basic variables when the nonbasic variables are set to 0. In our example, the first tableau will be written as shown, thus $s_1 = 100$, $s_2 = 5000$, and $P = 0$ when x_1 and x_2 are nonbasic variables (are set to 0).

$$
\begin{array}{ccccccc}
x_1 & x_2 & s_1 & s_2 & P & \text{constants} & \text{basis} \\
\left(\begin{array}{cccccc}
3 & \textcircled{5} & 1 & 0 & 0 & 100 \\
200 & 100 & 0 & 1 & 0 & 5000 \\
-40 & -80 & 0 & 0 & 1 & 0
\end{array}\right) &
\begin{array}{c}
s_1 \\[6pt]
s_2 \\[6pt]
P
\end{array}
\end{array}
$$

The second tableau, formed by pivoting on the (1, 2)-entry, is:

$$
\begin{array}{l}
\\
r_1/5 \\
-20r_1 + r_2 \\
16r_1 + r_3
\end{array}
\begin{array}{ccccccc}
x_1 & x_2 & s_1 & s_2 & P & \text{constants} & \text{basis} \\
\left(\begin{array}{cccccc}
.6 & 1 & .2 & 0 & 0 & 20 \\
140 & 0 & -20 & 1 & 0 & 3000 \\
8 & 0 & 16 & 0 & 1 & 1600
\end{array}\right) &
\begin{array}{c}
x_2 \\
s_2 \\
P
\end{array}
\end{array}
$$

In this second tableau $x_2 = 20$, $s_2 = 3000$, and $P = 1600$ when x_1 and s_1 are set to 0. Since there are no negative entries in the last row, we cannot increase the profit by increasing the value of any variable. We have reached the maximum value of P at 1600. The solution to the linear program is $x_2 = 20$ and $x_1 = 0$ (since x_1 is a nonbasic variable). The value of the slack variables is $s_1 = 0$ and $s_2 = 3000$. We will have \$3000 extra in the cost constraint. ∎

To summarize (starting with a tableau corresponding to a basic feasible solution),

1. *Pivot column*: Choose the column with the most negative entry in the bottom row, excluding the constant column. If no negative entry exists, you are done.
2. *Pivot row*: Compute the ratios of the constant column to the pivot column, excluding the bottom row. Choose the row corresponding to the smallest nonnegative ratio. If no nonnegative ratios exist, then there is no maximum.
3. *Pivot entry*: The entry in the pivot row and pivot column.
4. The **maximum** is reached when there are no negative entries in the bottom row, except possibly the constant column entry. The solution to the system of equations can be found by reading off the values of the basic variables from the last column, and taking the nonbasic variables to be 0. The solution to the linear program is the values of the x variables in this solution.

EXAMPLE 2

$$\max P = 12x_1 + 9x_2$$

$$x_1 + x_2 \leq 850$$

$$2x_1 + 3x_2 \leq 2200$$

$$x_1 + 2x_2 \leq 1400$$

$$x_1 \geq 0,\ x_2 \geq 0$$

The system of equations with slack variables is:

$$x_1 + x_2 + s_1 = 850$$

$$2x_1 + 3x_2 + s_2 = 220$$

$$x_1 + 2x_2 + s_3 = 1400$$

$$-12x_1 - 9x_2 + P = 0$$

The first tableau is:

x_1	x_2	s_1	s_2	s_3	P	constants	basis	ratios
①	1	1	0	0	0	850	s_1	$\dfrac{850}{1}$ smallest
2	3	0	1	0	0	2200	s_2	$\dfrac{2200}{11}$
1	2	0	0	1	0	1400	s_3	$\dfrac{1400}{1}$
−12	−9	0	0	0	1	0	P	

A feasible solution, corresponding to the corner point (0, 0), is $x_1 = 0$, $x_2 = 0$, $s_1 = 850$, $s_2 = 2200$, $s_3 = 1400$, $P = 0$, but it does not yield the maximum.

The second tableau formed by pivoting on the (1, 1)-entry is:

	x_1	x_2	s_1	s_2	s_3	P	constants	basis
	1	1	1	0	0	0	850	x_1
$-2r_1 + r_2$	0	1	−2	1	0	0	500	s_2
$-r_1 + r_3$	0	1	−1	0	1	0	550	s_3
$12r_1 + r_4$	0	3	12	0	0	1	10,200	P

$x_1 = 850$, $x_2 = 0$, $s_1 = 0$, $s_2 = 500$, $s_3 = 550$, $P = 10,200$ is a feasible solution, corresponding to the corner point (850, 0). $P = 10,200$ is the maximum, since no negative entries appear in the bottom row. ■

PRACTICE EXAMPLE 1

Find a solution to the following linear program, using the simplex method:

$$\max P = 3x_1 + 5x_2$$

$$x_1 + x_2 \le 8$$

$$2x_1 + 3x_2 \le 18$$

$$x_1 \ge 0, \; x_2 \ge 0.$$ ■

EXAMPLE 3

$$\max T = x_1 + 2x_2$$

$$x_1 \ge 3$$

$$x_2 \le 5$$

$$2x_1 + x_2 \le 14$$

$$x_2 \ge 0$$

In SMF form:

$$\max T = x_1 + 2x_2$$
$$-x_1 \le -3$$
$$x_2 \le 5$$
$$2x_1 + x_2 \le 14$$
$$x_2 \ge 0$$

With slack variables:

$$-x_1 + s_1 = -3$$
$$x_2 + s_2 = 5$$
$$2x_1 + x_2 + s_3 = 14$$
$$-x_1 - 2x_2 + T = 0$$

With all constants nonnegative:

$$x_1 - s_1 = 3$$
$$x_2 + s_2 = 5$$
$$2x_1 + x_2 + s_3 = 14$$
$$-x_1 - 2x_2 + T = 0$$

First tableau:

x_1	x_2	s_1	s_2	s_3	T	constants	basis
1	0	−1	0	0	0	3	s_1
0	1	0	1	0	0	5	s_2
2	1	0	0	1	0	14	s_3
−1	−2	0	0	0	1	0	T

The first basic solution of $x_1 = 0$, $x_2 = 0$, $s_1 = -3$, $s_2 = 5$, $s_3 = 14$, and $T = 0$, is not feasible since s_1 is negative. We need to pivot to get a basic feasible solution. Since the -1 appears in the s_1-column, we want to pivot s_1 out of the basis. Since the only 1 in the first row is in the x_1-column, the (1, 1)-entry becomes the pivot entry.

Second tableau:

	x_1	x_2	s_1	s_2	s_3	T	constants	basis	ratios
	1	0	-1	0	0	0	3	x_1	
	0	①	0	1	0	0	5	s_2	$\dfrac{5}{1}$
$-2r_1 + r_3$	0	1	2	0	1	0	8	s_3	$\dfrac{8}{1}$
$r_1 + r_4$	0	-2	-1	0	0	1	3	T	

In this pivot x_1 entered the basis, and s_1 left the basis. The basic solution is now $x_1 = 3$, $x_2 = 0$, $s_1 = 0$, $s_2 = 5$, $s_3 = 8$, and $T = 3$. This solution is feasible and corresponds to the corner point (3, 0). It does not yield the maximum, however. The bottom row has two negative entries, with -2 the most negative. The second column becomes the pivot column, and the second row the pivot row, since 5 is the smallest ratio. Therefore, the (2, 2)-entry is the pivot entry.

Third tableau:

	x_1	x_2	s_1	s_2	s_3	T	constants	basis	ratios
	1	0	-1	0	0	0	3	x_1	
	0	1	0	1	0	0	5	x_2	
$-r_2 + r_3$	0	0	②	-1	1	0	3	s_3	$\dfrac{3}{2}$
$2r_2 + r_4$	0	0	-1	2	0	1	13	T	

With this pivot x_2 entered the basis, and s_2 left the basis. The basic solution is $x_1 = 3$, $x_2 = 5$, $s_1 = 0$, $s_2 = 0$, $s_3 = 3$, and $T = 13$. This is a basic feasible solution and corresponds to the corner point (3, 5) in Figure 11.2. We have not reached the maximum, however. We need to pivot again, using the third column as the pivot column. Only one ratio exists and is non-negative, so we pivot on the (3, 3)-entry.

Fourth tableau:

	x_1	x_2	s_1	s_2	s_3	T	constants	basis
$\dfrac{r_3}{2} + r_1$	1	0	0	$-\dfrac{1}{2}$	$\dfrac{1}{2}$	0	4.5	x_1
	0	1	0	1	0	0	5	x_2
$\dfrac{r_3}{2}$	0	0	1	$-\dfrac{1}{2}$	$\dfrac{1}{2}$	0	1.5	s_1
$\dfrac{r_3}{2} + r_4$	0	0	0	$\dfrac{3}{2}$	$\dfrac{1}{2}$	1	14.5	T

In this pivot s_1 entered the basis, and s_3 left the basis. This is our last tableau. We have reached the maximum. The basic solution is $x_1 = 4.5$, $x_2 = 5$, $s_1 = 1.5$, $s_2 = 0$, $s_3 = 0$, and $T = 14.5$. This solution corresponds to the corner point $(4.5, 5)$, which yields a maximum value of $T = 14.5$.

Notice that in this example we pivoted to a starting corner point of $(3, 0)$, then to the corner point $(3, 5)$, and finally to the corner point $(4.5, 5)$ to get to the maximum. See Figure 11.2. This example differed from the previous two in that we could not start at $(0, 0)$ as a corner point. ∎

EXAMPLE 4

Using Practice Example 1 from Section 9.4:

$$\max P = 10x_1 + 8x_2 + 4x_3$$

$$15x_1 + 12x_2 + 8x_3 \le 1200$$

$$5x_1 + 4x_2 + 3x_3 \le 600$$

$$4x_1 + 4x_2 + 3x_3 \le 480$$

$$x_1 \ge 0,\ x_2 \ge 0,\ x_3 \ge 0$$

With slack variables:

$$15x_1 + 12x_2 + 8x_3 + s_1 = 1200$$

$$5x_1 + 4x_2 + 3x_3 + s_2 = 600$$

$$4x_1 + 4x_2 + 3x_3 + s_3 = 480$$

$$-10x_1 - 8x_2 - 4x_3 + P = 0$$

First tableau:

x_1	x_2	x_3	s_1	s_2	s_3	P	constants	basis	ratios
⑮	12	8	1	0	0	0	1200	s_1	80
5	4	3	0	1	0	0	600	s_1	120
4	4	3	0	0	1	0	480	s_3	120
−10	−8	−4	0	0	0	1	0	P	

↑

The basic feasible solution is $x_1 = 0$, $x_2 = 0$, $x_3 = 0$, $s_1 = 1200$, $s_2 = 600$, $s_3 = 480$, and $P = 0$, but it is not the maximum.

The x_1-column becomes the pivot column, and the first row the pivot row, since 80 is the smallest ratio. Therefore, x_1 enters the basis, and s_1 leaves the basis. Since the pivot entry is the $(1, 1)$-entry, the first column is made to look like $1-0-0-0$.

Second tableau:

	x_1	x_2	x_3	s_1	s_2	s_3	P	constants	basis
$\dfrac{r_1}{15}$	1	.8	.53	.07	0	0	0	80	x_1
$-\dfrac{1}{3}r_1 + r_2$	0	0	.33	$-.33$	1	0	0	200	s_2
$-\dfrac{4}{15}r_1 + r_3$	0	.8	.87	$-.27$	0	1	0	160	s_3
$\dfrac{2}{3}r_1 + r_4$	0	0	1.33	.67	0	0	1	800	P

There are no negative entries in the last row, therefore the maximum has been reached. The basic feasible solution is $x_1 = 80$, $x_2 = 0$, $x_3 = 0$, $s_1 = 0$, $s_2 = 200$, $s_3 = 160$, and $P = 800$. The maximum occurs at the corner point (80, 0) with value of \$800. The firm should produce only 80 toaster-ovens. ∎

Since we do not graph the feasible region in performing the simplex method, how do we recognize when the feasible region is unbounded, and no maximum exists? Consider Example 5 from Section 9.5:

EXAMPLE 5

$$\max P = x_1 + 3x_2$$
$$x_1 \leq 4$$
$$x_2 \geq 6$$
$$x_1 \geq 0$$

In SMF, the linear program becomes:

$$\max P = x_1 + 3x_2$$
$$x_1 \leq 4$$
$$-x_2 \leq -6$$
$$x_1 \geq 0$$

With slack variables:

$$x_1 + s_1 = 4$$
$$-x_2 + s_2 = -6$$
$$-x_1 - 3x_2 + P = 0$$

With positive constants:

$$x_1 + s_1 = 4$$
$$x_2 - s_2 = 6$$
$$-x_1 - 3x_2 + P = 0$$

First tableau:

	x_1	x_2	s_1	s_2	P	constants	basis	ratios
	1	0	1	0	0	4	s_1	does not exist
	0	①	0	−1	0	6	s_2	6
	−1	−3	0	0	1	0	P	

This first basic solution is not feasible with $x_1 = 0$, $x_2 = 0$, $s_1 = 4$, $s_2 = -6$, and $P = 0$. We have to pivot to get s_2 out of the basis. The only variable that can enter the basis is x_2, since it has the only nonzero entry in a variable column of the second row. Therefore, the (2, 2)-entry is the pivot entry.

Second tableau:

	x_1	x_2	s_1	s_2	P	constants	basis	ratios
	1	0	1	0	0	4	s_1	does not exist
	0	1	0	−1	0	6	x_2	negative
$3r_2 + r_3$	−1	0	0	−3	1	18	P	

The s_2-column should be the next pivot column, but there are no non-negative ratios to determine the pivot row. From our summary section, we see that the linear program has no solution. If you look at the feasible region as drawn in Figure 9.33, you will see that the feasible region is unbounded.

In general, if there is no pivot in the first tableau that will produce a feasible solution, then the feasible region is the empty set. If there are no nonnegative ratios, then the feasible region is unbounded and there is **no solution**.

Find a solution, if possible, to the following linear program:

$$\max P = 5x_1 + 7x_2$$
$$x_1 + x_2 \geq 5$$
$$x_2 \leq 8$$
$$x_1 \geq 0, x_2 \geq 0$$

In this section we applied the simplex method to solve maximization linear programs. In the next section we will see how we can convert minimization problems to maximization problems so that we can solve minimization linear programs by the same method.

CONCEPTS

pivot row
pivot column
determining the pivot element
determining when the maximum is reached
how to tell when a solution does not exist

SOLUTIONS TO PRACTICE EXAMPLES

1.

	x_1	x_2	s_1	s_2	P	constants	basis	ratios
	1	1	1	0	0	8	s_1	8
	2	③	0	1	0	18	s_2	6
	-3	-5	0	0	1	0	P	

	x_1	x_1	s_1	s_2	P	constants	basis
$r_1 - \dfrac{1}{3} r_2$	$\dfrac{1}{3}$	0	1	$-\dfrac{1}{3}$	0	2	s_1
$\dfrac{1}{3} r_2$	$\dfrac{2}{3}$	1	0	$\dfrac{1}{3}$	0	6	x_2
$r_3 + \dfrac{5}{3} r_2$	$\dfrac{1}{3}$	0	0	$\dfrac{5}{3}$	1	30	P

Solution: max $P = 30$, with $x_1 = 0$, $x_2 = 6$, $s_1 = 2$, and $s_2 = 0$.

2. max $P = 5x_1 + 7x_2$ $\qquad$ $-x_1 - x_2 + s_1 = -5$

$\qquad -x_1 - x_2 \leq -5$ $\qquad\qquad$ $x_2 + s_2 = 8$

$\qquad\qquad x_2 \leq 8$ $\qquad\qquad$ $-5x_1 - 7x_2 + P = 0$

$\qquad\qquad x_1 \geq 0, x_2 \geq 0$

Let x_1 enter the basis, and s_1 leave the basis to get a feasible solution:

x_1	x_2	s_1	s_2	P	constants
①	1	-1	0	0	5
0	1	0	1	0	8
-5	-7	0	0	1	0

	x_1	x_2	s_1	s_2	P	constants	basis	ratios
	1	1	-1	0	0	5	x_1	—
	0	1	0	1	0	8	s_2	—
$r_3 + 5r_1$	0	-2	-5	0	1	25	P	—

There are no ratios, therefore there is no pivot element, and thus, no solution; the feasible region is unbounded.

EXERCISES 11.2

1. First tableau:

x_1	x_2	x_3	s_1	s_2	s_3	P	constants
1	0	1	1	0	0	0	5
0	1	1	0	1	0	0	7
4	2	3	0	0	1	0	18
-3	-4	-2	0	0	0	1	0

   (a) What is the pivot column?
   (b) What are the ratios?
   (c) What is the pivot element?
   (d) What is the next tableau?
   (e) What is the basic solution from your new tableau? Is it feasible?

2. Answer questions (a)–(e) of Exercise 1 for the following tableau:

x_1	x_2	s_1	s_2	P	constants
1	2	1	0	0	8
0	1	5	1	0	3
0	-3	-1	0	1	8

3. Answer questions (a)–(e) of Exercise 1 for the following tableau:

x_1	x_2	x_3	s_1	s_2	s_3	T	constants
5	0	1	1	2	0	0	3
-2	1	2	0	3	0	0	8
1	0	-1	0	4	1	0	2
-1	0	-2	0	3	0	1	8

4. Answer questions (a)–(e) of Exercise 1 for the following tableau:

x_1	x_2	s_1	s_2	s_3	P	constants
0	2	1	-1	0	0	4
1	1	0	2	0	0	6
0	1	0	1	1	0	8
0	-1	0	4	0	1	6

5–11.   Finish the solutions to the linear programs set up in Exercises 9 through 15 of Section 11.1.

12.   Prove that no solution exists to the linear program whose second tableau is:

$$
\begin{array}{cccccc}
x_1 & x_2 & s_1 & s_2 & P & \text{constants} \\
\left(\begin{array}{c} 0 \\ -2 \\ -3 \end{array}\right. & \begin{array}{c} -1 \\ 0 \\ -4 \end{array} & \begin{array}{c} 1 \\ 0 \\ 0 \end{array} & \begin{array}{c} 0 \\ 1 \\ 0 \end{array} & \begin{array}{c} 0 \\ 0 \\ 1 \end{array} & \left.\begin{array}{c} 5 \\ 3 \\ 0 \end{array}\right)
\end{array}
$$

13.   Construct a maximization linear program with two variables and an unbounded feasible region, but where the maximum occurs at a corner point.

14.   Construct a maximization linear program with two variables and no feasible region.

11.3   *Minimization and Duality*

In the last section we developed the simplex method to solve maximization linear programming problems. However, some linear programs, as we have seen before, have an objective function that is to be minimized.

We can convert any minimization problem to a maximization problem using the following property of real numbers: The minimum of a set of numbers is the negative of the maximum of the set of negative numbers. For example, the minimum of the set $\{5, 7, 4, 3, 2, 9\}$ is 2, but the maximum of the set $\{-5, -7, -4, -3, -2, -9\}$ is -2. Thus, $-(-2) = 2$, the minimum. Therefore minimum $S = -\max(-S)$.

If we have the linear program:

$$\min C = x_1 + 2x_2$$
$$x_1 + x_2 \leq 5$$
$$2x_1 + 3x_2 \geq 12$$
$$x_1 \geq 0, x_2 \geq 0$$

we can solve the linear program:

$$\max P = -x_1 - 2x_2 = -C$$
$$x_1 + x_2 \leq 5$$
$$2x_1 + 3x_2 \geq 12$$
$$x_1 \geq 0, x_2 \geq 0$$

The point (x_1, x_2) that maximizes P, also minimizes C with value $-P$.

EXAMPLE 1

Apply the simplex method to solve this maximization problem:

SMF:
$$\max P = -x_1 - 2x_2$$
$$x_1 + x_2 \leq 5$$
$$-2x_1 - 3x_2 \leq -12$$
$$x_1 \geq 0,\ x_2 \geq 0$$

Slack variables:
$$x_1 + x_2 + s_1 = 5$$
$$-2x_1 - 3x_2 + s_2 = -12$$
$$x_1 + 2x_2 + P = 0$$

With positive constants:
$$x_1 + x_2 + s_1 = 5$$
$$2x_1 + 3x_2 - s_2 = 12$$
$$x_1 + 2x_2 + P = 0$$

First tableau:

	x_1	x_2	s_1	s_2	P	constants	basis
	1	1	1	0	0	5	s_1
	2	③	0	−1	0	12	s_2
	1	2	0	0	1	0	P

We do not have a feasible solution with $x_1 = 0$, $x_2 = 0$, $s_1 = 5$, $s_2 = -12$, and $P = 0$, so we must pivot s_2 out of the basis. Arbitrarily choose x_2 to enter the basis (we have a choice between x_1 and x_2). Therefore the pivot entry is the (2, 2) entry.

Second tableau:

		x_1	x_2	s_1	s_2	P	constants	basis	ratios
$-\dfrac{r_2}{3} + r_1$		$\dfrac{1}{3}$	0	1	$\dfrac{1}{3}$	0	1	s_1	3
$\dfrac{r_2}{3}$		$\dfrac{2}{3}$	1	0	$-\dfrac{1}{3}$	0	4	x_2	6
$-\dfrac{2}{3} r_2 + r_3$		$-\dfrac{1}{3}$	0	0	$\dfrac{2}{3}$	1	−8	P	

$x_1 = 0$, $x_2 = 4$, $s_1 = 1$, $s_2 = 0$, and $P = -8$ is a basic feasible solution, but it does not produce the maximum. The first column becomes the pivot column, and since 3 is the smallest ratio, the first row is the pivot row.

Third tableau:

	x_1	x_2	s_1	s_2	P	constants	basis
$3r_1$	1	0	3	1	0	3	x_1
$-2r_1 + r_2$	0	1	-2	-1	0	2	x_2
$r_1 + r_2$	0	0	1	1	1	-7	P

Since we have no negative entries in the bottom row except for the constant column, we have reached the maximum with the basic solutions, $x_1 = 3$, $x_2 = 2$, $s_1 = 0$, $s_2 = 0$, and $P = -7$. The corner point (3, 2) produces the maximum value of P at -7. Therefore, the minimum value of C is $-(-7) = 7$ at the corner point (3, 2). ■

Another way to solve minimization problems provides more insight into the maximization problems.

Every maximization linear program corresponds to a *dual* minimization linear program. If the maximization linear program has a solution, then so does the dual minimization linear program, and the value of the objective function at the optimum for each program is the same.

EXAMPLE 2

Consider the linear program:

$$\max P = -5x_1 + 12x_2$$
$$-x_1 + 2x_2 \leq 1$$
$$-x_1 + 3x_2 \leq 2$$
$$x_1 \geq 0, x_2 \geq 0$$

To construct the dual linear program, we introduce new variables, called dual variables, corresponding to each constraint. In this example we will have two dual variables, u_1 corresponding to the first constraint, and u_2 corresponding to the second constraint. The objective function for the dual linear program has the dual variables as variables and coefficients equal to the constants of the constraints. Here the objective function for the dual linear program is: min $C(u_1, u_2) = 1u_1 + 2u_2$.

The constraints of the dual linear program are formed from the constraints of the original problem in SMF. The coefficients of the u_1 variable in the constraints are the coefficients in the first constraint. Similarly, the coefficients of the u_i variable are the coefficients in the ith constraint. Each of the constraints of the dual minimization problem are $\geq$ constraints (**standard minimization form**, SmF). The constants of the dual constraints are the coefficients of the original objective function.

Since the constraints of our maximization problem are:

$$-x_1 + 2x_2 \leq 1$$

$$-x_1 + 3x_2 \leq 2$$

the constraints of the dual problem are:

$$-u_1 - u_2 \geq -5$$

$$2u_1 + 3u_2 \geq 12$$

As before, we always have the nonnegativity constraints. Therefore the dual linear program is:

$$\min C = u_1 + 2u_2$$

$$-u_1 - u_2 \geq -5$$

$$2u_1 + 3u_2 \geq 12$$

$$u_1 \geq 0, u_2 \geq 0$$

The minimum value of C is the same as the maximum value of P in the original linear program. We can read the values of the dual variables from the final tableau of the maximization problem.

Apply the simplex method to the maximization problem. Introduce slack variables:

$$-x_1 + 2x_2 + s_1 = 1$$

$$-x_1 + 3x_2 + s_2 = 2$$

$$5x_1 - 12x_2 + P = 0$$

First tableau:

x_1	x_2	s_1	s_2	P	constants	basis	ratios
-1	②	1	0	0	1	s_1	$\dfrac{1}{2}$
-1	3	0	1	0	2	s_2	$\dfrac{2}{3}$
5	-12	0	0	1	0	P	

The basic feasible solution $x_1 = 0$, $x_2 = 0$, $s_1 = 1$, $s_2 = 2$, and $P = 0$ is not the maximum. We need to pivot in the x_2-column and the first row. Therefore we pivot on the $(1, 2)$ entry.

Second tableau:

	x_1	x_2	s_1	s_2	P	constants	basis	ratios
$\dfrac{r_1}{2}$	$-\dfrac{1}{2}$	1	$\dfrac{1}{2}$	0	0	$\dfrac{1}{2}$	x_2	—
$-\dfrac{3}{2}r_1 + r_2$	$\dfrac{1}{2}$	0	$-\dfrac{3}{2}$	1	0	$\dfrac{1}{2}$	s_2	1
$6r_1 + r_3$	-1	0	6	0	1	6	P	

The basic feasible solution $x_1 = 0$, $x_2 = \frac{1}{2}$, $s_1 = 0$, $s_2 = \frac{1}{2}$, and $P = 6$ does not produce the maximum, either. We need to pivot on the x_1-column and the second row, the (2, 1) entry.

Third tableau:

	x_1	x_2	s_1	s_2	P	constants	basis
$r_2 + r_1$	0	1	-1	1	0	1	x_2
$2r_2$	1	0	-3	2	0	1	x_1
$2r_2 + r_3$	0	0	3	2	1	7	P

Since the bottom row is all nonnegative, the maximum has been reached. The basic feasible solution is $x_1 = 1$, $x_2 = 1$, $s_1 = 0$, $s_2 = 0$, and $P = 7$. From our statement about the dual linear program, $C = 7$ is the minimum value for the dual linear program.

Each dual variable corresponds to a constraint in the original linear program. The value of the ith dual variable appears at the bottom of the ith slack variable column in the final tableau. Thus, the value of u_1 is found at the bottom of the s_1-column, and the value of u_2 is found at the bottom of the s_2-column. Therefore, $u_1 = 3$ and $u_2 = 2$.

This minimization problem is the same one that we started the section with and solved by taking negatives. Compare the answers. ◼

To summarize, we have the following dual linear programs:

SMF	SmF
$\max P = c_1 x_1 + c_2 x_2 + \cdots + c_k x_k$	$\min C = b_1 u_1 + \cdots + b_l u_l$
$a_{11}x_1 + \cdots + a_{1k}x_k \le b_1$	$a_{11}u_1 + \cdots + a_{l1}u_l \ge c_1$
$\vdots$	$\vdots$
$a_{l1}x_1 + \cdots + ax_{lk} \le b_l$	$a_{1k}u_1 + \cdots + a_{lk}u_l \ge c_k$
$x_i \ge 0, \quad i = 1, 2, \ldots, k$	$u_j \ge 0, \quad j = 1, 2, \ldots, l$

PROPERTIES
1. **Von Neumann duality principle**   If one of a pair of dual linear programs has a solution then they both do and the values of the optimums are the same.
2. If one of a pair of dual linear programs has an unbounded feasible region then the other has the empty set as a feasible set.
3. The bottom row of the final tableau of the simplex method for the maximization program gives the solution to the dual minimization linear program. The value of the objective function is in the last row–last column entry, and the value of the ith dual variable is at the bottom of the ith slack variable column.

PRACTICE EXAMPLE 1

Write the dual of the linear program of Practice Example 1 of Section 11.2.   ■

EXAMPLE 3

As an example of an economic interpretation of the dual variables we will consider Example 4 of the last section. We wanted to know how many of each type of toaster to produce to maximize profit. We had the linear program:

$$\max P = 10x_1 + 8x_2 + 4x_3$$

$$15x_1 + 12x_2 + 8x_3 \le 1200$$

$$5x_1 + 4x_2 + 3x_3 \le 600$$

$$4x_1 + 4x_2 + 3x_3 \le 480$$

$$x_1 \ge 0,\ x_2 \ge 0,\ x_3 \ge 0$$

The final tableau was:

x_1	x_2	x_3	s_1	s_2	s_3	P	constants	basis
1	.8	.53	.07	0	0	0	80	x_1
0	0	.33	−.33	1	0	0	200	s_2
0	.8	.87	−.27	0	1	0	160	s_3
0	0	1.33	.67	0	0	1	800	P

The dual linear program is:

$$\min C = 1200u_1 + 600u_2 + 480u_3$$

$$15u_1 + 5u_2 + 4u_3 \ge 10$$

$$12u_1 + 4u_2 + 4u_3 \ge 8$$

$$8u_1 + 3u_2 + 3u_3 \ge 4$$

$$u_1 \ge 0,\ u_2 \ge 0,\ u_3 \ge 0$$

From the final tableau, we know that min $C = 800$ at $u_1 = .67$ (rounded from $\frac{2}{3}$), $u_2 = 0$, and $u_3 = 0$. These dual variables represent the increase in profit per unit increase in the constraint bounds. In other words, the profit will increase \$.67 for each additional minute of manufacturing time that could be made available. Adding an extra minute to either the assembly or packaging departments would not increase the profit. One interpretation of these results is that the company might be willing to pay up to \$.66 a minute for time in manufacturing. This does not mean that one should endlessly increase the number of minutes; only that the time can be increased as long as the same solution to the linear program exists.   ■

PRACTICE EXAMPLE 2   Find the dual variables for the problem of Practice Example 1, and give an economic interpretation.   ■

EXAMPLE 4   Recall the cereal problem of Section 9.4, Example 6:

$$\min C = 4x_1 + 3x_2$$
$$x_1 + x_2 \geq 2000$$
$$x_2 \leq 1200$$
$$.8x_1 - .2x_2 \geq 0$$
$$.9x_2 - .1x_1 \geq 0$$
$$x_1 \geq 0, \, x_2 \geq 0$$

In standard minimum form (SmF):

$$\min C = 4x_1 + 3x_2$$
$$x_1 + x_2 \geq 2000$$
$$-x_2 \geq -1200$$
$$.8x_1 - .2x_2 \geq 0$$
$$.9x_2 - .1x_1 \geq 0$$
$$x_1 \geq 0, \, x_2 \geq 0$$

We will find a solution to this linear program by finding a solution to the dual maximization problem.

$$\max P = 2000u_1 - 1200u_2$$
$$u_1 + .8u_3 - .1u_4 \leq 4$$
$$u_1 + u_2 - .2u_3 + .9u_4 \leq 3$$
$$u_1 \geq 0, \, u_2 \geq 0, \, u_3 \geq 0, \, u_4 \geq 0$$

Adding slack variables:

$$u_1 + .8u_3 - .1u_4 + s_1 = 4$$

$$u_1 - u_2 - .2u_3 + .9u_4 + s_2 = 3$$

$$-2000u_1 + 1200u_2 + P = 0$$

First tableau:

	u_1	u_2	u_3	u_4	s_1	s_2	P	constants	basis	ratios
	1	0	.8	−.1	1	0	0	4	s_1	4
	①	−1	−.2	.9	0	1	0	3	s_2	3
	−2000	1200	0	0	0	0	1	0	P	

The pivot entry is the (2, 1) entry.

Second tableau:

	u_1	u_2	u_3	u_4	s_1	s_2	P	constants	basis	ratios
$-r_2 + r_1$	0	①	1	−1	1	−1	0	1	s_1	1
	1	−1	−.2	.9	0	1	0	3	u_1	—
$2000r_2 + r_3$	0	−800	−400	1800	0	2000	1	6000	P	

We are still not at the maximum. The next pivot entry is the (1, 2) entry, since there is only one nonnegative ratio.

Third tableau:

	u_1	u_2	u_3	u_4	s_1	s_2	P	constants	basis
	0	1	1	−1	1	−1	0	1	u_2
$r_1 + r_2$	1	0	.8	−.1	1	0	0	4	u_1
$800r_1 + r_3$	0	0	400	1000	800	1200	1	6800	

The maximum of P occurs at the point with coordinates $u_1 = 4$, $u_2 = 1$, $u_3 = 0$, $u_4 = 0$, with a maximum value of 6800. Therefore the minimum value of C is 6800, also. The dual variables, the variables for the minimization program, are $x_1 = 800$ and $x_2 = 1200$, the numbers appearing at the bottom of the slack variable columns.

Since the inequalities in a minimum program are all $\geq$, we have **surplus variables** instead of slack variables for the constraints. We can compute these surplus variables by substituting x_1 and x_2 into the constraints:

$$x_1 + x_2 = 800 + 1200 = 2000 \text{ (no surplus)}$$

$$-x_2 = -1200 \text{ (no surplus)}$$

$$.8x_1 - .2x_2 = .8(800) - .2(1200) = 400 \text{ (surplus)}$$

$$-.1x_1 + .9x_2 = -.1(800) + .9(1200) = 1000 \text{ (surplus)}$$

We can also read the values of the surplus variables directly from the last tableau by reading the last entry in each of the original variable columns. u_1 corresponds to the first constraint, therefore the 0 at the bottom of the u_1-column is the value of the first surplus variable. Similarly, u_2 corresponds to the second constraint, therefore the value of the second surplus variable is 0; u_3 corresponds to the third constraint, therefore the third surplus variable is 400; and u_4 corresponds to the fourth constraint, therefore the fourth surplus variable is 1000. ∎

EXAMPLE 5

One of the classic linear programming problems involves choosing a diet from a set of foods that will provide all the minimum daily nutrient requirements and minimize the cost of the diet. As our last example, let us consider an updated version of the diet problem, where we now wish to minimize the number of calories, rather than cost. In fact, let us take the problem one step further, and assume we are limited to eating in one fast-food restaurant for the day. The restaurant serves only four foods; a Bigburger (hamburger with lettuce and tomato), french fries, 8 oz. milk, and apples. How much of each of the four foods should one eat to satisfy the minimum daily nutrient requirements and minimize the number of calories consumed? The table below gives data concerning the amount of each nutrient in a serving of the four foods, the minimum daily requirements of nutrients, and the number of calories in a serving of each food:

	Bigburger	8 oz. Milk	Apple	Fr. F.	Min. Daily Req.
Vitamin C	15	3	8	7	75 mgs
Vitamin A	2700	450	150	800	5000 mgs
Calcium	50	280	20	50	800 mgs
Iron	5.9	.2	.5	.3	12 mgs
Protein	25	9	1	2	60 mgs
Calories	350	165	75	100	(Merck Manual)

If we let:

x_1 = the number of Bigburgers to be eaten

x_2 = the number of glasses of milk to be drunk

x_3 = the number of apples to be eaten

x_4 = the number of servings of french fries to be eaten

we have the following linear program to minimize caloric intake:

$$\min C = 350x_1 + 165x_2 + 75x_3 + 100x_4$$

$$15x_1 + 3x_2 + 8x_3 + 7x_4 \geq 75$$

$$2700x_1 + 450x_2 + 150x_3 + 800x_4 \geq 5000$$

$$50x_1 + 280x_2 + 20x_3 + 50x_4 \geq 800$$

$$5.9x_1 + .2x_2 + .5x_3 + .3x_4 \geq 12$$
$$25x_1 + 9x_2 + x_3 + 2x_4 \geq 60$$
$$x_i \geq 0$$

To solve the problem, write the dual linear program, a maximization linear program:

$$\max P = 75u_1 + 500u_2 + 800u_3 + 12u_4 + 60u_5$$
$$15u_1 + 2700u_2 + 50u_3 + 5.9u_4 + 25u_5 \leq 350$$
$$3u_1 + 450u_2 + 280u_3 + .2u_4 + 9u_5 \leq 165$$
$$8u_1 + 150u_2 + 20u_3 + .5u_4 + u_5 \leq 75$$
$$7u_1 + 800u_2 + 50u_3 + .3u_4 + 2u_5 \leq 100$$
$$u_j \geq 0$$

The dual variables u_1, u_2, u_3, u_4, and u_5 correspond to the caloric saving that is afforded by decreasing the minimum daily requirement by one unit. For example, u_1 represents the number of calories that one would not have to consume if the minimum daily requirement of vitamin C is reduced 1 mg. Similarly, u_5 is the number of calories that would not have to be consumed if the minimum daily requirement for protein is decreased 1 g.

From another point of view, the dual variables represent the caloric saving if the nutrient is available in pure form as a tablet. For example, u_3 is the number of calories that would be saved if a 1 mg tablet of calcium was taken instead.

It should be clear to the student that trying to apply the simplex method to this problem would be very time consuming. We will look at the computer implementation of the simplex method in the next section and will provide the solution to this problem at that time.

CONCEPTS

dual linear program
dual variables
standard minimization form
Von Neumann duality principle
surplus variables

SOLUTIONS TO PRACTICE EXAMPLES

1. $\min C = 8u_1 + 18u_2$

$u_1 + 2u_2 \geq 3$

$u_1 + 3u_2 \geq 5$

$u_1 \geq 0,\ u_2 \geq 0$

2. Final tableau:

$$\begin{pmatrix} x_1 & x_2 & s_1 & s_2 & P & \text{constants} \\ \frac{1}{3} & 0 & 1 & -\frac{1}{3} & 0 & 2 \\ \frac{2}{3} & 1 & 0 & \frac{1}{3} & 0 & 6 \\ \frac{1}{3} & 0 & 0 & \frac{5}{3} & 1 & 30 \end{pmatrix} \quad \begin{matrix} \text{basis} \\ s_1 \\ x_2 \\ P \end{matrix}$$

The dual variables are $u_1 = 0$, $u_2 = \frac{5}{3}$, with min $C = 30$. The manager should be willing to pay up to \$1.66 a unit for more of constraint 2.

EXERCISES 11.3

Write the dual of each of the following linear programs.

1. max $P = x_1 + 2x_2$

    $x_1 + x_2 \le 5$

    $2x_1 + 3x_2 \le 12$

    $x_1 \ge 0, x_2 \ge 0$

2. max $T = x_1 + 3x_2 + x_3$

    $2x_1 + x_2 + x_3 \le 15$

    $x_1 - x_2 + x_3 \le 9$

    $3x_1 + 5x_2 - x_3 \le 18$

    $x_1 \ge 0, x_2 \ge 0, x_3 \ge 0$

3. max $P = 5x_1 + 3x_2 + x_3$

    $x_1 + x_3 \le 6$

    $x_2 + 2x_3 \le 8$

    $2x_1 + x_2 \le 5$

    $x_1 \ge 0, x_2 \ge 0, x_3 \ge 0$

4. max $W = x_1 + x_3$

    $x_1 + x_2 + x_3 \ge 6$

    $2x_1 - x_2 + 3x_3 \le 10$

    $3x_1 + 5x_2 + 2x_3 \le 18$

    $x_1 \ge 0, x_2 \ge 0, x_3 \ge 0$

5. min $C = 8x_1 + 10x_2$

$$3x_1 + 7x_2 \geq 15$$
$$2x_1 + x_2 \geq 8$$
$$x_1 \geq 0, x_2 \geq 0$$

6. min $C = x_1 + x_2 + x_3$

$$2x_1 + x_2 - x_3 \geq 8$$
$$x_1 + 5x_2 + x_3 \geq 7$$
$$4x_1 + 5x_2 + 3x_3 \geq 20$$
$$x_1 \geq 0, x_2 \geq 0, x_3 \geq 0$$

7. min $R = 100x_1 + 200x_2 + 50x_3$

$$3x_1 + 5x_2 + 20x_3 \leq 100$$
$$2x_1 + x_2 \geq 25$$
$$5x_2 + 7x_3 \geq 45$$
$$x_1 \geq 0, x_2 \geq 0, x_3 \geq 0$$

8. Use the simplex method to find the solution for the linear program in Exercise 1. What are the dual variables?

9. Use the simplex method to find the solution to the linear program in Exercise 2. What are the dual variables?

10. Find the solution to the linear program in Exercise 5 by first finding the solution to the dual.

11. Find the solution to the linear program in Exercise 6 by first finding the solution to the dual.

12. Find the dual of the program constructed in Exercise 13 in Section 11.2. What can be said about the feasible region of the dual?

13. Find the dual of the program constructed in Exercise 14 in Section 11.2. What can be said about the feasible region of this dual. Can you generalize?

14. An advertising agency has a client's money to invest in newspaper ads, television commercials, and magazine ads. The television commercials can be during prime time or not. The client wants to reach the young adult, middle age, and older person markets. From past research, the agency can determine the effectiveness of each type of advertising for each type of market. The effectiveness scores per dollar spent (on a range of 0–10) are given in the following table:

	Newspaper	Prime time TV	TV nonprime	Magazine
Young adult	8	9	2	6
Middle age	9	8	7	5
Older	5	10	8	3

The client insists on a total effectiveness of 25,000 for the young adult population, 30,000 for the middle age population, and 28,000 for the older population. How much money should be spent on each type of advertising to minimize the total cost?

11.4   *Using a Computer for the Simplex Method*

In the last two sections, we used the simplex method to find solutions to linear programs with two and three variables. In actual practice, most linear programs have more than two or three variables. However, applying the simplex method to programs with more than three variables becomes tedious and time consuming. Possibilities for error abound. Try to solve the maximization problem that is the dual of the diet problem without a computer!

Fortunately, for almost every computer on the market, we now have software available that implements the simplex method. The software programs only require you to enter the coefficients of the objective function, the coefficients and the constants in the constraints, and to name the variables.

EXAMPLE 1

Consider the dual of the diet problem:

$$\max P = 75u_1 + 5000u_2 + 800u_3 + 12u_4 + 60u_5$$

$$C1 \quad 15u_1 + 2700u_2 + 50u_3 + 5.9u_4 + 25u_5 \leq 350$$

$$C2 \quad 3u_1 + 450u_2 + 280u_3 + .2u_4 + 9u_5 \leq 165$$

$$C3 \quad 8u_1 + 150u_2 + 20u_3 + .5u_4 + u_5 \leq 75$$

$$C4 \quad 7u_1 + 800u_2 + 50u_3 + .3u_4 + 2u_5 \leq 100$$

$$u_j \geq 5$$

With slack variables and in a form to be transferred to the first tableau, we have:

$$15u_1 + 2700u_2 + 50u_3 + 5.9u_4 + 25u_5 + s_1 = 350$$

$$3u_1 + 450u_2 + 280u_3 + .2u_4 + 9u_5 + s_2 = 165$$

$$8u_1 + 150u_2 + 20u_3 + .5u_4 + u_5 + s_3 = 75$$

$$7u_1 + 800u_2 + 50u_3 + .3u_4 + 2u_5 + s_4 = 100$$

$$-75u_1 - 5000u_2 - 800u_3 - 12u_4 - 60u_5 + P = 0$$

The information from this linear program was entered into a computer, using a Hewlett-Packard software package. Both the first tableau and the last tableau are printed as part of the **computer output**. The numbers printed in the tableau are written with three decimal places multiplied by 10 to some power. For example, $1.500E+01$ means $1.500 \times 10^1 = 15.00$.

Similarly, $4.500E+02 = 4.500 \times 10^2 = 450$, and $2.00E-01 = 2.00 \times 10^{-1} = .2$. The solutions are given with five decimal place accuracy in the same form.

The variables are listed as either basic or nonbasic for each tableau. The underlined numbers correspond to the numbers in the last column of the tableau. The indication of lower bound or upper bound signifies that the nonbasic variable is set at its lower-bound or upper-bound level.

The printout for the first tableau is:

<u>INITIAL TABLEAU FOR PROBLEM MAX</u>
FOR PHASE 2

CONSTRAINT: C1   /BASIC VARIABLE: SLACK

```
1.500E+01   2.700E+03   5.000E+01   5.900E+00   2.500E+01   1.000E+00
0.000E+00   0.000E+00   0.000E+00                           3.500E+02
```

CONSTRAINT: C2   /BASIC VARIABLE: SLACK

```
3.000E+00   4.500E+02   2.800E+02   2.000E-01   9.000E+00   0.000E+00
1.000E+00   0.000E+00   0.000E+00                           1.650E+02
```

CONSTRAINT: C3   /BASIC VARIABLE: SLACK

```
8.000E+00   1.500E+02   2.000E+01   5.000E-01   1.000E+00   0.000E+00
0.000E+00   1.000E+00   0.000E+00                           7.500E+01
```

CONSTRAINT: C4   /BASIC VARIABLE: SLACK

```
7.000E+00   8.000E+02   5.000E+01   3.000E-01   2.000E+00   0.000E+00
0.000E+00   0.000E+00   1.000E+00                           1.000E+02
```

COST ROW:

```
-7.500E+01  -5.000E+03  -8.000E+02  -1.200E+01  -6.000E+01   0.000E+00
 0.000E+00   0.000E+00   0.000E+00                           0.000E+00
```

NOTE: THE UNDERLINED NUMBER IN EACH ROW REPRESENTS THE VALUE
      OF THE CORRESPONDING BASIC VARIABLE, EXCEPT IN THE COST
      ROW WHERE IT GIVES THE VALUE OF THE OBJECTIVE FUNCTION.

VARIABLE DEFINITIONS

VARIABLE NUMBER	VARIABLE NAME	BASIC OR NONBASIC	LOWER OR UPPER BOUND
1	U1	NONBASIC	LOWER
2	U2	NONBASIC	LOWER
3	U3	NONBASIC	LOWER
4	U4	NONBASIC	LOWER
5	U5	NONBASIC	LOWER
6	SLACK FOR CONSTRAINT C1	BASIC	
7	SLACK FOR CONSTRAINT C2	BASIC	
8	SLACK FOR CONSTRAINT C3	BASIC	
9	SLACK FOR CONSTRAINT C4	BASIC	

The solution to the maximization linear program is given next. In this example, the maximum value of P is $1.30894E+03 = 1.30894 \times 10^3 = 1308.94$, with solution set: $u_1 = 5.56578$, $u_2 = 0$, $u_3 = .500416$, $u_4 = 40.9309$, $u_5 = 0$, $s_1 = 0$, $s_2 = 0$, $s_3 = 0$, and $s_4 = 23.7395$.

```
SOLUTION ANALYSIS FOR PROBLEM MAX


THE SOLUTION IS BOTH FEASIBLE AND OPTIMAL.
THE MAXIMUM VALUE OF THE OBJECTIVE FUNCTION =   1.30894E+03
```

DECISION VARIABLES:

VARIABLE NAME	VARIABLE VALUE	BASIC OR NONBASIC	LOWER OR UPPER BOUND
U2	0.00000E+00	NONBASIC	LOWER
U5	0.00000E+00	NONBASIC	LOWER
U4	4.09309E+01	BASIC	
U3	5.00416E-01	BASIC	
U1	5.56578E+00	BASIC	

SLACK AND SURPLUS VARIABLES:

VARIABLE NAME	VARIABLE VALUE	BASIC OR NONBASIC	LOWER OR UPPER BOUND
SLACK FOR CONSTRAINT C3	0.00000E+00	NONBASIC	LOWER
SLACK FOR CONSTRAINT C2	0.00000E+00	NONBASIC	LOWER
SLACK FOR CONSTRAINT C1	0.00000E+00	NONBASIC	LOWER
SLACK FOR CONSTRAINT C4	2.37395E+01	BASIC	

Remember, we do not really want the solution to the maximization program, but we do want the solution to its dual minimization program (the diet program).

The minimization program is the dual of the maximization program:

$$\min C = 350x_1 + 165x_2 + 75x_3 + 100x_4$$

$$15x_1 + 3x_2 + 8x_3 + 7x_4 \geq 75$$

$$2700x_1 + 450x_2 + 150x_3 + 800x_4 \geq 5000$$

$$50x_1 + 280x_2 + 20x_3 + 50x_4 \leq 800$$

$$5.9x_1 + .2x_2 + .5x_3 + .3x_4 \geq 12$$

$$25x_1 + 9x_2 + x_3 + 2x_4 \geq 60$$

$$x_i \geq 0$$

Therefore, the variables can be read from the bottom row of the final tableau. The final tableau, as printed out, is:

FINAL TABLEAU FOR PROBLEM MAX

CONSTRAINT: C1   /BASIC VARIABLE: U4

```
 0.000E+00    4.838E+02    0.000E+00    1.000E+00    4.581E+00    2.015E-01
-9.245E-03   -3.744E-01    0.000E+00                              4.093E+01
```

CONSTRAINT: C2   /BASIC VARIABLE: U3

```
 0.000E+00    1.423E+00    1.000E+00    0.000E+00    3.144E-02   -9.245E-06
 3.670E-03   -1.359E-03    0.000E+00                              5.004E-01
```

CONSTRAINT: C3   /BASIC VARIABLE: U1

```
 1.000E+00   -1.505E+01    0.000E+00    0.000E+00   -2.399E-01   -1.257E-02
-8.598E-03    1.518E-01    0.000E+00                              5.566E+00
```

CONSTRAINT: C4   /BASIC VARIABLE: SLACK

```
 1.000E-11    6.890E+02    1.000E-10    0.000E+00    7.330E-01    2.801E-02
-1.206E-01   -8.823E-01    1.000E+00                              2.374E+01
```

COST ROW:

```
 0.000E+00    8.156E+02    0.000E+00    0.000E+00    2.130E+00    1.468E+00
 2.180E+00    5.805E+00    0.000E+00                              1.309E+03
```

NOTE: THE UNDERLINED NUMBER IN EACH ROW REPRESENTS THE VALUE
      OF THE CORRESPONDING BASIC VARIABLE, EXCEPT IN THE COST
      ROW WHERE IT GIVES THE VALUE OF THE OBJECTIVE FUNCTION.

VARIABLE DEFINITIONS

VARIABLE NUMBER	VARIABLE NAME	BASIC OR NONBASIC	LOWER OR UPPER BOUND
1	U1	BASIC	
2	U2	NONBASIC	LOWER
3	U3	BASIC	
4	U4	BASIC	
5	U5	NONBASIC	LOWER
6	SLACK FOR CONSTRAINT C1	NONBASIC	LOWER
7	SLACK FOR CONSTRAINT C2	NONBASIC	LOWER
8	SLACK FOR CONSTRAINT C3	NONBASIC	LOWER
9	SLACK FOR CONSTRAINT C4	BASIC	

The bottom row (cost row) of the final tableau has a number corresponding to each of the five u-variables. 1.468 is at the bottom of the first slack variable column, thus, $x_1 = 1.468$. 2.180 is at the bottom of the second slack variable column, therefore, $x_2 = 2.18$. 5.805 appears at the bottom of the third slack variable column, thus, $x_3 = 5.805$. Finally, 0 is at the bottom of the fourth slack variable column, therefore, $x_4 = 0$. In terms of our diet problem, these results tell us that if we eat one and a half hamburgers, 2.18 glasses of milk, 6 apples, and no french fries, we will satisfy the minimum daily nutrient requirements, and consume only 1309 calories. (We might still be hungry, however.)

The numbers appearing at the bottom of the u_j-variable columns correspond to the surplus of each nutrient that we would have when we consume this diet. Therefore, we would have no surplus of vitamin C, no surplus of calcium, and no surplus of iron. We would have surplus of 815.6 mg of vitamin A, and we would have a surplus of 2.13 g of protein.

Recall that the values of the dual u_j-variables correspond to the caloric saving if the ith constraint is decreased 1 unit, or if 1 unit is available in tablet form. Thus, $u_1 = 5.566$ implies a saving of 5.566 calories if the vitamin C requirement is reduced 1 mg. $u_3 = .5004$ implies a saving of .5004 calories if the calcium requirement is reduced 1 unit, or a 1 mg tablet of calcium is available. $u_4 = 40.93$ implies a saving of 40.93 calories if the iron requirement is reduced 1 mg or a 1 mg tablet of iron is available. No savings in calories is possible by changing the requirements for vitamin A or protein.

The output from the simplex method program also produces a **sensitivity analysis**. In other words, how sensitive to changes in the bounds on the constraints and values of the objective function is our maximum solution?

The output of the program breaks the changes in the coefficients of the variables of the objective function into two parts, the nonbasic variable coefficients and the basic coefficients. The output of this program says that if the coefficient of u_2, call it c_2, is in the following range: $-\infty \leq c_2 \leq 5815.6$, then the solution (corner point) to the linear program remains the same. Outside the range, the solution changes. Similarly, if c_5 is the coefficient of u_5, and $-\infty \leq c_5 \leq 62.13$, then the solution remains the same; if c_1 is the coefficient of u_1, and $36.76 \leq c_1 \leq 83.877$, then the solution remains the same; if c_3 is the coefficient of u_3, and $732.27 \leq c_3 \leq 5071.4$, then the solution remains the same; and if c_4 is the coefficient of u_4 and $11.535 \leq c_4 \leq 27.504$, then the solution remains the same.

SENSITIVITY ANALYSIS FOR PROGRAM MAX

OBJECTIVE FUNCTION COEFFICIENT
RANGE FOR NONBASIC VARIABLES:

VARIABLE NAME	LOWER LIMIT	COEFFICIENT VALUE	UPPER LIMIT
U2	-INFINITY	5.0000E+03	5.8156E+03
U5	-INFINITY	6.0000E+01	6.2130E+01

```
OBJECTIVE FUNCTION COEFFICIENT
RANGE FOR BASIC VARIABLES:


VARIABLE        LOWER           COEFFICIENT     UPPER
NAME            LIMIT           VALUE           LIMIT


U4              1.1535E+01      1.2000E+01      2.7504E+01
U3              7.3227E+02      8.0000E+02      5.0714E+03
U1              3.6760E+01      7.5000E+01      8.3877E+01


RIGHT-HAND-SIDE RANGE:


CONSTRAINT      LOWER           RHS             UPPER
NAME            LIMIT           B(I)            LIMIT


C1              1.4690E+02      3.5000E+02      7.9268E+02
C2              2.8652E+01      1.6500E+02      3.6192E+02
C3              3.8334E+01      7.5000E+01      1.0191E+02
C4              7.6261E+01      1.0000E+02      +INFINITY
```

The sensitivity analysis also provides for variations in the constants of the constraints, call them b_1, b_2, b_3, and b_4. If:

$$146.9 \leq b_1 \leq 792.68$$

$$28.652 \leq b_2 \leq 361.92$$

$$38.334 \leq b_3 \leq 101.91$$

$$76.261 \leq b_4 \leq \infty$$

then the solution to the linear program remains the same. Outside these ranges the solution changes.

This type of information is extremely useful to the business manager, since there may be daily fluctuations in the constants of the constraints and the coefficients of the objective function. As illustrated by our next example, a new solution may not have to be computed each time.

EXAMPLE 2   In Section 9.4, Exercise 10 asked the reader to set up a linear program to give a manufacturing schedule for handbags that would maximize profit. If

x_1 denotes the number of dozens of style-341 handbags
x_2 denotes the number of dozens of style-262 handbags
x_3 denotes the number of dozens of style-43 handbags
x_4 denotes the number of dozens of style-784 handbags
x_5 denotes the number of dozens of style-5–A handbags

then the linear program is:

$$\max P = 30x_1 + 40x_2 + 45x_3 + 25x_4 + 60x_5$$

$$3x_1 + 4x_2 + 2x_3 + 2x_4 + 5x_5 \leq 700$$

$$8x_1 + 3x_2 + 2x_3 + x_4 + 4x_5 \leq 600$$

$$2x_1 + x_2 + 3x_4 + 4x_5 \leq 400$$

$$6x_1 + 2x_3 + 4x_4 + 3x_5 \leq 900$$

$$4x_2 + 5x_3 + 6x_4 + 2x_5 \leq 300$$

$$x_1 + 7x_3 + 4x_4 + 3x_5 \leq 400$$

$$4x_1 + 7x_2 + 6x_3 + x_4 + 3x_5 \leq 1000$$

$$2x_1 + 4x_2 + 2x_3 + x_4 \leq 900$$

$$3x_1 + 4x_2 + 2x_4 + 4x_5 \leq 1600$$

$$x_1 \leq 100$$

$$x_2 \leq 50$$

$$x_3 \leq 90$$

$$x_4 \leq 70$$

$$x_5 \leq 30$$

$$x_1 \geq 0,\ x_2 \geq 0,\ x_3 \geq 0,\ x_4 \geq 0,\ x_5 \geq 0$$

Clearly, this is a linear program that you would not want to solve by hand. The Hewlett-Packard program provides for giving both lower and upper bounds on the variables at the outset. In this example the lower bounds are each 0 and the upper bounds are given as 100, 50, 90, 70, and 30 doz. for each of the five variables, respectively. Therefore, it suffices to use only the first nine constraints for the problem. At the completion of the final tableau, the nonbasic variables are each set equal to their lower bounds and their upper bounds, all combinations thereof to determine the optimal solution. As you can see from the printout, the value of x_5 at the maximum is the upper bound of x_5, namely 30, whereas the value of x_4 at the maximum is the lower bound for x_4, namely 0. The printout of the "solution" follows:

<u>INITIAL TABLEAU FOR PROBLEM TWO</u>
<u>FOR PHASE 2</u>

```
CONSTRAINT: C1        /BASIC VARIABLE: SLACK

  3.000E+00    4.000E+00   2.000E+00    2.000E+00    5.000E+00    1.000E+00
  0.000E+00    0.000E+00   0.000E+00    0.000E+00    0.000E+00    0.000E+00
  0.000E+00    0.000E+00                                          7.000E+02
```

```
CONSTRAINT: C2        /BASIC VARIABLE: SLACK

  8.000E+00    3.000E+00    2.000E+00    1.000E+00    4.000E+00    0.000E+00
  1.000E+00    0.000E+00    0.000E+00    0.000E+00    0.000E+00    0.000E+00
  0.000E+00    0.000E+00                                            6.000E+02

CONSTRAINT: C3        /BASIC VARIABLE: SLACK

  2.000E+00    1.000E+00    0.000E+00    3.000E+00    4.000E+00    0.000E+00
  0.000E+00    1.000E+00    0.000E+00    0.000E+00    0.000E+00    0.000E+00
  0.000E+00    0.000E+00                                            4.000E+02

CONSTRAINT: C4        /BASIC VARIABLE: SLACK

  6.000E+00    0.000E+00    2.000E+00    4.000E+00    3.000E+00    0.000E+00
  0.000E+00    0.000E+00    1.000E+00    0.000E+00    0.000E+00    0.000E+00
  0.000E+00    0.000E+00                                            9.000E+02

CONSTRAINT: C5        /BASIC VARIABLE: SLACK

  0.000E+00    4.000E+00    5.000E+00    6.000E+00    2.000E+00    0.000E+00
  0.000E+00    0.000E+00    0.000E+00    1.000E+00    0.000E+00    0.000E+00
  0.000E+00    0.000E+00                                            3.000E+02

CONSTRAINT: C6        /BASIC VARIABLE: SLACK

  1.000E+00    0.000E+00    7.000E+00    4.000E+00    3.000E+00    0.000E+00
  0.000E+00    0.000E+00    0.000E+00    0.000E+00    1.000E+00    0.000E+00
  0.000E+00    0.000E+00                                            4.000E+02

CONSTRAINT: C7        /BASIC VARIABLE: SLACK

  4.000E+00    7.000E+00    6.000E+00    1.000E+00    3.000E+00    0.000E+00
  0.000E+00    0.000E+00    0.000E+00    0.000E+00    0.000E+00    1.000E+00
  0.000E+00    0.000E+00                                            1.000E+03

CONSTRAINT: C8        /BASIC VARIABLE: SLACK

  2.000E+00    4.000E+00    2.000E+00    1.000E+00    0.000E+00    0.000E+00
  0.000E+00    0.000E+00    0.000E+00    0.000E+00    0.000E+00    0.000E+00
  1.000E+00    0.000E+00                                            9.000E+02

CONSTRAINT: C9        /BASIC VARIABLE: SLACK

  3.000E+00    4.000E+00    0.000E+00    2.000E+00    4.000E+00    0.000E+00
  0.000E+00    0.000E+00    0.000E+00    0.000E+00    0.000E+00    0.000E+00
  0.000E+00    1.000E+00                                            1.600E+03

COST ROW:

 -3.000E+01   -4.000E+01   -4.500E+01   -2.500E+01   -6.000E+01    0.000E+00
  0.000E+00    0.000E+00    0.000E+00    0.000E+00    0.000E+00    0.000E+00
  0.000E+00    0.000E+00                                            0.000E+00
```

NOTE: THE UNDERLINED NUMBER IN EACH ROW REPRESENTS THE VALUE
      OF THE CORRESPONDING BASIC VARIABLE, EXCEPT IN THE COST
      ROW WHERE IT GIVES THE VALUE OF THE OBJECTIVE FUNCTION.

VARIABLE DEFINITIONS

VARIABLE NUMBER	VARIABLE NAME	BASIC OR NONBASIC	LOWER OR UPPER BOUND
1	X1	NONBASIC	LOWER
2	X2	NONBASIC	LOWER

3	X3	NONBASIC	LOWER
4	X4	NONBASIC	LOWER
5	X5	NONBASIC	LOWER
6	SLACK FOR CONSTRAINT C1	BASIC	
7	SLACK FOR CONSTRAINT C2	BASIC	
8	SLACK FOR CONSTRAINT C3	BASIC	
9	SLACK FOR CONSTRAINT C4	BASIC	
10	SLACK FOR CONSTRAINT C5	BASIC	
11	SLACK FOR CONSTRAINT C6	BASIC	
12	SLACK FOR CONSTRAINT C7	BASIC	
13	SLACK FOR CONSTRAINT C8	BASIC	
14	SLACK FOR CONSTRAINT C9	BASIC	

SOLUTION ANALYSIS FOR PROBLEM TWO

THE SOLUTION IS BOTH FEASIBLE AND OPTIMAL.
THE MAXIMUM VALUE OF THE OBJECTIVE FUNCTION = 5.38398E+03

DECISION VARIABLES:

VARIABLE NAME	VARIABLE VALUE	BASIC OR NONBASIC	LOWER OR UPPER BOUND
X4	0.00000E+00	NONBASIC	LOWER
X5	3.00000E+01	NONBASIC	UPPER
X1	4.57576E+01	BASIC	
X2	1.28139E+01	BASIC	
X3	3.77489E+01	BASIC	

SLACK AND SURPLUS VARIABLES:

VARIABLE NAME	VARIABLE VALUE	BASIC OR NONBASIC	LOWER OR UPPER BOUND
SLACK FOR CONSTRAINT C2	0.00000E+00	NONBASIC	LOWER
SLACK FOR CONSTRAINT C5	0.00000E+00	NONBASIC	LOWER
SLACK FOR CONSTRAINT C6	0.00000E+00	NONBASIC	LOWER

```
SLACK FOR
CONSTRAINT
C1              2.85974E+02      BASIC
SLACK FOR
CONSTRAINT
C3              1.75671E+02      BASIC
SLACK FOR
CONSTRAINT
C4              4.59957E+02      BASIC
SLACK FOR
CONSTRAINT
C7              4.10779E+02      BASIC
SLACK FOR
CONSTRAINT
C8              6.81732E+02      BASIC
SLACK FOR
CONSTRAINT
C9              1.29147E+03      BASIC
```

The analysis of the solution for this example shows that the maximum profit is $P = \$5,383.98$ and comes from producing 45.75 dozen style-341 handbags, 12.81 dozen style-262 handbags, 37.74 dozen style-43 handbags, no style-784 handbags, and 30 dozen style-5–A handbags. There is a slack of 285.97 hours in the clicking department, a slack of 175.67 hours in the stitching department, and a slack of 459.95 hours in the finishing department. There is also a slack of 410.78 yards of backing fabric, a slack of 681.73 yards of lining fabric, and a slack of 1291.47 yards of accessory fabric. If the firm cannot produce a fractional part of a dozen of any style handbag, each of the first three quantities must be rounded down to the next integer. (Rounding down is necessary to maintain feasibility.) Therefore, the firm could produce 45 dozen style-341 handbags, 12 dozen style-262 handbags, 37 dozen style-43 handbags, no style-784 handbags, and 30 dozen style-5–A handbags. The profit will be reduced by $88.20 to $5,295.78. This solution is feasible, but it may not be optimal. Unfortunately, if integer solutions are required the problem becomes an integer programming problem, and certain integer programming techniques must be applied. Most of these techniques require first finding the solution to the linear programming problem, so all is not lost.

FINAL TABLEAU FOR PROBLEM TWO

```
CONSTRAINT: C1          /BASIC VARIABLE: SLACK

  0.000E+00     0.000E+00     0.000E+00     -1.247E+00    2.935E+00     1.000E+00
 -4.156E-01     0.000E+00     0.000E+00     -6.883E-01    3.247E-01     0.000E+00
  0.000E+00     0.000E+00                                               2.860E+02

CONSTRAINT: C2          /BASIC VARIABLE: X1

  1.000E+00     0.000E+00     0.000E+00     -3.030E-01    3.939E-01     0.000E+00
  1.212E-01     0.000E+00     0.000E+00     -9.091E-02    3.030E-02     0.000E+00
  0.000E+00     0.000E+00                                               4.576E+01

CONSTRAINT: C3          /BASIC VARIABLE: SLACK

  0.000E+00     0.000E+00     0.000E+00     2.874E+00     3.177E+00     0.000E+00
 -2.641E-01     1.000E+00     0.000E+00     -5.195E-02    1.126E-01     0.000E+00
  0.000E+00     0.000E+00                                               1.757E+02
```

```
CONSTRAINT: C4          /BASIC VARIABLE: SLACK

  0.000E+00    0.000E+00    0.000E+00    4.589E+00   -1.082E-01    0.000E+00
 -6.926E-01    0.000E+00    1.000E+00    5.195E-01   -4.589E-01    0.000E+00
  0.000E+00    0.000E+00                                           4.600E+02

CONSTRAINT: C5          /BASIC VARIABLE: X2

  0.000E+00    1.000E+00    0.000E+00    7.316E-01    3.463E-02    0.000E+00
  2.165E-02    0.000E+00    0.000E+00    2.338E-01   -1.732E-01    0.000E+00
  0.000E+00    0.000E+00                                           1.281E+01

CONSTRAINT: C6          /BASIC VARIABLE: X3

  0.000E+00    1.444E-13    1.000E+00    6.147E-01    3.723E-01    0.000E+00
 -1.732E-02    0.000E+00    0.000E+00    1.299E-02    1.385E-01    0.000E+00
  0.000E+00    0.000E+00                                           3.775E+01

CONSTRAINT: C7          /BASIC VARIABLE: SLACK

  0.000E+00   -1.000E-11    0.000E+00   -6.597E+00   -1.052E+00    0.000E+00
 -5.325E-01    0.000E+00    0.000E+00   -1.351E+00    2.597E-01    1.000E+00
  0.000E+00    0.000E+00                                           4.108E+02

CONSTRAINT: C8          /BASIC VARIABLE: SLACK

  0.000E+00    0.000E+00    0.000E+00   -2.550E+00   -1.671E+00    0.000E+00
 -2.944E-01    0.000E+00    0.000E+00   -7.792E-01    3.550E-01    0.000E+00
  1.000E+00    0.000E+00                                           6.817E+02

CONSTRAINT: C9          /BASIC VARIABLE: SLACK

  0.000E+00    0.000E+00    0.000E+00   -1.732E-02    2.680E+00    0.000E+00
 -4.502E-01    0.000E+00    0.000E+00   -6.623E-01    6.017E-01    0.000E+00
  0.000E+00    1.000E+00                                           1.291E+03

COST ROW:

  0.000E+00    0.000E+00    0.000E+00    2.284E+01   -3.004E+01    0.000E+00
  3.723E+00    0.000E+00    0.000E+00    7.208E+00    2.165E-01    0.000E+00
  0.000E+00    0.000E+00                                           5.384E+03
```

NOTE: THE UNDERLINED NUMBER IN EACH ROW REPRESENTS THE VALUE
      OF THE CORRESPONDING BASIC VARIABLE, EXCEPT IN THE COST
      ROW WHERE IT GIVES THE VALUE OF THE OBJECTIVE FUNCTION.

VARIABLE DEFINITIONS

VARIABLE NUMBER	VARIABLE NAME	BASIC OR NONBASIC	LOWER OR UPPER BOUND
1	X1	BASIC	
2	X2	BASIC	
3	X3	BASIC	
4	X4	NONBASIC	LOWER
5	X5	NONBASIC	UPPER
6	SLACK FOR CONSTRAINT C1	BASIC	
7	SLACK FOR CONSTRAINT C2	NONBASIC	LOWER
8	SLACK FOR CONSTRAINT C3	BASIC	

```
9               SLACK FOR
                CONSTRAINT
                C4              BASIC
10              SLACK FOR
                CONSTRAINT
                C5              NONBASIC        LOWER
11              SLACK FOR
                CONSTRAINT
                C6              NONBASIC        LOWER
12              SLACK FOR
                CONSTRAINT
                C7              BASIC
13              SLACK FOR
                CONSTRAINT
                C8              BASIC
14              SLACK FOR
                CONSTRAINT
                C9              BASIC
```

SENSITIVITY ANALYSIS FOR PROGRAM TWO

OBJECTIVE FUNCTION COEFFICIENT RANGE FOR NONBASIC VARIABLES:

VARIABLE NAME	LOWER LIMIT	COEFFICIENT VALUE	UPPER LIMIT
X4	-INFINITY	2.5000E+01	4.7835E+01
X5	2.9957E+01	6.0000E+01	+INFINITY

OBJECTIVE FUNCTION COEFFICIENT RANGE FOR BASIC VARIABLES:

VARIABLE NAME	LOWER LIMIT	COEFFICIENT VALUE	UPPER LIMIT
X1	2.2857E+01	3.0000E+01	1.0536E+02
X2	9.1667E+00	4.0000E+01	4.1250E+01
X3	4.3438E+01	4.5000E+01	1.2570E+02

RIGHT-HAND-SIDE RANGE:

CONSTRAINT NAME	LOWER LIMIT	RHS B(I)	UPPER LIMIT
C1	4.1403E+02	7.0000E+02	+INFINITY
C2	2.2250E+02	6.0000E+02	1.0475E+03
C3	2.2433E+02	4.0000E+02	+INFINITY
C4	4.4004E+02	9.0000E+02	+INFINITY
C5	2.4519E+02	3.0000E+02	4.5907E+02
C6	1.8525E+02	4.0000E+02	4.7400E+02
C7	5.8922E+02	1.0000E+03	+INFINITY
C8	2.1827E+02	9.0000E+02	+INFINITY
C9	3.0853E+02	1.6000E+03	+INFINITY

The final tableau gives the values of the dual variables. Each ith dual variable value occurs at the bottom of the ith slack variable column in the final tableau. Therefore, the value of the first dual variable, u_1, is the sixth entry of the cost (bottom) row, namely, $u_1 = 0$. Similarly, the value of the second dual variable, u_2, is the seventh entry of the cost row, namely, $u_2 = 3.723$. Continuing, $u_3 = 0$, $u_4 = 0$, $u_5 = 7.2$, $u_6 = .2165$, $u_7 = 0 = u_8 = u_9$. Economically, these values of the dual variables say that the firm should be willing to pay up to $3.72 an hour to get additional hours in the paring department, $7.20 a yard to get additional leather, and $.21 a yard to get additional main fabric. An increase of one unit in each of these constraints corresponds to an increase in profit of each of the previous amounts.

The sensitivity analysis tells us exactly by how many units we can change the constants on the constraints before the corner point (solution, except for P) that produces the maximum changes. Let b_i denote the constant for constraint i. Then the output tells us that if b_i falls in the following ranges, then the corner point remains the same (the optimal number of each handbag remains unchanged):

$$414.03 \leq b_1 \leq \infty$$

$$222.5 \leq b_2 \leq 1047.5$$

$$224.33 \leq b_3 \leq \infty$$

$$440.04 \leq b_4 \leq \infty$$

$$245.19 \leq b_5 \leq 459.07$$

$$185.25 \leq b_6 \leq 474$$

$$589.22 \leq b_7 \leq \infty$$

$$218.27 \leq b_8 \leq \infty$$

$$308.53 \leq b_9 \leq \infty$$

Outside these ranges, the optimal mix of handbags changes.

The sensitivity analysis of the objective function coefficients tells us that unless the profit contribution of style-784 goes beyond $47.835, the firm should not produce any of these handbags, and that unless the profit contribution of style-5–A handbags drops below $29.95, the firm should still produce the maximum allowable of 30 dozen of this style.

The ranges for the objective function coefficients for the first three styles, labeled c_1, c_2, and c_3, are given by:

$$\$22.857 \leq c_1 \leq \$105.36$$

$$\$9.1667 \leq c_2 \leq \$41.25$$

$$\$43.438 \leq c_3 \leq \$125.70$$

In other words, even a small upward change in profit from style-262, or a small downward change in profit from either style-341, or style-43 handbags changes the optimal mixture that should be constructed. ■

CONCEPTS

reading computer output of the simplex algorithm
sensitivity analysis

EXERCISES 11.4

1. The linear program for Exercise 6 in Section 9.4 is:

$$\max T = x_1 + x_2 + x_3$$
$$20x_1 + 15x_2 + 10x_3 \le 4800$$
$$5x_1 + 5x_2 + 8x_3 \le 1500$$
$$10x_1 + 5x_2 + 5x_3 \le 2500$$
$$x_1 \ge 0, x_2 \ge 0, x_3 \ge 0$$

where x_1 denotes the number of freshmen, x_2 denotes the number of under-graduates, and x_3 denotes the number of graduate students. Using the computer output below, answer each of the following questions:

(a) What is the maximum number of students that can be processed? How many of each type can be processed?

(b) What are the values of the dual variables? Give an interpretation of the dual variables.

(c) If b_1 represents the constant for the first constraint, how high can b_1 be before the corner point that determines the maximum changes? How low can it drop? Answer the same question for b_2 representing the constant of the second constraint and b_3 representing the constant of the third constraint.

<u>INITIAL TABLEAU FOR PROBLEM Ex. 1.</u>
FOR PHASE 2

CONSTRAINT: C1   /BASIC VARIABLE: SLACK

2.000E+01   1.500E+01   1.000E+01   1.000E+00   0.000E+00   0.000E+00
                                                      4.800E+03

CONSTRAINT: C2   /BASIC VARIABLE: SLACK

5.000E+00   5.000E+00   8.000E+00   0.000E+00   1.000E+00   0.000E+00
                                                      1.500E+03

CONSTRAINT: C3   /BASIC VARIABLE: SLACK

1.000E+01   5.000E+00   5.000E+00   0.000E+00   0.000E+00   1.000E+00
                                                      2.500E+03

```
COST ROW:

-1.000E+00   -1.000E+00   -1.000E+00   0.000E+00   0.000E+00   0.000E+00
                                                                0.000E+00
```

NOTE: THE UNDERLINED NUMBER IN EACH ROW REPRESENTS THE VALUE
      OF THE CORRESPONDING BASIC VARIABLE, EXCEPT IN THE COST
      ROW WHERE IT GIVES THE VALUE OF THE OBJECTIVE FUNCTION.

VARIABLE DEFINITIONS

VARIABLE NUMBER	VARIABLE NAME	BASIC OR NONBASIC	LOWER OR UPPER BOUND
1	X1	NONBASIC	LOWER
2	X2	NONBASIC	LOWER
3	X3	NONBASIC	LOWER
4	SLACK FOR CONSTRAINT C1	BASIC	
5	SLACK FOR CONSTRAINT C2	BASIC	
6	SLACK FOR CONSTRAINT C3	BASIC	

SOLUTION ANALYSIS FOR PROBLEM Ex. 1.

THE SOLUTION IS BOTH FEASIBLE AND OPTIMAL.
THE MAXIMUM VALUE OF THE OBJECTIVE FUNCTION =   3.00000E+02

DECISION VARIABLES:

VARIABLE NAME	VARIABLE VALUE	BASIC OR NONBASIC	LOWER OR UPPER BOUND
X3	0.00000E+00	NONBASIC	LOWER
X1	6.00000E+01	BASIC	
X2	2.40000E+02	BASIC	

SLACK AND SURPLUS VARIABLES:

VARIABLE NAME	VARIABLE VALUE	BASIC OR NONBASIC	LOWER OR UPPER BOUND
SLACK FOR CONSTRAINT C1	0.00000E+00	NONBASIC	LOWER
SLACK FOR CONSTRAINT C2	0.00000E+00	NONBASIC	LOWER
SLACK FOR CONSTRAINT C3	7.00000E+02	BASIC	

FINAL TABLEAU FOR PROBLEM Ex. 1.

CONSTRAINT: C1 /BASIC VARIABLE: X1

```
1.000E+00   0.000E+00  -2.800E+00   2.000E-01  -6.000E-01   0.000E+00
                                                            6.000E+01
```

CONSTRAINT: C2 /BASIC VARIABLE: X2

```
0.000E+00   1.000E+00   4.400E+00  -2.000E-01   8.000E-01   0.000E+00
                                                            2.400E+02
```

CONSTRAINT: C3 /BASIC VARIABLE: SLACK

```
0.000E+00   0.000E+00   1.100E+01  -1.000E+00   2.000E+00   1.000E+00
                                                            7.000E+02
```

COST ROW:

```
0.000E+00   0.000E+00   6.000E-01   0.000E+00   2.000E-01   0.000E+00
                                                            3.000E+02
```

NOTE: THE UNDERLINED NUMBER IN EACH ROW REPRESENTS THE VALUE
      OF THE CORRESPONDING BASIC VARIABLE, EXCEPT IN THE COST
      ROW WHERE IT GIVES THE VALUE OF THE OBJECTIVE FUNCTION.

VARIABLE DEFINITIONS

VARIABLE NUMBER	VARIABLE NAME	BASIC OR NONBASIC	LOWER OR UPPER BOUND
1	X1	BASIC	
2	X2	BASIC	
3	X3	NONBASIC	LOWER
4	SLACK FOR CONSTRAINT C1	NONBASIC	LOWER
5	SLACK FOR CONSTRAINT C2	NONBASIC	LOWER
6	SLACK FOR CONSTRAINT C3	BASIC	

SENSITIVITY ANALYSIS FOR PROGRAM Ex. 1.

OBJECTIVE FUNCTION COEFFICIENT
RANGE FOR NONBASIC VARIABLES:

VARIABLE NAME	LOWER LIMIT	COEFFICIENT VALUE	UPPER LIMIT
X3	-INFINITY	1.0000E+00	1.6000E+00

OBJECTIVE FUNCTION COEFFICIENT
RANGE FOR BASIC VARIABLES:

VARIABLE NAME	LOWER LIMIT	COEFFICIENT VALUE	UPPER LIMIT
X1	-INFINITY	1.0000E+00	1.0000E+00
X2	8.6364E-01	1.0000E+00	1.0000E+00

RIGHT-HAND-SIDE RANGE:

CONSTRAINT NAME	LOWER LIMIT	RHS B(I)	UPPER LIMIT
C1	4.5000E+03	4.8000E+03	5.5000E+03
C2	1.2000E+03	1.5000E+03	1.6000E+03
C3	1.8000E+03	2.5000E+03	+INFINITY

2. The linear program for Exercise 8 in Section 9.4 is:

$$\min C = 10x_1 + 12x_2 + 15x_3 + 8x_4$$

$$x_1 + x_2 \le 200$$

$$x_3 + x_4 \le 200$$

$$x_1 + x_3 \ge 150$$

$$x_2 + x_4 \ge 180$$

$$x_1 \ge 0,\ x_2 \ge 0,\ x_3 \ge 0,\ x_4 \ge 0$$

where x_1 denotes the amount shipped from warehouse 1 to terminal 1, x_2 denotes the amount shipped from warehouse 1 to terminal 2, x_3 denotes the amount shipped from warehouse 2 to terminal 1, and x_4 denotes the amount shipped from warehouse 2 to terminal 2.

(a) Write the linear program in standard minimum form.

(b) Write the dual of the linear program.

(c) The computer output for this dual maximization linear program is below. What is the solution to the maximization linear program?

(d) What is the minimum value of C?

(e) What is the solution to the original minimization problem?

(f) Give an economic interpretation to the values of the dual variable (maximum program).

(g) What are the values of the surplus variables for the minimization program constraints?

INITIAL TABLEAU FOR PROBLEM Ex. 2.
FOR PHASE 2

CONSTRAINT: C1   /BASIC VARIABLE: SLACK

-1.000E+00	0.000E+00	1.000E+00	0.000E+00	1.000E+00	0.000E+00
0.000E+00	0.000E+00				1.000E+01

```
CONSTRAINT: C2          /BASIC VARIABLE: SLACK

-1.000E+00    0.000E+00    0.000E+00    1.000E+00    0.000E+00    1.000E+00
 0.000E+00    0.000E+00                                           1.200E+01

CONSTRAINT: C3          /BASIC VARIABLE: SLACK

 0.000E+00   -1.000E+00    1.000E+00    0.000E+00    0.000E+00    0.000E+00
 1.000E+00    0.000E+00                                           1.500E+01

CONSTRAINT: C4          /BASIC VARIABLE: SLACK

 0.000E+00   -1.000E+00    0.000E+00    1.000E+00    0.000E+00    0.000E+00
 0.000E+00    1.000E+00                                           8.000E+00

COST ROW:

 2.000E+02    2.000E+02   -1.500E+02   -1.800E+02    0.000E+00    0.000E+00
 0.000E+00    0.000E+00                                           0.000E+00
```

NOTE: THE UNDERLINED NUMBER IN EACH ROW REPRESENTS THE VALUE
      OF THE CORRESPONDING BASIC VARIABLE, EXCEPT IN THE COST
      ROW WHERE IT GIVES THE VALUE OF THE OBJECTIVE FUNCTION.

VARIABLE DEFINITIONS

VARIABLE NUMBER	VARIABLE NAME	BASIC OR NONBASIC	LOWER OR UPPER BOUND
1	Y1	NONBASIC	LOWER
2	Y2	NONBASIC	LOWER
3	Y3	NONBASIC	LOWER
4	Y4	NONBASIC	LOWER
5	SLACK FOR CONSTRAINT C1	BASIC	
6	SLACK FOR CONSTRAINT C2	BASIC	
7	SLACK FOR CONSTRAINT C3	BASIC	
8	SLACK FOR CONSTRAINT C4	BASIC	

SOLUTION ANALYSIS FOR PROBLEM Ex. 2.

THE SOLUTION IS BOTH FEASIBLE AND OPTIMAL.
THE MAXIMUM VALUE OF THE OBJECTIVE FUNCTION = 2.94000E+03

DECISION VARIABLES:

VARIABLE NAME	VARIABLE VALUE	BASIC OR NONBASIC	LOWER OR UPPER BOUND
Y1	0.00000E+00	NONBASIC	LOWER
Y2	0.00000E+00	NONBASIC	LOWER
Y3	1.00000E+01	BASIC	
Y4	8.00000E+00	BASIC	

SLACK AND SURPLUS VARIABLES:

VARIABLE NAME	VARIABLE VALUE	BASIC OR NONBASIC	LOWER OR UPPER BOUND
SLACK FOR CONSTRAINT C1	0.00000E+00	NONBASIC	LOWER
SLACK FOR CONSTRAINT C4	0.00000E+00	NONBASIC	LOWER
SLACK FOR CONSTRAINT C2	4.00000E+00	BASIC	
SLACK FOR CONSTRAINT C3	5.00000E+00	BASIC	

FINAL TABLEAU FOR PROBLEM Ex. 2.

CONSTRAINT: C1   /BASIC VARIABLE: Y3

```
-1.000E+00   0.000E+00   1.000E+00   0.000E+00   1.000E+00   0.000E+00
 0.000E+00   0.000E+00                                       1.000E+01
```

CONSTRAINT: C2   /BASIC VARIABLE: SLACK

```
-1.000E+00   1.000E+00   0.000E+00   0.000E+00   0.000E+00   1.000E+00
 0.000E+00  -1.000E+00                                       4.000E+00
```

CONSTRAINT: C3   /BASIC VARIABLE: SLACK

```
 1.000E+00  -1.000E+00   0.000E+00   0.000E+00  -1.000E+00   0.000E+00
 1.000E+00   0.000E+00                                       5.000E+00
```

CONSTRAINT: C4   /BASIC VARIABLE: Y4

```
 0.000E+00  -1.000E+00   0.000E+00   1.000E+00   0.000E+00   0.000E+00
 0.000E+00   1.000E+00                                       8.000E+00
```

COST ROW:

```
 5.000E+01   2.000E+01   0.000E+00   0.000E+00   1.500E+02   0.000E+00
 0.000E+00   1.800E+02                                       2.940E+03
```

NOTE: THE UNDERLINED NUMBER IN EACH ROW REPRESENTS THE VALUE
      OF THE CORRESPONDING BASIC VARIABLE, EXCEPT IN THE COST
      ROW WHERE IT GIVES THE VALUE OF THE OBJECTIVE FUNCTION.

VARIABLE DEFINITIONS

VARIABLE NUMBER	VARIABLE NAME	BASIC OR NONBASIC	LOWER OR UPPER BOUND
1	Y1	NONBASIC	LOWER
2	Y2	NONBASIC	LOWER
3	Y3	BASIC	
4	Y4	BASIC	
5	SLACK FOR CONSTRAINT C1	NONBASIC	LOWER

```
6            SLACK FOR
             CONSTRAINT
             C2                BASIC
7            SLACK FOR
             CONSTRAINT
             C3                BASIC
8            SLACK FOR
             CONSTRAINT
             C4                NONBASIC        LOWER
```

SENSITIVITY ANALYSIS FOR PROGRAM Ex. 2.

OBJECTIVE FUNCTION COEFFICIENT
RANGE FOR NONBASIC VARIABLES:

VARIABLE NAME	LOWER LIMIT	COEFFICIENT VALUE	UPPER LIMIT
Y1	-INFINITY	-2.0000E+02	-1.5000E+02
Y2	-INFINITY	-2.0000E+02	-1.8000E+02

OBJECTIVE FUNCTION COEFFICIENT
RANGE FOR BASIC VARIABLES:

VARIABLE NAME	LOWER LIMIT	COEFFICIENT VALUE	UPPER LIMIT
Y3	0.0000E+00	1.5000E+02	2.0000E+02
Y4	0.0000E+00	1.8000E+02	2.0000E+02

RIGHT-HAND-SIDE RANGE:

CONSTRAINT NAME	LOWER LIMIT	RHS B(I)	UPPER LIMIT
C1	0.0000E+00	1.0000E+01	1.5000E+01
C2	8.0000E+00	1.2000E+01	+INFINITY
C3	1.0000E+01	1.5000E+01	+INFINITY
C4	0.0000E+00	8.0000E+00	1.2000E+01

NOTE: PLEASE CONSULT THE MANUAL FOR A PROPER
      INTERPRETATION OF THE SENSITIVITY ANALYSIS.

3. Try Exercises 1 and 2 on a computer at your school.

CHAPTER SUMMARY

SETTING UP A LINEAR PROGRAM FOR THE SIMPLEX ALGORITHM

1. Write the linear program in *standard maximum form*:

$$\max P = c_1 x_1 + c_2 x_2 + \cdots + c_n x_n$$

$$\text{constraints: } a_1 x_1 + a_2 x_2 + \cdots + a_n x_n \leq b$$

$$x_1 \geq 0, \; x_2 \geq 0, \ldots, x_n \geq 0$$

2. Introduce a *slack variable* for each constraint to create an equation:

$$a_1 x_1 + a_2 x_2 + \cdots + a_n x_n + s = b$$

3. If $b \leq 0$ then multiply the equation by -1.
4. Write the objective function with all variables to the left of the equal sign:

$$-c_1 x_1 - c_2 x_2 - \cdots - c_n x_n + P = 0$$

5. Write the augmented matrix for the system of equations formed from 2–4 above. Call it the *first tableau*. Use headings for the columns to keep track of the variables.

Starting with a tableau corresponding to a *basic feasible solution*:

1. *Pivot column*   Choose the column with the most negative entry in the bottom row, excluding the constant column. If no negative entry exists, you are done.
2. *Pivot row*   Compute the ratios of the constant column to the pivot column, excluding the bottom row. Choose the row corresponding to the smallest nonnegative ratio. If no nonnegative ratios exist, then there is no maximum.
3. *Pivot entry*   The entry in the pivot row and pivot column.
4. The *maximum* is reached when there are no negative entries in the bottom row, except possibly the constant column entry. The solution to the system of equations can be found by reading off the values of the basic variables from the last column, and taking the nonbasic variables to be 0. The solution to the linear program is the values of the x variables in this solution.

Duality can be illustrated by the following *dual linear programs*:

SMF	SmF

$$\max P = c_1 x_1 + c_2 x_2 + \cdots + c_k x_k$$

$$a_{11} x_1 + \cdots + a_{1k} x_k \le b_1$$

$$\cdot$$
$$\cdot$$
$$\cdot$$

$$a_{l1} x_1 + \cdots + a x_{lk} \le b_l$$

$$x_i \ge 0, \qquad i = 1, 2, \ldots, k$$

$$\min C = b_1 u_1 + \cdots + b_l u_l$$

$$a_{11} u_1 + \cdots + a_{l1} u_l \ge c_1$$

$$\cdot$$
$$\cdot$$
$$\cdot$$

$$a_{1k} u_1 + \cdots + a_{lk} u_l \ge c_k$$

$$u_j \ge 0, \qquad j = 1, 2, \ldots, l$$

PROPERTIES

1. *Von Neumann duality principle*: If one pair of dual linear programs has a solution then they both do and the values of the optimums are the same.
2. If one of a pair of dual linear programs has an unbounded feasible region then the other has the empty set as a feasible set.
3. The bottom row of the final tableau of the simplex method for the maximization program gives the solution to the dual minimization linear program. The value of the objective function is in the last row—last column entry, and the value of the ith dual variable is at the bottom of the ith slack variable column.

When a computer is available the solutions to both the linear program and its dual are given as output. A *sensitivity analysis* is given that aids in determining how much the coefficients of the objective function and the right-hand constants of the constraints can change without changing the solution.

REVIEW EXERCISES FOR CHAPTER 11

The linear program for Exercises 1 through 4 is:

$$\max P = 2x_1 + 3x_2 + x_3$$

$$x_1 + x_2 + x_3 \le 10$$

$$2x_1 + x_2 + x_3 \le 12$$

$$5x_1 + 2x_2 + 2x_3 \le 30$$

$$x_i \ge 0$$

1. Introduce slack variables and write the objective function in proper form to apply the simplex algorithm.

2. Write the first tableau. What variables are in the basis?

3. Choose a pivot element and indicate which variable goes out of the basis and which variable goes into the basis.

4. Find the second tableau.

5. Write the following program in standard maximum form:

$$\max T = 3x_1 + x_2$$
$$x_1 \geq 5$$
$$x_2 \leq 10$$
$$x_1 - x_2 \geq 8$$
$$x_2 \geq 0$$

6. Introduce slack variables for the system of constraints in Exercise 5.

Refer to the following tableau for Exercises 7 through 9:

$$
\begin{array}{ccccccc}
x_1 & x_2 & x_3 & s_1 & s_2 & s_3 & P \\
\left(\begin{array}{cccccc|c}
1 & -1 & 0 & 1 & 0 & -2 & 4 \\
0 & 2 & 0 & -1 & 1 & 1 & 6 \\
0 & 1 & 1 & 1 & 0 & 1 & 5 \\
0 & -3 & 0 & -1 & 0 & 2 & 20
\end{array}\right)
\end{array}
$$

7. What is the current solution? Is it optimal? Why?

8. Find the next tableau.

9. What is the solution now? Is it optimal? Why?

10–12. Answer Exercises 7 through 9 for the following tableau:

$$
\begin{array}{ccccccc}
x_1 & x_2 & x_3 & s_1 & s_2 & s_3 & P \\
\left(\begin{array}{cccccc|c}
2 & 0 & 2 & 1 & 0 & -1 & 27 \\
-1 & 0 & 2 & 0 & 1 & 0 & 0 \\
-1 & 1 & 1 & 0 & 0 & 1 & 0 \\
-100 & 0 & -110 & 0 & 0 & 60 & 0
\end{array}\right)
\end{array}
$$

13. Use the simplex algorithm to find the solution to the following linear program:

$$\max P = x_1 + 2x_2 + x_3$$
$$x_1 - x_2 + x_3 \leq 5$$
$$x_1 + x_3 \leq 8$$
$$2x_2 + x_3 \leq 10$$
$$x_i \geq 0$$

14–17. Use the simplex algorithm to find the solution to the linear programs in Chapter 9's Review Exercises.

18. Write the dual linear program for the linear program in Exercise 13.

19. Find the solution to the dual linear program of Exercise 18.

20. Use the simplex algorithm to find a solution to the following linear program or indicate why no solution exists:

$$\max P = 3x_1 + x_2 + 5x_3$$
$$x_1 \geq 7$$
$$x_1 + x_2 + x_3 \leq 15$$
$$x_2 + x_3 \leq 10$$
$$x_3 \geq 7$$
$$x_2 \geq 0$$

21. Write the dual linear program of the problem in Exercise 20. What can you say about the solution of the dual?

22. Use the simplex algorithm to find a solution to the following linear program, if one exists. If not, tell why one does not exist.

$$\max P = 3x_1 + 4x_2$$
$$x_1 + x_2 \geq 3$$
$$x_1 \leq 5$$
$$x_i \geq 0$$

23. In a computer implementation of the simplex algorithm, the following information was provided. Interpret the results and give the maximum value of the objective function.

$$x_3 = 0 \quad \text{nonbasic}$$
$$x_4 = 0 \quad \text{nonbasic}$$
$$x_1 = 2.3789E + 01 \quad \text{basic}$$
$$x_2 = 1.7645E + 01 \quad \text{basic}$$

Range of objective function coefficients:

Lower limit	Value	Upper limit
.5000E + 00	1	1.9200E + 10
1.4810E + 00	3	.3417E + 20

Right-hand side range:

Constraint	Lower limit	b	Upper limit
C1	3.0472E + 00	15	∞
C2	− ∞	20	3.7641E + 02

Game Theory

12

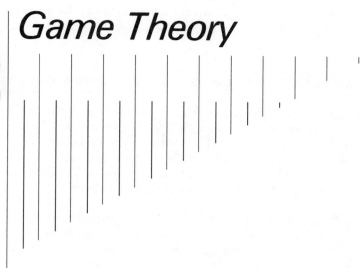

The origins of game theory go back to 1928 when John Von Neumann presented his theory to the Mathematical Society of Gottingen. As is the case with linear programming, it was during World War II that the theory was first put to practical use.

Game theory is concerned with the analysis of human behavior in conflict situations. The conflict can be between two or more individuals, or between an individual and forces of nature. If enough information is known, a mathematical analysis of a game can determine what is the best strategy (way to play) for each player. The analysis of games and alternate strategies can indicate to a player how he or she should act to accomplish particular goals. In games each player has different strategies available.

In this chapter, we present the essence of game theory and indicate the wide range of its applications. This chapter is appropriately at the end of the book, as game theory makes use of almost all of the mathematical techniques previously developed. In Sections 12.1 and 12.2 matrices are used to indicate essential information about a game, and matrix multiplication is used to calculate consequences of various strategies. As we will see in Sections 12.2 and 12.3, many games are played where the strategy is defined by probabilities. Graphing linear equations and linear programming techniques are used to find optimal strategies for such games. In the first three sections we consider exclusively two-person games, but in the last section we look at games involving more than two players. There we also return to some of the material discussed in Chapter 1 on voting choices and put this material in the context of a game.

It is hoped that by the end of this chapter the student will have a basic background in the theory of games, be able to recognize a situation or problem as a possible game, and be able to use the problem-solving skills developed here to find a solution or strategy for a solution to real-world problems.

12.1   *Introduction to Game Theory—Strictly Determined Games*

Competitive situations arise in business, economic, and political activities as well as in parlor or Las Vegas-type games. The players are groups, individuals, or nonspecific entities such as nature or the weather. In this section we will consider the simplest games and use matrices to help us determine the best strategies for each player. The first example is the game that started Von Neumann's analysis of games.

EXAMPLE 1   John and Mary play the game of matching pennies. Each child throws out a penny head up or tail up. If the pennies match, either both heads or both tails, John gains a penny. If they do not match Mary gains a penny. Neither player knows what the other player will do.   ■

EXAMPLE 2   ATT in the mid-eighties has to decide if it should enter the personal computer market, challenging other companies, IBM, in particular. The company has to decide if it will use its capital to launch a personal computer program or to upgrade its business computers. ATT's decision is based in part on what IBM will do with its capital. IBM has three choices: invest all in its business division; invest all in its personal computer division; or split its investment evenly between its personal computer division and its business division. Analysts for ATT and IBM determine that the profit in millions of dollars to ATT from these decisions is as given in the following table:

		IBM		
		Business	*Personal comp.*	*Half-half*
ATT	Business	6	8	5
	Personal comp.	10	2	4

The (1, 2)-entry 8 means that if ATT invests its money in its business computer division and IBM invest its money in its personal computer division, ATT will gain a profit of $8 million.   ■

EXAMPLE 3   A farmer has 180 acres of land and wants to plant corn or wheat. Corn requires a wetter climate than wheat. Unfortunately, it cannot be predicted in advance what the weather will be for a growing season. The farmer's income is determined by the combination of weather and crops as follows:

		Weather	
		Wet	Dry
Crop	Corn	10000	−2000
	Wheat	2000	8000

EXAMPLE 4   Delta and United both plan to add another city to their list of cities with nonstop flights from Boston. Minneapolis, Philadelphia, and St. Louis seem to be the best choice for each airline. If both airlines add Minneapolis to their list, then Delta will show a gain of $75,000 over United. If both add Philadelphia, Delta will show a gain of $50,000 over United. However, if both choose St. Louis, United will show a gain of $100,000 over Delta. If Delta chooses Philadelphia and United chooses either of the other two, Delta will show a profit of $200,000 over United. If Delta chooses Minneapolis and United chooses St. Louis or vice versa, then they are even. Finally, if United chooses Philadelphia, and Delta chooses Minneapolis, then Delta has a gain of $25,000 over United, but if Delta chooses St. Louis, United has a gain of $50,000 over Delta.

A **two-person game** is any competition or conflict between two opponents, called **players**. A **two-person zero-sum game** is any two-person game where the amount won (or gained) by one player is lost by the other player.

In two-person zero-sum games we will use a matrix, called a **payoff matrix**, to denote the gains and losses to player 1, called the **row player**. Gains will appear as positive entries in the matrix and losses will appear as negative entries in the matrix.

In Example 1 with matching pennies, if we call John player 1, we have the following payoff matrix, P:

$$P = \quad \text{John} \quad \begin{array}{c} \\ H \\ T \end{array} \begin{pmatrix} 1 & -1 \\ -1 & 1 \end{pmatrix}$$

Mary

H   T

The rows of a payoff matrix correspond to the choices for player 1, and the columns correspond to the choices for player 2. The (i, j)-entry is the gain to player 1 if player 1 chooses row i to play and player 2 chooses column j to play. Thus, a negative entry is a loss for the row player and a gain for the column player.

The table given in Example 2 can be converted to a payoff matrix for

Example 2 with ATT the row player and IBM the column player:

IBM

$$
\begin{array}{c}
& \text{Business} \quad\quad \text{Personal comp.} \quad\quad \text{half-half} \\
\text{ATT} \quad
\begin{array}{l}
\text{Business} \\
\text{Personal comp.}
\end{array}
\left(
\begin{array}{ccc}
6 & 8 & 5 \\
10 & 2 & 4
\end{array}
\right)
\end{array}
$$

The (2, 3)-entry 4 indicates a payoff or gain to ATT of $4 million if ATT invests its money in personal computer development and IBM splits its investment half and half. It is assumed that IBM loses $4 million if ATT gains $4 million.

Example 3 provides an example of a two-person game between an individual and nature. If the farmer is designated as player 1, the row player, and nature is player 2, the column player, then the payoff matrix is:

$$
P =
\begin{array}{c}
& \text{Wet} \quad\quad \text{Dry} \\
\begin{array}{l}
\text{Corn} \\
\text{Wheat}
\end{array}
\left(
\begin{array}{cc}
10000 & -2000 \\
2000 & 8000
\end{array}
\right)
\end{array}
$$

It is assumed that the farmer has only two choices, corn or wheat, and that the climate is either wet or dry.

In the last example, Example 4, each of the airlines has three choices. Designating Delta as player 1, and United as player 2 gives the following payoff matrix:

United

$$
\text{Delta}
\begin{array}{l}
\text{Philadelphia} \\
\text{Minneapolis} \\
\text{St. Louis}
\end{array}
\begin{array}{c}
\text{Philadelphia} \quad\quad \text{Minneapolis} \quad\quad \text{St. Louis} \\
\left(
\begin{array}{ccc}
50{,}000 & 200{,}000 & 200{,}000 \\
25{,}000 & 75{,}000 & 0 \\
-50{,}000 & 0 & -100{,}000
\end{array}
\right)
\end{array}
$$

PRACTICE EXAMPLE 1

Suppose $10 is set aside from previous games to be used in the penny-pitching game. If both toss a head then John wins $10, if both toss a tail no one wins any money, and if one tosses a head and the other a tail John wins $5. Write the payoff matrix for this game.

In each of these four games, player 1 must make a decision in the absence of any knowledge of player 2's choice. Player 1 would like to maximize its gain and player 2 would like to minimize its losses (or player 1's gain). In Example 2, ATT can get the greatest gain by investing in personal computer development, but only if IBM puts all of its investment in its business computer. ATT cannot be sure that IBM will do just that, however. If ATT puts its investment in business computers, it will always gain at least $5 million, no matter what IBM chooses to do, whereas if ATT invests in personal computer development it may gain only $2 million. ATT, to minimize the risk or maximize its guaranteed gain, should choose the largest of these guaranteed minimum payments, namely invest in its business computers. Similarly, IBM wants to minimize its risk, to minimize its losses. By investing in business computers it can lose at most $10 million; by investing in personal computers it can lose at most $8 million; and by splitting the investment, it can lose at most $5 million. Clearly, IBM wants to split its investment to minimize its losses.

In this example the best strategy (in terms of risk) for player 1, ATT, is row 1, and the best strategy for player 2, IBM, is column 3. The result, if both players employ their best strategy, is that ATT gains $5 million.

In a game with payoff matrix P, the row player can choose any of the rows of P and the column player can choose any of the columns of P. A player who makes the same choice each time the game is played is using a **pure strategy**. In terms of risk, the **best pure strategy** is the pure strategy that *guarantees* the greatest gain to the player, not knowing the other player's choice. The concept of best method to play is not based on the actual winnings *but rather on* the notion that a player does the best he can under the circumstances.

BEST PURE STRATEGY FOR THE ROW PLAYER

1. Determine the least element in each row of the payoff matrix.
2. Choose the row for which this least element is the largest.

In the ATT example we circle the least element in each row of P.

$$\begin{pmatrix} 6 & 8 & ⑤ \\ 10 & ② & 4 \end{pmatrix}$$

The largest of the circled elements is 5. ATT should choose row 1.

BEST PURE STRATEGY FOR THE COLUMN PLAYER

1. Determine the largest element in each column of the payoff matrix.
2. Choose the column for which this largest element is the smallest.

In the ATT example, we box the largest element in each column of P.

$$\begin{pmatrix} 6 & \boxed{8} & \boxed{5} \\ \boxed{10} & 2 & 4 \end{pmatrix}$$

The smallest of the boxed entries is 5. IBM should choose column 3.

Note that the entry 5 in the above example is simultaneously the least element in its row and largest element in its column. The row corresponding to this entry is the best pure strategy of the row player and the column corresponding to this entry is the best pure strategy for the column player.

> DEFINITION An entry of the payoff matrix that is simultaneously the least element in its row and the largest element in its column is called a **saddle point** for the game. A game that has a saddle point is called a **strictly determined game**, and the saddle point is called the **value** of the game. The value of the game is the largest payoff the row player can be guaranteed.

To find the best pure strategy for the farmer in Example 3, we circle the least element in each row and choose the largest of these elements.

$$
\begin{array}{c c}
 & \begin{array}{c c} \text{Wet} & \text{Dry} \end{array} \\
\begin{array}{c} \text{Corn} \\ \text{Wheat} \end{array} & \left(\begin{array}{c c} 10000 & \boxed{-2000} \\ \boxed{2000} & 8000 \end{array} \right)
\end{array}
$$

Since 2000 is the largest of the two circled elements, the farmer should choose row 2 and plant wheat.

However, this is not a strictly determined game. The element 2000 is not the largest in its column. There is no saddle point.

In Example 4, find a saddle point, if one exists.

$$
\begin{array}{c c c c}
 & P & M & S \\
P & \boxed{50,000} & \boxed{200,000} & \boxed{200,000} \\
M & 25,000 & 75,000 & ⓪ \\
S & -50,000 & 0 & \boxed{-100,000}
\end{array}
$$

The least element of each row is circled, and the largest element in each column is boxed. The largest of the circled elements is 50,000, and the smallest of the boxed elements is 50,000. Each airline should choose Philadelphia. The saddle point is 50,000, and the game is strictly determined. The value of the game is 50,000.

The matching pennies game of Example 1 is not strictly determined. As indicated in the payoff matrix, the largest of the circled elements is −1, and the smallest of the boxed elements is 1. In the next section we determine mixed strategies for games that are not strictly determined.

$$
\begin{array}{c c c}
 & H & T \\
H & \boxed{1} & \boxed{-1} \\
T & \boxed{-1} & \boxed{1}
\end{array}
$$

**PRACTICE
EXAMPLE 2**

Determine the best pure strategy for each player in the game for Practice Example 1. Is it strictly determined? If so, what is the value of the game?

■

In games that are not strictly determined, players may want to vary their strategy from play to play. In this case, each player is trying to determine the best mixed strategy, rather than the best pure strategy. In the next section we describe methods for determining mixed strategies.

CONCEPTS

two-person game
two-person zero-sum game
row player
best pure strategy for the row player
best pure strategy for the column player
saddle point

value
players
payoff matrix
pure strategy
strictly determined game

SOLUTIONS TO PRACTICE EXAMPLES

1.

$$
\begin{array}{c}
 \\
\text{John} \quad
\begin{array}{c}
H \\
T
\end{array}
\begin{array}{cc}
H & T
\end{array} \\
\end{array}
$$

$$
\text{John} \quad
\begin{array}{c}
H \\
T
\end{array}
\begin{pmatrix}
10 & 5 \\
5 & 0
\end{pmatrix}
$$

2.

$$
\text{Mary}
$$

$$
\text{John} \quad
\begin{array}{c}
H \\
T
\end{array}
\begin{pmatrix}
\boxed{10} & \boxed{5} \\
 & \boxed{0}
\end{pmatrix}
$$

John plays a head, Mary plays a tail. It is a strictly determined game with the value of 5.

EXERCISES 12.1

Each of the following matrices is the payoff matrix for a game. Determine the best pure strategies for the row player and for the column player. Find the value of the game if it is strictly determined.

1.
$$
\begin{pmatrix}
3 & -1 \\
1 & -2
\end{pmatrix}
$$

2.
$$
\begin{pmatrix}
10 & 20 \\
5 & 15
\end{pmatrix}
$$

3. $\begin{pmatrix} 0 & 4 & 2 \\ -4 & 0 & 3 \\ -2 & -3 & 0 \end{pmatrix}$

4. $\begin{pmatrix} 5 & -1 & 6 \\ -2 & 5 & -8 \\ 8 & -10 & 5 \end{pmatrix}$

5. $\begin{pmatrix} 1 & 2 & 3 \\ 4 & -1 & 1 \end{pmatrix}$

6. $\begin{pmatrix} 0 & -10 & 1 \\ -5 & 15 & 2 \\ 8 & 7 & 5 \end{pmatrix}$

7. $\begin{pmatrix} -3 & 6 \\ 6 & -4 \\ 2 & -8 \end{pmatrix}$

8. $\begin{pmatrix} 5 & 1 & 3 \\ 7 & -2 & -5 \end{pmatrix}$

9. Two children, Carol and Rose, play the game of shooting fingers. Each child presents from 0 to 5 fingers. If the sum of the fingers on the two hands is even Rose wins one dollar; if it is odd, then Carol wins one dollar. Write the payoff matrix for this game, determine optimal pure strategies, and the value of the game if it is strictly determined.

10. The game is the same as in Exercise 9, except that the payoff is the total number of fingers in dollars to Rose if the sum is even, and to Carol if the sum is odd.

11. Each of two presidential candidates must decide on the best time to broadcast an hour-long television spot. Each choose from 1, 2, or 3 days before the election. If they broadcast on the same day there is no gain to either candidate. If they do not broadcast on the same day, the one who broadcasts closest to the election has the advantage. If there is one day separating, the one who broadcasts closest to the election gains 30% of the uncommitted votes. If there are two days separating them, the one who broadcasts closest gains 50% of the uncommitted votes. Write the payoff matrix for the game. Determine when each should broadcast, and if the game is strictly determined, the value of the game.

12. A college professor just inherited $10,000. The professor wants to invest the money in either the stock market or a money-market account. If the economy is anti-inflationary, then the stock market will provide the professor with a gain of 16%, and the money market account will provide the professor with a gain of 9%. If the economy is inflationary then the stock market provides for a gain of 6% and the money-market account provides a gain of 12%. If the professor has to invest the money all in one place, where should it be invested? Is the game strictly determined?

13. For what values of a and b is the game with payoff matrix P strictly determined?

$$\begin{pmatrix} a & 0 \\ 0 & b \end{pmatrix}$$

14. During reconstruction of Boston's Southeast Expressway, a commuter must decide on a route into the city, either the expressway, bus, or subway. The decision must be made for each day the night before. The time saved by each method is determined by whether the day is nice or rainy. The average trip takes 45 minutes. The time saved on a nice day is 10 by expressway, 5 by bus, and 0 by subway. The time saved on a rainy day is -25 by expressway, -15 by bus, and 0 by subway. Write the payoff matrix for the game and determine the commuter's best pure strategy.

15. $$\begin{pmatrix} a & -b \\ -a & b \end{pmatrix}$$

If $a > 0$ and $b < 0$, then what has to be true for a to be the value of the game?

12.2   *Mixed Strategies*

Most of the time a game is not played just once, but is repeated many times. If the game is not strictly determined, player 2 wants to figure out player 1's pure strategy, and as we will see, may want to switch strategy from play to play. Often, one may not have to invest all one's money in one place, or plant all available acreage in one crop, etc. A mixed strategy corresponds, in these cases, to a division of the total into fractional parts. In this section we show how to use matrix multiplication to determine the expected value of a game with mixed strategies for each player. We also look at one technique for finding the best or optimal mixed strategy for each player.

EXAMPLE 1   Suppose two players each write one of the numbers 2, 3, or 5 on a sheet of paper. The papers are placed in the center of the table. The payoffs to player 1 are given in the following payoff matrix:

$$P = \begin{array}{c} \\ 2 \\ 3 \\ 5 \end{array} \begin{array}{ccc} 2 & 3 & 5 \\ \begin{pmatrix} 6 & -5 & 3 \\ -5 & 4 & 2 \\ -3 & -2 & 8 \end{pmatrix} \end{array}$$

The minimums for each row are -5, -5, and -3, the largest of which is -3. Player 1's pure strategy would be to always write a 5. Likewise, the maximum for the columns are 4, 6, and 8, the smallest of which is 4. Therefore, player 2's pure strategy would be to write the number 3 each time. Player 2 would gain two dollars from this combination of plays. Once player 2 realizes that player 1 is always writing the number 5, player 2 would switch to writing a 2, to increase the gain to three dollars. Once player 2 switched, player 1 would also switch to writing a 2 to get a gain of six dollars. This game is not strictly determined, therefore the players should mix their strategies from play to play, but by some randomly chosen method.

Let us look back at Example 1 in Section 12.1, the pitching pennies example. The payoff matrix is:

$$\begin{array}{cc} & \begin{array}{cc} \text{H} & \text{T} \end{array} \\ \begin{array}{c} \text{H} \\ \text{T} \end{array} & \left(\begin{array}{cc} 1 & -1 \\ -1 & 1 \end{array} \right) \end{array}$$

This game is not strictly determined. Suppose John plays heads half of the time and tails half of the time, mixing it so no one can guess which he will play next. If Mary plays heads then the expected payoff to John is $\frac{1}{2}(1) + \frac{1}{2}(-1) = 0$. If Mary plays tails the expected payoff to John is also $\frac{1}{2}(-1) + \frac{1}{2}(1)$. Even if Mary also plays heads half the time and tails half the time the expected payoff to John is $0 = \frac{1}{2}(0) + \frac{1}{2}(0)$. The **expected value** of the game is said to be 0. The row matrix $(\frac{1}{2} \quad \frac{1}{2})$ corresponding to the row player choosing row 1 half of the time and row 2 half of the time is the mixed strategy of the row player.

In general, if a payoff matrix has n rows and m columns then the row matrix $(r_1, r_2, \ldots, r_n)$ denotes the row player's mixed strategy and says that the row player chooses row i with probability r_i. Similarly, the column matrix:

$$\begin{pmatrix} c_1 \\ c_2 \\ \cdot \\ \cdot \\ \cdot \\ c_m \end{pmatrix}$$

denotes the column player's mixed strategy and says that the column player chooses column j with probability c_j. Note that $r_1 + r_2 + r_3 + \cdots + r_n = 1$ and $c_1 + c_2 + c_3 + \cdots + c_m = 1$.

Returning to the payoff matrix of Example 1, suppose player 1's strategy is $(\frac{1}{4} \quad \frac{1}{4} \quad \frac{1}{2})$.

$$P = \begin{array}{c} 2 \\ 3 \\ 5 \end{array} \begin{array}{c} \begin{array}{ccc} 2 & 3 & 5 \end{array} \\ \left(\begin{array}{ccc} 6 & -5 & 3 \\ -5 & 4 & 2 \\ -3 & -2 & 8 \end{array} \right) \end{array}$$

The expected payoff for player 1 depends on player 2's choice with a mixed strategy for each as follows:

If player 2 chooses 2, 1's expected payoff is:

$$\frac{1}{4}(6) + \frac{1}{4}(-5) + \frac{1}{2}(-3) = -\frac{5}{4}$$

If player 2 chooses 3, 1's expected payoff is:

$$\frac{1}{4}(-5) + \frac{1}{4}(4) + \frac{1}{2}(-2) = -\frac{5}{4}$$

If player 2 chooses 5, 1's expected payoff is:

$$\frac{1}{4}(3) + \frac{1}{4}(2) + \frac{1}{2}(8) = \frac{21}{4}$$

Now if player 2 chooses columns with strategy:

$$\begin{pmatrix} \frac{1}{4} \\ \frac{1}{2} \\ \frac{1}{4} \end{pmatrix}$$

then the expected payoff, or expected value of the game, is $E = \frac{1}{4}(-\frac{5}{4}) + \frac{1}{2}(-\frac{5}{4}) + \frac{1}{4}(\frac{21}{4}) = \frac{3}{8}$. Recall from Chapter 5 that we can compute these expected values as we did since player 2's choice of column is independent of player 1's choice of row. An easier way to have carried out the calculations above is to use matrix multiplication:

$$\begin{pmatrix} \frac{1}{4} & \frac{1}{4} & \frac{1}{2} \end{pmatrix} \begin{pmatrix} 6 & -5 & 3 \\ -5 & 4 & 2 \\ -3 & -2 & 8 \end{pmatrix} \begin{pmatrix} \frac{1}{4} \\ \frac{1}{2} \\ \frac{1}{4} \end{pmatrix} = \begin{pmatrix} -\frac{5}{4} & -\frac{5}{4} & \frac{21}{4} \end{pmatrix} \begin{pmatrix} \frac{1}{4} \\ \frac{1}{2} \\ \frac{1}{4} \end{pmatrix} = \frac{3}{8}$$

Given a payoff matrix P for a two-person, zero-sum game, a row matrix A listing the row player's strategy, and a column matrix B listing the column player's strategy, then the product $E = APB$ is the **expected value** of the game when strategies A and B are used. When it is important to denote the strategies A and B, E will be written as $E(P, A, B)$. It is assumed that the players choose the times to play each choice in some random way such as toss of a coin or roll of dice.

If the game is strictly determined and the players use a pure strategy determined by the saddle point, then the expected value is the value of the game as defined in Section 12.1. In this case the matrix A has a 1 in the entry corresponding to the row player's choice and 0's elsewhere, and the matrix B has a 1 in the entry corresponding to the column player's choice and 0's elsewhere. For example, in the ATT example:

$$P = \begin{pmatrix} 6 & 8 & 5 \\ 10 & 2 & 4 \end{pmatrix}, \qquad A = (1 \quad 0) \qquad \text{and} \qquad B = \begin{pmatrix} 0 \\ 0 \\ 1 \end{pmatrix}$$

$$E = APB = (1 \quad 0) \begin{pmatrix} 6 & 8 & 5 \\ 10 & 2 & 4 \end{pmatrix} \begin{pmatrix} 0 \\ 0 \\ 1 \end{pmatrix} = (6 \quad 8 \quad 5) \begin{pmatrix} 0 \\ 0 \\ 1 \end{pmatrix} = 5$$

PRACTICE EXAMPLE 1

If the row player uses the strategy of playing row 1 half the time and row 2 half of the time, and the column player plays column 1 one-quarter of the time and column 2 three-quarters of the time, what is the expected value for the game with the following payoff matrix?

$$P = \begin{pmatrix} 2 & 5 \\ 4 & 3 \end{pmatrix}$$

■

Suppose the farmer in Example 3 of Section 12.1 wants to determine an optimal mixed acreage allotment for wheat and corn. This is equivalent to finding the best mixed strategy for the farmer in the game. The probabilities of a wet and dry season, $\frac{3}{8}$ and $\frac{5}{8}$, respectively, can be determined from the *Farmer's Almanac*. These probabilities can be considered as the strategy of player 2, nature. If we let r_1 denote the proportion of land used for corn and r_2 the proportion of land used for wheat, we have $E = APB$, or:

$$E = (r_1 \quad r_2) \begin{pmatrix} 10000 & -2000 \\ 2000 & 8000 \end{pmatrix} \begin{pmatrix} \dfrac{3}{8} \\ \dfrac{5}{8} \end{pmatrix} = (r_1 \quad r_2) \begin{pmatrix} 2500 \\ 5750 \end{pmatrix}$$

$$E = 2500r_1 + 5750r_2$$

Since $r_1 + r_2 = 1$ and $0 \le r_1 \le 1$, we have:

$$E = 2500r_1 + 5750(1 - r_1) = 5750 - 3250r_1$$

E is largest when r_1 is as small as possible, namely when $r_1 = 0$. Therefore, $r_2 = 1$, and $E = 5750$. Given the mixed strategy of nature, the farmer should use a pure strategy of planting all wheat.

Usually one player cannot estimate the probabilities of the other player's mixed strategy as easily as the farmer did. We will now look at a way of determining mixed strategies when neither player knows the other's strategy.

EXAMPLE 2

Two manufacturers of cereal for children, Kellogg's and General Mills, want to purchase advertising time on Saturday morning television. They both want to appeal to the younger age group. The two most effective time periods are 8 A.M. and 9 A.M. A research consulting firm determines that the gain to Kellogg's for various choices of time slots is given by the following payoff matrix in thousands of dollars:

$$\begin{array}{c} \text{General Mills} \\ \begin{array}{cc} \text{8 A.M.} & \text{9 A.M.} \end{array} \end{array}$$

$$P = \quad \text{Kellogg's} \quad \begin{array}{c} \text{8 A.M.} \\ \text{9 A.M.} \end{array} \begin{pmatrix} -5 & 10 \\ 20 & -10 \end{pmatrix}$$

Let $A = (r_1 \quad r_2)$ be the mixed strategy for Kellogg's, and

$$B = \begin{pmatrix} c_1 \\ c_2 \end{pmatrix}$$

be the mixed strategy for General Mills. These probabilities indicate the proportion of weeks each chooses to use the 8 A.M. slot and the 9 A.M. slot. The matrix product:

$$AP = (r_1 \qquad r_2) \begin{pmatrix} -5 & 10 \\ 20 & -10 \end{pmatrix} = (-5r_1 + 20r_2 \qquad 10r_1 - 10r_2)$$

indicates an expected value $E_1 = -5r_1 + 20r_2$ to Kellogg's if General Mills uses the 8 A.M. slot and expected value $E_2 = 10r_1 - 10r_2$ to Kellogg's if General Mills uses the 9 A.M. slot. Since $r_2 = 1 - r_1$, these can be written as:

$$E_1 = -5r_1 + 20(1 - r_1) = -25r_1 + 20$$

and

$$E_2 = 10r_1 - 10(1 - r_1) = 20r_1 - 10$$

If we graph these two linear functions with r_1 the horizontal axis and E the vertical axis, keeping in mind that $r_1 \leq 1$, we have the graph shown in Figure 12.1.

Figure 12.1

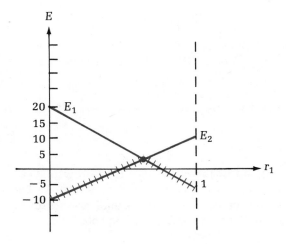

When $r_1 = 0$, $E_1 = 20$, and when $r_1 = 1$, $E_1 = -5$. When $r_1 = 0$, $E_2 = -10$, and when $r_1 = 1$, $E_2 = 10$.

As in the case of pure strategies, Kellogg's wants to choose its strategy so as to maximize its gain, no matter what General Mills chooses to do. The point of intersection of the two lines in Figure 12.1 corresponds to the point where the expected values are equal no matter what General Mills decides to do. The expected value at the point of intersection is also the maximum of the worst Kellogg's can do relative to General Mills' strategy as indicated by the hatched lines in Figure 12.1. Finding this point of intersection is similar to finding the maximum of the row minimums in determining pure strategies.

What is the point of intersection?

$$E_1 = -25r_1 + 20 \quad \text{and} \quad E_2 = 20r_1 - 10$$

Therefore:

$$-25r_1 + 20 = 20r_1 - 10$$

$$30 = 45r_1$$

$$r_1 = \frac{30}{45} = \frac{2}{3}.$$

Since:

$$r_2 = 1 - r_1, \qquad r_2 = \frac{1}{3}$$

$$E_2 = 20r_1 - 10 = 20\left(\frac{2}{3}\right) - 10 = \frac{10}{3}.$$

Therefore, Kellogg's should advertise at 8 A.M. two-thirds of the weeks (randomly chosen) and at 9 A.M. one-third of the weeks, for an expected gain of $\frac{10}{3}$ thousand dollars. ∎

> DEFINITION Let P be the payoff matrix of a two-person zero-sum game, and $E_{A'} = \min E(P, A', B)$ for all column strategies B.
>
> $$A = (r_1, r_2, \ldots, r_n)$$
>
> is an **optimal strategy for the row player** if $E_A \geq E_{A'}$ for all row strategies A'.

This is optimal in the sense that if the row player uses a nonoptimal strategy, then that player is expected to win less. The above procedure indicates how one can compute an optimal row strategy. The hatched lines in Figure 12.1 indicate the minimum expected value for all strategies A'.

The optimal mixed strategy for General Mills can be determined by looking at the matrix product:

$$PB = \begin{pmatrix} -5 & 10 \\ 20 & -10 \end{pmatrix} \begin{pmatrix} c_1 \\ c_2 \end{pmatrix} = \begin{pmatrix} -5c_1 + 10c_2 \\ 20c_1 - 10c_2 \end{pmatrix}$$

If Kellogg's advertises at 8 A.M. the expected value is $E_1 = -5c_1 + 10c_2$, and if Kellogg's advertises at 9 A.M., the expected value is $E_2 = 20c_1 - 10c_2$. Since $c_2 = 1 - c_1$, we get the linear functions: $E_1 = -5c_1 + 10(1 - c_1)$ $= -15c_1 + 10$ and $E_2 = 20c_1 - 10(1 - c_1) = 30c_1 - 10$. Graphing these functions on the same set of axes, and noting that $0 \leq c_1 \leq 1$, we get the graph shown in Figure 12.2:

Figure 12.2

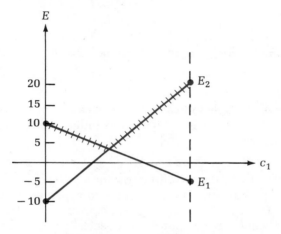

If $c_1 = 0$, then $E_1 = 10$, and if $c_1 = 1$, then $E_1 = -5$. If $c_1 = 0$, then $E_2 = -10$, and if $c_1 = 1$, then $E_2 = 20$.

General Mills wishes to minimize its losses to Kellogg's, thus it wants to find the minimum of the potential gains to Kellogg's, the hatched segments in Figure 12.2. Once again, this corresponds to finding the point of intersection of the two lines and is similar to finding the minimum of the column maximums in determining pure strategies.

The point of intersection is determined by equating the two functions for E:

$$-15c_1 + 10 = 30c_1 - 10$$

$$20 = 45c_1$$

$$c_1 = \frac{20}{45} = \frac{4}{9}$$

$$c_2 = 1 - c_1 = 1 - \frac{4}{9} = \frac{5}{9}$$

$$E = 30 \left(\frac{4}{9} \right) - 10 = \frac{10}{3}$$

Therefore, the optimal strategy for General Mills is to advertise four-ninths of the time at 8 A.M. and five-ninths of the time at 9 A.M. The expected value is $\frac{10}{3}$, the same as before. ∎

DEFINITION   Let P be a payoff matrix for a two-person zero-sum game, and $E_{B'} = \max E(P, A, B')$ for all row strategies A.

$$B = \begin{pmatrix} c_1 \\ c_2 \\ \cdot \\ \cdot \\ \cdot \\ c_m \end{pmatrix}$$

is an **optimal strategy for the column player** if $E_B \leq E_{B'}$, for all column strategies B'.

The above example indicates how one can compute an optimal column strategy. The hatched lines in Figure 12.2 indicate the expected value for all column strategies B'.

THEOREM   If P is the payoff matrix for a two-person zero-sum game, then an optimal strategy A for the row player always exists, an optimal strategy B for the column player always exists, and the expected values E computed with each are the same, and equal $E(P, A, B)$. In this case, $E(P, A, B)$ is defined to be the *value of the game*, and will be denoted $v(P)$.

PROCEDURE FOR FINDING OPTIMAL STRATEGIES IN GAMES WHERE EACH PLAYER HAS ONLY TWO CHOICES:

Row player

1. Compute:

$$(r_1 \quad r_2) \begin{pmatrix} a_{11} & a_{12} \\ a_{21} & a_{22} \end{pmatrix} = (r_1 a_{11} + r_2 a_{21} \quad r_1 a_{12} + r_2 a_{22})$$

2. Let $E_1 = r_1 a_{11} + r_2 a_{21}$ and $E_2 = r_1 a_{12} + r_2 a_{22}$.
3. Replace r_2 in each with $1 - r_1$.
4. Graph E_1 and E_2 on the same set of axis, remembering that $0 \leq r_1 \leq 1$.
5. Find the point of intersection of the two lines to get r_1 and E. $r_2 = 1 - r_1$.

Column player

1. Compute:

$$\begin{pmatrix} a_{11} & a_{12} \\ a_{21} & a_{22} \end{pmatrix} \begin{pmatrix} c_1 \\ c_2 \end{pmatrix} = \begin{pmatrix} a_{11}c_1 + a_{12}c_2 \\ a_{21}c_1 + a_{22}c_2 \end{pmatrix}$$

2. Let $E_1 = a_{11}c_1 + a_{12}c_2$ and $E_2 = a_{21}c_1 + a_{22}c_2$
3. Replace c_2 with $1 - c_1$ in both E_1 and E_2.
4. Graph E_1 and E_2 on the same set of axis, remembering that $0 \le c_1 \le 1$.
5. Find the point of intersection of the two lines to get c_1 and E. $c_2 = 1 - c_1$.

PRACTICE EXAMPLE 2

Find the optimal mixed strategies for the game with payoff matrix:

$$P = \begin{pmatrix} 2 & 5 \\ 4 & 3 \end{pmatrix}$$

■

EXAMPLE 3

A real estate developer owns a large tract of land in Montgomery Township in New Jersey. The developer purchased the land prior to a decision to extend I-295 through Montgomery Township and has waited five years for the courts to make a ruling on whether the road can be extended as planned, but can wait no longer. The availability of small-business loans at low interest rates ends at the end of the fiscal year. These loans are essential for any type of development that might be undertaken. The chart below gives the developer's profit for each choice, depending on whether the road is extended.

		Government	
		Highway	No highway
	Apartments	0	25,000
Developer	Shopping mall	35,000	15,000
	Houses	−10,000	20,000

If we set this problem up like the last one, the developer has three choices with probabilities r_1 for apartments, r_2 for a shopping mall, and r_3 for houses.

$$(r_1 \quad r_2 \quad r_3) \begin{pmatrix} 0 & 25 \\ 35 & -15 \\ -10 & 20 \end{pmatrix} = (35r_2 - 10r_3 \quad 25r_1 - 15r_2 + 20r_3)$$

in thousands of dollars. Therefore, we get two expected value functions:

$E_1 = 35r_2 - 10r_3$, and $E_2 = 25r_1 - 15r_2 + 20r_3$, both functions of three variables. If we use the fact that $r_1 + r_2 + r_3 = 1$, we can reduce the functions to functions of two variables, but no further. Therefore, graphing these functions requires graphing in three-dimensional space. Most problems of this type are more easily handled with linear programming techniques and the use of the simplex algorithm. ∎

However, the payoff matrix for this example has a characteristic that allows us to eliminate a row and hence use the graphing technique after all.

> DEFINITION   A **row** i is said to **dominate** another row j in a payoff matrix if each corresponding entry in row i is greater than or equal to each entry in row j.

In the payoff matrix for the development game of Example 3, row 1 dominates row 3, since $0 \geq -10$, and $25 \geq 20$.

$$P = \begin{pmatrix} 0 & 25 \\ 35 & -15 \\ -10 & 20 \end{pmatrix}$$

Since it can be assumed that a player will always choose to maximize his or her gain, and for all choices of the opponent, will do better with row i than row j, row j can be eliminated from the payoff matrix, when row i dominates row j.

> DEFINITION   A **column** i is said to **dominate** a column j if each entry in column i is less than or equal to each corresponding entry in column j.

In zero-sum games, since the payoff matrix gives the gains to the row player and losses to the column player, and the column player wishes to minimize his losses, he or she will always choose column i over column j if the entries in column i are less than or equal to the corresponding entries in column j, regardless of the row player's choices. Column j can therefore be eliminated in the payoff matrix when column i dominates column j.

> THEOREM   If **row i dominates row j (column i dominates column j)** in payoff matrix P, and P' is the matrix formed from P by removing row j (column j), then the value of the game determined by P' is the same as the value of the game determined by P, and the optimal strategies are the same.

If:

$$P = \begin{pmatrix} 1 & -5 & -2 \\ 2 & 0 & 7 \\ 7 & 5 & -1 \end{pmatrix}$$

then column 2 dominates column 1, since $-5 < 1$, $0 < 2$, and $5 < 7$,

$$P' = \begin{pmatrix} -5 & -2 \\ 0 & 7 \\ 5 & -1 \end{pmatrix}$$

and then to

$$P'' = \begin{pmatrix} 0 & 7 \\ 5 & -1 \end{pmatrix}$$

PRACTICE EXAMPLE 3

Use dominance to reduce each of the payoff matrices:

(a) $\begin{pmatrix} 1 & 3 & -1 \\ 4 & 4 & 2 \\ -6 & 1 & 5 \end{pmatrix}$ (b) $\begin{pmatrix} -5 & -3 & 2 \\ -1 & 0 & 4 \\ 4 & 1 & 3 \end{pmatrix}$ ■

Returning to our developer's dilemma, we see that the matrix:

$$P = \begin{pmatrix} 0 & 25 \\ 35 & -15 \\ -10 & 20 \end{pmatrix}$$

can be reduced to the matrix:

$$P' = \begin{matrix} \text{apts.} \\ \text{shop} \end{matrix} \begin{pmatrix} 0 & 25 \\ 35 & -15 \end{pmatrix}$$

by removing row 3, which is dominated by row 1.

We can now apply the graphical method to determine the optimal strategy for the developer. Let r_1 denote the proportion given to apartments and r_2 denote the proportion given to a shopping mall.

$$E = AP' = (r_1 \quad r_2) \begin{pmatrix} 0 & 25 \\ 35 & -15 \end{pmatrix} = (35 r_2 \quad 25 r_1 - 15 r_2)$$

If a highway is built, the expected value is $E_1 = 35 r_2$, and if the highway is not built, the expected value is $E_2 = 25 r_1 - 15 r_2$. Since $r_1 = 1 - r_2$, we get the linear functions: $E_1 = 35 r_2$ and $E_2 = 25(1 - r_2) - 15 r_2 = 25 - 40 r_2$. Graphing each of these functions on the same set of axes and remembering that $0 \leq r_2 \leq 1$, we have a graph as in Figure 12.3.

Figure 12.3

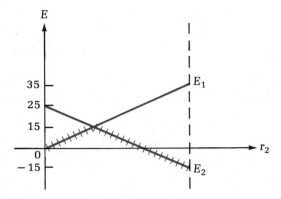

The point of intersection of the lines E_1 and E_2 determines the optimal strategy.

$$E = 35r_2 = 25 - 40r_2$$

$$75r_2 = 25$$

$$r_2 = \frac{25}{75} = \frac{1}{3}$$

$r_1 = 1 - r_2 = 1 - \frac{1}{3} = \frac{2}{3}$, and $E = 35(\frac{1}{3}) = \frac{35}{3}$ thousand dollars. Assuming that the tract of land can be split, the developer should allocate two-thirds of it to apartments and one-third of it to the shopping mall.

In the next section we use linear programming techniques to find optimal mixed strategies when the graphical method is too difficult.

CONCEPTS

expected value
row i dominates row j
column i dominates column j

procedure for finding optimal strategies
optimal strategy for row player
optimal strategy for column player

SOLUTIONS TO PRACTICE EXAMPLES

1. $\begin{pmatrix} \frac{1}{2} & \frac{1}{2} \end{pmatrix} \begin{pmatrix} 2 & 5 \\ 4 & 3 \end{pmatrix} \begin{pmatrix} \frac{1}{4} \\ \frac{3}{4} \end{pmatrix} = (3 \quad 4) \begin{pmatrix} \frac{1}{4} \\ \frac{3}{4} \end{pmatrix} = \frac{15}{4} = v$

2. $(r_1 \quad r_2) \begin{pmatrix} 2 & 5 \\ 4 & 3 \end{pmatrix} \begin{pmatrix} c_1 \\ c_2 \end{pmatrix}$

$$E_1 = 2r_1 + 4r_2 = 2r_1 + 4(1 - r_1) = -2r_1 + 4$$
$$E_2 = 5r_1 + 3r_2 = 5r_1 + 3(1 - r_1) = 2r_1 + 3$$

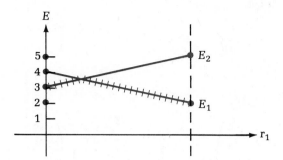

$$-2r_1 + 4 = 2r_1 + 3, \ r_1 = \frac{1}{4}, \ r_2 = \frac{3}{4}, \ \text{and} \ E = \frac{7}{2}$$

$$E_1 = 2c_1 + 5c_2 = 2c_1 + 5(1 - c_1) = 5 - 3c_1$$
$$E_2 = 4c_1 + 3c_2 = 4c_1 + 3(1 - c_1) = 3 + c_1$$

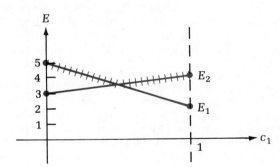

$$5 - 3c_1 = 3 + c_1, \ c_1 = \frac{1}{2}, \ c_2 = \frac{1}{2}, \ \text{and} \ R = \frac{7}{2}$$

3. (a) $\begin{pmatrix} 1 & 3 & -1 \\ 4 & 4 & 2 \\ -6 & 1 & 5 \end{pmatrix} \rightarrow \begin{pmatrix} 4 & 4 & 2 \\ -6 & 1 & 5 \end{pmatrix} \rightarrow \begin{pmatrix} 4 & 2 \\ -6 & 5 \end{pmatrix}$

(b) $\begin{pmatrix} -5 & -3 & 2 \\ -1 & 0 & 4 \\ 4 & 1 & 3 \end{pmatrix} \rightarrow \begin{pmatrix} -1 & 0 & 4 \\ 4 & 1 & 3 \end{pmatrix} \rightarrow \begin{pmatrix} -1 & 0 \\ 4 & 1 \end{pmatrix}$

EXERCISES 12.2

Determine the optimal row and column strategies for the games with the following payoff matrices:

1. $\begin{pmatrix} 3 & -4 \\ -5 & 1 \end{pmatrix}$ 2. $\begin{pmatrix} -2 & 8 \\ 0 & -3 \end{pmatrix}$

3. $\begin{pmatrix} 1 & 2 & 3 \\ 4 & -1 & 1 \end{pmatrix}$ 4. $\begin{pmatrix} 5 & -1 & 6 \\ -2 & 5 & 8 \end{pmatrix}$

5. $\begin{pmatrix} -3 & 6 \\ 6 & -4 \\ 2 & -8 \end{pmatrix}$ 6. $\begin{pmatrix} 5 & -1 \\ 0 & -4 \\ -8 & 0 \end{pmatrix}$

7. $\begin{pmatrix} 3 & -2 & 7 \\ -2 & 1 & -3 \end{pmatrix}$ 8. $\begin{pmatrix} 0 & 5 & -7 \\ -2 & 1 & 4 \end{pmatrix}$

Even though the payoff matrix of a game has a saddle point, if the column player is nature or an opponent that does not choose its plays, but probabilities of the column choices are known, then the best or optimal row player strategy must be determined using the column probabilities. Using the technique illustrated with the farmer and the *Farmer's Almanac*, find optimal strategies for the games in Exercises 9 through 12.

9. A student must decide whether to choose the usual grading system of A–F or a pass-fail system for a course. The student estimates that the probability of receiving an A is .3, a B is .3, a C is .2, a D is .1, and an F is .1. The student adds 4 points to the point hour count for an A, 3 points for a B, 2 points for a C, 1 point for a D, and no points for an F. On the pass-fail system, 3 points are given for a pass and 0 points for a fail. Which system should the student choose? Is your answer the same if on the pass-fail system pass means A, B, or C only?

10. The Lion's Club is trying to decide if they should have a fund-raising picnic. If it rains they will lose $2000, but if it is nice, they will gain $5000. The probability of rain for the day of the picnic is .2. Should they schedule the picnic? What if the probability of rain is .4?

11. A man is told that he has cancer, and he must decide whether or not to have an operation. The operation has a probability of .7 of success. He estimates a payoff matrix in terms of years to live as follows:

$$P = \begin{matrix} & \text{Success} & \text{No success} \\ \text{Operation} & \begin{pmatrix} 25 & 0 \\ \text{No operation} & 1 & 1 \end{pmatrix} \end{matrix}$$

What should he do?

12. A recently divorced woman must decide if she should sell the house she is living in now. The payoff matrix represents her gain for her choices. The probability that the economy will remain the same is .5, that it will improve is .2, and that it will worsen is .3. What should she do?

$$P = \begin{array}{c} \\ \text{Sell} \\ \text{Keep it} \end{array} \begin{array}{ccc} \text{Same} & \text{Improve} & \text{Worsen} \\ \left(\begin{array}{ccc} 100 & 300 & -200 \\ -200 & 0 & 200 \end{array}\right) \end{array}$$

Determine the optimal row and column strategies in Exercises 13 and 14.

13. A firm has two courses of action whose associated gains are believed to be dependent on which party is in control, provided a commitment is made prior to the election. The payoff matrix is as follows:

$$P = \begin{array}{c} \\ 1 \\ 2 \end{array} \begin{array}{cc} \text{Rep} & \text{Dem} \\ \left(\begin{array}{cc} 3 & -2 \\ -5 & 2 \end{array}\right) \end{array}$$

14. Two companies are considering locating in two towns, Des Moines and Ames. The payoffs for company 1 (losses for company 2) resulting from their choices are given in the payoff matrix, P:

$$P = \begin{array}{c} \\ \text{Des Moines} \\ \text{Ames} \end{array} \begin{array}{cc} \text{Des Moines} & \text{Ames} \\ \left(\begin{array}{cc} 0 & 1000 \\ 2000 & -1000 \end{array}\right) \end{array}$$

15. Let:

$$P = \begin{pmatrix} a & b \\ c & d \end{pmatrix}$$

be the payoff matrix for a two-person zero-sum game. Compute formulas for the optimal row strategy and for the optimal column strategy.

12.3   *Mixed Strategies Through Linear Programming*

In this section we use **linear programming techniques** to find optimal mixed strategies for players in two-person zero-sum games.

EXAMPLE 1   An investor is considering the purchase of two stocks. Stock A is an over-the-counter stock that is considered speculative, stock B is from the American exchange and is considered moderately conservative, and stock C is from the New York exchange and is considered very conservative. If the economy is strong, stock A will increase 20%, stock B will increase 10%, and stock C will increase 3%. If the economy is weak, stock A will remain the same, stock B will increase 3%, and stock C will increase 5%. Determine the optimal mixed strategy for the investor.

The payoff matrix is:

$$P = \begin{array}{c} \\ A \\ B \\ C \end{array} \begin{array}{cc} \text{Strong} & \text{Weak} \\ \begin{pmatrix} 20 & 0 \\ 10 & 3 \\ 3 & 5 \end{pmatrix} \end{array}$$

One should routinely check to see if any game is strictly determined before attempting to find a mixed strategy. If the game is strictly determined, then the best pure strategy is the best strategy. The row minimums in this example are 0 and 3, with a largest equal to 3. The column maximums are 20 and 5, with a least one equal to 5. There is no saddle point, therefore, the game is not strictly determined.

No row dominates any other row, nor does any column dominate any other column.

The investor wants to determine an optimal mixed strategy (r_1, r_2, r_3) for the game.

$$(r_1, r_2, r_3) \begin{pmatrix} 20 & 0 \\ 10 & 3 \\ 3 & 5 \end{pmatrix} = (20r_1 + 10r_2 + 3r_3, 3r_2 + 5r_3)$$

If the economy is strong, then $E_1 = 20r_1 + 10r_2 + 3r_3$ is the expected value. If the economy is weak, then the expected value is $E_2 = 3r_2 + 5r_3$. The investor wants to find the maximum of the minimum of

$$\{20r_1 + 10r_2 + 3r_3, 3r_2 + 5r_3\}$$

where

$$r_1 + r_2 + r_3 = 1, 0 \leq r_1 \leq 1, 0 \leq r_2 \leq 1, 0 \leq r_3 \leq 1$$

If we let $v = \min \{20r_1 + 10r_2 + 3r_3, 3r_2 + 5r_3\}$, then $v > 0$, since at least one of r_1, r_2, or r_3 must be positive. We want to maximize v, or equivalently minimize $\frac{1}{v}$. Also, since v is a minimum, $20r_1 + 10r_2 + 3r_3 \geq v$ and $3r_2 + 5r_3 \geq v$. Dividing each inequality by v, we get two inequalities:

$$\frac{20r_1}{v} + \frac{10r_2}{v} + \frac{3r_3}{v} \geq 1$$

$$\frac{3r_2}{v} + \frac{5r_3}{v} \geq 1$$

Since $r_1 + r_2 + r_3 = 1$, $\frac{r_1}{v} + \frac{r_2}{v} + \frac{r_3}{v} = \frac{1}{v}$.

We introduce new variables x_1, x_2, and x_3, with $x_1 = \frac{r_1}{v}$, $x_2 = \frac{r_2}{v}$, and

$x_3 = \frac{r_3}{v}$. We have a linear program:

$$\min \frac{1}{v} = x_1 + x_2 + x_3$$

$$20x_1 + 10x_2 + 3x_3 \geq 1$$

$$3x_2 + 5x_3 \geq 1$$

$$x_1 \geq 0, \ x_2 \geq 0, \ x_3 \geq 0$$

The simplex algorithm handles maximization problems, therefore, we need to find the dual of this linear program:

$$\max T = u_1 + u_2$$

$$20u_1 \leq 1$$

$$10u_1 + 3u_2 \leq 1$$

$$3u_1 + 5u_2 \leq 1$$

$$u_1 \geq 0, \ u_2 \geq 0$$

Since the dual is a two-variable program, the solution can be found either graphically or by using the simplex algorithm. Ultimately, we want the solution to the minimization program. If we use the simplex algorithm, we can read the values of the x_i's from the bottom row of the last tableau. Adding slack variables, we get:

$$20u_1 + s_1 = 1$$

$$10u_1 + 3u_2 + s_2 = 1$$

$$3u_1 + 5u_2 + s_3 = 1$$

$$-u_1 - u_2 + T = 0$$

The first tableau is:

u_1	u_2	s_1	s_2	s_3	T	constants	ratios
20	0	1	0	0	0	1	
10	3	0	1	0	0	1	$\frac{1}{3}$
3	5	0	0	1	0	1	$\frac{1}{5}$ min
-1	-1	0	0	0	1	0	

The second tableau is:

u_1	u_2	s_1	s_2	s_3	T	constants	basis	ratios
20	0	1	0	0	0	1	s_1	$\dfrac{1}{20}$
$\dfrac{41}{5}$	0	0	1	$-\dfrac{3}{5}$	0	$\dfrac{2}{5}$	s_2	$\dfrac{2}{41}$ min
$\dfrac{3}{5}$	1	0	0	$\dfrac{1}{5}$	0	$\dfrac{1}{5}$	u_2	$\dfrac{1}{3}$
$-\dfrac{2}{5}$	0	0	0	$\dfrac{1}{5}$	1	$\dfrac{1}{5}$	T	

The third, and last, tableau is:

u_1	u_2	s_1	s_2	s_3	T	constants	basis
0	0	1	$-\dfrac{100}{41}$	$\dfrac{60}{41}$	0	$\dfrac{1}{41}$	s_1
1	0	0	$\dfrac{5}{41}$	$-\dfrac{3}{41}$	0	$\dfrac{2}{41}$	u_1
0	1	0	$-\dfrac{3}{41}$	$\dfrac{10}{41}$	0	$\dfrac{7}{41}$	u_2
0	0	0	$\dfrac{2}{41}$	$\dfrac{7}{41}$	1	$\dfrac{9}{41}$	T

Therefore, $u_1 = \frac{2}{41}$, $u_2 = \frac{7}{41}$, and $T = \frac{9}{41}$ from the right-hand column. From the bottom row, $x_1 = 0$, $x_2 = \frac{2}{41}$, and $x_3 = \frac{7}{41}$. Also, $\frac{1}{v} = \frac{9}{41}$, thus $v = \frac{41}{9}$. Since:

$$\frac{r_1}{v} = x_1, \ r_1 = x_1 v = 0(v) = 0$$

$$\frac{r_2}{v} = x_2, \ r_2 = x_2 v = \frac{2}{41}\left(\frac{41}{9}\right) = \frac{2}{9}$$

$$\frac{r_3}{v} = x_3, \ r_3 = x_3 v = \frac{7}{41}\left(\frac{41}{9}\right) = \frac{7}{9}$$

The investor's optimal investment strategy is $(0, \frac{2}{9}, \frac{7}{9})$; two-ninths of the money invested in stock B and seven-ninths of the money invested in stock C. ∎

Suppose the payoff matrix in the last example was for a game where the column player could choose its moves. To compute the optimal strategy for the column player, we look at:

$$\begin{pmatrix} 20 & 0 \\ 10 & 3 \\ 3 & 5 \end{pmatrix} \begin{pmatrix} c_1 \\ c_2 \end{pmatrix} = \begin{pmatrix} 20c_1 \\ 10c_1 + 3c_2 \\ 3c_1 + 5c_2 \end{pmatrix}$$

The column player wants to minimize the maximum of the elements of the set $\{20c_1, 10c_1 + 3c_1, 3c_1 + 5c_2\}$. If we let $v' = \max\ \{20c_1, 10c_1 + 3c_2, 3c_1 + 5c_2\}$, then:

$$20c_1 \leq v'$$

$$10c_1 + 3c_2 \leq v'$$

$$3c_1 + 5c_2 \leq v'$$

Since v' is also positive, dividing by v' yields:

$$\frac{20c_1}{v'} \leq 1$$

$$\frac{10c_1}{v'} + \frac{3c_2}{v'} \leq 1$$

$$\frac{3c_1}{v'} + \frac{5c_2}{v'} \leq 1$$

Minimizing v' is the same as maximizing $\frac{1}{v'}$. Replacing $\frac{c_1}{v'}$ with y_1, $\frac{c_2}{v'}$ with y_2, since $c_1 + c_2 = 1$, we get:

$$\max \frac{1}{v'} = y_1 + y_2$$

$$20y_1 \leq 1$$

$$10y_1 + 3y_2 \leq 1$$

$$3y_1 + 5y_2 \leq 1$$

$$y_1 \geq 0,\, y_2 \geq 0$$

But this is exactly the same linear program we just found the solution to using the simplex method. The y's were called u's and $\frac{1}{v'}$ is T. The linear program used to find the optimal strategy for the column player is the dual of the linear program to find the optimal strategy for the row player. Therefore, we already know the solution:

$$c_1 = y_1 v = u_1 v = \frac{2}{41} \left(\frac{41}{9} \right) = \frac{2}{9}$$

$$c_2 = y_2 v = u_2 v = \frac{7}{41} \left(\frac{41}{9} \right) = \frac{7}{9}$$

Thus, the optimal mixed strategy for the column player is to choose column 1 two-ninths of the time, and choose column 2 seven-ninths of the time.

In this last example we relied very heavily on the fact that v, the value of the game, was positive so we could divide by v. If every entry in the payoff matrix is positive, then v will be positive, since at least one r_i is positive.

SUMMARY

If $(r_1, r_2, \ldots, r_n)$ represents the optimal mixed strategy for the row player and:

$$\begin{pmatrix} c_1 \\ c_2 \\ \cdot \\ \cdot \\ \cdot \\ c_m \end{pmatrix}$$

represents the optimal mixed strategy for the column player in a two-person zero-sum game with payoff matrix:

$$P = \begin{pmatrix} a_{11} & a_{12} & \cdots & a_{1m} \\ a_{21} & a_{22} & \cdots & a_{1m} \\ \cdot & \cdot & & \cdot \\ \cdot & \cdot & & \cdot \\ \cdot & \cdot & & \cdot \\ a_{n1} & a_{n2} & \cdots & a_{nm} \end{pmatrix}$$

all of whose entries are positive, then the numbers r_i and c_j can be found by solving the pair of dual linear programs:

$$\max T = y_1 + y_2 + \cdots + y_m$$

$$a_{11}y_1 + a_{12}y_2 + \cdots + a_{1m}y_m \leq 1$$

$$a_{21}y_1 + a_{22}y_2 + \cdots + a_{2m}y_m \leq 1$$

$$\vdots \qquad \vdots \qquad \qquad \vdots$$

$$a_{n1}y_1 + a_{n2}y_2 + \cdots + a_{nm}y_m \leq 1$$

$$y_i \geq 0$$

and

$$\min R = x_1 + x_2 + \cdots + x_n$$

$$a_{11}x_1 + a_{21}x_2 + \cdots + a_{n1}x_n \geq 1$$

$$a_{12}x_1 + a_{22}x_2 + \cdots + a_{n2}x_n \geq 1$$

$$\begin{matrix} \cdot & \cdot & \cdot \\ \cdot & \cdot & \cdot \\ \cdot & \cdot & \cdot \end{matrix}$$

$$a_{1m}x_1 + a_{2m}x_2 + \cdots + a_{nm}x_n \geq 1$$

$$x_i \geq 0$$

where $v = \frac{1}{T}$, $r_i = x_i v$, and $c_j = y_j v$.

PROCEDURE

1. Use the simplex method to find the solution to the maximization program to get T and the y_j. The value of the game is $v = \frac{1}{T}$.
2. $c_j = y_j v$ is the optimal column strategy.
3. Read the solutions for the x_i as the solutions for the dual variables in the bottom row of the final tableau in Step 1.
4. $r_i = x_i v$ is the optimal row strategy.

PRACTICE EXAMPLE 1

Write the pair of linear programs to be solved to find the optimal strategies for the game with payoff matrix:

$$P = \begin{pmatrix} 1 & 4 & 5 \\ 12 & 1 & 3 \\ 5 & 8 & 1 \end{pmatrix}$$

What happens if all the entries in the payoff matrix are not positive?

EXAMPLE 2

Peter and Paul play a game where each writes one of the numbers 1, 4, or 7. If they match, there is no payoff. If they do not match, then the one with the higher number wins in dollars the sum of the two numbers shown. The payoff matrix for this game is:

$$\begin{array}{c} & & \text{Paul} \\ & & \begin{matrix} 1 & \quad 4 & \quad 7 \end{matrix} \\ \text{Peter} \begin{matrix} 1 \\ 4 \\ 7 \end{matrix} & \begin{pmatrix} 0 & -5 & -8 \\ 5 & 0 & -11 \\ 8 & 11 & 0 \end{pmatrix} = P \end{array}$$

This game is strictly determined, with the (3, 3)-entry 0 as saddle point. Each player should write the number 7, and the value of the game is 0.

The most negative entry in the payoff matrix is -11. Therefore, if we add 12 to every entry of P, all entries will be positive. We will get a new payoff matrix:

$$P' = \begin{pmatrix} 12 & 7 & 4 \\ 17 & 12 & 1 \\ 20 & 23 & 12 \end{pmatrix}$$

P' is also the payoff matrix of a strictly determined game with optimal pure strategy for the row player of playing row 3, and for the column player of playing column 3. The value of this game is $12 = v(P) + 12$. ∎

> **THEOREM** If P is a payoff matrix for a two-person zero-sum game and P' is the matrix formed from P by adding k to each entry of P, then $v(P) = v(P') - k$, and the optimal strategies for the game determined by P are the same as the optimal strategies for the game determined by P'.

PRACTICE EXAMPLE 2

For each of the payoff matrices, find a new payoff matrix whose game has the same optimal strategies as the original, and all of whose entries are positive:

(a) $\begin{pmatrix} -4 & 5 & 7 \\ 3 & -4 & 9 \\ -11 & 3 & -3 \end{pmatrix}$ (b) $\begin{pmatrix} 2 & -9 & 7 \\ -13 & -5 & 9 \\ 8 & -6 & -2 \end{pmatrix}$ ∎

EXAMPLE 3

The Democratic and Republican candidates for president must decide which states to visit the last day before the election. They each narrow the choices down to New York with 36 electoral votes, Pennsylvania with 25 electoral votes, and California with 47 electoral votes. It is predicted that unless something changes the mind of the electorate, California is still a toss-up, New York will go Democratic, and Pennsylvania will go Republican. An independent agency computes a payoff matrix of gains for the Republican candidate as follows:

Democratic

		CA	NY	PA	
	CA	24	11	22	
Republican	NY	-11	18	11	$= P$
	PA	-22	-11	12	

To find the optimal strategies for each candidate using linear programming, we need to add 23 to each entry of P to get a new payoff matrix:

$$P' = \begin{pmatrix} 47 & 34 & 45 \\ 12 & 41 & 34 \\ 1 & 12 & 35 \end{pmatrix}$$

Since row 1 dominates row 3, P' can be reduced to:

$$P'' = \begin{pmatrix} 47 & 34 & 45 \\ 12 & 41 & 34 \end{pmatrix}$$

The Republican candidate need not visit Pennsylvania at all. The value of P will be 23 less than the value of P''.

Apply the simplex algorithm to find a solution of the linear program corresponding to P'':

$$\max T = y_1 + y_2 + y_3$$

$$47y_1 + 34y_2 + 45y_3 \leq 1$$

$$12y_1 + 41y_2 + 34y_3 \leq 1$$

$$y_i \geq 0$$

Recall that the y_i's determine the Democratic candidate's strategy, and the dual variables determine the Republican candidate's strategy.

Adding slack variables:

$$47y_1 + 34y_2 + 45y_3 + s_1 = 1$$

$$12y_1 + 41y_2 + 34y_3 + s_1 = 1$$

$$-y_1 - y_2 - y_3 + T = 0$$

First tableau:

y_1	y_2	y_3	s_1	s_2	T	constants	basis	ratios
㊼	34	45	1	0	0	1	s_1	$\dfrac{1}{47}$
12	41	34	0	1	0	1	s_2	$\dfrac{1}{12}$
-1	-1	-1	0	0	1	0	T	

$\uparrow$

Second tableau:

y_1	y_2	y_3	s_1	s_2	T	constants	basis
1	.723	.957	.021	0	0	.021	y_1
0	(32.324)	22.516	$-.252$	1	0	.748	s_2
0	$-.277$	$-.043$	.021	0	1	.021	T

$\uparrow$

Third and last tableau:

y_1	y_2	y_3	s_1	s_2	T	constants	basis
1	0	.453	.0266	$-.0233$	0	.00437	y_1
0	1	.6966	$-.0078$	.0309	0	.023	y_2
0	0	.150	.0188	.0086	1	.02737	T

Therefore,

$$v(P'') = \frac{1}{T} = \frac{1}{.02737} = 36.536$$

$$c_1 = y_1 v = .00437(36.536) = .16$$

$$c_2 = y_2 v = .023(36.536) = .84$$

$$c_3 = y_3 v = 0(36.536) = 0$$

$$r_1 = x_1 v = .0188(36.536) = .69$$

$$r_2 = x_2 v = .0085(36.536) = .31$$

$$v(P) = v(P'') - 23 = 36.536 - 23 = 13.536$$

Neither candidate should visit Pennsylvania at all. The Republican candidate should spend 69% of the day in California and 31% of the day in New York. The Democratic candidate should spend 16% of the day in California and 84% of the day in New York, admittedly difficult to do with the distance between them. The value of the game is 13.536 electoral votes. ◼

PRACTICE EXAMPLE 3   Use linear programming techniques to find the optimal mixed strategies for the game with payoff matrix:

$$\begin{pmatrix} 3 & -6 \\ -5 & 4 \end{pmatrix}$$

◼

In the next section we consider general n-person games.

CONCEPT

linear programming techniques

SOLUTIONS TO PRACTICE EXAMPLES

1. max $T = y_1 + y_2 + y_3$

    $y_1 + 4y_2 + 5y_3 \leq 1$

    $12y_1 + y_2 + 3y_3 \leq 1$

    $5y_1 + 8y_2 + y_3 \leq 1$

    $\qquad\qquad y_i \geq 0$

    min $R = x_1 + x_2 + x_3$

    $x_1 + 12x_2 + 5x_3 \geq 1$

    $4x_1 + x_2 + 8x_3 \geq 1$

    $5x_1 + 3x_2 + x_3 \geq 1$

    $\qquad\qquad x_i \geq 0$

2. (a) $\begin{pmatrix} 8 & 17 & 19 \\ 15 & 8 & 21 \\ 1 & 15 & 9 \end{pmatrix}$ (b) $\begin{pmatrix} 16 & 5 & 21 \\ 1 & 9 & 23 \\ 22 & 8 & 12 \end{pmatrix}$

3. $P = \begin{pmatrix} 3 & -6 \\ -5 & 4 \end{pmatrix} \xrightarrow{+7} \begin{pmatrix} 10 & 1 \\ 2 & 11 \end{pmatrix} = P'$

    max $T = y_1 + y_2$

    $10y_1 + y_2 \leq 1$

    $2y_1 + 11y_2 \leq 1$

    $\qquad\quad y_i \geq 0$

    $y_1 = \dfrac{5}{54}, y_2 = \dfrac{4}{54}, T = \dfrac{1}{6}, v' = 6$

    $c_1 = \left(\dfrac{5}{54} \right)(6) = \dfrac{5}{9}, c_2 = \left(\dfrac{4}{54} \right)(6) = \dfrac{4}{9}$

    $x_1 = \dfrac{1}{12}, x_2 = \dfrac{1}{12}$

    $r_1 = \left(\dfrac{1}{12} \right)(6) = \dfrac{1}{2}, r_2 = \left(\dfrac{1}{12} \right)(6) = \dfrac{1}{2}$

    $v = v' - 7 = -1$

EXERCISES 12.3

Find optimal row and column strategies for each of the games with payoff matrices:

1. $\begin{pmatrix} 2 & 3 & 4 \\ 1 & 7 & 2 \\ 3 & 1 & 3 \end{pmatrix}$

2. $\begin{pmatrix} -1 & 3 & 6 \\ 9 & 4 & 1 \\ 0 & 1 & 8 \end{pmatrix}$

3. $\begin{pmatrix} 1 & 8 \\ 2 & 1 \\ 5 & 2 \end{pmatrix}$

4. $\begin{pmatrix} 2 & 7 \\ 3 & 4 \\ -2 & 5 \end{pmatrix}$

5. $\begin{pmatrix} 3 & 0 & 6 \\ 0 & 1 & 3 \end{pmatrix}$

6. $\begin{pmatrix} 9 & -4 & 2 \\ -6 & -1 & 0 \end{pmatrix}$

7. $\begin{pmatrix} 3 & 7 \\ 4 & 2 \\ 6 & 1 \\ 8 & 3 \end{pmatrix}$

8. $\begin{pmatrix} 0 & 9 \\ 1 & 8 \\ 7 & 2 \\ 1 & 0 \end{pmatrix}$

9. $\begin{pmatrix} -3 & -5 & -2 \\ 0 & 7 & 2 \\ -6 & 8 & 1 \end{pmatrix}$

10. $\begin{pmatrix} 3 & 5 & 6 \\ 0 & -4 & 9 \\ 1 & 2 & -3 \end{pmatrix}$

11. In a card game a person can pass, play and bet $10, or play and bet $100. A lucky player will win the hand and win double what was bet. An unlucky player forfeits the bet. There is a $20 charge to get in the casino. Write a payoff matrix for this game representing the player's gains. Find the optimal strategy for the player.

12. A student can solve a problem in 60 minutes without a book, and in 10 minutes with a book from the library. The book may or may not be in the library. Going to the library takes 20 minutes. What should the student do?

12.4 General Games

In this section, we look at games that are played by an arbitrary number of players, called n-person games. In Chapter 1 we introduced some of these games as examples in our discussion of sets. In these games, the players try to reach an agreement about possible outcomes. A solution to an n-person game can be viewed as a prediction of the set of outcomes that can occur when the game is played. Players will be allowed to cooperate and form coalitions if it is to their benefit.

Each game has a finite set, I, of players, and any subset S of I will be called a **coalition**—a group of players acting together to achieve a goal. The **value of a coalition**, S, denoted $v(S)$, is the largest payoff the coalition can guarantee itself. Thus, the value v is a function that associates to every subset of players a real number. We require that the function v satisfy two properties:

1. $v(\varnothing) = 0$
2. $v(S \cup T) \geq v(S) + v(T)$ if $S \cap T = \varnothing$

Condition 2 says that two disjoint groups working together do at least as well as the two groups working separately and then pooling their payoffs. This second condition is called **superadditivity**.

EXAMPLE 1   The owner of a large tract of land, player 1, has two and only two prospective buyers for the land: one who plans to build a shopping mall, player 2, and one who plans to build a housing development, player 3. The land is currently worth $1 million to the owner as is. Player 2 considers the land to be worth $2 million, and player 3 considers the land to be worth $1.5 million. To define the value of the game, we need to assign a real number to each subset of $I = \{1, 2, 3\}$. These subsets are: $\varnothing$, $\{1\}$, $\{2\}$, $\{3\}$, $\{1, 2\}$, $\{1, 3\}$, $\{2, 3\}$, and $\{1, 2, 3\}$. Condition 1 requires that $v(\varnothing) = 0$. Since player 1 already owns the land worth $1 million, $v(\{1\}) = \$1$ million. By themselves, or together, players 2 and 3 can do nothing since they do not have the land. Therefore, $v(\{2\}) = v(\{3\}) = v(\{2, 3\}) = 0$. Players 1 and 2 can form a coalition with player 1 agreeing to sell the land to player 2, thus $v(\{1, 2\}) = \$2$ million. Similarly, we have $v(\{1, 3\}) = \$1.5$ million. Player 1 can agree to sell the land to the highest bidder, so $v(\{1, 2, 3\}) = \$2$ million. In summary:

$$v(\varnothing) = 0$$

$$v(\{1\}) = \$1 \text{ million}$$

$$v(\{2\}) = v(\{3\}) = v(\{2, 3\}) = 0$$

$$v(\{1, 3\}) = \$1.5 \text{ million}$$

$$v(\{1, 2\}) = v(\{1, 2, 3\}) = \$2 \text{ million}$$

Condition 2 for a value function is satisfied. For example, $v(\{1, 2\}) = 2 \geq v(\{1\}) + v(\{2\}) = 1 + 0$. Therefore v is a value function of the game.

We would like to know whether player 1 makes a sale and if so, at what price. This example generalizes to any two-buyer market.

If we apply common sense to solving the problem, we would see that since player 2 is the stronger player (has more to gain), player 2 can outbid player 3, but will have to bid over the value to player 3 of the coalition $\{1, 3\}$. Therefore, the price of the property will be between $1.5 million and $2 million. We will see mathematically that this is indeed the solution to the game. First, let us look at a few more examples.

EXAMPLE 2   A majority of the 100 U.S. senators must vote favorably to pass a particular piece of legislation. The players in this game are the 100 senators. We can define the payoff of the game to be 1 if the bill passes and 0 otherwise. Therefore, the value function is:

$$v(S) = \begin{cases} 1 & \text{if } S \text{ has more than 50 elements} \\ 0 & \text{if } S \text{ has 50 or less elements} \end{cases}$$

We will want to know under what conditions a coalition is likely to form, and if so which ones. ∎

EXAMPLE 3   An agency of the federal government has offered 10 states $6 million for development of waste treatment facilities provided the states can agree on a distribution of the money. If no agreement is reached, the federal government will hold the money. The players in this game are the 10 states, and:

$$v(S) = \begin{cases} 6 \text{ million} & \text{if } S \text{ is } I, \text{ the whole set} \\ 0 & \text{otherwise} \end{cases}$$ ∎

EXAMPLE 4   Each of eight states has toxic wastes that it must dump in another state. The set of players for the game is the set of eight states. If S is any proper subset of the set of players I, then as a group they can decide to dump their toxic wastes in a state not in the coalition S. For example, suppose states 1 through 6 group together. They can decide to split their toxic wastes between states 7 and 8, and 7 and 8 undoubtedly will dump theirs in states 1 through 6. However, the coalition consisting of the whole set of players has no place to dump the wastes outside the set. If each state has 1 unit of toxic wastes to be dumped, then the value of a coalition is the negative of the number of states not in the coalition for all coalitions not equal to I or $\varnothing$. In our example above the value of the coalition $\{1, 2, 3, 4, 5, 6\}$ is -2 and the value of the coalition $\{7, 8\}$ is -6. Therefore, we can write the value function for subsets with k elements as:

$$v(S) = \begin{cases} 0 & \text{if } k = 0 \\ -8 & \text{if } k = 8 \\ k - 8 & \text{if } 0 < k < 8 \end{cases}$$

If we defined the value of a subset to be the number of units dumped outside the coalition, superadditivity would be violated, for $v(I) = 0 < v(S) + v(T)$, $S \neq \varnothing$.

We want to determine which coalitions could be formed. ∎

PRACTICE   Each of six countries has the means to destroy any one of the others. If the
EXAMPLE 1   players are the six countries, determine a value function for the game. ∎

A game can have various possible outcomes. A **solution to a game** gives the set of possible outcomes. We will represent an outcome by a row matrix that lists the payoffs to each player, $(x_1, x_2, \ldots, x_n)$ where x_i is the payoff to player i. The payoff of the game is the value of the whole set. An outcome is a distribution of the payoff among the players. We assume that a player will not accept a payoff unless it is at least as good as what he or she can assure him or herself. Therefore, for each i, $x_i \geq v(\{i\})$. Since a solution ascribes or imputes a payoff for each player, the term imputation is used.

DEFINITION An **imputation** of a game, with players 1, 2, ..., n, is an outcome $(x_1, x_2, \ldots, x_n)$ such that:

(1) $x_1 + x_2 + \cdots + x_n = v(\{1, 2, \ldots, n\})$
(2) $x_i \geq v(\{i\})$ for each $i = 1, 2, \ldots, n$

In Example 1 the imputations are all row matrices (x_1, x_2, x_3) such that:

$$x_1 \geq 1 \text{ million}$$

$$x_2 \geq 0, \ x_3 \geq 0$$

$$x_1 + x_2 + x_3 = 2 \text{ million}$$

In Example 2, the imputations are all row matrices $(x_1, x_2, \ldots, x_{100})$ such that:

$$x_i \geq 0 \text{ each } i$$

$$x_1 + x_2 + \cdots + x_{100} = 1$$

The imputations for Example 3 on the waste treatment facility are the row matrices $(x_1, x_2, \ldots, x_{80})$ such that:

$$x_i \geq 0 \text{ for each } i$$

$$x_1 + x_2 + \cdots + x_{80} = 6$$

The more complicated example of states' toxic waste dumping has imputations $(x_1, x_2, \ldots, x_8)$ such that:

$$x_i \geq v(\{i\}) = -7 \text{ for each } i$$

$$x_1 + x_2 + \cdots + x_8 = -8$$

We want to designate those imputations of a game that are best in some sense. In particular, we want to designate those imputations for which no other imputation is better.

DEFINITION The **core** of a game with value function v consists of all imputations such that for any subset $S \neq \varnothing$, the sum of the payoffs to members of S is greater than or equal to the value of the coalition S.

Listing the nonempty subsets, S, for the two-market game of Example 1, and the values of these subsets, gives conditions for an imputation to be in the core:

Subsets	$v(S)$	Conditions
$\{1\}$	1	$x_1 \geq 1$
$\{2\}$	0	$x_2 \geq 0$
$\{3\}$	0	$x_3 \geq 0$
$\{1, 2\}$	2	$x_1 + x_2 \geq 2$
$\{1, 3\}$	1.5	$x_1 + x_3 \geq 1.5$
$\{2, 3\}$	0	$x_2 + x_3 \geq 0$
$\{1, 2, 3\}$	2	$x_1 + x_2 + x_3 \geq 2$

But we already know that $x_1 + x_2 + x_3 = 2$, since (x_1, x_2, x_3) is an imputation, which satisfies the first three conditions. Combining $x_1 + x_2 \geq 2$ with $x_1 + x_2 + x_3 = 2$, implies that $x_3 = 0$, and $x_1 + x_2 = 2$. Since $x_3 = 0$ and $x_1 + x_3 \geq 1.5$, we have $x_1 \geq 1.5$, as well as $x_1 \leq 2$. Therefore we can completely describe the core for this game. It is the set of imputations: $C = \{(x_1, x_2, x_3) \mid 1.5 \leq x_1 \leq 2, x_2 = 2 - x_1, x_3 = 0\}$. Note that this is the same as our commonsense solution to the game. The core indicates that player 1 receives a payoff of between \$1.5 and \$2 million and therefore will sell the land to player 2 for a price between \$1.5 and \$2 million. Player 2 ends up with the land which is worth \$2 million minus the price paid to player 1. Player 3 was eliminated from the bargaining and has no payoff. Thus, when the core is nonempty, the core provides a set of outcomes for the game, or a solution to the game. There are, however, other ways to determine the solution of a game.

In Example 2, for an imputation $(x_1, x_2, \ldots, x_{100})$ to be in the core, the sum of any 51 or more of the x_i's must be greater than or equal to 1. In particular, $x_1 + x_2 + \cdots + x_{100} - x_i \geq 1$. Also, the total sum,

$$x_1 + x_2 + \cdots + x_{100} = 1$$

Subtracting these two inequalities yields:

$$
\begin{aligned}
x_1 + x_2 + \cdots + x_{100} - x_i &\geq 1 \\
- \quad x_1 + x_2 + \cdots + x_{100} \quad\ &= 1 \\
\hline
0 - x_i &\geq 0
\end{aligned}
$$

or $x_i \leq 0$, for each $i = 1, 2, \ldots, 100$. Since $v(\{i\}) = 0$, we know that $x_i \geq 0$ as well. Thus $x_i = 0$ for each i. But this contradicts the fact that the sum is equal to 1. Therefore, there is no imputation in the core. The core is $\varnothing$. Thus, if the core is used to determine a solution of a game, there is no solution to this game.

On the opposite end of the spectrum, we have the core for Example 3. The 10 states must all unite for the federal government to grant them any money. Therefore for $S \neq I$, $v(S) = 0$. For an imputation $(x_1, x_2, \ldots, x_{10})$ to be in the core, $x_i \geq 0$, for each $i = 1, 2, \ldots, 10$, and $x_1 + x_2 + \cdots + x_{10} = 6$, the same conditions imposed by the definition of an imputation. Therefore, the core consists of all imputations of the game. Each imputation is an outcome, or solution, of the game.

Finally, the core for the waste-dumping example is the empty set. Recall that when a coalition S has k elements, the value is defined by:

$$v(S) = \begin{cases} 0 & \text{if } k = 0 \\ -8 & \text{if } k = 8 \\ k - 8 & \text{if } 0 < k < 8 \end{cases}$$

Since the core consists of imputations $(x_1, x_2, \ldots, x_8)$, we must have $x_1 + x_2 + \cdots + x_8 = -8$ and $x_i \geq v(\{i\}) = -7$ for each i. To be in the core, $x_1 + x_2 + \cdots + x_7 \geq -1$, since $v(\{1, 2, 3, 4, 5, 6, 7\}) = -1$. Now:

$$x_1 + x_2 + \cdots + x_7 + x_8 \geq -1 + x_8$$
$$-8 \geq -1 + x_8$$
$$-7 \geq x_8$$

Therefore, $x_8 = -7$. Similarly, $x_i = -7$, for each i. Now the sum of the x_i's is -56, not -8, as required. Therefore, the core has no elements. There is no solution to the game.

PRACTICE EXAMPLE 2

Find the core for the game given in Practice Example 1.   ■

EXAMPLE 5

In Chapter 1, we looked at many examples of coalition formation where the members of a committee have different numbers of votes. Consider a committee with four members $\{1, 2, 3, 4\}$ where the members have 7, 4, 2, and 1 votes, respectively. A simple majority of 8 votes is required to pass a piece of legislation. We can view this situation as a four-person game with value function defined by:

$$v(S) = \begin{cases} 1 & \text{if } S \text{ has 8 or more votes among its members} \\ 0 & \text{otherwise} \end{cases}$$

The set of imputations consists of all (x_1, x_2, x_3, x_4) such that $x_i \geq 0$, and $x_1 + x_2 + x_3 + x_4 = 1$. If we list the subsets containing ·more than one member, with its number of votes, its values, and related inequalities, we have:

S	Votes	v(S)	Inequality
$\{1, 2\}$	11	1	$x_1 + x_2 \geq 1$
$\{1, 3\}$	9	1	$x_1 + x_3 \geq 1$
$\{1, 4\}$	8	1	$x_1 + x_4 \geq 1$
$\{2, 3\}$	6	0	$x_2 + x_3 \geq 0$
$\{2, 4\}$	5	0	$x_2 + x_4 \geq 0$
$\{3, 4\}$	3	0	$x_3 + x_4 \geq 0$
$\{1, 2, 3\}$	13	1	$x_1 + x_2 + x_3 \geq 1$
$\{1, 2, 4\}$	12	1	$x_1 + x_2 + x_4 \geq 1$
$\{1, 3, 4\}$	10	1	$x_1 + x_3 + x_4 \geq 1$
$\{2, 3, 4\}$	7	0	$x_2 + x_3 + x_4 \geq 0$
$\{1, 2, 3, 4\}$	we already have $x_1 + x_2 + x_3 + x_4 = 1$		

Combining $x_1 + x_2 + x_3 \geq 1$ with $x_1 + x_2 + x_3 + x_4 = 1$, we have $x_4 = 0$. Similarly, combining $x_1 + x_2 + x_4 \geq 1$ with $x_1 + x_2 + x_3 + x_4 = 1$, we have $x_3 = 0$. Finally, combining $x_1 + x_3 + x_4 \geq 1$ with $x_1 + x_2 + x_3 + x_4 = 1$, we have $x_2 = 0$. Since the sum is 1, we must have $x_1 = 1$. Therefore, the core consists of the single imputation $(1, 0, 0, 0)$. Player 1 does not have enough votes to pass any legislation alone, but without Player 1 no legislation passes. As described in Chapter 1, this committee member possesses a veto. ▪

As we indicated before, the core is only one way to determine a solution to a game. The concept of stable set, which we will not describe here, is an alternative way of defining a solution (see Shubik 1985 or Roberts 1979). The Shapley-Shubik Power index as described in Chapter 4.3 is a special case of the Shapley value of a game used to determine solutions of a game (see Shubik 1985).

CONCEPTS

coalition	value of a coalition
superadditivity	solution to a game
imputation	core

SOLUTIONS TO PRACTICE EXAMPLES

1.
$$v(S) = \begin{cases} 0 & \text{if } S = I = 6 \text{ countries} \\ 0 & \text{if } S = \varnothing \\ -k & \text{if } S \text{ has } k \text{ elements, } 0 < k < 6 \end{cases}$$

2. The core is the set $(x_1, x_2, \ldots, x_i)$ such that $x_i \geq -1$ and $x_1 + x_2 + \cdots + x_6 = 0$. Therefore, $x_i = 0$, for each i. A payoff must be 0 or -1 as a country is either alive or dead. The only coalition that should be formed is the whole set coalition.

EXERCISES 12.4

1. Show that for a game with players 1, 2, and 3:

$$v(S) = \begin{cases} 0 & \text{if } S = \emptyset, \{1\}, \{2\}, \{3\}, \{2, 3\}, \{1, 3\} \\ 2 & \text{if } S = \{1, 2\} \\ 3 & \text{if } S = \{1, 2, 3\} \end{cases}$$

is a value function.

2. A three-person game has value function:

$$v(S) = \begin{cases} 1 & \text{if } S = \{1, 2\}, (2, 3), \text{ or } \{1, 2, 3\} \\ 0 & \text{otherwise} \end{cases}$$

Find the core.

3. Is the following a value function for a three-person game?

$$v(S) = \begin{cases} 0 & \text{if } S = \emptyset \\ -1 & \text{if } S = \{1\}, \{2\}, \{3\} \\ 3 & \text{if } S = \{1, 2\} \text{ or } \{1, 3\} \\ 2 & \text{if } S = \{1, 2, 3\} \\ 4 & \text{if } S = \{2, 3\} \end{cases}$$

If so, find the core.

4. If $I + I = \{1, 2, 3, 4\}$, and:

$$v(S) = \begin{cases} 0 & \text{if } S = \emptyset \text{ or } S = \{i\} \\ \dfrac{(i + j)}{10} & \text{if } S = \{i, j\} \\ \dfrac{(i + j + k)}{10} & \text{if } S = \{i, j, k\} \\ 1 & \text{if } S = I \end{cases}$$

Explicitly write out the value of each subset and determine the core.

5. A three-person subcommittee of the finance committee must determine if various bills should go on for full committee vote. A majority of members voting in favor is sufficient for the bill to be passed on to the full committee. Determine a value function for this game, and the core.

6. Five communities must decide if they wish to join together to create a common water supply. The present cost of water for community i is c_i, and the cost to a coalition of communities S is $c(S)$. Therefore, the value function is: $v(S) =$ (sum of the c_i for members of S) $- c(S)$. An imputation is the savings to the whole community of forming a common water supply. The cost to community i for a common water supply is $c_i - x_i$. Practically speaking, what is meant by an imputation being in the core?

7. A committee consists of three senators and three representatives. For a bill to pass in the committee, at least two senators and two representatives must approve it. Write a value function for this game, and determine the core.

CHAPTER SUMMARY

In this chapter we looked at games—any competition or conflict between opponents, people, nature, or organizations. In a two-person zero-sum game there are two players and the amount won by one player is lost by the other player.

A two-person game is usually described by a payoff matrix that indicates the gains for the row player. When a player plays the same row (or column) every time the game is played, the player is using a pure strategy. To minimize the risk, the row player finds the maximum of the row minimums, and the column player finds the minimum of the column maximums. In this way each player maximizes his or her guaranteed gain. When the entry of the matrix that is the minimum of the row maximums is the same as the entry that is the minimum of the column maximums, that entry is called the *saddle point* for the game, and the *value* of the game.

If P is the payoff matrix for a two-person zero-sum game then the row player's mixed strategy can be given by a row matrix A, and the column player's mixed strategy can be given by a column matrix B, and the *expected value* of the game is the matrix product $E = APB$. The mixed strategies of each are matrices whose entries are probabilities, the sum of whose entries is 1.

Sometimes a payoff matrix can be simplified by removing rows, and/or columns. A row of a matrix dominates another row if each entry of the first row is greater than or equal to the corresponding entry of the second row. A column of a matrix dominates another column if each entry of the first column is less than or equal to the corresponding entry of the second column. In these cases, the smaller row and/or the larger column can be removed and the payoff matrix is reduced.

Optimal mixed strategies for each player can be computed using the techniques of linear programming or by graphing. These calculations are tedious to carry out by hand, but can be implemented with ease on a computer.

The last section looks at n-person games. Here the theory is more complicated and the notion of a solution not as well defined, but certain conditions need to be satisfied. If I is a set of players, then any subset S is a *coalition*. The value of a coalition S, denoted $v(S)$, is the largest payoff a coalition S can *guarantee* itself. The value function v must satisfy two conditions:

1. $v(\varnothing) = 0$
2. $v(S \cup T) \geq v(S) + v(T)$ if $S \cap T = \varnothing$

An *imputation* of a game with players $1, 2, \ldots, n$ is an outcome, or payoff distribution $(x_1, x_2, \ldots, x_n)$ such that:

1. $x_1 + x_2 + \cdots + x_n = v(\{1, 2, \ldots, n\})$
2. $x_i \geq v(\{i\})$ for each $i = 1, 2, \ldots, n$

One attempt to define a solution to a game is given by computing the core of a game. The *core* consists of all imputations such that for any subset $S \neq \varnothing$, the sum of the payoffs to members of S is greater than or equal to the value of the coalition S.

REVIEW EXERCISES FOR CHAPTER 12

1. Peter and Pam each have three cards, a 5, a 7, and a 10. Each selects a card and simultaneously they lay their card face up on the table. If they play the same card no payment is made. If they play different cards, then the one with the higher card gets that number of dollars.
    (a) Write the payoff matrix for this game.
    (b) Determine the best pure strategy for each player.
    (c) If the game is strictly determined what is the saddle point and the value of the game?

2. Reduce the matrix in Exercise 1 by domination.

3. $P = \begin{pmatrix} -4 & 15 \\ 10 & -2 \end{pmatrix}$

    is the payoff matrix for a game. What is the best pure strategy for each player? Is the game strictly determined?

4. Two neighboring discount department stores are trying to compete for sales of a weed-eater. Stores A and B both have the choice of giving a 10% discount or a 20% discount. The percentage of sales A will get given their choices is listed below in the payoff matrix. Find the best pure strategy for each store:

    $$
    \begin{array}{cc}
     & B \\
    \begin{array}{c} \\ A \end{array} &
    \begin{array}{cc}
    10\% & 20\% \\
    \begin{array}{c} 10\% \\ 20\% \end{array}
    \begin{pmatrix} .5 & .2 \\ .8 & .5 \end{pmatrix}
    \end{array}
    \end{array}
    $$

5. A game is defined by the matrix:

$$\begin{pmatrix} 2 & -3 & 2 \\ -4 & 2 & 3 \\ -4 & 1 & 1 \end{pmatrix}$$

Reduce the matrix by domination and find the best mixed strategy for the row player by graphing.

6. Find the value of the game whose payoff matrix is:

$$\begin{pmatrix} 1 & 0 \\ 0 & -1 \end{pmatrix}$$

7. Show that the best mixed strategy for both players is $(\frac{1}{3}, \frac{1}{3}, \frac{1}{3})$ in the game whose payoff matrix is:

$$\begin{pmatrix} 0 & 1 & -1 \\ -1 & 0 & 1 \\ 1 & -1 & 0 \end{pmatrix}$$

8. The row player uses the mixed strategy $(\frac{2}{5}, \frac{1}{5}, \frac{2}{5})$ and the column player uses the mixed strategy:

$$\begin{pmatrix} \frac{1}{2} \\ \frac{1}{4} \\ \frac{1}{4} \end{pmatrix} \quad \begin{pmatrix} 1 & -1 & 3 \\ -2 & 0 & 2 \\ -4 & 2 & -1 \end{pmatrix} = P$$

With these strategies, what is the expected value of the game?

9. The row player uses the mixed strategy $(\frac{3}{4}, \frac{1}{8}, \frac{1}{8})$ and the column player uses the mixed strategy:

$$\begin{pmatrix} \frac{3}{5} \\ \frac{1}{5} \\ \frac{1}{5} \end{pmatrix}$$

in the game in Exercise 8. What is the expected value now?

10. Two friends, Rebecca and Jennifer, go to dinner, and each tosses a coin to see who pays for dinner. If both throw heads or both throw tails, then Rebecca pays. If they throw differently, then Jennifer pays. Write the payoff matrix for this game. Find the optimal strategy for each.

11. Determine the best strategy for the column player in the game whose payoff matrix is:

$$\begin{pmatrix} 1 & 3 \\ 3 & 1 \\ 5 & 2 \end{pmatrix}$$

12. Two players play the Cat and Mouse game. Each independently chooses a mouse, a cat, a tiger, or an elephant, and simultaneously they reveal their choices. A cat chases a mouse for a score of 1, a tiger chases a cat for a score of 2, an elephant chases a tiger for a score of 3, and a mouse chases an elephant for a score of 4. Other combinations score 0.
(a) Write the payoff matrix for this game.
(b) Solve the Cat and Mouse game by finding the best strategy for each player.

13. One thousand lottery tickets are sold at $1 each. There are two prizes, one of $400 and one of $100. You are the row player and you have two choices, to buy a ticket or not to buy a ticket. Fate is the column player and there are three choices: you win $400, you win $100, you lose your $1.
(a) Write the payoff matrix for this game.
(b) Using probability theory, determine the strategy of the column player.

14. Determine your best strategy for the game in Exercise 14.

15. Colonel Peters has three divisions to defend two mountain passes. He will defend successfully against equal or smaller strength, but lose against superior forces. The enemy has two divisions. The battle is lost if either pass is captured. Neither side has advance informaton on the disposition of the opponent's divisions. Assume that the worth of overall victory is 1 and that that of defeat is −1. Write the payoff matrix for this game. (Hint: Denote the choices by (a, b) where a is the number deployed to pass 1 and b is the number deployed to pass 2. Colonel Peters has four choices and the enemy has three choices.)

16. Find the best strategy for Colonel Peters and the best strategy for the enemy.

17. In the Australian government, each of the six states gets one vote and the federal government gets three votes. Five votes are needed to pass legislation. Write a value function for this game of seven players, and find the core ($v = 0$ or 1 only).

18. In the Italian Chamber of Deputies, there are four parties, one with 225 votes, one with 198 votes, one with 73 votes, and one with 42 votes. There are 270 votes necessary to pass any legislation. Write a value function for this game and compute the core.

Answers to Odd-Numbered Exercises

Chapter 1

Exercises 1.1

1. Republicans = {Ford, Reagan}; Democrats = {Carter, Humphrey, Mondale}; Possible pairs in November election must include one Republican and one Democrat:

    {Ford, Carter},   {Ford, Humphrey},   {Ford, Mondale}
    {Reagan, Carter},   {Reagan, Humphrey},   {Reagan, Mondale}

    So there are *six* different pairs to question the voters about.

3. $A = \{a, b, c, d, e\}$ each member has one vote

    (a)   Simple majority required, total votes = 5; Simple majority requires 3 votes

    Winning coalitions:
    Minimal: $\{a, b, c\}$, $\{a, b, d\}$, $\{a, b, e\}$, $\{a, c, d\}$, $\{a, c, e\}$, $\{a, d, e\}$,
    $\{b, c, d\}$, $\{b, c, e\}$, $\{b, d, e\}$, $\{c, d, e\}$

    Nonminimal: $\{a, b, c, d\}$, $\{a, b, c, e\}$, $\{a, b, d, e\}$, $\{a, c, d, e\}$, $\{b, c, d, e\}$,
    $\{a, b, c, d, e\}$

    Blocking coalitions: None

    (b)   Two-thirds vote required = 4 votes

    Winning coalitions:
    Minimal: $\{a, b, c, d\}$, $\{a, b, c, e\}$, $\{a, b, d, e\}$, $\{a, c, d, e\}$, $\{b, c, d, e\}$

    Nonminimal: $\{a, b, c, d, e\}$

    Blocking coalitions: $\{a, b\}$, $\{a, c\}$, $\{a, d\}$, $\{a, e\}$, $\{b, c\}$, $\{b, d\}$, $\{b, e\}$,
    $\{c, d\}$, $\{c, e\}$, $\{d, e\}$, $\{a, b, c\}$, $\{a, b, d\}$, $\{a, b, e\}$, $\{a, c, d\}$, $\{a, c, e\}$,
    $\{a, d, e\}$, $\{b, c, d\}$, $\{b, c, e\}$, $\{b, d, e\}$, $\{c, d, e\}$

5. Minimal winning coalitions: must include all five permanent members and exactly four other members. Blocking coalitions: any set with at least one but less than all five of the permanent members; any set of seven or more of the other members.

7. Federal government: *two* votes. Let the set be represented by {g, s1, s2, s3, s4, s5, s6} where g represents the federal government and s1–s6 represent the six states. Needed to win = 5 votes. Federal government makes the decision in case of 4–4 tie.

    Minimal winning coalitions: {s1, s2, s3, s4, s5},   {s1, s2, s3, s4, s6},   {s1, s2, s3, s5, s6},
    {s1, s2, s4, s5, s6},   {s1, s3, s4, s5, s6},   {s2, s3, s4, s5, s6},   {g, s1, s2},   {g, s1, s3},
    {g, s1, s4},   {g, s1, s5},   {g, s1, s6},   {g, s2, s3},   {g, s2, s4},   {g, s2, s5},
    {g, s2, s6},   {g, s3, s4},   {g, s3, s5},   {g, s3, s6},   {g, s4, s5},   {g, s4, s6},
    {g, s5, s6}

Federal government: *three* votes. Needed to win: 5 votes

Minimal winning coalitions: same as above

9. $A = \{S1, S2, S3, R1, R2, R3\}$. Needed to win = at least two senators and at least two representatives

Minimal winning coalitions: $\{S1, S2, R1, R2\}$, $\{S1, S2, R1, R3\}$, $\{S1, S2, R2, R3\}$,
   $\{S1, S3, R1, R2\}$, $\{S1, S3, R1, R3\}$, $\{S1, S3, R2, R3\}$, $\{S2, S3, R1, R2\}$,
   $\{S2, S3, R1, R3\}$, $\{S2, S3, R2, R3\}$

Blocking coalitions: $\{S1, S2, R1\}$, $\{S1, S2, R2\}$, $\{S1, S2, R3\}$, $\{S1, S3, R1\}$,
   $\{S1, S3, R2\}$, $\{S1, S3, R3\}$, $\{S2, S3, R1\}$, $\{S2, S3, R2\}$, $\{S2, S3, R3\}$,
   $\{S1, R1, R2\}$, $\{S2, R1, R2\}$, $\{S3, R1, R2\}$, $\{S1, R1, R3\}$, $\{S2, R1, R3\}$,
   $\{S3, R1, R3\}$, $\{S1, R2, R3\}$, $\{S2, R2, R3\}$, $\{S3, R2, R3\}$

11. $A = \{a, b, c, d\}$. The power set of A has $2^4 = 16$ elements.

$P(A) = \{\emptyset,$ $\{a\},$ $\{b\},$ $\{c\},$ $\{d\},$ $\{a, b\},$ $\{a, c\},$ $\{a, d\},$ $\{b, c\},$
   $\{b, d\},$ $\{c, d\},$ $\{a, b, c\},$ $\{a, b, d\},$ $\{a, c, d\},$ $\{b, c, d\},$ $\{a, b, c, d\}\}$

13.   A situation such as a set $\{a, b, c, d\}$ with vote distribution 3, 1, 1, 1 with three votes needed to win could produce $\{a\}$ and $\{b, c, d\}$, both winning coalitions.

15.   It is not possible to determine the number needed to win in Exercise 8. Each combination of one member from $\{a, b\}$ and one member from $\{x, y\}$ must be a winning coalition. However, if each single member has more than half the number of votes needed to win then $\{a, b\}$, for example, would be a winning coalition.

Exercises 1.2

1. $F =$ freshmen
   $B =$ business majors

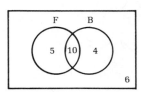

6 students are nonfreshmen and nonbusiness majors $= (F \cup B)'$

25 students $-$ 15 freshmen $=$ 10 nonfreshmen F'

25 students $-$ 14 business majors $=$ 11 nonbusiness majors B'

11 nonbusiness majors $-$ 6 nonfreshmen, nonbusiness majors $=$ 5 freshmen nonbusiness majors $F - B$

10 nonfreshmen $-$ 6 nonfreshmen, nonbusiness majors $=$ 4 nonfreshmen business majors $B - F$

14 business majors $-$ 4 nonfreshmen, business majors $=$ 10 freshmen business majors $F \cap B$

There are 10 freshmen business majors.

3. A has 16 elements
   B has 10 elements
   $A \cup B$ has 20 elements

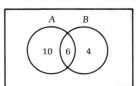

Since $A \cup B$ has 20 elements and A has 16 elements then B must have 4 elements that are not in A. $B - A$ has 4 elements. (Or $A \cup B$ has 20 elements and B has 10 elements so A must have 10 elements that are not in B. $A - B$ has 10 elements.) B has 10 elements and $B - A$ has 4 elements so $A \cap B$ must have 6 elements. (Or A has 16 elements and $A - B$ has 10 elements so $A \cap B$ must have 6 elements.)

5. Survey of 100 people in Hanover:

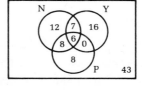

6 read all three magazines	
14 read *Newsweek* and *People*	$14 - 6 = 8$
6 read *Yankee* and *People*	$6 - 6 = 0$
13 read *Newsweek* and *Yankee*	$13 - 6 = 7$
22 read *People*	$22 - 14 = 8$
29 read *Yankee*	$29 - 13 = 16$
33 read *Newsweek*	$33 - 21 = 12$

Read some of these three magazines: $12 + 7 + 6 + 8 + 16 + 8 = 57$
Read none of these magazines: $100 - 57 = 43$

(a) How many read none of the three? $100 - 57 = 43$ (b) How many read only one of the magazines? $12 + 16 + 8 = 36$ (c) How many read *Newsweek* and *Yankee* but not *People*? 7

7. Survey of 1000 businesspeople:

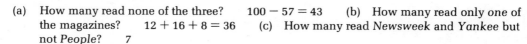

200 walked

300 took the subway

450 drove a car

50 drove a car and walked

10 took the subway and walked

60 drove a car and took the subway

10 drove a car, took the subway, and walked

$60 - 10 = 50$ drove a car and took the subway; did not walk

$10 - 10 = 0$ took the subway and walked; did not drive a car

$50 - 10 = 40$ drove a car and walked; did not take the subway

$450 - (50 + 10 + 40) = 350$ used car only

$300 - (50 + 10) = 240$ used subway only

$200 - (40 + 10) = 150$ walked only

(a) none of the three ways: $1000 - (350 + 50 + 10 + 40 + 240 + 150) = 1000 - 840 = 160$
(b) only drove a car: $450 - (50 + 10 + 40) = 350$
(c) only *one* of the three modes of transportation: $350 + 240 + 150 = 740$

9. 36 children surveyed:

   20 sixth graders

   18 sixth graders wanted to take a language

    8 seventh graders did not want to take a language

   Sixth graders and their complement; Those who want to take a language and their complement

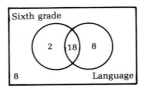

   How many seventh graders wanted to take a language?

   Total number of students − sixth graders = 36 − 20 = 16 seventh graders

   Seventh graders − seventh graders who did not want to take a language =
   16 − 8 = 8 seventh graders who did want to take a language

   How many sixth graders did not want to take a language?   20 − 18 = 2

Exercises 1.3

1. Three-base DNA chains that begin with A and end with G: {ATG, ACG, AAG, AGG}

3. Choose any ten of these fourteen possible code numbers:

   three element codes: 000   001   010   100   011   101   110   111

   two element codes: 00   01   10   11

   one element codes: 0   1

5. $S = \{1, 2, 3, 4, 5\}$ "There are at least two defective chips" $= \{2, 3, 4, 5\}$

7. (a) $S = \{c, o, m, p, u, t, e, r, n, s\}$ (b) Vowel chosen $= \{o, u, e\}$ (c) Letter preceding m in
   the alphabet chosen $= \{c, e\}$

9. (a) $S = \{AH, AD, AC, AS, JH, JD, JC, JS, QH, QD, QC, QS, KH, KD, KC, KS\}$
   where

                 A = ace, J = jack, Q = queen, K = king
               H = heart, D = diamond, C = club, S = spade

   (b) Red queen drawn $= \{QH, QD\}$ (c) Spade or diamond is drawn $= \{AS, JS, QS, KS, AD,$
   $JD, QD, KD\}$ (d) Any king or jack of clubs $= \{KH, KD, KC, KS, JC\}$

11. f = current owner-farmer. $100,000
    s = shopping center developer. $200,000
    h = housing developer. $300,000

    $A = \{f, s, h\}$

Coalitions	Monetary Gain	Winning if Monetary Gain > 0
{f, s, h}	$300,000	winning
{f, s}	$200,000	winning
{f, h}	$300,000	winning
{s, h}	$0	not winning
{f}	$100,000	winning
{s}	$0	not winning
{h}	$0	not winning

Exercises 1.4

1. Total votes cast $= 36$; Plurality winner: B_2 wins with 13 first place votes; Simple majority: No one received 19 or more first place votes needed for a simple majority winner; With run-off procedure; top two: B_2 and B_1

	B_1	B_1	B_2
	B_2	B_2	B_1
Votes cast	12	11	13

    B_1 wins with $12 + 11 = 23$ votes.

3. Total votes cast $= 33$; Plurality method: A_1 wins with 15 first place votes; Simple majority: No one received 17 first place votes needed for simple majority winner; With run-off procedure:

	A_1	A_1	A_3	A_3
	A_3	A_3	A_1	A_1
Votes cast	12	3	10	8

    A_3 wins with 18 votes (to 15 votes for A_1).

5. The two procedures could possibly result in different candidates being elected. For example:

	A	A	A	A	A	A		B	B	B	B	B	B
	B	B	C	C	D	D		A	A	C	C	D	D
	C	D	B	D	B	C		C	D	A	D	A	C
	D	C	D	B	C	B		D	C	D	A	C	A
Votes cast	5	5	6	6	5	6		6	6	6	6	6	6

	C	C	C	C	C	C		D	D	D	D	D	D
	A	A	B	B	D	D		A	A	B	B	C	C
	B	D	A	D	A	B		B	C	A	C	A	B
	D	B	D	A	B	A		C	B	C	A	B	A
Votes cast	5	5	5	5	5	5		1	1	1	1	5	5

    B wins Part (a) (58 for B to 55 for A). C wins Part (b) (59 for C to 54 for A).

7. A_2 over A_1 with 28
    A_3 over A_2 with 22
    A_3 over A_1 with 17
    A_3 would be declared the winner by the condorcet criterion.

9. Play-offs for sports events often use a method close to the one described but usually pair the team that came out first at the end of the season with the one that came out fourth, and pair the teams that came out second and third at the end of the season. The pairing described, however, does make it more likely that the candidates (teams) that came out first and second will both be in the final election.

Chapter 2

Exercises 2.1

1.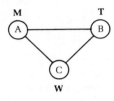

    or any other combination
    of different days

3.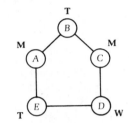

    3 days

5.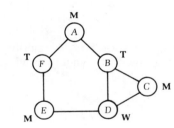

    3 days

7.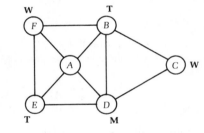

    3 days

9.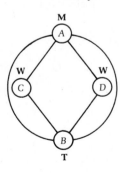

    3 days

11.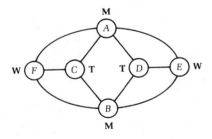

    3 days

13.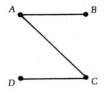

or other possible
variations such as:

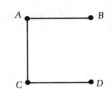

15.

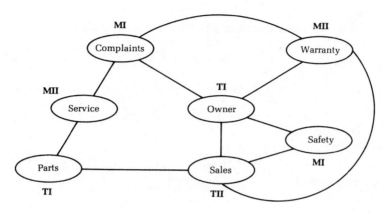

17. (a)

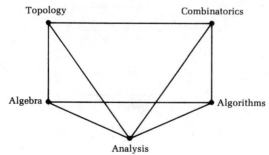

(b)

Time slot	Courses
I	Analysis
II	Algebra — Combinatorics
III	Topology — Algorithms

Exercises 2.2

1. Can be drawn as described:

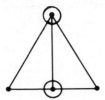 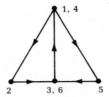

3. Cannot be drawn as described; 4 vertices with an odd number of edges meeting at the vertices:

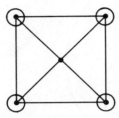

5. Can be drawn as described:

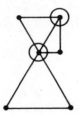 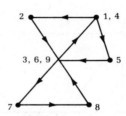

7.

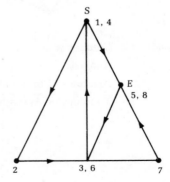

9.

11.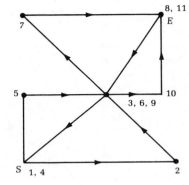

13. Walk described is possible:

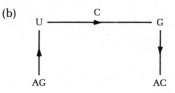

15. Walk described is not possible; *A* and *B* are both meeting places for an odd number of vertices.

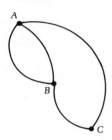

In Exercises 17 through 20 vertices represent rooms and outdoors and edges represent doorways.

17. Walk described is possible:

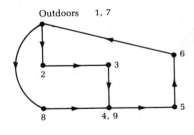

19. Walk described is possible:

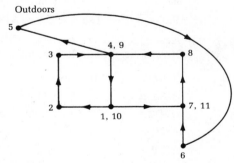

21. AGCUGAC   23. UGACGAUG or UGAUGACG? (last vertex is not labeled)

25. UGGCAUGC or UGCAUGGC

27. (a) *G fragments*   *U-C fragments*   (b)
      AC   C
      AG   AG-U
      U-C-G   G-AC

    (c) RNA chain: AGUCGAC

29.　(a)　*G fragments*　　*U-C fragments*　　(b)

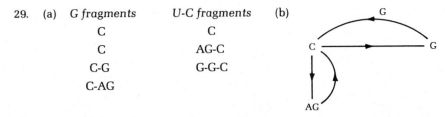

G fragments	*U-C fragments*
C	C
C	AG-C
C-G	G-G-C
C-AG	

(c)　need to find starting point for RNA chain—must start at C:
RNA chain: CAGCGGC or CGGCAGC

Exercises 2.3

1.　*Route*　　　　　*Cost*
　　ABCDA　　　$50 + 30 + 80 + 70 = 230$

3.　ADEBCA　　　$50 + 40 + 70 + 100 + 73 = 333$

5.　ABCEDA　　　$40 + 30 + 100 + 120 + 50 = 340$

7.　(a)　*Route*　　(b)　*Cost*
　　　ABCDA　　　　$60 + 70 + 50 + 55 = 235$
　　　ABDCA　　　　$60 + 100 + 50 + 50 = 260$
　　　ACBDA　　　　$50 + 70 + 100 + 55 = 275$
　　　ACDBA　　　　$50 + 50 + 100 + 60 = 260$
　　　ADBCA　　　　$55 + 100 + 70 + 50 = 275$
　　　ADCBA　　　　$55 + 50 + 70 + 60 = 235$

　　(c)　Paths of least cost: *ABCDA* or *ADCBA* cost $= 235$

　　(d)　Nearest neighbor rule gives: *ACDBA* cost, $50 + 50 + 100 + 60 = 260$.
　　　　Nearest neighbor rule does not give a path of least cost.

9.　(a)　*Route*　　(b)　*Cost*
　　　ABCDA　　　　$60 + 60 + 70 + 70 = 260$
　　　ABDCA　　　　$60 + 100 + 70 + 50 = 280$
　　　ACBDA　　　　$50 + 60 + 100 + 70 = 280$
　　　ACDBA　　　　$50 + 70 + 100 + 60 = 280$
　　　ADBCA　　　　$70 + 100 + 60 + 50 = 280$
　　　ADCBA　　　　$70 + 70 + 60 + 60 = 260$

　　(c)　Paths of least cost: *ABCDA*, *ADCBA* cost $= 260$

　　(d)　Nearest neighbor rule gives: *ACBDA* cost 280.
　　　　Nearest neighbor rule does not give a path of least cost.

11. (a) *Route* (b) *Cost*

   ABCDA $200 + 100 + 200 + 100 = 600$

   ABDCA $200 + 300 + 200 + 300 = 1000$

   ACBDA $300 + 100 + 300 + 100 = 800$

   ACDBA $300 + 200 + 300 + 200 = 1000$

   ADBCA $100 + 300 + 100 + 300 = 800$

   ADCBA $100 + 200 + 100 + 200 = 600$

   (c) Paths of least cost: *ABCDA* or *ADCBA* cost $= 600$

   (d) Nearest neighbor rule gives: *ADCBA* cost, $100 + 200 + 100 + 200 = 600$
   Nearest neighbor rule does give a path of least cost.

13. (a) *Route* (b) *Cost*

   ABCDEA $50 + 80 + 50 + 60 + 400 = 640$

   ABCEDA $50 + 80 + 150 + 60 + 100 = 440$

   ABDCEA $50 + 50 + 50 + 150 + 400 = 700$

   ABDECA $50 + 50 + 60 + 150 + 60 = 370$

   ABECDA $50 + 60 + 150 + 50 + 100 = 410$

   ABEDCA $50 + 60 + 60 + 50 + 60 = 280$

   ACBDEA $60 + 80 + 50 + 60 + 400 = 650$

   ACBEDA $60 + 80 + 60 + 60 + 100 = 360$

   ACDBEA $60 + 50 + 50 + 60 + 400 = 620$

   ACDEBA $60 + 50 + 60 + 60 + 50 = 280$

   ACEBDA $60 + 150 + 60 + 50 + 100 = 420$

   ACEDBA $60 + 150 + 60 + 50 + 50 = 370$

   ADBCEA $100 + 50 + 80 + 150 + 400 = 780$

   ADBECA $100 + 50 + 60 + 150 + 60 = 420$

   ADCBEA $100 + 50 + 80 + 60 + 400 = 690$

   ADCEBA $100 + 50 + 150 + 60 + 50 = 410$

   ADEBCA $100 + 60 + 60 + 80 + 60 = 360$

   ADECBA $100 + 60 + 150 + 80 + 50 = 440$

   AEBCDA $400 + 60 + 80 + 50 + 100 = 690$

   AEBDCA $400 + 60 + 50 + 50 + 60 = 620$

   AECBDA $400 + 150 + 80 + 50 + 100 = 780$

   AECDBA $400 + 150 + 50 + 50 + 50 = 700$

   AEDBCA $400 + 60 + 50 + 80 + 60 = 650$

   AEDCBA $400 + 60 + 50 + 80 + 50 = 640$

   (c) Paths of least cost: *ABEDCA* or *ACDEBA* cost $= 280$

   (d) Nearest neighbor rule gives: *ABDCEA* cost, $50 + 50 + 50 + 150 + 400 = 700$
   Nearest neighbor rule does not give a path of least cost.

15. *ABCD* cost $= 3 + 2 + 12 = 17$ or *ADBC* cost $= 7 + 8 + 2 = 17$

17. $ADCB$ cost $= 80 + 300 + 120 = 500$ **19.** $ABCD$ cost $= 20 + 30 + 50 = 100$

21. Hamiltonian path: passes through each vertex once and only once. For example, Amato to Nichols to Widmer to Mauro to Downing to Collins to Owen or Amato to Nichols to Owen to Collins to Downing to Mauro to Widmer

23.

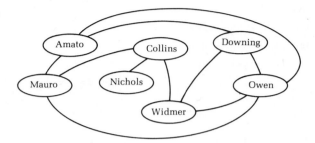

Hamiltonian path: for example,   Nichols to Collins to Mauro to Amato to Downing to Owen to Widmer (Note: Nichols must be on one end of the path and Collins must be next to Nichols.)

25.

Amato	Nichols	Widmer	Mauro	Downing	Collins	Owen
1	2	3	4	5	6	7

Table II

27.

Nichols	Collins	Mauro	Amato	Downing	Owen	Widmer
1	2	3	4	5	6	7

Table II

Exercises 2.4

1.

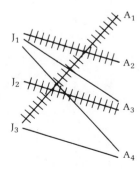

J_1: A_2
J_2: A_3
J_3: A_1

3.

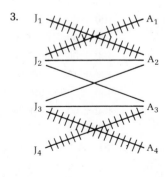

J_1: A_2
J_2: A_1
J_3: A_4
J_4: A_3

5.

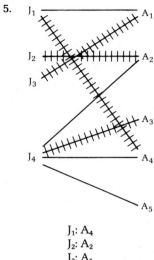

J_1: A_4
J_2: A_2
J_3: A_1
J_4: A_3 (or A_5)

7.

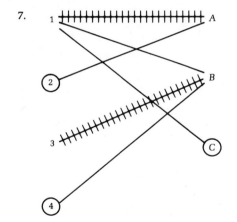

Alternating path:
C to 1 to A to 2

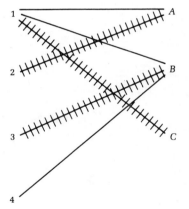

No alternating path;
largest number of edges
in any matching $= 3$.

9.

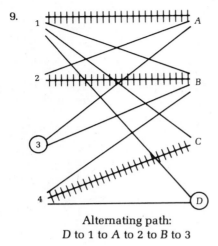

Alternating path:
D to 1 to A to 2 to B to 3

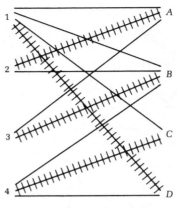

No alternating path;
largest number of edges
in any matching = 4.

11.

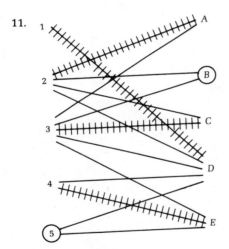

No alternating path; largest number of edges in any matching = 4.

13.

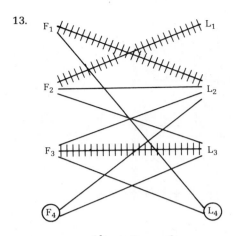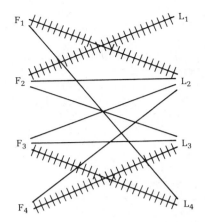

Alternating path:
F_4 to L_3 to F_3 to L_4

No alternating path

Store: F_1 in L_2, F_2 in L_1, F_3 in L_4, F_4 in L_3

15. (Edge = not on the committee)

Committees   *Reviewers*

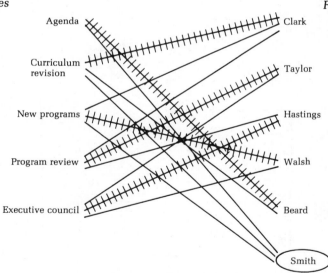

No alternating path; largest number of edges in any matching = 5.

Committee	Reviewer
Agenda	Beard
Curriculum revision	Clark
New programs	Walsh
Program review	Taylor
Executive council	Hastings

Exercises 2.5

1. 6

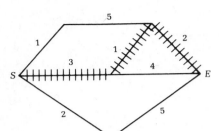

3. 7

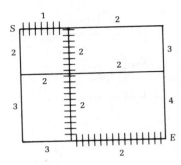

5. 9

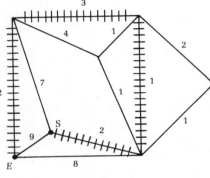

7.

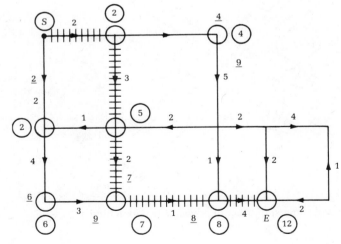

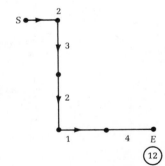

9.

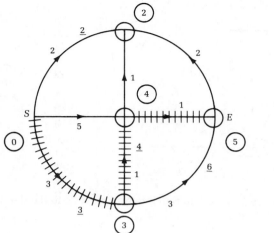

11.

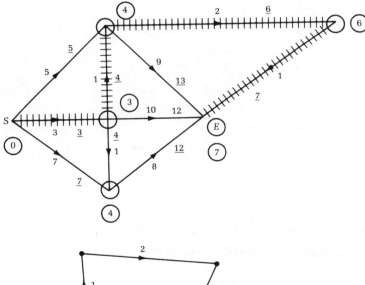

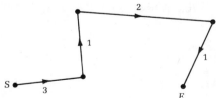

13.

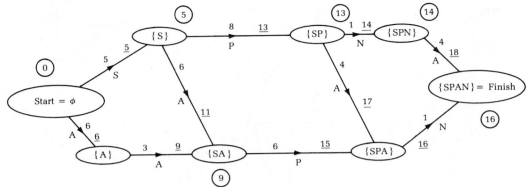

Order of steps that minimizes production time: A to S to P to N (Assemble to Sand to Protective coating to Name plate); Time = 16 minutes

Chapter 3

Exercises 3.1

1. (a)   •
        a

   (b)   •————•
        a b

   (c)

3. A disconnected graph such that $e = n - 1$

   For example:
   $n = 4$
   $e = 3$

   or
   $n = 6$
   $e = 5$

5. A tree with $n = 100$ vertices has $e = n - 1 = 100 - 1 = 99$ edges.

7. (a)   Not a tree because 1-2-3-5-1 is a circuit   (b)   A tree   (c)   Not a tree because it is not connected

9. An example of a forest:

Exercises 3.2

1. Yes, the tree shown in Practice Example 3.1 is a binary tree.

3. Yes, the tree is a binary tree.   5. $2^{5+1} - 1 = 2^6 - 1 = 64 - 1 = 63$ vertices

7. $S = \{324, 478, 213, 987, 387, 187, 921\}$
    187, 213, 324, 387, 478, 921, 987
      1   2   3   4   5   6   7

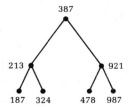

9. Insert the file number 98:

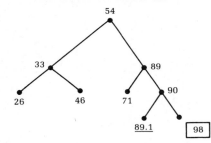

11. $S = \{8, 9, 2, 4, 27, 41, 23, 46, 32, 92, 67, 88, 34\}$

  2, 4, 8, 9, 23, 27, 32, 34, 41, 46, 67, 88, 92
  1   2   3   4   5   6   7   8   9   10   11   12   13

15 is closest.

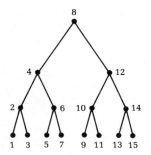 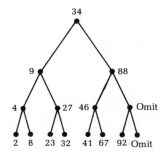 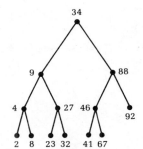

Exercises 3.3

1. Bridge: $\{d, e\}$

3. No bridges

5. For example:

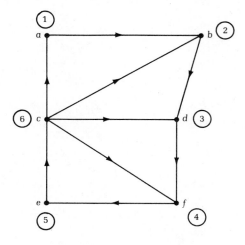

7. For example:

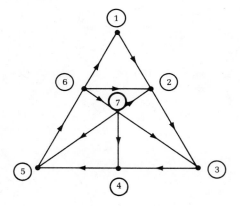

9. For example:

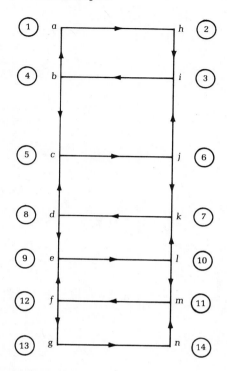

Exercises 3.4

1.

$\{a, e\}$	$\{a, d\}$	$\{e, d\}$	$\{e, b\}$	$\{a, b\}$	$\{e, c\}$	$\{a, c\}$	$\{b, c\}$	$\{d, b\}$	$\{d, c\}$
5	7	7	8	10	10	11	12	15	20

$\{a, e\}$ 5
$\{a, d\}$ 7
$\{e, b\}$ 8
$\{e, c\}$ $\underline{10}$
Weight =   30

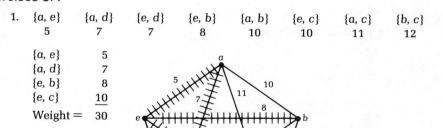

3.

{a, b}	{a, j}	{b, i}	{j, i}	{b, c}	{i, h}	{c, h}	{c, d}	{d, g}	{h, g}
7	7	8	8	8	9	9	9	10	10

{d, e}	{g, f}	{e, f}
10	11	11

{a, b}	7
{a, j}	7
{b, i}	8
{b, c}	8
{i, h}	9
{c, d}	9
{d, g}	10
{d, e}	10
{g, f}	11
Weight =	69

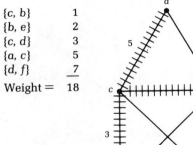

5.

{c, b}	{b, e}	{c, d}	{b, d}	{c, e}	{a, c}	{a, b}	{d, f}	{e, f}	{d, e}
1	2	3	3	4	5	6	7	8	9

{c, b}	1
{b, e}	2
{c, d}	3
{a, c}	5
{d, f}	7
Weight =	18

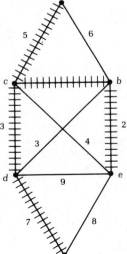

7.

{B, E}	{E, D}	{A, B}	{A, D}	{A, E}	{B, C}	{E, C}	{D, C}
1	1	2	2	2	2	2	2

{B, E}	1
{E, D}	1
{A, B}	2
{B, C}	2
Weight =	6

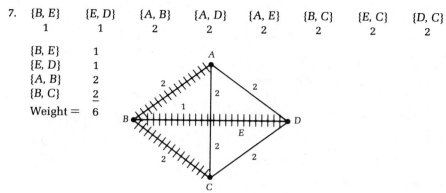

9.

{F, G}	{G, H}	{H, I}	{A, B}	{B, C}	{D, E}	{E, F}	{A, I}	{A, C}	{A, H}
90	90	90	100	100	100	100	150	200	200

{C, D}	{E, H}	{D, F}	{D, H}	{B, E}	{B, G}
200	200	300	300	400	400

{F, G}	90
{G, H}	90
{H, I}	90
{A, B}	100
{B, C}	100
{D, E}	100
{E, F}	100
{A, I}	150
Cost =	820

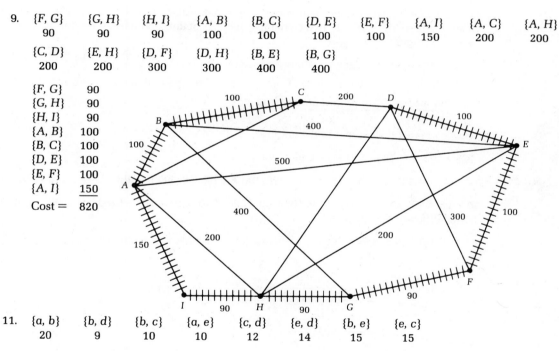

11.

{a, b}	{b, d}	{b, c}	{a, e}	{c, d}	{e, d}	{b, e}	{e, c}
20	9	10	10	12	14	15	15

{a, b}	20
{b, d}	9
{b, c}	10
{a, e}	10
Weight =	49

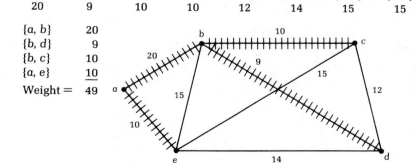

Chapter 4

Exercises 4.1

1. | choices for governor | choices for lt. governor | choices for state treasurer |
    |---|---|---|
    | 5 | × 6 | × 3 | = 90

    90 slates of endorsed candidates are possible.

3. $2 \times 2 \times 2 \times 3 \times 3 = 72$ ways to fill out the answer sheet

5. $7 \times 6 \times 5 = 210$ different messages are possible

7. $2^{10} = 1024$ ways to fill out the answer sheet

9. There are $2^5 = 32$ five-element sequences of dots and dashes. Ten of these are used to encode the ten digits so $32 - 10 = 22$ five-element sequences of dots and dashes are *not* used to encode the digits.

11. (a) $3 \times 2 = 6$ ways to get from Home to Granny's

    (b) $3 \times 2 \times 2 \times 3 = 36$ ways to get from Home to Granny's and back Home

13. | ways and means | appropriations | agenda | education | finance |
    |---|---|---|---|---|
    | 3 | × 2 | × 1 | × 2 | × 2 | =

    24 ways to label the vertices in the graph

15. $3 \times 3 \times 2 \times 1 = 18$ ways to wash the floor

17. $100 + 435 = 535$ possible delegates if OR; $100 \times 435 = 43,500$ possible delegates if AND

19. $(26 \times 26 \times 10) + (26 \times 26 \times 10 \times 10) + (26 \times 26 \times 10 \times 10 \times 10) = 6760 + 67,600 + 676,000 = 750,360$ different license plates

21. $(3 \times 4 \times 10) + (4 \times 3) + (4 \times 10) + 4 = 120 + 12 + 40 + 4 = 176$ different meals are possible

Exercises 4.2

1.

3.

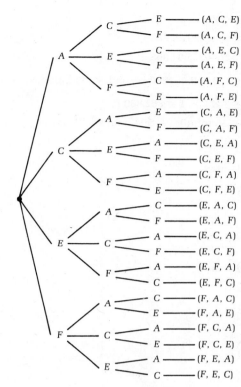

5.

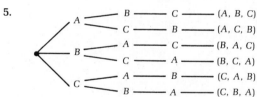

7. $P(3, 2) = 3 \times 2 = 6$ 9. $P(4, 3) = 4 \times 3 \times 2 = 24$

11. $P(4, 4) = 4! = 4 \times 3 \times 2 \times 1 = 24$

13. $P(7, 2) = 7 \times 6 = 42$

15. $P(10, 2) = 10 \times 9 = 90$

17. $P(9, 3) = 9 \times 8 \times 7 = 504$

19. $N = 6$ $k = 6$
$P(6, 6) = 6! = 6 \times 5 \times 4 \times 3 \times 2 \times 1 = 720$

21. (a) $N = 7$ $k = 3$ $P(7, 3) = 7 \times 6 \times 5 = 210$

 (b) $N = 12$ $k = 3$ $P(12, 3) = 12 \times 11 \times 10 = 1320$

 (c) $N = N$ $k = 3$ $P(N, 3) = N \times (N - 1) \times (N - 2)$

23. $N = 5$ $k = 3$ $P(5, 3) = 5 \times 4 \times 3 = 60$

25. $N = 7$ $k = 3$ $P(7, 3) = 7 \times 6 \times 5 = 210$

27. (a) $P(12, 7) = 12 \times 11 \times 10 \times 9 \times 8 \times 7 \times 6 = 3,991,680$

 (b) $12 \times 12 \times 12 \times 12 \times 12 \times 12 \times 12 = 12^7 = 35,831,808$

29. (a) $P(7, 4) = 7 \times 6 \times 5 \times 4 = 840$ (b) $840 \times 2 = 1680$ seconds $= 28$ minutes

31. (a) $P(9, 9) = 9! = 9 \times 8 \times 7 \times 6 \times 5 \times 4 \times 3 \times 2 \times 1 = 362,880$

 (b) $362,880 \times 5 = 1,814,400$ seconds $= 30,240$ minutes $= 504$ hours $= 21$ days

Exercises 4.3

1. A Ⓑ C B Ⓐ C C Ⓐ B

 A Ⓒ B B C Ⓐ C B Ⓐ

 $SS(A) = 4 \div 6 = 2/3$
 $SS(B) = SS(C) = 1/6$

3. Ⓐ B C B Ⓐ C C Ⓐ B

 Ⓐ C B B C Ⓐ C B Ⓐ

 $SS(A) = 6 \div 6 = 1$
 $SS(B) = SS(C) = 0$

5. A Ⓑ C B Ⓐ C C Ⓐ B

 A Ⓒ B B C Ⓐ C B Ⓐ

 $SS(A) = 4 \div 6 = 2/3$
 $SS(B) = SS(C) = 1/6$

7. A Ⓑ C B Ⓐ C C Ⓐ B

 A Ⓒ B B Ⓒ A C Ⓑ A

 $SS(A) = 2 \div 6 = 1/3$
 $SS(B) = 2 \div 6 = 1/3$
 $SS(C) = 2 \div 6 = 1/3$

9. A Ⓑ C D B Ⓐ C D C Ⓐ B D D A Ⓑ C

 A Ⓑ C D B Ⓐ D C C Ⓐ D B D A Ⓒ B

 A Ⓒ B D B Ⓒ A D C Ⓑ A D D B Ⓐ C

 A Ⓒ D B B Ⓒ D A C Ⓑ D A D B Ⓒ A

 A D Ⓑ C B D Ⓐ C C D Ⓐ B D C Ⓐ B

 A D Ⓒ B B D Ⓒ A C D Ⓑ A D C Ⓑ A

 $SS(A) = 8 \div 24 = 1/3$
 $SS(B) = 8 \div 24 = 1/3$
 $SS(C) = 8 \div 24 = 1/3$
 $SS(D) = 0$

11. A (B) C D   B (A) C D   C (A) B D   D A (B) C
    A (B) D C   B (A) D C   C (A) D B   D A (C) B
    A (C) D B   B C (A) D   C B (A) D   D B (A) C
    A (C) D B   B C (D) A   C B (D) A   D B (C) A
    A D (B) C   B D (A) C   C D (A) B   D C (A) B
    A D (C) B   B D (C) A   C D (B) A   D C (B) A

SS(A) = 10 ÷ 24 = 5/12
SS(B) = 6 ÷ 24 = 1/4
SS(C) = 6 ÷ 24 = 1/4
SS(D) = 2 ÷ 24 = 1/12

13. A (B) C D   B (A) C D   C (A) B D   D A (B) C
    A (B) D C   B (A) D C   C (A) D B   D A (C) B
    A (C) B D   B C (A) D   C B (A) D   D B (A) C
    A (C) D B   B C (D) A   C B (D) A   D B (C) A
    A D (B) C   B D (A) C   C D (A) B   D C (A) B
    A D (C) B   B D (C) A   C D (B) A   D C (B) A

SS(A) = 10 ÷ 24 = 5/12
SS(B) = 6 ÷ 24 = 1/4
SS(C) = 6 ÷ 24 = 1/4
SS(D) = 2 ÷ 24 = 1/12

15. A (B) C D   B (A) C D   C (A) B D   D A (B) C
    A (B) D C   B (A) D C   C (A) D B   D A (C) B
    A (C) B D   B (C) A D   C (B) A D   D B (A) C
    A (C) D B   B (C) D A   C (B) D A   D B (C) A
    A D (B) C   B D (A) C   C D (A) B   D C (A) B
    A D (C) B   B D (C) A   C D (B) A   D C (B) A

SS(A) = 8 ÷ 24 = 1/3
SS(B) = 8 ÷ 24 = 1/3
SS(C) = 8 ÷ 24 = 1/3
SS(D) = 0

17. $5! = 120$ permutations
     A is pivotal when A is in the third or fourth place.
     A is in the third place in $4 \times 3 \times 2 \times 1 = 24$ permutations.
     A is in the fourth place in $4 \times 3 \times 2 \times 1 = 24$ permutations.
     So A is pivotal in $24 + 24 = 48$ permutations.

$$SS(A) = 48 \div 120 = \tfrac{2}{5}$$
$$1 - \tfrac{2}{5} = \tfrac{3}{5}$$
$$SS(B) = SS(C) = SS(D) = SS(E)$$
$$4 \times SS(B) = \tfrac{3}{5} \text{ so } SS(B) = \left(\tfrac{3}{5}\right)\left(\tfrac{1}{4}\right) = \tfrac{3}{20}$$
$$SS(B) = SS(C) = SS(D) = SS(E) = \tfrac{3}{20}$$

19. $5! = 120$ permutations
     A is pivotal when A is in the second, third, or fourth place.
     A is in the second place in $4 \times 3 \times 2 \times 1 = 24$ permutations.
     A is in the third place in $4 \times 3 \times 2 \times 1 = 24$ permutations.
     A is in the fourth place in $4 \times 3 \times 2 \times 1 = 24$ permutations.
     So A is pivotal in $24 + 24 + 24 = 3 \times 24 = 72$ permutations.

$$SS(A) = 72 \div 120 = \tfrac{3}{5}$$
$$1 - \tfrac{3}{5} = \tfrac{2}{5}$$
$$SS(B) = SS(C) = SS(D) = SS(E)$$
$$4 \times SS(B) = \tfrac{2}{5} \text{ so } SS(B) = \left(\tfrac{2}{5}\right)\left(\tfrac{1}{4}\right) = \tfrac{1}{10}$$
$$SS(B) = SS(C) = SS(D) = SS(E) = \tfrac{1}{10}$$

21. $6! = 720$ permutations
     A is pivotal when A occurs in the third or fourth place.
     Each of these can happen in $5 \times 4 \times 3 \times 2 \times 1 = 120$ ways.
     So A is pivotal in $2 \times 120 = 240$ permutations.

$$SS(A) = 240 \div 720 = \tfrac{1}{3}$$
$$1 - \tfrac{1}{3} = \tfrac{2}{3}$$
$$SS(B) = SS(C) = SS(D) = SS(E) = SS(F)$$
$$5 \times SS(B) = \tfrac{2}{3} \text{ so } SS(B) = \left(\tfrac{2}{3}\right)\left(\tfrac{1}{5}\right) = \tfrac{2}{15}$$
$$SS(B) = SS(C) = SS(D) = SS(E) = SS(F) = \tfrac{2}{15}$$

Exercises 4.4

1. $C(3, 2) = (3 \times 2) \div (2 \times 1) = 3$ 3. $C(5, 3) = (5 \times 4 \times 3) \div (3 \times 2 \times 1) = 10$

5. $C(7, 3) = (7 \times 6 \times 5) \div (3 \times 2 \times 1) = 35$ 7. $C(10, 2) = (10 \times 9) \div (2 \times 1) = 45$

9. $C(8, 3) = (8 \times 7 \times 6) \div (3 \times 2 \times 1) = 56$ 11. $C(9, 4) = (9 \times 8 \times 7 \times 6) \div (4 \times 3 \times 2 \times 1) = 126$

13. (a) $\{A\}, \{B\}, \{C\}$ (b) $\{A, B\}, \quad \{A, C\}, \quad \{B, C\}$ (c) $\{A, B, C\}$

15. (a) $C(5, 1) = 5 \div 1 = 5$

    (b) $C(5, 2) = (5 \times 4) \div (2 \times 1) = 10$

    (c) $C(5, 3) = (5 \times 4 \times 3) \div (3 \times 2 \times 1) = 10$

    (d) $C(5, 4) = (5 \times 4 \times 3 \times 2) \div (4 \times 3 \times 2 \times 1) = 5$

    (e) $C(5, 5) = (5 \times 4 \times 3 \times 2 \times 1) \div (5 \times 4 \times 3 \times 2 \times 1) = 1$

17. $C(6, 3) = (6 \times 5 \times 4) \div (3 \times 2 \times 1) = 20$ committees are possible

19. (a) $C(7, 3) = (7 \times 6 \times 5) \div (3 \times 2 \times 1) = 35$ groups

    (b) $C(12, 3) = (12 \times 11 \times 10) \div (3 \times 2 \times 1) = 220$ groups

    (c) $C(N, 3)$ groups

21. (a) $C(10, 2) = (10 \times 9) \div (2 \times 1) = 45$ different sets of two prize-winning tickets are possible

    (b) $C(50, 2) = (50 \times 49) \div (2 \times 1) = 1225$ different sets of two prize-winning tickets are possible

    (c) $C(100, 2) = (100 \times 99) \div (2 \times 1) = 4950$ different sets of two prize-winning tickets are possible

23. (a) $C(10, 4) = (10 \times 9 \times 8 \times 7) \div (4 \times 3 \times 2 \times 1) = 210$ different dinner specials are possible

    (b) $C(30, 4) = (30 \times 29 \times 28 \times 27) \div (4 \times 3 \times 2 \times 1) = 27,405$ different dinner specials are possible

    (c) $C(50, 4) = (50 \times 49 \times 48 \times 47) \div (4 \times 3 \times 2 \times 1) = 230,300$ different dinner specials are possible

25. $C(10, 5) = (10 \times 9 \times 8 \times 7 \times 6) \div (5 \times 4 \times 3 \times 2 \times 1) = 252$ groups of five students each if being in group A is not the same as being in group B (perhaps by being assigned to different rooms where what room a group is assigned matters)

    If being in group A is the same as being in group B (if room assignments do not matter) then there are $252 \div 2 = 126$ groups of 5 students

27. $C(10, 2) \times C(22, 3) = 45 \times 1540 = 69,300$ different committees are possible

29. $C(6, 3) \times C(5, 1) \times C(3, 1) = 20 \times 5 \times 3 = 300$ different teams are possible

31. $C(10, 4) \times C(6, 3) \times C(3, 3) = 210 \times 20 \times 1 = 4200$ different ways to give out the toys

33. $C(10, 7) = C(10, 3) = 120$ ways to choose the three incorrect questions
    There are $2^3 = 8$ ways to answer three questions incorrectly.
    There are $120 \times 8 = 960$ ways to get 7 questions correct.

35. $C(25, 4) = 12,650$ total number of samples of 4 apples from 25

    (a) $C(20, 4) = 4845$ samples with only good apples

    (b) $C(5, 1) \times C(20, 3) = 5 \times 1140 = 5700$ samples with 3 good apples

    (c) $C(5, 4) + [C(5, 3) \times C(20, 1)] + [C(5, 2) \times C(20, 2)] + [C(5, 1) \times C(20, 3)] =$
    $5 + [10 \times 20] + [10 \times 190] + [5 \times 1140] = 5 + 200 + 1900 + 5700 = 7805$ samples with one or more rotten apples

    or total number of samples − samples with only good apples = $12,650 - 4845 = 7805$ samples with one or more rotten apples

37. (a) $2^{10} = 1024$ ways to fill out the answer sheet (two possible answers to each of 10 questions)   (b) $C(10, 8) + C(10, 9) + C(10, 10) = C(10, 2) + C(10, 1) + C(10, 0) = 45 + 10 + 1 = 56$ ways to fill out the answer sheet

Exercises 4.5

1. (a) $P(E) = \# (E) \div \# (S) = \frac{3}{5}$ (b) $P(F) = \# (F) \div \# (S) = \frac{3}{5}$ (c) $P(E') = \# (E') \div \# (S) = \frac{2}{5}$
    (d) $P(F') = \# (F') \div \# (S) = \frac{2}{5}$ (e) $P(E \cup F) = \# (E \cup F) \div \# (S) = 5 \div 5 = 1$
    (f) $P(E \cap F) = \# (E \cap F) \div \# (S) = \frac{1}{5}$

3. $S = \{1, 2, 3, 4, 5, 6, 7, 8, 9, 10, 11, 12\}$
    (a) $E = \{10\}$ $P(E) = \frac{1}{12}$ (b) $E = \{7\}$ $P(E) = \frac{1}{12}$ (c) $E = \{2, 4, 6, 8, 10, 12\}$
    $P(E) = 6 \div 12 = \frac{1}{2}$ (d) $E = \{1, 3, 5, 7, 9, 11\}$ $P(E) = 6 \div 12 = \frac{1}{2}$ (e) $E = \{4, 5, 6, 7, 8, 9,$
    $10, 11, 12\}$ $P(E) = 9 \div 12 = \frac{3}{4}$ (f) $E = \{9, 10, 11, 12\}$ $P(E) = 4 \div 12 = \frac{1}{3}$
    (g) $E = \{1, 2, 3, 4, 5\}$ $P(E) = \frac{5}{12}$

5. (a) $S = \{(a, b), (a, 1), (a, 2), (a, 3), (b, 1), (b, 2), (b, 3), (1, 2), (1, 3), (2, 3)\}$
    $\# (S) = C(5, 2) = 10$

    (b) $E = \{(a, b)\}$ $\# (E) = C(2, 2) = 1$
    $P(E) = \frac{1}{10}$

    (c) $F = \{(1, 2), (1, 3), (2, 3)\}$ $\#(F) = C(3, 2) = 3$
    $P(F) = \frac{3}{10}$

    (d) $G = \{(a, 1), (a, 2), (a, 3), (b, 1), (b, 2), (b, 3)\}$
    $\# (G) = C(2, 1) \times C(3, 1) = 2 \times 3 = 6$
    $P(G) = 6 \div 10 = \frac{3}{5}$

    (e) $H = \{(a, b), (a, 1), (a, 2), (a, 3), (b, 1), (b, 2), (b, 3)\}$
    $\# (H) = $ number of pairs with two letters $+$ number of pairs with only one letter
    $= C(2, 2) + [C(2, 1) \times C(3, 1)]$
    $= 1 + [2 \times 3] = 1 + 6 = 7$
    $P(H) = \frac{7}{10}$

7. $\# (S) = C(7, 2) = 21$
    (a) $\# (E) = C(2, 2) = 1$ (b) $P(E) = 1 - (1 \div 21) = 20 \div 21 = .95$
    $P(E) = 1 \div 21 = .05$

    (c) $\# (E) = $ number of pairs with the vacation to Hawaii
    $= C(1, 1) \times C(6, 1)$
    $= 1 \times 6 = 6$
    $P(E) = 6 \div 21 = .29$

9. (a) $\# (S) = C(52, 2) = 1326$ (b) $\# (S) = C(11, 2) = 55$
    $\# (E) = [C(4, 1) \times C(16, 1)]/2 = 32$ $\# (E) = [C(2, 1) \times C(5, 1)]/2 = (2 \times 5)/2 = 5$
    $P(E) = 32 \div 1326 = 16 \div 663 = .024$ $P(E) = 5 \div 55 = .091$

    (c) $\# (S) = 9$
    $\# (E) = 5$
    $P(E) = \frac{5}{9}$

11. $\#(S) = 7^4 = 2401$

 (a) $E =$ the set of blanks in which no floor is listed twice (b) $1 - .35 = .65$
 $\#(E) = 7 \times 6 \times 5 \times 4 = 840$
 $P(E) = 840 \div 2401 = .35$

13. $\#(S) =$ number of ways to fill out the answer sheet
 $= 2^{10} = 1024$
 $\#(E) =$ number of ways to get 7 or more correct
 $= C(10, 7) + C(10, 8) + C(10, 9) + C(10, 10)$
 $= 120 + 45 + 10 + 1$
 $= 176$
 $P(E) = 176 \div 1024 = 11 \div 64 = .172$

15. $\#(S) =$ number of ways to select 4 from 20
 $= C(20, 4)$
 $= 4845$

 (a) $\#(E) = C(15, 4) = 1365$ (b) $\#(E) = 4845 - 1365 = 3480$
 $P(E) = 1365 \div 4845 = .282$ $P(E) = 3480 \div 4845 = .718$
 or $1 - .282 = .718$

17. $C(50, 3) = 19,600$ different ways to choose 3 winning tickets

 (a) $1 - [C(47, 1) \div C(50, 1)] = 1 - (47 \div 50) = 1 - .94 = .06$

 (b) $1 - [C(47, 4) \div C(50, 4)] = 1 - (178,365 \div 230,300) = 1 - .774 = .226$

 (c) $1 - [C(47, 10) \div C(50, 10)] = 1 - [(5.178 \times 10^9) \div (1.027 \times 10^{10})] = 1 - .504 = .496$

Chapter 5

Exercises 5.1

1. $2/5 + 1/2 + 1/10 = 2/10 + 5/10 + 1/10 = 8/10 = 1$; Not a probability space. 3. All $\geqslant 0$, sum $= 1$; A probability space. 5. All $\geqslant 0$, sum $= 1$; A probability space.

7. $P(\{a, b\}) = P(\{a\}) + P(\{b\})$
 $1/4 \quad\quad = 1/12 + P(\{b\})$
 $P(\{b\}) \quad = 1/4 - 1/12 = 3/12 - 1/12 = 2/12 = 1/6$
 $P(\{b\}) \quad = 1/6$

 $P(\{a\}) + P(\{b\}) + P(\{c\}) + P(\{d\}) = 1$
 $1/12 + 1/6 + 5/12 + P(\{d\}) = 1$
 $P(\{d\}) = 1 - (1/12 + 1/6 + 5/12) = 1 - (1/12 + 2/12 + 5/12)$
 $\quad\quad = 1 - 8/12 = 4/12 = 1/3$
 $P(\{d\}) = 1/3$

9.

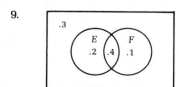

$P(F) = .5$
$P(E \cap F) = .4$

11.

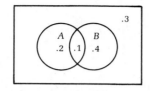

$P(A) = .3$
$P(B) = .5$

13. $P(E \cup F) = P(E) + P(F) - P(E \cap F)$
    $.8 \qquad = .5 + .5 - P(E \cap F)$
    $P(E \cup F) = 1 - .8 = .2$

15. $P(A \cup V) = P(A) + P(V) - P(A \cap V)$
    $0 \qquad = .5 + P(V) - .2$
    $P(V) \quad = .9 - .5 + .2$
    $P(V) \quad = .6$

17. $P(\text{spinner stops when pointing to a region numbered 3 or 4}) = \frac{3}{8}$

19. (a) $P(\text{bill is less than \$30}) = .01 + .18 + .2 + .2 = .59;$ (b) $P(\text{bill is \$30 or more}) = .30 + .03$
    $+ .03 + .05 + .03 = .41$ Or $1 - .59 = .41$

21. $P(\{G\}) \quad = 60 \div 85 = 12/17 \qquad P(\{Y\}) = 5 \div 85 = 1/17$
    $P(\{R\}) \quad = 20 \div 85 = 4/17$
    $P(\{G, Y\}) = P(\{G\}) + P(\{Y\}) = 12/17 + 1/17 = 13/17$

23. $F = \text{freshman} \qquad B = \text{business major}$

    $P(F) \qquad = .714$
    $P(B) \qquad = .857$
    $P(F \cup B) = 1 - .057 = .943$

    $P(F \cup B) = P(F) + P(B) - P(F \cap B)$
    $.943 \qquad = .714 + .857 - P(F \cap B)$
    $P(F \cap B) = .628$

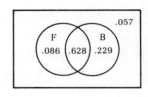

The probability that a person picked at random from the class is a freshman not majoring in business is .086.

25. $W = \text{women}$
    $R = \text{regular coffee}$
    Total number surveyed $= 50 + 35 = 85$

    33 favored decaffeinated (includes 27 women and 6 men)

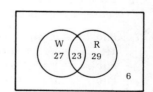

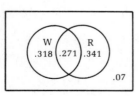

P(a person selected at random from the survey
favored regular coffee) $= .271 + .314 = .612$

or

total number surveyed − number favoring decaffeinated =
number favoring regular coffee
$85 − 33 = 52$ favored regular coffee

P(a person selected at random from the survey
favored regular coffee) $= 52/85 = .612$

27. (a) #S $= C(14, 5) = 2002$

     #E $=$ no. committees with either 3 men and 2 women or 2 men and 3 women

         $= C(8, 3) \times C(6, 2) + C(8,2) \times C(6, 3)$

         $= 56 \times 15 + 28 \times 20$

         $= 840 + 560$

         $= 1400$

     $P(E) = 1400 \div 2002 = 700 \div 1001 = .699$

  (b) $P(E) = 560 \div 1400 = 140 \div 350 = 14 \div 35 = .4$

Exercises 5.2

1. $P(E/F) = P(E \cap F) \div P(F) = .6 \div .8 = .75$

3. (a) P(the machine accepts a counterfeit bill) $= P(A/C) = P(A \cap C) \div P(C) = 2/200 \div 50/200 = 2 \div 50 = 1/25 = .04$ (b) P(a bill accepted by the machine is legal) $= P(L/A) = P(L \cap A) \div P(A) = 118/200 \div 120/200 = 118 \div 120 = .98$ (c) $P(A/L) = $ P(a legal bill is accepted by the machine) $= P(A \cap L) \div P(L) = 118/200 \div 150/200 = 118/150 = .787$ (d) $P(C/R) = $ P(a bill rejected by the machine is counterfeit) $= P(C \cap R) \div P(R) = 48/200 \div 80/200 = 48/80 = .6$

5. (a) $P(B) = 100 \div 200 = .5$ (b) $P(B/A) = P(B \cap A) \div P(A) = 48/200 \div 60/200 = 48 \div 60 = .8$
(c) Yes

7. If E and F are independent, $P(E \cap F) = P(E)P(F); P(E \cap F) = P(E)P(F) = (.6)(.8) = .48$

9. If E, F, and G are independent, $P(E \cap F \cap G) = P(E)P(F)P(G); P(E \cap F \cap G) = P(E)P(F)P(G) = (.8)(.5)(.6) = .24$

11. HA $=$ Home Alert system   HS $=$ Home Security system
One Home Security system: $P(HS) = .999$
Two Home Alert systems
Probability at least one of the two detects a burglar:

$$P(HA \cup HA) = P(HA) + P(HA) - P(HA \cap HA)$$
$$= .99 + .99 - P(HA) P(HA)$$
$$= .99 + .99 - P(.99)(.99)$$
$$= .99 + .99 - .9801$$
$$= .9999$$

So two Home Alert systems give greater protection against burglars than one Home Security system.

13. P(a defective part goes undetected through both machines) $= 1 - (.9)(.9) = 1 - .81 = .19$

15. $P(\text{burning out}) = .08$ $P(\text{not burning out}) = .92$

$P(\text{1 out of 1 burn out}) = C(1, 1)\,(.08)^1\,(.92)^0 = .08$
$P(\text{at least 1 of 1 does not burn out}) = 1 - .08 = .92$

$P(\text{2 out of 2 burn out}) = C(2, 2)\,(.08)^2\,(.92)^0 = .0064$
$P(\text{at least 1 of 2 does not burn out}) = 1 - .0064 = .9936$

$P(\text{3 out of 3 burn out}) = C(3, 3)\,(.08)^3\,(.92)^0 = .000512$
$P(\text{at least 1 of 3 does not burn out}) = 1 - .000512 = .999488$

$P(\text{4 out of 4 burn out}) = C(4, 4)\,(0, 8)^4\,(.92)^0 = .000041$
$P(\text{at least 1 of 4 does not burn out}) = 1 - .00041 = .999956$

So **4** light bulbs are needed.

17. $P(\text{a six}) = \frac{1}{6}$ $P(\text{not a six}) = \frac{5}{6}$

$P(\text{no six in 4 rolls of a die}) = C(4, 0)\left(\frac{1}{6}\right)^0\left(\frac{5}{6}\right)^4 = .4822531$

19. (a) $P(\text{no double 6 in 1 roll}) = C(1, 0)\left(\frac{1}{6}\right)^0\left(\frac{35}{36}\right)^1$

$P(\text{no double 6 in 10 rolls}) = C(10, 0)\left(\frac{1}{6}\right)^0\left(\frac{35}{36}\right)^{10}$

$P(\text{no double 6 in 20 rolls}) = C(20, 0)\left(\frac{1}{6}\right)^0\left(\frac{35}{36}\right)^{20}$

$P(\text{no double 6 in 30 rolls}) = C(30, 0)\left(\frac{1}{6}\right)^0\left(\frac{35}{36}\right)^{30}$

Number of rolls of a pair of dice	Probability you win	Probability you lose
1	.9722	.0278
10	.7545	.2455
20	.5693	.4307
30	.4295	.5705

(b) The smallest number of times the dice have to be rolled in order for the probability of your losing to be greater than the probability of your winning is between 20 and 30.

Number of rolls of a pair of dice	Probability you win	Probability you lose
21	.5534	.4466
22	.5381	.4619
23	.5231	.4769
24	.5086	.4914
25	.4945	.5055

The smallest number of times the dice have to be rolled for the probability of your losing to be greater than the probability of your winning is 25.

21. $P(S) = \frac{3}{4}$ $P(F) = \frac{1}{4}$

(a) P(exactly three successes in five trials) $= C(5, 3) (.75)^3 (.25)^2 = (10) (.421875) (.0625) = .2637$

(b) P(more than three successes in five trials) $= P$(4 or 5 successes in five trials) $= C(5, 4) (.75)^4 (.25)^1$ $+ C(5, 5) (.75)^5 (.25)^0 = (5) (.3164063) (.25) + (.2373047) = .3955078 + .2373047 = .6328125$
P(more than three successes in five trials) $= .6328$

(c) P(more than one success in five trials) $= 1 - P$(no successes or one success in five trials) $= 1 - (C(5, 0) (.75)^0 (.25)^5 + C(5, 1) (.75)^1 (.25)^4) = 1 - (.0009766 + .0146484) = 1 - .015625 = .9844$
or P(2 or 3 or 4 or 5 successes in five trials) $= C(5, 2) (.75)^2 (.25)^3 + C(5, 3) (.75)^3 (.25)^2 + C(5, 4)$ $(.75)^4 (.25)^1 + C(5, 5) (.75)^5 (.25)^0 = .0878906 + .2637 + .3955 + .2373 = .9844$

23. P(defective) $= .01$ P(not defective) $= .99$

(a) P(fewer than three defective chips out of 25) $= P$(none or 1 or 2 defective chips out of 25) $=$ $C(25, 0) (.01)^0 (.99)^{25} + C(25, 1) (.01)^1 (.99)^{24} + C(25, 2) (.01)^2 (.99)^{23} = .7778 + .1964 + .0238 = .998$

(b) P(more than two defective chips out of 25) $= 1 - P$(fewer than three defective chips out of 25) $= 1 - .998 = .002$

25. P(correct) $= .5$ P(not correct) $= .5$
P(8 or more correct out of 10) $= P$(8 or 9 or 10 correct out of 10) $= C(10, 8) (.5)^8 (.5)^2 + C(10, 9) (.5)^9 (.5)^1$ $+ C(10, 10) (.5)^{10} (.5)^0 = (45) (.0039063) (.25) + (10) (.0019531) (.5) + (1) (.0009766) (1) = .0439453 +$ $.0097656 + .009766 = .0546875$
The probability the person gets eight or more correct is .0547.

27. P(success) $= .5$ P(not a success) $= .5$

(a) P(8 patients out of 10) $= C(10, 8) (.5)^8 (.5)^2 = (45) (.0039063) (.25) = .0439453 = .0439$

(b) P(more than 7 out of 10) $= P$(8 or 9 or 10 out of 10) $= C(10, 8) (.5)^8 (.5)^2 + C(10, 9) (.5)^9 (.5)^1 + C(10,$ $10) (.5)^{10} (.5)^0 = (45) (.0039063) (.25) + (10) (.0019531) (.5) + (1) (.0009766) (1) = .0439453 +$ $.0097656 + .0009766 = .0546875 = .0547$

(c) P(more than 15 out of 20) $= P$(16 or 17 or 18 or 19 or 20 out of 20) $= C(20, 16) (.5)^{16} (.5)^4 + C(20,$ $17) (.5)^{17} (.5)^3 + C(20, 18) (.5)^{18} (.5)^2 + C(20, 19) (.5)^{19} (.5)^1 + C(20, 20) (.5)^{20} (.5)^0 = (4845) (.0000153)$ $(.0625) + (1140) (.0000076) (.125) + (109) (.000001) + (20) (.000001) + (1) (.000001) = .0046206 +$ $.001083 + .0019 + .0000191 + .000001 = .0059136 = .0059$

29. P(opposed) $= .4$ P(favor) $= .6$

P(3 or more opposed to the bill out of five) $=$
P(3 or 4 or 5 opposed to the bill out of 5) $=$
$C(5, 3) (.4)^3 (.6)^2 + C(5, 4) (.4)^4 (.6)^1 + C(5, 5) (.4)^5 (.6)^0 =$
$(10) (.064) (.36) + (5) (.0256) (.6) + (1) (.01024) (1) =$
$.2304 + .0768 + .01024 = .31744 = .3174$

Exercises 5.3

1. $P(C) = (.2) (.5) + (.8) (.7) = .1 + .56 = .66$ 3. $P(A/C) = P(A \cap C) \div P(C) = .1 \div .66 = .1515$

5. $P(A/D) = P(A \cap D) \div P(D) = .1 \div .34 = .2941$ 7. $P(A) = (.7) (.1) + (.3) (.7) = .07 + .21 = .28$

9. $P(C) = (.7) (.5) + (.3) (.1) = .35 + .03 = .38$ 11. $P(F/A) = P(F \cap A) \div P(A) = .21 \div .28 = .75$

13. $P(F/B) = P(F \cap B) \div P(B) = .06 \div .34 = .1765$ 15. $P(F/C) = P(F \cap C) \div P(C) = .03 \div .38 = .0789$

17.

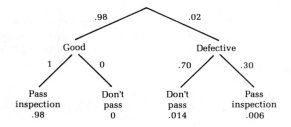

(a) $P(\text{Pass}) = P(G \cap \text{Pass}) + P(D \cap \text{Pass}) = .98 + .014 = .994 \ (99.4\%)$

(b) $P(D/\text{Pass}) = P(D \cap \text{Pass}) \div P(\text{Pass}) = .006/.986 = .00609$

19.

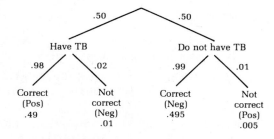

(a) $P(T \cap C) + P(NT \cap C) = .49 + .495 = .985$

(b) $P(T/\text{Pos}) = P(T \cap \text{Pos}) \div P(\text{Pos}) = .49 \div (.01 + .495) = .49 \div .495 = .989899 = .9899$

(c) $P(NT/\text{Neg}) = P(NT \cap \text{Neg}) \div P(\text{Neg}) = .495 \div (.01 + .495) = .495 \div .505 = .9802$

21.

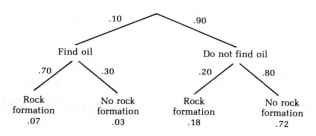

$$P(\text{Oil}/\text{Rock formation}) = P(\text{Oil} \cap \text{Rock formation}) \div P(\text{Rock formation})$$
$$= .07 \div (.07 + .18) = .07 \div .25 = .28$$

23.

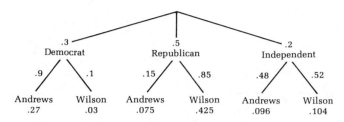

$P(\text{Andrews}) = .27 + .075 + .096 = .441$
$P(\text{Wilson}) = .03 + .425 + .104 = .559$
Based on the poll and distribution of voters by party Wilson will win the election.

25.

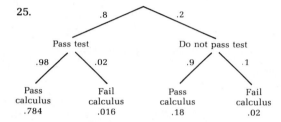

(a)   Fraction that pass calculus when they take the course $= .784 + .18 = .964$

(b) $P(\text{Do not pass test/Fail calculus}) = P(\text{Do not pass test} \cap \text{Fail calculus})/P(\text{Fail calculus}) = .02/(.02 + .016) = .02/.036 = .5556$

27.   (a)   Coin flipped once: $P(\text{Heads}) = .5$
         $P(\text{Two-headed/Heads}) = P(\text{Two-headed} \cap \text{Heads})/P(\text{Heads}) = .5/(.5 + .25) = .5/.75 = .6667$

      (b)   Coin flipped three times: $P(\text{Heads}) = .015625$
         $P(\text{Two-headed/Heads}) = P(\text{Two-headed} \cap \text{Heads})/P(\text{Heads}) = .5/(.5 + .0078125) = .5/.5078125 = .9846$

      (c)   Coin flipped five times: $P(\text{Heads}) = .0004883$
         $P(\text{Two-headed/Heads}) = P(\text{Two-headed} \cap \text{Heads})/P(\text{Heads}) = .5/(.5 + .0004883) = .5/.50004883 = .9990$

29. $P(A_j/B) = P(A_j \cap B)/P(B)$
      Equation 1: $P(B) = P(A_1 \cap B) + \cdots + P(A_k \cap B)$
      $P(A_j/B) = P(A_j \cap B) \div (P(A_1 \cap B) + \cdots + P(A_k \cap B))$
      Formula: $P(E \cap F) = P(E) \, P(F/E)$ so $P(A_j \cap B) = P(A_j) \, P(B/A_j)$ and $P(A_j/B) = P(A_j) \, P(B/A_j) \div (P(A_1)P(B/A_1) + \cdots + P(A_k) \, P(B/A_k))$

Exercises 5.4

1.

x	Probability	Product
10	.8	8
−20	.2	−4

   $4 = $ expected value of X

3.

x	Probability	Product
10	.2	2
20	.5	10
−100	.3	−30

-22 = expected value of X

5.

Gain	Probability	Product
40,000 − 500 = 39,500	.2	7,900
− 500	.8	−400

$7,500 = expected profit per bid

7.

Gain	Probability	Product
50,000 − 1,200 = 48,800	.1	4,800
− 1,200	.9	−1,080

$3,800 = architect's expected profit

9.

Gain	Probability	Product
100	.995	99.5
100 − 10,000 = −9,900	.005	−49.5

$50 = expected gain per policy for the insurance company

11. (a)

Loss	Probability	Product
500	.01	5
400	.04	16
300	.35	105
200	.30	60
100	.25	25
0	.05	0

$211 = expected loss after the security measures are implemented

(b) Loss $600 per week without the security measures
Loss $221 per week with the security measures, which cost $200 per week

$600 − $221 = $379
$379 − $200 = $179 saved per week by implementing the security measures

13.

Gain	Probability	Product
1	.25	.25
1	.25	.25
100	.25	25
5,000	.25	1259

$1,275.50 = expected winnings per game

15.

Gain	Probability	Product
$6 - 4 = 2$	1/6	.3333333
$5 - 4 = 1$	1/6	.1666667
$4 - 4 = 0$	1/6	0
$3 - 4 = -1$	1/6	−.1666667
$2 - 4 = -2$	1/6	−.3333333
$1 - 4 = -3$	1/6	−.5

$\$-.50$ = expected profit per play

17.

No. Sets owned	No. Sets rented	Profit	Probability	Product	Expected profit
14	14	280	.2	56	$56
15	14	$280 - 5 = 275$	.2	55	
	15	300	.3	90	$145
16	14	$280 - 10 = 270$	.2	54	
	15	$300 - 5 = 295$	.3	88.5	
	16	320	.3	96	$238.50
17	14	$280 - 15 = 265$	.2	53	
	15	$300 - 10 = 290$	.3	87	
	16	$320 - 5 = 315$	.3	94.5	
	17	340	.2	68	$302.50

19. Consider losing 5 games in a row:

Game	Bid	Total losses after game
1	$1	$1
2	$2	$3
3	$4	$7
4	$8	$15
5	$16	$31

Possible gain is $1 if you win any of the first 5 games and $−31 if you lose the 5 games. Probability of losing 5 games = $(.5)^5$ = .03125

Winnings	Probability	Product
1	.96875	.96875
−31	.03125	−.96875

0 = expected winnings

Chapter 6

Exercises 6.1

1. (a) $A \times B = \{(1, 3), (1, 4), (2, 3), (2, 4)\}$ (b) $A \times B = \{(1, 1), (1, 2), (2, 1), (2, 2)\}$
   (c) $A \times B = \{(1, 1), (1, 2)\}$ (d) $A \times B = \{(1, 1), (2, 1)\}$

3. The set of outfits he can form from his shirts and pants.

5. $\{(CM, 1.98), (C, 1.95), (BA, 1.64), (MG, 1.36)\}$

7.

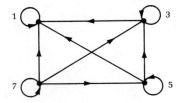

9. $R = \{(1541, 249), (Dual, 649), (Single, 349), (8050, 979)\}$

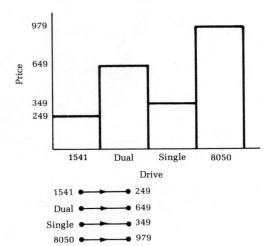

Exercises 6.2

1. (a) −4,800   (b) −3,600   (c) 0   (d) 6,000   (e) 114,000

3. Function,   not one-to-one,   onto.

5. Function,   one-to-one,   onto.

7. Function,   one-to-one,   onto.

9. Function,   one-to-one,   not onto.

11. Function,   one-to-one,   not onto.

13. Not a function

15. (Only for 5, 6, 7, 11)
    For 5, the inverse is

$B \longrightarrow A$

$(a) \longrightarrow 0$

For 7, the inverse is $\{(b, a) \; b^2 = a^2 \text{ and } B = A = \mathcal{N} \}$
For 6, $\{(b, a) \mid b = a \text{ and } B = A = \mathcal{N} \}$
For 11, $B = A = \mathcal{N}$

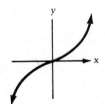

17. $R(x) = 48x$
    $P(x) = R(x) - C(x)$

19. $\{C: C \in \mathcal{N} \ \& \ C = 15x_1 + 20x_2 + 1000, x_1 \in \mathcal{N}, x_2 \in \mathcal{N} \}$

21. $C(0) = 1,000,$ $C(50) = 1,000,$ $C(100) = 1,000,$ $C(300) = 3,000$

23. $IQ(10, 12) = 120,$ $IQ(15, 15) = 100$

Exercises 6.3

1. $x + 15y = 650$ 3. $x + y = 1100$

5. $x - 10y = 20$ 7. $y = \frac{25}{2}x - 25$

9–11. For 7, the intercepts are $(0, -25)$ and $(2, 0)$ 13. $C(0) = 1{,}000$, $C(100) = 3{,}000$

15. $n + 41 = 4p$

17. $P_G(x) = x(x - 1)(x - 2)^2(x - 3)$
x choices for a, $(x - 1)$ choices for b,
$(x - 2)$ choices for d and c, $(x - 3)$ choices for e

Exercises 6.4

1. Equivalence relation   3. Equivalence relation

5. Not an equivalence relation since it is not transitive

7. Equivalence relation   9. Equivalence relation

11. Not an equivalence relation since it is not symmetric   13. Equivalence relation

15. For 7, the equivalence classes are the books that have the same number of pages.
For 9, the equivalence classes are persons who own the same computer.
For 13, the equivalence classes are squares that have the same area.
For 1, $C_1 = \{1, 3\}$, $C_3 = \{3, 1\}$
For 3, $C_3 = \{3, 4\}$, $C_4 = \{4, 3\}$, $C_5 = \{5, 6\}$, $C_6 = \{6, 5\}$

17. Corresponds to equivalence relation

19. Does not correspond to equivalence relation since it is not reflexive

21. Does not correspond to equivalence relation since it is not reflexive

23. $R = \{(a, b) \mid a \,\&\, b$ are both registered voters and in the same party or no party affiliations$\}$

Exercises 6.5

For 1. No   3. No   5. No   7. No   9. No   11. Linear order   13. No
17. No   19. No   21. No

23. Score $(a) = 2$,   Score $(b) = 0$
Score $(c) = 1$,   Score $(d) = 3$
The winner is d.
There is a Hamiltonian path: $d - a - c - b$.

25. Score $(a) = 1$,   Score $(b) = 3$ Score $(c) = 2$,   Score $(d) = 4$,   Score $(e) = 0$
The winner is d. There is a Hamiltonian path: $d - b - c - a - e$.

27. Guttman scale is:

29. tires 1; gear shift 2; wheels 3; pedals 4; handle bars 5; frame 6.

Review Exercises

1.

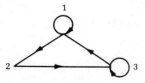

3. $\{(50, 1500), \quad (52, 1000), \quad (54, 800), \quad (60, 500)\}$

5. $C(0) = 560, \quad C(10) = 2560, \quad C(15) = 3560, \quad C(20) = 4560$

7. A function, one-to-one, onto   9. $C(x) = 8x + 1000$
$R(x) = 16x$
$P(x) = 16x - 8x - 1000 = 8x - 1000$

11. $x - 16y + 60 = 0$ 13. $P_G(x) = x(x - 1)(x - 2)^3$
$P_G(3) = 6, \quad P_G(4) = 96$

15. Equivalence relation   17. Partial order   19. Equivalence relation

21. No, since $(B, A) \in R$ but $(A, B) \notin R$, i.e., not symmetric.

23.

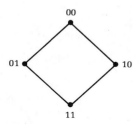

Linear order that contains the partial order is

$$\underbrace{11}_{\text{level 0}}, \quad \underbrace{01, 10}_{1}, \quad \underbrace{00}_{2}.$$

Chapter 7
Exercises 7.1

1. $(\$1000)(.06) = \$60$ 3. $(\$800)(.08) = \$64$

5. (a) $(\$2000)(.10) = \$200$ (b) $\$2000 + \$200 = \$2200$

7. (a) ($1000)(.09) = $90   (b) $1000 + $90 = $1090

9. (a) 3 months   (b) .06 ÷ 4 = .015   11. (a) 6 months   (b) .12 ÷ 2 = .06

13. .08 ÷ 4 = .02   ($1000)(1.02) = $1020   15. .07 ÷ 12 = .0058333   ($600)(1.058333) = $603.50

17. B_{12} = ($500)(1.02)^{12} = $634.12   19. B_5 = ($10,000)(1.12)^5 = $17,623.42

21. B_4 = ($800)(1.0125)^4 = $840.76   23. B_4 = ($12,000)(1.065)^4 = $15,437.60

25. $1000 deposited for two years at 12% per year interest compounded:
  (a) yearly   ($1000)(1.12)^2 = $1254.40   (b) semiannually   ($1000)(1.06)^4 = $1262.48
  (c) quarterly   ($1000)(1.03)^8 = $1266.77   (d) monthly   ($1000)(1.01)^{24} = $1269.73
  (e) weekly   ($1000)(1.0023077)^{104} = $1270.90

27. $1,000 = B_0 (1.0066667)^{12} B_0 = $1,000 ÷ 1.0829995 = $923.36

29. $10,000 = B_0 (1.09)^{10} B_0 = $10,000 ÷ 2.3673637 = $4,224.11

31. $100,000 = B_0 (1.01)^{360} B_0 = $100,000 ÷ 35.949642 = $2,781.67

33. $20,000 = B_0 (1.0066667)^{240} B_0 = $20,000 ÷ 4.9268029 = $4,059.43

35. $1 deposited for 200 years at 8% per year interest compounded:
  (a) yearly   ($1)(1.08)^{200} = $4,838,949.59   (b) semiannually   ($1)(1.04)^{400} =
  $6,506,324.50   (c) monthly   ($1)(1.0066667)^{2,400} = $8,426,588.25

Exercises 7.2

1. (a) interest = ($500)(.09 ÷ 12) = ($500)(.0075) = $3.75
    (b) balance = $500 + $3.75 + $20 = $523.75

3. (a) interest = ($350)(.005) = $1.75
    (b) balance = $350 + $1.75 + 25 = $376.75

5. (a) interest = ($800)(.0058333) = $4.67
    (b) balance = $800 + $4.67 + $50 = $854.67

7. (a) interest = ($1000)(.10) = $100
    (b) balance = $1000 + $100 + $100 = $1200

9. (a) interest = ($10,000)(.01) = $100
    (b) balance = $10,000 + $100 − $5000 = $5100

11. (a) interest = ($7000)(.04) = $280
     (b) balance = $7000 + $280 − $150 = $7130

13. B_0 = $100
     B_1 = ($100)(1.0041667) + $20 = $100.42 + $20 = $120.42
     B_2 = ($120.42)(1.0041667) + $20 = $120.92 + $20 = $140.92
     B_3 = ($140.92)(1.0041667) + $20 = $141.51 + $20 = $161.51

15. $B_0 = \$1000$
   $B_1 = (\$1000)(1.0058333) + \$100 = \$1005.83 + \$100 = \$1105.83$
   $B_2 = (\$1105.83)(1.0058333) + \$100 = \$111.28 + \$100 = \$1212.28$
   $B_3 = (\$1212.28)(1.0058333) + \$100 = \$1219.35 + \$100 = \$1319.35$

17. $B_0 = \$351$
   $B_1 = (\$351)(1.0058333) + \$50 = \$353.05 + \$50 = \$403.05$
   $B_2 = (\$403.05)(1.0058333) + \$50 = \$405.40 + \$50 = \$455.40$
   $B_3 = (\$455.40)(1.0058333) + \$50 = \$458.06 + \$50 = \$508.06$

19. $B_0 = \$278$
   $B_1 = (\$278)(1.005) + \$30 = \$279.39 + \$30 = \$309.39$
   $B_2 = (\$309.39)(1.005) + \$30 = \$310.94 + \$30 = \$340.94$
   $B_3 = (\$340.94)(1.005) + \$30 = \$342.65 + \$30 = \$372.65$

21. $B_0 = \$400$
   $B_1 = (\$400)(1.05) - \$100 = \$420 - \$100 = \$320$
   $B_2 = (\$320)(1.05) - \$100 = \$336 - \$100 = \$236$
   $B_3 = (\$236)(1.05) - \$100 = \$247.80 - \$100 = \$147.80$

23. $B_0 = \$500$
   $B_1 = (\$500)(1.05) - \$75 = \$525 - \$75 = \$450$
   $B_2 = (\$450)(1.05) - \$75 = \$472.50 - \$75 = \$397.50$
   $B_3 = (\$397.50)(1.05) - \$75 = \$417.38 - \$75 = \$342.38$

25. $B_2 = (500 + 100 \div .12)(1.12)^2 - 100 \div .12$
   $= (500 + 833.33)(1.2544) - 833.33$
   $= (1,333.33)(1.2544) - 833.33$
   $= 1,672.53 - 833.33$
   $= \$839.20$

27. $B_4 = (2000 + 100 \div .05)(1.05)^4 - 100 \div .05$
   $= (2,000 + 2000)(1.2155063) - 2000$
   $= (4,000)(1.2155063) - 2000$
   $= 4,862.025 - 2000$
   $= \$2862.03$

29. $B_{24} = (750 + 100 \div .0058333)(1.0058333)^{24} - 100 \div .0058333$
   $= (750 + 17,142.857)(1.149806) - 17,142.857$
   $= (17,892.857)(1.149806) - 17,142.857$
   $= 20,573.315 - 17,142.857$
   $= \$3430.46$

31. $B_8 = (593 + 75 \div .0066667)(1.0066667)^8 - 75 \div .0066667$
   $= (593 + 11,250)(1.0545945) - 11,250$
   $= (11,843)(1.0545945) - 11,250$
   $= 12,489.563 - 11,250$
   $= \$1239.56$

33. $B_3 = (10,000 + -1,000 \div .12)(1.12)^3 - (-1000 \div .12)$
   $= (10,000 - 8333.3333)(1.404928) + 8,333.3333$
   $= (1666.667)(1.404928) + 8333.3333$
   $= 2341.5467 + 833.3333$
   $= \$10,674.88$

35. $B_4 = (1,000 + -100 \div .02)(1.02)^4 - (-100 \div .02)$
   $= (1,000 - 5,000)(1.0824322) + 5,000$
   $= (-4,000)(1.0824322) + 5,000$
   $= -4,329.7286 + 5,000$
   $= \$670.27$

37. Note: no initial deposit was given—assume 0.
   $B_7 = (0 + 25,000 \div .10)(1.10)^7 - 25,000 \div .10$
   $= (250,000)(1.9487171) - 250,000$
   $= 487,179.28 - 250,000$
   $= \$237,179.28$

39. $B_{20} = 2,000,000 = (C + C \div .04)(1.04)^{20} - C \div .04$
   $= 2,000,000 = (C + 25\ C)(2.19911231) - 25\ C$
   $= 2,000,000 = (26\ C)(2.19911231) - 25\ C$
   $= 2,000,000 = 56.969201\ C - 25\ C$
   $= 2,000,000 = 31.969201\ C$
   $C = 2,000,000 \div 31.969201 = 62,560.212$
   Each deposit must be \$62,560.21.

41. (a) $1,000,000 = (3,500 + C \div .12)(1.12)^{30} - C \div .12$
      $1,000,000 = (3500 + 8.3333333\ C)(29.959922) - 8.3333333\ C$
      $1,000,000 = 104,859.73 + 249.66602\ C - 8.3333333\ C$
      $8,951,140.27 = 241.33767\ C$
      $C = 8951.40.27 \div 241.33267 = \$3,709.15$
   (b) $1,000,000 = (3,500 + C \div .12)(1.12)^{35} - C \div .12$
      $1,000,000 = (3,500 + 8.3333333\ C)(52.799619) - 8.3333333\ C$
      $1,000,000 = 184,798.67 + 439.99683\ C - 8.3333333\ C$
      $815,201.33 = 431.66349\ C$
      $C = 815,201.33 \div 431.66349 = \$1,888.51$

43. $0 = (B_0 + -50,000 \div .12)(1.12)^{20} - (-50,000 \div .12)$
   $0 = (B_0 + 416,666.67)(9.6462931) + 416,666.67$
   $0 = 9.6462931\ B_0 - 4,019,288.8 + 416,666.67$
   $3,602,622.1 = 9.6462931\ B_0$
   $B_0 = 3,602,622.1 \div 9.6462931 = \$373,472.18$

Exercises 7.3

	Payment	Interest	Principal payment	Remaining principal
1.	2	57.02	113.87	4,773.57
3.	3	582.43	39.33	49,883.37
	171	345.70	276.06	29,355.54

5.

15	38.49	132.40	3,166.54
18	32.75	138.14	2,668.94
24	23.92	146.97	1,903.19

Totals for
the year   393.63   1,657.05

7. $P_{12} = (7{,}000 - 100 \div .0125)(1.0125)^{12} + 100 \div .0125$
$= (7{,}000 - 8{,}000)(1.1607545) + 8{,}000$
$= (-1{,}000)(1.1607549) + 8{,}000$
$= -1{,}160.75 + 8{,}000$
$= \$6{,}839.25$

9. $P_{12} = (25{,}000 - 300 \div .0108333)(1.018333)^{12} + 300 \div .0108333$
$= (25{,}000 - 27{,}692.31)(1.1380325) + 27{,}692.31$
$= (-2692.31)(1.1380325) + 27{,}692.31$
$= -3063.94 + 27{,}692.31$
$= \$24{,}628.37$

11. $0 = (1{,}000 - M \div .0125)(1.0125)^{12} + M \div .0125$
$0 = ((.0125)(1000) - M)(1.1607545) + M)$
$0 = 14.509431 - 1.1607545\,M + M$
$0 = 14.509431 - .1607545\,M$
$M = 14.50943 \div .1607545 = \$90.26$

13. $0 = (25{,}000 - M \div .0091667)(1.0091667)^{96} + M \div .0091667$
$0 = ((.0091667)(25{,}000) - M)(2.4012541) + M)$
$0 = 550.2894 - 1.401254\,M$
$M = 550.2894 \div 1.4012541 = \$392.71$

15. $0 = (P_0 - 60 \div .0175)(1.0175)^{36} + 60 \div .0175$
$0 = (.0175\,P_0 - 60)(1.8674073) + 60$
$0 = .0326796\,P_0 - 112.04444 + 60$
$0 = .0326796\,P_0 - 52.044436$
$P_0 = 52.044436 \div .0326796 = \$1{,}592.57$

17. $0 = (P_0 - 800 \div .0116667)(1.0116667)^{120} + 800 \div .0116667$
$0 = (.0116667\,P_0 - 800)(4.0224705) + 800$
$0 = .046929\,P_0 - 3{,}217.9764 + 800$
$0 = .046929\,P_0 - 2{,}417.9764$
$P_0 = 2{,}417.9764 \div .046929 = \$51{,}524.19$

19. $.2\,S = 2{,}500;\ S = 12{,}500$ Largest possible sticker price from the down payment
$0 = (P_0 - 250 \div .0108333)(1.0108333)^{48} + 250 \div .0108333$
$0 = (.0181711\,P_0 - 250)(1.6773304) + 250$
$0 = .0191711\,P_0 - 419.33261 + 250$
$0 = .0181711\,P_0 - 169.33261$
$P_0 = 169.33261 \div .0181711 = 9{,}318.80$
The couple can afford to borrow up to \$9,318.80 to finance 80% of the sticker price.
$.8\,S = 9{,}318.80;\ S = 11{,}648.50.$ So the couple can afford to buy a new car with a sticker price
of \$11,648.50 or less.

21. (a) $0 = (P_0 - 800 \div .01)(1.01)^{240} + 800 \div .01$
     $0 = (.01\, P_0 - 800)(10.892554) + 800$
     $0 = .0189255\, P_0 - 8714.043 + 800$
     $0 = .1089255\, P_0 - 7914.043$
     $P_0 = 7,914.043 \div .1089255 = 72,655.558$
     With a 20-year mortgage the couple can afford to borrow $72,655.56.

    (b) $0 = (P_0 - 800 \div .01)(1.01)^{360} + 800 \div .01$
     $0 = (.01\, P_0 - 800)(35.949642) + 800$
     $0 = .3594964\, P_0 - 28,759.713 + 800$
     $0 = .3594964\, P_0 - 27,959.713$
     $P_0 = 27,959.713 \div .3594964 = 77,774.669$
     With a 30-year mortgage the couple can afford to borrow $77,774.70.

23. $490,000 - $60,000 = $430,000$
    $0 = (430,000 - M \div .03)(1.03)^{32} + M \div .03$
    $0 = (12,900 - M)(2.5750828) + M$
    $0 = 33,218.568 - 2.5750828\, M + M$
    $0 = 33,218.568 - 1.5750828\, M$
    $M = 33,218.568 \div 1.5750828 = 21,090.046$
    The quarterly payment is $21,090.05

25. (a) $0 = (3500 - M \div .10)(1.10)^4 + M \div .10$
     $0 = (350 - M)(1.4641) + M$
     $0 = 512.435 - 1.4641\, M + M$
     $0 = 512.435 - .4641\, M$
     $M = 512.435 \div .4641 = 1104.1478$
     The yearly payment is $1104.15

    (b)

Payment	Interest	Principal payment	Remaining principal
0	0	0	3500
1	350	754.15	2745.85
2	274.59	829.56	1916.29
3	191.63	912.52	1003.77
4	100.38	1003.77	0
Total	916.60	3500	

Chapter 8

Exercises 8.1

1. $a_3 = 15,$ $a_4 = 31,$ $a_5 = 63$ 3. $a_3 = 6,$ $a_4 = 10,$ $a_5 = 16$ 5. $c_3 = 6,$ $c_4 = 10,$ $c_5 = 15$ 7. $d_3 = 16,$ $d_4 = 8,$ $d_5 = 4$ 9. $a_3 = 2,$ $a_4 = 2,$ $a_5 = 2$

11. (a) 40 degrees   (b) $\frac{400}{9}$ degrees

13. (a) 100 milligrams   (b) $A_k = 100 \left(\frac{9}{10}\right)^k,$ $k = 0, 1, 2, 3, \ldots$
    (c) (i) $A_1 = 90$ milligrams
         $A_2 = 81$ milligrams
         $A_3 = 72.9$ milligrams

15. (a) (i) 16 grains   (b) 2^{k-1} grains for the kth square   (c) (i) $s_1 = 1$
      (ii) 32 grains   (ii) $s_2 = 3$

    (iii) $s_3 = 7$

    (iv) $s_4 = 15$

    (v) $s_5 = 31$

(d) $s_k = 2s_{k-1} + 1$ (e) $s_{64} = 2^{64} - 1$

17. (a) $C_k = \frac{k(k+1)}{2}$ (b) (i) $A_k = \frac{k(k+1)}{2}$

$C_{k+1} = \frac{(k+1)(k+2)}{2}$ (ii) $A_k = 1 + \frac{k(k+1)}{2}$

$= \frac{(k+1)k}{2} + \frac{2(k+1)}{2}$

$= C_k + (k+1)$

Exercises 8.2

1. $x_k = 5(2^k) - 1$ 3. $x_k = \frac{20}{9} + \frac{7}{9}(0.1)^k$ 5. $x_k = 100 - 50(-1)^k$ 7. $x_k = 3x_{k-1} + 1$

9. $x_k = 0.8x_{k-1} + 3$ 11. 57,881.25   13. (a) 90 units   (b) 72.9 units   (c) 20.59 units

15. 8,300 years   17. $x_k = (1.02)x_{k-1} - 1000$ 19. $x_k = \frac{17}{19}x_{k-1} + \frac{130}{19}$

21. $\because x_k - x_{k-1} = A(R - x_{k-1})$ 23. (a) $X_k = 70{,}000 + \frac{3}{10}x_{k-1}$ (b) 97,300

$\therefore x_k = (1-A)x_{k-1} + AR$

Plug into $x_k = \frac{b}{1-a} + (x_0 - \frac{b}{1-a})a^k$

where $a = 1 - A$, $b = AR$

We get $x_k = R + (x_0 - R)(1 - A)^k$

Exercises 8.3

1. $B_k = B_0(1+i)^k$ 3. $\because C_k = 2C_{k-1} + 1, C_1 = 1$ 5. $\frac{1-2^7}{1-2} = 2^7 - 1 = 127$

$\therefore 1 = 2C_0 + 1 \rightarrow C_0 = 0$

Plug $a = 2, b = 1$, and $C_0 = 0$ into

$x_k = \frac{b}{1-a} + (x_0 - \frac{b}{1-a})a^k$

$= 2^k - 1$

7. 1111   9. 5.977   11. (a) $r\left(\frac{1-a^{k+1}}{1-a}\right)$ (b) $\frac{6560}{2187}$

Chapter 9

Exercises 9.1

1. $2x_1 + 3x_2 = 6$
Intercepts: $(0, 2), (3, 0)$

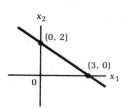

3. Intercepts: $(0, 5)$, $(3, 0)$

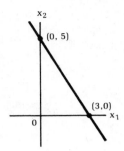

5. Intercepts: $(0, 2)$, $(8, 0)$

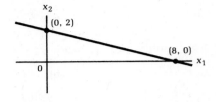

7.

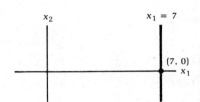

9.

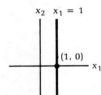

11.

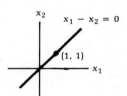

13.

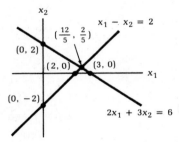

15.

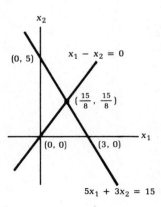

17.

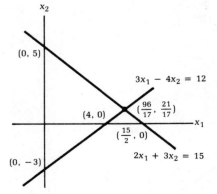

Exercises 9.2

1. $x_1 = 8$, $\quad x_2 = 15$ $\qquad$ 3. $x_1 = 5$, $\quad x_2 = 10$ $\qquad$ 5. $x_1 = 12$, $\quad x_2 = 4$ $\qquad$ 7. $x_1 = 225/13$,
$x_2 = 19/13$ $\qquad$ 9. x_1 = the number of rat experiments
$\qquad\qquad\qquad\quad x_2$ = the number of mouse experiments
$\qquad\qquad\qquad\quad x_1 = 2x_2$
$\qquad\qquad\qquad\quad 5x_1 = 8x_2 = 90$
$\qquad\qquad\qquad\quad x_1 = 10 \qquad x_2 = 5$

11. x_1 = units of task 1 $\qquad x_2$ = units of task 2
$3x_1 + 4x_2 = 10$
$1000\,x_1 + 1500\,x_2 = 3500$
$x_1 = 2 \qquad x_1 = 1$

13. $x = 225$ $\qquad\qquad\qquad$ 15. $x = 25 \qquad y\,(R = C) = 87.5$
$y = (R = C) = 562.5$

Exercises 9.3

1.

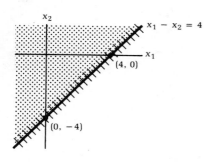

3.

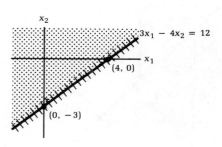

5.

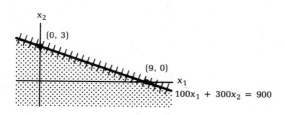

7.

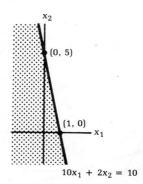

9.

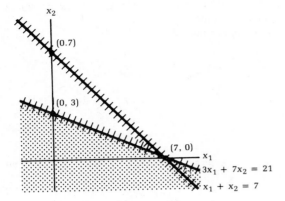

11.

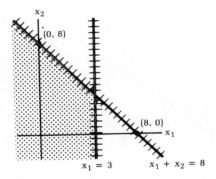

13.

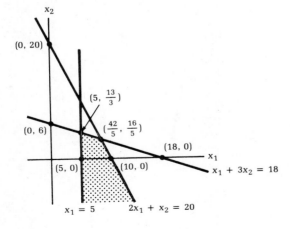

15. x_1 = money to invest in stock A
     x_2 = money to invest in stock B
     $x_1 + x_2 \leqslant 100{,}000$

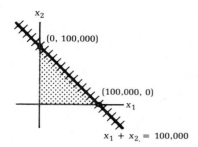

17. x_1 = ounces of A
     x_2 = ounces of B
     $1.0x_1 + 1.5x_2 \geqslant 10$

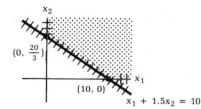

Exercises 9.4

1. max $P = 15{,}000\, x_1 + 10{,}000\, x_2$ x_1 = no. of colonials
    $300\, x_1 + 180\, x_2 \leqslant 18{,}000$ x_2 = no. of ranches
    $40{,}000\, x_1 + 30{,}000\, x_2 \leqslant 3{,}600{,}000$
    $x_1 \geqslant 0, \qquad x_2 \geqslant 0$

3. max $P = x_1 + 2x_2$ x_1 = no. of type 1 lizards
    $3x_1 + x_2 \leqslant 60$ x_2 = no. of type 2 lizards
    $x_1 + 2x_2 \leqslant 40$
    $x_1 \geqslant 0, \qquad x_2 \geqslant 0$

5. max $P = 12x_1 + 8x_2$ x_1 = no. of bracelets
    $10x_1 + 5x_2 \leqslant 100$ x_2 = no. of pins
    $6x_1 + 8x_2 \leqslant 96$
    $x_1 \geqslant 0, \qquad x_2 \geqslant 0$

7. x_1 = no. assigned day 1   7–3
    x_2 = no. assigned day 1   3–11
    x_3 = no. assigned day 1   11–7
    x_4 = no. assigned day 2   7–3
    x_5 = no. assigned day 2   3–11
    x_6 = no. assigned day 2   11–7
    x_7 = no. assigned day 3   7–3
    x_8 = no. assigned day 3   3–11
    x_9 = no. assigned day 3   11–7

$$\max V = 10(x_1 + x_4 + x_7) + 8(x_2 + x_5 + x_8) + 5(x_3 + x_6 + x_9)$$
$$x_1 + x_2 + x_3 + x_4 + x_5 + x_6 + x_7 + x_8 + x_9 \leqslant 50$$

$x_1 \geqslant 4$	$x_4 \geqslant 3$	$x_7 \geqslant 5$
$x_2 \geqslant 4$	$x_5 \geqslant 3$	$x_8 \geqslant 4$
$x_3 \geqslant 3$	$x_6 \geqslant 2$	$x_9 \geqslant 3$

9. $\max P = 55x_1 + 250x_2$ x_1 = no. of letter-quality printers
   $1500x_1 + 750x_2 \leqslant 19{,}500$ x_2 = no. of matrix-dot printers
   $x_1 \geqslant 3$
   $x_2 \geqslant 0$

Exercises 9.5

1. $x_1 = 0$, $x_2 = 2$ or $x_1 = 2$, $x_2 = 1$

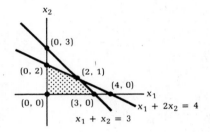

	$P = x_1 + 2x_2$
(0, 0)	0
(3, 0)	3
(2, 1)	4 } max
(0, 2)	4

3. $(x_1 = 5, \quad x_2 = 0)$

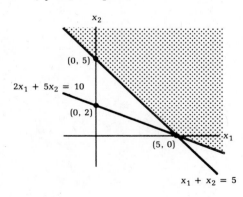

	$C = 3x_1 + 4x_2$
(0, 5)	20
(5, 0)	15 min

5. $x_1 = 0$ $x_2 = 6$

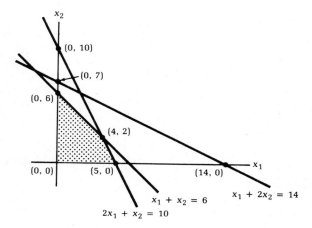

	$P = 30x_1 + 40x_2$	
(0, 0)	0	
(5, 0)	150	
(0, 6)	240	max
(4, 2)	200	

7.   min $C(x_1\ x_2) = 4x_1 + 3x_2$
   $x_1 + x_2 \geqslant 2{,}000$
   $x_2 \leqslant 1{,}200$
   $0.8x_1 - 0.2x_2 \geqslant 0$
   $0.9x_2 - 0.1x_1 \geqslant 0$
   $x_1 \geqslant 0$
   $x_2 \geqslant 0$

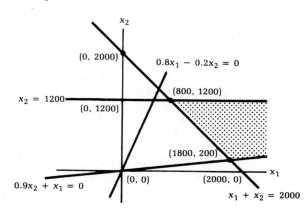

	$C = 4x_1 + 3x_2$	
(800, 1,200)	6,800	min
(1,800, 200)	7,800	

$x_1 = 800$
$x_2 = 1{,}200$

9. $x_1 = $ oil through route 1
    $x_2 = $ oil through route 2
    min $P(x_1\ x_2) = 15x_1 + 10x_2$
    $x_1 + x_2 = 10{,}000$
    $x_1 + 2x_2 \leqslant 16{,}000$
    $5{,}000 \geqslant x_1 \geqslant 0,\ x_2 \geqslant 0$

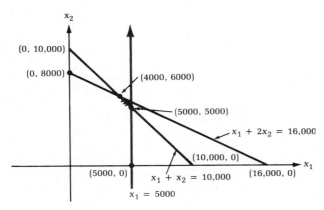

	$P = 15x_1 + 10x_2$	
(4,000, 6,000)	120,000	min
(5,000, 5,000)	125,000	

$x_1 = 4{,}000$
$x_2 = 6{,}000$

11. $x_1 = $ alfalfa (ton)
    $x_2 = $ corn (ton)
    max $P(x_1\ x_2) = 200\ x_1 + 250x_2$
    $3x_x + 2x_1 \leqslant 900$
    $x_1 + x_2 \leqslant 400$
    $x_1 \geqslant 0,\ x_2 \geqslant 0$

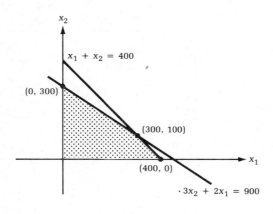

	$P = 200x_1 + 250x_2$	
(0, 300)	75,000	
(300, 100)	85,000	max
(400, 0)	80,000	
(0, 0)	0	

13. x_1 = number of letter quality printers
     x_2 = number of matrix dot printers
     max $P(x_1\ x_2) = 55x_1 + 250x_2$
     $1500x_1 + 750x_2 \leqslant 19500$
     $0 \leqslant x_2, \qquad x_1 \geqslant 3$

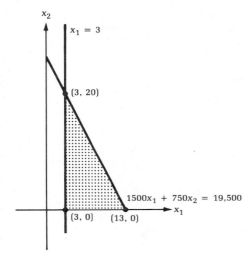

	$P = 55x_1 + 250x_2$	
(3, 20)	5,165	max
(3, 0)	165	
(13, 0)	715	

Chapter 10

Exercises 10.1

1. (i) $R_1(A) = (1 \quad 3 \quad 5)$ (ii) $C_2(A) = \begin{pmatrix} 3 \\ 4 \end{pmatrix}$ (iii) $A_{1,\,3} = 5$ (iv) the (2, 1)-entry = 2

3. (i) $R_3(A) = (3 \quad -2)$ (ii) $C_1(A) = \begin{pmatrix} 1 \\ 4 \\ 3 \end{pmatrix}$ (iii) $A_{2,\,1} = 4$ (iv) the (3, 2)-entry = -2

5. $A = \begin{pmatrix} 2 & 4 & 4 & 1 \\ 0 & -1 & 5 & -1 \\ 7 & 2 & 3 & 2 \end{pmatrix}$

7. $A = \begin{pmatrix} 1 & 1 & 1 & 0 \\ 0 & 0 & 1 & 1 \\ 0 & 0 & 0 & 1 \\ 0 & 0 & 0 & 1 \end{pmatrix}$

9. $A = \begin{pmatrix} 1 & 1 & 0 \\ 1 & 0 & 1 \\ 0 & 1 & 0 \end{pmatrix}$

11.
$$A = \begin{pmatrix} 0 & 0 & 1 & 2 \\ 0 & 0 & 2 & 1 \\ 1 & 2 & 0 & 0 \\ 2 & 1 & 0 & 0 \end{pmatrix}$$

13.

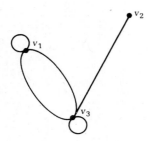

15.
$$A = \begin{pmatrix} 1 & 0 & 0 & 0 \\ 0 & 1 & 1 & 0 \\ 0 & 1 & 0 & 1 \\ 0 & 1 & 0 & 1 \end{pmatrix}$$

17. (a)
$$A = \begin{pmatrix} 0 & 0 & 0 & 0 \\ 1 & 0 & 0 & 1 \\ 1 & 1 & 0 & 1 \\ 1 & 0 & 0 & 0 \end{pmatrix}$$

(b) The ith players' score equals the sum of the entries of the ith row.

Player I's score $= 0$
Player II's score $= 2$
Player III's score $= 3$
Player IV's score $= 1$

Exercises 10.2

1. $\begin{pmatrix} 6 & 3 \\ 2 & 11 \end{pmatrix}$ 3. $\begin{pmatrix} 12 \\ 2 \\ -7 \end{pmatrix}$ 5. $\begin{pmatrix} 0 & 1 \\ -1 & 1 \\ -1 & 1 \end{pmatrix}$

7. (13) 9. (25) 11. (6) 13. $\begin{pmatrix} 3 \\ 5 \end{pmatrix}$ 15. $\begin{pmatrix} 3 & 4 \\ 6 & 8 \end{pmatrix}$ 17. $\begin{pmatrix} -7 & -8 \\ 23 & 34 \end{pmatrix}$

19. $\begin{pmatrix} -30 & -45 \\ 20 & 30 \end{pmatrix}$ 21. $\begin{pmatrix} 3 & -6 \\ 7 & 9 \end{pmatrix}$ 23. $(5 \quad -1 \quad 2)$ 25. $\begin{pmatrix} 1 & 0 & 0 \\ 0 & 1 & 0 \\ 0 & 0 & 1 \end{pmatrix}$

27. $\begin{pmatrix} 1 & 0 \\ 0 & 1 \end{pmatrix}$ 29. $\begin{pmatrix} 2 & 2 \\ 2 & 2 \end{pmatrix}$

31. $\begin{aligned} x_1 + 2x_2 &= 7 \\ 4x_1 - 3x_2 &= 5 \end{aligned}$ 33. $\begin{aligned} x_1 + 2x_2 - x_3 &= 0 \\ 3x_1 + 5x_2 - 2x_3 &= 1 \end{aligned}$

35. $\begin{pmatrix} 1 & 1 \\ 2 & -3 \end{pmatrix} \begin{pmatrix} x_1 \\ x_2 \end{pmatrix} = \begin{pmatrix} 4 \\ 11 \end{pmatrix}$ **37.** $\begin{pmatrix} 1 & 1 & -1 \\ 2 & -1 & 3 \\ 3 & 1 & -5 \end{pmatrix} \begin{pmatrix} x_1 \\ x_2 \\ x_3 \end{pmatrix} = \begin{pmatrix} 0 \\ 4 \\ 63 \end{pmatrix}$

39. Total amount $= (70 \quad 100 \quad 50) \begin{pmatrix} 5 \\ 9 \\ 2 \end{pmatrix} = 1350$

41. (i)
$$A = \begin{pmatrix} 0 & 0.5 & 0 \\ 0 & 0 & 0.7 \\ 4 & 0 & 0 \end{pmatrix}$$

  (ii) $(a_{k+3} \quad b_{k+3} \quad c_{k+3}) = P_{k+3} = P_{k+2}A = P_{k+1}A^2 = P_k A^3$

$$= (a_k \quad b_k \quad c_k) \begin{pmatrix} 0 & 0.5 & 0 \\ 0 & 0 & 0.7 \\ 4 & 0 & 0 \end{pmatrix}^3$$

$$= (a_k \quad b_k \quad c_k) \begin{pmatrix} 1.4 & 0 & 0 \\ 0 & 1.4 & 0 \\ 0 & 0 & 1.4 \end{pmatrix}$$

$$= (1.4a_k \quad 1.4b_k \quad 1.4c_k)$$

43. (a) $A^2 = \begin{pmatrix} 0 & 0 & 1 \\ 0 & 0 & 0 \\ 0 & 0 & 0 \end{pmatrix}$ (b) $A + A^2 = \begin{pmatrix} 0 & 1 & 2 \\ 0 & 0 & 1 \\ 0 & 0 & 0 \end{pmatrix}$ (c) Power of $s_1 = 3$
Power of $s_2 = 1$
Power of $s_3 = 0$

Exercises 10.3

1. $D(2) = (0.74 \quad 0.26)$
$D(3) = (0.774 \quad 0.226)$
$D(4) = (0.7774 \quad 0.2226)$

3. $D(2) = (0.1 \quad 0.9)$
$D(3) = (0.28 \quad 0.72)$
$D(4) = (0.244 \quad 0.756)$

5. $D(2) = (0.31 \quad 0.28 \quad 0.41)$
$D(3) = (0.299 \quad 0.283 \quad 0.418)$
$D(4) = (0.2997 \quad 0.2778 \quad 0.4225)$

7. $D = \left(\frac{7}{9} \quad \frac{2}{9}\right) = (0.778 \quad 0.4225)$ **9.** $D = (0.25 \quad 0.75)$

11. $D = \left(\frac{15}{51} \quad \frac{14}{51} \quad \frac{22}{51}\right) = (0.294 \quad 0.275 \quad 0.431)$ **13.** $D = \left(\frac{2}{7} \quad \frac{5}{7}\right) = (0.286 \quad 0.714)$

15. $D = \left(\frac{10}{11} \quad \frac{1}{11}\right) = (0.909 \quad 0.091)$ **17.** (a) $T = \begin{pmatrix} 0.97 & 0.03 \\ 0.12 & 0.88 \end{pmatrix}$ (b) (i) 88.5%
(ii) 87.23%
(iii) 86.14%

19. (a) $T = \begin{pmatrix} 0.9 & 0.1 \\ 0.05 & 0.95 \end{pmatrix}$ (b) (i) $(0.39 \quad 0.61)$
(ii) $(0.3815 \quad 0.6185)$
(iii) $\left(\frac{1}{3} \quad \frac{2}{3}\right)$

21. (a) $T = \begin{pmatrix} 0.95 & 0.05 \\ 0.35 & 0.65 \end{pmatrix}$ (b) 87.5%

23. (a) $(0.5 \quad 0.5)$ (b) All the states: $(x \quad 1-x), x \in [0,1]$

25.   Proof: Suppose

$$(x \quad 1-x) \begin{pmatrix} a & 1-a \\ b & 1-b \end{pmatrix} = (x \quad 1-x)$$

then we have

$$ax + b(1-x) = x$$
$$(1-a)x + (1-b)(1-x) = 1-x$$

Since T is nonzero, $a - b \neq 1$ (note: $0 < a, b < 1$),

there exists one and only one $x = \dfrac{b}{1-a+b}$

satisfying the above equations.

$$D = \left(\dfrac{b}{1-a+b} \quad \dfrac{1-a}{1-a+b} \right)$$

Exercises 10.4

1. $\begin{pmatrix} 1 & 2 & 1 \\ 0 & 2 & -1 \end{pmatrix}$ 3. $\begin{pmatrix} 1 & -1 & 1 & 3 \\ 0 & 6 & 3 & -8 \\ 0 & 3 & 9 & 3 \end{pmatrix}$ 5. $\begin{pmatrix} 1 & 1 & -1 & -7 \\ 0 & 2 & -7 & -21 \\ 0 & 8 & -1 & -24 \end{pmatrix}$

7. $x_1 = 3$ 9. $x_1 = 20$ 11. $x_1 = 2$ 13. $x_1 = 1$ 15. $x_1 = 3$ 17. $x_1 = -1$
    $x_2 = -1$ $x_2 = 40$ $x_2 = 5$ $x_2 = 7$ $x_2 = 2$ $x_2 = -1$
                                            $x_3 = -1$ $x_3 = 2$ $x_3 = 10$ $x_3 = 2$

19. $x_1 = 7$ 21. $x_1 = 6$ 23. $a = 3$ 25. $p(x) = 3x^2 + 4x - 1$
     $x_2 = 3$ $x_2 = 3$ (x_1: food I, x_2: food II) $b = 4$ $p(3) = 222$
     $x_3 = -5$ $c = -1$

Exercises 10.5

1. $x_1 = 1 - 2x_3$ 3. $x_1 = 3 - 2x_3$ 5. $x_1 = \dfrac{8}{3} - \dfrac{2}{3}x_3$ 7. $x_1 = 11 - 7x_3$ 9. $x_1 = x_4$
    $x_2 = 3 + x_3$ $x_2 = 5 - x_3$ $x_2 = -\dfrac{5}{3} - \dfrac{1}{3}x_3$ $x_2 = 8 - 5x_3$ $x_2 = 5 - x_4$
                                                                                                                      $x_3 = 2$

11. (a) $x_1 = 10 - 2x_3$ (b) (i) $x_1 = 10$ (ii) $x_1 = 4$
          $x_2 = 9 - 3x_3$ $x_2 = 9$ $x_2 = 0$
                                        $x_3 = 0$ $x_3 = 3$ (x_1: food F_1; x_2: food F_2; x_3: food F_3)

13. (a) $x_1 = 50 + x_4$ (b) $x_1 = 50$
          $x_2 = 100 - x_4$ $x_2 = 100$
          $x_3 = 300 - 2x_4$ $x_3 = 300$
                                  $x_4 = 0$ (x_1: sofa; x_2: chair; x_3: table; x_4: desk)

15. $x_{11} = 30 - x_{21}$ Shipping schedule of least cost:

$x_{12} = x_{21} + x_{23}$ $x_{11} = 30$

$x_{13} = 45 - x_{23}$ $x_{12} = 0$

$x_{22} = 50 - x_{21} - x_{23}$ $x_{13} = 45$

$x_{21} = 0$

$x_{22} = 50$

$x_{23} = 0$

(x_{ij}: the number of machines shipping from warehouse i to store j)

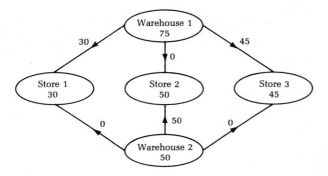

Exercises 10.6

1. $\begin{pmatrix} -9 & 2 \\ 5 & -1 \end{pmatrix}$ 3. $\begin{pmatrix} 5 & -2 \\ -7 & 3 \end{pmatrix}$ 5. $\begin{pmatrix} -1 & -1 & 2 \\ 2 & 1 & -2 \\ -1 & 0 & 1 \end{pmatrix}$ 7. $\begin{pmatrix} 1 & 0 & -1 \\ 1 & -1 & 1 \\ -2 & 2 & -1 \end{pmatrix}$

9. $\begin{pmatrix} -14 & -2 & 15 & -12 \\ 8 & 1 & -8 & 6 \\ -4 & 0 & 4 & -3 \\ 1 & 0 & -1 & 1 \end{pmatrix}$ 11. (a) $\begin{pmatrix} x_1 \\ x_2 \end{pmatrix} = \begin{pmatrix} 23 \\ -12 \end{pmatrix}$ (b) $\begin{pmatrix} x_1 \\ x_2 \end{pmatrix} = \begin{pmatrix} -17 \\ 10 \end{pmatrix}$

13. (a) $\begin{pmatrix} x_1 \\ x_2 \\ x_3 \end{pmatrix} = \begin{pmatrix} 4 \\ -3 \\ 1 \end{pmatrix}$ (b) $\begin{pmatrix} x_1 \\ x_2 \\ x_3 \end{pmatrix} = \begin{pmatrix} -3 \\ 5 \\ -2 \end{pmatrix}$

15. Proof:

$$\begin{pmatrix} a & b \\ c & d \end{pmatrix} \begin{pmatrix} d/D & -b/D \\ -c/D & a/D \end{pmatrix} = \begin{pmatrix} \frac{ab - bc}{D} & \frac{-ab + ab}{D} \\ \frac{cd - cd}{D} & \frac{-bc + ad}{D} \end{pmatrix} = \begin{pmatrix} 1 & 0 \\ 0 & 1 \end{pmatrix}$$

17. $I - A = \begin{pmatrix} 0.70 & -0.10 \\ -0.20 & 0.98 \end{pmatrix}$ 19. $I - A = \begin{pmatrix} 0.98 & -0.50 \\ -0.10 & 0.95 \end{pmatrix}$

   $(I - A)^{-1} = \begin{pmatrix} 1.4715 & 0.1502 \\ 0.3003 & 1.0511 \end{pmatrix}$ $(I - A)^{-1} = \begin{pmatrix} 1.0783 & 0.5675 \\ 0.1135 & 1.1124 \end{pmatrix}$

21.   (a)

    (b)

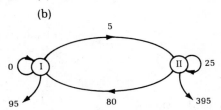

    (c) $\begin{pmatrix} 5 \\ 105 \end{pmatrix}$ (d) $\begin{pmatrix} 95 \\ 395 \end{pmatrix}$ (e) $A = \begin{pmatrix} 0 & 0.01 \\ 0.80 & 0.05 \end{pmatrix}$ (f) $AX = \begin{pmatrix} 5 \\ 105 \end{pmatrix}$

    (g) $X - AX = \begin{pmatrix} 95 \\ 395 \end{pmatrix}$

23.   (a)

    (b)

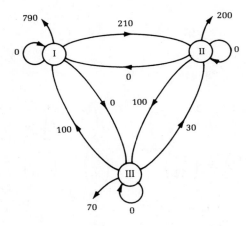

    (c) $\begin{pmatrix} 210 \\ 100 \\ 130 \end{pmatrix}$ (d) $\begin{pmatrix} 790 \\ 200 \\ 70 \end{pmatrix}$ (e) $A = \begin{pmatrix} 0 & 0.70 & 0 \\ 0 & 0 & 0.50 \\ 0.10 & 0.10 & 0 \end{pmatrix}$ (f) $AX = \begin{pmatrix} 210 \\ 100 \\ 130 \end{pmatrix}$

    (g) $X - AX = \begin{pmatrix} 790 \\ 200 \\ 70 \end{pmatrix}$

25. $(I - A)^{-1} = \begin{pmatrix} 1.1830 & 0.0121 \\ 0.5553 & 1.0261 \end{pmatrix}$

    (a)   Total output of autos = \$60.360 billion   (b)   Increase of \$5.553 billion in the total
          Total output of steel = \$130.375 billion   output of steel

27.
$$(I - A)^{-1} = \begin{pmatrix} 1.389 & .329 & .891 \\ .163 & 1.325 & .312 \\ .299 & .336 & 1.705 \end{pmatrix}$$

(a) $\begin{pmatrix} 29.229 \\ 14.26 \\ 30.581 \end{pmatrix} \begin{matrix} N \\ M \\ E \end{matrix}$ (b) $\Delta X = \begin{pmatrix} 2.561 \\ -0.0315 \\ 2.6885 \end{pmatrix} \begin{matrix} N \\ M \\ E \end{matrix}$

Chapter 11

Exercises 11.1

1. $-10x_1 - 7x_2 \leqslant -25$

3. $4x_1 + 5x_2 \leqslant 10$
   $-4x_1 + 5x_2 \leqslant -10$

5. $-x_1 - x_2 \leqslant -12$

7. $\max S = 2x_1 + 7x_2$
   $2x_1 + 3x_2 \leqslant 10$
   $-x_1 + x_2 \leqslant -5$
   $x_1 - 5x_2 \leqslant -6$
   $x_1 \geqslant 0 \qquad x_2 \geqslant 0$

9. $\max P = 3x_1 + 9x_2$
   $-x_1 - x_2 \leqslant -5$
   $2x_1 - 3x_2 \leqslant 7$
   $-x_1 \leqslant -4$
   $x_1 \geqslant 0 \qquad x_2 \geqslant 0$

   $-x_1 - x_2 + s_1 = -5$
   $2x_1 - 3x_2 + s_2 = 7$
   $-x_1 + s_3 = -4$

   $x_1 + x_2 - s_1 = 5$
   $2x_1 - 3x_2 + s_2 = 7$
   $x_1 - s_3 = 4$
   $-3x_1 - 9x_2 + P = 0$

   First tableau:

   $$\begin{pmatrix} x_1 & x_2 & s_1 & s_2 & s_3 & P & \text{constants} \\ 1 & 1 & -1 & 0 & 0 & 0 & 5 \\ 2 & -3 & 0 & 1 & 0 & 0 & 7 \\ 1 & 0 & 0 & 0 & -1 & 0 & 4 \\ -3 & -9 & 0 & 0 & 0 & 1 & 0 \end{pmatrix}$$

11. $\max T = x_1 + x_2 + x_3$
    $-x_1 - 2x_2 - 3x_3 \leqslant -4$
    $2x_1 + 3x_2 + x_3 \leqslant 15$
    $-x_1 + x_2 + x_3 \leqslant 0$
    $x_1 \geqslant 0 \qquad x_2 \geqslant 0 \qquad x_3 \geqslant 0$

    or

    $-x_1 - x_2 - x_3 + T = 0$
    $x_1 + 2x_3 + 3x_3 - s_1 = 4$
    $2x_1 + 3x_2 + x_3 + s_2 = 15$
    $-x_1 + x_2 + x_3 + s_3 = 0$
    $x_1 \geqslant 0 \qquad x_2 \geqslant 0 \qquad x_3 \geqslant 0$

First tableau:

x_1	x_2	x_3	s_1	s_2	s_3	T	constants
1	2	3	−1	0	0	0	4
2	3	1	0	1	0	0	15
−1	1	1	0	0	1	0	0
−1	−1	−1	0	0	0	1	0

13. $2x_1 + x_2 + s_1 = 4$
$x_2 + 3x_3 + s_2 = 7$
$x_1 + x_3 + s_3 = 6$
$-x_1 - x_2 - x_3 + W = 0$

First tableau:

x_1	x_2	x_3	s_1	s_2	s_3	W	constants
2	1	0	1	0	0	0	4
0	1	3	0	1	0	0	7
1	0	1	0	0	1	0	6
−1	−1	−1	0	0	0	1	0

15. x_1 = pounds of 90% lean hamburg; x_2 = pounds of 80% lean hamburg

$$\max P = 1.59\,x_1 + 1.39\,x_2$$
$$0.9\,x_1 + 0.8\,x_2 \leqslant 1000$$
$$0.1\,x_1 + 0.2\,x_2 \leqslant 200$$
$$x_1 \geqslant 0 \qquad x_2 \geqslant 0$$

First tableau:

x_1	x_2	s_1	s_2	P	constants
0.9	0.8	1	0	0	1000
0.1	0.2	0	1	0	200
−1.59	−1.39	0	0	1	0

Exercises 11.2

1. (a) Pivot column:
$$\begin{pmatrix} 0 \\ 1 \\ 2 \\ -4 \end{pmatrix}$$

(b) Ratios:
$7 \div 1 = 7$
$18 \div 2 = 9$

(c) Pivot element:
1

(d) Next tableau:

	x_1	x_2	x_3	s_1	s_2	s_3	P	constants
	1	0	1	1	0	0	0	5
	0	1	1	0	1	0	0	7
$2r_2 + r_3$	4	0	1	0	−2	1	0	4
$4r_2 + r_4$	−3	0	2	0	4	0	1	28

(e) Basic solution: $x_1 = 0$ $\qquad x_2 = 7$ $\qquad x_3 = 0$ $\qquad s_1 = 5$ $\qquad s_2 = 0$ $\qquad s_3 = 4$ $\qquad p = 28$;
It is feasible.

3. (a) Pivot column: (b) Ratios: (c) Pivot element:

$$\begin{pmatrix} 1 \\ 2 \\ -1 \\ -2 \end{pmatrix}$$

$3 \div 1 = 3$
$8 \div 2 = 4$
$2 \div -1 = -2$

1

(d) Next tableau:

	x_1	x_2	x_3	s_1	s_2	s_3	T	constants
	5	0	1	1	2	0	0	3
$2r_1 + r_2$	-12	1	0	-2	-1	0	0	2
$r_1 + r_3$	6	0	0	1	6	1	0	5
$2r_1 + r_4$	9	0	0	2	7	0	1	14

(e) Basic solution: $x_1 = 0$ $x_2 = 2$ $x_3 = 3$ $s_1 = 0$ $s_2 = 0$ $s_3 = 5$ $p = 14$;
It is feasible.

5. No maximum   7. $x_1 = 5$ $x_2 = 0$ $x_3 = 5$ $P = 10$ 9. $x_1 = 0$ $x_2 = 4$

$x_3 = 1$ $P = 5$ 11. $x_1 = \dfrac{10{,}000}{9}$ $x_2 = 0$ $P = \dfrac{10{,}000}{9} \times 1.59 = 176.67$

Exercises 11.3

1. $\min C = 5u_1 + 12u_2$
$u_1 + 2u_2 \geqslant 1$
$u_1 + 3u_2 \geqslant 2$
$u_1 \geqslant 0,\qquad u_2 \geqslant 0$

3. $\min C = 6u_1 + 8u_2 + 5u_3$
$u_1 + 2u_3 \geqslant 5$
$u_2 + u_3 \geqslant 3$
$u_1 + 2u_2 \geqslant 1$
$u_1 \geqslant 0,\qquad u_2 \geqslant 0,\qquad u_3 \geqslant 0$

5. $\max P = 15u_1 + 8u_2$
$3u_1 + 2u_2 \leqslant 8$
$7u_1 + u_2 \leqslant 10$
$u_1 \geqslant 0,\qquad u_2 \geqslant 0$

7. $\max P = -100u_1 + 25u_2 + 45u_3$
$-3u_1 + 2u_2 \leqslant 100$
$-5u_1 + u_2 + 5u_3 \leqslant 200$
$-20u_1 + 7u_3 \leqslant 50$
$u_1 \geqslant 0,\qquad u_2 \geqslant 0,\qquad u_3 \geqslant 0$

9. First tableau:

x_1	x_2	x_3	s_1	s_2	s_3	T	constants
2	1	1	1	0	0	0	15
1	-1	1	0	1	0	0	9
3	5	-1	0	0	1	0	18
-1	-3	-1	0	0	0	1	0

Second tableau:

x_1	x_2	x_3	s_1	s_2	s_3	T	constants
1.4	0	1.2	1	0	-0.2	0	11.4
1.6	0	0.8	0	1	0.2	0	12.6
0.6	1	-0.2	0	0	0.2	0	3.6
0.8	0	-1.6	0	0	0.6	1	10.8

Final tableau:

$$
\begin{array}{cccccccc}
x_1 & x_2 & x_3 & s_1 & s_2 & s_3 & T & \text{constants} \\
\frac{7}{6} & 0 & 1 & \frac{5}{6} & 0 & \frac{-1}{6} & 0 & \frac{19}{2} \\
\frac{4}{6} & 0 & 0 & \frac{-4}{6} & 1 & \frac{2}{6} & 0 & 3.48 \\
\frac{5}{6} & 1 & 0 & \frac{-1}{6} & 0 & \frac{1}{6} & 0 & 5.88 \\
\frac{16}{6} & 0 & 0 & \frac{8}{6} & 0 & 0.28 & 1 & 29.04
\end{array}
$$

So the solution is $x_1 = 0$, $x_2 = 5.88$, $x_3 = 9.5$, $T = 29.04$;

dual variables $u_1 = \frac{8}{6}$, $u_2 = 0$, $u_3 = 0.28$.

11. dual:

$$\max P = 8u_1 + 7u_2 + 20u_3$$
$$2u_1 + u_2 + 4u_3 \leqslant 1$$
$$u_1 + 5u_2 + 5u_3 \leqslant 1$$
$$-u_1 + u_2 + 3u_3 \leqslant 1$$
$$u_1 \geqslant 0, u_2 > 0, u_3 > 0$$

First tableau:

$$
\begin{array}{cccccccc}
u_1 & u_2 & u_3 & s_1 & s_2 & s_3 & P & \text{constants} \\
2 & 1 & \boxed{4} & 1 & 0 & 0 & 0 & 1 \\
1 & 5 & \boxed{5} & 0 & 1 & 0 & 0 & 1 \\
-1 & 1 & 3 & 0 & 0 & 1 & 0 & 1 \\
-8 & -7 & -20 & 0 & 0 & 0 & 1 & 0
\end{array}
$$

Second tableau:

$$
\begin{array}{cccccccc}
u_1 & u_2 & u_3 & s_1 & s_2 & s_3 & P & \text{constants} \\
\boxed{\frac{6}{5}} & -3 & 0 & 1 & \frac{-4}{5} & 0 & 0 & \frac{1}{5} \\
\frac{1}{5} & 1 & 1 & 0 & \frac{1}{5} & 0 & 0 & \frac{1}{5} \\
\frac{-8}{5} & -2 & 0 & 0 & \frac{-3}{5} & 1 & 0 & \frac{2}{5} \\
-4 & 13 & 0 & 0 & 4 & 0 & 1 & 4
\end{array}
$$

Final tableau:

$$
\begin{array}{cccccccc}
u_1 & u_2 & u_3 & s_1 & s_2 & s_3 & P & \text{constants} \\
1 & \frac{-5}{2} & 0 & \frac{5}{6} & \frac{-4}{6} & 0 & 0 & \frac{1}{6} \\
0 & \frac{3}{2} & 1 & \frac{-1}{6} & \frac{2}{6} & 0 & 0 & \frac{1}{6} \\
0 & -6 & 0 & \frac{4}{3} & \frac{-5}{3} & 1 & 0 & \frac{2}{3} \\
0 & 3 & 0 & \frac{10}{3} & \frac{4}{3} & 0 & 1 & \frac{24}{5}
\end{array}
$$

So dual solution: $u_1 = \frac{1}{6}$, $u_2 = 0$, $u_3 = \frac{1}{6}$, $P = \frac{24}{5}$

The solution: $x_1 = \frac{10}{3}$, $x_2 = \frac{4}{3}$, $x_3 = 0$, $C = \frac{24}{5}$

13. For example: Min $C = 10u_1 - 5u_2$

$$u_1 - u_2 \leqslant 2$$
$$u_1 - u_2 \leqslant 1$$
$$u_1 \geqslant 0$$
$$u_2 \geqslant 0$$

The feasible region is unbounded.

If the feasible region of the original is the empty set then the feasible region of the dual is unbounded and if the feasible region of the original is unbounded then the feasible region of the dual is the empty set.

Exercises 11.4

1. (a) max $T = 300$

   $x_1 = 60$ $x_2 = 240$ $x_3 = 0$

   (b) $u_1 = 0$ $u_2 = .2$ $u_3 = 0$

   Economically, this means that the university should be willing to pay 20¢ a minute to get an extra minute of time in the sign-ups department, since this will mean an increase in the total number of students processed.

   (c) $4500 < b_1 < 5500$

   $1200 < b_2 < 1600$

   $1800 < b_3 < \infty$

Chapter 12

Exercises 12.1

1. Row 1 is the best pure strategy for the row player. Column 2 is the best pure strategy for the column player. The value of the game is –1.

3. Row 1 is the best pure strategy for the row player. Column 1 is the best pure strategy for the column player. The value of the game is 0.

5. Row 1 is the best pure strategy for the row player. Column 2 is the best pure strategy for the column player. This is not a strictly determined game.

7. Row 1 is the best pure strategy for the row player. Columns 1 and 2 are equivalent for the column player. This is not a strictly determined game.

9. Payoff matrix:

Rose

	0	1	2	3	4	5
0	−1	1	−1	1	−1	1
1	1	−1	1	−1	1	−1
2	−1	1	−1	1	−1	1
3	1	−1	1	−1	1	−1
4	−1	1	−1	1	−1	1
5	1	−1	1	−1	1	−1

Carol

There is not an optimal pure strategy, and this is not a strictly determined game.

11. Payoff matrix:

$$\begin{pmatrix} 0 & 0.3 & 0.5 \\ -0.3 & 0 & 0.3 \\ -0.5 & -0.3 & 0 \end{pmatrix}$$

Both of them should broadcast one day before the election. The value of the game is 0.

13. $a > 0 > b$ [in this case, the saddle point is the entry (1, 2)]

    $b > 0 > a$ [in this case, the saddle point is the entry (2, 1)]

    $v = 0$

15. $a < -b$

Exercises 12.2

1. $r_1 = \frac{6}{13}$, $\quad r_2 = \frac{7}{13}$, $\quad c_1 = \frac{5}{13}$, $\quad c_2 = \frac{8}{13}$, $\quad E = -\frac{17}{13}$ 3. $r_1 = \frac{5}{6}$, $\quad r_2 = \frac{1}{6}$, $\quad c_1 = \frac{1}{2}$, $c_2 = \frac{1}{2}$, $\quad E = \frac{3}{2}$ 5. $r_1 = \frac{10}{19}$, $\quad r_2 = \frac{9}{19}$, $\quad c_1 = \frac{10}{19}$, $\quad c_2 = \frac{9}{19}$, $\quad E = \frac{24}{19}$ 7. $r_1 = \frac{3}{8}$, $r_2 = \frac{5}{8}$, $\quad c_1 = \frac{3}{8}$, $\quad c_2 = \frac{5}{8}$, $\quad E = -\frac{1}{8}$ 9. He should choose the grading system of A–F. He should then choose pass-fail. 11. He should choose the operation. 13. $r_1 = \frac{7}{12}$, $r_2 = \frac{5}{12}$, $\quad c_1 = \frac{1}{3}$, $\quad c_2 = \frac{2}{3}$, $\quad E = -\frac{1}{3}$

15. $r_1 = \frac{d - c}{(a + d) - (b + c)}$

$r_2 = \frac{a - b}{(a + d) - (b + c)}$

$C_1 = \frac{d - b}{(a + d) - (b + c)}$

$C_2 = \frac{a - c}{(a + d) - (b + c)}$

$E = \frac{ad - bc}{}$

Exercises 12.3

1. $r_1 = 0$, $\quad r_2 = \frac{1}{4}$, $\quad r_3 = \frac{3}{4}$;   3. $r_1 = 0.3$, $\quad r_2 = 0$, $\quad r_3 = 0.7$
$c_1 = \frac{3}{4}$, $\quad c_2 = \frac{1}{4}$, $\quad c_3 = 0$; $c_1 = 0.4$, $\quad c_2 = 0.6$
$v = \frac{10}{4}$ $v = 3.8$

5. $r_1 = \frac{1}{4}$, $\quad r_2 = \frac{3}{4}$, $\quad r_3 = 0$ 7. $r_1 = \frac{5}{9}$, $\quad r_2 = 0$, $\quad r_3 = 0$, $\quad r_4 = \frac{4}{9}$
$c_1 = \frac{1}{4}$, $\quad c_2 = \frac{3}{4}$, $\quad c_3 = 0$ $c_1 = \frac{4}{9}$, $\quad c_2 = \frac{5}{9}$
$v = \frac{3}{4}$ $v = \frac{47}{9}$

9. This is a strictly determined game.
Row 2 is the best pure strategy for the row player.
Column 1 is the best pure strategy for the column player.
The value of the game is 0.

11. Payoff matrix:

$$\begin{array}{c} \\ \text{pass} \\ \text{play } \$10 \\ \text{play } \$100 \end{array} \begin{array}{cc} \text{L} & \text{W} \\ \begin{pmatrix} -20 & -20 \\ 0 & -30 \\ 180 & -220 \end{pmatrix} \end{array}$$

The best strategy for the player is to pass.

Exercises 12.4

1. Proof: (1) $v(\emptyset) = 0$
(2) $0 = v(\{2, 3\}) \geqslant v(\{2\}) + v(\{3\}) = 0$
$0 = v(\{1, 3\}) \geqslant v(\{1\}) + v(\{3\}) = 0$
$2 = v(\{1, 2\}) \geqslant v(\{1\}) + v(\{2\}) = 0$
$3 = v(\{1, 2, 3\}) \geqslant v(\{1\}) + v(\{2\}) + v(\{3\}) = 0$
$v(\{1, 2\}) + v(\{3\}) = 2$
$v(\{1\}) + v(\{2, 3\}) = 0$
$v(\{1, 3\}) + v(\{2\}) = 0$

3.   This is not a value function. $v(\{1, 2, 3\}) = 2 \neq v(\{1\}) + v(\{2, 3\}) = -1 + 4 = 3$

5. $v(S) = \begin{cases} 0 \text{ if } S = \emptyset, \{1\}, \{2\}, \{3\} \\ 1 \text{ if } S = \{1, 2\}, \{2, 3\}, \{1, 3\}, \{1, 2, 3\} \end{cases}$

   Core is empty.

7.   Let $I = \{1, 2, 3, 4, 5, 6\}$

   $v(S) = \begin{cases} 0 \text{ if } S = \emptyset, \{i\}, \{i, j\}, \{i, j, k\}; (1 \leqslant i, j, k \leqslant 6) \\ \qquad \{1, 2, 3, m\}, \{n, 4, 5, 6\}, (4 \leqslant m \leqslant 6, \;\; 1 \leqslant n \leqslant 3) \\ 1 \text{ otherwise} \end{cases}$

   The core of this game is empty.

Review Exercises

1.   (a)   Payoff matrix:

$$\begin{pmatrix} 0 & -7 & -10 \\ 7 & 0 & -10 \\ 10 & 10 & 0 \end{pmatrix}$$

   (b)   The best pure strategy for each player is to select the card 10.

   (c)   The saddle point is the (3.3)-entry. The value of the game is 0.

3.   This game is not strictly determined.

$$r_1 = \tfrac{12}{31}, \qquad r_2 = \tfrac{19}{31}, \qquad c_1 = \tfrac{17}{31}, \qquad c_2 = \tfrac{14}{31}, \qquad E = \tfrac{142}{31}$$

5. $P' = \begin{pmatrix} 2 & -3 \\ -4 & 2 \end{pmatrix}$

$$r_1 = \tfrac{6}{11}, \quad r_2 = \tfrac{5}{11}, \quad r_3 = 0, \quad E = \tfrac{8}{11}$$

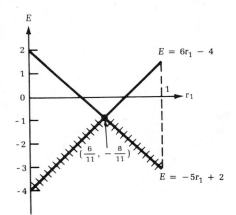

7.   Proof: Add 2 to each entry of the original payoff matrix to get P':

$$P' = \begin{pmatrix} 2 & 3 & 1 \\ 1 & 2 & 3 \\ 3 & 1 & 2 \end{pmatrix}$$

Then use the simplex method to get the solution:

$$\begin{pmatrix} 2 & 3 & 1 & 1 & 0 & 0 & 0 & 1 \\ 1 & 2 & 3 & 0 & 1 & 0 & 0 & 1 \\ \boxed{3} & 1 & 2 & 0 & 0 & 1 & 0 & 1 \\ -1 & -1 & -1 & 0 & 0 & 0 & 1 & 0 \end{pmatrix} \longrightarrow$$

$$\begin{pmatrix} 0 & \boxed{\frac{7}{3}} & \frac{-1}{3} & 1 & 0 & \frac{-2}{3} & 0 & \frac{1}{3} \\ 0 & \frac{5}{3} & \frac{7}{3} & 0 & 1 & \frac{-1}{3} & 0 & \frac{2}{3} \\ 1 & \frac{1}{3} & \frac{2}{3} & 0 & 0 & \frac{1}{3} & 0 & \frac{1}{3} \\ 0 & \frac{-2}{3} & \frac{-1}{3} & 0 & 0 & \frac{1}{3} & 1 & \frac{1}{3} \end{pmatrix} \longrightarrow$$

$$\begin{pmatrix} 0 & 1 & \frac{-1}{7} & \frac{3}{7} & 0 & \frac{-2}{7} & 0 & \frac{1}{7} \\ 0 & 0 & \boxed{\frac{18}{7}} & \frac{-5}{7} & 1 & \frac{1}{7} & 0 & \frac{3}{7} \\ 1 & 0 & \frac{5}{7} & \frac{-1}{7} & 0 & \frac{3}{7} & 0 & \frac{2}{7} \\ 0 & 0 & \frac{-3}{7} & \frac{2}{7} & 0 & \frac{1}{7} & 1 & \frac{3}{7} \end{pmatrix} \longrightarrow$$

$$\begin{pmatrix} 0 & 1 & 0 & x & x & x & x & \frac{1}{6} \\ 0 & 0 & 1 & \frac{-5}{18} & \frac{7}{18} & \frac{1}{18} & 0 & \frac{1}{6} \\ 1 & 0 & 0 & x & x & x & x & \frac{1}{6} \\ 0 & 0 & 0 & \frac{1}{6} & \frac{1}{6} & \frac{1}{6} & 1 & \frac{1}{2} \end{pmatrix} \longrightarrow$$

Therefore, we get $r_1 = r_2 = r_3 = c_1 = c_2 = c_3 = \frac{1}{3}$.

9. $E = \frac{3}{8}$ 11. $r_1 = \frac{3}{5}$, $r_2 = 0$, $r_3 = \frac{2}{5}$
$c_1 = \frac{1}{5}$, $c_2 = \frac{4}{5}$
$E = \frac{13}{5}$

13. (a) Payoff matrix:

$$\begin{matrix} 399 & 99 & -1 \\ 0 & 0 & 0 \end{matrix}$$

(b) You should never buy the ticket.

15. Payoff matrix:

	(0, 2)	(1, 1)	(2, 1)
(0, 3)	1	-1	-1
(1, 2)	1	1	-1
(2, 1)	-1	1	1
(3, 0)	-1	-1	1

The best strategy for Colonel Peters is (0, 1/2, 1/2, 0).

17. Let $I = \{1, 2, 3, 4, 5, 6, 7\}$
$$v(S) = \begin{cases} 0 \text{ if } S = \emptyset, \{i\}, \{i, j\}, \{i, j, k\}, (i, j, k \neq 7), \{i, j, k, l\} \, (i, j, k, \neq 7) \\ 1 \text{ otherwise} \end{cases}$$
The core of the game is empty.

References

Adler, I. "The Consequences of Constant Pressure in Phyllotaxis." *J. Theoretical Biology* 65 (1977): 29–77.

Aho, A. V., Hopcroft J. E., and Ullman, J. D. *The Design and Analysis of Computer Algorithms*. Reading, Mass.: Addison Wesley, 1974.

Appel, K., and Haken, W. "The Four-Color Problem." *Mathematics Today: Twelve Informal Essays*, Springer Verlag (1978): 153–180.

Arrow, K. *Social Choice and Individual Values*, 2nd ed., New Haven, Conn.: Yale University Press, 1963.

Balaban, A. T., ed. *Chemical Applications of Graph Theory*. New York: Academic Press, 1976.

Berman, L. S. "Development of Input-Output Statistics." In *Input-Output in the United Kingdom*, proceedings of the 1968 Manchester Conference, edited by W. F. Grossling, London: Frank Cass, 1970.

Birkhoff, G. D., and Lewis, D. C. "Chromatic Polynomials." *Trans. Amer. Math Soc. 60* (1946): 355–451.

Boesch, F., and Tindall, R. "Robbins Theorem for Mixed Graphs." *Amer. Math Monthly* 87 (1980): 716–719.

Bondy, J. A., and Murty, U. S. R. *Graph Theory with Applications*. Elsevier, New York/London: Macmillan, 1976.

Bradley, S., Hax, A., and Magnanti, T. *Applied Mathematical Programming*. Reading, Mass.: Addison Wesley, 1977.

Brams, S. J., and Fishburn, P. C. *Approval Voting*. Boston: Birkhauser, 1983.

Branson, W. H., and Litvack, J. M. *Macroeconomics*, 2nd ed., New York: Harper and Row, 1981.

Cayley, A. "On the Mathematical Theory of Isomers." *Philos Mag. 67* (1874): 444–446.

———. "A Theorem on Trees." *Quart. J. Math. 23* (1889): 376–378.

Christofides, N. *Graph Theory: An Algorithmic Approach*. New York: Academic Press, 1979.

Chvatal, V. *Linear Programming*. New York: W. H. Freeman, 1983.

Cohen, J. E. *Food Webs and Niche Space*. Princeton, N. J.; Princeton University Press, 1978.

Coxeter, H. S. M. *Introduction to Geometry*. New York: John Wiley & Sons, 1961.

Cozzens, M. B., and Porter, R. *Recurrence Relations—Counting Backwards*. Lexington, Mass.: HIMAP Module 2, COMAP, 1986.

Cozzens, M. B., and Roberts, F. S. "T-Colorings of Graphs and the Channel Assignment Problem." *Congressus Numeratum 35* (1982): 191–208.

Dawes, R. M. *Fundamentals of Attitude Measurement*. New York: John Wiley & Sons, 1972.

Deo, N. *Graph Theory with Applications to Engineering and Computer Science*. Englewood Cliffs, N. J.: Prentice Hall, 1974.

Dewdney, A. K. "Computer Recreations." *Scientific American* (November 1984): 19–28.

Edmonds, J. "The Chinese Postman Problem." *Oper. Res.* 13 Suppl. 1 (1965): 373.

Edmonds, J., and Johnson, E. L. "Matching Euler Tours and the Chinese Postman." *Math Program.* 5 (1973): 88–124.

Gamow, G. *One, Two, Three . . . Infinity.* New York: Mentor Books, New American Library, 1954.

Graham, R. I., and Hell, P. "On the History of the Minimum Spanning Tree Problem." Mimeographed, Bell Laboratories, Murray Hill, N.J., (1982) to appear in the *Annals of the History of Computing.*

Harary, F. *Graph Theory.* Reading, Mass.: Addison Wesley, 1969.

Hutchinson, G. "Evaluation of Polymer Sequence Fragment Data Using Graph Theory." *Bull. Math Biophys.* 31 (1969): 541–562.

Kemeny, J. G., and Snell, J. L. *Mathematical Models in the Social Sciences.* New York: Blaisdell, 1962. Reprinted by MIT Press, Cambridge, Mass., 1972.

Kirchhoff, G. "Uber die Auflosung der Gleichungen, auf welche man bei der Unterschung der linearen Verteilung galvanischer Strome gefuhrt wird." *Ann. Phys. Chem.* 72 (1847): 497–508.

Knuth, D. E. *The Art of Computing, Vol. 3, Sorting and Searching.* Reading, Mass.: Addison Wesley, 1973.

Konig, D. *Theorie des endlichen und unendlichen Graphen.* Leipzig: Akademische Verlagsgesellschaft, 1936. Reprinted by Chelsea, New York, 1950.

Kruskal, J. B. "On the Shortest Spanning Tree of a Graph and The Travelling Salesman Problem." *Proc. Amer. Math. Soc.* 7 (1956): 48–50.

Leftwich, R., and Eckert, R. *The Price System and Resource Allocation,* 8th ed., New York: The Dryden Press, 1982.

Leontief, W. *Input-Output Economics.* New York: Oxford University Press, 1966.

⸺ . "The Structure of the U.S. Economy." *Scientific American* 212, no. 4 (April 1965): 25–35.

Levy, H., and Lessman, R. *Finite Difference Equations.* New York: Macmillan, 1961.

Liu, C. L. *Topics in Combinatorics.* Washington, D.C.: Mathematical Association of America, 1972.

Luce, R. D., and Raiffa, H. *Games and Decisions.* New York: John Wiley & Sons, 1957.

Malkevitch, J. *The Mathematical Theory of Elections.* Lexington, Mass.: HIMAP Module 1, COMAP, 1985.

Malkevitch, J., and Meyer, W. *Graphs, Models, Finite Mathematics.* Englewood Cliffs, N.J.: Prentice Hall, 1974.

Miller, R. L. *Economics Today,* 5th ed., New York: Harper and Row, 1985.

Moon, J. W. "Various proofs of Cayley's Formula for Counting Trees." In *A Seminar on Graph Theory,* edited by F. Harary, 70–78. New York: Holt, Rinehart, and Winston, 1967.

Mosteller, F., and Wallace, D. *Inference and Disputed Authorship: The Federalist.* Reading, Mass.: Addison Wesley, 1984.

Nova Adventures in Science, Reading, Mass.: Addison Wesley, 1982.

Ore, O. "Note on Hamilton Circuits." *Amer. Math Monthly* 67 (1960): 55.

Pai, A., and Roberts, H. M. *Genetics, Its Concepts and Implications.* Englewood Cliffs, N.J.: Prentice Hall, 1981.

Papadimitriou, C. H., and Steiglitz, K. *Combinatorial Optimization Algorithms and Complexity.* Englewood Cliffs, N.J.: Prentice Hall, 1982.

Prim, R. C. "Shortest Connection Networks and Some Generalizations." *Bell Syst Tech. J.* 36 (1957): 1389–1401.

Read, R. C. "An Introduction to Chromatic Polynomials." *J. Comb. Theory* 4 (1968): 52–71.

Reingold, E. M., and Tarjan, R. E. "On a Greedy Heuristic for Complete Matching." *SIAM J. Comput.* 10 (1981): 676–681.

Roberts, F. S. *Applied Combinatorics.* Englewood Cliffs, N.J.: Prentice Hall, 1984.

———. *Discrete Mathematical Models, with Applications to Social, Biological, and Environmental Problems.* Englewood Cliffs, N.J.: Prentice Hall, 1976.

———. *Graph Theory and its Applications to Society.* NSF-CBMS Monograph, No. 29, Philadelphia: SIAM, 1978.

Shapley, L. S. "Measurement of Power in Political Systems." In *Game Theory and its Applications,* edited by W. F. Lucas, vol. 24 (1981): 69–81. Providence, R.I.: American Mathematical Society.

Sherbert, D. R. *Difference Equations with Applications,* Lexington, Mass.: UMAP module 322, COMAP, 1980.

Shier, D. "Testing for Homogeneity using Minimum spanning Trees." *UMAP J.* 3 (1982): 273–283.

Shubik, M. *Game Theory in the Social Sciences, Concepts and Solutions.* Cambridge, Mass.: MIT Press, 1984.

Simmons, D. M. *Linear Programming for Operations Research.* Cambridge, Mass.: W. R. Grace and Co., 1972.

Stevens, P. *Patterns in Nature.* Boston: Little, Brown and Co.

Tucker, A. *Applied Combinatorics.* New York: Wiley, 1980.

Von Neumann, J., and Morgenstern, O. *Theory of Games and Economic Behavior.* New York: John Wiley & Sons, 1944.

Index

Addition of matrices, 429
Addition method for solving
   equations, 373–376
Algorithm, 88
   depth first search and one-
      way street assignment, 123
   Dijkstra's, 88
   Eulerian circuit, 53
   matching, 81
   minimum spanning tree, 131
   search, 116
   simplex algorithm, 522
Amortization schedule, 311
Annuity, 300
Antisymmetric relation, 275
Approval voting, 28
Arrow's Impossibility Theorem,
   29
Augmented matrix, 463

Balance, 294
Basic feasible solution, 525
Basic solution, 525
Basic variables, 525
Bayes' theorem, 218
Bernoulli trials, 207, 234
Binary search tree, 115
Binary tree, 115, 137
Bipartite graph, 81
Bits, 19
Bond graph, 105
Borda count, 26
Bounded set, 407
Bridge, 122

Carbon
   dating, 343
      radioactive, 341
Cartesian product, 242
Chess, 328
Chromatic polynomial, 265

Circuit, 106
   Eulerian, 53
   Hamiltonian, 65
Coalition, 2, 615, 623
   minimal winning, 3
   value of, 22, 615
   winning, 2, 22
Codes, 17
   binary, 19
$C(N, k)$, 164
Column, 420
   matrix, 422
   dominant (in a game), 598
Combination, 164, 182
Complement of a set, 4, 5
Complete (strongly complete)
   relation, 276
Compound interest, 293
Computer output of a linear
   program, 557–560
Conditional probability, 200,
   234
Condorcet criterion, 27
Connected graph, 106
Constraints, 393
Consumer Price Index,
   350
Cooling, 344
Core of a game, 617, 623
Cost function, 252
Counting, 143
   combinations, 164
   DNA chains, 143
   permutations, 151
   product rule, 143
   subsets, 144
   sum rule, 145

Decay, radioactive, 341
Decision tree, 107
De Morgan's Laws, 20–21

Deposit, 294
Depth-first search and one-way
   street assignment algorithm,
   123
Determinant of a 2-by-2 matrix,
   499
Difference equation, 326
   solution, 352
Dijkstra's algorithm, 88
Directed graph, 45
   food web, 45
   of a relation, 243
Distribution matrix, 449
   steady state, 453
DNA chains, number of,
   143
Dominance relation, 445
Dominant rows and columns,
   598
Dual linear programs, 547
Dual variables, 547

Edge, 38
Element of a set, 2
Empty set, 2
Entry, 420
Equiprobable probability
   space, 189
Equivalence classes, 272
Equivalence relation,
   272
Euler, 49
Eulerian
   circuit, 53
   path, 52
Event, 20, 172, 182, 186
   independent, 200
   simple, 186
Expected value, 225, 234
   of a game, 590
Experiment, 19, 171

Feasible region (set), 403
Fibonacci, 328
  numbers, 331
  sequence, 328
Final demand, 502
Fixed cost, 252
Four-color problem, 43
Function, 247
  cost, 252
  inverse, 254
  linear, 258
  of several variables, 253
  one-to-one, 248
  onto, 248
  quadratic, 262
Functional notation, 249
Fundamental Theorem of Linear
  Programming, 408

Game, 581–623
  expected value of, 590
  linear programming solution,
    603–612
  n-person, 614–620
  strictly determined, 585
  two-person, 583
  two-person zero-sum, 583
Gauss-Jordan elimination, 463,
  514
Geometric series, 357
Graph, 45
  bipartite, 81
  coloring of a, 41, 264
  competition, 45
  directed, 45
  input-output, 500
  matching in a, 80
  matrix of a, 423
  path in a, 49
Guttman scaling, 281

Hamiltonian
  circuit, 65
  path, 65
Hasse diagram, 279
Heating, 344
Homogeneous bimetallic object,
  132
Horizontal line test, 252

Identity matrix, 438
Image of a function, 249
Imputation, 617
Independent events, 203, 234
Individual retirement account
  (IRA), 309
Inequality, 380
  linear, 380
  graph of, 380–381
  graph of system of, 384–389
Inflation, 340
Initial
  balance, 294
  condition, 328
  deposit, 294
Input-Output, 249, 491
  demand, 502
  graph, 500
  matrix, 501
  models, 491
Insert procedure, 118
Installment
  loan, 315
  payment, 315
Intercepts, 260, 362
Interest, 291, 300, 311, 321
  compound, 293
  due, 310
  earned, 294
  period, 293
  rate, 292
Intersection of two sets, 5
Inverse of a function, 254
Inverse of a matrix, 492, 515
  2-by-2, 499
Iteration, 352

Königsburg bridge problem, 51
Kruskal's Algorithm, 131

Leontief model, 500
Level of a tree, 115
Linear function, 258
Linear order, 276
Linear programs, 393
  diet, 483
  dual, 547
  feasible region of, 403
  for games, 603, 608–609
  geometrical method for, 408

simplex method, 522
solution of, 393
standard maximum form, 522
standard minimum form, 549
transportation, 479
Loan, 315

Majority winner, 25
Markov chain, 451, 514
  states, 450
  steady state, 453
Matching, 80
Matrix, 420
  addition, 429
  augmented, 463
  coefficient, 440
  columns, 420
  determinant of a 2-by-2, 499
  distribution, 449
  of a dominance relation, 445
  edge, 423
  entry, 420
  equality, 422
  of a graph, 423
  incidence, 423
  identity, 438
  input-output, 501
  inverse, 492, 499, 515
  multiplication, 433, 435
  payoff, 583, 622
  reduced, 477
  of a relation, 423
  rows, 420
  size, 422
  square, 438
  subtraction, 429
  and systems of equations, 439
  of a tournament, 445
  transition, 449
Minimum spanning tree, 105, 130
Minimum spanning tree
  algorithm, 131
Model
  heating-cooling, 344
  input-output, 491
  of Markov chain, 451
  population growth, 343, 444
  radioactive decay, 341
  spread of information-disease,
    345

Multiplication of matrices, 433, 435

Nearest neighbor rule, 66
Newton's law, 344
n-person games, 614–620
Nonnegativity constraints, 393

Objective function, 393
Orientation of a graph, 121
Output flow graph, 501

Partial order, 279
Partition of a set, 217, 272
Path, 49
    alternating, 82
    Eulerian, 49, 52
Payoff matrix, 583, 622
Permutation, 149, 182
    formula, 151
PERT networks, 280
Pivot
    column, 534, 536
    element, 535, 536
    row, 535, 536
Pivotal member, 156
Players in a game, 583
Plurality winner, 25
$P(N, k)$, 152
Population growth, 343, 444
Power set, 4
    number of elements in, 144
Preference, 25, 241, 278
    ballot, 25
    orders, 25
Principal
    payment, 311, 322
    remaining, 310, 322
Probability, 171, 183, 189
    conditional, 200, 448
    equiprobable, 189
    space, 189
    tree, 214
    Venn diagrams, 192
Problem
    assignment, 78
    counting, 70
    diet, 483
    existence, 70
    four-color, 43
    Königsberg bridge, 51

matching, 78
optimization, 70
scheduling, 38
shortest route, 86
transportation, 479
traveling salesman, 65
Product rule, 143, 182

Radioactive
    carbon, 342
    decay, 341
Random variable, 225
Recurrence relation, 327
    solution, 352
Reduced matrix, 477, 514
Reflexive relation, 270
Regular annuity, 300
Relation, 242
    antisymmetric, 275
    complete, 276
    dominance, 445
    equivalence, 272
    linear order, 276
    matrix of a, 423
    on a set, 243
    recurrence, 327
    reflexive, 270
    strongly complete, 276
    symmetric, 271
    transitive, 271
RNA chain, 19, 56
    fragments, 19, 56
Robbins's Theorem, 122
Row, 420
    dominant, 598
    matrix, 422
    operations, 465, 515
Run-off procedure, 25

Saddle point, 585
Sample space, 20, 172, 182, 186
Scheduling problems, 38, 148
Search algorithm, 116–117
Sensitivity analysis, 561
Sequence, 326
    Fibonacci, 328
Set, 2
    cartesian product, 242
    complement of, 5
    element of, 2

empty set, 2
intersection of two, 5
partition, 217
power set, 4
solution set, 371
subset, 2
union of two, 5
Venn diagram of, 5, 9
Shapley-Shubik power index, 157, 182
Shortest route problems, 86
Simple event, 20, 186
Simplex algorithm, 522
Sinking fund, 305
Size of a matrix, 422
Slack variables, 523
Slope of a line, 259
Solution of difference equations, 354
Solution for a linear program, 393
Solution set, 371
Spanning tree, 124, 137
Square matrix, 438
Standard maximum form, 522
Standard minimum form, 547
States of a Markov chain, 450
Steady state distribution, 453
Strategy for games, 585–597
    best pure, 585
    optimal for column player, 596
    optimal for row player, 594
    procedures for, 596–597
Strictly determined games, 585
Strongly connected, 121
Subsets, 2
    number of, 144
    power set, 4
    proper, 2
Substitution method for solving equations, 376–377
Subtraction of matrices, 429
Sum rule, 145, 182
Superadditivity, 615
Surplus variables, 522
Survey sampling, 8–15
Symmetric relation, 271
Systems of equations, 371
    coefficient matrix, 440

matrix of, 439, 463
solving, 373–377, 462, 476

Tableau, 524
Total output, 502
Tournament, 277
matrix of, 445
Tower of Hanoi, 332
Transition matrix, 449
Transitive relation, 271
Traveling salesman problem, 65, 147
Tree, 105–111, 137, 329, 432
binary, 115, 137
binary search tree, 115

decision tree, 107
level of, 115
minimum spanning tree, 105, 130
probability, 214, 447
spanning tree, 124, 137
Triangular number, 338
Two-person game, 583
Two-person zero-sum game, 583

Union of sets, 5

Value of a coalition, 615
Value of a game, 585

Variables
basic, 525
cost, 252
dual, 547
independent and dependent, 249
nonbasic, 525
slack, 522
surplus, 552
Venn diagram, 5
and probability, 192
Vertex, 38
Vertical line test, 251
Von Neumann duality principle, 550

COUNTING

Permutations:

$$P(N, k) = \underbrace{N \times (N - 1) \times (N - 2) \times \cdots (N - k + 1)}_{k \text{ terms}}$$

Combinations:

$$C(N, k) = \frac{P(N, k)}{k!}$$

PROBABILITY

$$P(E) = 1 - P(E')$$

$$P(E \cup F) = P(E) + P(F) - P(E \cap F)$$

Conditional probability:

$$P(E/F) = \frac{P(E \cap F)}{P(F)}$$

Independent events:

$$P(E \cap F) = P(E)P(F)$$

Bernoulli trials:

$$P(k \text{ successes in } N \text{ trials}) = C(N, k) \, (P(S))^k (P(F))^{N-k}$$

DIFFERENCE EQUATIONS AND FINANCE

The difference equation $x_k = ax_{k-1} + b$ has solution:

$$x_k = \frac{b}{1 - a} + \left(x_0 - \frac{b}{1 - a} \right) a^k$$

provided $a \neq 1$.

Compound interest:

$$B_k = B_0(1 + i)^k$$

where

i = interest rate per interest period
B_0 = initial balance
B_k = balance after k interest periods